HANDBOOK ON TEACHING AND LEARNING IN POLITICAL SCIENCE AND INTERNATIONAL RELATIONS

Handbook on Teaching and Learning in Political Science and International Relations

Edited by

John Ishiyama
University of North Texas, USA

William J. Miller
Flagler College, USA

Eszter Simon
Masaryk University, Czech Republic

Edward Elgar
PUBLISHING

Cheltenham, UK • Northampton, MA, USA

© John Ishiyama, William J. Miller and Eszter Simon 2015

All rights reserved. No part of this publication may be reproduced, stored in a retrieval system or transmitted in any form or by any means, electronic, mechanical or photocopying, recording, or otherwise without the prior permission of the publisher.

Published by
Edward Elgar Publishing Limited
The Lypiatts
15 Lansdown Road
Cheltenham
Glos GL50 2JA
UK

Edward Elgar Publishing, Inc.
William Pratt House
9 Dewey Court
Northampton
Massachusetts 01060
USA

A catalogue record for this book
is available from the British Library

Library of Congress Control Number: 2014954941

This book is available electronically in the **Elgar**online
Social and Political Science subject collection
DOI 10.4337/9781782548485

ISBN 978 1 78254 847 8 (cased)
ISBN 978 1 78254 848 5 (eBook)

Typeset by Servis Filmsetting Ltd, Stockport, Cheshire
Printed and bound in Great Britain by T.J. International Ltd, Padstow

Contents

List of figures	viii
List of tables	ix
List of boxes	x
List of contributors	xi
Introduction John Ishiyama, William J. Miller and Eszter Simon	xxii

PART I CURRICULUM AND COURSE DESIGN

1 Best practices in the American undergraduate political science curriculum 3
   E. Fletcher McClellan

2 Capstone courses and senior seminars as culminating experiences in undergraduate political science education 16
   Paul E. Sum

3 Teaching politics to practitioners 28
   John Craig

4 Best practices in professional development in graduate education 35
   Clodagh Harris

5 Distance and online course design 47
   J. Simon Rofe

6 Student and civic engagement: cultivating the skills, efficacy and identities that increase student involvement in learning and in public life 60
   J. Cherie Strachan

7 Curricular and program assessment techniques in the USA 74
   Kerstin Hamann

8 Performance assessment in Europe 85
   Alasdair Blair

9 Course-based assessment and student feedback 95
   William J. Miller

10 Multidisciplinary approaches to teaching political science 111
    Brenda Kauffman

11 Promoting information literacy and information research 121
    Stephen Thornton

12 Internationalization of the curriculum (Bologna Process) 132
    Erkki Berndtson

13	Promoting employability and jobs skills via the political science curriculum *Simon Lightfoot*	144

PART II TEACHING SUBJECT AREAS

14	After the apocalypse: a simulation for Introduction to Politics classes *Wendy L. Watson, Jesse Hamner, Elizabeth A. Oldmixon and Kimi King*	157
15	Teaching conflict and conflict resolution *Agnieszka Paczynska*	173
16	Teaching about diversity issues *Boris E. Ricks*	185
17	Teaching gender politics *Fiona Buckley*	196
18	Teaching graduate research methods *Mitchell Brown*	208
19	Teaching undergraduate research methods *Cristina Leston-Bandeira*	221
20	Teaching political theory *Matthew J. Moore*	233
21	Teaching controversial topics *David Malet*	244
22	Teaching at the community college: faculty role, responsibilities and pedagogical techniques *Erin Richards*	255
23	Teaching international relations *Rebecca Glazier*	265

PART III IN-CLASS TEACHING TECHNIQUES

24	Effective syllabus design *John Ishiyama and Robert G. Rodriguez*	279
25	Integrating technology into the classroom *Gabriela Pleschová*	291
26	War, peace and everything in between: simulations in international relations *Victor Asal, Chad Raymond and Simon Usherwood*	304
27	Developing your own in-class simulations: design advice and a 'commons' simulation example *Mark A. Boyer and Elizabeth T. Smith*	315

28	Group work in political science: how to get collaboration into the classroom *Bobbi Gentry*	327
29	Designing team-based learning activities *Andreas Broscheid*	340
30	Experiential education in political science and international relations *Elizabeth A. Bennion*	351
31	Best practices in Problem-Based Learning *Heidi Maurer*	369
32	Developing student scholars: best practices in promoting undergraduate research *James M. Scott*	384
33	Teaching international relations with film and literature: using non-traditional texts in the classroom *Jennifer K. Lobasz and Brandon Valeriano*	399
34	Promoting course based writing in the discipline *Brian Smentkowski*	410
35	Best practices in undergraduate lecturing: how to make large classes work *Kinga Kas and Elizabeth Sheppard*	422
36	Political science and the scholarship of teaching *Jeffrey L. Bernstein*	434
37	Getting students to talk: best practices in promoting student discussion *Michael P. Marks*	444

Index   455

Figures

5.1	Salmon's five-stage model of online learning	53
30.1	Kolb's experiential learning cycle	355
31.1	The PBL cycle	371
32.1	Approaches to undergraduate research	385
32.2	Undergraduate research in context	396

Tables

2.1	Percentage of programs that have culminating experiences as part of their undergraduate curricula	22
5.1	Example e-tivity	55
9.1	Action verbs corresponding with Bloom's Revised Taxonomy	99
9.2	Sample rubric	105
9.3	Example student learning outcome data inserted on reporting sheet	107
9.4	Met/not met	107
9.5	Total score	107
9.6	Average score	108
9.7	Three multiple choice and one true/false give outcome no. 1	108
13.1	Graduate skills sought by UK employers (in %)	147
14A.1	Grading rubric	170
14A.2	Teaching assistant rubric—total across all 5 categories = 75	171
14A.3	Peer (student) rubric—total across all 5 categories = 25	172
18.1	Substance of courses across degree levels	214
18.2	Journal articles (single and co-authored) by current and recent doctoral students	216
19.1	Ten recommendations for successful undergraduate methods teaching	222
27.1	A non-random sampling of some recently published simulations	318
30.1	Eight principles of good practice – an example (professor: Elizabeth Bennion, Indiana University South Bend; courses: American Politics, Elections and Voting Behavior)	358
30.2	Categorization of experiential learning activities	359
30.3	Definitions of experiential learning activities	360
32.1	Issues and choices in undergraduate research programs	386
32.2	Strategies for support of undergraduate research	395
33.1	Films and IR	402

Boxes

9.1	Example learning outcomes for three courses	100
11.1	Politics research trail	127
11.2	Information literacy workshop	128
24.1	Example of basic information to be included in the syllabus	283
24.2	Example of course description	283
24.3	Example of resources to be included in the syllabus	284
24.4	Sample syllabus	286
27.1	Summary of simulation development requirements	317
27.2	A commons simulation: international fishery management	321
31.1	PBL assignment example: learning about decision-making in a politics course	374
31.2	PBL assignment example 2: learning about basics of international law in an international relations course	374
31.3	Assignment example: 'why institutions'	376
31.4	Assignment example: 'EU institutions'	377
31.5	Assignment example: 'Maastricht Treaty' (too descriptive)	378
31.6	Assignment example: 'Maastricht Treaty' (revised)	379

Contributors

Victor Asal, SUNY-Albany, USA
Victor Asal is Director of the Center for Policy Research and an associate professor in the Department of Political Science at the University at Albany, State University of New York. In addition to his work on the use of simulations and games as pedagogical tools to teach political science he also does research on political violence and political discrimination.

Elizabeth A. Bennion, Indiana University South Bend, USA
Elizabeth A. Bennion, Professor of Political Science and Campus Director of the American Democracy Project at Indiana University South Bend, earned her BA in American Studies from Smith College, and her MA and PhD in Political Science at the University of Wisconsin–Madison. Bennion teaches courses in American politics with an emphasis on political behavior. She has received numerous teaching and service awards, and her grant-supported scholarship has been published in multiple books and academic journals. Bennion is co-editor of the book *Teaching Civic Engagement: From Student to Active Citizen* and co-founder of the Intercampus Consortium for SoTL Research. She conducts large-scale, national field experiments testing innovative approaches to civic education and engagement. Bennion also hosts 'Politically Speaking', a weekly PBS public affairs show on WNIT-TV.

Erkki Berndtson, University of Helsinki, Finland
Erkki Berndtson is Senior Lecturer in Political Science at the University of Helsinki. He has been a visiting scholar at the universities of Gothenburg (1973), Chicago (1983), California, Berkeley (1990) and Harvard (1990). He has also held the titles of Editor-in-Chief of *Politiikka*, a journal of the Finnish Political Science Association (1985–86), a member of the Executive Committee of the Nordic Political Science Association (1981–93), President of the Finnish Political Science Association (1995–99) and a member of the Executive Council of the European Political Science Network (2002–05). Currently, he is a chair of the IPSA Research Committee on 'The Study of Political Science as a Discipline'. His research interests include the history of political science and the politics of higher education.

Jeffrey L. Bernstein, Eastern Michigan University, USA
Jeffrey L. Bernstein is Professor of Political Science at Eastern Michigan University, where he has been on the faculty since 1997. He holds a BA from Washington University and an MA and PhD from the University of Michigan. His research interests include public opinion and political behavior, citizenship education, and the scholarship of teaching and learning. Bernstein was a 2005–06 Carnegie Scholar with the Carnegie Foundation for the Advancement of Teaching in Palo Alto, California. He is co-editor and contributing author of *Citizenship Across the Curriculum* (Indiana University Press, 2010) and of numerous scholarly articles and book chapters, many co-authored with the kind of remarkable students who make being an academic so much fun, and so rewarding.

Alasdair Blair, De Montfort University, UK

Alasdair Blair is Jean Monnet Professor of International Relations, Head of the Department of Politics and Public Policy, and Director of the Jean Monnet Centre of European Governance at De Montfort University, Leicester, UK. In 2006 he was awarded a National Teaching Fellowship. His main research and teaching interests are British foreign policy, European integration, and teaching and learning in Politics and International Relations. He is the author of 11 books and numerous articles and book chapters. His most recent book is *Britain and the World since 1945* (Routledge, 2015). In 2014 he received the Political Studies Association Politics Learning and Teaching Prize for the best learning and teaching article published in the journal *Politics* in 2012–13.

Mark A. Boyer, University of Connecticut, USA

Mark A. Boyer is Board of Trustees Distinguished Professor and Director of the Environmental Studies Program at the University of Connecticut. His current research focuses on environmental policy and particularly climate change adaptation. He also very much enjoys developing simulations and problem-based learning exercises to stimulate student learning.

Andreas Broscheid, James Madison University (JMU), USA

Andreas Broscheid is Associate Professor of Political Science at James Madison University. His work centers on American, particularly judicial, politics, European Union interest groups, the scholarship of teaching and learning, and faculty development. His publications include articles in *European Union Politics*, the *Journal of European Public Policy* and the *Law & Society Review*. An empirical study of Team-Based Learning in a large introductory political science class is forthcoming in the *Journal of Political Science Education*. From 2011 through 2013, Andreas Broscheid was a faculty associate at JMU's Center for Faculty Innovation. He received his PhD from Stony Brook University.

Mitchell Brown, Auburn University, USA

Mitchell Brown, PhD, is an associate professor in the Department of Political Science at Auburn University, and is a member of the department's MPA and PhD faculty. Dr. Brown is the author of numerous publications, including *Applied Research Methods in Public and Non-Profit Organizations* (2014) with Dr. Kathleen Hale, and 'Cross-Integration of Community, Research, and the Classroom: Extensions of a National Evaluation' in *Scholarship in Action: Community, Leaders and Citizens* (2013). She is the recipient of several research and teaching awards, among them the 2013 Student Government Association (SGA) Outstanding Faculty Award for the College of Liberal Arts at Auburn University.

Fiona Buckley, University College Cork (UCC), Ireland

Fiona Buckley is a lecturer in the Department of Government, UCC, Ireland. Her research and teaching areas include gender politics, Irish politics, and the scholarship of teaching and learning. She is co-editor (with Yvonne Galligan) of *Politics and Gender in Ireland: The Quest for Political Agency* (Routledge, 2015). Within the area of teaching and learning, Fiona has researched experiential learning in political science and the use of online discussion forums and Twitter in teaching.

John Craig, Higher Education Academy, UK
John Craig is Assistant Director at the Higher Education Academy in the UK. He is Chair of the Political Studies Association Teaching and Learning Specialist Group and a member of the editorial board of the *Journal of Political Science Education*. He has taught Politics at the University of Huddersfield, University of Leeds, Teesside University and the Open University. He was awarded a National Teaching Fellowship in 2009.

Bobbi Gentry, Bridgewater College, USA
Bobbi Gentry is a scholar of Teaching and Learning who focuses on improving student engagement in the classroom through simulations, policy problem/solution proposals and research projects. She is also a youth voting scholar and does extensive research in political identity development. As a political psychologist, Dr. Gentry applies psychological methods to understanding political phenomena including leadership, political participation and youth involvement. She has written on topics of Political Science education such as service learning and improving student writing. Her current work on the Scholarship of Teaching and Learning includes assessment of performance learning, curriculum review in higher education and identity development in the Political Science classroom.

Rebecca Glazier, University of Arkansas, Little Rock, USA
Rebecca Glazier is an assistant professor at the University of Arkansas at Little Rock. She joined the faculty of the Political Science Department there in 2009, after completing her PhD at the University of California, Santa Barbara. Rebecca's research agenda addresses issues of religion, framing and US foreign policy. She is particularly interested in how religion motivates political action, and has published research on the role of providential religious beliefs in the process. Rebecca also studies the Scholarship of Teaching and Learning and has published articles on various teaching strategies, including simulations, satire and smartphone apps. She has a substantive interest in the Middle East and coordinated the Middle Eastern Studies Program at UALR from 2012–14.

Kerstin Hamann, University of Central Florida, USA
Kerstin Hamann (PhD Washington University) is Professor of Political Science at the University of Central Florida. She is currently the Editor-in-Chief of the *Journal of Political Science Education*. Prof. Hamann's books include *Assessment in Political Science* (co-edited with John Ishiyama and Michelle Deardorff); *The Politics of Industrial Relations: Labor Unions in Spain*; *Parties, Elections, and Policy Reform in Western Europe: Voting for Social Pacts* (with John Kelly); and *Democracy and Institutional Development: Spain in Comparative Political Perspective* (co-edited with Bonnie N. Field). Her research on Spanish politics, comparative industrial relations, and the Scholarship of Teaching and Learning has been widely published in book chapters and journals such as *Comparative Politics*, *Comparative Political Studies*, *PS: Political Science & Politics*, *Journal of Political Science Education*, *British Journal of Industrial Relations*, *West European Politics*, *European Journal of Industrial Relations*, *South European Society & Politics*, *Industrial & Labor Relations Review* and *College Teaching*, among others.

Jesse Hamner, University of North Texas, USA
Dr. Jesse Hamner is the Director of Research and Assessment at the UNT Libraries, Adjunct Professor of Political Science, and Technical Director for the Social Conflict in

Africa (SCAD) project. His research and teaching interests include hydropolitics, civil war, research methods and data science.

Clodagh Harris, University College Cork (UCC), Ireland
Dr. Clodagh Harris is a senior lecturer in the Department of Government, UCC. Her research interests include deliberative and participatory democracy, democratic innovations, and the Scholarship of Teaching and Learning. She established and convenes with Dr. Brid Quinn (University of Limerick) the teaching and learning specialist group of the Political Studies Association of Ireland (PSAI) and sits on the committee that awards the PSAI prize for excellence in teaching. She served on the International Scientific Advisory Board of Ireland's first Citizens' Assembly and was an international observer for the G1000 Belgian Citizens' Summit. She was also a member of the Academic and Legal Advisory group of Ireland's Constitutional Convention. She has published in international journals such as *Representation, European Political Science* and the *Journal of Political Science Education*.

John Ishiyama, University of North Texas, USA
John Ishiyama is University Distinguished Research Professor of Political Science at the University of North Texas. He is also the Editor-in-Chief for the *American Political Science Review* and Director of the National Science Foundation's Research Experience for Undergraduates Program in Conflict Management and Peace Science at the University of North Texas. He is the author or editor of seven books and author or co-author of 130 journal articles and book chapters on democratization, party politics, ethnic politics, and post-communist Russian, European and African politics. He has also written widely on curriculum development, educational opportunity and educational assessment.

Kinga Kas, American Girne University, Cyprus
Kinga Kas received her PhD in Political Science at the Corvinus University of Budapest. She taught undergraduate and graduate courses as well in the field of Political Science and International Relations at the Eotvos Lorand University of Budapest and at the Girne American University of North Cyprus. She has been involved in projects dealing with issues related to the teaching of Political Science and is a founding member of the standing group on Teaching and Learning Politics in the European Consortium for Political Research (ECPR). She is the author of several related papers and is co-editor of the book *Teaching Theory and Academic Writing* (Budrich Verlag, 2008).

Brenda Kauffman, Flagler College, USA
Dr. Kauffman earned her PhD in Political Science from Auburn University, a master's degree in Liberal Arts and Philosophy from Spring Hill College, a bachelor's in Philosophy and Religious Studies from Georgia State University, and an associate's degree in Liberal Arts and Sciences from Penn State University. Her areas of specific interest include environmental politics, international organizations and international political economy.

Kimi King, University of North Texas, USA
Dr. Kimi King has taught for over twenty-five years at four different universities and is the recipient of multiple teaching and service awards. Her teaching and research interests

include American institutions, as well as constitutional and international humanitarian law. She has published both empirical and pedagogical works ranging from the courts, presidential power and foreign policy to the role of gender in sexual violence cases before war crimes tribunals. Her use of classroom simulations dates back to the first class she taught, and she has been using some variation of engaged learning ever since. Her proudest accomplishment is her amazing family, who support her teaching and zombie addictions.

Cristina Leston-Bandeira, University of Hull, UK
Cristina Leston-Bandeira is a senior lecturer at the School of Politics, Philosophy and International Studies, University of Hull, UK. She has written on active learning, online learning and research methods teaching. She is the recipient of numerous awards in recognition of the quality and innovation of her teaching, such as a National Teaching Fellowship from the UK Higher Education Academy.

Simon Lightfoot, University of Leeds, UK
Simon Lightfoot is a senior lecturer in European Politics at the University of Leeds, UK. He is editor (with Cathy Gormley-Heenan) of *Teaching Politics and International Relations* (Palgrave, 2012) and is on the editorial board of the *Journal of Contemporary European Research*. He is a National Teaching Fellow and holds a University Student Education Fellowship from the University of Leeds. In 2009 he won the Political Studies Association's Bernard Crick Prize for Outstanding Teaching.

Jennifer K. Lobasz, University of Delaware, USA
Jennifer K. Lobasz, PhD (University of Minnesota, 2012) is an assistant professor at the University of Delaware, with a joint appointment in the Department of Political Science and International Relations and the Department of Women and Gender Studies. Her teaching and research interests include critical international relations theories, gender and global governance, religion and politics, and trafficking in persons. Prof. Lobasz currently serves as President of the International Studies Association – Northeast.

David Malet, University of Melbourne, Australia
David Malet is Senior Lecturer in International Relations at the University of Melbourne. Previously he was the founding Director of the Center for the Study of Homeland Security at Colorado State University. From 2000 to 2003 he served as a defense and foreign policy aide to United States Senate Majority Leader Tom Daschle. His dissertation research on transnational militant recruitment was published as *Foreign Fighters* (Oxford University Press, 2013). During 2011–14, he led a study funded by the US Environmental Protection Agency to analyze the use of social media in public risk communications following bioterrorist incidents. After student-teaching at a Massachusetts high school, he earned a BS in Education and a teacher certification.

Michael P. Marks, Willamette University, USA
Michael P. Marks is a professor of Politics at Willamette University in Salem, Oregon, where he teaches courses on international relations and comparative politics. He received his MA and PhD in Government from Cornell University. Prof. Marks is the author of three books, including *The Prison as Metaphor: Re-Imagining International Relations* and most recently *Metaphors in International Relations Theory*. His current

research and writing interests include the use of metaphors in international relations theory, pedagogical techniques and the role of the media in politics.

Heidi Maurer, Maastricht University, the Netherlands
Dr. Heidi Maurer is an assistant professor in European Studies at the Department of Political Science at the Faculty of Arts and Social Sciences at Maastricht University. She has been the 2012/13 Austrian Marshall Plan Foundation Fellow at the Center for Transatlantic Relations (CTR) at the School for Advanced International Studies (SAIS) at Johns Hopkins University in Washington DC. Heidi's research interests focus on EU foreign policymaking and European diplomacy. Since joining Maastricht University, she has also engaged actively in research about alternative teaching methods and in particular Problem-Based Learning. With Simon Lightfoot she co-edited a 2014 special issue on 'Old and New Tools for Student Engagement' in *European Political Science*.

E. Fletcher McClellan, Elizabethtown College, USA
E. Fletcher McClellan is Dean of Faculty and Professor of Political Science at Elizabethtown College, Elizabethtown PA, USA. Before becoming Dean, he served as Interim Provost, Associate Dean of Faculty and Chair of the Department of Political Science at Elizabethtown. His principal areas of interest are the American presidency, public administration and democratic theory. He contributed to the APSA monograph *Assessment in Political Science* (2010) and has delivered numerous conference presentations on teaching and learning in political science. He served on the executive council of the Political Science Education section of APSA. He holds a bachelor's degree in Government from Franklin and Marshall College, a master's degree in Political Science from East Tennessee State University and a doctorate in Political Science from the University of Tennessee–Knoxville.

William J. Miller, Flagler College, USA
William J. Miller is the Director of Institutional Research and Effectiveness at Flagler College, where he also teaches in both Political Science and Public Administration. He received his PhD from the University of Akron in 2010 in Urban Studies and Public Affairs. Previous education has included a master's degree in Applied Politics from the Ray C. Bliss Institute for Applied Politics at the University of Akron, an MA in Political Science from Ohio University and a BA from the Ohio University Honors Tutorial College. He focuses his research on campaigns and elections, public opinion toward public policy and events (especially attitudes within the Muslim world), and the pedagogy of political science. His research appears in *Journal of Political Science Education*, *Journal of Political Marketing*, *Studies in Conflict & Terrorism*, *International Studies Quarterly*, *Nonproliferation Review*, *Afro-Americans in New York Life and History*, *Journal of South Asian and Middle Eastern Studies*, *American Behavioral Scientist*, *PS: Political Science & Politics*, and *Journal of Common Market Studies*.

Matthew J. Moore, California Polytechnic State University, USA
Matthew J. Moore is Associate Professor of Political Science at California Polytechnic State University in San Luis Obispo, CA. He received a PhD in Political Science from the Johns Hopkins University in 2004. His specialty is political theory, and he has published on value pluralism, theories of legal interpretation, the philosophy of Ludwig Wittgenstein, political theory as a discipline and Buddhist political thought.

Elizabeth A. Oldmixon, University of North Texas, USA
Elizabeth A. Oldmixon is Associate Professor of Political Science at the University of North Texas. She is formerly a Fulbright Scholar at University College Cork (Fall 2010) and an American Political Science Association Congressional Fellow (2001–02). Her research and teaching interests include legislative policymaking, religion and politics, and Irish, Israeli and American politics.

Agnieszka Paczynska, George Mason University, USA
Agnieszka Paczynska is Associate Professor at the School for Conflict Analysis and Resolution, George Mason University and Co-Principal Investigator of the FIPSE-funded Undergraduate Experiential Learning Project (UELP). She is the co-editor of the book series Studies in Conflict, Justice, and Social Change (Ohio University Press). Her research interests include the relationship between economic and political change and conflict, distributive conflicts, the relationship between globalization processes and local conflicts, and post-conflict reconstruction policies. She is the author of *State, Labor, and the Transition to a Market Economy: Egypt, Poland, Mexico and the Czech Republic* (Penn State University Press, 2013, updated edition) and has published in the *Review of International Political Economy*, *New Political Science*, *PS: Political Science & Politics* and *Eastern European Politics and Societies*, among others.

Gabriela Pleschová, Comenius University in Bratislava, Slovakia
Gabriela Pleschová teaches at the Department of East Asian Studies at Comenius University in Bratislava. Her background is in Political Science, and in 2012 she graduated from the MSc program in Education (Higher Education) offered by Oxford University. Since 2004, she has been coordinating workshops and other development activities for beginner teachers in higher education. Currently she serves as the Chairperson of the ECPR standing group Teaching and Learning Politics as well as a member of the editorial board of the *Journal of Political Science Education*. She is co-editor with Eszter Simon of *Teacher Development in Higher Education: Existing Programs, Program Impact and Future Trends*, which was published by Routledge in 2012. In 2013 she become Senior Fellow of the Higher Education Academy.

Chad Raymond, Salve Regina University, USA
Chad Raymond is Associate Professor of Political Science and International Relations at Salve Regina University, where he teaches in the undergraduate Political Science and Global Studies majors and in the graduate program in International Relations. He has a PhD in Political Science from the University of Hawai'i at Manoa and bachelor's and master's degrees in the same field from MIT. His research interests and publications fall into two general areas: the political economy of development, especially as applied to Asia and the Middle East, and evaluating the effectiveness of teaching methods used in the university classroom. He is the managing editor of the Active Learning in Political Science blog at http://activelearningps.wordpress.com.

Erin Richards, Cascadia College, USA
Erin Richards earned a master's degree and completed doctoral coursework in Political Science at Washington State University. She has been teaching in the Washington State Community College system since 2005, and joined Cascadia Community College in 2007 where she is a Senior I Tenured faculty member. She served on the planning committee

for the APSA Teaching and Learning Conference, is a current member of the APSA Political Science Education section council and is the 2013–14 President of the Pacific Northwest Political Science Association. Her teaching interests include American government, state and local government, and women in politics. She also teaches International Relations, Comparative Government, Introduction to Politics, and any other course that needs teaching.

Boris E. Ricks, California State University, Northridge, USA
Boris E. Ricks is an associate professor of political science at California State University, Northridge. Prof. Ricks specializes in urban politics, state and local politics, racial and ethnic politics, environmental justice, public policy, political leadership, public administration, and health disparities. He is a former Andrew Mellon Postdoctoral Fellow in the Politics Department at Pomona College (2004–06). He is also former Assistant Professor of Political Science at the University of Missouri, Kansas City (2006–08). He received his PhD from the University of Southern California (MA in Political Science), Master of Public Administration (MPA) from the University of Mississippi and Bachelor of Science (Honors) in Criminal Justice from Mississippi Valley State University. Ricks is an advocate of Civic Engagement. His scholarly research has appeared in the following publications: *National Political Science Review*, *Journal of American Ethnic Studies*, *Journal of Rhetoric and Public Affairs* and the *Encyclopedia of African American Religion and Politics*, not to mention several book chapters, book reviews, monographs and technical reports. Prof. Ricks has been awarded several research grants including the prestigious Robert Wood Johnson Foundation Award, CSUN-RIMI Research Grant and CSBS Summer Research Grant.

Robert G. Rodriguez, Texas A&M University–Commerce, USA
Robert G. Rodriguez is an assistant professor of political science at Texas A&M University–Commerce. Prof. Rodriguez teaches courses in comparative and American politics, and is the recipient of two All-Texas A&M System Student Recognition Awards for Teaching Excellence. He has also been named 'Faculty of the Year' by the A&M–Commerce Office of Hispanic Outreach and Student Programs, and was nominated for the Paul W. Barrus Distinguished Faculty Award for Teaching as well as an A&M–Commerce Faculty Senate Teaching-Classroom Award. His research focuses on Latin American politics in addition to the intersections between politics and sports in the USA and abroad. In 2009, he published a book entitled *The Regulation of Boxing: A History and Comparative Analysis of Policies among American States*.

J. Simon Rofe, SOAS, University of London, UK
J. Simon Rofe is Senior Lecturer in the Centre for International Studies and Diplomacy at SOAS, University of London. He is Founding Chair of the British International Studies Association Learning and Teaching Working Group (https://sites.google.com/site/bisaltwg/), and a founding member of the ECPR Standing Group (SG) on Teaching and Learning Politics. His pedagogic research focuses upon the application of Technology, Online and Distance Learning. His publications include 'The IR Model and E-moderating', a case study in Gilly Salmon, *E-Moderating: The Key to Teaching and Learning Online*, 3rd edition (Routledge Falmer, 2011) and 'The "IR model": A Schema for Pedagogic Development through the Integration of Learning Technologies into

Distance Learning (DL) Programmes in International Relations', *European Political Science*, 10(1) (2011). His broader research interests lie in the field of US Diplomacy and Foreign Relations in the twentieth century.

James M. Scott, Texas Christian University, USA
James M. Scott is Herman Brown Chair and Professor of Political Science at Texas Christian University, and he specializes in foreign policy analysis and international relations. He is the author of seven books and more than sixty articles, book chapters, review essays and other publications. He has been conference organizer and President of both the International Studies Association's Foreign Policy Analysis section and the ISA's Midwest region. He has also been a two-time winner of the ISA-Midwest's Klingberg Award for Outstanding Faculty Paper. Since 1996 he has received over two dozen awards from students and peers for teaching, research and research mentoring. He directed the Democracy Interdependence and World Politics Summer Research Program, a National Science Foundation Research Experience for Undergraduates, from 2005–14. He is currently an associate editor of *Foreign Policy Analysis*. In 2012, he received the Quincy Wright Distinguished Scholar Award from the ISA-Midwest for outstanding scholarship and service.

Elizabeth Sheppard, University of Tours, France
Elizabeth Sheppard is Associate Professor and Head of the International Relations Program at François Rabelais University, Tours, France where she teaches International Relations and American Studies. She is heavily invested in teaching and learning innovation, particularly in large lecture classes, and is involved with the ECPR Standing Group on Teaching and Learning. She has written a number of articles on the subject, notably on the use of simulations and technology in the classroom.

Eszter Simon, Masaryk University, Czech Republic
Eszter Simon is Postdoctoral Fellow at Masaryk University in the Czech Republic and recurring Visiting Professor in the Center for North American Studies at the Economics University in Bratislava, Slovakia. Her research interest includes counterinsurgency, foreign policy analysis, American foreign policy, and Central European politics. Currently, she researches the role of communication technology in superpower conflicts. She has also been active in teaching and learning issues, co-editing a book about instructional development (*Teacher Development in Higher Education*, Routledge), publishing articles in *Journal of Political Science Education* and *European Political Science*, and teaching at ECPR's Teaching and Learning Politics Summer School.

Brian Smentkowski, Appalachian State University, USA
Brian Smentkowski (Ph.D. 1993, Political Science, University of Kentucky) is Associate Director of Faculty and Academic Development and Research Professor of Government and Justice Studies at Appalachian State University. He previously was Associate Professor of Political Science, Associate Dean of the College of Liberal Arts, and Co-Directing Faculty Associate of the Center for Scholarship in Teaching and Learning at Southeast Missouri State University. He has presented and published widely in political science and faculty development, with recent works appearing in *Transformative Dialogues, International Journal of Teaching and Learning in Higher Education*, and *Tea Party Effects on the 2010 US Senate Elections*. He is co-author of *Misreading the Bill of*

Rights (2015) with Kirby Goidel and Craig Freeman. His current teaching and research interests investigate the nexus of law, politics, and social justice, as well as the scholarship of teaching, learning, and engagement.

Elizabeth T. Smith, University of South Dakota, USA
Elizabeth T. Smith is an associate professor of political science and the Associate Director of the Farber Center for Civic Leadership at the University of South Dakota. Her teaching focuses on American politics and public administration and her research interests center on public participation in political and civic life.

J. Cherie Strachan, Central Michigan University, USA
J. Cherie Strachan received her doctorate in Political Science from the State University of New York at Albany in 2000. She is currently Director of the Women and Gender Studies Program, Co-Director of the Civic Engagement Division and Professor of Political Science at Central Michigan University. She is the author of *High-Tech Grassroots: The Professionalization of Local Elections*, as well as numerous articles and book chapters. Her recent publications focus on the role of civility in a democratic society, as well as on college-level civic education interventions intended to enhance students' civic skills and identities. Her applied research, which focuses on facilitating student-led deliberative discussion sessions and on enhancing campus civil society, has resulted in an affiliation with the Kettering Foundation. She can be reached at strac1jc@cmich.edu.

Paul E. Sum, University of North Dakota, USA
Paul E. Sum is Professor and Chair of Political Science at the University of North Dakota. Sum's research addresses citizen mobilization in post-communist countries, especially Romania. His publications investigate voting behavior and other forms of political participation, public opinion, civil society development and political parties of the radical right. A dedicated teacher, Sum also has published a number of studies on assessment of student learning outcomes in higher education. He has served as a consultant and evaluator for a number of agencies including the OSCE, US Department of State, World Bank and the Romanian Ministry of Education.

Stephen Thornton, Cardiff University, UK
Stephen Thornton is Senior Lecturer and Programme Director, Politics at the Department of Politics and International Relations, Cardiff University, UK. He has published widely on the topic of information literacy in the Politics classroom in both Europe and the USA. He does write about other subjects too, his latest book being *Demolishing Whitehall: Leslie Martin, Harold Wilson and the Architecture of White Heat* (co-written with Adam Sharr, Ashgate, 2013).

Simon Usherwood, University of Surrey, UK
Dr. Simon Usherwood is Associate Dean for Learning and Teaching in the Faculty of Arts and Human Sciences, University of Surrey. His background is in Comparative and European Politics, on which he has taught and published extensively. Pedagogically, his primary interest is in the use of simulation games in higher education, which he has used widely, including in courses on negotiation. As well as research publications in this field, he has also produced various web-based resources. He is a regular contributor to the Active Learning in Political Science blog.

Brandon Valeriano, University of Glasgow, UK
Brandon Valeriano is a senior lecturer in global security at the University of Glasgow in the School of Social and Political Sciences. Dr. Valeriano's main research interests include investigations of the causes of conflict and peace as well as the study race/ethnicity from the international perspective. Ongoing research explores interstate rivalry, classification systems of war, arms buildups, cyber conflict, popular culture and foreign policy, and Latino foreign policy issues. He recently published a book on the origins of rivalry (*Becoming Rivals*, Routledge, 2012) and a book on China, Tibet and Hollywood (Palgrave, 2012). His main focus is on two forthcoming books, *Cyber Hype versus Cyber Reality* at Oxford University Press and *Russian Coercive Diplomacy* at Palgrave.

Wendy L. Watson, University of North Texas, USA
Dr. Wendy L. Watson is a senior lecturer and pre-law advisor at the University of North Texas. Her research and teaching interests include constitutional law, judicial process, quantitative methods, and issues of equal access to justice for the economically disadvantaged.

Introduction
John Ishiyama, William J. Miller and Eszter Simon

THE IMPORTANCE OF TEACHING AND LEARNING IN POLITICAL SCIENCE

While education departments have long studied methods of teaching, strategies for implementing high-impact practices, tactics for assessment and the design of syllabi and various other course materials in their efforts to train future primary and secondary teachers, other academic disciplines have failed to focus on such skills—even in doctoral programs. Faculty in political science spent their college careers learning about the discipline. Across the subfields, higher education has shown a remarkable ability to produce subject-matter experts. Today's instructors unquestionably leave graduate school knowing a great deal about *what* they will be expected to teach, but, without taking education courses of their own volition, do they know *how* to teach it? While some programs have begun making concerted efforts to train teachers—as well as scholars—it still seems normal for students to enter academia with only minor experience as teaching assistants without formalized training. As a result, they are forced to teach themselves how to teach, typically relying on their own past experiences and the advice of those around them. In short, they learn as they go.

Nonetheless, the importance of teaching and learning has undeniably grown in the discipline in the past decade. National, regional and international political science conferences have recognized the value (in terms of both pedagogy and scholarship) of teaching and learning, and consequently have allocated time for tracks devoted to looking at what and how political scientists teach. For example, the Teaching and Learning Politics Group of the European Consortium of Political Research (ECPR) had five pedagogy-focused panels at its 2012 conference in Bordeaux; and the Annual Meeting of the Midwest Political Science Association featured 11 panels covering teaching and learning in Chicago in 2014. At these conferences, best practices and ideas are disseminated and discussed in an effort to improve pedagogy within the political science classroom.

Moreover, the pedagogy of political science and international relations has become a conference theme in its own right. Eleven years ago, the American Political Science Association (APSA) hosted the inaugural Teaching and Learning Conference in Washington, DC. Recognizing the importance of the teacher–scholar model, APSA brought in 40 political scientists and graduate students to discuss approaches, techniques and methodologies for increasing student attainment in the political science classroom. Following this small pilot meeting, the conference celebrated its tenth anniversary in February 2014 with more than 300 attendees. Europe followed suit with the first Europe-wide teaching and learning conference for political scientists in Maastricht in June 2014, jointly organized by ECPR, the British International Studies Association (BISA), the Political Studies Association (PSA) in the UK and the UACES (the academic association for contemporary European Studies).

It has not been only through conferences that teaching and learning research has been shared with the discipline, however. In January 2005, the first issue of the *Journal of Political Science Education* was published, under the direction of John Ishiyama and Marijke Breuning at Truman State University. Held under the Undergraduate Education Section of APSA (with nearly 450 members), the journal has become an invaluable resource for instructors hoping to increase their understanding of evidence-based teaching techniques and curricular innovations. Other US-based journals (e.g. the *Journal of Public Affairs Education*, the *eJournal of Public Affairs*, *Perspectives on Political Science*) have similarly looked at issues concerning teaching and learning. While these journals have dedicated themselves to studying pedagogy in political science and international relations, *PS: Political Science & Politics* and *European Political Science* have long made efforts to include teaching and learning research in their publications. In Europe, the ECPR journal, *European Political Science*, not only regularly publishes articles on pedagogical issues, but, similarly to the British journal, *Politics*, produced a special teaching and learning issue in 2013.

For faculty, this new direction reflects a desire to improve teaching techniques and curriculum decisions—all in the effort to improve student learning within political science and international relations programs. Perhaps even more importantly, this line of research has permitted faculty who are asked to focus primarily on teaching to maintain a strong research agenda without having to stretch themselves thin worrying about pedagogical research being undervalued. Teaching and learning research, rather, may be viewed as even more valuable in teaching-centered institutions. In short, the past ten years have demonstrated a recognized effort to better understand political science pedagogy.

Nonetheless, while our discipline has taken great strides in the past decade to give value to the scholarship of teaching and learning, conference presentations and journal articles tend to focus more on the results of pedagogical experiments than the nuts and bolts of how to transfer them into other classrooms. Indeed, they already presuppose a certain level of pedagogical knowledge. As a result, they may not, on face value, be as useful for new instructors or those searching for new inspiration and ideas after years of teaching. Moreover, conference papers and journal articles disseminate information regarding whether some method successfully impacted student learning, but less attention is typically paid to applicability to different settings and procedures for applying the method to another classroom. Other efforts, such as the biannual ECPR Teaching and Learning Summer School, are more helpful in this respect, but they can only impact a small number of scholars at a time.

GOALS OF THE HANDBOOK

We find it important to reach out to as many as our colleagues as possible. Therefore, this handbook aims to speak to all faculty in political science and international relations—from those nervously entering a classroom for the first time in their lives to those who seemingly etched their first lecture on a stone tablet. Authors have been asked to write to both a novice and experienced audience and to attempt to provide concrete examples of best practices as much as possible. Given our stated concerns regarding the pedagogical preparation of new instructors in political science and international relations, the scope of the book is intended to allow first-time instructors to read on a particular topic, understand its importance and pull useful ideas that could be utilized within their own classroom. We do not suggest that these chapters represent an exhaustive coverage of any particular topic. Instead, we recognize that different faculty who read will have their own ideas or tidbits related to the material covered. In this way, we simply hope that the handbook will serve as a base on which faculty (both rookies and veterans alike) can build. In others words, knowing that much of what faculty in political science and international relations do in the classroom has been borrowed and adapted from others, we hope that the handbook will succeed in planting seeds and introducing new strategies and tactics of learning that will spur further innovation. In addition, his handbook has been designed to account for teaching at institutions of various levels—from small, private liberal arts colleges in the USA to research-intensive universities across Europe. And we have attempted to assure that materials can be taken and used in instructors' own classrooms.

APPROACH OF THE HANDBOOK

This handbook is committed to the principles of student-centered education, in which instructors move beyond traditional lecture-style information delivery toward a more participatory and interactive learning environment. Thus, learning no longer focuses on information transfer and instructors cease to be the sage on the stage. Rather, they become a guide on the students' side.

The popularity of student-centered instruction in the past decades stems from its superior ability over traditional lecturing or teacher-centered instruction in fostering both the motivation and the preparation of students. As such, it has proven more effective in fostering deep learning. Deep learning, as opposed to surface learning, points beyond the mere memorization of information and aims to enable students to understand and reflect on the meaning of new information, relate it to previous knowledge, practice and experience, and to differentiate between evidence and information (Ramsden 1988; Weimer 2002).

Much of the pedagogical research related to political science and international relations has focused on student-centeredness and such deep learning. While the imparting of content knowledge remains highly relevant, there are increased calls for adequately preparing students to be able to read, write and exercise sound critical thinking. Deep learning can be fostered only by developing students' skills as well as subject knowledge. Additionally, given the fundamental ideals surrounding the study of government and politics, our particular discipline is one in which writing, reading and creative thinking should play a fundamental role when determining successful student outcomes. And students should leave with a sense of self-efficacy, prepared and able to apply these skills to the content knowledge disseminated throughout their time in school or to new information shared at their workplace.

Thus student-focused education actively involves students in the learning process. Political science and international relations is well suited to assure students have numerous opportunities to apply their classroom knowledge. Given the significant number of governmental bodies, non-profit organizations and agencies impacting political decisions across the world, it is not surprising that internships are a ripe learning opportunity for students in political science and international relations. In many cases, undergraduates can undertake numerous internships over their academic careers (at varying levels and branches of government) in an effort to discover where they believe they would most enjoy attempting to work post graduation.

Nor are these internships necessarily tied to the student's individual country. Study-abroad opportunities permit students to experience government work in other nations (or with international organizations). Through these experiences, students become active participants in their education and gain knowledge that cannot be simply explained in a textbook or via a lecture. While internships and study abroad are prime examples of deep learning, they may not be possible for all students. Simulations held within a class can help provide students with a more practical understanding of what they are studying. Model United Nations, Model Arab League and mock legislatures are regularly used campus wide, while numerous other class-based simulations have been created to help make politics real for students.

Likewise, students in political science and international relations can easily participate in community-integrated learning (also referred to as community service, experiential learning or service learning). In this environment, colleges and universities partner with organizations within their community to give students opportunities to exercise classroom knowledge in projects designed to assist some facet of life in their society. Beyond helping town–gown relationships, the projects offer the students the potential for great meaning. If community-integrated learning is not possible in a given context, political science and international relations opens numerous doors for extracurricular activities for students to participate in—including, but not limited to, guest speakers, public meetings and campaign events. Lastly, political science and international relations have proven to be fertile ground for both capstone projects within disciplines and more generalized undergraduate research. As a discipline that is impacted hourly by events in the world, political science and international relations offer regular opportunities for new questions and techniques—not all of which require a graduate degree or formal methods of training to be meaningfully explored.

When students 'learn by doing' inside or outside the classroom, their motivation and preparation, which are crucial for learning to take place, are likely to improve markedly. Moreover, since learning-centered instruction assumes different levels of knowledge and skills on the part of the learners, it can be a successful resolution of the instructor's dilemma of often having to teach three courses at once for the average, advanced and struggling students. It does so by recognizing that everyone brings different knowledge and skills to the learning process and that learning is—or can be—a joint, interpersonal effort (Huba and Freed 2000, p. 33).

Student-centered instruction requires a conceptual change from both the instructors and the students. When successful, such conceptual change covers the five cornerstones of student-centered education. First, the balance of power shifts from the instructors toward the students so that power is shared. Second, such a shift redefines the role of instructors into one in which they are primarily responsible for creating a successful learning environment and assessing whether learning is taking place, rather than whether teaching is well received. They become guides for students to reach a predetermined outcome. Third, instructors no longer use assessment merely to grade students, but also to provide feedback and guidance in the learning process. Fourth, students' responsibility for their own learning increases. Finally, in this framework the function of content knowledge also changes, in that, besides establishing the foundation for further learning, it also becomes a means through which skills are developed (Weimer 2002; Huba and Freed 2000; Blumberg 2009).

OVERVIEW OF SECTIONS

The chapters that follow have been broken into three sections. In the opening section, authors examine the macro-level of pedagogy in political science and international relations: curriculum and course design. Topics covered include undergraduate curriculum design, capstone courses, graduate curriculum design, professional development, distance learning, civic engagement, program assessment, performance assessment, course-based assessment, multidisciplinarity, information literacy, the Bologna Process and promoting employability and job skills. The second section of the handbook moves to a meso-level, examining particular subject areas within political science and international relations. Subject areas examined in this section include the introduction to politics course, conflict, diversity, gender politics, undergraduate and graduate research methods, political theory, controversial topics, two-year institutions, international relations and teaching practitioners. These chapters provide broad overviews of strategies and tactics proven effective in the classroom. The final section takes us to the micro-level, focusing on techniques within the classroom that have the potential to be successful in assuring student learning. Techniques discussed include designing a syllabus, integrating technology, designing simulations, group work, team-based learning, problem-based learning, undergraduate research, experiential learning, utilizing literature and film, course-based writing, lecturing and classroom management, conducting scholarship related to teaching and learning and promoting student discussion.

CONCLUSION

In short, this handbook has been compiled in order to fill a noted gap in the political science and international relations literature: it is a comprehensive, discipline-specific guide for faculty interested in becoming better teachers. While the past decade has brought forth a flurry of academic scholarship related to teaching and learning, graduate students and current faculty still must largely rely on materials prepared by non-political scientists when trying to hone their craft in the classroom. The handbook has been put together with the intention of being accessible regardless of years in the classroom, type of institution or familiarity with the concepts covered. In short, we hope that readers of our handbook will emerge better teachers.

REFERENCES

Blumberg, P. (2009), *Developing learner-centered teaching: a practical guide for faculty*, San Francisco, CA: Jossey-Bass.

Huba, M.E. and Freed, J.E. (2000), *Learner-centered assessment on college campuses: shifting the focus from teaching to learning*, Boston, MA: Allyn & Bacon.

Ramsden, P. (1988), 'Studying learning: improving teaching', in P. Ramsden (ed.), *Improving learning: new perspectives*, London: Kogan Page, pp. 13–31.

Weimer, M. (2002), *Learner-centered teaching: five key changes to practice*, San Francisco, CA: Jossey-Bass.

PART I

CURRICULUM AND COURSE DESIGN

1. Best practices in the American undergraduate political science curriculum
E. Fletcher McClellan

This chapter describes various models for organizing the undergraduate political science major.[1] Though debate and discussion of the proper goals and structure of the political science curriculum go back to the founding of the discipline (Ishiyama, Breuning and Lopez 2006), the present review focuses on activities in the USA since the 1980s to reform the major.

Curriculum reform efforts in political science have taken place in the midst of reform waves in higher education. The circumstances surrounding the last reform effort sponsored by the American Political Science Association (APSA), the 1991 'Wahlke Report' on liberal education and the political science major (Association of American Colleges 1990; Wahlke 1991), are illustrative. After several years of studies criticizing academic majors as loosely organized collections of distribution requirements and faddish electives (Association of American Colleges 1985; Zemsky 1989), the Association of American Colleges (AAC) called on disciplinary associations to formulate recommendations to 'strengthen study-in-depth' (Association of American Colleges 1990). In response, APSA appointed a task force with John Wahlke from the University of Arizona as chair. Sharing AAC's view that depth of understanding cannot be reached 'merely by cumulative exposure to more and more subject matter', the authors of the political science report set out to design a model that featured sequential learning, 'building on blocks of knowledge that lead to more sophisticated understanding . . . leaps of imagination . . . and efforts at synthesis' (Association of American Colleges 1990, p. 131).

Following a similar process, three distinct curricular frameworks in the discipline have developed since the Wahlke Report. The drive for greater student civic and political engagement began with the service-learning movement of the late 1980s and 1990s (Battistoni and Hudson 1997). Outcomes-based curricula grew as part of the assessment movement, which evolved from external demands for accountability (National Commission on Excellence in Education 1983; National Governors Association 1986) and increased interest in student learning within the academy (Study Group on Conditions of Excellence in Education 1984; McClellan 2009). More recently, the successor to AAC, the Association of American Colleges and Universities (AAC&U), spearheaded the use of 'high-impact practices' (HIPs) as a means to broaden and deepen student attainment of 'essential learning outcomes' (Kuh 2008).

Despite the array of curricular models with high potential for increasing student learning, the political science curriculum at most institutions remains organized by distribution requirements. After describing the four alternatives to the distribution model and their status in the discipline, the final section of this chapter will address the question of why the political science curriculum appears impervious to change.

THE DISTRIBUTION MODEL AND CURRICULUM REFORM BEFORE 1990

Judging from the occasional reports on the political science curriculum commissioned by APSA over the past century, leaders in the discipline recommended different goals and approaches to the undergraduate major at different times. From the early 1900s through the 1930s, the consensus view was that the major should instill in students substantive knowledge of governmental institutions and practical training for public service. World War II brought about a fundamental shift in thinking, leading to numerous reports criticizing the descriptive and practical approach and favoring curriculum reforms that would promote critical thinking and other intellectual skills (Ishiyama, Breuning and Lopez 2006).

Influenced no doubt by the Cold War, curriculum reformers in the early 1950s advocated responsible citizenship as the goal of political science education. The APSA report, *Goals for Political Science*, emphasized skill development and citizenship training through an integrated curriculum with fewer courses. Critics of the report did not dispute the objective of producing critical thinkers, but disagreed with harnessing liberal learning to civic education (Fesler et al. 1951).

Although reform efforts stirred vigorous debate within the profession, they had little discipline-wide impact, according to a review conducted by Ishiyama, Breuning and Lopez (2006). Even the authors of APSA reports acknowledged the difficulty of imposing a standard curriculum on departments of different sizes residing in different types of institutions. Furthermore, the number of recognized subfields in the discipline grew from four in 1915 to eight during World War II to 60 in the early 1970s (Association of American Colleges 1990).[2]

If anything resembling a standard for the political science major existed in the years leading to the Wahlke Report, it was the distribution model. An APSA survey of departments in 1987–88 showed that only one-half of departments required an introduction-to-politics course. More often, departments required several introductory courses – American government, comparative politics, international relations and political theory, respectively – and a choice of upper-level courses in all or most of the same subfields plus a methods course (Association of American Colleges 1990). Less than a quarter of departments required courses in other subfields such as public administration, public policy and public law.

Looking at the 1987–88 survey results, the Wahlke task force condemned what it called a collective picture of 'disparate and unstructured practices aptly described . . . as not so much experiences in depth as they are bureaucratic conveniences' (Association of American Colleges 1990, p. 134). This harsh critique not only reflected the negative tone of 1980s national studies toward the lack of coherence in liberal arts majors, but it echoed previous reform analyses in political science. More strongly than prior studies in the discipline, however, Wahlke attempted to link curricular integrity to liberal learning.

THE BUILDING-BLOCK MODEL, CRITICAL THINKING AND THE WAHLKE REPORT

The Wahlke panel proposed a sequential model upon which students would build increasingly sophisticated structures of knowledge and develop intellectual skills. According to the report, the goal of the curriculum was not to produce 'good citizens' or train future government workers; rather, political science instruction should turn 'politically interested and concerned students into politically literate college graduates, whatever their career plans or other interests' (Association of American Colleges 1990, p. 134).

Intended not as a model curriculum but as guidelines for political science programs to work toward the aims and objectives of liberal education, the Wahlke Report recommended the following structure for the major:

- a common introductory course (ideally, introduction to politics, but if departmental capacity was limited, introduction to American government taught in comparative context);
- a capstone experience in the senior year, such as a senior seminar or research project, which would give students the opportunity to integrate and synthesize prior learning; and
- exposure to analytical approaches and methods of inquiry, normative and empirical, through a specific scope and methods course, an applied course such as public policy, or across the curriculum (Association of American Colleges 1990).

Interestingly, the report took care not to recommend specific subfields for the major or anything that would smack of a distribution requirement. Instead, the task force proposed that students be introduced to a common set of core topics such as ethical dimensions of government, the role of law and public policy (Association of American Colleges 1990).[3] By organizing learning experiences on those topics in traditional courses or through other vehicles, departments would enable students to acquire the knowledge and skills necessary to read, comprehend and analyze contemporary political texts.

The underlying assumption of the Wahlke Report was that curricular coherence led to higher student achievement, and a line of research supports that claim. Breuning, Parker and Ishiyama (2001) showcased the positive effects (favorable exit interviews and surveys, insightful portfolios, nationally normed exam results above the national average) of the Truman State program, which is highly structured (introductory and capstone courses, methods sequence, seven or eight required courses) and integrated (writing, speaking, critical thinking and research skills are developed and assessed throughout the major). Ishiyama and Hartlaub (2003) compared two differently organized political science programs and discovered that the more structured program (Truman State) was better at developing abstract and critical thinking skills. Ishiyama (2005b) examined political science curricula at 32 colleges and universities, and found that programs arranged more along the guidelines of the Wahlke Report (more common courses, senior capstone and early methods course) produced greater learning in terms of better political science field test scores than did less structured programs.

Despite the evidence in support of the building-block model, the Wahlke Report had limited impact on the discipline as a whole. Exploring the websites of 193 Midwestern political science programs, Ishiyama (2005a) determined that only 18 percent had a common introductory course, methods course and capstone experience, approximating the Wahlke model. Political science programs in combined departments were less likely to require all three elements of the approach, a finding that suggested resource limitations as one explanation for the Wahlke Report's small footprint.

On the other hand, the inability or unwillingness of most departments to embrace the Wahlke Report did not mean that the study was inconsequential. The report's call for more authentic means of evaluating program effectiveness, beyond job and graduate placement rates, presaged outcomes assessment activities in political science over the next two decades (McClellan 2009). Additionally, Wahlke asserted the importance of context in political studies, calling upon faculty to supply the comparative, international, and ethnic and cultural diversity backgrounds of subject matter in all relevant courses (Association of American Colleges 1990). Most importantly for the purpose of this study, the idea of organizing the political science major into building blocks, analogous to natural science curricula, continues to be the Holy Grail for many curriculum reformers.

THE POLITICAL ENGAGEMENT MODEL AND CIVIC EDUCATION

Civic education and involvement have been traditional emphases of political science since the beginnings of the discipline. Internships in government and politics are features of many if not most political science programs. Indeed, the entire fields of public administration and public policy have their origins in training students for government work and public problem-solving. More generally, the profession has justified the value of a political science degree in part by its capacity to develop the knowledge and skills needed to lead and serve the community.

The discipline has not always privileged civic involvement in the political science curriculum, as noted above, but interest was rekindled in the late 1980s and early 1990s with the rise of the service-learning movement and the establishment of national service programs (Battistoni 2013). In 1996 APSA president Elinor Ostrom initiated the association's commitment by establishing a task force on civic education, and a year later, political scientists contributed a volume to the American Association for Higher Education (AAHE) series on service learning in the disciplines (Battistoni and Hudson 1997).

The cause of promoting civic and political involvement among young adults has acquired greater urgency in the past two decades, with studies showing declining social capital with each new generation (Putnam 2000), decreasing youth voting turnout through 2000, and increasing political distrust (Harward and Shea 2013). The situation was exacerbated by the harsh ideological and partisan rhetoric of the Gingrich–Clinton years, and has escalated during the George W. Bush and Obama presidencies. Political engagement advocates were further discouraged when surveys indicated that political interest and activity among young adults declined despite increased volunteer service activities (Sax 2004). Some studies revealed that students preferred community service to political participation as a way to solve social problems (Creighton and Harwood 1993).

Within the political science discipline, some scholars criticized a curriculum that was at best ambivalent about the significance of political participation (McCartney 2013). To counter pessimism about the effectiveness of civic education efforts, the Carnegie Foundation and other foundation supporters launched the Political Engagement Project (PEP) in the early 2000s (Colby et al. 2007).

The PEP researchers studied over 1000 undergraduates who participated in 21 different political programs and courses between 2001 and 2005. Each of the courses and programs included at least one 'pedagogy of engagement', such as service-learning projects, internships, meetings with political leaders or participation in simulations such as Model UN. Administering pre- and post-tests to the students, Colby and colleagues found increased levels of political knowledge, skills and motivation to participate in politics or government. The increases were larger among students who entered these programs or courses with low levels of political interest. Furthermore, these changes in political understanding took place without significant differences in the students' partisan and ideological orientations (Colby et al. 2007).

Efforts to promote political engagement (PE) accelerated with the establishment of the American Democracy Project in 2003 by the American Association of State Colleges and Universities (AASCU) in partnership with the *New York Times*. Now involving 250 universities, the project sponsors many forms of civic involvement including voter education, special days of action and reflection such as Constitution Day, and community service projects. Within this larger project nine state universities are involved in the continuing Carnegie PEP (American Association of State Colleges and Universities 2013).

The 2012 release of *A Crucible Moment* by a national task force appointed by AAC&U and the US Department of Education continued the momentum for PE. Higher education institutions were put on notice to take 'essential actions' to promote civic and political engagement (National Task Force on Civic Learning and Democratic Engagement 2012). The following year, APSA released *Teaching Civic Engagement: From Student to Active Citizen*, the culmination of 15 years of disciplinary work (McCartney, Bennion and Simpson 2013).

Though PE activity has undoubtedly increased at the course level, there is little widespread information about political science departments that have successfully integrated political engagement in their programs or indeed made PE the primary goal in their curricula. To be sure, there are interdisciplinary majors, minors and certificates in civic engagement, some housed in political science (Meinke 2013). Among political science curricula, however, there are only a few recorded examples of how departments have structured PE activities to develop knowledge, skills and dispositions toward effective political action (McHugh and Mayer 2013; Smith and Graham 2014). Consequently, it is probably premature to call PE a fully developed curriculum model at this point, but the potential is there.

THE OUTCOMES-BASED MODEL, DEVOLUTION AND STANDARDIZATION

With the surge of interest in political engagement over the last decade, the debate within the discipline has arisen as to what the goals and techniques of political science education should be. The sharpness of this dispute is not obvious at first glance. Almost all members of the profession support the idea that political science should advance liberal learning, and almost all believe it is appropriate to teach citizen duties in some pedagogical situations (Hunter and Brisbin 2003). Even the Wahlke Report, which downplayed citizenship training, stated that all students should have the opportunity to experience real-life political situations off campus through internships, participation in electoral politics or study abroad (Association of American Colleges 1990).

However, few faculty members would question their obligation to teach critical thinking skills, while a 2003 survey of APSA members revealed that fewer than half of them believed it was their duty to provide civic education (Hunter and Brisbin 2003). Further evidence of this divide can be shown by looking at the learning outcomes statements of political science departments. Before we explore this issue, let us examine how an outcomes-based approach to the political science curriculum compares with the distributive, building-block and PE models.

Outcomes assessment in political science comes down to four questions for departments and individual instructors. First, what should political science undergraduates know and be able to do? Second, what are the best ways to promote student achievement of desired knowledge and skills? Third, by what standards and means can we measure the extent to which students are achieving what we want them to learn? Finally, how can we use student achievement evidence to improve political science programs and individual instruction? (Deardorff, Hamann and Ishiyama 2009).

By focusing on student learning, outcomes-based models are neutral as to whether a building-block, distribution or other curriculum structure is optimal for students. Indeed, a pure outcomes approach would be indifferent to the traditional course, credit-hour and seat-time model. Whatever structure or mode of instruction promotes the most learning at a reasonable cost is best, though critics argue the model in practice serves different agendas and has meant 'at the least cost' (Bennett and Brady 2012). The explosion of online or connected learning programs, including Massively Open Online Courses (MOOCs), and the rising interest in competency-based or mastery-learning modules stem from these premises (Fain 2014; Jankowski et al. 2013).

As to which curricular goals political scientists value most, the outcomes model in the USA devolves the responsibility to departments to decide what is appropriate for their programs. With some degree of variation across regional accrediting agencies, institutions are permitted to define the learning goals appropriate to their missions (Young, Cartwright and Rudy 2014). Within constraints set by the accrediting body and individual colleges or universities, academic departments have autonomy to define program and course outcomes.

Looking at learning outcomes in political science departmental websites, we can get a sense of the diversity of the discipline around the issue of curriculum goals. Only tentative generalizations can be made, since only around one-quarter of a random sample of departments, including those in doctoral-granting institutions, provided clear learning outcomes on the Web (Young, Cartwright and Rudy 2014). Focusing on a sample of baccalaureate degree-only programs in political science, McClellan and Maurer (2014) found that 37 percent listed outcomes. The remainder did not provide any learning objectives (24 percent) or provided vague goals in narrative style (39 percent).[4]

Within that group of BA-separate programs with specific outcomes, nearly all departments specified the acquisition of concepts, models and factual knowledge in the discipline as a learning objective (McClellan and Maurer 2014). Eighty percent of programs promoted the development of fundamental skills such as writing, researching, and critical and analytical thinking. Reflecting the lower priority among political scientists of fostering political engagement, slightly less than one-half of departments mentioned political involvement, effective citizenship or civic engagement as outcomes. Relatedly, specific experiential learning activities such as study abroad and internships were cited as goals in one-quarter of the sampled programs. Over 40 percent of programs stated an outcome of preparation for graduate or professional school, public service jobs or careers in general.[5]

Thus the outcomes-based model provides departments with the flexibility to define learning goals and objectives, the structure of the curriculum and the mode of instruction. Assessment pioneers such as Alverno College and King's College in Pennsylvania have specified competency levels for intellectual skills and, in Alverno's case, effective citizenship. Typically, these institutions have constructed matrices and rubrics to track individual and program success in achieving desired competencies at different stages of the college career (Banta et al. 1996).

Although assessment practice is decentralized in political science and the USA generally, there are efforts to bring about greater standardization of outcomes across institutions. As an example of an important US initiative, AAC&U developed so-called VALUE (Valid Assessment of Learning in Undergraduate Education) rubrics for 15 competencies as part of its Liberal Education for America's Promise (LEAP) project. The competencies were derived from the LEAP 'essential learning outcomes' (National Leadership Council and Liberal Education for America's Promise 2007). Not only were intellectual and practical (teamwork and problem-solving) skills included, but there were also rubrics for intercultural competence and civic engagement (Rhodes 2010). AAC&U formed partnerships with several state higher education systems and public liberal arts colleges to align transfer policies around the idea of competencies.

It is possible, therefore, that the language and assessment of some outcomes favored by political science departments could be regularized. For the foreseeable future, though, the widespread use of the outcomes-based model will reflect and even reinforce the lack of curricular consensus within the discipline.

THE HIGH-IMPACT PRACTICES MODEL AND STUDENT ENGAGEMENT IN POLITICAL SCIENCE

To promote student mastery of the LEAP learning outcomes and competencies, AAC&U strongly encourages institutions to adopt 'high-impact' educational practices. These activities include first-year seminars, learning communities, writing-intensive courses, undergraduate research, cross-cultural experiences such as study abroad, community-based learning, internships, and capstone courses and projects (Kuh 2008). What makes these experiences impactful is that, when done well, they engage students and bring to life effective principles of teaching and learning: high learning expectations, faculty–student interaction, student time on task, frequent feedback on student performance, peer cooperation, and respect for diversity and different ways of knowing (Kuh 2008; Pascarella and Blaich 2013).

The student engagement research links HIPs to use of deep (higher-order, integrative, reflective) learning experiences as reported by first-year and senior students in the National Survey of Student Engagement (NSSE) (Kuh 2008; Kuh and O'Donnell 2013). These experiences are in turn correlated with positive gains in self-reported learning (Kuh 2008; Kuh and O'Donnell 2013) and direct measures of critical thinking and orientation toward continuous intellectual development, according to the Wabash National Study (Pascarella and Blaich 2013).

The effectiveness of HIPs in promoting learning is good news for political science. According to NSSE, senior political science majors are far more likely than majors in other disciplines to study abroad, participate in internships and complete a capstone course or experience (National Survey of Student Engagement 2010). Around one-half of political science majors are involved in capstones, a higher proportion (along with history) than in any other major (National Survey of Student Engagement 2010). The 40 percent of political science majors who study abroad far exceeds the national average of 14 percent (Kuh and O'Donnell 2013). As for other HIPs, political science ranks in the middle of all majors with regard to students conducting research with a faculty member and engaging in service learning (National Survey of Student Engagement 2010).

In fact, many political science students are likely to participate in multiple HIPs during the college career, which should give the discipline an advantage in making claims about the value of a political science education. A strong, positive relationship exists between students' cumulative participation in multiple HIPs and self-reported gains in deep learning (Finley and McNair 2013). Moreover, there is considerable literature in political science detailing the positive learning effects of specific engaging experiences such as first-year learning communities (Huerta 2004), civic engagement and service learning (Battistoni and Hudson 1997; McCartney, Bennion and Simpson 2013), internships (McLauchlan 2013), and undergraduate research (Ishiyama and Breuning 2003). Most of these studies document the impact of a particular experience or program at a single institution on student learning of knowledge and skills.

This research provides promising opportunities for reform in the political science major. Departments can strengthen student learning by organizing packages of HIPs. With the possible exception of capstone courses, which are often required in the major, political science programs routinely offer HIPs such as internships as opportunities, and advise students to enroll in such programs. However, departments could require specific HIPs or a choice of HIP options for all majors in order to maximize learning for all political science students. This would especially benefit groups such as first-generation students, transfers, African Americans and Hispanics, who are underrepresented participants in some HIPs and who register greater learning gains from HIP participation than do the rest of the population (Kuh 2008; Kuh and O'Donnell 2013; Finley and McNair 2013).

Unfortunately, it is difficult to find examples of political science departments making efforts to provide multiple HIPs to all students and documenting the possible cumulative effects on student learning. As part of a university initiative to implement HIPs to promote student learning of LEAP outcomes, the University of Wisconsin–Whitewater is conducting such an enterprise (Johnson 2012). By offering a first-year seminar, writing-intensive course, pre-law learning community and internship program, the department aims to have nearly all majors participate in more than one HIP. The effects of these experiences on retention, self-reported learning and student satisfaction are mixed so far, at the beginning stages of the program.

To be sure, requiring or increasing the opportunities for political science students to engage in HIPs is easier said than done. Study abroad can be a costly option for students (and institutions). Activities such as undergraduate research supervision are time intensive for faculty. So too are the placement and oversight of students in internships and service-learning experiences, although strong administrative support can assume some of the workload. As the final section will explore, this raises the question of whether there are sufficient incentives for political science faculty to focus on teaching rather than research (McCartney 2013). When the choice involves curriculum change or teaching activities that are perceived as demanding and time-consuming, the conflict becomes even more acute.

THE PERSISTENCE OF THE DISTRIBUTION MODEL AND THE FUTURE OF CURRICULUM REFORM

In their review of the history of curriculum reform in the discipline, Ishiyama, Breuning and Lopez (2006) say the story is one of 'continuity and (little) change'. It is hard to disagree. The building-block model proposed by the Wahlke Report was not widely adopted. Few departments organize their curricula around civic and political engagement, though its various pedagogies have increased appeal and demonstrated effectiveness (McCartney, Bennion and Simpson 2013). Outcomes-based models are widespread and provide departments with the flexibility to prioritize educational goals and structure their programs and pedagogies accordingly, but they do not appear to have produced much in the way of curricular innovation. High-impact practices are extensively used in the discipline but are largely viewed as program options rather than as essentials.[6]

This leaves the distribution model as winner and still champion of the political science curriculum title. In its defense, the model has more going for it than just administrative convenience. There is a building-block pattern in having students take a series of introductory subfield courses, followed by upper-level courses in the same areas. This structure may not promote higher-order skills such as integrated learning, but knowledge acquisition and skill development take place nonetheless. Students in political science are ranked highly in analytical reasoning and critical thinking (Jones 1992; Pascarella and Terenzini 2005). In the controversial study *Academically Adrift*, which assessed critical thinking and writing competency as measured by the Collegiate Learning Assessment (CLA), social science students, including political science majors, outscored students in the arts, humanities and professional programs, and nearly equaled natural science and mathematics majors (Arum and Roksa 2010).

Still, critics of the distribution approach argue that a sequential or engagement model can do a better job of promoting deeper learning. As supporting evidence for alternative models accumulates, why does the discipline appear so resistant to curricular change? Ishiyama, Breuning and Lopez (2006) suggest four reasons. First, the structure of incentives in the profession favor research productivity over quality teaching, particularly if teaching involves a large commitment of time. This has particularly hampered efforts to promote civic education and engagement (McCartney 2013).

Second, disciplinary leaders have held negative attitudes toward curriculum reform in general and civic education in particular. Third, past curriculum reform efforts have been dominated by scholars from large research institutions, ignoring faculty from undergraduate teaching institutions who could contribute the most and have the most at stake (Ishiyama, Breuning and Lopez 2006).

The fourth reason – no institutional forums existed to discuss ideas for curriculum reform or teaching and learning generally – is less true today than a decade ago. Stimulated by the activities of the APSA Teaching and Learning Committee and the Political Science Education section, the establishment of the APSA Teaching and Learning Conference in 2004, and new publication outlets such as the *Journal of Political Science Education*, there is increased interest in the scholarship of teaching and learning (SoTL) among political scientists (Craig 2014).

These discipline-wide activities should produce a robust literature on curriculum reform. So far, unfortunately, this has not been the case. Instead, most SoTL research has focused on course-level teaching interventions (Craig 2014). Reasons for this might include the greater ease with which individual faculty can conduct such research and the difficulty of comparing curricular models empirically. Regardless of the explanation, the dearth of discussion about the state of the political science major from those who have had the greatest scholarly and professional interest is disappointing.

Curriculum inertia in political science can be explained not only by the structure and norms of the discipline, but also by market pressures and increased oversight of colleges and universities by federal and state regulators and regional accreditors. It may be that institutional or departmental control of academic programs has been overridden by curriculum mandates and efficiency-driven initiatives from external stakeholders (Slaton 2014). In other words, even if a political science department wanted to change its major requirements in order to promote greater learning or engagement, it might not have the decisional autonomy or resources to accomplish the change.

Nevertheless, interest in political science curriculum reform is increasing once again (Ishiyama, Breuning and Lopez 2006; Mealy 2013). If APSA commissions another blue-ribbon panel, it will have to take into account extraordinary changes surrounding higher education, the discipline within the profession and, as this review has described, the emergence of new alternatives to traditional ways of organizing the curriculum.

The biggest obstacle to curriculum reform remains the inability of the discipline to come to an agreement on the goals of political science education. If no agreement can be reached, it might be best for the next 'report to the profession' to admit candidly that there is no one right way to organize the political science major. Then we can proceed to identify the curricular and pedagogical conditions under which different goals can be achieved. This may be the way to avoid the failures of past reform efforts, and provide our students with the best chances for success.

NOTES

1. An earlier version of this chapter appeared as: McClellan, E. Fletcher and Brianna Maurer (2014), 'After Wahlke: new models for organizing the undergraduate political science major and the prospects for

reform', presented at the American Political Science Association Teaching and Learning Conference, 7–9 February 2014, Philadelphia, PA.
2. As of 2013, there are 43 organized sections in APSA. In addition, the program for the 2013 annual APSA meeting lists 69 related groups.
3. Some of the core topics, however, are similar to introductory courses in subfields such as political theory.
4. Following the finding that PhD-granting institutions are less responsive to outcomes assessment demands (Young, Cartwright and Rudy 2014), McClellan and Maurer (2014) focused on BA-granting departments only.
5. The contour of these findings is similar to that described by Ishiyama and Breuning (2008). In their analysis of the learning outcomes from 50 political science department assessment plans (which included graduate degree-granting institutions), they found that two-thirds of departments mentioned knowledge of theories, political institutions and processes, and around 60 percent mentioned intellectual skills such as critical thinking and writing. Only 24 percent listed effective citizenship as an outcome, and 22 percent mentioned an objective of promoting career goals. On the other hand, the McClellan and Maurer (2014) findings suggest greater departmental attention, at least among undergraduate programs, to political engagement and career outcomes.
6. This study recognizes that there are more curricular frameworks than the five presented here. For example, values-based models can point curricular structure, offerings and pedagogy toward a particular ideal such as social justice. Often these values will be derived from an institution's educational mission, as is the case with faith-based colleges. In their survey of outcomes in political science programs, McClellan and Maurer (2014) found 15–20 percent of programs contained value-oriented or faith-based outcome statements. The models presented in this chapter were those that are either widely used (distribution model), widely discussed in the discipline (building-block and political engagement), or widely found in the literature on student learning (outcomes and high-impact practices).

REFERENCES

American Association of State Colleges and Universities (2013), 'American democracy project', available at http://www.aascu.org/programs/ADP/ (accessed 19 July 2013).
Arum, Richard and Josipa Roksa (2010), *Academically Adrift: Limited Learning on College Campuses*, Chicago, IL: University of Chicago Press.
Association of American Colleges (1985), *Integrity in the College Classroom: A Report to the Academic Community*, Washington, DC: Association of American Colleges.
Association of American Colleges (1990), 'Political Science', in *Liberal Learning and the Arts and Sciences Major: Volume Two – Reports from the Fields*, Washington, DC: Association of American Colleges, pp. 131–49.
Banta, Trudy W., Jon P. Lund, Karen E. Black and Frances W. Oblander (eds) (1996), *Assessment in Practice: Putting Principles to Work on College Campuses*, San Francisco, CA: Jossey-Bass.
Battistoni, Richard (2013), 'Preface', in Alison Rios Millett McCartney, Elizabeth A. Bennion and Dick Simpson (eds), *Teaching Civic Engagement: From Student to Active Citizen*, Washington, DC: American Political Science Association, pp. xiii–xvi.
Battistoni, Richard M. and William E. Hudson (eds) (1997), *Experiencing Citizenship: Concepts and Models for Service-Learning in Political Science*, Washington, DC: American Association for Higher Education.
Bennett, Michael and Jacqueline Brady (2012), 'A radical critique of the learning outcomes assessment movement', *Radical Teacher*, **94** (Fall), 34–47.
Breuning, Marijke, Paul Parker and John T. Ishiyama (2001), 'The last laugh: skill building through a liberal arts curriculum', *PS: Political Science & Politics*, **34** (3), 657–61.
Colby, Anne, Elizabeth Beaumont, Thomas Ehrlich and John Corngold (2007), *Educating for Democracy: Preparing Undergraduates for Responsible Political Engagement*, San Francisco, CA: Jossey-Bass.
Craig, John (2014), 'What have we been writing about? Patterns and trends in the scholarship of teaching and learning in political science', *Journal of Political Science Education*, **10** (1), 23–36.
Creighton, J.A. and Richard C. Harward (1993), *College Students Talk Politics*, Dayton, OH: Kettering Foundation.
Deardorff, Michelle D., Kerstin Hamann and John Ishiyama (eds) (2009), *Assessment in Political Science*, Washington, DC: American Political Science Association.
Fain, Paul (2014), 'Going all in on proficiencies', available at http://www.insidehighered.com/news/2014/02/14/university-maine-presque-isle-drops-grades-proficiencies-across-its-curriculums (accessed 14 February 2014).

Fesler, James, Louis Hartz, John H. Hallowell, Victor G. Rosenblum, Walter H.C. Laves, W.A. Robson and Lindsay Rogers (1951), 'Goals for political science: a discussion', *American Political Science Review*, **45** (December), 996–1024.

Finley, Ashley and Tia McNair (2013), *Assessing Underserved Students' Engagement in High Impact Practices*, Washington, DC: Association of American Colleges and Universities.

Harward, Brian M. and Daniel M. Shea (2013), 'Higher education and the multiple modes of engagement', in Alison Rios Millett McCartney, Elizabeth A. Bennion and Dick Simpson (eds), *Teaching Civic Engagement: From Student to Active Citizen*, Washington, DC: American Political Science Association, pp. 21–40.

Huerta, Juan Carlos (2004), 'Do learning communities make a difference?', *PS: Political Science & Politics*, **37** (April), 291–6.

Hunter, Susan and Richard A. Brisbin Jr (2003), 'Civic education and political science: a survey of practices', *PS: Political Science & Politics*, **33** (4), 759–63.

Ishiyama, John (2005a), 'Examining the impact of the Wahlke report: surveying the structure of the political science curriculum at liberal arts colleges and universities in the Midwest', *PS: Political Science & Politics*, **35** (March), 71–4.

Ishiyama, John (2005b), 'The structure of an undergraduate major and student learning: a cross-institutional study of political science programs at thirty-two colleges and universities', *The Social Science Journal*, **42**, 359–66.

Ishiyama, John and Marijke Breuning (2003), 'Does participation in undergraduate research affect political science students?', *Politics & Policy*, **31** (1), 163–80.

Ishiyama, John and Marijke Breuning (2008), 'Assessing assessment: examining the assessment plans at 50 political science departments', *PS: Political Science & Politics*, **41** (January), 167–70.

Ishiyama, John, Marijke Breuning and Linda Lopez (2006), 'A century of continuity and (little) change in the undergraduate political science curriculum', *American Political Science Review*, **100** (November), 659–65.

Ishiyama, John and Stephen Hartlaub (2003), 'Sequential or flexible? The impact of differently structured political science majors on the development of student reasoning', *PS: Political Science & Politics*, **36** (1), 83–6.

Jankowski, Natasha, Pat Hutchings, Peter Ewell, Jillian Kinzie and George Kuh (2013), 'The Degree Qualifications Profile: what it is and why we need it now', *Change: The Magazine of Higher Learning*, **45** (6), 6–14.

Johnson, Susan M. (2012), 'Incorporating high impact practices into a political science curriculum', presented at the annual meeting of the Western Political Science Association, 22–24 February 2012, Portland, OR.

Jones, Elizabeth A. (1992), 'Is a core curriculum best for everybody?', in James L. Ratcliff (ed.), *Assessment and Curriculum Reform*, San Francisco, CA: Jossey-Bass, pp. 37–46.

Kuh, George D. (2008), *High Impact Practices: What They Are, Who Has Access to Them, and Why They Matter*, Washington, DC: Association of American Colleges and Universities.

Kuh, George D. and Ken O'Donnell (2013), *Ensuring Quality & Taking High-Impact Practices to Scale*, Washington, DC: Association of American Colleges and Universities.

McCartney, Alison Rios Millett (2013), 'Teaching civic engagement: debates, definitions, benefits, and challenges', in Alison Rios Millett McCartney, Elizabeth A. Bennion and Dick Simpson (eds), *Teaching Civic Engagement: From Student to Active Citizen*, Washington, DC: American Political Science Association, pp. 9–20.

McCartney, Alison Rios Millett, Elizabeth A. Bennion and Dick Simpson (eds) (2013), *Teaching Civic Engagement: From Student to Active Citizen*, Washington, DC: American Political Science Association.

McClellan, E. Fletcher (2009), 'An overview of the assessment movement', in Michelle D. Deardorff, Kerstin Hamann and John Ishiyama (eds), *Assessment in Political Science*, Washington DC: American Political Science Association, pp. 39–58.

McClellan, E. Fletcher and Brianna Maurer (2014), 'After Wahlke: new models for organizing the undergraduate political science major and the prospects for reform', presented at the American Political Science Association Teaching and Learning Conference, 7–9 February 2014, Philadelphia, PA.

McHugh, Mary and Russell Mayer (2013), 'The different types of experiential learning offered in a political science department: a comparison of four courses', in Alison Rios Millett McCartney, Elizabeth A. Bennion and Dick Simpson (eds), *Teaching Civic Engagement: From Student to Active Citizen*, Washington, DC: American Political Science Association, pp. 353–68.

McLauchlan, Judithanne Scourfield (2013), 'Learning citizenship by doing: integrating political campaign internships into political science coursework', in Alison Rios Millett McCartney, Elizabeth A. Bennion and Dick Simpson (eds), *Teaching Civic Engagement: From Student to Active Citizen*, Washington, DC: American Political Science Association, pp. 279–96.

Mealy, Kimberly A. (2013), '2013 APSA Teaching and Learning Conference track summaries', *PS: Political Science & Politics*, **46** (3), 343–63.

Meinke, Timothy (2013), 'Learning objectives and outcomes of an interdisciplinary minor in civic engagement', in Alison Rios Millett McCartney, Elizabeth A. Bennion and Dick Simpson (eds), *Teaching Civic Engagement: From Student to Active Citizen*, Washington, DC: American Political Science Association, pp. 337–52.

National Commission on Excellence in Education (1983), *A Nation at Risk: The Imperative for Educational Reform*, Washington, DC: US Government Printing Office.

National Governors Association (1986), *A Time for Results: The Governors' 1991 Report on Education*, Washington, DC: National Governors Association.

National Leadership Council for Liberal Education and America's Promise (2007), *College Learning for the New Global Century*, Washington, DC: American Association of Colleges and Universities.

National Survey of Student Engagement (2010), *Major Differences: Examining Student Engagement by Field of Study – Annual Results 2010*, Bloomington, IN: Indiana University Center for Postsecondary Research.

National Task Force on Civic Learning and Democratic Engagement (2012), *A Crucible Moment: College Learning and Democracy's Future*, Washington, DC: American Association of Colleges and Universities.

Pascarella, Ernest T. and Charles Blaich (2013), 'Lessons from the Wabash national study of liberal arts education', *Change: The Magazine of Higher Learning*, **45** (2), 6–15.

Pascarella, Ernest and Patrick T. Terenzini (2005), *How College Affects Students: Vol. 2. A Third Decade of Research*, San Francisco, CA: Jossey-Bass.

Putnam, Robert (2000), *Bowling Alone: The Collapse and Revival of American Community*, New York: Simon & Schuster.

Rhodes, Terrel L. (ed.) (2010), *Assessing Outcomes and Improving Achievement: Tips and Tools for Using Rubrics*, Washington, DC: Association of American Colleges and Universities.

Sax, L.J. (2004), 'Citizenship development and the American college student', *New Directions for Institutional Research*, **122**, 65–80.

Slaton, Amy E. (2014), 'Competency vs. open-ended inquiry', available at http://www.insidehighered.com/views/2014/02/21/essay-questions-benefits-rush-competency-based-education (accessed 21 February 2014).

Smith, Michael and The Honorable Bob Graham (2014), 'Teaching active citizenship: a companion to the traditional political science curriculum', *PS: Political Science & Politics*, **47** (3), 703–9.

Study Group on the Conditions of Excellence in American Higher Education (1984), *Involvement in Learning: Realizing the Potential of American Higher Education*, Washington, DC: National Institute of Education.

Wahlke, John C. (1991), 'Liberal learning and the political science major: a report to the profession', *PS: Political Science & Politics*, **24** (March), 48–60.

Young, Candace C., Debra K. Cartwright and Michael Rudy (2014), 'To resist, acquiesce, or internalize: departmental responsiveness to demands for outcomes assessment', *Journal of Political Science Education*, **10** (1), 3–22.

Zemsky, Robert (1989), *Structure and Coherence: Measuring the Undergraduate Curriculum*, Washington, DC: Association of American Colleges.

2. Capstone courses and senior seminars as culminating experiences in undergraduate political science education
Paul E. Sum

Capstone courses and senior seminars mark a transition for students and programs alike: students beginning their professional lives or pursuing graduate studies and faculty reflecting on successes and shortcomings among students in the graduating class (Hunter et al. 2012, p.xii). Such courses encourage students to synthesize and evaluate their university experience. At the same time, they present an opportunity for program assessment. In this respect, capstones elicit reflection from both students and faculty regarding how the many pieces of an undergraduate education fit together. Capstone experiences also round out a sequence of high-impact practices that enrich higher education endeavors and form the final stage of student development (Brownell and Swaner 2010).

Although other vehicles, such as senior theses, senior portfolio construction and required internships, might provide similar opportunities for student development and assessment, capstone courses and seminars are the most effective (Boyer 1987; Henscheid 2012). They are also the most frequently used culminating experience in higher education, with political science following the trend. In this chapter, I discuss the purposes of these culminating experiences for students and faculty. I then describe the frequency and characteristics of culminating experiences that American undergraduate political science programs use. I conclude with a discussion of best practices in designing and implementing capstones and seminars for a political science curriculum.

CAPSTONE COURSES AND SENIOR SEMINARS IN A POLITICAL SCIENCE CURRICULUM

Culminating experiences might be structured into a curriculum in many ways, including capstone courses, senior seminars, thesis projects, portfolio assembly, comprehensive subject examinations, internships and service-learning requirements, along with a host of career services opportunities. Of these, capstone courses and senior seminars are the most commonly used (Henscheid 2000; Levine 1998). Padgett and Kilgo (2012, p.11) find that 89 percent of all capstone experiences are course based.

In political science, the Wahlke Report called for greater intentionality in curriculum design (Wahlke 1991). The report recommended that political science undergraduate programs develop a sequential approach to their curricula so that concepts and methods build logically upon one another, with a capstone experience serving as the culmination. Evidence suggests that utilization of this approach increases knowledge of the discipline among political science graduates (Ishiyama 2005a, p.364). Critical thinking and problem-solving skills are also enhanced through a curriculum with a sequential design culminating in a capstone (Ishiyama and Hartlaub 2003, p. 85). Political science undergraduate programs responded to the call, with 39.9 percent (the plurality) using capstone courses or senior seminars as culminating experiences (Ishiyama 2005b, p. 72; Ishiyama 2009, p. 67). I focus on course-based delivered capstones because of the frequency of their use.

The difference between a capstone and a seminar is primarily one of opportunity to design depth and breadth into the course (Smith 1998, p. 90). A typical capstone course provides an overview of discipline themes, a review of sub-disciplines and a discussion of how to bridge gaps among theory, empirical observation and personal practice. A senior seminar, alternatively, is often narrower in focus with attention placed on one of the sub-disciplines of political science (e.g. political theory), a fundamental topic that spans sub-disciplines (e.g. human rights) or an interdisciplinary course that links the major to general education goals (e.g. politics and the arts). Instructors teaching a senior seminar often select an overriding theme around which the integrative process will be organized. Because of their somewhat limited scope, senior seminars tend to be more intensely focused in terms of subject matter.[1] However, capstones and seminars are united by two shared goals: student development and assessment (Rowles et al. 2004).

Capstones as Student Development

Capstone courses or senior seminars provide an outstanding forum for student development. They facilitate a process through which a student reflects widely on his or her experiences as an undergraduate. Thus student development through these courses does not hinge on the acquisition of new knowledge or skills but on conceptual internalization and integration.

Ideally, synthesis across the curriculum will be achieved as students begin to connect the dots of their own learning. Students refine their own understanding of the world as they contemplate how things they learned in one course (or other collegiate context) paved the way for greater understanding and success in another course (or other collegiate context). Connections among concepts gained from general education courses, political science courses and the wide array of other personal and professional experiences expand students' cognitive skills. The impact on students will vary widely because of the diversity they have experienced in their undergraduate careers, even within a common major such as political science.

Capstone courses and senior seminars take different forms and have dramatically different purposes depending on institutional context. 'They involve lectures, discussions, practica, independent study, and every conceivable combination thereof. They are taught by individual faculty, faculty teams, off-campus professionals, students, and anyone else you can imagine' (Levine 1998, p. 55). However, these courses and seminars share goals of depth and breadth of knowledge integrated within the major and linked to general education goals. The process is at the core of what is referred to as 'learning transfer'.

Transfer of learning is widely considered the highest goal for any educational setting. The term can be defined as the ability of students to take what is learned in the classroom and successfully apply it to similar situations outside the course context, extending to other courses as well as to students' professional lives (Marini and Genereux 1995).

Ideally, transfer creates a chain reaction so that prior learning positively impacts new learning; failure to achieve learning transfer is often tantamount to program failure. Capstones set the stage for this aspect of student development to continue into a lifelong learning endeavor. The implications are that lofty mission goals, such as student acquisition of ethics or civics, can be initiated through a program that instills this long-term aspiration and equips students to refine these characteristics for decades to come.

A key feature of a sequential curriculum is a culminating experience that leads to synthesis. A capstone course or senior seminar is explicitly integrative in purpose, meaning that it is designed to connect knowledge in the major discipline to the rest of a student's education, as determined by the mission statement of the program, as well as the broader institutional mission of the college or university (Ratcliff 1992). Mission-driven, a capstone course provides a political science perspective to a student's overall experience in higher education. In this respect, a capstone course or senior seminar might begin with a frank discussion of what it means to be a political scientist and how do we, as political scientists, think about the world differently compared to students who followed other disciplines? Capstone courses and senior seminars also synthesize the major sub-fields of the discipline through common conceptual themes, so that we, as political scientists, might ask how power, ideology, citizenship or legitimacy operates across the discipline sub-fields. Furthermore, a capstone serves as an impetus to provide students with a practical orientation to the discipline (Hauhart and Grahe 2010, p. 4). In other words, capstones open the door to discussing how we, as political scientists, apply the lessons from our discipline most effectively in our personal and professional lives.

The 'we' is important because capstone experiences signal a blurring of the division between faculty and student as undergraduates transition to their post-graduation lives. Synthesis does not stop with the past but looks to students' futures, so that the capstone should give attention to the transition to post-academic life, including consideration of personal and professional aspirations. For this reason, exercises in résumé writing and career development are sometimes included in capstones, less so in the more focused seminars. Capstone courses may also include service-learning, internship requirements or other forms of experiential learning that build a more tangible bridge to the future (Turner 2013).

The centerpiece for many capstones and senior seminars is the writing of a major research paper. Among these courses, 71.9 percent include a major project and 75.1 percent require an oral presentation (Henscheid 2000, p. 95). This trend is in keeping with the Carnegie Foundation recommendation that capstone experiences include a significant writing assignment that encapsulates conceptual, methodological and ethical themes from the major, as well as a public presentation of the project for critical review and discussion (Boyer 1987).

Major projects and presentations conducted through a capstone or seminar differ from a stand-alone senior thesis requirement in two important ways. First, expectations for a senior thesis often exceed those for a capstone course or senior seminar in terms of the depth in which the topic is pursued. Second, senior theses tend to incorporate a mentoring role for faculty who work one-on-one with the student (Ishiyama 2005b, p. 75). Generally, those teaching capstone courses and seminars advise and evaluate all course papers. The practice limits the amount of individualized attention that can be given to students. The strength of capstone courses and seminars is their ability to offer integrative experiences linked to structured discussions and in-class activities (Sum and Light 2010). Moreover, the emphasis on integrative learning found in capstones and seminars promises 'to bridge—at last—the long-standing cultural divide in which one set of disciplines, the arts and sciences, has been regarded as intellectual but not practical, while the professional fields are viewed as practical, but for that very reason, inherently illiberal' (Schneider 2004, p. 9). Even when a thesis is required 'approximately half (55.3%) of all project-based experiences were linked to one or more courses' (Padgett and Kilgo 2012, p. 11). Thus many stand-alone senior theses resemble a course-based model.

Choosing the form that a culminating experience will take interacts with more general curriculum debates that continue within political science (Ishiyama, Breuning and Lopez 2006). One debate centers on the balance a curriculum strikes between substantive knowledge of the discipline and skill sets, such as analytic thinking and effective communication. A second debate considers the relative weight that civic education should take in the curriculum. Capstone courses and seminars offer a unique opportunity for students to internalize the importance of civic engagement and civic literacy, should a department choose to design the course this way (Turner 2013, p. 3). For example, Johansson et al. (2008) found the capstone experience helped to cement an emerging civic identity among political science students, which was a recognized goal within a number of Swedish political studies departments. Thus capstones and seminars are flexible enough so that a program can be designed to put its best foot forward, articulating its core mission values. Capstones are an attractive option for many political science programs as a vehicle through which student development is finalized.

Capstones as Assessment

Capstone courses and senior seminars are attractive because they can so easily facilitate program assessment, which has become an imperative in higher education. Assessment is defined as 'the systematic collection, review, and use of information about educational programs, undertaken for the purpose of improving student learning and development' (Palomba and Banta 1999, p. 4). As an iterative process, assessment provides data on student learning outcomes. Faculty members use assessment output to evaluate the extent to which learning goals are being met. Assessment data then guides decisions to make changes to instruction or program design, the so-called 'closing-the-loop' stage. Assessment is a continuous process that faculty can and should embrace; however, it is vitally important for the department to undertake the assessment process collectively. Assessment needs to become part of an ongoing conversation among colleagues regarding how program mission goals and student learning outcomes are achieved (Massy, Graham and Short 2007).

Most political science programs have made assessment a priority (Ishiyama 2009). Demands for greater accountability, such as that articulated in the 2006 Spellings Commission Report, indicate a loss of public faith that institutions of higher learning are delivering on their promises of student learning outcomes, while, at the same time, the costs of education have ballooned. This crisis in legitimacy is not new, being identifiable as early as the mid-1980s; however, the response from the academy has been disjointed (Young 2009, p. 117).

Capstone experiences can be designed in different ways in order to accommodate a wide range of assessment tools that capture different student learning goals in different programs (Wagenaar 1993). The artifacts produced during a capstone course or senior seminar, such as a research paper and presentation, are natural objects for assessment and can connect directly to program goals. In this way, capstone experiences become excellent forms of summative assessment (Earl 2004). Nearly half of the institutions that offer capstone courses do so with the expressed purpose of assessing student learning outcomes (Henscheid 2000).

The relative flexibility of a capstone course or seminar does not make developing assessment measures any easier. In political science, mission goals sometimes include elements that are difficult to measure. For example, mission goals might include statements regarding ethical behavior, commitment to public service or engaged citizenship. The challenge of measuring such concepts begins with a departmental conversation regarding their meaning so that faculty members can voice their vision. The result may well be a rewritten mission statement that specifies a more modest goal, but this is what the call for accountability is about: demonstrating that students receive what programs claim they provide. Thus assessment links directly to the mission, and the capstone experience becomes the vehicle through which departments verify that students meet the mission goals.

Capstone experiences also offer an excellent opportunity to incorporate student participation in the assessment process. 'Through capstone courses, *students* take that second look at their own learning throughout their college experiences, and during the course of this look provide invaluable information to faculty about the quality of instruction and of programs' (Black and Hundley 2004, p. 3). Capstone courses and senior seminars provide an ideal setting to reintroduce students to the program mission goals and engage them as conscious partners in the assessment process. Student input can constructively add to the process through indirect assessment activities based on their perceptions and recollections. Indirect assessment might take place through course mapping exercises that ask students to identify courses where they gained specific skills and knowledge or open-ended surveys that ask students to convey what they felt were pivotal learning moments in their undergraduate careers (Sum and Light 2010, p. 525).

Students can also contribute, and learn from, direct forms of assessment. For example, students might engage in peer review of research papers through an assessment rubric, or score each other's oral presentations. In this way, capstone assessment moves from strictly summative in nature to include formative (assessment *for* learning). Capstone experiences might extend to assessment *as* learning activities as well. For example, requiring students to lead substantive discussions on major political science concepts allows for assessment by the instructor, but also becomes an aspect of student development as they synthesize what they have learned. It should not be surprising that capstone courses are regularly incorporated into political science undergraduate programs (Ishiyama 2009, p. 67). Below, I address the extent to which political science programs utilize culminating experiences as part of the core curriculum.

CAPSTONES AND SEMINARS IN POLITICAL SCIENCE

Institutions of higher learning, as a whole, have responded positively to the calls for enhancing student senior experiences and becoming more systematic in program evaluation. Capstone courses and senior seminars have been an important part of that response. The 1999 National Survey of Senior Seminars and Capstone Courses found that these forms of a culminating experience were the most widely used.

> More than 70 percent of sample respondents reported that senior seminars and capstone courses are discipline or department based [with] 75 percent used to foster integration and synthesis within the academic major, promote integration and connections between the academic major and the work world, and improve seniors' discipline-specific career preparation and preprofessional development. (Henscheid 2008, p. 83)

By 2011, nearly all institutions of higher learning offered capstone courses of some form to students, with 35.4 percent of the institutions in the sample reporting that every graduate has passed through a senior capstone experience (Padgett and Kilgo 2012, p. 5).

Discipline-specific figures regarding the use of capstones and senior seminars show that gaps still exist. For example, a study of psychology and sociology programs shows that 61 percent of the sample offer capstone courses (Hauhart and Grahe 2010, p. 8). In political science, the frequencies have been somewhat lower. Surveying political science programs, Ishiyama (2005b, p. 72) finds that 39.9 percent of political science programs require a senior seminar or capstone experience. Kelly and Klunk (2003, p. 453) report that 39.6 percent of political science programs utilize a capstone course for assessment purposes.

Survey instruments, such as those used by the studies referenced above, may suffer from selection bias since departments that are focused on learning assessment or believe the department has done a good job in this area may be overrepresented (Kelly and Klunk 2003, p. 451). With this possibility in mind, I approached the problem somewhat differently, drawing a sample from the list of those departments that maintain institutional membership in the American Political Science Association. APSA institutional members consist of a wide variety of departments and programs immune to the possibility of selection bias noted above.[2]

The APSA website provides a sampling frame of institutional members and their web links. Most departments were easily accessed on the Web and provided undergraduate program degree requirements and often course descriptions. I noted whether a program required a capstone course or senior seminar. I also noted if programs required students to write a senior thesis. Finally, I tallied other forms of culminating experiential requirements, including internships, student portfolios, service-learning activities or a major field examination.

Table 2.1 shows the results according to the highest degree in political science awarded. Departments that offer a PhD degree in political science make up the first category. A second category includes departments that offer an MA. Lastly I considered departments that offer no degree higher than a BA or a BS in political science. This third category included two types of programs: those that were exclusively political science departments and those that combined political science with other disciplines, commonly history, sociology or geography.

Table 2.1 Percentage of programs that have culminating experiences as part of their undergraduate curricula

Highest degree awarded	Seminar or capstone	Senior thesis	Other	Total	N
PhD	18.7	11.2	4.5	34.4	126
MA	33.3	11.3	5.3	50.0	150
BA/BS separate	48.4	13.0	4.9	66.3	184
BA/BS combined	51.3	11.0	5.5	67.9	109
All institutions	38.7	12.0	5.1	55.7	569

PhD-granting institutions total 134 on the APSA website, while there are 161 MA-granting institutions. Because of the relatively low numbers, I decided to review each of these programs. The process yielded minimal missing data due to a department not offering an undergraduate degree, not providing program requirements online or not maintaining functional websites. The final number of institutions reviewed was 126 PhD-granting departments and 150 departments that grant an MA as the highest political science degree. For BA-/BS-granting programs, the APSA lists 774 that are either separate departments (489) or combined-discipline departments (285). Because of this larger number, I drew a sample proportionately across these two types, numbering 300. Of these, seven departments either were not accessible via their websites or did not provide information about their requirements for undergraduate curriculum, resulting in a sample size of 293.[3]

The results show that capstone courses and senior seminars are the most common culminating experiences used by political science programs, with 38.7 percent listing such a requirement. The result is strikingly similar to those found in similar studies, lending to the validity of the figure. When we consider any form of culminating experience, 55.7 percent of APSA member institutions employ such a requirement.

The type of political science department, defined by the highest degree awarded, influences the likelihood of capstone courses or senior seminars. The use of capstones and seminars is not uniform across types of programs, with less than 20 percent of PhD-granting departments requiring one, while nearly half of the BA or BS departments require a capstone or seminar and MA-granting institutions fall in between. The pattern is very similar to that found in psychology and sociology, with capstones being used in 75 percent of programs with BA/BS as the highest degree awarded, 56 percent for MA programs and 22 percent in departments that offer a PhD (Hauhart and Grahe 2010, p. 8).

The type of department does not seem to matter with regard to other forms of culminating experiences. Approximately 12 percent of departments require a senior thesis and about 5 percent mandate some other form of requirement, such as an internship, service-learning activity, portfolio assemblage or major field examination. The difference between separate and combined BA or BS programs was minimal and well within the margin of error for forms of culminating experiences.

Two findings stand out. First, the use of capstone courses and senior seminars does not seem to have expanded over the years. There is sound evidence regarding the positive pedagogical gains associated with capstones, and many voices throughout the academy have called for their use (Gardner and Van der Veer 1998; Henscheid 2012, p. 93). Despite this, the number of political science departments using capstones in 2013 does not differ significantly from the figure for 2003. Second, the type of department matters. The reason relates in part to the extent to which faculty have become specialized; capstones require faculty who are generalists. Faculty can become focused on their own courses, perhaps a very limited number of undergraduate offerings in a research-intensive PhD department, growing away from the undergraduate degree program (Smith 1998, p. 85). PhD-granting institutions, by their very nature, gravitate much more toward fields of specialization because of the need for greater expertise offered to graduate students and the much larger faculties that are required to offer a doctorate. Additionally, according to the 2010–11 APSA Department Survey, PhD-granting institutions are much more likely to have political science enrollments that exceed 2000 students (81 percent for public institutions; 57 percent for private institutions), compared to those departments that offer only a BA or BS degree in political science (28 percent for public institutions; 3 percent for private institutions).[4]

TOWARD BEST PRACTICES

Capstone courses and senior seminars serve both students and faculty. As an aspect of student development, they integrate undergraduate knowledge and experiences, and promote student transition into the professional world. For faculty, capstones and senior seminars facilitate summative assessment, which provides an opportunity to determine the strengths and weaknesses of a program. For both, capstone experiences are reflective and oriented toward the future through evaluation of the past.

Although capstone experiences share these general characteristics, course content is as varied as the departments and programs that use them. Many programs organize a capstone around the production of a research paper that students present to the group. Research projects serve multiple purposes in student development, including synthesizing discipline themes, promoting critical analysis of a problem and refining written communication skills. Organized as simulated academic conferences, with the instructor serving as chair and discussant, oral presentations of student research facilitate discussions of broad discipline themes. With awareness of student learning objectives, rubrics for critical thinking and effective communication can be applied to theses and presentations as evidence of student skill sets. However, any number of activities might be part of a capstone course, depending on program learning goals and one's ability to assess. Some capstones include mandatory public service projects that are coupled with structured group discussions regarding such matters as purpose and effectiveness of their activities. Reflective essays and journals provide additional opportunities for student development and program assessment. Capstone courses might include students teaching a discussion section of one of the program's first-year survey courses. Learning through teaching is an effective way to encourage students to consider their former selves (sitting in that same survey course in some cases), reflecting on the most important things they have learned since then (Sum and Light 2010). Capstone courses might also include structured debates, which again force students to consider broad themes in political science and are ready-made artifacts for assessment. With forethought, rubrics can be developed for any capstone activity so that programs can capture the extent to which students have acquired the relevant skill sets.

The physical characteristics of departments also differ substantially in terms of number of enrollments, student–faculty ratios, depth and breadth of course offerings, and resource availability. Departmental cultures vary considerably, often reinforced through the relative weight afforded teaching and learning endeavors of faculty. For these reasons, and the many other points of variance across political science programs, it is not possible to advance a template for an ideal capstone experience. However, we might identify a number of sound practices that should be considered when designing or assessing a capstone experience, the main one being 'alignment'.

Alignment refers to the compatibility of different components of an educational endeavor, which might operate on a course or program level. Course alignment seeks compatibility among the student learning goals for the course, the teaching and learning activities of the course and the process through which goals will be assessed (Biggs 1999). Successful capstone courses and senior seminars achieve course-level alignment. If the goal is to provide an opportunity for students to synthesize their experiences in the major, the capstone must include learning activities that promote this reflection and assessment tools that capture the extent to which students achieve this goal. Course alignment should be at the heart of the decision whether to offer a capstone course, senior seminar or some other vehicle, with careful consideration as to what goals faculty want to achieve with the culminating experience.

Program alignment seeks compatibility among the capstone experience goals, wider institutional goals (e.g. program, department, college and university) and summative assessment procedures (Jacobs 2004). Successful capstone experiences need to be designed to reflect the wider institutional goals. Consideration must be given to how program and broader institutional goals are achieved so that assessment measures and techniques can be better calibrated (Massy 2003).

Course and program alignment in the development of capstone experiences can be difficult. The broad goals of integration and synthesis are difficult to match to teaching and learning techniques used by otherwise specialized faculty, pushing instructors out of their comfort zone (Levine 1998, p. 54). Assessing these goals can be equally challenging since 'synthesis' is an ambiguous, if not subjective, term. Program alignment poses additional challenges. Within many departments, fundamental understandings of mission goals remain unresolved, producing awkward silences or vocal frustration when broached. Program alignment forces these departmental issues to the fore. Constructive communication is needed for capstone implementation. Indeed, program alignment leads to increased collegiality and greater willingness among faculty to collaborate (Uchiyama and Radin 2009).

Program alignment must also address wider college and university goals. Sometimes a disjuncture exists between university administrative initiatives and departmental practices. The development of a capstone experience forces departments to consider this wider context. If a capstone experience is to successfully integrate student experiences, the wider goals of general education and university expectations must be taken into account.

Inherent in these questions of program alignment is a question of scope: is it possible to capture the entirety of an undergraduate experience? Designing a course that reaches too far will likely lack the depth of exploration sought in a capstone experience. Indeed, many departments choose to offer senior seminars that address only a sub-discipline of political science so that more attention can be given to synthesizing students' experiences. However, a focus that is too narrow limits the opportunities for synthesis. Thus departments must find a balance that is compatible with their mission.

The above refers to 'design quality' for capstone experiences. However, attention should also be given to 'implementation quality' (Massy, Graham and Short 2007, pp. 31–3). The implementation of capstone courses must occur in most cases with existing personnel and financial resources. The costs might be quite substantial in large departments since capstone courses and senior seminars will be more effective if class sizes are small. If multiple sections are offered, or faculty rotated year to year, the design of the course may change dramatically if the department has not clearly identified parameters around the culminating experience. Capstones may travel many roads but programs should aim for consistency. Thus, regardless of will, departments need the resources to implement successful capstones.

In the end, students and faculty benefit from including a capstone course or senior seminar within the curriculum. Students have the opportunity to reflect on their university experience and see why political science can be rightly referred to as a discipline, and how the discipline fits into a larger liberal arts approach. They also have an opportunity to engage in learning transfer, applying things they have learned to new contexts. For students, capstone experiences can bridge the gap between their academic and professional careers, providing a step toward lifelong learning. For faculty, capstone experiences are also a time to reflect. Program components can be reviewed and a number of alignment issues considered. Capstone experiences should provide the impetus for departmental communication and allow faculty to consider how they contribute to the major. For both, culminating experiences are not ends in themselves but new beginnings.

NOTES

1. I draw the distinction here for analytic clarity. In political science, however, we seldom see such a rigid distinction. Instead, the terms are frequently used interchangeably and in combination. For example, at Winthrop College, the political science program refers to a '*Capstone Senior Seminar*' (http://www.winthrop.edu/uploadedFiles/cas/politicalscience/PLSC490-001-KedrowskiAndVanAller.pdf), whereas at Bowen University, the term is '*Senior Capstone Seminar*' (http://bowen.pages.tcnj.edu/files/2010/10/POL498_Syllabus.pdf).
2. It is still quite possible that APSA membership contains a selection bias according to resource endowment or willingness to remain 'active' within the professional discipline in this way. I cannot deny this possibility, but my results are consistent with comparable studies that have utilized surveys.
3. The sample produced a margin of error of +/– 4.61 percent at the 95 percent confidence interval for BA- or BS-granting departments.
4. See https://www.apsanet.org/media/dsp/Enrollment1011APSA.pdf for a full overview of political science enrollments by department.

REFERENCES

Biggs, John (1999), *Teaching for Quality Learning at University*, Buckingham, UK: Society for Research in Higher Education and Open University Press.

Black, Karen E. and Stephen P. Hundley (2004), 'Capping off the curriculum', *Assessment Update*, **16** (1), 3.

Boyer, Ernest L. (1987), *College: The Undergraduate Experience in America*, New York: Harper & Row.

Brownell, Jayne E. and Lynn E. Swaner (2010), *Five High-Impact Practices: Research on Learning Outcomes, Completion, and Quality*, Washington, DC: Association of American Colleges and Universities.

Earl, Lorna M. (2004), *Assessment as Learning: Using Classroom Assessment to Maximize Student Learning*, Thousand Oaks, CA: Corwin.

Gardner, John N. and Gretchen Van der Veer (1998), 'The emerging movement to strengthen the senior experience', in John N. Gardner and Gretchen Van der Veer (eds), *The Senior Year Experience: Facilitating Integration, Reflection, Closure, and Transition*, San Francisco, CA: Jossey-Bass, pp. 3–20.

Hauhart, Robert C. and Jon E. Grahe (2010), 'The undergraduate capstone course in the social sciences: Results from a regional survey', *Teaching Sociology*, **38** (1), 4–17.

Henscheid, Jean M. (2000), *Professing the Disciplines: An Analysis of Senior Seminars and Capstone Courses*, Columbia, SC: University of South Carolina, National Resources Center for the First-Year Experience and Students in Transition.

Henscheid, Jean M. (2008), 'Institutional efforts to move seniors through and beyond college', *New Directions for Higher Education*, **144**, 79–87.

Henscheid, Jean M. (2012), 'Senior seminars and capstone courses', in Mary Stuart Hunter, Jennifer R. Keup, Jillian Kinzie and Heather Maietta (eds), *The Senior Year: Culminating Experiences and Transitions*, Columbia, SC: National Resource Center for the First Year Experience & Students in Transition, pp. 91–109.

Hunter, Mary Stuart, Jennifer R. Keup, Jillian Kinzie and Heather Maietta (2012), 'Introduction', in Mary Stuart Hunter, Jennifer R. Keup, Jillian Kinzie and Heather Maietta (eds), *The Senior Year: Culminating Experiences and Transitions*, Columbia, SC: National Resource Center for the First Year Experience & Students in Transition, pp. xi–xxiii.

Ishiyama, John (2005a), 'The structure of an undergraduate major and student learning: A cross-institutional study of political science programs at thirty-two colleges and universities', *Social Science Journal*, **42**, 359–66.

Ishiyama, John (2005b), 'Examining the impact of the Wahlke Report: Surveying the structure of the political science curricula at liberal arts and sciences colleges and universities in the Midwest', *PS: Political Science & Politics*, **38** (1), 71–5.

Ishiyama, John (2009), 'Comparing learning assessment plans in political science', in Michelle D. Deardorff, Kristin Hamann and John Ishiyama (eds), *Assessment in Political Science*, Washington, DC: The American Political Science Association, pp. 61–75.

Ishiyama, John and Stephen Hartlaub (2003), 'Sequential or flexible? The impact of differently structured political science majors on the development of student reasoning', *PS: Political Science & Politics*, **36** (1), 83–6.

Ishiyama, John, Marijke Breuning and Linda Lopez (2006), 'A century of continuity and (little) change in the undergraduate political science curriculum', *American Political Science Review*, **100** (4), 659–65.

Jacobs, Heidi H. (2004), *Getting Results with Curriculum Mapping*, Alexandria, VA: Association for Supervision and Curriculum Development.

Johansson, Kristina, Helene Hård af Segerstad, Håkan Hult, Madeleine Abrandt Dahlgren and Lars Owe Dahlgren (2008), 'The two faces of political science studies – junior and senior students' thoughts about their education and their future profession', *Higher Education*, **55**, (6), 623–36.

Kelly, Marisa and Brian E. Klunk (2003), 'Learning assessment in political science departments: Survey results', *PS: Political Science & Politics*, **36** (3), 451–5.

Levine, Arthur (1998), 'A president's personal and historical perspective', in John N. Gardner and Gretchen Van der Veer (eds), *The Senior Year Experience: Facilitating Integration, Reflection, Closure, and Transition*, San Francisco, CA: Jossey-Bass, pp. 51–9.

Marini, Anthony and Randy Genereux (1995), 'The challenge of teaching for transfer', in Anne MacKeough, Judy Lee Lupart and Anthony Marini (eds), *Teaching for Transfer: Fostering Generalization in Learning*, Mahwah, NJ: Lawrence Erlbaum Associates, pp. 1–19.

Massy, William F. (2003), *Honoring the Trust: Quality and Cost Containment in Higher Education*, San Francisco, CA: Jossey-Bass.

Massy, William F., Steven W. Graham and Paula Myrick Short (2007), *Academic Quality Work: A Handbook for Improvement*, Bolton, MA: Anker Publishing.

Padgett, Ryan D. and Cindy A. Kilgo (2012), *2011 National Survey of Senior Capstone Experiences: Institutional-Level Data on the Culminating Experience*, Columbia, SC: National Resource Center for the First Year Experience & Students in Transition.

Palomba, Catherine A. and Trudy W. Banta (1999), *Assessment Essentials: Planning, Implementing, Improving Assessment in Higher Education*, San Francisco, CA: Jossey-Bass.

Ratcliff, James L. (1992), 'What we can learn from coursework patterns about improving the undergraduate curriculum', *New Directions for Higher Education*, **54**, 5–22.

Rowles, Connie J., Daphene Cyr Koch, Stephen P. Hundley and Sharon J. Hamilton (2004), 'Toward a model for capstone experiences: Mountaintops, magnets, and mandates', *Assessment Update*, **16** (1), 1–2.

Schneider, Carol G. (2004), 'Practicing liberal education: Formative themes in the reinvention of liberal learning', *Liberal Education*, **90** (2), 6–11.
Smith, Barbara Leigh (1998), 'Curricular structures for cumulative learning', in John N. Gardner and Gretchen Van der Veer (eds), *The Senior Year Experience: Facilitating Integration, Reflection, Closure, and Transition*, San Francisco, CA: Jossey-Bass, pp. 81–94.
Sum, Paul E. and Steven A. Light (2010), 'Assessing student learning outcomes and documenting success through a capstone course', *PS: Political Science & Politics*, **43** (3), 523–31.
Turner, Charles C. (2013), 'State of the community: Students as political consultants', paper presented at the American Political Science Association Teaching and Learning Conference, Long Beach, California, 8–10 February, available at http://papers.ssrn.com/sol3/papers.cfm?abstract_id=2202397 (accessed 25 February 2014).
Uchiyama, Kay Pippin and Jean L. Radin (2009), 'Curriculum mapping in higher education: A vehicle for collaboration', *Innovative Higher Education*, **33**, 271–80.
Wagenaar, Theodore C. (1993), 'The capstone course', *Teaching Sociology*, **21**, 209–14.
Wahlke, John C. (1991), 'Liberal learning and the political science major: A report to the profession', *PS: Political Science & Politics*, **24** (1), 48–60.
Young, Candace C. (2009), 'Program evaluation and assessment: Integrating methods, processes, and culture', in Michelle D. Deardorff, Kristin Hamann and John Ishiyama (eds), *Assessment in Political Science*, Washington, DC: The American Political Science Association, pp. 117–39.

3. Teaching politics to practitioners
John Craig

Political science is generally taught as a non-vocational subject. While those who study it may aspire to pursue careers as politicians, diplomats, civil servants or pollsters, they do not generally have direct experience of these roles. Neither do political science courses generally provide the type of tailored preparation for practice that would be common in areas such as medicine or architecture. Students may be actively involved in politics as citizens and use the knowledge and skills that they develop through the study of politics in these activities. However, with the exception of those undertaking an internship, the nearest that many students will come to the professional world of politics is participation in a simulation. While simulations generally aim to recreate the experience of working in a political environment, for the most part students study the practice of politics from a distance, through reading, listening, debate and discussion.

The distinguishing feature of teaching politics to practitioners is the identity of the students. They are practitioners. They work in politics, government and related areas in their professional lives. As a result, the knowledge, skills and motivations that they bring to their studies will be different from those of people who do not share their experiences. From a student-centered learning perspective, practitioners form a distinct type of student and the design of the learning experiences provided should reflect their particular needs. This chapter will explore how this can be achieved. It will begin by exploring the different types of practitioner who may engage in the study of politics and consider some of the motivating factors involved. It will then examine aspects of curriculum design for practitioner-focused courses, before identifying a number of pedagogic strategies that have proved successful in this context.

PRACTITIONERS: WHO ARE OUR STUDENTS?

While there are a number of different types of practitioner who will engage in the study of politics, perhaps the most common type is those who might be termed career bureaucrats. Despite the recent tendency towards the pejorative use of this term, it remains the best encompassing label for the variety of public managers, administrators, civil servants and salaried officials found at different levels of government in different states. In the Weberian sense of the term, they generally share the characteristics of being appointed on merit to a structured hierarchy through which they aim to progress during the course of their careers on the basis of expertise and performance (Hughes 2003). Some countries have long histories of bureaucrats studying public administration programs and, although in parts of the world this has been in decline, globally the number of programs is growing (Miller 2012, pp. 10–12). These range from more generalist programs, such as Masters in Public Administration (MPA), which are designed for professionals from a range of public services, to more specialist courses for particular groups such as career diplomats (Hemery 2002), district officials (Dzimbiri 2007) and local government employees (Craig 2010).

While probably the largest group, bureaucrats are by no means the only types of practitioner who study politics. Wrage (2012) writes about his experiences of teaching ethics and international relations to midshipmen at the US Naval Academy in Annapolis, and Brown and Syme-Taylor (2012) report on their teaching experiences within a military staff college in Northern Europe. Harding and Whitlock (2013) outline the work that they have undertaken with policy analysts working in the area of mass atrocity prevention. There are also cases in which the practitioners are politicians. For example, Hale (2013) reports on a number of courses for elected local councilors provided by universities in the UK, while Pindani (1999) explores development programs for parliamentarians in Malawi, focused on democratic culture and governance. This list of different types of practitioner is by no means exhaustive, being primarily a reflection of what is reported in the academic literature. Nevertheless, it begins to demonstrate the diverse contexts and roles of practitioners who engage in the study of politics.

The motivations for engaging in the study of politics are likewise equally diverse. While individual learners may engage in learning in pursuit of their own personal and career aspirations, contextual factors can also be identified. Quinn (2013, p. 7) identifies the emergence of New Public Management and changing relationships between the state, market and society as creating new demands on public sector managers. In this context, many managers have sought to engage in programs to support their career development. Indeed, such changes also have implications for elected officials, with Hale (2013, p. 544) identifying the growing expectations for local councilors to undertake the multiple roles of 'budget-holders', 'go-betweens', 'troubleshooters', 'negotiators', 'judge/filters', 'democratic champions' and 'advocates for their communities' as creating greater demands for greater development opportunities. In the context of professional military education Klinger (2004) identifies changes in the post-cold war international systems as generating new demands for practitioner education. She identifies the increasing involvement of the US military in peacetime engagements alongside the challenges of nation building and global terrorism as creating a need for military officers to have a deeper understanding of international relations and regional politics.

The final aspect to highlight in relation to practitioners as students is that they tend to be relatively old in comparison with other groups of students. Given that many of those who engage with such programs are mid-career professionals, this should not be surprising, but what may be considered of relevance in this context is the educational literature on adult learners. Summarizing this literature, Rogers (2002) points to a number of characteristics that may be of particular relevance in the context of practitioner education. First, adult learners are identified as bringing a more developed set of values and experiences to the learning process than younger learners. This ties in with the point made in the opening section of this chapter, but which can be further unpacked here, for it can present both opportunities and challenges. In terms of the first, there may be a reservoir of examples and first-hand experiences from which students can draw in their discussion of issues. Utilizing this can be particularly effective as a means of valuing students' existing knowledge and building their confidence in the learning process. However, it can also present a challenge, where first-hand experience of a particular area has provided the student with a partial understanding of a topic that needs to be unpicked and explored before further learning can progress.

Other factors that have been identified as relevant to adult learners include a greater goal orientation from the learner in relation to what they want to gain from the process; a more self-directed approach to study; and an orientation towards integrating their learning from different contexts and experiences. To what extent these characteristics are reflected in any particular group will vary, but may be useful points of reference in considering the needs and preferences of learners.

WHAT TO TEACH: ISSUES OF CURRICULUM DESIGN

In designing the curriculum for practitioner-focused politics courses, instructors will generally take account of the professional contexts from which the students are drawn and seek to ensure that what is taught addresses the developmental needs of the learners. In some cases the focus will be on the development of specialist knowledge that may be considered to be of particular vocational value and relevance for practitioners. In these cases, the curriculum may emphasize particular sub-fields such as public policy analysis. In other cases, the impetus for engagement will be to broaden the knowledge and conceptual repertoire of learners. These situations will more often result in a curriculum that draws on elements of political theory or political philosophy. While these two approaches can be presented as alternatives, they may in practice exist side by side within an overall program of study. Indeed, as outlined in the following section, the design of the program can actively encourage students to explore the linkages between these two aspects.

The balance between knowledge and skills development is a further aspect in which the design of courses may differ. Both the approaches considered in the preceding paragraph focus on extending the knowledge of the learners, whether in depth or breadth. An alternative approach is that outlined by Hemery (2002), which aims to develop the skills sets of diplomats in the areas of leadership, negotiation, communication and the exercise of judgment. While such skills may be considered to be generic and applicable to management and leadership development in any organizational context, it is often the specificity of the political context that determines the types of tactics and strategies that can be employed. It is in this vein that Anderson (2002) identifies the need to teach political skills as an essential aspect of public administration education. He points to the skill needed when working within environments of political uncertainty and partisanship, and those needed to facilitate citizen engagement in democratic processes.

A third factor that may come into play in designing a curriculum for practitioners is the potential role of those who employ the students. This is likely to be strongest where a course is offered as part of a professional development program within a particular organization, but may also be a factor in cases where an employer is interested in sponsoring employees to engage in a program or where there are other drivers for engagement such as accreditation requirements. While all partnership arrangements will present particular sets of challenges and opportunities that have to be negotiated, the wider-context academic–practitioner relationships that have emerged within the discipline will also require negotiation. Writing in the context of public administration, Bogason and Brans

(2008) identify a number of challenges such as differences in vocabulary and terminology between academics and practitioners that can make discussion of shared areas of interest difficult. More generally, they identify the tensions between what has been termed Mode One and Mode Two knowledge by Gibbons et al. (1994). Mode One knowledge is that generally held and developed within the academic sphere, bound together within disciplines that value particular concepts and epistemologies. Mode Two, by contrast, is characterized as emerging from practice and application, and is more eclectic and transdisciplinary in nature. It is the bridging of these two worlds of knowledge that is essential not only for successful collaborations, but also for the construction of a curriculum that will meet the needs of students as they move between them.

HOW TO TEACH: EFFECTIVE PEDAGOGIES FOR PRACTITIONERS

In determining the types of teaching that will be most effective in supporting the learning of practitioners a number of factors need to be taken into account. The first is that, while most practitioners may share the typical characteristics set out earlier, each group will have its own particular needs that the educator should aim to identify and address. Notwithstanding this, as Kuh (2008) argues, there are several characteristics that high-impact educational practices tend to share, such as directing student effort into purposeful activities and providing opportunities to interact with faculty and peers. In this respect, the approach to teaching practitioners is no different from that of teaching any other student. The question is, rather, what particular approaches are successful in supporting practitioners to engage in effective learning behaviors. Finally, it should be acknowledged that all teaching takes place within constraints of time, space and resource. While the examples explored will not be suitable in all contexts, the underlying approaches that they illustrate are highly adaptable and can be developed for different circumstances.

A starting point for exploring the ways in which this can be achieved is to draw together a number of the points made earlier in the chapter. As practitioners, students will possess first-hand knowledge and experience of the areas in which they have served during their careers. Indeed, on the rich points of detail, the expertise of the practitioner will on many occasions surpass that of the academic who has studied the institution as an outsider. In addition, the adult learning literature suggests that learners can be engaged by strategies that draw this existing knowledge into the learning process and develop the links between different aspects of learning. As such, approaches that can effectively utilize these in the learning process have the potential to be effective in engaging learners. However, such an approach is not without its challenges. As noted earlier, students' experiences will inevitably be partial and may need to be unpacked and explored for their learning value to become fully realized. For these experiences to become more than pre-existing or background knowledge for the student, they need to be counterposed to other forms of knowledge encountered within the course (Usher 1993). There are several different ways in which this can be conceptualized. Barnett (1997) writes of the process of critical reflection that challenges learners to engage with theoretical and societal issues in examining their own experiences and actions. Quinn (2013) explores the concepts of reflexivity in the context of public administration education as an approach to facilitate practitioners in developing a critical understanding of their professional roles. Across these approaches the shared intention is to support a process in which practitioners can look afresh at what has become familiar to them in their roles and develop a critical approach to their practice.

One approach to operationalizing the process of critical reflection is to ask students to engage with academic texts and explore the relationship between the insights offered in the texts and their perceptions of their own roles and organizations. Rowe (2013) reports on his use of Lipsky's (1980) work *Street-level Bureaucracy*. The book examines how street-level bureaucrats, such as police officers, social workers and housing officers, operate on a day-to-day basis through local interpretations, rules of thumb and other uncodified practices. For students undertaking such roles, the introduction to a conceptual framework that can be used to analyze the issues that they experience in their professional lives can be valuable. Developing such links can help to overcome the potential alienation that some practitioners may experience in relation to the more theoretical content. Where the relevance and usefulness of such content can be demonstrated to learners, engagement is likely to be enhanced. It can also be an effective means of integrating different elements of the curriculum that are focused on more specialist learning with those that are oriented towards more general education. In addition, such exercises can form the bases for assignments undertaken by students. Inviting a student to read a paper on a topic such as policy implementation and to critically examine this within the context of their own organization can provide the opportunity for critical analysis of both the organizational practices and the adequacy of the literature for analyzing the issue.

Case-based learning provides an alternative approach that is well suited to the needs of practitioners. While this term is used to describe a range of approaches, in this context it refers to learning activities that present students with a problem-based scenario that they work through with other learners. The cases usually require the group to come to some type of decision in a situation in which there is no 'right answer'. Wrage (2012) reports on his use of such cases to teach ethics in international relations to US Navy personnel. Each case presents the students with a situation such as that of an intelligence officer aware of violent abuse within a prison. In working through the cases, students are introduced to three different perspectives: realist, idealist and constructivist. As such, they are able to develop an understanding of these key theoretical approaches within the context of concrete examples. Craig and Hale (2008) examine the use of case-based learning in the context of courses for local government bureaucrats. The cases that they used were focused on more grass-roots issues such as the management of community organizations. Students reported that engagement in these cases supported them in making links between different elements of the curriculum and prompted them to explore how a conceptual framework introduced in other parts of the course might be utilized to analyze the issues. Case-based learning can also provide learners with a further opportunity to draw upon their own experiences in thinking through the scenarios. The group deliberations around each case can be an effective prompt for students to draw parallels with situations that they have experienced previously and to begin to analyze the degree of comparison and lessons learnt.

A variation on the use of pre-existing scenarios is for practitioners to write their own cases and share these with other students. Alkadry and Miller (2002) outline their experiences in using this approach with MPA students. They argue that engaging learners in a process of storytelling can help them to explore and articulate the experiences that they bring to the course. In addition, they suggest that the cases that emerge can provide a more humanized account of public management that can be used with wider groups of students to challenge academic writing that takes a more rationalist approach.

The emphasis on the practitioner as a producer of knowledge can be further developed by approaches that engage students in undertaking work-based projects and research. Such approaches have the advantage of engaging practitioner experience as an ongoing and developing resource, rather than as static background knowledge that students have brought with them to the program. Work-based projects can take many forms. Craig (2010) reports on the year-long professional project undertaken by learners working in local government. In this case, the practitioners were asked to identify a public service improvement initiative that they would undertake within their workplace, lead the implementation of the project and report on the outcomes of this. In both the scoping of the project and the project report, students were prompted and supported in using the academic literature to interrogate and analyze the issues that arose and the solutions that were pursued. One of the advantages of such an approach is that it can result in improved outcomes for service users. Apart from the social good that results, it can also provide an effective way in which to bridge the academic–practitioner divide by demonstrating the value that can be generated through collaboration.

CONCLUSION

As reflected in this chapter, practitioner education is a wide and varied field. Nevertheless, in all cases there exist opportunities to draw upon and to develop the experience that the student brings to the program of study. In this way, the identity of the student as a practitioner is acknowledged and put to use as a valuable resource within the learning process. The range of methods through which this can be achieved has been discussed here, but the list is not exhaustive; it can at least describe some effective ways in which this can be put into practice.

REFERENCES

Alkadry, M.G. and Miller, H.T. (2002), 'Reading case studies vs. writing them: how to engage practitioner students?', in S. Nagel (ed.), *Teaching Public Administration and Public Policy*, New York: Snova Books, pp. 73–82.
Anderson, J. (2002), 'An essay on teaching politics as the core of public administration: the missing piece', in S. Nagel (ed.), *Teaching Public Administration and Public Policy*, New York: Snova Books, pp. 3–13.
Barnett, R. (1997), *Higher Education: A Critical Business*, Buckingham, UK: The Society for Research in Higher Education and the Open University Press.
Bogason, P. and Brans, M. (2008), 'Making public administration teaching and theory relevant', *European Political Science*, **7** (1), 84–97.
Brown, K.E. and Syme-Taylor, V. (2012), 'Women academics and feminism in professional military education', *Equality, Diversity and Inclusion: An International Journal*, **31** (5/6), 452–66.
Craig, J. (2010), 'Practitioner-focused degrees in politics', *Journal of Political Science Education*, **6** (4), 391–404.

Craig, J. and Hale, S. (2008), 'Implementing problem-based learning in politics', *European Political Science*, **7** (2), 165–74.

Dzimbiri, L.B. (2007), 'Public administration training in Botswana: the case of the district commissioners and districts officers', *Teaching Public Administration*, **27** (1), 15–28.

Gibbons, M., Limoges, C., Nowotny, H., Schartzman, S., Scott, P. and Trow, M. (1994), *The New Production of Knowledge: The Dynamics of Research in Contemporary Societies*, London: Sage.

Hale, S. (2013), 'Education for modernisation? The impact of higher education member development programmes on councilors' perceptions and performance of their roles', *Local Government Studies*, **39** (4), 541–61.

Harding, T.B. and Whitlock, M.A. (2013), 'Leveraging Web-based environments for mass atrocity prevention', *Simulation and Gaming*, **44** (1), 94–117.

Hemery, J. (2002), '"Educating diplomats" in academics, practitioners, and diplomacy: an IPS Symposium on the Theory and Practice of Diplomacy', *International Studies Perspectives*, **3** (2), 139–75.

Hughes, O. (2003), *Public Management and Administration: An Introduction*, 3rd edn, Basingstoke, UK: Palgrave Macmillan.

Klinger, J. (2004), 'Academics and professional military education', *Academic Exchange Quarterly*, **8** (2), 264–8.

Kuh, G. (2008), *High-Impact Educational Practices: What They Are, Who Has Access to Them, and Why They Matter*, Washington, DC: Association of American Colleges and Universities.

Lipsky, M. (1980), *Street-Level Bureaucracy: The Dilemmas of the Individual in Public Services*, New York: Russell Sage Foundation.

Miller, K.J. (2012), 'The future of the discipline: trends in public sector management', in J. Diamond and J. Liddle (eds), *Critical Perspectives on International Public Sector Management, Vol. 1 – Emerging and Potential Trends in Public Management: An Age of Austerity*, Bingley, UK: Emerald, pp. 1–24.

Pindani, D.G. (1999), 'Capacity building for effective governance: some thoughts on the Malawi Parliamentary Training Programme', *Teaching Public Administration*, **19** (2), 22–32.

Quinn, B. (2013), 'Reflexivity and education for public managers', *Teaching Public Administration*, **31** (1), 6–17.

Rogers, A. (2002), *Teaching Adults*, 3rd edn, Maidenhead, UK: Open University Press.

Rowe, M. (2013), 'Going back to the street: revisiting Lipsky's street-level bureaucracy', *Teaching Public Administration*, **30** (1), 10–18.

Usher, R. (1993), 'Experiential learning or learning from experience: does it make a difference?', in David Boud, Ruth Cohen and David Walker (eds), *Using Experience for Learning*, Buckingham, UK: The Society for Research in Higher Education and the Open University Press, pp. 169–80.

Wrage, S. (2012), 'Teaching ethics at a military academy', *International Studies Perspectives*, **13** (1), 21–5.

4. Best practices in professional development in graduate education
Clodagh Harris

INTRODUCTION

Analyses of professional development in political science education have traditionally focused on undergraduate students. However, changes in the postgraduate labor market as well as advances in the nature and delivery of postgraduate programs have required faculty to pay greater attention to professional development in graduate education (Listokin and McKeever 2011).

It is recognized that the approaches, techniques and tools used in the professional development of undergraduate students may not be 'as well suited for graduate students' in terms of preparing them for an academic career (Obst et al. 2010, p. 571), which requires developing a specialized skill set they will need as researchers, teachers and contributors to the faculty and the wider community (service).

This chapter explores developments in the professionalization of graduate education with reference to best practices in North America and Europe. It focuses on the following developments in political science and international relations: doctoral education; teacher training; mentoring; and mobility, all of which can prepare a student for a future academic career. It also includes a discussion of the role played by professional associations in developing and supporting disciplinary best practice. Finally, it concludes with some recommendations for the future of graduate professional development programs. It is important to note that this chapter focuses primarily on developing graduates' professional skills for the academic labor market rather than other forms of employment.

DEVELOPMENTS IN THE PROFESSIONALIZATION OF GRADUATE EDUCATION: PREPARING GRADUATES FOR FACULTY LIFE

Doctoral Education

Doctoral training programs have been an important step in the professionalization of the discipline as they play a key role in socializing graduates in the profession and preparing them for an academic career, particularly as researchers.

Such programs are relatively heterogeneous as they reflect institutional and departmental research capacities and expertise. However, there is agreement on key criteria and core principles. In its 2009 report on accreditation of doctoral training centers (DTCs) and doctoral training units (DTUs), the UK's Economic and Social Research Council (ESRC) emphasizes high-quality doctoral training that focuses on core social science research methods training (both qualitative and quantitative) and core disciplinary-specific training. Similarly the American Political Science Association (APSA) Task Force on Graduate Education (2004) recommends that students are introduced to a wide range of political science approaches and issues in their first years of graduate study and are provided with more in-depth training in a specific research area in later years. The organizations have also issued guidelines and recommendations on training that develop graduates' general research skills (bibliographic, ICT, language), teaching and other work experience skills, networking skills, research management skills, professional ethics and training to maximize the impact of their research (ESRC 2009; APSA 2004).

Meeting these guidelines can prove problematic for smaller institutions. Solutions have seen students participating in courses run by other departments in the university (e.g. linguistic courses) and/or the development of partnerships with neighboring universities offering a different range of expertise in the discipline. Denmark's POLFORSK program, which uses inter-institutional collaboration in the development and delivery of a high-quality doctoral training program, provides an excellent example of how a small community of political scientists can provide PhD students with access to specialized courses as well as opportunities to participate in a wider network of early career researchers in their field (Löfgren et al. 2010, p. 420). Alternatively, students who wish to hone specialist research skills not available in their home institution can do so by attending summer schools in research methods, for example the ECPR summer schools in Essex and Ljubljana, or by participating in the Travelling scholar (US) or Erasmus (EU) mobility programs that offer students the opportunity to study in another institution for six months/one year for credit.

Despite common ground on the curricula of doctoral training programs, there are differences between North America (the USA in particular) and Europe in their provision. Until recently the lack of formal training was one of the distinctive differences between the European and the American doctorate (Mény 2010). However, in the last ten to 15 years a 'revolution' has taken place at the doctoral level in Europe (Mény 2010, p. 16). The UK has been at the front of this so-called revolution with the establishment of doctoral or graduate schools. This process was further standardized and professionalized with the publication of the ESRC guidelines in 2009.

However, this has not been the case for all doctoral training programs offered across Europe. It is argued that they are 'extremely heterogeneous' (Mény 2010, p. 17), as some concentrate on training in methods while others focus on theory (Mair 2009, p. 146). Also student experiences of doctoral training can range from structured taught courses with supervision to a program that involves individual supervision alone. This is reflected in the European University Association (EUA) report (2007), which shows that 49 percent of doctoral programs employ a mix of taught courses plus individual supervision; 29 percent have established doctoral schools and 22 percent of the programs use only individual supervision (EUA 2007 report cited in Goldsmith and Goldsmith 2010, p. 69).

Yet how successful are doctoral training programs in preparing graduates for faculty life? The days when a good-quality PhD was sufficient to secure an academic post are gone. In the current academic labor market a well-prepared candidate is 'likely to have completed a Ph.D. to have one or more publications, particularly in international refereed journals, and to have some teaching and postdoc experience' (Mair 2009, p. 148). Stefuriuc (2009) concurs, arguing that an academic position requires 'a combination of a good thesis, a good record of teaching experience and a list of high standard publications' (p. 140).

These observations on the need to have published in peer-reviewed journals are supported by Hesli et al.'s (2006) finding, which shows that graduates 'employed as a faculty member at a college or university are significantly more likely to have published articles prior to graduating' (p. 320). A number of approaches to prepare and support graduates to publish in high-impact journals have emerged. Some institutions organize seminars on how to get published and provide resources on publishing for staff and students – for example, the Academic Publishing office of the London School of Economics (LSE).[1] Others, such as the Howe Writing Center at Miami University (Ohio) use writing groups and boot camps for graduate students and faculty.[2] Such seminars and boot camps could be offered for credit as part of structured taught doctoral programs or as an additional support to students whose program involves individual supervision alone. At a departmental or school level, the inclusion of graduate students in research cluster activities can provide them with publishing advice and support. Some departments house professional journals and are in a position to employ graduate students, thereby giving them valuable experience of publishing from an editorial perspective. Yet successfully negotiating the early years of faculty employment also depends on a range of other skills.

Thorlakson (2009) notes that 'the strategies for success rely on a range of teaching, research, managerial and networking skills that we likely did not develop during our doctoral years' (p. 162). For her part, Stefuriuc (2009) recognizes that an academic post involves 'attracting research funds, developing collaborative research, networking, managing research projects, supervising students and complying with a host of administrative demands' (p. 140).

These features are not likely to be developed as part of graduate programs whose primary focus is the development of researchers. It is argued that they do not offer sufficient preparation for academic life, particularly in different types of institutions of higher education (Gaff et al. 2003). Studies show that 50 percent of all doctoral graduates in the USA pursue academic careers, yet only 25 percent of academic posts are in research universities (Hoffer et al. 2002; Berger et al. 2001, both cited in Gaff et al. 2003). Thus approximately three-quarters of doctoral graduates will secure faculty positions in institutions with a different mission from their graduate one (Gaff et al. 2003). These figures are higher in political science, where 72 percent of doctoral graduates become faculty (Nerad and Cerny, cited in Ishiyama et al. 2010) and 'only 26 to 35 percent of faculty positions in political science are located in doctoral granting departments' (Ishiyama et al. 2013, p. 34).

The points discussed above raise some pertinent issues for graduate professional development both for those who have graduated from a taught doctoral training program and those whose doctoral experience is one of individual supervision alone. They highlight the need for an holistic approach to the preparation of graduates for an academic career, one that incorporates teacher training, mobility and mentoring. This holistic perspective was incorporated in the Preparing Future Faculty (PFF) program, an American initiative designed to better prepare graduate and postdoctoral students for faculty life in a variety of academic institutions. Although the external funding for the program has expired, it has been embedded in some universities, most notably Duke University's Graduate School. It is to these other elements of the holistic approach to graduate professional development that this chapter now turns.

Teacher Training

As observed by Ishiyama, Miller and Simon in the introduction to this handbook, future faculty exiting doctoral programs may find themselves with an expertise in *what* they teach but without the skills or experience of *how* to teach it. However, in recent times, moves to professionalize university teaching, through the provision of teacher training courses for faculty and graduate students, have sought to redress this anomaly.

This need to prepare graduates for a teaching career was stressed in the 2004 report of the APSA Task Force on Graduate Education, which called on departments to prepare their students to 'be not simply political scientists, but also teachers of political science'. Emphasizing the need for 'teacher–scholars' (Ishiyama et al. 2010, p. 516), it calls on departments 'to set up formal mechanisms to help graduate students become better instructors' (2004, p. 132).

This is also referred to in the ESRC (2009) guidelines, which state:

> Students undertaking teaching or other employment-related responsibilities should receive appropriate training and support. The training provided should be indicated in proposals for DTC or DTU accreditation. It is beneficial to research students if they can obtain teaching experience, for example with seminar groups, or any other work that helps develop personal and professional skills. (p. 20)

In 1997 only 44 percent of PhDs who entered the academic labor market had prior teaching experience (Dolan et al. 1997, in Buehler and Marcum 2007), and Ishiyama (2011) reckons that 'this number is likely even smaller now' (p. 3). These participation rates are mirrored to an extent in the provision and uptake of teacher training courses.

Research conducted by Dolan et al. (1997) found that 'of the graduate programs in the United States, only 55 percent offer a teaching seminar. From that same pool, only 41 percent of the graduate schools actually require students to attend these courses' (cited in Buehler and Marcum 2007, p. 22). More recent figures compiled by Ishiyama et al. (2010) found that, of the 122 PhD-granting political science departments in the USA (practitioner programs excluded), 41 had a graduate-level course on teaching political science, and, of these, 28 required that some of the students took the course. For 13 of them participation was optional. This could prove problematic for the discipline when we consider that up to two-thirds of all new jobs in the discipline in the USA are teaching positions (Ishiyama 2010, cited in Obst et al. 2010, p. 571).

From the European perspective, Pleschová and Simon (2009) find 'that about half of EU institutions offering Ph.D. programs also provide some form of teacher training' (p. 233). This European trend has been led by Belgium, Ireland, the UK and the Nordic countries (Pleschová and Simon 2013; Renc Roe and Yarkova 2013). Their research highlights 'the positive impact of teacher training on the quality of teaching and learning as well as the positive valuation of training by more than two-thirds of PhD students in our sample', and concludes that teacher training should be more 'widely available' (Pleschová and Simon 2009, p. 233). This is supported by a recent study of a teacher development course offered by the Central European University's (CEU) Curriculum Resource Centre. Based in Budapest, Hungary, the CEU is a graduate university that offers international programs primarily in the humanities and social sciences (Renc Roe and Yarkova 2013). An evaluation of the 'teaching in higher education' course offered to graduate students as part of their doctoral program finds that it 'manages to develop basic teaching and course design skills and begins the formation of a more confident, self-reflexive teaching persona' (Renc Roe and Yarkova 2013, p. 31). As the CEU does not offer undergraduate programs, the graduates participating in these programs gain experience as teaching assistants (TAs) on MA courses. Also the university endeavors to 'loan' its students to neighboring universities where they can teach on undergraduate programs.

In contrast, other research shows that most graduate programs are not sufficiently preparing their doctoral students for a career as teachers (Gaff et al. 2003; Buehler and Marcum 2007). A study by Gaff et al. (2003, p. 3) found that, while some graduate programs offer teacher training and teaching experience, these experiences are not always well structured and do not adequately tackle issues such as 'assessment, different types of student learning, the pedagogy of the discipline, curricular innovations, the impact of technology on education, or the variety of teaching styles that might be helpful with students from different racial, ethnic, or cultural backgrounds'. In their comparative analysis of graduates' teaching philosophies and behavior, Buehler and Marcum (2007) found dissonance in graduate instructors' knowledge and practice.

Scholars have recommended formal mentoring systems for teacher training and greater evaluation and supervision of graduate instructors (APSA 2004; Buehler and Marcum 2007). According to Buehler and Marcum (2007), evaluation should occur in the classrooms of both the professor and the graduate student instructor (GSI). APSA (2004) also emphasizes apprentice-style methods of teacher training 'serving as a TA/GSI under a fine, experienced undergraduate teacher is an excellent way to learn how to teach, especially when combined with departmental seminars and monitoring practices focused on teaching' (p. 132.)

Mentoring and apprentice-style approaches to teacher training have been employed innovatively and successfully in Miami University (Ohio) and Baylor University (Texas) respectively in a manner that has not placed a 'strain on resources or faculty time' (Ishiyama et al. 2010, p. 521).

Adopting shadowing and mentoring techniques, the Baylor program developed an active teacher training course that gives graduate instructors a structured, supported and meaningful teaching experience. As a small university, it decided against developing a specific course on teaching in political science, and 'apprenticed' graduate students to senior faculty instead. The graduate instructors' levels of responsibility increase as they progress in their studies; for example, in year four they are assigned a course to teach. Also the assignments are devised in accordance with the needs of the graduate student and not the faculty/department, and they choose their 'apprenticeship' course (Ishiyama et al. 2010; Ishiyama et al. 2013).

Like Baylor, Miami University does not offer an explicit graduate teacher training course, with graduate instructors, as in other departments/universities, working as teaching assistants. However, when teaching independent courses, they are required to participate in the College Professor Training Program offered by the university's teaching and learning center, thereby using existing campus services (Ishiyama et al. 2010, p. 521). The program provided by the center is quite comprehensive. It includes teacher training, program design and diversity training as well as workshops on recruitment and retention, student life, administration and teaching aids. Unlike the Baylor program, participation is voluntary (Ishiyama et al. 2010).

The PFF program (PFF4 included APSA and four PhD-awarding American political science departments) also endeavored to enhance teacher training and the preparation of graduates for academic careers, particularly at institutions that are primarily focused on teaching (Gaff et al. 2003; Ishiyama et al. 2013). The University of Illinois Chicago serves as an example of best practice in this regard. Its PFF director, Dick Simpson, developed two new courses: 'introduction to the political science profession' (required course for all new PhD entrants) and 'teaching political science' (required course for teaching assistants) that were embedded in the doctoral program in political science. These sequential courses were offered through the university's Council for Excellence in Teaching and Learning (CETL), which also awarded a certificate to those who took the 'teaching political science' course, participated in three CETL workshops and developed a teaching portfolio (Gaff et al. 2003, p. 38).

Developments in the professionalization of teacher training are to be welcomed. Yet have they impacted positively on the academic employment rates of PhD graduates? Research shows some mixed results. In their study of teacher training course impact on placement rates, Ishiyama et al. (2013) found that the courses had 'little effect on enhancing the placement of graduates, even at political science departments that emphasized teaching over research' (p. 50). What they did discover, however, was that the research productivity of the graduate's department 'still remains the best predictor of job placement' (Ishiyama et al. 2009, p. 7; Ishiyama et al. 2013). They speculate that this might be because graduates of highly research-productive departments have more opportunities to work as research assistants and publish, or because the 'hiring' teaching department based its judgment on the reputation of the graduates' PhD department.

In the European context, it is difficult to come to such conclusions as further research on graduate placement rates from European doctoral programs is needed. Indeed, it can be safely speculated that practice across Europe is heterogeneous in this regard, varying from country to country and from institution to institution.

Ishiyama et al. (2009) conclude that, while a teacher training course may not improve a graduate's placement chances, teaching experience is vital, as in their view it is 'a much better indicator of preparedness for teaching than is one's course work, and is likely to impact more on a hiring decision than what appears on a transcript' (p. 8). Also, by putting such emphasis on graduate employability we risk overlooking the possibility that the first years of an academic's career may be eased if they have teaching skills and some classroom experience.

These early 'pressure cooker' years of faculty life, which usually require quality research output, strong teaching practice as well as service to the university, the community and the discipline, can also be supported through the development of good mentoring relationships.

Mentoring

Traditionally used to introduce and socialize new students and faculty to a department, mentoring can benefit graduate students by providing them with information and advice on a variety of issues such as teaching, networking, publishing, funding opportunities, tenure and promotion, as well as fostering a stronger sense of involvement (Bennion 2004; Boyle and Boice 1998; Monroe 2003).

Research on mentoring shows that graduate instructors found teacher training received through mentoring to be more effective than that gained from campus seminars or specific departmental training (Jones 1993, cited in Boyle and Boice 1998). Graduate students who undergo intensive mentoring produce more research output and advance more quickly in their careers than those who do not (Girves and Wemmerus 1998). Also, a strong mentoring relationship affects the chances of the graduate student becoming a faculty member (Hesli et al. 2006).

For graduate students, mentoring can play a key role in the successful completion of their doctorate, acting as an effective tool against attrition (Hesli et al. 2003a). Also, it has been shown that 'the single best predictor of level of dissatisfaction with the graduate student experience is whether the graduate student received sufficient encouragement, mentoring, and consultation from faculty' (Hesli et al. 2003a, p. 459). This research also reveals a gendered dimension to the availability of sufficient mentoring, with women registering lower levels of satisfaction. This may be partly a consequence of the fact that women graduates' mentoring relationships are 'less established and also less likely to be with same sex mentors' (Heinrich 1991, cited in Hesli et al. 2003b, p. 801).

Traditional mentoring programs link more experienced political scientists with graduate students, usually within the same department, and can take a couple of formats. It may be 'natural, spontaneous mentoring', or systematic (Boyle and Boice 1998, p. 159). Natural mentoring tends to benefit those in more privileged positions such as white men, while women and racial/ethnic minorities are better supported by systematic mentoring processes (Boyle and Boice 1998). Mindful of this, the APSA Task Force on Mentoring, established in 2002, examined issues of 'recruitment, retention, and integration of women and people of color in the profession' (APSA Task Force on Mentoring website). It focused on mentoring initiatives for new entrants to the discipline, namely graduate students and early career faculty and developed APSA's mentoring program, which includes an array of mentoring resources such as a database that gives young scholars access to a mentor outside of their home institution.

There has been a move to develop diverse forms of mentoring relationships, and Bennion (2004) advises that 'it is wise for interested young scholars to seek multiple mentoring relationships' (p. 112) that may include mentoring relationships with more senior faculty members in another field, or in the same field but at a different university. She also advocates peer mentoring in which peers can 'explore personal and academic dilemmas as well as a better balance and integration between one's professional and personal lives' (ibid.). This form of mentoring offers advantages to all political scientists and is of particular importance for women and racial/ethnic minorities (ibid., pp. 112–13).

Another, more traditional mentoring relationship is the tutoring role played by graduate students in teaching and supporting undergraduates. There has been little research on this long-established scholarly role. However, a recent study of a program that assigned undergraduate students a faculty and a graduate student mentor found that 'everyone's [undergraduate and graduate students'] teaching and learning needs were met simultaneously, effectively, and efficiently' (Ishiyama 2011, p. 9). It concluded by highlighting 'the importance of providing graduate students with the opportunity to develop their own teaching and mentoring styles, by providing faculty assistant activities that go beyond the formalistic teacher training that is found at many Ph.D. granting departments' (ibid.). This form of mentoring not only enhances the graduate students' teaching skills but also offers them important service experience.

Mentoring, particularly systematic mentoring, has been shown to work and can be organized in a variety of formats to ensure that an excessive burden is not placed on faculty members (particularly female and racial/ethnic minority members). Also, it is considered good practice that graduate students and early career faculty develop a variety of mentoring relationships. Research has shown that such relationships, if structured properly, can enhance a graduate's early career faculty member's professional prospects.

Mobility programs can also play an important role in this regard by offering graduate students and early career faculty international mentoring experiences.

Mobility

Recent employment trends in the discipline show that US PhDs are more likely to be employable in both the North American and European academic job markets (Stefuriuc 2009; Mair 2009). Yet, even with this increased migration from the USA to Europe, few graduate programs in the USA prepare students for a faculty position abroad (Jenne 2009).

As an American alumna working in Europe, Jenne (2009) suggests that graduate students from North American universities wishing to secure an academic post in Europe would 'do well to attend European conferences in their field and forge ties with US centers and departments that are already integrated in European scholarly networks' (p. 172).

Mobility programs can facilitate this. They have been established in North America and Europe to fund student and faculty travel to another institution (national or international) to research and teach. They allow graduate and postdoctoral students to 'build a network that will clearly be far more solid than one can hope to achieve by regular conference participation alone' (Stefuric 2009, p. 141).

Numerous mobility programs are available to graduate and postdoctoral students as well as faculty, and offer opportunities to access unique library collections, follow specialized courses of study, work closely with international experts in their discipline, participate in academic life in another institution and network with colleagues elsewhere.

For graduate students specializing in comparative studies and international relations, in particular, mobility schemes can facilitate essential field work.

Some of the mobility schemes available to graduate students include:

- Marie Curie Fellowships;[3]
- the Fulbright program;[4]
- Erasmus partnerships;[5]
- the Travelling Scholar Program of the Committee on Institutional Cooperation (CIC).[6]

Marie Curie Fellowships are EU research grants that are open to researchers regardless of nationality, age, experience or field of research to gain experience abroad and in the private sector, and to complete and/or continue their training.

Another internationally renowned scheme is the Fulbright program (financed by the US State Department). It offers graduate students and young professionals the opportunity to continue their education or professional development abroad. The Fulbright US student program offers funding for US citizens to study abroad and the Fulbright foreign student program provides scholarships for students from other countries to study in the USA.

The European Union's Erasmus program supports partnerships between higher-education institutions in Europe and a range of countries around the world. It grants scholarships to students (undergraduate and postgraduate) and staff (administrative and academic) to study, research and/or teach in another partner institution.

Finally, in the USA the Travelling Scholar Program of the CIC allows doctoral students to spend up to a full academic year at another CIC institution to follow a specialized course of study, conduct research in specific library collections or to have access to advanced equipment or laboratories.

Mobility programs can help prepare future faculty by providing training, research and networking opportunities for graduate students. Yet professional associations, in particular their graduate associations, can make a significant contribution in this regard.

Role for Professional Associations

More and more political science associations are mindful of the role they can play in the professional development at all levels in their discipline. They recognize their responsibility to prepare the next generation of faculty for professional life. As Gaff et al. (2003, p. 46) observe,

> for at least two decades, the humanities and social science disciplinary societies [APSA is one of the societies mentioned] have recognized that supporting and disseminating research is not enough to serve the discipline adequately. Through various mechanisms, each of these societies also emphasizes the importance of teaching and learning, professional and career development of faculty members and graduate students, educational innovations, and knowledge of larger trends affecting higher education and the institutions in which their specializations are practiced.

In political science, APSA, its regional associations, the PSA (Political Studies Association, UK) and the ECPR (the European Consortium for Political Research) lead the field in terms of advancing and supporting the professionalization of the discipline through:

- the provision of summer schools (e.g. the ECPR biannual summer school on teaching and learning as well as summer schools on social science data analysis and methods and techniques in Colchester and Ljubljana);
- publishing peer-reviewed scholarly research including research on the scholarship of teaching and learning;
- organizing conferences. Stefuriuc (2009) advises graduate students and early career faculty that it is 'worthwhile attending panels about the profession, professional development roundtables and the various receptions organized by publishers, graduates and other sub-groups of professional organizations' (p. 142);

- funding for conference attendance – thereby facilitating international mobility and networking that may lead to research collaboration;
- the organization of graduate associations that convene workshops, conferences and facilitate networking. Also, they provide an opportunity for professional service through sitting on the graduate association committee, convening the graduate conference and/or editing the graduate association newsletter; and
- the development of graduate education and mentoring policies (APSA).

Moreover, as discussed by Ishiyama, Miller and Simon in their introduction to this handbook, the professional associations have played a key role in recognizing the importance of the scholarship of teaching and learning in political science.

CONCLUSION

In preparing future faculty, graduate education programs should provide students with opportunities to develop and publish high-quality research, and offer them structured, supported and evaluated teaching experience as well as some service experience.

This chapter has explored professional development in graduate education with reference to international examples of best practice in doctoral education, teacher training, mentoring and mobility programs. It has also included a brief discussion of the supporting role played in all of these by professional associations. Although the examples are presented in individual sections, their interdependency is recognized, and an holistic approach to graduate education is advocated. For example, producing quality research may lead to a publication in a high-impact journal, but it can also enhance teaching through research-led teaching approaches. Also, research and teaching may provide service experiences for students through the use of community integration research methods and community-integrated (or service) learning.[7]

Mindful that universities and faculty vary in terms of resources and mission, this chapter nonetheless finds in favor of:

- formal taught doctoral programs;
- structured, supported and evaluated teaching experience, preferably accompanied by accredited teacher training;
- multiple systematic mentoring relationships;
- international mobility for the development of research skills; fostering mentoring relationships; diverse teaching experiences; and networking opportunities;
- publication supports in the form of publishing seminars, writing circles/boot camps and the like; and
- active participation in professional associations, through participation in conferences, workshops, summer schools, specialist groups, committees and so on.

Finally, recognizing their significant contribution to the professionalization of the discipline and the development of graduate education, in particular, this chapter calls on the larger professional associations to establish graduate education committees, and organize professional development workshops or 'cafés' at their annual conferences.

It is clear that much has been done in terms of the professionalization of graduate education in the discipline, but without further research in this area it is difficult to ascertain how effective these approaches are and what more can be done to prepare future political scientists for academic life.

NOTES

1. http://www.lse.ac.uk/researchAndExpertise/academicPublishing/home.aspx.
2. http://writingcenter.lib.muohio.edu/?page_id=896.
3. For more information see http://ec.europa.eu/research/mariecurieactions/ (accessed 27 June 2013).
4. For more information see http://eca.state.gov/fulbright (accessed 27 June 2013).
5. For more information see http://ec.europa.eu/education/external-relation-programmes/mundus_en.htm (accessed 27 June 2013).
6. For more information see http://www.cic.net/projects/shared-courses/traveling-scholar-program/introduction (accessed 27 June 2013).
7. For an example of service learning in the graduate classroom see Harris (2010).

REFERENCES

APSA Task Force on Graduate Education (2004), 'Report to the Council', *PS: Political Science & Politics*, **38**, 129–35.

APSA Task Force on Mentoring, available at http://www.apsanet.org/content_2473.cfm (accessed 27 June 2013).

Bennion, Elizabeth A. (2004), 'The importance of peer mentoring for facilitating professional and personal development', *PS: Political Science & Politics*, **38**, 111–13.

Boyle, Peg and Bob Boice (1998), 'Systematic mentoring for new faculty teachers and graduate teaching assistants', *Innovative Higher Education*, **22** (3), 157–79.

Buehler, Melissa J. and Anthony S. Marcum (2007), 'Looking into the teaching crystal: graduate teaching and the future of political science', *Journal of Political Science Education*, **3**, 21–38.

Economic and Social Research Council (ESRC) (2009), 'Postgraduate and training guidelines', available at http://www.esrc.ac.uk/_images/Postgraduate_Training_and_Development_Guidelines_tcm8-2660.pdf (accessed 27 June 2013).

Gaff, Jerry G., Anne S. Pruitt-Logan, Leslie B. Sims and Daniel D. Denecke (2003), *Preparing Future Faculty in the Social Sciences and Humanities*, Washington, DC: Council of Graduate Schools and Association of American Colleges and Universities.

Girves, J.E. and V. Wemmerus (1988), 'Developing models of graduate student degree progress', *Journal of Higher Education*, **59**, 163–89.

Goldsmith, Mike and Chris Goldsmith (2010), 'Teaching political science in Europe', *European Political Science*, **9** (S1), 61–71.

Harris, Clodagh (2010), 'Active democratic citizenship and service learning in the postgraduate classroom', *Journal of Political Science Education*, **6** (3), 227–44.

Hesli, Vicki L., Evelyn C. Fink and Diane Duffy (2003a), 'Mentoring in a positive graduate student experience: survey results from the Midwest region, Part I', *PS: Political Science & Politics*, **36**, 457–60.

Hesli, Vicki L. Evelyn C. Fink and Diane Duffy (2003b), 'The role of faculty in creating a positive graduate student experience: survey results from the Midwest region, Part II', *PS: Political Science & Politics*, **36**, 801–4.

Hesli, Vicki L., Jacqueline DeLaat, Jeremy Youde, Jeanette Mendez and Sang-shin Lee (2006), 'Success in graduate school and after: survey results from the Midwest region, Part III', *PS: Political Science & Politics*, **39** (2), 317–25.

Ishiyama, John (2011), 'Teaching as learning: engaging graduate students in the active learning of teaching and mentoring', *Science*, **333** (6045), 1037–9.

Ishiyama, John, Christine Balerezo and Tom Miles (2009), 'Do graduate student teacher training courses affect placement rates?', paper prepared for delivery at the 2009 Annual Meeting of the American Political Science Association, 3–6 September, Toronto, ON, Canada.

Ishiyama, John, Tom Miles and Christine Balarezo (2010), 'Training the next generation of teaching professors: a comparative study of PhD programs in political science', *PS: Political Science & Politics*, **43**, 515–22.

Ishiyama, John, Alexandra Cole, Angela D. Nichols, Kerstin Hamann and Kimberley Mealy (2013), 'Graduate student teacher-training courses, job placement and teaching awards in the United States', in Eszter Simon and Gabriela Pleschová (eds), *Teacher Development in Higher Education*, New York and Abingdon, UK: Routledge, pp. 34–53.

Jenne, Erin J. (2009), 'Preparing for an academic career in Europe: the perspective of a North American', *European Political Science*, **8** (2), 168–74.

Listokin, Siona and Robert McKeever (2011), 'APSA teaching and learning conference track summaries, track: graduate education and professional development', *PS: Political Science & Politics*, **45**, 658–9.

Löfgren, K., E. Sørensen and F. Bjerke (2010), 'Lessons learned from the Danish national PhD programme POLFORSK', *European Political Science*, **9** (3), 420–27.

Mair, P. (2009), 'The way we work now', *European Political Science*, **8** (2), 143–50.

Mény, Y. (2010), 'Political science as a profession', *European Political Science*, **9** (S1), 11–21.

Monroe, Kristen R. (2003), 'Mentoring in political science', *PS: Political Science & Politics*, **36** (1), 93–6.

Obst, Kirsten, Nancy Wright, Heather Edwards and Katherine Brown (2010), 'APSA teaching and learning conference track summaries track: graduate education and professional development', *PS: Political Science & Politics*, **43** (3), 571–2.

Pleschová, Gabriela and Eszter Simon (2009), 'Teacher training for political science PhD students in Europe: determinants of a tool for enhanced teaching in higher education', *Journal of Political Science Education*, **5**, 233–49.

Pleschová, Gabriela and Eszter Simon (2013), 'What we know and fail to know about the impact of teacher development', in Eszter Simon and Gabriela Pleschová (eds), *Teacher Development in Higher Education*, New York and Abingdon, UK: Routledge, pp. 1–16.

Renc Roe, Joanna and Tatiana Yarkova (2013), 'Preparing doctoral students for a teaching career: the case of an international university with a history of regional engagement', in Eszter Simon and Gabriela Pleschová (eds), *Teacher Development in Higher Education*, New York and Abingdon, UK: Routledge, pp. 19–33.

Stefuriuc, Irina (2009), 'Building an academic profile – considerations for graduate students embarking on an academic career in political science in Europe', *European Political Science*, **8** (2), 138–42.

Thorlakson, Lori (2009), 'Collective wisdom: advice to new entrants to the profession', *European Political Science*, **8** (2), 162–7.

5. Distance and online course design
J. Simon Rofe

INTRODUCTION: THE CONTEXT MATTERS

As today's students arrive at university, one of the first things they will do, without thought to what they might consider their 'learning', is to exchange a raft of information with their peers – through various forms of social media. This means that they will be online, communicating with each other before they arrive at their first class. Distance learning (DL) students may never arrive at a 'classroom'. Yet, whatever the mode of their distance learning delivery, they will almost certainly converse with their peers by some means, probably online, and with equal likelihood beyond the confines of their academic programs. The potential impact on their learning experience is not always fully understood by teachers or more broadly by universities, though there is some exciting work being done in exploring this relationship (Shirky 2013a). As a professor of education wrote in 2005, '[i]t is perhaps a chastening thought for teachers and lecturers to think that what we do not consciously plan for may have a more profound influence on our students than all our well-intentioned efforts' (Humes 2005). While the activities of students in this regard may form a hidden curriculum in higher education, governments responsible for national education policies and university management have increasingly seen both online and distance learning as providing opportunities to manage the costs of tertiary education, broaden participation and facilitate universities' impact on wider society (Snyder 1970).

In recent times, the possibilities provided by MOOCs (Massive Open Online Courses) have given rise to much editorial comment and considerable opportunities for universities to operate in non-traditional markets despite the fact that 'most MOOCs reiterate the ancient form of the lecture', and fail to 'signal much of a leap in pedagogy' (Shirky 2013b; see also Shirky 2009). Nonetheless, MOOC is the educational buzzword de jour.[1] Educational writer Clay Shirky (2013b) observes, '[i]t's impossible to understand what's happening with MOOCs without understanding what's happened to higher education in general'. That is to say, the context matters.

This has particular relevance to the study at a distance or online because both terms are regularly misused by being conflated with each other, or with other 'new' approaches to student learning. In addressing the attributes of good distance and online learning, the chapter will provide an assessment of the contributory factors that influence the successful deployment of these forms of learning. In short order, they are: the enthusiasm and/or motivation of the instructor; the technology at the instructors' disposal; the involvement/acquiescence of faculty in the immediate departmental environment; the interests of the institution's higher management in the success of the endeavor; the financial support involved; and finally the qualities of the student body. Recognizing how these factors relate to each other in the specific environment in which an individual finds himself or herself will be important in the successful deployment of any distance or online program.

With such a variety of influencing factors, alongside our students' communicating online from the outset of their studies, and managers seeking to embrace new technology, those working in universities globally face a challenging milieu.[2] The question that teachers of political science and international relations confront is how to meaningfully comprehend the ramifications of designing worthwhile and engaging online and distance courses while reconciling the requirement to produce world-class research and excellence in student learning. As Gormley-Heenan and Lightfoot (2012) note, the 'traditional divide within the profession between teaching and research' is one that will become increasingly untenable in responding to the demands of the profession in the twenty-first century (p. 2).

In delving into distance and online learning a little deeper, it is the job of this chapter to outline the main contours of each form, providing the parameters to their definitions, and the distinctions between them. The chapter will then look at a number of approaches to learning, referencing Bloom's *Taxonomy*, the work of Gilly Salmon and, specifically to our field, the 'IR Model', before offering some concluding thoughts.

What follows is not prescription. The extent to which learners – both teachers and students – engage with the principles and the practical advice that follows is up to the individual and will reflect their individual approach to course design and teaching. What matters, as ever, is thinking about the learning objective and the tools one would choose to deploy to achieve this. So whether a class includes data sets, document analysis, role play, simulations (see chapters 26 and 27), multiple choice tests, research papers, collaborative projects or essay writing, there is no learning objective that cannot be achieved in a meaningful fashion in an online or distance environment. When this is done well it is not because those who do it have necessarily acquired separate distinct skills based solely on working online or at a distance; it is because they have applied the sound pedagogic principles.

In harmony with the objectives of this handbook, this chapter contends that it is the 'learning' in distance or online learning that is important. It is not distance or online 'teaching'. The goal of our collective scholarly endeavors is the achievement of 'learning' on the part of students, not necessarily the 'teaching' on the part of instructors. As such, it is worth considering Paul Ramsden's (2003) argument that higher education is 'about changing the ways in which learners understand, or experience or conceptualize the world around them' (p. 78). Equally, as Ramsden often quotes from Whitehead (1927), university is about 'the imaginative acquisition of knowledge'. Be imaginative. The scope provided by distance or online learning makes it all the more exciting for instructors and students alike. These realms mean class size is not restricted by the availability of lecture halls, or that learning takes place at 10.00 on Tuesday morning because that is when the timetable dictates. There are opportunities to engage in learning without these constraints.

Most colleagues embarking on distance or online teaching will have had some experience of campus-based teaching, be that convening seminars, giving lectures or running tutorials. These skills are indistinguishable from those needed for distance and online teaching, but it does not mean they are the 'same'. A necessary translation process converts good face-to-face learning to distance and online. Without recognizing the need to 'translate', good campus learning materials can have poor learning outcomes at a distance or online. That said, to translate learning materials need not be very onerous or costly in terms of time or money, but it does need to be done sensitively. One of the attributes of the successful IR Model, which will be discussed later, is its ability to adapt existing campus courses and materials to distance and online.

Online learning is not simply taking teaching materials such as lecture slides and putting them 'on the Web'. There is no difference between depositing such materials online and sending them in the mail, or indeed in putting a book in a library. On their own these actions are inadequate for providing an engaging student experience when exciting alternatives exist. While all three may offer 'knowledge', and have the capacity to provide some measure of learning, this is the case only rarely; the intervention of teachers is needed to stimulate intellectual engagement and curiosity that allow students to achieve higher-level learning. It is the nature of such 'intervention' – in class or online or at a distance – that may vary and will be outlined here.

To be imaginative distance and online instructors, scholars of political science and international relations should remember Ramsden's (2003) salient advice to university teachers: 'to become a good teacher, first you must understand your student's experience of learning' (p. xiii). It is therefore important to consider the distance and online student in his or her own right. These students lack the same coherence in terms of demography that typifies campus-based classes. Age ranges, gender balance, financial support, levels of prior knowledge and professional experience are at a greater variance than in traditional student bodies, and, thus, course designers should consider these factors – particularly the requirement for flexibility. Indeed, one of the appeals of these modes of learning is the flexibility for students to learn in a manner that fits with their own circumstances, so that they can interact with the program on their own terms. When it comes to course design, programs must be flexible enough to meet the requirements of professional work-based learners, those who may never have encountered 'traditional' university teaching, those returning to study after a number of years in a different realm, non-native speakers and others facing individual challenges to studying. Catering to all of these different constituents is a challenge, but one that distance and online learning can meet in ways not always available in a campus-based environment.

PRINCIPLES AND DEFINITIONS

The principles of good course design apply whenever thought is given to crafting an educational experience. Distance and online course design is no different. Careful consideration of class, module or program learning objectives, and the application of the appropriate means to achieve them in an engaging and intellectually challenging student-focused manner, must surely be our goal (see chapters 1–4). To comprehend how the goal of engaging our students can be achieved in the realm of distance and online learning, let us explore the terms and provide some working definitions. This is important because to be a good teacher one needs to understand the topography of higher education in which any distance or online learning program operates.

Distance learning is a form of learning where the learner–teacher relationship is dislocated by geography, with particular implications for the synchronicity of learning. A recent digest of the literature on distance learning summarizes distance learning as follows: 'some form of instruction occurs between two parties (a learner and an instructor), it is held at different times and/or places, and uses varying forms of instructional materials' (Moore, Dickson-Dean and Gaylen 2011, p. 130). Typically, though not universally, it is the learner who is remote from the teacher who is in turn part of an established higher education institution (HEI). Distance learning dates back at least two centuries, when postal services provided the mode of physical delivery of learning materials in print form as 'correspondence learning' (the approach still forms the basis of some distance learning). Distance learning has employed various other new technologies as they have developed (telegraph, telephone, radio, television), and latterly the Internet. The use of the Internet, especially, has transformed the opportunities for distance and online learning, moving it beyond its institutional origins in the UK to be a global phenomenon.[3]

Online learning is any form of learning that involves use of online materials, typically from the World Wide Web (www). As an information repository, the Web holds a huge variety of resources to learn from, but there are also numerous online materials dedicated to assisting learners and teachers, catering for almost every individual. Almost universally, HEIs have a dedicated virtual learning environment (VLE) (sometimes known as a learning platform), which can provide a framework for both online and distance learning.

Distance learning and online learning are distinct: one can be a distance learner without being online (though that is increasingly rare); and one can learn online while being on a campus-based program. Nonetheless, the terms are sometimes conflated and misunderstood, often by those directing colleagues to undertake such endeavors. Research by Moore, Dickson-Dean and Gaylen (2011) 'show[s] great differences in the meaning of foundational terms that are used in the field' (p. 134). Further, beyond the specific circumstantial factors outlined at the outset of the chapter, the terms have particular national, cultural and institutional meanings that influence the context in which they operate.[4]

While such definitional distinctions will be helpful, and familiar to scholars in the discipline, it is probable that students new to the discipline will not see them. Indeed, they probably do not need to. A 2007 report on the learner's perspective on e-learning found that students were, unsurprisingly, '[b]lending the use of familiar personal technologies – such as iPods, MySpace or mobile phones – with institutionally based technologies and traditional practice – such as VLEs, face-to-face classes and lectures – in ways that make learning more efficient, spontaneous and meaningful' (JISC 2007, p. 24). That students will construct meaning from the context in which their learning takes place is (nearly always) a goal of our intervention as teachers in terms of our subject matter, and so we should consider the mode of their learning in a similar light.

Equally, it is worth remembering that the medium of learning may not be as important for the students as it may appear to scholars charged with designing courses. That is not to excuse poor design, but to say that traditional, campus-based students may well undertake aspects of their program by distance learning and/or online learning without acknowledging these modes of delivery. Undertaking a multiple choice test during an evening, providing class feedback, fulfilling a research project, or simply visiting a library off campus may be tasks common to learning online, at a distance or in a classroom with chalk and a blackboard.

The challenges of establishing common usage of terms, even within the relatively heterogeneous educational environments of the USA, the UK and continental Europe, illustrate once more the salience of the principle that thoughtful pedagogic design is just that, whether the medium is a traditional campus-based classroom, at a distance or online.

APPROACHES TO AND METHODS OF DISTANCE AND ONLINE LEARNING

Designing a program online or at a distance is a challenge; guidance may be found in returning to a classic source of pedagogic learning: Benjamin Bloom's *Taxonomy of Educational Objectives: The Classification of Educational Goals* (Bloom 1956). The chapter will then consider the canon of work by Professor Gilly Salmon, a globally recognized expert in e-learning as applied to distance and online learning, before looking at a practical example of a mode of online/distance learning: the IR Model devised by this author. These are arbitrary choices, given the constraints of space here, but they have been selected as exemplars because they engage with the issues relevant to distance learning and online course design in a thought-provoking and practical fashion.

Bloom's original purpose was to provide a schema for experts in assessment – 'examiners' – but he incidentally made a huge contribution to educators across the world. Much debated, the *Taxonomy* has been through a number of subsequent iterations across the domains of learning (cognitive – knowledge, affective – attitude and psychomotor – skills) aimed to achieving higher-order thinking.[5] It has stood the test of repeated investigation, and recent interpretations have demoted 'evaluation' from the apex of the taxonomy and replaced it with 'creating', replacing nouns with verbs. The former emphasizes the goal of the educational enterprise as higher-level learning, while the latter describes 'learners' thinking processes rather than behaviors' (Shank 2013). The most relevant adaptation for those involved in online and distance learning is the revision by Andrew Churches (2007), 'Bloom's Digital Taxonomy', first published, appropriately, as a wiki. Churches' work emphasizes the Taxonomy as geared towards 'problem and project based learning where the student must work through the entire process of development and evaluation'. It is this developmental and associated collaborative aspect that lends itself so well to the distance and online environments when married with careful course design, such as that promoted by the three Ds of 'Design, Development and Delivery', as espoused in the IR Model (Rofe 2011a, p.104). To reiterate, it is the 'learning' that matters in distance and online learning, and Bloom's *Taxonomy* in all its various guises provides an epistemological foundation that reminds us as teachers to be cognizant of working towards the higher-level learning objectives we profess as the goal of our programs and courses.

The marriage of thorough course design and collaboration in achieving higher-order thinking is certainly evident in the work of Gilly Salmon. Salmon's work has introduced two key concepts that have proved invaluable to distance and online course designers. The first is the concept of 'e-tivities'. An e-tivity is a framework for online, active and interactive learning following a format that states clearly its 'Purpose'; the 'Task' at hand; the contribution or 'Response' type; and the 'Outcome' (Salmon 2002). The second concept that Salmon introduces in online and distance course design is that of 'e-moderating'. This method is dialogical in emphasizing discussion of ideas and sharing of opinions among peers, with the teacher as facilitator of the discourse; and so the teacher becomes, in Alison King's (1993) phrase, 'the guide on the side' rather than the 'sage on the stage'. Given that this is the goal of a typical seminar discussing the environmental policies of the G20, just-war theory or the ethnic composition of post-colonial states, the skill set will be familiar to teachers of political science and international relations, even if the term is new. To be clear, e-moderating is about facilitating student learning; requiring the appropriate and thoughtful intervention on the part of the teacher with the requisite skills; importantly this can happen asynchronously. The notion of asynchronous learning allows for students to develop at their own pace in circumstances that best suit them, and is particularly important to distance and online learners. In this respect Salmon's work acknowledges the principle of the 'flip classroom' (Educause 2012), which is to value student/teacher interaction to facilitate problem solving rather than transmission of knowledge. The outcome of the effective deployment of e-tivities and e-moderating can be to outstrip the most stimulating learning experiences on-campus, with value added by considered contributions from all students.

Important to all of Salmon's work is the ancillary place of technology in the delivery of learning materials. This chapter has consciously not dwelled on particular pieces of technology or software that can contribute to student learning (see Chapter 25). That is not to say technology is superfluous to learning; it can be very important, and can do seemingly 'magical' things, but it should not be the master of the learning. There is a risk to learning for both students and teachers in being captivated by the next new technology. Put another way, technology, new or old, is only as effective as the teacher who uses it.

Underpinning both e-tivities and e-moderating is Salmon's five-stage model of online learning (Figure 5.1). This model provides a framework for learners who may be absolute beginners to progress to become competent online learners. Further, for the purposes of orientation, it does not take a huge leap of intellectual faith to map the trajectory of Bloom's *Taxonomy* onto the steps of Salmon's model 'knowledge construction' and 'development' consummate with 'evaluating' and 'creating' (see Figure 5.1).

Salmon's model provides a routemap for effective e-learning that can be applied to distance and online learning. It begins (at stage 1 at the base of the flight of steps) by blending students' access to learning and their – varying – technological skills. As such, students are seamlessly learning the skills they need to succeed and their subject matter. The second stage is about students establishing their own online identities, and at stage 3 there is a sharing of those identities in the appropriate distance or online environment. During the first three stages, increasing levels of cooperation can be seen in the student body as they form ties that assist their individual learning and lead into group interactions in stage 4, as full-scale collaboration occurs. The level of mutual support students receive from their peers means they are able to take meaningful steps as independent learners by this point in their evolution as e-learners. Importantly, '[e]ach stage requires participants to master certain technical skills (shown in the bottom left of each step). Each stage calls for different e-moderating skills (shown on the right top of each step)' (Rofe 2011a).[6] For those considering adopting this model, it is important to note the 'interactivity bar' running along the right of the flight of steps; it indicates the intensity of the commitment required by those undertaking e-moderating. The commitment is not consistent, as in a weekly campus-based class; instead the e-moderator's intervention takes place at the most appropriate juncture to facilitate learning.

Distance and online course design 53

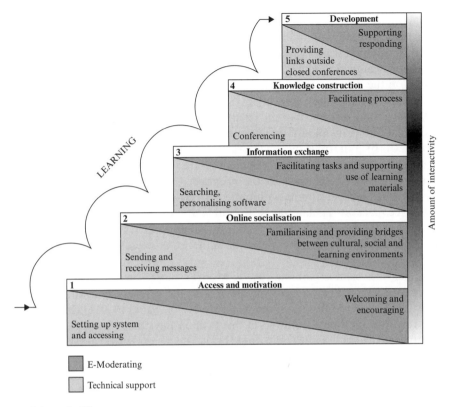

Source: Salmon (n.d)[7].

Figure 5.1 Salmon's five-stage model of online learning

While the contribution to pedagogic thinking of Bloom and Salmon applies respectively to the whole field of education, and then to e-learning, this chapter will now explore one approach with this heritage firmly in the field of political science and international relations.

Applicable to distance and/or online learning, the 'IR Model' is a schema of pedagogic design and development, where IR is a reference to the discipline of international relations *and* 'intellectual reflection' on performance by teachers and learners alike (Rofe 2011a). For teachers in higher education, the IR Model provides an innovative model for program and module design by encouraging a holistic approach to course design, development and delivery: the three Ds necessary for high-quality and sustainable provision. For the learner, the IR Model delivers an outstanding 'student experience' based on high levels of engagement and, importantly, student attainment. For example, in a number of modules taught online and in traditional form on campus for modules with the same learning objectives, student attainment has been higher by between 5 and 10 percent for those distance/online modules following the IR Model approach. The Model has been widely acknowledged: it is 'a very worthwhile contribution resulting from what was obviously close engagement with issues of best-practice, pedagogy and philosophy of

L[earning] & T[eaching]' (Reviewer, European Political Studies 2010). Particularly noteworthy is the affirmation of an involved student experience, with one observer noting 'I have been struck by just how good the DL experience has been for students. Because of the careful pedagogical design ... the students remained actively engaged throughout and, based on the posting in the online forums, clearly enjoyed the experience' (Simon Kear, Learning Technologist, University of Leicester, April 2010).

The IR Model delivers outstanding results to students through the application of well-founded pedagogic principles of good course design with a focus on the student experience (Rofe 2011b). What this means in practical terms, aided by the Salmon model, is a consistent planned approach to each element of an online or distance program. In turn, this means a uniform format across the program, comparable forms of assessment in terms of the task and their timing within the course, and, most importantly, appropriate and timely feedback at regular stages. In online and distance learning there is risk that students will become disorientated by inconsistent approaches to their learning; leading to disengagement from the process and the subject, subsequent poor performance and ultimately withdrawal.

The longer answer in explaining the IR Model's success in delivering a high-quality learning experience online and at a distance is in the careful application of Salmon's work, and especially the five-stage model (Rofe 2011c; Salmon 2011). Individual international relations modules operating in this fashion have been developed with a series of six 'e-tivities'. These e-tivities map onto the five-stage model and are aligned to a progressive assessment regime. Critical for student learning is the way each of the e-tivities builds cumulatively towards a final module assessment, providing formative feedback – 'feed forward' (Nicol and Macfarlane-Dick 2004), and giving students the opportunity to develop key skills individually and collaboratively, which in turn fulfill the module's learning objectives (Rofe 2011a). Furthermore, in line with stages 4, and particularly 5, of the Salmon model, students can learn from each other through higher-order peer-to-peer learning.

An example e-tivity is provided below from a diplomatic studies module (see Table 5.1), which asks students to access the university's online library provision, provide bibliographical references, and contribute to the relevant discussion forum with a 200-word analysis of their peer's composition. The outcome is clearly stated for the student.

On the IR Model any number of e-tivities can be deployed, addressing the five stages of Salmon's model and covering any range of academic tasks: a book analysis, a pop quiz, a literature review or an essay. The configuration of the assessment regime is crucial to the planning needed to allow students to prosper. Experience suggests that the most effective configuration of e-tivities as enablers of student attainment is to have six e-tivites across a module, the first being purely formative, and then five blending formative and summative qualities. E-tivities 2, 3 and 5 carry 5 percent of the overall module mark, while e-tivity 4 carries 15 percent and the final assessment 70 percent.

Other aspects to consider in online and distance course design through the IR Model should include issues such as student accessibility, student-generated materials, the utilization of technology and overall student support. The IR Model allows for distance or online students to access their learning materials at multiple different points, which is significant for a student cohort lacking the homogeneity of their campus-based cousins bound by timetables and room allocations. The careful deployment of a variety

Table 5.1 Example e-tivity

Purpose	To access e-resources and use a bibliographic database to find articles from an academic journal through the online library.
Task	Watch the tutorial on retrieving information from the online library. Using an appropriate database, search for articles relating to 'Diplomacy'. Produce a bibliography containing **two articles** chosen by you that are both available through the University's online library. Write a short paragraph of no more than 200 words to accompany your bibliography, telling your colleagues why these particular articles are worth reading and what they will gain from using your bibliography. Post the bibliography and its rationale in the e-tivity 2 Forum.
Respond	Return to the e-tivity 2 Forum and explore a bibliography recommended by one of your colleagues. Post a reply under this entry, giving your thoughts on the selection of articles that were recommended to you. How useful and interesting did you find this selection? Could you recommend an article to add to this bibliography? **Submit *both* forum entries to TurnItIn no later than 11:59 pm on the date of the submission**. E-tivity submission dates are detailed in the Study Calendar.
Outcome	You will be able to search the University's databases, identify and access and evaluate appropriate academic journal articles, and present the required bibliographic information accurately.

We recommend you spend a minimum of 2 hours on this e-tivity, and as much time as you are able participating in the Forum.

of e-tivities with varying weightings in terms of their assessment, and the amount of time needed to complete them, means that students are able to exploit their individual approaches to learning, and provides structure to learners studying at a distance or online. These features give a framework to a body of students learning online or at a distance, and so provide a sense of a shared learning experience rather than one of isolation. The meaningful development of student-generated course content also helps in this regard. As can be seen in the example e-tivity above, students are asked to build collectively a bibliography, and discuss its merits. Importantly, access to these resources is retained throughout a student's registration so they can use them as a reference tool in their future studies. The flexibility of the IR Model is also evident here in preventing any students from feeling as if they have 'missed out' and thus becoming disheartened by having to 'catch up'.

As a mode of distance and online course design, the IR Model also makes innovative, imaginative and, most importantly, appropriate use of relevant technology. Again it is only through appropriately deployed technology that students will be able to make the most of their learning experience. Starting from the assumption that students may bring minimal IT skills to their study of politics and IR, and little experience of university VLEs, a module's early e-tivities combine developing knowledge of the subject matter with enhancing key skills enabling students to complete their studies, and, crucially for their success, the confidence to use them. This is seen clearly in the example e-tivity above, which familiarizes students with some of the literature in the field while giving them experience of using a library database, working with their peers and developing skills they will need in their future studies. To recap, in each of the elements that comprise the IR Model's approach the learner is recognized as an integral part. Opportunities for reflection are offered in a number of ways, and allow students to engage in their individual learning journey as part of their personal development plan. It is with this in mind that the IR Model promotes 'accessible and powerful learning experiences' in a 'pedagogically thrilling' fashion (Reviewer, European Political Studies, 2010).

CONCLUDING THOUGHTS

'[T]he corporal and Colonel Korn both agreed that it was neither possible nor necessary to educate people who never questioned anything'. Somewhat perversely, these words from Joseph Heller's timeless novel *Catch-22* illustrate the value of being inquisitive in any setting, and this is especially true for those in higher education. As Heller's book was first published in 1961, Lord Lionel Robbins was appointed by British Prime Minister Harold Wilson to review higher education in the UK. His eponymous report, published after considerable international consultation two years later, stated that '[h]igher education should attract, and in some measure create, students who will make demands upon their teachers, and teachers who can both satisfy those demands and stimulate further curiosity and intellectual energy' (Robbins 1963, p. 170). Distance and online learning are another means to stimulate and engage learners' 'curiosity and intellectual energy' (Robbins 1963). They provide the means of being imaginative and experimenting in the teaching of political science and international relations.

To be clear, scholars of political science and international relations, as a discipline, are blessed. We are blessed by the fact that the issues that influence the challenges of twenty-first-century higher education are germane to what appears on our syllabus, whatever our particular field of expertise. To varying degrees, topics including political and ideological interests, a range of actors from the local to global and negotiations between them, and resource management and decision making, typically manifest themselves in some form or other whether one's course is in political philosophy, strategic studies, comparative politics or foreign policy analysis (see the 2013 special issue of *International Studies Review*, especially for Simmons 2013). This is 'good news', and gives us something of a competitive advantage in a 'marketplace' of disciplines. Nevertheless, to stop there and rest content with that knowledge would be to do an injustice to our discipline and to the students who study it.

This chapter is not a manifesto for distance or online learning; the reality is that as teachers in the field we already engage to varying degrees with the concepts of learning online or at a distance. While we may not always acknowledge this explicitly, we are fortunate that so much of our teaching, and research, and research into teaching, can be done in this fashion. Recognizing this, as scholars of politics and international studies, allows us to contribute to fundamental questions about traditional campus-based universities.

A 2013 report by the Institute for Public Policy Research concerning the 'revolution ahead' in higher education concluded the 'traditional multipurpose university with a combination of a range of degrees and a modestly effective research program has had its day. The traditional university is being unbundled' (Institute for Public Policy Research 2013). Shirky (2013b) agrees that 'the demand for complex knowledge far outstrips our ability to provide it via current colleges and universities'. It is in this light that MOOCs are currently receiving such attention as an often misplaced moniker for the exciting realm of distance and online learning. A cautionary word to end: Sir John Daniel sagely notes that '[w]hile the hype about MOOCs presaging a revolution in higher education has focused on their scale, the real revolution is that universities with scarcity at the heart of their business models are embracing openness' (Daniel 2012). It is the issues surrounding 'openness' that give scholars of political science and international relations opportunities to use their subject-matter expertise, however tangential it may at first appear, to contribute to the discourse about learning in higher education.

NOTES

1. MOOC as an abbreviation fails to distinguish between xMOOCs and cMOOCs: the former, the 'recent' (since 2012) contribution by the likes of Coursera, Udacity as private companies with antecedents in leading universities, and edX Harvard–MIT partnership; and cMOOCs foreshadowing these with a 'collectivist' approach to learning.
2. The economic dimension to distance education is adroitly outlined by Ormond Simpson (2002), who points to the motivations for economic return (return on investment) as the prime driver for investment in these approaches (rather than their potential to enhance student learning). The important implication here is that this will trump individual interest and endeavors, with strategic decisions being fed down to operatives such as lecturers, especially newly appointed ones deemed to be 'in touch' with the student ranks they recently left.
3. In the UK distance learning in these various guises has been associated with two institutions: first, the University of London International Programmes (http://www.londoninternational.ac.uk/uk), given a Royal Charter in 1858 and thus the first university to provide distance learning degrees; and second, the Open University (http://www.open.ac.uk/), established in 1969 and with over 250000 enrolled students. This is the single largest HEI in the UK and one of the biggest in the world.
4. Other terms need to be referenced here, as they can have a material influence on the task of designing a distance or online course: e-learning; blended learning; m-learning; and, in a professional context, Web-based training (WBT). E-learning can be considered as 'learning facilitated and supported through the use of information and communications technology' (JISC n.d.). As with all of these terms, other definitions exist. Bernard Luskin (2010) suggests that 'The "e" in e-learning means much more than "electronic" when applied to e-learning – think instead of a big "E" for "exciting, energetic, engaging, extended" learning'. As such, it may be considered distinct in part from online learning by virtue of the information and communication technology (ICT) not necessarily being online (admittedly, unlikely).

    'Blended learning' refers to an approach that brings together, or blends, traditional campus-based modes of learning with online and/or e-learning and/or distance learning. 'M-learning' is shorthand for mobile learning. According to UNESCO (n.d.), it 'offers modern ways to support learning process through mobile devices, such as handheld and tablet computers, MP3 players, smartphones and mobile phones'. The International Association for Mobile Learning (n.d.) lists a collection of mobile learning resources. Finally Web-based training (WBT) refers to the Web-based delivery of professional training. While for scholars the temptation is to eschew training for education, it is highly likely that at least part of our professional development training as scholars will be delivered as part of a WBT package.
5. Sources on Bloom are plentiful. The revised texts of recent years include Bloom (1994), Anderson et al. (2000) as well as Anderson and Krathwohl (2001).
6. E-moderation is a necessary element of any forum discussion if it is to achieve particular learning objectives. It can be achieved on a self-policing basis among experienced users, although a quasi-independent e-moderator can be employed as an 'associate tutor' (the equivalent of a graduate teaching assistant) to guide and support learning in our forums. See Salmon (2004, pp. 54–5) for a rubric of the skills for an e-moderator.

7. Work on this website is licensed under a Creative Commons Attribution-NonCommercial-NoDerivs 3.0 Unported License.

REFERENCES

Anderson, L. and D.R. Krathwohl (2001), *Taxonomy for Learning, Teaching and Assessing: A Revision of Bloom's Taxonomy of Educational Objectives*, New York: Longman.

Anderson, L.W., D.R. Krathwohl, Peter W. Airasian, Kathleen A. Cruikshank, Richard E. Mayer, Paul R. Pintrich, James Raths and Merlin C. Wittrock (eds) (2000), *A Taxonomy for Learning, Teaching, and Assessing: A Revision of Bloom's Taxonomy of Educational Objectives*, Boston, MA: Allyn & Bacon.

Bloom, Benjamin S. (ed.) (1956), *Taxonomy of Educational Objectives: The Classification of Educational Goals*, Boston, MA: Allyn & Bacon.

Bloom, Benjamin S. (1994), 'Reflections on the development and use of the taxonomy', in Lorin W. Anderson and Lauren A. Sosniak (eds), *Bloom's Taxonomy: A Forty-Year Retrospective*, Chicago, IL: National Society for the Study of Education.

Churches, Andrew (2007), 'Bloom's Digital Taxonomy', available at http://edorigami.wikispaces.com/Bloom's+Digital+Taxonomy and http://edorigami.wikispaces.com/file/view/bloom's+Digital+taxonomy+v3.01.pdf (both accessed 26 May 2013).

Daniel, Sir John (2012), 'Making sense of MOOCs: musings in a maze of myth, paradox and possibility', available at http://www.academicpartnerships.com/docs/default-document-library/moocs.pdf?sfvrsn=0 (accessed 23 February 2013).

Educause Learning Initiative (2012), '7 things you should know about ... flipped classrooms', available at http://net.educause.edu/ir/library/pdf/eli7081.pdf (accessed 4 July 2013).

Gormley-Heenan, Cathy and Simon Lightfoot (eds) (2012), *Teaching Politics and International Relations*, Basingstoke, UK: Palgrave Macmillan.

Humes, Walter (2005), 'Never discount the hidden curriculum', *Times Education Supplement*, **25**, 25 February 2005 (last updated 12 May 2008), available at http://www.tes.co.uk/article.aspx?storycode=2076639 (accessed 26 December 2013).

Institute for Public Policy Research (2013), 'An avalanche is coming: higher education and the revolution ahead', available at http://www.ippr.org/images/media/files/publication/2013/04/avalanche-is-coming_Mar2013_10432.pdf (accessed 22 July 2013).

International Association for Mobile Learning (n.d.), 'Biblio', available at http://www.iamlearn.org/biblio (accessed 22 March 2013).

JISC (Joint Information Systems Committee) (2007), 'In their own words: exploring the learner's perspective on e-learning', available at http://www.jisc.ac.uk/media/documents/programmes/elearningpedagogy/iowfinal.pdf (accessed 22 March 2013).

JISC (Joint Information Systems Committee) (n.d.), 'E-learning programme', available at http://www.jisc.ac.uk/whatwedo/themes/elearning.aspx (accessed 2 March 2013).

King, Alison (1993), 'From sage on the stage to guide on the side', *College Teaching*, **41** (1), 30–35.

Luskin, Bernard (2010), 'Think "Exciting": e-learning and the big "E"', *EDUCAUSE Quarterly*, available at http://www.educause.edu/ero/article/think-exciting-e-learning-and-big-e (accessed 2 March 2013).

Moore, Joi L., Camille Dickson-Deane and Krista Galyen (2011), 'e-Learning, online learning, and distance learning environments: are they the same?', *Internet and Higher Education*, **14** (2), 129–35.

Nicol, David and Debra Macfarlane-Dick (2004), *Rethinking Formative Assessment in HE: A Theoretical Model and Seven Principles of Good Feedback Practice*, Heslington, UK: Higher Education Academy.

Ramsden, Paul (2003), *Learning to Teach in Higher Education*, London: Routledge Falmer.

Robbins, Lord Lionel (1963), *Higher Education Report of the Committee appointed by the Prime Minister under the Chairmanship of Lord Robbins*, London: Her Majesty's Stationery Office, available at http://www.educationengland.org.uk/documents/robbins/index.html (accessed 26 April 2013).

Rofe, J. Simon (2011a), 'The "IR Model": a schema for pedagogic design and development in international relations distance learning (DL) programmes', *European Political Science*, **9** (4), 103–17.

Rofe, J. Simon (2011b), 'Something that works: the IR Model's approach to technology', in Steven Curtis and J. Simon Rofe (eds), *Does the Medium Matter? IT-Assisted Learning and Teaching in International Relations and Politics – Why Social Science Matters*, Issue 5, C-SAP Publications.

Rofe, J. Simon (2011c), 'The IR Model and e-moderating', in Gilly Salmon (ed.), *E-Moderating: The Key to Teaching and Learning Online*, 3rd edn, New York and London: Routledge Falmer, pp. 57–9.

Salmon, Gilly (2002), *E-tivities: The Key to Active Online Learning*, New York and London: Routledge Falmer.

Salmon, Gilly (2004), *E-Moderating: The Key to Teaching and Learning Online*, 2nd edn, New York and London: Routledge Falmer.
Salmon, Gilly (n.d.), 'Five-stage model', available at http://www.gillysalmon.com/five-stage-model.html (accessed 9 May 2014).
Shank, Hillary (2013), 'eLearning Guild Research: reconsidering Bloom's Taxonomy (Old AND New)', available at http://www.learningsolutionsmag.com/articles/1105/ (accessed 26 May 2013).
Shirky, Clay (2013a), 'How to save college', The Awl, available at http://www.theawl.com/2013/02/how-to-save-college (accessed 14 April 2014).
Shirky, Clay (2013b), 'MOOCs and economic reality', *The Chronicle of Higher Education*, available at http://chronicle.com/blogs/conversation/2013/07/08/moocs-and-economic-reality/.
Simmons, Beth A. (2013), 'Preface: international relationships in the information age', *International Studies Review*, **15** (1), 1–4.
Simpson, Ormond (2002), *Supporting Students in Open and Distance Learning, Open and Flexible Learning*, London: Routledge.
Snyder, Benson R. (1970), *The Hidden Curriculum*, New York: Alfred A. Knopf.
UNESCO (n.d.), 'Mobile learning', available at http://www.unesco.org/new/en/unesco/themes/icts/m4ed/ (accessed 21 March 2013).
Whitehead, Alfred North (1927), 'Universities and their function', available at https://webspace.utexas.edu/hcleaver/www/330T/350kPEEwhiteheadunivfxtable.pdf (accessed 26 May 2013).

6. Student and civic engagement: cultivating the skills, efficacy and identities that increase student involvement in learning and in public life
J. Cherie Strachan

INTRODUCTION

Today, higher education institutions are called upon to advance two goals: increase student learning and success rates; and cultivate citizens capable of sustaining democracy. These goals are complementary. The same pedagogical approaches and institutional characteristics that predict our students' success also promote their long-term participation in public life. Both academic success and citizenship are advanced when students are engaged as active members of a learning community – especially when that community not only structures opportunities for meaningful engagement, but cultivates the shared norm that taking advantage of such opportunities is expected.

The underpinning goals of both the student engagement movement (which ultimately depends on shaping students' academic identities and intrinsic motivations for undertaking scholarly endeavors as learners) and the civic engagement movement (which ultimately depends on shaping students' civic identities and intrinsic motivations for undertaking public work as citizens) are normative. Both depend on cultivating preferred identities and norms in order to mold student behavior in ways that will yield desired outcomes – in-depth learning and academic achievement on the one hand, higher rates of civic and political participation and voting on the other. Unlike those of the civic engagement movement, however, the goals of the student engagement movement are almost universally shared across academia, which helps to disguise their prescriptive nature. Meanwhile, the goal of transforming students into good citizens is controversial, even in the USA, where higher education's civic mission has, perhaps, the most explicit roots. Yet universal access to public education is linked to stable democracy, in part because such access helps to reduce economic inequality, but also because high-quality education tends to cultivate individual traits long associated with good citizenship, in particular: trust in others; trust in government; proficiency in civic skills; and a strong sense of political efficacy (Rothstein 2011; Verba et al. 1995). Given concerns over eroded and/or limited opportunities to cultivate these traits in more natural political settings (Hooghe and Stolle 2003; Putnam 2000, 2002; Rothstein 2011; Skocpol 2003; Uslaner 2002), however, those concerned with sustaining healthy levels of participation in established democracies and with increasing participation in emerging democracies may find a viable alternative by embracing the civic mission of higher education.

Given that the recent civic engagement movement initially emerged in the USA, this chapter examines the role that American higher education institutions have played in both the student engagement and civic engagement movements. However, the overarching goal is to provide an overview of the parallel pragmatic and normative underpinnings of these movements, as well as to describe the overlapping best practices that can be used to motivate all students to actively engage in learning, as well to actively engage in their civic and political communities.

STUDENT ENGAGEMENT AND STUDENTS' SUCCESS IN THE US CONTEXT

US colleges and universities have always cared about student graduation rates, persistence and success. Yet when only a fraction of the American public pursued an advanced degree, students were much more likely to arrive on campus in possession of the two traits associated with persistence and success – academic preparation and motivation (Adelman 2004; Pascarella and Terenzini 1991, 2005).

Initially, the private colleges founded when America was still a British colony provided religious education for the sons of America's elite, white families (Addis 2003; Brickman 1972). Now, most colleges and universities focus on secular, academic instruction, and welcome a far more diverse group of students that includes not only the less privileged, but also women and minorities (Nemec 2006; Lazerson 1988; Fass 1989). In short, more people from a wider array of backgrounds are now going to college. These demographic trends, in combination with the financial pressure to maintain high enrollment, make it unlikely that today's US student body will comprise exclusively selected, well-prepared and highly motivated students (Keller 2001; Kuh 2001a).

At the same time, increasing the percentage of college graduates has become an important federal- and state-level public policy goal. According to Kuh et al. (2005a, p. 7), 'Nearly everyone agrees that persistence and educational attainment rates, as well as the quality of student learning, must improve if post-secondary education is to meet the needs of our nation and our world'. Historically, however, higher education scholars estimated that only 50 percent of enrolled US students completed a baccalaureate degree within four years (Braxton 2000; Pascarella and Terenzini 1991, 2005; Tinto 1993). In short, US higher education institutions are being called upon to increase student success rates, at the same time that they are tasked with enrolling a wider swathe of students who, for a variety of reasons, are less prepared for the challenges of post-secondary education. These reasons include not only poor academic preparation, but more students with lower socioeconomic and first-generation college status, not to mention increasing numbers of non-traditional and commuter students.

Faculty and administrators cannot remedy poor academic preparation, but can bolster student motivation to close this gap. Fortunately, longstanding research indicates that what students are willing to do while they are on campus is one of the best ways to predict their success – and more importantly one that can trump poor preparation. In short, student engagement, or the amount of time and effort students expend on learning-related academic, interpersonal and extracurricular experiences, is the most effective way to improve their scholarly and personal growth while in college (Astin 1991; Chickering and Reisser 1993; Kuh et al. 1991, 2005a; Pascarella and Terenzini 1991, 2005). As Pascarella and Terenzini (2005, p. 602) argue, '[s]tudents are not passive recipients of institutional efforts to "educate" or "change" them, but rather bear a major responsibility for any gains derived from their post-secondary experience'.

Yet encouraging students to assume this responsibility can be challenging. This frustration is exacerbated, moreover, when instructors are committed to traditional pedagogy that conceptualizes teaching as mere information transfer. Professors wedded to this approach typically rely on detailed lectures, expect students to comprehend and recall the information, and blame unmotivated students when this process 'breaks down' (Harward and Shea 2013, p. 30). When students are provided with opportunities and are clearly expected to shift from superficial or strategic learning to deep learning, they are much more likely to take responsibility for their own education (Bain and Zimmerman 2009). Moreover, at-risk students benefit the most from the high-impact educational practices of experiential, engaged or active pedagogy (Kuh 2008). Thus college and university officials should ensure that institutional and classroom practices facilitate student engagement rather than stifle it. Ideally, 'if faculty and administrators use principles of good practice to arrange the curriculum and other aspects of the college experience, students would ostensibly put forth more effort' (Kuh et al. 2005a, p. 9).

Chickering and Gamson (1987), in their now classic article 'Seven principles for good practice in undergraduate education', provided a preliminary checklist, which has served as the building block for higher education research identifying best practices for motivating students. These practices are now assessed, as 'Clusters of Effective Practices', in the National Survey of Student Engagement. The NSSE begins by assessing whether institutions require students to engage in challenging intellectual and creative work, as well as whether their educational experiences include active, collaborative learning. Examples of the first include the amount of time students spend reading scholarly materials, writing papers and using higher-order thinking skills. Examples of the latter include not only participating in classroom discussions and presentations, but also working together outside of the classroom, joining forces on a community project, or tutoring other students. Additional educational experiences assessed by the NSSE include student interactions with faculty members outside of the classroom, ranging from informal discussions to formal collaboration on research projects or service committees, as well as exposure to enriching or 'high-impact' educational experiences such as internships, community service, study abroad, capstone projects and extracurricular activities (Kuh et al. 2005a, 2005b).

These questions tap into whether college experiences are providing students not only with experiences that cultivate adequate substantive knowledge and skills (e.g. reading, writing and critical thinking), but also with experiences that cultivate self-efficacy, or the sense that they can apply knowledge and skills in meaningful, effective ways beyond the context of a particular classroom (e.g. mastery and deep learning).

More importantly, the NSSE also attempts to assess whether these student experiences are provided in a supportive environment where the entire campus community is purposefully oriented toward student learning and success. This final element is important, as it speaks to institutional culture. A precursor for establishing the types of policies and classroom practices that promote student engagement is to cultivate an institutional culture that makes student learning a priority (Kuh and Whitt 1988). Indeed, the schools that are most effective at promoting student engagement rely on socializing mechanisms (such as rituals, traditions and ceremonies) that reify shared norms and communicate the high value placed on student learning (Kuh and Whitt 1988). Institutional culture is important for two reasons. First, all of the practices referenced above require faculty and staff to expend considerable time, energy and resources, and to coordinate their behavior toward a common goal – which is unlikely to happen unless they also share norms and values that drive their choices. While active pedagogies are increasingly promoted as best (or 'high-impact') practices (Kuh 2008), many US professors continue to reenact the traditional approaches to teaching, as few were trained to incorporate active learning as part of their own graduate education (Beaumont and Battistoni 2006; Rimmerman 2011). Hence current undergraduates still expect to find the 'sage on the stage' imparting objective truth and wisdom at the head of their classrooms, and risk-adverse students, focused on passing exams, are inclined to reward these traditional instructors (as long as they are also sufficiently entertaining) with high evaluation scores. Further, while all schools recognize teaching and service, the unspoken (and sometimes explicit) message that many new professors receive is that publications are the true 'coin' of the 'academic realm'. Some professors may avoid adjusting their teaching – either because incorporating active learning is in fact more time-consuming and will distract from their research agendas, or even because they are afraid that they will appear to be too student-focused (McKeachie and Svinicki 2006). In short, it is easier for faculty members to incorporate active learning approaches when their institution culture supports their efforts – and especially when their institution has embraced the Boyer Model of Scholarship (Boyer 1990), which values the scholarship of teaching and learning (SoTL) alongside the scholarship of discovery.

Second, and perhaps more importantly, a cohesive institutional culture consistently communicates to students the importance of engaged learning. Even when good teaching occurs, students are much more likely to respond when performance expectations are consistently high and clearly communicated (Education Commission of the States 1995; Kuh 2001b; Kuh et al. 1991; Miller 2009; Pascarella 2001).

When a cohesive institutional culture results in a clear, consistent message, shared norms and values are likely to be internalized by the students themselves. At this point, students will be engaged and motivated not merely because professors expect it, but because they will have internalized the identity of engaged learners. Students spend far more time with each other than they do with professors or staff, and their peers also have a much greater, lasting influence on their attitudes, values and behaviors (Bean 1985; Chickering 1974; Kuh and Umbach 2004; Pascarella 1984, 1985). Moreover, a supportive student culture can extend learning and engagement beyond the classroom to experiences over which students have greater influence: co-curricular activities. The more students participate in campus academic and social organizations, the more their persistence increases; they are more apt to have higher levels of academic achievement, and they are less likely to drop out (Pascarella and Terenzini 2005). This type of involvement is especially important for minority students in the USA, who often experience micro-aggressions and a negative campus climate when they enroll at predominantly white institutions, as well as for first-generation college students, who often find the transition to college difficult.

Interviews with undergraduates enrolled at 'involving colleges', which are known for the quality of their out-of-class activities, reveal how intensely influential such experiences can be. Students described interactions with one another as the 'high points of their undergraduate experience' and recognized that 'their peers influence them in ways that faculty members or classes never could' (Kuh et al. 1991, p.192). Yet it is also important to note that peer groups can undermine, but be equally influential on, students' engagement, learning and personal development (Astin 1977; Chickering 1974; Pascarella 1985). Just as in broader civil society, groups that provide individual members with personal resources through bonding social capital can cultivate otherwise undesirable outcomes. Hence colleges and universities should aspire to achieve the status of an 'involving college', with a student culture that reinforces rather than undermines the importance of engaged learning (Kuh et al. 1991).

Summary

In short, professors who prefer active pedagogy and high-impact teaching now have access to an increasing number of resources. Higher education research provides insight into effective practices, which professors can review to enhance their own pedagogy. Those who lack a supportive environment can engage in long-term, strategic efforts to embed support for engaged learning within their institutional and student culture (Kuh et al. 2005b). In the meantime, however, the link between active pedagogy, student engagement and deepening concerns over student retention and graduation rates should bolster support for engaged teaching – not only on US campuses but in any academic setting with heightened concerns for retention and graduation rates.

CIVIC ENGAGEMENT AND STUDENTS' CITIZENSHIP

These same trends are influencing the role higher education plays in US civic education. While many of the earliest US colleges and universities were private institutions, politicians faced with an increasing enfranchisement in a mass democracy soon realized that an educated citizenry was a valuable public good (Addis 2003). As such, the number of public colleges and universities expanded, and public institutions were expected to carry on the tradition of character development initiated by their predecessors (Rudolph 1990; Thelin 2004). In particular, American institutions were expected to 'foster enlightened civic and political leadership' (Hartley 2011, p. 28). Of course, the need for such leadership is not restricted to the USA. Higher education institutions in all modern democracies find themselves called on to provide both leaders and citizens who help to balance the need for informed decision-making with concerns over mass political participation. Yet this priority was marginalized in the USA after World War II, as the number of institutions proliferated, the type of students attending college was dramatically transformed, and curricular offerings shifted to focus on meeting the needs of an increasingly diverse economy (Hartley 2011, p. 28). US colleges and universities began to emphasize individual intellectual and professional development over character development. Even in the discipline of political science, which was founded with the explicit normative agenda of improving democratic governance, scholars questioned (and continue to question) whether the goal of transforming students into good (i.e. active) citizens is appropriate. As the director of the American Political Science Association, Michael Brintnall, notes, '[t]here is broad agreement that civic engagement is a social responsibility, but it has become less certain whether it is a professional or a disciplinary responsibility' (Brintnall 2013, p. xi).

By the 1980s, frustration with this skeptical view of character development, along with growing concern that students, mirroring broader societal trends, were increasingly focused on their own individual advancement at the expense of their public obligations, culminated in efforts to revitalize the civic mission of American higher education (Bellah et al. 1985; Bloustein 1999). The resulting civic engagement movement is grounded in John Dewey's ([1916] 1966, 1933, 1938) approach to cultivating good citizens through experiential learning. The contemporary version of this pedagogy has been labeled 'service learning', and it aspires to link students' classroom learning with relevant, meaningful experiences in their communities. The teaching approaches advocated by the citizen engagement movement are high-impact practices that cultivate student engagement, mastery and deep learning, with the added expectation that students will also assume responsibility for their civic obligations in a democratic society.

A small group of advocates launched Campus Compact, an organization to support higher education institutions incorporating this approach, in 1985. One measure of the movement's success is the increasing awareness and use of service learning at all educational levels. Another is the institutionalization of support for this approach on US college campuses, in higher education professional associations and even in US public policy.

Many campuses, for example, now highlight service learning by housing it within a center or institute, which is also charged with providing professional development for faculty and with reaching out to community partners. From 1992 until 2011 (when the program's budget was cut), such efforts were often eligible for financial support through the national Learn and Serve America program. Professional associations founded to advocate this approach to civic education continue to thrive. Campus Compact now has 1200 members, and approximately one-third of the student body on member campuses is enrolled in service-learning courses each year.[1] Meanwhile, the American Association of State Colleges and Universities (AASCU) launched the American Democracy Project to support civic engagement efforts at four-year institutions, and its success has recently inspired The Democracy Commitment, intended to provide similar programming and support for US community colleges.[2] The Carnegie Foundation for the Advancement of Teaching (CFAT) now provides public recognition as an incentive for colleges and universities to embrace this approach with its new Community Engagement classification. Applications for this voluntary classification were accepted for the first time in 2010, and 196 campuses across the country demonstrated sufficient commitment to civic engagement to earn CFAT's classification (CFAT 2012).

The civic engagement movement has often targeted administrators, based on the assumption that committed presidents and provosts can do far more to promote change on their campuses than individual faculty members. When these senior officers look for partners on campus, they often turn to political science – where department mission statements and professors' personal convictions often embrace the task of cultivating informed, active citizens (Frank 2013). Not all political scientists recognize this responsibility, as some remain convinced that the key to advancing the discipline within the academy is to focus on traditional scholarship. Others position civic education within liberal political theory, focusing on providing students with substantive political knowledge, and questioning whether colleges, particularly publicly funded institutions, ought to cultivate students' normative civic identities. Yet, even though civic engagement and service learning have not been wholeheartedly embraced, American political scientists such as Harry Boyte were early supporters of the civic engagement movement, while others such as Richard Battistoni (2002) and Battistoni and William Hudson (1987) provided important early resources for implementing and assessing service learning.

As Battistoni (2000) called on political science to remain at the forefront of the movement, the discipline had already responded (and continues to do so). Initially, the American Political Science Association (APSA) founded the Teaching and Learning Section in the 1990s, and the number of SoTL and civic engagement articles appearing in *PS: Political Science* began to increase until they became a regular feature in 'The Teacher' section. In 1997, professors engaged in SoTL research founded their own section, which was has since been renamed 'The Political Science Education' section. In 2005, a peer-reviewed journal, *The Journal of Political Science Education*, was launched, and in 2004 APSA initiated its Teaching and Learning Conference. These outlets guarantee that the increasing numbers of political scientists engaged in SoTL and civic engagement research will have an outlet for their work. Further evidence that citizen engagement is coming to fruition within the discipline is provided by Allison Rios Millet McCartney et al.'s (2013) edited collection, *Teaching Civic Engagement: From Student to Active Citizen*, as well as by the newly launched Consortium for Inter-Campus SoTL Research, which will facilitate members' abilities to conduct well-designed, peer-reviewed SoTL and civic engagement research across their collective campuses.[3]

These efforts are grounded in the normative belief that higher education is responsible for transforming students into active citizens. Yet, just as efforts to promote student engagement have become more important for pragmatic reasons in the USA, so too have citizen engagement efforts. Prominent higher education scholars, for example, are concerned that public support for higher education has waned because our institutions are increasingly disconnected from average citizens and that the benefits of higher education are now more often framed as a private benefit for individual students than as a collective good (Saltmarsh and Hartley 2011). As this mindset continues to take root, public support for higher education could simply evaporate. Saltmarsh and Hartley (2011) believe that the only public institutions that will survive will be those that cultivate authentic democratic engagement (rather than hierarchical, expert–client relationships) with community partners. Hence practicing pedagogies of engagement will not only produce the engaged citizens democracy requires, but should help to raise the profile of political science during a time of ever-shrinking resources and fiscal constraint.

Moreover, public officials are now joining the call for higher education institutions to cultivate healthy civic – and increasingly explicitly political – engagement among America's youngest citizens. Such calls (Bok 2006; Boyer 1987; Carnegie Corporation of New York 2003; Colby et al. 2003; Colby et al. 2007; Ehrlich et al. 2000; Galston 2001) were initially triggered by young voters' poor turnout at the polls, as well as their general declining interest in politics – all of which hit disconcerting, historic lows throughout the 1990s and early 2000s (Wattenberg 2012; Zukin et al. 2006).[4] As president of the American Political Science Association in the mid-1990s, Elinor Ostrom responded to these concerns by calling for a renewed commitment to civic education within the discipline. She established the APSA Task Force on Civic Education (1998, p. 636), which went on to conclude that 'levels of political knowledge, political engagement and political enthusiasm are so low as to threaten the vitality and stability of democratic politics in the United States'.

Young people's rejection of traditional politics occurred despite the civic engagement movement's success in institutionalizing service learning, increasing youth concern about broader social issues and heightening rates of youth volunteerism. Some observers find these patterns sufficiently reassuring, because they find volunteerism to be an acceptable alternative to explicitly political participation (Dalton 2008). Others express deep concern that young citizens are purposefully avoiding traditional politics and turning to face-to-face volunteerism and political consumerism (which involves both boycotting and 'buy-cotting' products) as a replacement (Zukin et al. 2006) – for while such behaviors are valuable in and of themselves, healthy democracies require higher levels of explicitly political participation. Volunteering, these critics would point out, can supplement voting, but cannot be seen as an acceptable alternative to voting. In particular, Boyte (1991, p. 765) warned that college 'appears to leave students without concepts or language to explore what is political about their lives' – a warning that was confirmed when more than half of graduating college seniors reported that their college experience had little or no effect on their plans to vote in the future (Kuh and Umbach 2004). In short, in the same way that student engagement advocates would not be satisfied if students improved their scholarly skills and abilities, but did not use them to achieve higher levels of academic achievement, civic engagement advocates will not be satisfied until students use newly gained civic skills and political efficacy to actively influence political decision-making.

When the Obama campaigns' targeted mobilization of young people in 2008 and in 2012 helped to reverse these low voter turnout patterns, scholars and pundits breathed a collective sigh of relief – only to have their concerns reignited when it became clear that these spikes were contextual. As numerous public opinion polls, as well as the ensuing midterm, special and primary elections have revealed, paying attention to politics and voting have not yet become consistent habits for many American young people (Harward and Shea 2013, pp. 22–4).

Hence reformers most committed to the agenda of explicit political socialization are not satisfied with the accomplishments of the citizen engagement movement, and now argue for renewed vigor, new approaches and even new terminology (shifting from the term 'citizen engagement' to 'democratic engagement') in an effort to democratize the culture of higher education (Saltmarsh and Hartley 2011).

Similar concerns inspired the National Task Force on Civic Learning and Democratic Engagement, a joint project of the US Department of Education and the American Association of Colleges and Universities (AACU). The Task Force's report, *A Crucible Moment: College Learning and Democracy's Future*, provides the most explicit call yet for higher education to promote students' 'democratic engagement'. Professors who choose to pursue this agenda will not need to start from scratch, as the citizen engagement movement has already produced a rich scholarship of teaching and learning that not only describes well-designed teaching practices, but documents their effectiveness (Battistoni 2002; Battistoni and Hudson 1987; McCartney et al. 2013).

In particular, the Political Engagement Project (PEP), a cross-campus effort to collect data undertaken by scholars affiliated with the CFAT, offers important insights into promoting political engagement (Colby et al. 2007; Beaumont 2013). As Beaumont

(2013) highlights, PEP findings provide three important responses for critics of political education. These are, first, that such efforts can be effective in cultivating students' political engagement; second, that these outcomes can be accomplished without imposing a particular ideological or partisan bias; and, third, that such efforts do not widen the 'democratic achievement gap' as they have a consistently higher impact on politically disengaged students. (Note that this third finding mimics the effect of high-impact practices on low-achieving students' levels of student engagement and success.)

The PEP project assessed whether students were gaining the political understanding and skills essential for active citizenship in a democracy. In addition, it tracked improvements in students' motivation to participate in politics, as well as their likelihood of participating in the future (Colby et al. 2007; Beaumont 2013). Note that these desired outcomes mirror those measured in the broader student engagement literature. The college experience must initially provide students with adequate substantive knowledge and skills, laying the foundation for deep, transformative learning as students come to realize that they can (and should) apply these in meaningful and effective ways beyond the classroom. These positive outcomes were most likely to occur when students had opportunities to participate within a politically active community, acquire and practice political action skills, engage in political discourse, and collaborate with other students in racially pluralist contexts (Beaumont 2013). More specific examples of experiential learning that can be used to cultivate civic engagement include: discussion of controversial political issues in settings ranging from classrooms to social networking sites; and service-learning projects in the local community, ranging from internships in political settings, simulations of political decision-making and participation in campus student organizations.[5] Again, it should come as no surprise that these types of learning opportunities fall into the category of high-impact teaching practices that bolster student engagement more generally (Kuh 2008).

Even with high-impact practices, no single class or activity can transform passive students into engaged learners. Yet if the entire campus is oriented toward promoting engagement, students' experiences inside and outside of the classroom will have cumulative, influential effects. Discrete engaged practices are important, but they are much more effective when they overlap and complement one another (Kuh et al. 1991, 2005a, 2005b). Similarly, a single civic engagement class or activity, no matter how well designed, cannot transform students into active citizens. This type of reinforcement is obviously much more apt to occur when the institutional culture on campus supports and rewards the faculty and staff who are responsible for implementing civic engagement activities. Recognizing that institutional culture is essential for advancing their goals, the authors of *A Crucible Moment* (2012, p. 14) urge, 'every college and university to foster a civic ethos that governs campus life, makes civic literacy a goal for every graduate, integrates civic inquiry within majors and general education, and advances civic action as lifelong practice'. This advice is important not only in the USA, but everywhere where higher education is expected to help cultivate an active and engaged citizenry.

Further, just as the long-term goal of active pedagogy is to cultivate students' identities as engaged learners, the goal of civic engagement pedagogy is to cultivate students' civic identities (Gentry 2013). Hence reformers cannot underestimate, once again, how important both the student culture and the campus equivalent of civil society – student groups and organizations – will be in advancing civic engagement goals. Extracurricular group activities have consistently proved a better predictor of adult political participation than classroom learning. Student government and non-athletic clubs – where students use democratic decision-making and produce tangible outcomes – are ideal, because they help students learn to think of themselves as the type of people who pay attention to public issues and who are capable of resolving them (Hooghe and Stolle 2003; Ladewig and Thomas 1987; Yates and Youniss 1998; Youniss et al. 1997; Verba et al. 1995). Recent work in political science has renewed interest in civic duty, providing more in-depth understanding of how it sustains participation, as well as the environments that cultivate it (Campbell 2006). In short, when young people are members of a community that expects political participation, and if their peers impose social sanctions when this expectation is not met, adolescents will internalize norms of civic obligation – and will be intrinsically motivated to participate in public life throughout their lives (Campbell 2006). Yet there is no guarantee that student culture and co-curricular groups will reinforce healthy civic norms. Indeed, groups that cultivate high levels of bonding social capital can undermine tolerance and inclusion, even as they provide members with civic skills and political efficacy (Sidanius et al. 2010; Strachan 2008; Strachan and Owens 2011; Strachan and Senter 2013). Hence efforts to transform institutional culture in support of civic engagement goals should also extend to efforts to transform student culture and campus civil society.

Summary

In short, professors committed to civic engagement pedagogy also now have access to more resources than ever before. The tradition of SoTL research provides well-documented insight into best practices, which can be used to enhance teaching effectiveness. Meanwhile, those who lack a supportive campus environment can work to foster a 'civic ethos' within their institutional and student cultures. In the meantime, however, prominent calls for higher education to promote citizenship can be used to bolster support for civic engagement pedagogy on our campuses.

CONCLUSION

This review of student and civic engagement suggests that the time is ripe to reframe the underlying purpose of pursuing a degree on a traditional college campus. Scholars and administrators who care about the future of higher education would be wise to seize this opportunity. In the past, universities could make credible claims that the substantive knowledge they passed on to students was not available elsewhere in society. One could reasonably argue that administrators recruited teams of specialists so that students could come to campus to learn objective truth and received wisdom from these experts, conveniently gathered together in one location. Yet the rise in alternative sources of expert information – including for-profit institutions, distance education and even the very existence of the Internet – threatens the credibility of this narrative. If college-level learning is primarily about information transfer and rote memorization, the unique benefits of attending a traditional college campus become increasingly hard to defend. If college is about processing and memorizing information, traditional campuses can easily be replaced by the most affordable and convenient ways of accessing that information.

Despite the popularity of the narrative described above, even among many academics, colleges and universities have always been more than a convenient confluence of expertise. Traditional campuses have always provided students with the opportunity to become members of a distinct learning community – a place where incoming students can find faculty mentors and supportive peer networks, both of which provide opportunities for engaged, interactive and transformative learning. Descriptions of this ideal, engaged learning community are embedded in institutional mission statements across the globe. Some colleges and universities, those with a close link between their espoused and enacted mission (Kuh et al. 2005a, p. 26), have simply done a better job of cultivating and sustaining an ideal learning community. In order to succeed in meeting the current challenges of enhancing student learning and persistence while promoting good citizenship, more institutions will need to follow suit by first acknowledging and then celebrating both the normative and communal underpinnings of a good education. The current push for student engagement and civic engagement on campus offers an ideal opportunity to do so.

NOTES

1. A description of Campus Compact's history and current activities can be found on the organization's web page at http://www.compact.org/.
2. More details about these programs can be found at http://www.aascu.org/programs/ADP/ and http://www.aascu.org/programs/adp/democracycommitment/.
3. To learn more about the Consortium or to join, go to http://is.gd/SOTL_Consortium or contact the co-founders, Elizabeth Bennion (ebennion@iusb.edu) and J. Cherie Strachan (strac1jc@cmich.edu).
4. See Harward and Shea (2013), pp. 22–4, for an overview of these patterns.
5. See McCartney et al. (2013) for detailed descriptions of how these and other specific pedagogical approaches have been implemented.

REFERENCES

Addis, C. (2003), *Jefferson's Vision for Education, 1760–1845*, New York: Peter Lang.
Adelman, C. (2004), *Principal Indicators of Student Academic Histories in Postsecondary Education, 1972–2000*, Washington, DC: US Department of Education, Institute of Educational Sciences.
American Political Science Association Task Force on Civic Education in the 21st Century (1998), 'Expanded articulation statement: a call for reactions and contributions', *PS: Political Science & Politics*, **31** (3), 636–8.
Astin, A.W. (1977), *Four Critical Years*, San Francisco, CA: Jossey-Bass.
Astin, A.W. (1991), *Assessment for Excellence: The Philosophy and Practice of Assessment and Evaluation in Higher Education. American Council on Education Series on Higher Education*, Washington, DC and New York: American Council on Education and Macmillan.
Bain, K. and Zimmerman, J. (2009), 'Understanding great teaching', *Peer Review*, **11** (2), 9–12.
Battistoni, R.M. (2000), 'Service learning in political science: an introduction', *PS: Political Science & Politics*, **33** (3), 614–16.
Battistoni, R.M. (2002), *Civic Engagement across the Curriculum: A Resource Book for Service Learning Faculty in all Disciplines*, Providence, RI: Campus Compact.
Battistoni, R.M. and Hudson, W.E. (eds) (1997), *Experiencing Citizenship: Concepts, and Models for Service Learning in Political Science*, Washington, DC: American Association for Higher Education.
Bean, J.P. (1985), 'Interaction effects based on class level in an explanatory model of college student dropout syndrome', *American Educational Research Journal*, **22**, 35–64.

Beaumont, E. (2013), 'Political learning and democratic capacities: some challenges and evidence of promising approaches', in A.R.M. McCartney, E.A. Bennion and D. Simpson (eds), *Teaching Civic Engagement: From Student to Active Citizen*, Washington, DC: American Political Science Association, pp. 41–56.

Beaumont, E. and Battistoni, R.M. (2006), 'Beyond Civics 101: rethinking what we mean by civics education', *Journal of Political Science Education*, **2** (3), 441–7.

Bellah, R., Madsen, W.M., Swidler, A. and Tipton, S.M. (1985), *Habits of the Heart: Individualism and Commitment in American Life*, Los Angeles, CA: University of California Press.

Bloustein, E.J. (1999), 'Community service: a new requirement for the educated person', in B. Barber and R.M. Battistoni (eds), *Education for Democracy*, Dubuque, IA: Kendall/Hunt, pp. 489–94.

Bok, D. (2006), *Our Underachieving Colleges*, Princeton, NJ: Princeton University Press.

Boyer, E.L. (1987), *College: The Undergraduate Experience in America*, Princeton, NJ: Carnegie Foundation for the Advancement of Teaching.

Boyer, E.L. (1990), *Scholarship Reconsidered. The Priorities of the Professoriate*, San Francisco, CA: Jossey-Bass.

Boyte, H. (1991), 'Community service and civic education', *Phi Delta Kappan*, **72** (10), 765–7.

Braxton, J.M. (2000), *Rethinking the Departure Puzzle: New Theory and Research on College Retention*, Nashville, TN: Vanderbilt University Press.

Brickman, W.W. (1972), 'American higher education in historical perspective', *Annals of the American Academy of Political and Social Science*, **404**, 31–43.

Brintnall, M. (2013), 'Foreword', in A.R.M. McCartney, E.A. Bennion and D. Simpson (eds), *Teaching Civic Engagement: From Student to Active Citizen*, Washington, DC: American Political Science Association, pp. xi–xii.

Campbell, D.E. (2006), *Why We Vote: How Schools and Communities Shape our Civic Life*, Princeton, NJ: Princeton University Press.

Carnegie Corporation of New York (2003), *The Civic Mission of Schools*, New York: Carnegie Corporation of New York.

Carnegie Foundation for the Advancement of Teaching (2012), 'Community engagement classification', available at http://classifications.carnegiefoundation.org/descriptions/community_engagement.php (accessed 30 September 2012).

Chickering, A.W. (1974), *Commuting versus Resident Students: Overcoming Educational Inequalities of Living off Campus*, San Francisco, CA: Jossey-Bass.

Chickering, A.W. and Gamson, Z.E. (1987), 'Seven principles for good practice in undergraduate education', *AAHE Bulletin*, **39** (7), 3–7.

Chickering, A.W. and Reisser, L. (1993), *Education and Identity*, San Francisco, CA: Jossey-Bass.

Colby, Anne, Beaumont, Elizabeth, Ehrlich, Thomas and Corngold, Josh (2007), *Educating for Democracy: Preparing Undergraduates for Responsible Political Engagement*, San Francisco, CA: Jossey-Bass.

Colby, Anne, Ehrlich, Thomas, Beaumont, Elizabeth and Stephens, Jason (2003), *Educating Citizens: Preparing America's Undergraduates for Lives of Moral Responsibility*, San Francisco, CA: Jossey-Bass.

Dalton, R.J. (2008), *The Good Citizen: How a Younger Generation is Reshaping American Politics*, Washington, DC: CQ Press.

Dewey, J. (1933), *How we Think: A Restatement of the Relation of Reflective Thinking to the Educative Process*, Boston, MA: DC Heath.

Dewey, J. ([1916] 1966), *Democracy and Education: An Introduction to the Philosophy of Education*, New York: Free Press.

Education Commission of the States (1995), *Making Quality Count in Undergraduate Education*, Denver, CO: Education Commission of the States.

Ehrlich, T. (ed.) (2000), *Civic Responsibility and Higher Education*, Phoenix, AZ: The American Council on Education and Oryx Press.

Fass, P.S. (1989), *Outside In: Minorities and the Transformation of American Education*, New York: Oxford University Press.

Frank, P.E. (2013), 'Political science faculty as models of political engagement', in A.R.M. McCartney, E.A. Bennion and D. Simpson (eds), *Teaching Civic Engagement: From Student to Active Citizen*, Washington, DC: American Political Science Association, pp. 87–100.

Galston, W.A. (2001), 'Political knowledge, political engagement, and civic education', *Annual Review of Political Science*, **4**, 217–34.

Gentry, B. (2013), 'Bridging adolescent engagement and adult engagement: a theory of political identity', in A.R.M. McCartney, E.A. Bennion and D. Simpson (eds), *Teaching Civic Engagement: From Student to Active Citizen*, Washington, DC: American Political Science Association, pp. 57–72.

Hartley, M. (2011), 'Idealism and compromise and the civic engagement movement', in J. Saltmarsh and M. Hartley (eds), *'To Serve a Larger Purpose': Engagement for Democracy and the Transformation of Higher Education*, Philadelphia, PA: Temple University Press, pp. 27–48.

Harward, B.M. and Shea, D.M. (2013), 'Higher education and multiple modes of engagement', in A.R.M. McCartney, E.A. Bennion and D. Simpson (eds), *Teaching Civic Engagement: From Student to Active Citizen*, Washington, DC: American Political Science Association, pp. 21–40.

Hooghe, M. and Stolle, D. (2003), *Generating Social Capital: Civil Society and Institutions in Comparative Perspective*, New York: Palgrave Macmillan.

Keller, G. (2001), 'The new demographics of higher education', *The Review of Higher Education*, **24** (3), 219–35.

Kuh, G.D. (2001a), 'College students today: why we can't leave serendipity to chance', in P. Altback, P. Gumport and B. Johnstone (eds), *In Defense of the American University*, Baltimore, MD: The Johns Hopkins University Press.

Kuh, G.D. (2001b), 'Assessing what really matters to student learning', *Change*, May/June, 10–17.

Kuh, G.D. (2008), *High Impact Educational Practices: What They Are, Who has Access to Them, and Why They Matter*, Washington, DC: Association of American Colleges and Universities.

Kuh, G.D., Kinzie, J., Schuh, J. and Whitt, E.J. (2005a), *Student Success in College: Creating Conditions that Matter*, San Francisco, CA: Jossey-Bass.

Kuh, G.D., Kinzie, J., Schuh, J. and Whitt, E.J. (2005b), *Assessing Conditions to Enhance Educational Effectiveness*, San Francisco, CA: Jossey-Bass.

Kuh, G.D., Schuh, J.H. and Whitt, E.J. (1991), *Involving Colleges: Successful Approaches to Fostering Student Learning and Personal Development outside of the Classroom*, San Francisco, CA: Jossey-Bass.

Kuh, G.D. and Umbach, P.D. (2004), 'College and character: insights from the National Survey of Student Engagement', *New Directions for Institutional Research*, **112**, 37–54.

Kuh, G.D. and Whitt, E.J. (1988), *The Invisible Tapestry: Culture in American Colleges and Universities. ASHE-ERIC Higher Education Report No 1*, Washington, DC: Association for the Study of Higher Education.

Ladewig, H. and Thomas, J.K. (1987), *Assessing the Impact of 4-H on Former Members*, College Station, TX: Texas Tech University.

Lazerson, M. (1998), 'The disappointments of success: higher education after World War II', *Annals of the American Academy of Political and Social Science*, **559**, 64–76.

McCartney, A.R.M., Bennion, E.A. and Simpson, D. (eds) (2013), *Teaching Civic Engagement: From Student to Active Citizen*, Washington, DC: American Political Science Association.

McKeachie, W.J. and Svinicki, M. (2006), *McKeachie's Teaching Tips: Strategies, Research and Theory for College and University Teachers*, 12th edn, Independence, KY: Cengage Learning.

Miller, R. (2009), 'Connecting beliefs with research on effective undergraduate education', *Peer Review*, **11** (2), 4–8.

National Task Force on Civic Learning and Democratic Engagement (2012), *A Crucible Moment: College Learning and Democracy's Future*, Washington, DC: Association of American Colleges and Universities.

Nemec, M.R. (2006), *Ivory Towers and Nationalist Minds: Universities, Leadership, and the Development of the American State*, Ann Arbor, MI: The University of Michigan Press.

Pascarella, E.T. (1984), 'Reassessing the effects of living on-campus versus commuting to college: a causal modeling approach', *Review of Higher Education*, **7**, 247–60.

Pascarella, E.T. (1985), 'College environmental influences on learning and cognitive development', in J.C. Smart (ed.), *Higher Education Handbook of Theory and Research*, vol. 1, New York: Agathon, pp. 1–62.

Pascarella, E.T. (2001), 'Identifying excellence in undergraduate education: are we even close?', *Change*, **33** (3), 19–23.

Pascarella, E.T. and Terenzini, P.T. (1991), *How College Affects Students*, San Francisco, CA: Jossey-Bass.

Pascarella, E.T. and Terenzini, P.T. (2005), *How College Affects Students: A Third Decade of Research*, San Francisco, CA: Jossey-Bass.

Putnam, R.D. (2000), *Bowling Alone: The Collapse and Revival of American Community*, New York: Simon & Schuster.

Putnam, R.D. (2002), *Democracies in Flux: The Evolution of Social Capital in Contemporary Societies*, New York: Oxford University Press.

Rimmerman, C. (2011), 'Service-learning and public policy', in C. Rimmerman (ed.), *Service-learning in the Liberal Arts: How and Why it Works*, Lanham, MD: Lexington, pp. 71–84.

Rothstein, B. (2011), *The Quality of Government: Corruption, Social Trust, and Inequality in International Perspective*, Chicago, IL; University of Chicago Press.

Rudolph, F. (1990), *American College and University: A History*, Athens, GA: University of Georgia Press.

Saltmarsh, J. and Hartley, M. (eds) (2011), *To Serve a Larger Purpose: Engagement for Democracy and the Transformation of Higher Education*, Philadelphia, PA: Temple University Press.

Sidanius, J., Levin, S., Van Laar, C. and Sears, D.O. (2008), *The Diversity Challenge: Social Identity and Intergroup Relations on the College Campus*, New York: Russell Sage.

Skocpol, T. (2003), *Diminished Democracy: From Membership to Management in American Civil Life*, Norman, OK: The University of Oklahoma Press.

Strachan, J. Cherie (2008), 'Using the classroom to cultivate student support for participation in campus life', *Journal of Political Science Education*, **4** (1), 21–41.
Strachan, J.C. and Owens, C.T. (2011), 'Learning civic norms outside of the classroom: diversity and campus associational life', *Journal of Political Science Education*, **7** (4), 464–82.
Strachan, J.C. and Senter, M. (2013), 'Student organizations and civic education on campus: the Greek system', in A.R.M. McCartney, E.A. Bennion and D. Simpson (eds), *Teaching Civic Engagement: From Student to Active Citizen*, Washington, DC: American Political Science Association, pp. 385–402.
Thelin, J.R. (2004), *A History of American Higher Education*, Baltimore, MD: Johns Hopkins University Press.
Tinto, V. (1993), *Leaving College: Rethinking the Causes and Cures of Student Attrition*, 2nd edn, Chicago, IL: University of Chicago Press.
Uslaner, Eric (2002), *The Moral Foundations of Trust*, New York: Cambridge University Press.
Verba, S., Schlozman, K.L. and Brady, H.E. (1995), *Voice and Equality: Civic Volunteerism in American Politics*, Cambridge, MA: Harvard University Press.
Wattenberg, Martin P. (2012), *Is Voting for Young People?*, 3rd edn, New York: Pearson.
Yates, M. and Youniss, J. (1998), 'Community service and political identity development in adolescence', *Journal of Social Issues*, **54** (3), 495–52.
Youniss, J., McLellen, J.A. and Yates, M. (1997), 'What we know about engendering civic identity', *American Behavioral Scientist*, **40** (5), 620–31.
Zukin, C., Keeter, S.A., Jenkins, K. and Delli Carpini, M.X. (2006), *A New Engagement? Political Participation, Civic Life and the Changing American Citizen*, New York: Oxford University Press.

7. Curricular and program assessment techniques in the USA
Kerstin Hamann

Curricular and program assessment have become increasingly important tasks for political science and international relations departments[1] in institutions of higher learning across the USA. Program and curricular assessment matter for several reasons. Perhaps most importantly, when done well, assessment furnishes insights into what students have learned or what they know, which, in turn, is instrumental in informing departments as they strive to improve their curriculum and instruction. Empirical data about student learning are crucial in identifying areas of strengths and weaknesses in programs, and are therefore core for devising strategies to improve student learning. At the same time, assessment has become increasingly important because in many colleges and universities it is required for accreditation purposes; satisfies demands by legislators to provide evidence of student learning and, consequently, is considered a good investment of taxpayers' money; and is requested by parents who want to know whether the college of choice for their children will ensure that they will graduate equipped with adequate types of knowledge and skill sets to prepare them for future careers and a fulfilled life (see Suskie 2007).

Faculty members and administrators charged with assessment have a variety of resources available to assist them in designing the assessment process. Books and websites on assessment include discussions concerning the use of assessment, detailed descriptions of the necessary steps for a meaningful assessment process, as well as different examples and illustrations that help guide the choice of assessment tools.[2] Yet, at the same time, the discipline-specific literature addressing programmatic assessment in political science and international relations is by and large still quite limited, perhaps a reflection of the fact that political science as a discipline is a relative latecomer to the assessment movement (McClellan 2009; Smoller 2004). Frequently, literature on assessment in the discipline showcases assessment plans in specific departments or programs as case studies; these case studies, although valuable, cannot always be readily applied in different departmental contexts. More recent advances in the Scholarship of Teaching and Learning (SoTL) in the discipline have provided some valuable examples of classroom and course assessment that can usefully be integrated into program assessment processes, but as such these studies are for the most part not designed with programmatic assessment in mind. Valuable examples of classroom and course assessment in political science and international relations are regularly published in disciplinary journals, especially the *Journal of Political Science Education*,[3] *PS: Political Science & Politics* and *International Studies Perspectives*. At the same time, a few studies have analyzed the use of different tools designed for program assessment in the discipline and thus provide a guide map of different assessment strategies (e.g. Deardorff et al. 2009a; Ishiyama 2009; Ishiyama and Breuning 2008; Kelly and Klunk 2003). The APSA Teaching and Learning

Conference regularly offers tracks and conference papers on program assessment and brief track summaries are published in *PS: Political Science & Politics*.[4]

This chapter provides a brief introduction to the assessment process in general, presents an overview of commonly used assessment practices in political science departments and offers some guidelines on developing an assessment program.

ESSENTIALS OF THE ASSESSMENT PROCESS

Program assessment can be defined as

> a means for focusing our collective attention, examining our assumptions, and creating a shared academic culture dedicated to continuously improving the quality of higher learning. Assessment requires making expectations and standards for quality explicit and public; systematically gathering evidence on how well performance matches these expectations and standards; analyzing and interpreting the evidence; and using the resulting information to document, explain, and improve performance. (Angelo 1995, p. 11)

Although there is no consensus on a definition of assessment, other definitions are similar, for example

> the **systematic and ongoing** method of **gathering, analyzing and using information** from various sources about a program and measuring program outcomes in order **to improve student learning**. This is done through obtaining a good understanding of what the program's graduates know, what they can do with this knowledge and what they value as a result of this knowledge. (University of Central Florida 2006, p. 3, emphasis in the original)

Thus assessment serves several purposes. For many political science departments, assessment is a response to external demands and consequently primarily an exercise that satisfies the mandate by administrators, regional accreditation bodies, or legislatures to assess student learning. At the same time, assessment is also a useful tool to set departmental or programmatic expectations for what students are supposed to learn or which skills they are expected to develop as they progress through their curriculum; and to analyze what students have learned at different stages of their college career (most commonly, assessment plans focus on what students know or how well they perform on certain skills near the time they graduate). These insights won from the assessment process can help departments estimate the need for additional courses and future hires, structure advising practices, stimulate mapping of the curriculum, think about sequencing skill development – for example different types of writing assignments, analytical skills, or presentation skills – over the course of a college career, help structure course offerings and schedules, form partnerships with other units (such as career centers) on campus, form closer relationships with internship sites and future employers, and so on. In sum, assessment results ideally lead to curricular changes that, in turn, target improvements in student learning. Consequently, most descriptions and general 'how to' guides on assessment emphasize the assessment process as a 'loop' or circle, where insights gained from the program assessment feed back into curricular design.

Commonly, the 'best-practice' assessment sequence is described as having several components that build sequentially on each other. The sequence begins with establishing a set of departmental or programmatic learning objectives; learner objectives, for their part, need to be closely aligned with the departmental or programmatic mission, which, in turn, should be aligned with the mission of the college and institution. Unless it is clear what the students are expected to learn, it is difficult, if not impossible, to design measures to assess student learning. The learner objectives then inform a set of measures to gauge what students have actually learned, or what they know, or what they can do. Data need to be collected and analyzed to evaluate student learning. The results of the data analysis then serve as the basis for curricular revisions designed to improve student learning – or 'closing the loop' (see, e.g., Kelly and Klunk 2003, p. 451). Assessment is thus a continuous process designed to measure and improve student learning on a set of selected objectives. It is most useful if it forms the empirical basis for changes in the curriculum or program that aim to increase student learning in areas where assessment has identified weaknesses.

In practice, assessment efforts have indeed turned out to be useful tools for revising program structures and curricular offerings, as well as course contents. While there is little research on the effectiveness of assessment for improving instruction in political science and international relations, Kelly and Klunk's (2003) study reports that 19 percent of the responding departments revised their major requirements, while others (4 percent) developed new majors, tracks, or emphases. Other departments changed or introduced course sequencing, requiring students to take specific courses at a specified time in their college career – for example, demanding that students take a research methods course early on in their college career rather than as seniors. Departments also added courses to their curricular offerings to address learning deficiencies in some areas or subfields, for example in international relations. Another way of addressing weaknesses discovered through assessment was to change course contents, for example in research methods courses (Kelly and Klunk 2003, p. 454). These data confirm that assessment, when done well and used to close the loop, can play a useful role in reviewing and revising curricula and programs (see also Smoller 2004).

CURRENT ASSESSMENT PRACTICES IN POLITICAL SCIENCE DEPARTMENTS

The assessment practices used by political science departments in the USA vary widely and depend on several factors, including the purpose of the assessment, assessment rules and guidelines mandated by the institution, the state or regional accreditation bodies, the size of the institution and the program/department, and available resources at the institutional, department and program levels. For example, departments or programs with a relatively small number of students may embrace the opportunity to assess a freshman seminar and a capstone course to trace gains in student knowledge and skills, while departments with a large number of majors and a significant proportion of transfer students from two-year institutions may not offer these types of courses that provide a seminar-like experience; therefore they have to rely on other ways to measure student learning in the program. The mission and curriculum of the department are important considerations also when assessment plans are developed, since the learner objectives that drive the assessment should be geared to match the mission and the curriculum of a particular program. For example, learner outcomes – and therefore the relevant assessment objectives and measures – are likely different for departments in a small private liberal arts college, a faith-based college and a program at a large public institution. Some departments may make experiential learning, such as community engagement and service learning, an integral part of their mission and curriculum, while others may emphasize early research experiences or focus on skills, such as critical thinking or written communication skills. Some departments strive to place their alumni in graduate or postgraduate professional schools, while others attempt to prepare them for employment upon graduation. These variations in program missions should ideally be reflected in course curricula, which in turn provide the basis for designing learner outcomes that are targeted in the assessment project.

Survey data from 213 colleges and universities, as reported in Kelly and Klunk (2003), confirm that departments indeed exhibit considerable variation when they adopt their learning objectives, reflecting diversity in missions and learner outcomes in the discipline. More than half of the responding departments reported that they had adopted learning objectives relating to theories and analytical approaches, critical thinking and writing skills; almost as many departments (40–50 percent) stated learner objectives concerning subfields, international dimension, the design and conduct of research; between 30 and 40 percent had adopted learning objectives related to quantitative approaches, normative approaches, reading skills, presentation skills and information technology skills. Other learning objectives were concerned with ethnic/gender/cultural dimensions, practical experience and others (Kelly and Klunk 2003, p. 452). If these stated learning objectives are at all related to the department's mission, it is evident that both the mission and the consequent learning objectives vary greatly across departments, and not all departments have clearly stated objectives for different areas of political science instruction. Consequently, not one type of assessment fits every program; instead, assessment tools need to be chosen carefully, keeping in mind the goals as well as the resources and constraints related to developing and implementing an assessment plan. It is therefore necessary to gain a thorough understanding of the range of tools available for assessing student learning, and to pick the appropriate tools carefully to develop a good match with the program.[5]

Kelly and Klunk's (2003) findings are echoed in a study by Ishiyama (2009)[6] that identifies departments' and programs' learner objectives. Coding the assessment plans of 70 political science programs of US colleges and universities that are publicly available online, Ishiyama finds that the most commonly reported learning goals were critical thinking (68.1 percent), knowledge of fields in political science and written communication skills (66.7 percent each) and knowledge of theories pertaining to political science (65.2 percent), followed by knowledge of political institutions and processes (63.8 percent) and methods and research skills (62.3 percent). Oral communication and presentation skills are listed in over half of the assessment plans (53.6 percent). Less frequently mentioned goals are citizenship and career, each of which was listed as a learning goal in about one-quarter of the assessment plans, and cultural diversity (17.4 percent) and ethics/values (11.6 percent). Again, these results demonstrate that, while there is some commonality in terms of what political science programs across the country strive to teach their students, there is also considerable variation. These results also illustrate that individual assessment plans do not necessarily cover the entire range of learning objectives pursued in a department, but perhaps comprise a rather selective list of objectives that is analyzed in the assessment process. It is quite common, and in fact good practice, to focus on particular and selective objectives for assessment, identify weaknesses, design and implement a plan to address these weaknesses, and, once student learning has improved in that area, rotate to a different objective or set of objectives to target other areas of the curriculum.

What, then, are some of the most common tools used by political science departments? Several surveys conducted over the last decade or so have shown that departments employ a large variety of assessment methods and tools. Kelly and Klunk (2003) found in their survey that the most commonly used assessment tool was the senior capstone course, employed by 39.6 percent of responding departments. Other tools in practice included (listed here in descending order of frequency) faculty observations, exit interviews, survey of students, a senior research project, a portfolio, a post-test, a pre-test/post-test and other unspecified tools.

Ishiyama (2009, p. 67) also finds that departments commonly use a variety of assessment tools. Listed in descending order of frequency, these tools include a graduating survey/questionnaire, which about half of all departments in the study employ; analysis of student grades/performance; senior seminar/capstone; a comprehensive exam; a senior thesis; a senior exit interview; a portfolio; random reading of student papers; student course evaluations; alumni surveys and interviews; and a syllabus analysis (7.1 percent). Again, the array of assessment methods illustrates that departments have a toolkit of methods available and can pick depending on needs and resources. Ishiyama (2009) illustrates that there is also some variation in the number of assessment tools in place, ranging from 0 to 6 in his sample. In identifying patterns of assessment tools used by different types of departments, perhaps most significantly he finds that political science departments located in small institutions and those that offer a Bachelor's degree only are more likely than departments in larger institutions and those offering a graduate degree to employ 'external' assessment techniques. Such techniques are not generated by regular course work, but instead require additional work to gather data, such as graduating senior interviews or portfolio analyses. Again, these findings suggest that the institutional context, including degree program, mission and resources, matters for designing assessment plans.

SOME GUIDELINES FOR EFFECTIVE PROGRAM ASSESSMENT

Most departments and faculty charged with developing an assessment plan are likely to be primarily concerned with the specifics of developing and implementing such a plan – for example, which measures to choose and how to collect the data. However, as has been frequently pointed out, the first step is to get departmental consensus on the mission of the program and the desired learning outcomes. Assessment is sometimes met with resistance from faculty for several reasons (see Deardorff and Folger 2009, p. 77). For one, assessment tends to be a task that is added to faculty members' to-do lists, often without granting new resources or compensation, and is thus commonly regarded as a burden, especially when class sizes increase while budgets are cut in many institutions. In many cases, the need for assessment is not identified through discussion among faculty, but is imposed externally on departments and faculty, adding to the list of chores faculty are charged with. Furthermore, professors may worry that, rather than student learning, it is their own teaching that is being assessed. In other words, what if assessment reveals that students do not actually learn much in their class(es)? The fear is that the professor may be blamed for lackluster student performance, which in turn could have potential consequences when it comes to promotion, tenure or even teaching awards. Similarly, departments on the whole may be concerned about the consequences of poor assessment results for the future of the department. Especially in times of constrained resources, departments may fear that the demonstration of lack of student accomplishments will have negative consequences if the administration is interested in using assessment for the purpose of decisions on resource allocation rather than with the aim of improving student learning. It is thus crucial that everyone involved in the assessment process is aware of its purpose, knows who will read the results, and what the results will be used for by department chairs and university administrators. Program assessment is done best when it focuses exclusively on student learning and when resulting evidence of poor student performance is used to improve teaching and learning in a constructive rather than in a punitive way. Given common faculty resistance to assessment, several strategies can help institutionalize assessment in departments and programs, and align them with those of the college and the institution.[7] For instance, some studies point to the importance of faculty buy-in and a bottom–up approach to designing effective assessment, suggesting that assessment is most effective when it becomes part of the departmental culture shared by all faculty (e.g. Deardorff and Folger 2009; Hill and Pastors 2009).

Departments charged with, or committed to, designing assessment programs from scratch are faced with complex choices. They have to consider available resources (financial as well as time constraints on faculty and resources that could be provided by the university), the number of students in the program, programmatic missions, mandates on what the assessment process may have to include and so forth. For example, the State of Florida's Board of Governors mandates that all BA degree programs at public universities provide assessment of Academic Learning Compacts in three areas: discipline-specific knowledge, skills, attitudes and behaviors; communication; and critical thinking. Given this mandate, some universities have made these Academic Learning Compacts part of the regular program assessment process.[8] Departments then need to assign appropriate learning objectives and measures in each of these three mandated areas. Thus it is important that departments are aware of external and university assessment mandates and demands as they design their assessment plans.

Young (2009) provides a useful approach to developing a plan for program assessment. She presents an array of assessment tools that can be tailored to respond to departmental needs and resources. Some types of data may be available through university offices, while others are already available at the level of the department, and yet others can be collected by faculty. For example, it may be useful for departments to begin by 'taking stock' at a macro-level and analyze program data as a first step. This can include data such as student–faculty ratio; graduation and retention rates; the number of majors over time; the percentage of students who enroll in experiential classes, such as service learning, internships, or participate in a study abroad experience; and placement of graduating seniors. Attitudinal and self-assessment data can also be helpful for program assessment and can be obtained by distributing surveys to students (perhaps at different stages in their college career and as they are graduating), internship sites, employers and so on. These surveys can gauge, for example, how well students and employers think that the program has prepared the students for the workplace or for graduate/law school, or what the biggest weaknesses in the program are perceived to be. Programs can also build assessment tools into their courses, for instance by assigning research projects or papers that can then be coded for writing and analytical skills. Another possibility is to administer exams to students to evaluate their knowledge, such as the Educational Testing Service (ETS) major field test or a locally developed test.[9] If the program is large, using a sample of the student population may be a useful approach.

In thinking about which particular assessment tools to use, assessment coordinators may want to classify them into several categories, each with specific advantages and disadvantages.[10] Institutional data, such as Grade Point Averages (GPAs), demographic background of the students, and length of time to graduation are helpful in developing a macro-level picture of the student body and may reveal patterns that help identify scheduling problems or weaknesses in student advising. For example, graduation and retention rates may indicate that students have to postpone graduation because required courses are not offered frequently enough, or more sections need to be offered; alternatively, the advising system may need improvement so that students can be guided to the courses needed to graduate in a timely fashion. This information can help with decisions on course scheduling or advising practices. On the other hand, these types of data tend to reveal little, if anything, about specific student learner outcomes.

Data derived from sources such as course syllabi can provide crucial information concerning the extent to which the departmental mission is linked to course offerings. To illustrate, if a program strives to equip its students with excellent communication skills, but the bulk of the courses have few or no writing assignments and opportunities for oral presentations are scarce, this information will be crucial in identifying weak links between the program mission and the actual curriculum. At the same time, syllabi reflect what professors teach rather than what students learn (Ishiyama 2009, p. 62). In order to get specific information about what students have learned, student learning itself must be assessed.

Student learning is commonly gauged through either indirect or direct measures. Indirect measures include surveys, such as exit interviews or surveys with graduating seniors, alumni or internship supervisors. These surveys prompt the student to report what they think they have learned. Items such as 'I gained a solid understanding of the political institutions and processes in the USA', or 'I understand the fundamental theories in international relations', along with a scaled answer expressing levels of agreement, are typical. They are also useful in gaining information concerning prospects for careers after graduation. In addition, surveys are sometimes convenient as they are often cost-effective and easy to administer, and, once set up, can be used for consecutive years. Clearly, despite the limitations to students' self-assessed competencies and knowledge, student perceptions of their knowledge or skills gained are important for many different reasons. Alumni satisfaction is a meaningful resource for many departments as it relates to student recruitment, departmental reputation and potential for future monetary donations to the department. Students also often have a good understanding of what they have learned during their college career. These indirect measures can therefore be useful if interpreted with appropriate caution. However, they also have obvious drawbacks as they do not directly measure knowledge, learning or skills.

Direct measures can provide information about student learning either through the work that students complete as part of their course assignments; additional measures of learning outcomes that are 'embedded' in regular coursework; or through external tools such as comprehensive exams, locally administered disciplinary tests (either locally developed or nationally normed reference tests, such as the ETS field test). For example, if students are required to write a research paper during their college career, such papers can be used to assess subject knowledge as well as written communication skills. Rubrics help standardize the scoring of student work on a set of learning outcomes, such as the correct use of political science terminology, understanding of core concepts, demonstration of familiarity with appropriate citation conventions and reference styles, and writing skills, such as proper use of grammar, punctuation and structure of the paper (see Stevens and Levi 2005).[11] In order to develop a useful assessment plan, departmental faculty should decide what they want students to learn or be able to do during their college career. This includes both knowledge and skills.

One of the problems of collecting useful data to inform program assessment is that this process often requires additional resources, such as faculty members' time to design and analyze comprehensive tests administered to students, money to purchase existing nationally normed tests, and staff time to contact students and to administer exit surveys for graduating seniors. Some departments may therefore prefer to use classroom assessments, or parts of classroom assessments, as sources of information for their program assessments. Classroom assessments provide countless opportunities to gather and analyze data on selected learning objectives.

To maximize the utility of course assessment as a part of program assessment, it may be necessary to engage in curriculum mapping (see Ewell 2013). In other words, it is important to know which skills and knowledge should be assessed from a particular course in the context of the entire curriculum. What are students taught in particular courses? How individual courses fit into the overall curriculum has a bearing on selecting which aspects of the coursework can meaningfully contribute to program assessment. This is important to know prior to deciding which courses can usefully inform program assessment. Taking a good look at course syllabi in the context of the curriculum as a whole may also stimulate a productive departmental discussion about what the distribution of skills and knowledge across the different courses in the curriculum should look like, and if the structure of the curriculum makes sense or should be revised in light of this discussion.

In addition to regularly scheduled classes, internships and other experiential learning contexts may also provide useful data for assessment purposes. Many departments offer internships to promote student engagement, professionalization, practical experience and so forth. Depending on their specific requirements, internships lend themselves to contributing to departmental assessment. For example, if a stated learner objective of the program is to prepare students for the job market, internships can be evaluated by the extent to which they achieve this goal through an assessment of student work, such as a reflective journal that discusses practical work experience; surveys with internship supervisors; or surveys with students at the end of their internship (see also Donahue and Ishiyama 2009). Learning experiences that emphasize civic engagement lend themselves to assessing learning objectives related to citizenship as well as an understanding of political processes at different levels.[12]

In sum, departments have many options to design an effective and meaningful assessment plan. When done well, the assessment process can make a contribution towards identifying weak spots in the curriculum and thereby assist in improving curricula and student learning. Even when assessment is externally imposed rather than demanded by faculty, it can still be a useful process that benefits students and improves programs.

CONCLUSION

Assessment may seem a daunting, and perhaps thankless, task. However, when done well and taken seriously, it can be a valuable tool in supporting faculty members' goals of providing their students with the best possible educational experience. Assessment can assist departments in clarifying and supporting their mission and in thinking strategically about curricula and instruction. Furthermore, as higher education in general, and political science more specifically, has come under attack by politicians and the public in recent years, assessment can have a second function as it documents the 'worth of our programs to external constituents' (Suskie 2007, p. 102). Through assessment, political science as a discipline can demonstrate what political science education can add to educating the public on matters of public interest, and what contribution it makes to having an educated and engaged citizenry.[13] Thus assessment can be used beyond the confines of programs and departments to explain the value of political science education more generally, and to demonstrate the value of such an education for the public.

Assessment demands resources and faculty time. However, it also provides opportunities to benefit faculty or at least ease the cost of time invested in assessment. The 'Scholarship of Assessment' (Deardorff et al. 2009b, pp. 7–8) and the Scholarship of Teaching and Learning offer opportunities to publish studies on assessment, either on program assessment, as the literature in this field is starting to grow in the discipline, or on classroom and course assessments, as is common in SoTL research. Articles in peer-reviewed disciplinary journals on aspects of assessment and teaching bridge what may be an externally mandated exercise with valued disciplinary scholarship based on empirical research. Journals in political science and international relations that publish in the field of SoTL and assessment include the *Journal of Political Science Education*, *International Studies Perspectives* and *PS: Political Science & Politics* (see Hamann et al. 2009). Thus assessment may be one of the links between teaching, research and service that proves beneficial to the students, the faculty and the department.

NOTES

1. Many political science departments house international relations programs, and international relations departments face many of the same challenges regarding assessment as political science departments. I thus treat assessment in political science and international relations as one exercise.
2. Several useful publications on assessment are listed at http://www.apsanet.org/content_65552.cfm?navID=846 and in handbooks and guidelines published by universities' institutional effectiveness or assessment offices, such as http://oeas.ucf.edu/doc/acad_assess_handbook.pdf (University of Central

Florida, 2006) or http://cet.usc.edu/resources/teaching_learning/assessment_learning.html (University of Southern California, n.d.), among many others, which can be adapted for specific disciplines and programs (see also Banta et al. 2009; Huba and Freed 2000; Pusateri et al. 2000; Suskie 2009). The general literature on assessment and assessment tools is relatively large; some useful guides include Angelo and Cross (1993) on classroom assessment techniques, or Bean (2011) on constructing and assessing writing assignments.
3. See, for example, the *Journal of Political Science Education*'s special issue on Simulations in Political Science, which includes several classroom assessments from the use of simulations in international relations courses (*Journal of Political Science Education*, **9** (2), 2013).
4. The track summaries are also available online; for example the summaries for the 2012 Teaching and Learning Conference can be found at http://www.apsanet.org/media/2012%20TLC%20Track%20 Summaries.pdf. See Young et al. (2012) for the summary for the program assessment track.
5. The American Political Science Association hosts a companion website (http://www.apsanet.org/content_62699.cfm) to Deardorff et al. (2009) that links to an array of assessment plans and resources used in political science departments in a variety of institutions of higher learning.
6. Ishiyama's (2009) study incorporates the data and findings by Ishiyama and Breuning (2008).
7. The University of Central Florida's assessment guidelines state explicitly that '[i]n order for program assessment to be successful, the department must reach a consensus on the goals of the program and have an understanding of what the program is trying to accomplish, as well as how the goals are addressed in the curriculum. The goals of a program or unit must be consistent with those of the school or college, and ultimately with the goals of the institution. It is necessary to ensure that agreement is reached on the mission statement before developing program goals' (UCF 2006, pp. 20–21). See also AAHE (1996) for underlying procedures of best practices.
8. This is the case, for example, at the University of Central Florida. See http://www.oeas.ucf.edu/alc/academic_learning_compacts.htm for Academic Learning Compacts.
9. These examples draw heavily on Young (2009, pp. 122–3).
10. See Wright (2005) for an inventory of possible assessment tools with detailed lists of advantages and disadvantages.
11. Stevens and Levi also provide guidance on constructing rubrics on their website at http://www.introductiontorubrics.com/.
12. For examples and templates for assessing civic engagement courses and components, see the companion website to McCartney et al. (2013), available at http://community.apsanet.org/TeachingCivicEngagement/SupplementalMaterials/AssessmentEvaluations.
13. See, for example, the chapters in McCartney et al. (2013) for examples of how political science engages students as citizens.

REFERENCES

American Association for Higher Education (AAHE) (1996), 'Nine Principles of Good Practice for Assessing Student Learning', available at http://www.academicprograms.calpoly.edu/pdfs/assess/nine_principles_good_practice.pdf (accessed 17 January 2014).
Angelo, Thomas A. (1995), 'Reassessing Assessment: Embracing Contraries, Bridging Gaps, and Resetting the Agenda', *AAHE Bulletin*, **47** (8), 10–14.
Angelo, Thomas A. and K.P. Cross (1993), *Classroom Assessment Techniques: A Handbook for College Teachers*, 2nd edn, San Francisco, CA: Jossey-Bass.
Banta, Trudi, Elizabeth A. Jones and Karen E. Black (2009), *Designing Effective Assessment: Principles and Profiles of Good Practice*, San Francisco, CA: Jossey-Bass.
Bean, John C. (2011), *Engaging Ideas: The Professor's Guide to Integrating Writing, Critical Thinking, and Active Learning in the Classroom*, San Francisco, CA: Jossey-Bass.
Deardorff, Michelle and Paul Folger (2009), 'Making Assessment Matter: Structuring Assessment, Transforming Departments', in Michelle D. Deardorff, Kerstin Hamann and John Ishiyama (eds), *Assessment in Political Science*, Washington, DC: American Political Science Association, pp. 77–95.
Deardorff, Michelle D., Kerstin Hamann and John Ishiyama (eds) (2009a), *Assessment in Political Science*, Washington, DC: American Political Science Association.
Deardorff, Michelle D., Kerstin Hamann and John Ishiyama (2009b), 'Introduction', in Michelle D. Deardorff, Kerstin Hamann and John Ishiyama (eds), *Assessment in Political Science*, Washington, DC: American Political Science Association, pp. 3–15.
Donahue, Veronica and John Ishiyama (2009), 'The Critical Portfolio: Facilitating the Reflective

Political Science Student in the Experiential Portfolio', in Michelle D. Deardorff, Kerstin Hamann and John Ishiyama (eds), *Assessment in Political Science*, Washington, DC: American Political Science Association, pp. 217–34.

Ewell, Peter T. (2013), 'The Lumina Degree Qualifications Profile (DQP): Implications for Assessment', *National Institute for Learning Outcomes Assessment*, Occasional Paper No. 16, January, available at http://www.learningoutcomesassessment.org/documents/EwellDQPop1.pdf (accessed 17 January 2014).

Hamann, Kerstin, Philip H. Pollock and Bruce M. Wilson (2009), 'Who SoTLs Where? Publishing the Scholarship of Teaching and Learning in Political Science', *PS: Political Science & Politics*, **42** (4), 729–35.

Hill, Jeffrey S. and Charles R. Pastors (2009), 'Who Will be the Assessment Champion? And Other Conditions for a Culture of Assessment', in Michelle D. Deardorff, Kerstin Hamann and John Ishiyama (eds), *Assessment in Political Science*, Washington, DC: American Political Science Association, pp. 97–115.

Huba, M.E. and J.E. Freed (2000), *Learner-Centered Assessment on College Campuses – Shifting the Focus from Teaching to Learning*, Boston, MA: Allyn & Bacon.

Ishiyama, John (2009), 'Comparing Learning Assessment Plans in Political Science', in Michelle D. Deardorff, Kerstin Hamann and John Ishiyama (eds), *Assessment in Political Science*, Washington, DC: American Political Science Association, pp. 61–75.

Ishiyama, John and Marijke Breuning (2008), 'Assessing Assessment: Examining the Assessment Plans at 50 Political Science Departments', *PS: Political Science & Politics*, **41**, 167–70.

Kelly, Marisa and Brian E. Klunk (2003), 'Learning Assessment in Political Science Departments: Survey Results', *PS: Political Science & Politics*, **36**, 451–5.

McCartney, Alison Rios Millet, Elizabeth A. Bennion and Dick Simpson (2013), *Teaching Civic Engagement: From Student to Active Citizen*, Washington, DC: American Political Science Association.

McClellan, Fletcher (2009), 'An Overview of the Assessment Movement', in Michelle D. Deardorff, Kerstin Hamann and John Ishiyama (eds), *Assessment in Political Science*, Washington, DC: American Political Science Association, pp. 39–58.

Pusateri, Thomas (comp.) with assistance from Jane Halonen, Bill Hill and Maureen McCarthy (2009), *The Assessment CyberGuide for Learning Goals and Outcomes*, 2nd edn, American Psychological Association Educational Directorate, available at http://www.apa.org/ed/governance/bea/assessment-cyberguide-v2.pdf (accessed 17 January 2014).

Smoller, Fred (2004), 'Assessment Is Not a Four-Letter Word', *PS: Political Science & Politics*, **37**, 871–4.

Stevens, Dannelle D. and Antonia J. Levi (2005), *Introduction to Rubrics: An Assessment Tool to Save Grading Time, Convey Effective Feedback, and Promote Student Learning*, Sterling, VA: Stylus.

Suskie, Linda (2007), 'Some Thoughts and Suggestions on Assessing Student Learning', *PS: Political Science & Politics*, **40** (1), 102.

Suskie, Linda (2009), *Assessing Student Learning: A Common Sense Guide*, 2nd edn, San Francisco, CA: Jossey-Bass.

University of Central Florida (2006), *Program Assessment Handbook: Guidelines for Planning and Implementing Quality Enhancing Efforts of Program and Student Learning Outcomes*, available at http://oeas.ucf.edu/assessment/support/acad_assess_handbook.pdf (accessed 17 January 2014).

University of Southern California Center for Excellence in Teaching (n.d.), *Assessment of Learning – Overview*, available at http://cet.usc.edu/resources/teaching_learning/assessment_learning.html (accessed 17 January 2014).

Wright, Barbara (2005), 'Assessment Methods – A Close-Up Look', available at apsanet.org/imgtest/Methodscloseup2.doc (accessed 17 January 2014).

Young, Candace C. (2009), 'Program Evaluation and Assessment: Integrating Methods, Processes, and Culture', in Michelle D. Deardorff, Kerstin Hamann and John Ishiyama (eds), *Assessment in Political Science*, Washington, DC: American Political Science Association, pp. 117–39.

Young, Candace, Jill Abraham Hummer, Daniel Mulcare and Tara N. Parsons (2012), 'Curricular and Program Assessment', *PS: Political Science & Politics*, **45** (3), 527–8, available at http://www.apsanet.org/media/2012%20TLC%20Track%20Summaries.pdf (accessed 17 January 2014).

8. Performance assessment in Europe
Alasdair Blair

The manner by which students are assessed is a central factor in determining the nature of their learning experience. Over the last two decades there has been a gradual shift in the engagement of the political science (PS) and international relations (IR) academic community with regard to teaching and learning practices. This has been reflected in greater attention being attached to the methods by which students are taught and assessed. As far as assessment is concerned, this has been reflected in a growing body of literature that has championed the use of innovative methods such as simulation exercises (Raymond and Usherwood 2013), problem-based learning (Archetti 2012) and placement learning (Curtis et al. 2009; Harris 2012). Articles such as these stress the value of introducing teaching and assessment methods that go beyond traditional classroom teacher-centered approaches that are often supported by assessment practices involving the likes of essays and exams. As has been rehearsed before in numerous books and articles, teacher-centered methods have a tendency to reinforce a surface-learning approach where student performance is influenced by their capacity to craft well-written essays and their ability to recall information in an examination format.

The shift to a more varied assessment diet has in this context been influenced by an increasing awareness of the need to develop individual student understanding and to ensure that assessment tasks encourage the sort of deep learning that adequately prepares students for future employment. For some academics this has resulted in emphasis on students undertaking learning and assessment that is aligned to the real world. In the USA this has been part of a trend that has emphasized the significance of experiential learning, of which service learning has been viewed as an important means of engaging students in developing a sense of civic awareness (see, e.g., Jacoby et al. 1996; McCartney et al. 2013). This contrasts with a European context where there has been less of a theoretical and conceptual discussion about the nature of service learning and civic engagement. Instead, at a European level greater attention has been attached to particular innovations in teaching and learning, such as simulations and placements, rather than a more conceptual and theoretical shift in the curriculum as a whole. In this context, European scholars have for the most part viewed these interventions as a means of enhancing student learning rather than as a method of reconnecting a university to its neighborhood and/or developing its graduates with a sense of civic awareness. For European scholars, the argument has often been framed within the context of how to make the subject matter 'real'. To this end, students of public administration are recognized to gain greater awareness of local governance in the UK by undertaking a placement activity in a local council where the combination of the close-up observation of local politics and the writing of an assessment task relating to the placement brings the subject matter alive. In the teaching and learning literature this is referred to as 'authentic assessment' (Ashford-Rowe et al. 2014).

In the European context, performance assessment is an extension of this focus on authentic assessment, stressing assessment tasks that entail students demonstrating their learning through some form of activity and performance, for example presentations, simulations, role-plays, placements and the submission of portfolios, all of which enable students to actively showcase their knowledge and understanding of the subject matter. For European scholars, the critical dimension here appears to be how student learning is deepened in specific modules rather than the manner by which universities have transformed their system of education to address social problems and serve national purposes (Boyer 1990). While this state of affairs may be viewed as unsurprising, given that European universities are located in different countries with distinct national traditions and systems of education, it is also the case that at a more general level PS and IR academics in Europe and elsewhere appear to be less engaged in broader conceptual and theoretical discussions on teaching and learning. In looking at these issues in more detail, it is noticeable that, of the 1600 articles listed in May 2014 in the International Political Education Database (IPED) that is supported by the Teaching and Learning Specialist Group of the UK Political Studies Association (PSA), none specifically dealt with either the topic of performance assessment or authentic assessment. Of the reasons for this state of affairs, it is notable that the authors from a PS and IR background tend to provide reflective accounts of teaching innovations that they have introduced into their own modules. For PS and IR scholars, such studies have the benefit of providing useful and adaptable accounts of what worked in terms of a particular module innovation. The tendency for studies to be focused at the module level has meant that, with the exception of a few articles such as Buckley et al. (2011) and Rofe (2011), far less has been written about the methods of assessment that might be most appropriately used across the totality of an undergraduate and/or postgraduate degree program. Moreover, the only textbook devoted to the subject of assessment from a PS and/or IR perspective is the edited volume by Deardorff et al. (2009). Consequently, as I previously observed in a study of the UK system,

> as far as assessment is concerned, this has meant that there has been less attention devoted to critically analyzing the appropriateness, reliability and validity of assessment practices from the perspective of the Politics discipline. This is despite the fact that a general theme of the last decade has been a need to look more closely – and in some cases re-evaluate – assessment methods for undergraduate students in particular. (Blair and McGinty 2012, pp. 106–7)

This chapter seeks to make an inroad into this lacuna by focusing on the issue of performance assessment from a European perspective, and in so doing it seeks to locate discussion of performance assessment within a holistic position of an overall program of studies, whose focus is the undergraduate curriculum. Such a study is, however, informed within the context that there are nevertheless distinct traditions relating to teaching and learning at the European level. This is an issue that Eszter Simon (2014) has highlighted in her investigation into the teaching of research methods within the higher education system in Hungary. She notes that within Europe there is a broad distinction between those countries that follow a more student-centered path, such as the UK, Ireland, Sweden, Belgium, the Netherlands and Sweden, and those that employ more of a didactic approach. Such differences in turn impact on the nature of innovation in teaching and learning and the European countries where there appears to be the greatest discussion taking place. This is evidenced by a survey of teaching and learning articles published by *European Political Science* (*EPS*), which is the leading European-focused journal for teaching and learning from the PS and IR community. Of the 34 teaching and learning articles published in *EPS* between 2008 and 2013, 19 were written by UK academics. Of the remaining articles, 4 were from the USA, 3 from Ireland, 3 from the Netherlands and 1 each from Belgium, Canada, Denmark, Italy, Germany and Finland (one article was co-authored from academics in Netherlands and Finland). The dominance of UK-based academics in teaching and learning reflects the UK's broader strength in PS in Europe, with studies noting that the UK has more professors of PS, more organizational units and more members in its professional association – the PSA – than can be found in any other European country (Berndtson 2013, p. 445).

The purpose of setting out these points is threefold. The first is to note that any reference to just a single European method would be misleading because of the very nature of the differences between the countries concerned. The second is to highlight the dominance of work relating to the teaching and learning of PS and IR that comes from higher education systems that have a student-centered approach to teaching. The third is to emphasize the structural and environmental factors that inform, shape and equally act as barriers to any enhancement of teaching and learning. Taking these points as our guide, this chapter proceeds as follows. First, it provides an overview of the subject matter of performance assessment, noting its significance for both students and staff. Second, it discusses issues relating to the structuring and implementation of performance assessment. Third, it evaluates the challenges that come from such changes. Finally, it presents a concluding argument that all PS and IR degree programs should embed performance assessment as a means of ensuring that students have a deeper knowledge of the subject matter and obtain the necessary skills and capabilities that enable them to be successful learners and meet the challenges of a competitive working environment.

ASSESSMENT ACROSS THE CURRICULUM

Although it is widely acknowledged that 'assessment is the most significant prompt for learning' (Boud 1995, p. 36), one of the most overlooked and yet at the same time crucial aspects of any degree program is the method of assessment used. In broad terms, assessment falls into two camps. The first type focuses on specific tasks, such as writing an essay or undertaking an end-of-term exam, where clearly defined areas of competence are being tested. The second type tests a broader range of competences, such as placements; this type is known as performance assessment. In the former, students have very little control over the learning environment and the manner by which they are judged: a student can either write an essay well or they cannot. By contrast, assessments that engage with student performance both permit and actively foster student engagement and control over the assessment exercise by virtue of the performance element. Of the two types of assessment, the former offers a strong element of comparability in student performance because a great deal of emphasis is given to standardized processes for assessment and grading. This is despite the fact that not all students may be aware of the principles behind the assessment and that there can be considerable problems with such methods: for example, essays and exams are themselves prone to the problem of unreliable marking (Brown 2010, pp. 279–81) and students do not always receive feedback on their performance in a timely manner that improves future performance (Blair et al. 2013a). Coursework such as essays has also been subject to criticism because of its tendency to encourage student dishonesty through plagiarism and because students found guilty of such practices are often faced with punitive sanctions. On the other hand, performance assessments can be subject to criticism because they offer a more loosely defined learning experience and assessment method. For example, no two placements will ever be the same. Yet, because performance assessments permit an appreciation of student skills and competencies, with a strong emphasis on feedback through the practice of 'doing', it is also the case that such assessments can provide a clearer sense to students of their understanding of the subject and the level of their own performance. Such real-world teaching and learning also acts as a barrier to plagiarism. Performance assessment has the additional advantage of offering opportunities for students from non-social-science backgrounds to succeed given that they tend not to be trained in the skills of essay writing to the same level as social-science students. This is an important and often overlooked issue, given that changes to university curricula often result in strategic initiatives to widen student learning opportunities, such as by permitting an engineering student to undertake a PS module.

For performance assessment to be effective it has to be part of a balanced approach to teaching and learning. In this sense, the introduction of a performance-based aspect of assessment needs to be viewed within the overall context of a degree program. The significance of this point is that the assessment methods that underpin a degree program are rarely uppermost in the minds of faculty, whose energies are more often focused at the module level. It could be argued that this is hardly surprising, given that the primary responsibility of faculty is their own teaching. Yet this is a problematic state of affairs on a number of fronts. Chief among these is that, when assessment is focused purely at the module level, it is by its very nature bounded by the confines of the module. This is an issue that relates both to modules taught over one term or semester and modules taught across the whole academic year, as controls are inevitably set on the number of hours studied and the weighting of individual assessments. In such circumstances, methods of assessment tend to be focused on teaching the knowledge within one individual module rather than looking at knowledge learned across a program.

STRUCTURING AND IMPLEMENTING PERFORMANCE ASSESSMENT

This section examines the issue of performance assessment in more detail by looking in turn at the use of portfolios, placements, presentations and simulations. Whichever the method used, it is important that faculty and students do not view performance assessment as being an easier option. Because performance assessment is different, it invariably involves a higher level of time and effort by faculty in preparing the groundwork and in supporting students in their program of study. Students too should not think that performance assessment, with its absence of exams, is an easier option, because for students to succeed they need to be actively engaged in the learning process throughout their program of studies.

Taking these case studies in turn, at face value portfolios offer a straightforward mechanism of introducing performance assessment into a module because the focus is on what the student has learned. Some observers may think this merely requires students to be tasked with collecting evidence of their learning. Yet if this is such a simple task, it should be noted that there is little evidence of portfolios being used in the teaching of PS and IR. This contrasts with other subjects, notably art, dance, design, music and engineering, where portfolios are an integral element of the assessment of the degree program. At first glance, the argument for this divide is that these subjects lend themselves to such an approach, with emphasis attached to a student producing a tangible object through a process of creativity. This in itself is problematic, because such a viewpoint automatically creates divisions between subject disciplines in terms of assessment rubrics and suggests that PS and IR do not produce anything tangible or creative. But such an approach does not reflect the fact that many elements of a PS and IR degree program require creativity, such as the construction of a PowerPoint presentation, the production of a poster and the use of photographs and video as visual imagery. Moreover, in the absence of a portfolio such creativity is further lost in a grading system where student performance is reflected in a structure that characterizes achievement on the lines of 'A', 'B', 'C' and so on. Significantly, however, such a system and record of achievement says little about the capabilities of the student in question and has been subject to significant criticism relating to problems of measurement accuracy (Yorke 2011). It is for this reason that students from such disciplines as art are asked at interview to present their portfolio: it provides a 'real' example of what they are able to do.

The argument here is that, for PS and IR, portfolios can provide a higher level of information about the skills and knowledge that a student has achieved, while also allowing measurement of performance (and progress) across the totality of the degree program. But if this is the case, it still does not address the issue of what such a portfolio should contain. Once again, the example of art and design is straightforward in that a student is likely to present their collection of drawings. The issue here, then, is to consider what a PS and IR portfolio should (and should not) contain. One approach to addressing this challenge is to consider the learning outcomes that govern the degree program as a whole and to link one (or more) of the outcomes to the portfolio exercise. This could be achieved, for example, by focusing on a student's knowledge of theory. Once it has been decided what the portfolio should contain, it is then important to think about its purpose and use. This might include whether the portfolio will be used as a formative or a summative piece of assessment. For PS and IR there is an argument that a portfolio should be used as a record of achievement and performance across all years of a degree program, as this could give a clear sense of the student's progress. This would still necessitate submission dates to be agreed for the portfolio work and feedback (including grades) to be provided to students as part of a developmental process.

Apart from the academic benefits outlined above, portfolios could also have the advantage of establishing continuity of student experience and could assist in providing a framework for integrating the learning experience of students taking programs of study, such as joint honors, where there can often be a disjointed learning experience. Portfolios might also go some way to tackling such issues as personal tutoring, where there is often a disjuncture between what universities aim to provide in terms of support and guidance and the reality of the student experience. In this manner, an academic allocated to supervise the portfolio could double as the personal tutor. From a student's perspective, one of the important advantages of portfolios is that they give them ownership over their program of study and act as a method of slow learning. Students also have to make judgments about what goes in (and what is left out of) the portfolio, while at the same time encouraging creativity in terms of the components that students use to demonstrate their learning.

Whereas portfolios allow students to showcase the progress in their learning, placements offer the opportunity to engage in the real world of politics and to apply to everyday situations the learning that students have undertaken in class, as well as to bring into the class lessons learned from the placement. Until relatively recently placements were viewed as the sort of learning experience that was relevant to the likes of a business studies degree, and which would be taken as part of a sandwich year. Although there are identifiable benefits from this approach in terms of providing students with an extended placement experience, it nevertheless has its limitations in terms of its suitability for all learners. The reason for this is that extended placements limit the opportunity for students to take up the experience as a result of such factors as the logistics of the placement. The question then is: how can a placement experience be inserted into a degree program of study without the year-long requirement? The argument here is that placements need only be for a short period of one or two weeks for students to gain sufficient benefit to impact on their studies (albeit with the likelihood of the placement being organized on the basis of one or two days per week so as to fit around other modules). This allows a placement to become part of the assessment component of an individual module and in so doing creates a linkage between the practice of 'doing' and 'learning' the subject matter.

That is not to say that such placements are straightforward, most notably because, whereas sandwich placements require students to find their own placement, the opposite is often the case in short placements, where the logistics of finding and negotiating with suitable providers is left to the university. This inevitably places a considerable burden on academic and/or administrative staff, who need to meet with placement providers to ensure suitable placements. After a suitable placement has been found, the question to be considered is the nature of the assessment task that can measure the performance. One method of doing this is to use a reflective blog, which, in a similar manner to that of a portfolio, also enables an assessment of the progress and learning that a student has made over the period of the placement. A possible problem with this form of assessment is that students might not automatically make the link between a blog and coursework such as essays. One way of rectifying this is to use another piece of assessment, such as an essay, which could incorporate research undertaken during the placement.

Presentations offer an opportunity for students to demonstrate their verbal reasoning skills and to respond to questions in front of an audience. While such higher-level skills help students to defend an academic argument, their position in the curriculum has tended to be viewed within the context of seminar discussions. And although the majority of universities endeavor to make a virtue of such practices, student performance and engagement in seminars can often be patchy. By contrast, formal presentations offer an opportunity for students to present to an audience. Such a task is probably best reserved for an upper-level module, whereby student confidence would have been developed in the likes of seminar discussion in lower-level modules. For presentations to work well, students need to be given classes in managing stress, dealing with nerves, effective preparation, use of body language, as well as examples of how presentations are undertaken within the world of politics. This linkage between assessment and the curriculum is critical because all too often students are given tasks such as presentations, but are ill-prepared to perform them. Apart from preparing students effectively to undertake a presentation, consideration also needs to be given to how their work will be graded. This requires a different set of grade descriptors from that of an essay, including such factors as eye contact, engaging with the audience and responding to questions.

Students can also present their work by producing a poster and defending its academic content. Such an approach is similar to that of a poster presentation format in an academic conference; it assists in reinforcing a research element in the undergraduate curriculum. In this way, poster presentations work well with extended research projects and final-year dissertations where students have undertaken significant academic work. From an assessment perspective, poster presentations can be used as one component of the module assessment and thereby assist in reducing the risk that student performance rests on just one assessment component. Poster presentations can also act as a vehicle for showcasing student work and create an informal environment of peer learning where students can review the work of others.

Finally, while simulations are recognized by scholars as an important means of providing students with real-world learning that assists in preparing them for future employment, they are a method of assessment that students often find to be the most complex. In part this reflects the fact that the newness of the exercise can create some anxiety. Consequently, any simulation exercise requires students to be educated in the practice and skills needed for the simulation and not just the subject matter. One consequence of this is that simulation exercises, as with many other elements of performance assessment, require a trade-off to be made between academic content in terms of subject delivery and the need to provide students with the support, guidance and advice to undertake the simulation. From the point of view of faculty, simulations require significant effort in terms of designing the exercise, and also result in higher levels of discussion and correspondence with students as opposed to more tried and tested approaches (exams). Consideration also has to be given to methods of assessment and their impact where students are operating as a group. As described in extensive detail elsewhere, group work can be subject to criticism because students do not always make an equal input and, as such, freeloading can occur. It should also be borne in mind that the method of assessment may affect the potential for grade inflation in the assessment exercise. As assessment is on performance, it is important that additional staff take part in the exercise to ensure accuracy of marks awarded. Thus the method of instruction and assessment is potentially more labor costly.

CHALLENGES OF CHANGE

A move to performance assessment is not without its challenges and difficulties; therefore several factors need to be taken into consideration when making changes to patterns and methods of assessment. Just as in the real world of politics, universities and academic departments have elites and established hierarchical orders, and thus challenging the established order can be problematic, for example with regard to career progression.

In looking at these issues in more detail, there are five key considerations, namely institutional frameworks, leadership, locality, time and space, and environment.

Institutional frameworks matter because they provide the context in which degree programs are structured within universities. For example, while there is a large body of literature that emphasizes the value of introducing a short placement as one element of an assessment component within a module (Curtis and Blair 2010), such changes are harder to make in modules that take place over one semester. The reason for this is that there are challenges in terms of preparing students to undertake such a task. This is not to say that placements cannot be undertaken successfully within a module delivered within a semester. Rather, their successful implementation depends on preparing the students (as in earlier modules) and arranging time for the placements. This often means that placements occur in the teaching period after Christmas, when there is greater flexibility in terms of providing the necessary space for students, such as through holidays and reading weeks.

Leadership is also an important factor, as it determines whether teaching and learning is taken seriously and the extent to which innovative approaches to assessment are encouraged and supported. Given the fact that university staff (administrators and academic faculty) tend to work for one university for a considerable period of time, there can emerge both established hierarchical orders within departments and at the same time cultures resistant to change. This can make it more difficult for innovation to be supported as established procedures and 'ways of working' exist. For education innovators, this can in turn result in curriculum changes involving performance assessment being primarily located in their own modules. However, the difficulty here is that, for performance assessment to impact on student learning in a positive manner, it ideally needs to be part of a broader reform of the curriculum.

Locality is important in that, where an element of performance is introduced into an assessment regime, it needs to be determined whether such a change can be successfully implemented. To give an example, the introduction of a placement as a method of assessment inevitably requires the creation of sufficient opportunities for students. In this context, the locality of some universities can make it easier (near a large town/city with a wide variety of employers) or near impossible (a campus-based university located in a rural/small town setting with relatively few employers) to achieve.

Time and space must be taken into consideration in relation to the resources needed to support change. Performance assessments are invariably more time consuming than traditional assessment formats. Thus, whereas essays and exams fit within established rubrics of university operations (such as methods of assignment hand-in, feedback sheets and timetabling arrangements), this is less so for performance assessments. For example, presentations require additional class sessions and suitable room arrangements when classes are timetabled at the start of an academic year. In the case of simulation exercises, where an activity requires multiple rooms to be booked for different delegation groups, this can often mean that such activities can take place only at the end of a teaching period.

Finally, the broader internal and external environment is critical. The economic crisis that has affected many European nations particularly badly since 2008 has in turn resulted in a reduction in public financial support for universities and a greater focus on employability by students and university leaders. In practical terms, this has meant that many universities have tasked their faculty to implement curriculum changes. But while such objectives are well intentioned, they can lead to more rapid and less considered changes being made that do not always result in an integrated approach to curriculum development. These issues are more complex in a competitive higher education environment where there is less scope for policy failure; this can lead to a conservative approach to innovation because of the broader risks in terms of student and university league table performance. In addition, external exogenous events (such as austerity and local finance difficulties) can be used as the rationale for change even in universities where there is less need for such change.

CONCLUSION

These examples show that one of the fundamental benefits of performance assessment is that it shifts the focus of teaching and learning away from a model that focuses on the grades that students achieve, to instead providing a system that gives a more engaged and authentic picture of student achievement. For this to happen, performance assessment must be meaningful, credible and realistic (and thereby authentic). In this context, authentic assessment involves tasks that students are made aware of, with far less reliance attached to methods that involve, for example, unknown exam questions. Not only does this aid deep learning; it crucially provides a context in which to enhance the feedback that students receive. One of the most common criticisms that students make of feedback is that assessment practices that focus on essays and exams do not provide a developmental environment for feedback to enhance future performance. This is the result of a number of factors, including feedback not being provided in a timely fashion, little or no feedback being given on exams and the fact that students are not always able to fully understand the significance of the feedback provided. The last factor can be influenced by the fact that feedback is often delivered in a written manner of academic discourse that students do not always have access to (Blair et al. 2013c). In this respect, one of the benefits of performance assessment is that it necessitates a dialogue between students and academic staff so as to clarify the requirements of assessment tasks and therefore assist in creating feedback dialogues (Blair et al. 2013b). Such an approach is similar to the process of scaffolding that Vygotsky (1978) argued takes place through interaction when less competent learners benefit from more skilful peers. The argument here is that this approach enables students to complete tasks that seemed initially to be beyond their learning, but that, once completed, enable them to become more successful learners. It is in this context that performance assessment can have a positive impact on the student learning experience and bridge the gap between the demarcated lines of summative and formative assessment by establishing a holistic approach to teaching, learning and assessment.

REFERENCES

Archetti, C. (2012), 'Friend or foe? Problem-based learning (PBL) in political communication', *European Political Science*, **11** (4), 551–66.

Ashford-Rowe, K., Herrington, K. and Brown, C. (2014), 'Establishing the critical elements that determine authentic assessment', *Assessment and Evaluation in Higher Education*, **39** (2), 205–22.

Berndtson, E. (2013), 'Contradictions of the Bologna Process: academic excellence versus political obsessions', *European Political Science*, **12** (4), 440–47.

Blair, A. and McGinty, S. (2012), 'Feedback-dialogues: exploring the student perspective', *Assessment & Evaluation in Higher Education*, **38** (4), 466–76.

Blair, A., Curtis, S., Goodwin, M. and Shields, S. (2013a), 'What feedback do students want?', *Politics*, **33** (1), 66–79.

Blair, A., Curtis, S. and McGinty, S. (2013b), 'Is peer feedback an effective approach for creating dialogue in politics?', *European Political Science*, **12** (1), 102–15.

Blair, A., Curtis, S., Goodwin, M. and Shields, S. (2013c), 'The significance of assignment feedback: from consumption to construction', *European Political Science*, **12** (2), 231–44.

Boud, D. (1995), *Enhancing Learning through Self-assessment*, London: Kogan Page.

Boyer, E.L. (1990), *Scholarship Reconsidered: Priorities of the Professoriate*, San Francisco, CA: The Carnegie Foundation for the Advancement of Teaching/Jossey-Bass.

Brown, G.T.L. (2010), 'The validity of examination essays in higher education: issues and responses', *Higher Education Quarterly*, **64** (3), 276–91.

Buckley, F., Harris, C., O'Mullane, M. and Reidy, T. (2011), 'Developing a political science curriculum for non-traditional students', *European Political Science*, **10**, 248–58.

Curtis, S., Axford, B., Blair, A., Gibson, C., Huggins, R. and Sherrington, P. (2009), 'Making short placements work', *Politics*, **29** (1), 62–70.

Curtis, S. and Blair, A. (2010), 'Experiencing politics in action: democratizing placement learning and politics as a vocation', *Journal of Political Science Education*, **6** (4), 369–90.

Deardorff, M.D., Hamann, K. and Ishiyama, J. (2009), *Assessment in Political Science*, Washington, DC: American Political Science Association.

Harris, C. (2012), 'Expanding political science's signature pedagogy: the case for service learning', *European Political Science*, **11** (2), 175–85.

Jacoby, B. and associates (1996), *Service-Learning in Higher Education: Concepts and Practices*, San Francisco, CA: Jossey-Bass.

Raymond, C. and Usherwood, S. (2013), 'Assessment in simulations', *Journal of Political Science Education*, **9** (2), 157–67.

Rios Millett McCartney, A., Bennion, E.A. and Simpson, D. (eds) (2013), *Teaching Civic Engagement: From Student to Active Centre*, Washington, DC: American Political Studies Association.

Rofe, J.S. (2011), 'The "IR Model": a schema for pedagogic design and development in international relations distance learning programmes', *European Political Science*, **10** (1), 103–17.

Simon, E. (2014), 'Teaching political science research methods in Hungary: transferring student-centred teaching practices into a subject-focused academic culture', *European Political Science*, **13**, 78–95.

Vygotsky, L.S. (1978), *Mind and Society: The Development of Higher Mental Processes*, Cambridge, MA: Harvard University Press.

Yorke, M. (2011), 'Summative assessment: dealing with the "measurement fallacy"', *Studies in Higher Education*, **36** (3), 251–73.

9. Course-based assessment and student feedback
William J. Miller

While programmatic assessment is becoming an increasingly essential task for departments hoping to maintain accreditation and please various internal and external stakeholders, for an individual faculty member course-based assessment is also vitally important. Faculty members need to know the strengths and weaknesses of student performance within their courses, along with their own skills in fostering student learning. By objectively examining student knowledge gains and deficiencies, along with utilizing course-level instructor feedback to improve teaching strategies and tactics, faculty can help foster an environment that permits students to reach (and even stretch) their potential.

WHY ASSESSMENT?

Despite the genuine excitement surrounding assessment expressed by politicians, education boards and administrators, faculty have yet to fully realize the benefits of looking at student performance. The typical faculty complaints follow one of two paths: (1) assessment data is not meaningfully used to improve anything; or (2) assessment data is used only to criticize faculty. Unfortunately, in the early days of assessment, it was difficult to say these faculty members were wrong. More recently, however, assessment data is being recognized as an important component in determining how higher education is helping students prepare for careers. By taking assessment seriously, faculty assure they are teaching what they want students to learn, helping students understand course-level expectations, engaging students in their own learning and providing valuable information regarding courses and curriculum.

Assessment is not grading. Many faculty, when faced with completing assessments, believe grades and outcomes are one and the same. While grades may reflect a student's overall performance in a course, they do not allow for a thorough investigation of how well students are doing with different pieces of the course. In short, grades are too holistic to allow for individual threads to be examined to the degree necessary in solid assessment. For well-intentioned instructors, it is quite natural to want to track learning.

Wright (1991) defines assessment as a learner-centered, teacher-directed approach designed to improve student learning in the classroom. It is systematic and involves some level of analysis. It is not enough for the good teacher simply to assume that students are learning what is being presented. Well-designed class-based assessment measures provide the necessary data to adequately judge student learning.

A guiding principle of assessment should be constructive alignment (Biggs 1999). It is the underpinning concept behind the current requirements for program specification, declarations of learning outcomes and the use of criterion-based assessment. According to constructive alignment, students construct meaning from what they do to learn and the teacher should be aligning planned learning activities with the learning outcomes within a course. In practice, faculty will begin with stated course learning outcomes that are clearly conveyed to students. Course activities should be designed to emphasize these outcomes (while building on the existing skill sets of students) and the results on these activities should be assessed to determine whether outcomes are being met. Then, most importantly, pedagogy and learning should be examined for possible ways to improve outcome performance. The basic premise of the whole system is that the curriculum is designed so that the learning activities and assessment tasks are aligned with the learning outcomes that are intended in the course. This means that the system is consistent.

To begin planning for meaningful course-based assessment, faculty should consider three questions:

1. What do you want students to learn in this course?
2. What have previous students learned?
3. How can you help students learn what you want them to?

After devoting time and thought to these questions, it is possible to begin planning for assessment by writing out student learning outcomes for the course, mapping out tools that can measure these outcomes and determining how to collect and use the data meaningfully (Tan 1992). For any particular course, a faculty member should begin by looking at current tools used in the classroom. As discussed earlier, grading and assessing are two separate activities. Palomba and Banta (1999) remind faculty that, in the planning process, materials generated in a classroom should be closely examined to determine what goals they are accomplishing and how they can be used to evaluate outcomes and teaching effectiveness. Ultimately, the goal is to establish learning goals, measure the extent to which students meet the said goals and tweak pedagogy to encourage greater accomplishment of goals.

THE ACTIVITIES OF ASSESSMENT

Establishing Goals and Outcomes

In Chapter 8, Kerstin Hamann discussed program-level assessment. In many cases, the goals set at the program level will lead to the development of a curriculum map, which in turn will dictate what course-level goals will look like. Goals should be big and broad, consisting of general terminology and reflecting what skills students should develop in a class. Being explicit in the establishment of goals will help assure the direction of your course and provide the greatest potential for meaningful assessment to occur. A simple way is to start by identifying the key academic goals on which students have progressed by the time they leave the course. Think about your current assignments and activities, determine what factual knowledge the course is responsible for, consider skill attainment and even reflect on previous difficulties for students. While a program may have three to five goals for students, each course will have specific outcomes that relate back to course goals, demonstrating how each course fits into the program as a whole through a curriculum map.

While goals can be broad and theoretical, outcomes should be SMART—specific, measurable, achievable, realistic and time-bound. Through outcomes, students and outside stakeholders should be able to clearly delineate how they will demonstrate success in accomplishing stated learning goals (Ohia 1995). Again, focusing on a few questions will help faculty to draft meaningful outcomes. First, go back to your list of course goals and determine specific things students can do during your course to show that they are achieving the goal. Second, assume the role of an outside accreditor and figure out what you want to see students doing to be considered as meeting a goal. And last, intuitively, as an instructor, trust your instinct to determine how you can tell when students are grasping material and creating outcomes that demonstrate it.

Solid outcomes will focus on what students know and are able to do. Political science, like all disciplines, has a body of core knowledge that students must learn in order to be successful, as well as a core set of applications of that knowledge in professional settings. These are observable and measurable actions or behaviors. They reflect the curriculum, the discipline and faculty expectations; as these elements evolve, learning outcomes change. They are recent (reflect current knowledge and practice in the discipline), relevant (relate logically and significantly to the discipline and the degree) and rigorous (degree of academic precision and thoroughness that the outcome requires in order to be met).

Many educators have been exposed to Bloom's Taxonomy at some point during their careers. While the original 1964 Taxonomy—consisting of knowledge, comprehension, application, analysis, synthesis and evaluation—is still useful, Bloom's Revised Taxonomy serves as an accepted description of the dimensions of knowledge and cognitive skills used to formulate meaningful outcome measures (Anderson and Krathwohl 2001). Good student learning outcomes will strive to measure at different levels. The Revised Taxonomy contains the following levels:

1. Remembering: can the student recall/remember information?
2. Understanding: can the student explain ideas or concepts?
3. Applying: can the student use the information in a new way?
4. Analyzing: can the student distinguish between different parts?
5. Evaluating: can the student justify a stance or decision?
6. Creating: can the student create a new product or point of view?

Any of these levels may be appropriate for a given course; however, the level of course, expected difficulty and the role the course plays in the overall curriculum may dictate whether particular student learning outcomes are suitable or not. For example, an introductory course may focus more on remembering and understanding while capstone courses devote more effort to evaluating and creating.

Some faculty will inadvertently blur the line between outcomes and outputs. Outputs describe and count what is done and whom is reached, and represent products or services produced. Processes deliver outputs: what is produced at the end of a process is an output. For example, in a student recruitment process the output might be ten new students. At the end of a degree program the output might be a certain number of graduates.

An outcome, on the other hand, is a level of performance or achievement. It may be associated with a process or its output. Outcomes imply measurement—quantification—of performance. Here are two examples: (1) after attending a study abroad program, students' intercultural competency improved by 20 percent as measured by the Intercultural Development Inventory (IDI); (2) as a result of increased external funding, five departments increased the number of undergraduate research opportunities by 20 percent over the previous reporting period.

This distinction is important, especially in the development and review of student learning outcomes. While most higher education institutions seek to measure both outcomes and outputs, the focus is on outcomes. For example, while a program will produce a number of new graduates (the output), it must have a measure of the quality of the graduates as defined by the college or discipline (the outcome). Effective outcomes describe, in measurable terms, these quality characteristics by defining expectations for graduates' knowledge, critical thinking and communication.

Writing Goals and Outcomes

While determining the content of goals and outcomes may seem daunting, the writing of these important assessment tools is equally challenging. The number one key to good outcome assessment is measurability, and measurability means an active verb that describes an observable behavior, process or product. Before discussing good verbs, we will examine a list of words and phrases that should never appear in goals or outcomes.

1. Understand: understanding is an internal process that is indicated by demonstrated behaviors and is nearly impossible to assess objectively in a direct fashion.
2. Appreciate or value: again, these are internal processes that are indicated by demonstrated behaviors closely tied to personal choice or preference.
3. Become familiar with: focuses assessment on the process of gaining familiarity, not on being familiar with.
4. Learn about or think about: not observable. These rely entirely on self-reported activities.
5. Become aware of or gain awareness of: as before, these verbs focus assessment on gaining, not actually demonstrating, awareness.
6. Demonstrate the ability to: focuses assessment on ability, not on the achievement or demonstration of a skill.

All of the above troublesome verbs or predicate phrases muddy the assessment waters by presenting potentially indirect outcomes.

In Table 9.1, however, I present a list of direct action verbs, which lend themselves to easier, more usable assessment.

To make the table even more useful, the verbs are designed to correspond with Bloom's Taxonomy. As such, the expectations increase as the Taxonomy level becomes more demanding. Considering what has been discussed about assessment so far, consider the following examples of good and bad outcomes from various disciplines.

1. Art
    - Bad: Students will be familiar with culture and the relationship of art making.
    - Good: Students will be able to identify the formal elements and principles of art that apply to the creation and discussion of an artwork.

Table 9.1 Action verbs corresponding with Bloom's Revised Taxonomy

Arrange	Classify	Calculate	Combine	Appraise	Create
Define	Describe	Construct	Figure	Argue	Assemble
Locate	Identify	Classify	Find	Assess	Compose
Recall	Indicate	Estimate	Sketch	Defend	Create
Recite	Organize	Illustrate	Solve	Estimate	Design
Describe	Interpret	Interpret	Predict	Judge	Devise
Repeat	Illustrate	Appraise	Change	Predict	Formulate
Identify	Reorganize	Contrast	Survey	Qualify	Invent
Select	Translate	Criticize	Compare	Rate	Manage
Quote	Paraphrase	Diagnose	Diagram	Support	Modify
Label	Summarize	Identify	Examine	Critique	Organize
Copy	Transform		Test	Recommend	Plan
List	Discuss		Modify		Prepare
Name	Explain				Produce
State	Defend				Propose
	Compare				Set up
	Report				Verify
	Restate				Construct
	Review				Develop
	Rewrite				

2. History
   - Bad: Students should be able to understand significant trends, movements and events in European history.
   - Good: Students will be able to compare and contrast historical perspectives of our world and describe the contributions of these historical perspectives.

3. Psychology
   - Bad: Students should know the historically important systems of psychology.
   - Good: Students should be able to recognize and articulate the foundational assumptions, central ideas and dominant criticisms of the psychoanalytic, Gestalt, behaviorist, humanistic and cognitive approaches to psychology.

At many institutions, including Flagler College, each course is required to have three outcomes that directly relate to one of the program outcomes. Fewer than three outcomes make it difficult to assure progression along Bloom's Taxonomy, while more make the course feel too crowded and force faculty into devoting energy to relatively small concepts. Looking specifically at course outcomes, examine the three shown in Box 9.1.

These outcomes were developed collectively by all faculty teaching the particular course and are re-examined annually (along with student data) to determine whether changes are required or advisable.

> BOX 9.1   EXAMPLE LEARNING OUTCOMES FOR THREE COURSES
>
> **POS200: INTRODUCTION TO POLITICAL SCIENCE**
>
> 1) Students completing this course will be able to describe and explain the basic concepts and elements of political science and their interconnections.
> 2) Students completing this course will be able to analyze and assess both the classic and contemporary issues confronted by students of politics.
> 3) Students successfully completing this course will be able to understand, appreciate and evaluate multiple perspectives on politics and power. They will also be required to critically assess and develop their own political and social values and defend those values in both intellectual and academic terms.
>
> **POS332: SCOPE AND METHODS IN POLITICAL SCIENCE**
>
> The primary aim of the course is to enable students to understand, appreciate and critique diverse empirical research. In addition, it aims to provide students with the tools and knowledge necessary to conduct sophisticated independent work in political science.
>
> 1) Students will be able to describe, identify and explain the terminology, classifications, methods and trends in the study of political science.
> 2) Students will be required to think critically about issues and questions in their political world. They will have to formulate, explain and defend their own thesis question relating to their chosen field of political science research.
> 3) Students will apply what they learn about methods of research in political science through the use of statistical software to analyze political data and ultimately through to the production of their own research proposal.
>
> **POS470: SENIOR SEMINAR**
>
> Students who successfully complete the Senior Seminar will:
>
> 1) Read analytically, think critically and organize political ideas in oral and written form so that their knowledge can be communicated both intelligently and intelligibly.
> 2) Write effectively, with clarity and with intellectual judgment.
> 3) Articulate their ideas effectively and professionally through oral presentation.

WHEN AND HOW TO ASSESS

Direct assessments of student learning are those that provide for direct examination or observation of student knowledge or skills against measurable performance indicators. Examples of direct assessment include, but are not limited to, quizzes, tests, inventories, team/group projects, standardized tests, licensure exams, internships, service-learning projects, case studies, simulations and portfolios. Indirect assessments are those that ascertain the opinion or self-report of the extent or value of learning experiences. Indirect assessments include, but are not limited to, quantitative data such as enrollments, questionnaires, honors, awards, scholarships, interviews, focus groups, employer satisfaction measures, retention/graduation rates and job/graduate school placement data. The balance of direct and indirect measures should be appropriate for the course and program, with over half of each outcome measured using direct assessments.

When considering how to measure student learning outcomes it may be helpful to think in terms of assessment methods and instruments. The assessment method is the general type of tool you will use to assess the student learning outcome. Do your students typically take exams? Would you get a clearer sense of whether they accomplished learning outcomes from a written assignment or oral presentation? Once you have decided on the best general method of assessing student learning outcomes, you can then develop or retrofit existing instruments to measure them. The instrument, then, is the actual assignment, quiz, exam or project you will use to complete the assessment. This is what you give to them, and what they complete for you. So, the first step is to determine the method you want to use and the second step is to develop the actual instrument.

First, consider the range of methods relevant to your discipline, course and desired learning outcome. What are the general ways students reveal what they know or what they can do? What do you already do in your course that can be used for successful assessment? Note that the most common assessment methods include, but are not limited to:

- tests/examinations
  —multiple choice, short answer, essay
- formal writing assignments
  —research papers, reaction papers, creative writing assignments
- performances
  —oral presentations, demonstrations
- portfolios
  —collated, aggregate representations of student work.

Once there is a decision on the method, it is time to shift to the instrument. Think about moving from a general idea to a specific, implementable representation of it. As an example: for a given class it may be decided that the most effective way (method) to measure student performance (related to an outcome) is to have students do an oral presentation in class. In-class presentation is the general method, and the assessment instrument might be stated and measured as an in-class oral presentation that requires the students to identify (or reveal) X, Y and Z (certain specific types of information or skills).

There are several nuanced considerations when choosing an assessment method to assure it aligns with the particular learning outcome. First, for outcomes that would be placed at the lower end of Bloom's Taxonomy, faculty should avoid overloading with multiple choice and true/false questions. Beyond encouraging only surface learning, it is difficult to measure analysis, creation or appraisal with such simplistic tools. While they are quick to grade, the key to assessment is proper utilization of tools. That said, assessment should also not be so cumbersome as to demotivate faculty from wanting to do a solid job. In a class of 100 students with no grading assistance, term papers may not be the most appropriate mechanism. It is hoped, however, that administrations will be aware of higher-level courses having higher-level outcomes and cap students at a manageable number in response.

Assessment can be done at a specific moment or over an extended period. It is important to explore ways to determine whether to assess student learning at a particular point in time or throughout the semester. Whether you assess student learning on a longer-term basis or 'at the moment' really depends on what you are trying to evaluate and find out. Do you want to look at learning in a general sense, measure knowledge gain over the course of the term or focus on snippets of material? Considering such questions will help determine the type of assessment you may want to utilize.

Assessments can be either formative or summative (Hanna and Detmer 2004). Formative assessments are ongoing assessments, reviews and observations in a classroom. Teachers use formative assessment to improve instructional methods and student feedback throughout the teaching and learning process. For example, if a faculty member observes that some students do not grasp a concept, he/she can design a review activity or use a different instructional strategy. Likewise, students can monitor their progress with periodic quizzes and performance tasks. The results of formative assessments are used to modify and validate instruction. Summative assessments, on the other hand, are typically used to evaluate the effectiveness of instructional programs and services at the end of an academic year or at a predetermined time. The goal of summative assessments is to make a judgment of student competency when an instructional phase is complete. Summative evaluations are used to determine if students have mastered specific competencies and to identify instructional areas that need additional attention. Thus formative assessments help students identify strengths and weaknesses, and faculty to see when students struggle, while summative assessments evaluate learning against some standard.

A variety of methods exist for faculty seeking to assess student learning at one specific point in time. Every instructor can identify key concepts within a course. Assessing the extent to which students understand these key concepts can be especially helpful in gauging whether they are 'getting' course content, or moving through the semester without a solid base of understanding of important fundamental concepts. This information can also help you find out whether to slow down, move faster or adjust your syllabus to accommodate disparities in learning. Some of the most common ways to assess at a point in time include:

- Primary trait analysis: To conduct PTA, the instructor: (1) breaks down individual components, or primary traits, of an assignment that are key to meeting assignment requirements; (2) identifies levels of achievement for each trait; and (3) constructs a grid (rubric) on which student achievement is scored.
- Minute paper: Several minutes before the end of class, you might stop your lecture or end the discussion to ask students to take one or two minutes to answer, in writing, several questions about the day's work. These questions might include 'What is the most important thing you learned in today's class?' or 'Do you still have questions about the material we covered today?' Students respond on a sheet of paper and hand it in before leaving.
- Muddiest point: Administered during or at the end of a lecture or class discussion, the muddiest point exercise asks students to think about what went on in class that day and to write about what was the (least clear) point.
- Punctuated lecturing: Students listen, stop, reflect, write and provide feedback on the spot on how they are learning from a lecture or a demonstration.
- Polling: Create a short survey (one or two questions) and ask students to complete it and hand it in.
- Reading response: The reading reaction paper forces students to slow down the reading process and asks them to think about what they have read.

Ideally, by using some combination of these, faculty will be able to judge student progress toward meeting goals and outcomes at any given point within a semester. It is important to remember as well that any of these assessment techniques can be used as assessments for learning as much as of learning. Thus the process can be as important as the end result.

Tracking student achievement over time is one of the best ways that you, as the instructor, can document that students are really accomplishing what you intend. Course goals are sometimes vague and difficult to quantify. Specific objectives that outline what a student must do to demonstrate completion of course goals make it easier to observe whether or not such goals have been achieved. Incorporating classroom assessment into your teaching and curriculum design facilitates specific documentation of results that clearly demonstrate student learning from the beginning of the semester until the end of the course. Examples of longer-term assessments include:

- Systematic assignment progression: This refers to a group of assignments that has been scheduled throughout the semester to track student progress on specific learning objectives as they occur. These often (or may) focus on one particular learning objective the instructor is particularly interested in studying. Each assignment is connected both to the one before and to the one after to maintain a formal record of student progress.
- Pre-/post-testing: A pre-test survey can be used at the beginning of the semester to capture the extent of student knowledge and understanding about key course concepts they will study that semester. Using a follow-up post-test (either the same as the pre-test or somewhat different) at the end of the semester and comparing results from the two can be an effective way to demonstrate student achievement over time.
- Portfolio analysis: This looks at student work over a period of time and evaluates the extent of learning based on the progression of the work from the first assignment until the last. At the classroom level, this might include a series of writing assignments of increasing difficulty or all work that the student has produced for a particular course.

Faculty should remember a few key pieces of information when designing and completing assessments. First, they should aim to include as many embedded assessments as possible. After all, using methods already in place for evaluation of student performance in the course is an efficient way to assess outcomes. Second, they should plan on multiple approved methods per course so they can have flexibility based on the particular students and classroom climate. While outcomes assessment differs from grading, both benefit from multiple measures. Multiple measures assure we play to the strength of all students (those who can write, answer multiple choice questions and communicate effectively, for example) and allow them to have an off day without risking their grade. Basing everything—whether a grade or an outcome—on one data point, consequently, is of some concern.

Rubrics

A rubric is an assessment tool that lists the criteria for a piece of work or what counts (Goodrich 1997; Popham 1997). Rubrics are useful for a variety of reasons: first, they allow assurances of reliability and validity of grades and, second, they allow graders to quickly peruse each essay and assign the corresponding score (Andrade 2000; Payne 2003). Thus they allow for consistency, effectiveness and efficiency. Since rubrics are used to assure validity and reliability, each student should receive the same score regardless of when their assignment is graded, and the score should be able to be duplicated. Rubric development is not a simple process. Faculty must be clear in determining the expectations and scoring criterion for each assignment. It is up to the instructor whether students are given the rubric prior to completing an assignment or whether it is simply used to assess performance. Table 9.2 presents an example rubric. When designed properly, the rubric should allay student questions, minimize the need for written comments and communicate clear standards for students.

Tracking Outcomes

When considering how data will be tracked by an instructor, there are three standard practices to choose from: single assessment; multiple assessments tracked by student; and multiple assessments tracked by method utilized. In this section, each is presented.

Single assessments are the most direct and simple. They use one single assessment to determine if a student has met some stated outcome. For example, perhaps the outcome is: 'Students will be able to identify the difference between presidential and parliamentary government.' A single exam question, a paper, a project or presentation could be used to demonstrate mastery. However the faculty choose to assess and whatever barometer is set to measure success, the data to be reported are simply (1) the number of students who were assessed, that is, who took the exam and so on, and (2) the number who met the outcome. Table 9.3 provides an example of a single assessment report.

When considering multiple assessments tracked by student, the assumption is that the faculty will be using more than one measure for the same outcome during the length of the course. Perhaps a test question, project and essay will all be used to see if a student is meeting a given course outcome. For every student, the instructor should record the score achieved for each student (or at least an indication of meeting or not meeting the outcome). Tables 9.4, 9.5 and 9.6 show three different ways to record progress and prepare for data reporting. In Table 9.4, met/not met is tracked and the faculty member stipulates that a student must meet the outcome in two of the three assessments to be considered successful.

Table 9.5, on the other hand, shows tracking by actual score, with a minimum score of 230 points required for the overall outcome to be claimed as met.

Lastly, Table 9.6 looks at score percentages with an 80 percent average necessary for success.

The final approach to reporting course outcomes is using multiple assessments tracked by method. Rather than looking at every student individually, this approach aggregates students together and looks at aggregate performance measures. The total number of students who attempted the assessment item and the number of students who met it should be recorded. Faculty will determine the final student score by dividing the number attempted or number met by the number of assessments. An example is presented in Table 9.7, with four assessment items (three multiple choice and one true/false). The number of students who attempted the assessment and the

Table 9.2 Sample rubric

Budget Project Grading Rubric

	Exceptional	Good	Adequate	Limited	Unacceptable
Title Page	Present with all information required (2)	Present with most information required (1)	Present with some information required (1)	Present with minimal information required (0)	Not present (0)
Table of Contents	Present with all information required (3)	Present with most information required (2)	Present with some information required (1)	Present with minimal information required (0)	Not present (0)
Background/ History of Agency and Community	Provides detailed background of agency and community (5)	Provides background of agency and community and highlights most necessary information (4)	Provides information about agency and community but does not highlight all needed information (3)	Provides information but lacks detail and does not cover full background of agency and community (1)	Provides inadequate information (0)
Overview of Agency	Provides detailed overview of agency (5)	Provides overview of agency and highlights most necessary information (4)	Provides information about agency but does not highlight all needed information (3)	Provides information but lacks detail and does not cover full overview of agency (1)	Provides inadequate information (0)
Budgetary Overview	Provides clear overview of budget processes discussed and complete budget (including discussion of overall vision for the department/ agency and how the budget serves that vision, provides an analysis of the environment and all variables influencing this budget, selection of budgetary format, summary of the proposed budget) (10)	Provides nearly all of the required information related to clear overview of budget processes discussed and complete budget (8)	Provides most of the required information related to clear overview of budget processes discussed and complete budget (6)	Provides some of the required information related to clear overview of budget processes discussed and complete budget (4)	Provides inadequate information related to clear overview of budget processes discussed and complete budget (2)

Table 9.2 (continued)

Budget Project Grading Rubric

	Exceptional	Good	Adequate	Limited	Unacceptable
Revenues	Provides a thoughtful, complete analysis of all revenues (including describing all sources and specific revenue levels) (25)	Provides nearly all of the required information regarding revenues (8)	Provides most of the required information regarding revenues (6)	Provides some of the required information regarding revenues (4)	Provides inadequate information regarding revenues (2)
Appropriations/ Expenditures	Provides a thoughtful, complete analysis of all appropriations/ expenditures (including operating and capital along with debt where necessary) (25)	Provides nearly all of the required information regarding appropriations/ expenditures (8)	Provides most of the required information regarding appropriations/ expenditures (6)	Provides some of the required information regarding appropriations/ expenditures (4)	Provides inadequate information regarding appropriations/ expenditures (2)
Strengths/ Limitations	Demonstrates clear understanding of the strengths/limitations of both the budget and the techniques selected (10)	Demonstrates understanding but fails to fully explain strengths/limitations (8)	Demonstrates some understanding but fails to fully explain strengths/limitations (6)	Demonstrates minimal understanding and fails to fully explain strengths/limitations (4)	Provides inadequate information (2)
Conclusion	Present with all information required (3)	Present with most information required (2)	Present with some information required (1)	Present with minimal information required (0)	Not present (0)
Appendices	Present with all information required (2)	Present with most information required (1)	Present with some information required (1)	Present with minimal information required (0)	Not present (0)
Professionalism of Writing and Presentation	The writing is free of errors and clear (10)	The writing is nearly free of errors and almost uniformly clear (8)	There are occasional errors, but they don't represent a major distraction or obscure meaning (6)	The writing has many errors and the reader is distracted by them (4)	There are so many errors that meaning is obscured. The reader is confused and stops reading (2)

Table 9.3 Example student learning outcome data inserted on reporting sheet

PS200	SLO	Outcome	No. Assessed	No. met
	SLO 1	Student will be able to identify two varieties of avocado	32	27
	SLO 2	Student will be able to recite the Jabberwocky	31	6
	SLO 3	Student will be able to recognize 5 Olympic athletes	32	32

Table 9.4 Met/not met

Student	Test question	Poster project	Essay question	2/3 = Meets
Doe, Jane	met	met	met	Met
Doe, John	met	not met	met	Met
Student, Sam	not met	not met	met	Not met
Student, Sarah	met	not met	did not take	Not met
Student, Sylvester	met	met	did not take	Met
Student, Sydney	did not take	met	did not take	Not met
Class			Assessed =	*6
			Met =	*3

Note: *Reported data.

Table 9.5 Total score

Student	Test question	Poster project	Essay question	Total score	Above 230 = Meets
Doe, Jane	84	95	68	247	Met
Doe, John	91	69	82	242	Met
Student, Sam	67	66	82	215	Not met
Student, Sarah	90	62	0	152	Not met
Student, Sylvester	92	80	0	172	Not met
Student, Sydney	0	97	0	97	Not met
Class				Assessed =	*6
				Met =	*2

Note: *Reported data.

number who met the outcome are recorded. Ultimately, divide the total number by four and end up with a student equivalent number of how many tried and met the outcome.

The proper assessment recording and reporting format will depend on the course, the students, the department, the program and the particular faculty member. The above discussion and explanation will prove a solid background, however.

Table 9.6 Average score

Student	Test question	Poster project	Essay question	Average score	Above 80% = Meets
Doe, Jane	84	95	68	82.3	Met
Doe, John	91	69	82	80.7	Met
Student, Sam	67	66	82	71.7	Not met
Student, Sarah	90	62	0	50.7	Not met
Student, Sylvester	92	80	0	57.3	Not met
Student, Sydney	0	97	0	32.3	Not met
Class				Assessed = Met =	*6 *2

Note: *Reported data.

Table 9.7 Three multiple choice and one true/false give outcome no. 1

Assessment	MC Q1	MC Q2	MC Q3	T/F Q1	Total number	No. of assessment activities	Final student score (rounded)
No. of students attempting	45	43	44	45	177	4	*44
No. of students meeting	40	38	36	45	159	4	*39

Note: *Reported data.

STUDENT EVALUATIONS OF INSTRUCTION

To this point, the chapter has focused solely on measuring student performance in meeting goals and outcomes in courses. However, equally important are student perceptions of their own learning, their faculty and their courses. The underlying assumptions regarding teaching center on the idea that effective teaching can most easily be assessed through measuring student perceptions of their learning. This learning should be based on progress toward specific objectives chosen by you, the instructor.

How student course evaluations fit into the assessment cycle is a key component of improving instructional delivery, with the larger goal of enhancing student learning. Above all, these evaluations help us tell if students are successfully learning what they should be from a particular course. Course evaluations allow for the collection of feedback, which permits interpretations of results, learning, reflection, discussion and ultimately improvement in future semesters.

With a plethora of both internally developed and marketed products available for use in course evaluations today, it is difficult to identify a least common denominator. However, nearly all course evaluations share a few components: self-assessments of progress on objectives, overall assessments of the course and overall assessments of the instructor. Prior to the conclusion of a semester (or in its immediate aftermath), an instructor should take time to type out a fairly detailed account of how each course went. Items to be considered include student interest, reactions to assessment tools, changes made in course set-up and/or delivery, tone of the classroom and any mitigating factors that could artificially inflate or deflate subjective or objective portrayals of student progress on goals and outcomes. When available or permitted, faculty should include course-specific questions covering any areas of interest (student feedback on assignments, textbooks or lecture delivery styles, for example) to assure maximum information gained.

CLOSING THE LOOP: MAKING ASSESSMENT WORK

Any type of assessment will be strengthened if students are actively engaged in the process. Faculty should be direct and allow students to know what their results are, how you interpreted them and what your response will be. Angelo and Cross (1993, p. 32) write:

> Students are unlikely to realize the value of assessment, or of self-assessment, unless faculty make them explicitly aware of it through instruction and modeling. When students are helped to see the useful ways that classroom assessment can inform teaching and learning, they are much more likely to participate fully and positively.

As Wright (1991, p. 585) puts it, classroom assessment has the potential to increase 'interest in learning and change attitudes and behaviors' when students become more involved, self-reflective learners. But, faculty must not forget Palomba and Banta (1999, p. 346), who remind us that the assessment process should 'help create high expectations for students as well as provide opportunities for synthesizing experiences, for active learning and for prompt feedback'.

Whether considering student course evaluations or progress on outcomes and goals, it is essential that students feel that the information they are providing is being used for some purpose—hopefully improvement. Defining and collecting assessment data is only part of the process. Understanding what the data tell you and deciding what to do with the results once you have gathered them are equally important. Regardless whether our goal is linked to classroom-based improvement, departmental reviews, institution-wide requirements or initiatives of accrediting bodies, it is important to close the loop and clearly delineate what changes will be made based on results. Knowing why you are assessing is key to deciding what to do with the data after you collect them. Farmer and Napieralski (1997), after all, remind us that effective assessment must begin with the real concerns of the stakeholders and result in useful information and recommendations related to the purpose of the assessment.

REFERENCES

Anderson, L.W. and D.R. Krathwohl (2001), *A taxonomy for learning, teaching and assessing: A revision of Bloom's Taxonomy of educational objectives*, New York: Longman.

Andrade, H.G. (2000), 'Using rubrics to promote thinking and learning', *Educational Leadership*, **57** (5), 13–18.
Angelo, T.A. and K.P. Cross (1993), *Classroom assessment techniques: A handbook for college teachers*, San Francisco, CA: Jossey-Bass.
Biggs, J. (1999), *Teaching for quality learning at university*, Buckingham, UK: SRHE and Open University Press.
Bloom, B.S. (1964), *Taxonomy of educational objectives: The classification of educational goals, by a committee of college and university examiners*, New York: Longman.
Farmer, D.W. and E.A. Napieralski (1997), 'Assessing learning in programs', in J.G. Gaff and J.L. Ratcliff (eds), *Handbook of the undergraduate curriculum*, San Francisco, CA: Jossey-Bass, pp. 591–607.
Goodrich, H. (1997), 'Understanding rubrics', *Educational Leadership*, **54** (4), 14–17.
Hanna, G.S. and P.A. Dettmer (2004), *Assessment for effective teaching: Using context-adaptive planning*, Boston, MA: Pearson.
Ohia, U.O. (1995), 'Connections among assessment, testing, and faculty development', *Assessment Update*, **7** (4), 9.
Palomba, C.A. and T.W. Banta (1999), *Assessment essentials*, San Francisco, CA: Jossey-Bass.
Payne, D.A. (2003), *Applied educational assessment*, Belmont, CA: Wadsworth.
Popham, J.W. (1997), 'What's wrong—and what's right—with rubrics', *Educational Leadership*, **55** (2), 72–5.
Tan, D.L. (1992), 'A multivariate approach to the assessment of quality', *Research in Higher Education*, **33** (2), 205–27.
Wright, B.D. (1991), 'Discipline-based assessment: The case of sociology', *AAHE Bulletin*, **44** (3), 14–16.

10. Multidisciplinary approaches to teaching political science
Brenda Kauffman

In essence, taking a multidisciplinary approach to studying theories and issues in political science involves the inclusion of diverse academic disciplines. While it may seem intuitive that issues of political concern naturally involve a variety of factors, such as economic realities, cultural elements, historical events or sociological dynamics, critically evaluating the issues from these disciplines requires thoughtful analysis and attention to fundamental principles found in the respective disciplines. This chapter will develop a plan for teaching students using theories and methods from multiple disciplines and will include examples of how disciplines can be brought together in the classroom to tackle a single theme. For this we will focus on the elements of a learning community that work well to introduce students to the process of looking at the world through multiple theoretical lenses. Such an approach aims to be comprehensive, coherent and consistent. Students should develop the ability to conceptualize and analyze challenging problems by studying and engaging in a variety of academic work through multiple disciplines.

FUNDAMENTALS OF LEARNING COMMUNITIES

While learning communities are typically aimed at freshman students in order to engage them with challenging multidisciplinary approaches early in their academic careers, they are certainly not limited to them (Kuh et al. 2010). In fact an increasing number of programs are instituting learning communities aimed at upper-level students because the multidisciplinary approach has so much to offer (Fink 2013). Students at any level should be exposed to diverse points of view and, as they progress in their academic careers, they will thereby be able to make stronger connections and more in-depth critical analyses. These learning environments will not only equip them with the essential tools for successful and meaningful work, but also make them better able to see the purpose behind the method, as well as better able to identify relevant and import questions, assess the validity of assumptions, recognize various points of view, evaluate data, distinguish different points of view, better interpret inferences and judge implications and consequences (Zhao and Kuh 2004).

Situations and issues of the real world are multifaceted and require students to acquire and apply knowledge from several different disciplines in order to be able to fully comprehend the complexity of the solutions (Barkley, Cross and Major 2014). Political issues tend to have a variety of factors that impact their outcomes, such as religious, cultural, social, scientific or economic concerns that vary among disparate interest groups. Issues such as the Israeli–Palestinian conflict, climate change or civil rights are often divisive in nature not because of a simple bifurcation of opinions, but because of many varied opinions that must be studied with diverse perspectives and methods. Some relevant disciplines that integrate well include economics, history, business, literature and philosophy.

In order to facilitate successful integration of different disciplines into the classroom there must be some planning and forethought as to how to introduce different methodologies and theories to the students. The information must be presented so that the students can ascertain the connections. Students must have the opportunity to practice making these connections, which can be achieved best through in-class discussions and writing assignments. Ideally students can be exposed to a dialogue between faculty from different disciplines engaged in a conversation concerning a single issue. Developing thoughtful tools for assessment is also a critical element. Students should be able to provide clarity, accuracy, relevance, depth, breadth, logic and significance when demonstrating what they have learned in the course. The learning community environment is ideal for cultivating and enhancing the students' abilities to draw connections and to critically analyze complicated problems.

Approaches to multidisciplinary teaching will naturally vary according to the theories and methodologies used to cover single topics. For example, studying theories about the development and maintenance of healthy political communities from a political and economic perspective will be fundamentally different from approaching the same issue from a philosophical and political perspective. Determining which perspectives will be focused on is the first part of the planning (Tinto 1995). Whether one is going to deliver the course individually and incorporate the various approaches will also be significant. In the case of the learning community approach two or more professors work together to create effective strategies for combining their disciplines. Each would bring to the discussion the language and methods relevant to their fields. It is tremendously beneficial for students to be exposed to various perspectives, especially when looking at the same set of problems or issues. It is also a useful exercise for faculty who might not otherwise step outside their own respective fields.

Political science and economics often use similar theoretical and even methodological approaches, but professionals within these disciplines may not always see clearly how the approach of the other can be useful in teaching about specific issues. While a political scientist and an economist may both want to determine which policies are best to implement during economic crises, they will rely on different starting assumptions. Simply stated, for political scientists policies are largely based on the political process and for economists are based much more on models. So, two instructors who endeavor to teach students both approaches would start by developing a plan to cover equally the important elements of politics such as the structures, institutions, actors, stakes and goals of policy as well as the gathering and developing of data for creating various economic models.

The ultimate goal of the learning community is successful integrated learning, but the process is clearly multidisciplinary. Students should be able to draw the connections across disciplines while simultaneously recognizing the distinctions found within them. To build further on the political and economic illustration, a good example of a sample assignment would be to build up the two disciplines in several class sessions and then present a case such as the 2008 global recession and housing crisis. Students could then apply the theories and models from the different disciplines to give a more complete picture of some of the causes of the crisis. Furthermore, they may be able to make predictions for future events or suggest policies that could prevent future crises. For an even more multidisciplinary approach, students could be introduced to the theories and methods of the social science disciplines such as sociology, psychology or anthropology to learn about how the social, psychological or cultural factors of a society might influence political and economic outcomes.

EXAMPLE CONNECTIONS AND ASSIGNMENTS

To illustrate in more detail what a course covering both economics and politics might look like, consider the following example of a course description for a learning community that combines 'Introduction to Political Science' and 'Macroeconomics':

> The course provides students with an interdisciplinary view of the U.S. economy and how it relates to the overall global economy. We are living in an increasingly globalized environment and national economies are more interdependent than ever before. Given this interdependence, events in one economy usually have ripple effects throughout the world. Economic phenomena, such as the global financial crisis of 2008–2010, often trigger policy responses. Much debate over economic policy, may it be in Washington D.C., London, Beijing, or Tokyo, centers around the appropriate role of government in the economy. In this Learning Community, students will learn to analyze the motivations behind economic policies and they will critically evaluate their effects, domestically as well as internationally. Ultimately, this course serves to make students better global citizens by integrating the principles of economics, politics, international relations, history, and geography into a coherent narrative about the global economy and the linkages that exist among countries.

An integrated class project that ensures that students apply the disciplines independently as well as drawing connections between them is an effective measure of their understanding. Such a project could involve group work or independent research. At the freshman level it can sometimes be difficult to assign extensive research papers, given varying levels of writing and analytical abilities. However, dividing the project into more manageable short pieces with a final product that integrates them achieves much better results. To begin, students could be assigned to choose three countries and research their political structures. They should be able to identify the institutions and main actors in the government, as well as the type of political and economic structures present.

A second paper might focus on gathering important economic information about their countries, such as gross domestic product, level of development, currency, unemployment rates, income gap, main exports and imports, important industries, debts and deficits. This would enable them to look at these same countries from an economic point of view. It would help to shape their ability to recognize that the world is complex and multidimensional, and, when examined from only one perspective, it is fractured. Finally the students would have to engage in more complicated research to discover which kinds of policies their respective states instituted to deal with the recession. They would then have to analyze the effectiveness of the policies. These short papers could be combined to present a broader answer to the initial question. The critical concern with these and any of the writing assignments is that the students learn how to write evidence-based papers substantiated with relevant source materials used for the class. The more opportunities students have to engage in developing their writing skills, the better. When students can see that research writing is the development of evidence-based writing, then, as they progress through their college careers, they will be better prepared for such work.

Utilizing current events in the classroom and looking at them from multidisciplinary approaches is an excellent way to challenge students to think from multiple points of view. Political science as a discipline lends itself well to cross-examinations from fields such as economics, literature, history or philosophy. Students will surely be able to better appreciate the relevance of political science and remain interested and enthusiastic about pursuing it academically when they are given challenging and interesting opportunities to apply the theories and to relate them to other fields. The outcome of education should be the creation of well-informed active citizens who can see themselves as integral parts of the whole community. Too often in academia students are not introduced to more than the perspective of their major discipline, especially once they have completed the required general education courses. Multidisciplinary approaches allow for a more nuanced learning process. Often students are so preoccupied with the business of checking off boxes that move them closer to a degree and to finding a job that they simply do not have the time or the inclination to take courses not on their checklist. This is another reason why teaching with a multidisciplinary approach is vital.

Considering the popularity of business majors at many institutions and the relationships between politics and business, these two disciplines also work well together in the classroom. Many students are attracted to studying the relationships between entrepreneurship and politics. A class in politics and entrepreneurship could be designed to provide a cultural, historical, philosophical and social scientific overview of the concept and importance of the connection between politics and business. Ideas from the humanities and the social sciences from across the centuries could be explored and connected to the evolution of American social and business life. By examining the words and ideas of writers, historians and philosophers who have written about intellectual and social forces that have influenced the development of America's political economy, students will be able to see that contemporary challenges affecting business and government have deep roots. This is significant considering the often contentious political debates that seem to dominate much of the contemporary dialogue surrounding regulation and tax policies.

A class such as this could incorporate a number of small writing assignments to help students develop ideas about more challenging concepts such as freedom and the pursuit of happiness, freedom and the rule of law, the threats to freedom from dishonorable politicians and entrepreneurs, as well as the links between political and economic freedom. Students often need to be pushed to explore theoretical or philosophical concepts, and providing a practical application for them makes the process easier. If they learn to see how the many varied theories can be applied to things that impact their daily lives, they will be better able to relate the abstract with the practical. If they can draw connections between the ideas that helped to establish the principles and laws that created the structures of modern society and the way these structures impact their personal decisions about what to buy or where to live or what to study in college, then they will surely find the whole experience more meaningful.

At the crossroads of business, economics and politics, students can be challenged to make connections between where, how and by whom the goods they consume are produced. Consumers in the modern global economy are largely unaware of the long commodity chains that gave rise to the t-shirt they are wearing or the fish they are eating. They are equally unaware of the political institutions and actors that play significant roles in determining how goods and services move about the planet. They are oblivious to how much of an influence they could have as citizens if they were actively engaged not just as consumers of goods and services but as individuals who clearly understand the impact their choices make on the world. This is true for political, economic and environmental reasons.

Environmental studies provide yet another dimension to help students see the usefulness of taking a multidimensional approach to understanding global or national issues. Instructors can incorporate guest lectures from the various disciplines or they can work closely with colleagues to develop their own lesson plans or utilize the wealth of reliable resources. In any policy-making process basic processes naturally occur. Most often, before any policy is even considered, an issue has to be identified. When it comes to environmental issues and problems, identification can come from a myriad of places. Individuals as concerned citizens, interest groups, environmental agencies or scientists who discover environmental challenges might define a problem and endeavor to set the agenda for policy.

The role that science plays in environmental policy is critical. With more young people becoming increasingly aware of the environmental realities of the world, there is a significant opportunity for the discipline of political science to help them navigate their way through the complexities of finding solutions. Whether it is climate change, deforestation, species extinction, the loss of biodiversity or looming resource scarcities, clear understanding of the problem requires exploring the scientific data as well as the political will and political obstacles to making policy. Students of political science need to be aware that politics is quite often reactive and, regardless of all the principles and institutions that they may learn about in their courses, including the constitutional powers of government, politics does not occur in a vacuum.

An example of an assignment that could be used to help students see how scientists and policy makers approach issues would be to teach them how to collect relevant data in the field and then to use those data to make policy recommendations. The key learning objective for this assignment would have to incorporate all of the other factors involved in policy making. In other words, students should be able to take into consideration all the agenda-setting and issue-defining problems that are present when politicians want to make policies regulating or addressing environmental factors. So, even if students have spent time in the field collecting data on an endangered species or a threatened habitat, the policy recommendation would have to factor in the economic, social and political costs and benefits of addressing the issue.

Another potential assignment integrating science and political science could look similar to the economics assignment, where students would do one paper establishing the political elements of a particular environmental policy and a second paper discussing the available scientific data concerning the issue. They could then evaluate whether or not the policy is good and whether it is likely to be an effective response to the issue. These kinds of exercises place a greater value on academic challenge and force students to rise to the challenge. Making politics relevant, interesting and challenging is critical to keeping majors actively engaged. It is especially effective when students are exposed to common readings that can be understood and analyzed from the different disciplines.

Sometimes it may be that the same story means something different to the environmental scientist than to the political scientist, and the true challenge is to determine how to reconcile these differences.

In addition to science, there are many other factors to consider when discussing environmental politics. One of the biggest factors impacting policy, environmental or otherwise, is culture. The choices individuals make every day are enormously important. This is true not only for environmental issues but for many other political issues. The things people believe, the assumptions on which they build their arguments and derive their conclusions, in many ways determine the course of their lives and all the things they will do along the way. Culture influences what people eat, what they wear, and what they choose to do for a living. Introducing anthropology and its many theories and methodologies is immeasurably valuable in broadening the scope of the study of political science.

Assignments that require students to incorporate both the theories and approaches of anthropology and political science could cover a very wide range of topics. The various areas of society, such as ethnology, technology and ideologies, as well as important methods of media transmission, are all elements that must be factored into any important discussion of politics. Students could engage in the collection of ethnographic information as they would do in a cultural anthropology course. If this course is combined with an introduction to political science course, the information then could be examined to see how it relates to political discourse. Another example of an assignment could be for students to examine the origin and development of political societies using the theories of anthropology as well as the theoretical perspectives of political science. Political institutions have existed in a variety of forms for much of human history. The evolution of the central authority that keeps peace and order in a society has deep anthropological roots. Political institutions should not be taken for granted. While students may spend a great deal of time covering these topics from an historical or philosophical point of view, their evolution and development go far beyond such views. Additionally, there are places in the world where no such institutions have emerged and been sustained. While there are likely to be social, political, historical, environmental and economic factors that offer explanations, there are also important cultural elements that are legitimate, if not always politically favorable, to explore.

History is in many ways the starting place for all disciplines. However, teaching history as part of political science and introducing students to the discipline of history requires a more deliberate approach. There are many historical events to draw upon for useful material. Some examples include exploration, revolutions, nationalism, wars, colonialism, decolonization and class struggles. Each of these topics has major historical significance, but has also specifically impacted global politics. Much of the globalization discussion today hinges on developing a deeper and more complete understanding of how these historical events occurred and what role they continue to play. Students could approach these issues from both disciplines by first establishing a solid foundation in the events themselves. They could write a paper discussing the context of the events and the main actors involved. They could then evaluate the same events in relation to how they shaped the political culture. Politics do not happen in a vacuum and have never done so. If students can grasp the meaning of this, then they may be better prepared to identify the various factors that are relevant to contemporary politics. The more students are required to read and think and write across disciplines, the better.

Fields such as philosophy and literature also enhance the presentation of political concepts for students and promote the benefits of multidisciplinary approaches. For example, political theory as a subfield of political science will be evaluated and incorporated into a political science program differently than it would in a philosophy program. While philosophy may focus more on how the political philosophers capture ideas about human nature or drives such as passions and aversions, the political scientist will see how those various notions about human nature create political structures and institutions, and furthermore how they arise, are sustained or why they sometimes fail. In all of the examples discussed thus far, writing exercises are the best way to assess the connections and development of ideas students are acquiring through the various multidisciplinary approaches.

From the Greeks to the Germans to the postmodernists, various ideas have been offered by philosophers and theorists to explain the human condition, and while the philosopher may be seeking the greater truth, if one is to be found, the political scientist will look to see how these ideas shaped changing political systems and led to democracies, monarchies, totalitarian regimes or variations of them. Philosophical inquiry is critically important for political inquiry. A closer look at ethical concerns and moral agency, as can be discovered through philosophical methodology and applied to political discourse, is especially valuable for the study and instruction of political science. The best approach would be to provide a number of opportunities and occasions for students to practice making ethical judgments of issues, based on different ethical theories to which they have been introduced.

Similarly, great works of literature may be best understood and explained by a professor of English, yet literature has given rise to valuable and important political ideas that have transformed societies. Literature has inspired people across time and space to rally against tyrannical regimes or to oppose broken social systems. It has also been extremely relevant as a medium for discussing and identifying social problems and evaluating other dominant social paradigms. It is useful in helping to discover why people behave the way they do in the political sphere. A course with political science and literature could examine issues of criminality, law and justice through the perspectives of political science and literary study. Beginning with fundamental questions of politics, such as 'Is the law just?', the course could explore theories of crime and punishment both in their application to political institutions and practices and in their expression in literature and film. Subtopics of the course could include: criminality and identity (race, class and gender); the death penalty; discipline and punishment through the authority of the state; and issues of law and criminality in international contexts. Authors to be studied could include political theorists—such as Henry David Thoreau, Martin Luther King, Karl Marx and Michel Foucault—and literary figures, ranging from the continental authors Albert Camus and Franz Kafka to the American novelists Nathaniel Hawthorne and Richard Wright. Films might include classics, such as *Anatomy of a Murder* and *Taxi Driver*, and recent cinema set in international contexts, such as *Syriana* and *Argo*.

The writing assignments could focus on these themes and require students to make academic arguments analyzing the materials from both disciplines. They would have to be able to identify the themes, ideas and concepts, as well as technical aspects of the writing from a literary point of view, as well as how it addresses the political issue. Evaluation would be based on their level of thoughtfulness in assessing both the quality and the relevance of the materials. Students sometimes do not even see the obvious political elements that are present in literature or even in pop culture. When exposed to such approaches, they not only develop better critical thinking skills but also a greater appreciation of the diverse media through which politics manifests itself. Science fiction literature also provides a tremendous amount of material for analysis from both a literary and political perspective.

Another interesting possibility would be to examine religious literature and politics. One specific approach would be to examine religious literature and writings independently for their contribution to the tenets of the religion, to culture, to society and to literature. Then, from a political perspective, the class could study the political structures and regimes that were present during the time and place of the writing. When these two perspectives are brought together, often the effects of the role that the politics played in establishing or preserving the religion are made evident. Students who are exposed to this kind of multidisciplinary approach look at two things that are quite often primary drivers of society but are at times in conflict. They can use enhanced knowledge and understanding to make more sense of the debates. One of the issues concerning political science is how to help students make reasoned arguments and acknowledge the source of the assumptions on which they base these arguments. In contemporary rhetoric, politics and religion are too often seen as two opposing forces. A course that introduces students to both perspectives helps them connect and can only make future discourse better. If society is to escape the extreme divides it now faces, this is essential.

Significant sociological concerns, which are increasingly scrutinized when measuring the well-being of a political community, present another useful multidisciplinary teaching opportunity. Qualitative measures of human life such as privacy, access to information, access to nutritious food, literacy rates, access to the Internet or to community associations need to be examined by the political scientist. Introducing students to the theories and methods of sociological study will help them to see these more abstract notions of human well-being with greater clarity.

WHY MULTIPLE DISCIPLINES?

The larger social questions that often seem to require public response are much more easily addressed using the more comprehensive multidisciplinary approach. For example, why are addiction and violence so prevalent in a society? What are the strengths and weaknesses of the education system? How can and should political figures respond to these issues? Students could be asked to examine a case study regarding one of these social problems using the kinds of research tools sociologists use. They could then, consistent with the other efforts to bring in multiple perspectives, be asked to recommend policies aimed at addressing the problems. They would do this by following the process established in this chapter. Through a series of readings, class discussions and writing assignments, they would gain valuable insights and become familiar with the various tools necessary to deal with social problems.

While the writing assignments that have been suggested are crucial to helping students cultivate their academic skills, the value of in-class discussions deserves separate attention. An enormous amount of recent literature suggests that this generation of students is more concerned about getting a job than any previous generation of college students. This presents a real problem for institutions that are promoting the value of learning for its own sake. This also applies to disciplines that have come under recent scrutiny for their relevance in higher education. While not quite as scrutinized as the humanities, social science fields like political science are often challenged to prove their value and place in academia.

This is where the importance of the in-class discussion is particularly meaningful. This is the chance that the professor has to engage the students and challenge them to think critically about more than just the job they hope to acquire after college, but to think about the role they will play in society and their obligations and duties as a citizen. Political science classes are the perfect setting for such discussions, and when students are able to see how interconnected the world is, they might take their role in it much more seriously.

CONCLUSION

If the study of political science and the role of political science instructors is ideally to prepare future citizens to be equipped to fulfill the duties of citizenship, then the true complexity of the world must be made clear. The ultimate goal should be to foster higher-order thinking. Students must be given more information than just the basic structures, theories and relevant actors in politics. They must be given the tools and the insight to look beyond and more deeply into the issues they will face. Too often students move through the checklists of their academic careers without ever truly questioning the status quo they are being initiated into. Perhaps one of the most important elements of the multidisciplinary approach is that it might be the best hope of helping students to challenge themselves as individuals and to see themselves and the problems of society as part of a larger whole.

When data show how little the average American actually knows about the issues, it is more important than ever to change the dynamics of higher education and to embrace and cultivate new perspectives. Citizenship should never be reduced to the act of voting, paying taxes, serving on a jury, registering for military service and obeying the laws. It should create more than mere consumers connected only through market activities and establish true members of a community. Bridging academic gulfs is one significant mechanism for creating and establishing an ability in students to make future connections on their own. If politics, as Aristotle described it, is the business of the community, then the members of the community must be well informed. Contemporary society seems to place a heavy emphasis on the individual, who often measures his/her worth by material possessions. Contemporary society is also in many ways composed of uninformed and politically apathetic unengaged citizens. The structures and institutions of this society need to be better understood and more closely scrutinized.

Political, economic and social structures change. How they change is determined by the forces that move them. In an increasingly complex globalized world, the student of political science must be aware of multiple dimensions of reality and various approaches to problem solving. The future of the discipline, if it is going to remain relevant in an uncertain shift in college and university curricula and platforms, will require instructors who continue to cultivate their own skills and establish collegial relations with fellow faculty members from different departments. While transferring valuable critical thinking and writing skills is fundamental to any discipline, political science has a unique opportunity to build on many different theories and methodologies to prepare students to honestly engage with their world and to be prepared for the task of addressing the many political issues of their lives. Students need to learn not just the technical methods of political science and other disciplines, but the higher end these methods can achieve. The achievement of an intellectual capacity enables analysis of whole systems and not simply the deconstruction of their parts.

BIBLIOGRAPHY

Barkley, E.F., K.P. Cross and C.H. Major (2014), *Collaborative Learning Techniques: A Handbook for College Faculty*, San Francisco, CA: John Wiley & Sons.
Fink, L.D. (2013), *Creating Significant Learning Experiences: An Integrated Approach to Designing College Courses*, San Francisco, CA: John Wiley & Sons.
Kuh, G.D., J. Kinzie, J.H. Schuh and E.J. Whitt (2010), *Student Success in College: Creating Conditions That Matter*, San Francisco, CA: John Wiley & Sons.
Tinto, V. (1995), 'Learning Communities, Collaborative Learning, and the Pedagogy of Educational Citizenship', *AAHE Bulletin*, **47** (7), 11–13.
Zhao, C.M. and G.D. Kuh (2004), 'Adding Value: Learning Communities and Student Engagement', *Research in Higher Education*, **45** (2), 115–38.

11. Promoting information literacy and information research
Stephen Thornton

INTRODUCTION

For many, access to information – political or otherwise – is no longer a problem. In less than a generation the Internet has provided easy admission to an almost limitless repository of data. Moreover, for those suitably connected, this revolution has radically changed information behaviors. Faced with a novel concept to fathom, where once a trip to the reference library would have been the common response, a quick browse using Google or a brief consultation with 'Dr' Wikipedia has become the new default. This is understandable given that both the ubiquitous search engine and the popular open-access encyclopedia often provide almost instant information gratification. More recently still, other features of 'new media' such as social networking sites and blogs have also become established information resources for a substantial proportion of college students (Head and Eisenberg 2011).

A sizable number of scholars and other commentators on the human condition have examined the opportunities and problems presented by the superabundance of information made available through a variety of media, mostly of a technological flavor. The tendency has been to focus on the behavior of the generation of learners with little or no recollection of life before the World Wide Web, a cohort often awarded such epithets as the 'Google Generation' or – to use Marc Prensky's (2001, p. 1) famous expression – 'digital natives'. For some, such as Prensky, this digital revolution is a wholly positive phenomenon, one to be embraced to the extent of discarding established teaching methods to accommodate something close to a new species of enhanced learner: students used to 'the instantaneity of hypertext, downloaded music, phones in their pockets, a library on their laptops, beamed messages and instant messaging' (Prensky 2001, p. 3). Others are less sanguine about these developments, not least the arrival of 'a library on their laptops'. For example, though acknowledging the rich benefits digital technology has provided in terms of widening access to information that would otherwise be the preserve of a particular elite, Tara Brabazon has warned that the popularity of, in particular, Google has also created severe problems; prominent among these, she argues, is the facilitation in a growing proportion of students of 'laziness, poor scholarship and compliant thinking' (Brabazon 2007, p. 15). Others have made a different criticism, suggesting that commentators such as Prensky have indulged in rampant overgeneralization, with Susan Herring (2008) making the point that many students entering higher education are not, as the digital native label suggests, *au fait* with all aspects of these new technologies and, moreover, that this characterization of an entire generation often seems to include a strong element of idealized wish-fulfillment on the part of older technophiles.

In recent years one particularly interesting development at the heart of this debate has been the introduction of the notion of 'information obesity', a term popularized by Andrew Whitworth (2009). Whitworth – who has a background in critical theory – suggests that the nature of information in the twenty-first century is such that it is increasingly difficult for many people to maintain some semblance of critical discrimination. Whitworth, making links to the expansion of physical obesity in some parts of the world, suggests that the sheer quantity of information now available is a significant factor driving this sclerosis of critical facilities, but other important factors include a perceived decline in the general quality of this information as commercial pressures to consume certain types of information – generally of the least 'nutritious' variety – have increased (Whitworth 2009, p. xi). Thus, the argument goes, Google and Wikipedia are the information world's equivalent of large fast-food restaurant chains, providing tasty, convenient and heavily marketed wares which, if devoured too often and too greedily, can cause grave damage to consumers' critical facilities. This danger – that it is becoming increasingly difficult for many in society, the 'information obese', to filter out the superficial, biased and possibly bogus information from that traditionally regarded as rich and authentic – appears particularly acute for students of political science and international relations, disciplines that appear to attract individuals and media outlets that prefer not to taint their analyses of events with either empirical evidence or cogent reasoning.

Regarding empirical evidence, there is an increasing body of literature that suggests a sizable proportion of students are developing symptoms of 'information obesity'; for example, as the large-scale studies conducted by Head and Eisenberg indicate, despite being part of the so-called 'digital native' generation and often skilled at finding a quick information fix online, many current students do struggle 'with processing all that the sites served up to them', and, in particular, find it difficult to sort the relevant from the irrelevant (Head and Eisenberg 2011, p. 19). Though far from abundant and generally small-scale, there are further studies that focus explicitly on the information behaviors of politics and international relations students. For example, Jonathan Cope and Richard Flanagan, after studying students taking an American politics class, were able to categorize four ideal types of information user: the Believer, the Cynic, the Opportunistic Surfer and the Discerning Analyst, of which only one – the far from overpopulated group of Discerning Analysts – demonstrated traits that distinguish critical and reflective consumers of information (Cope and Flanagan 2013, p. 4). More common were the Believers, who tended to accept truth claims without the burden of critical evaluation, and were prone to comments such as '[I] like . . . Wikipedia the most. Not only because it could give a basic understanding about things I was looking for, [but also because] it is not bias[ed]' (ibid., p. 14). Equally common were the Cynics, who thought all information was untrustworthy, and thus 'refused to judge the veracity of claims or to make a strong interpretive argument based on the information found in research' (ibid., p. 15). Cope and Flanagan's identification of the Believers and the Cynics brings to mind Alfred Korzybski's celebrated saying: 'there are two ways to slide easily through life: to believe everything or to doubt everything – both ways save us from thinking' (quoted in Ruggiero 2011, p. 101).

Another group with information issues identified by Cope and Flanagan were 'the Opportunistic Surfers' (2013, p. 15). Unlike the Believers and the Cynics, members of this group were aware that certain information sources could be more reliable than others, but were not prepared to explore widely, rarely venturing beyond a tightly circumscribed list of sources. Indeed, the Opportunistic Surfers display a characteristic noted by Head and Eisenberg in their much larger, multidisciplinary study, namely that one common response to the rapid expansion of available information is to retreat to a 'small set of common information sources – close at hand, tried and true' (Head and Eisenberg 2009, p. 3). The result, as Cope and Flanagan point out, is that the ease and familiarity of these few sources encourage this group to satisfy the requirements of any given assignment 'without having to dig too deep, or having to develop more complicated analytical arguments based on an evaluation of a range of sources' (Cope and Flanagan 2013, p. 17). Similar findings have been reported among groups of students studying political science modules in the UK (Thornton 2010).

INFORMATION LITERACY

Thus it appears – despite the hopes of optimists such as Prensky – that the mammoth expansion in the availability of information, in a variety of forms, has created serious problems. Moreover, as Brabazon (2007) warned some years ago, there is growing evidence that many students, despite the digital native moniker, are actually floundering in an environment of such superabundant online information that some – including students of political science and international relations – are showing clear symptoms of information obesity. Fortunately, for many years, there has been an antidote commonly prescribed to combat this affliction: information literacy.

It was nearly 40 years ago that Paul Zurkowski, at that time president of the Information Industry Association in the USA, coined the phrase 'information literacy', though it was not until the end of the 1980s, as electronic resources threatened the supremacy of printed material in the information world, that the concept gained traction beyond a narrow coterie of information specialists. This was symbolized by the formation of the American Library Association (ALA) Presidential Committee on Information Literacy in 1987, which, two years later, produced probably the most influential definition of the concept: to describe an individual as information literate, they 'must be able to recognize when information is needed and have the ability to locate, evaluate and use effectively the needed information' (ALA 1989).

Since that time there have been many attempts to refine this definition. For example, in 1999, the UK-based Standing Conference of National and University Libraries (SCONUL) added extra layers, or – to use their term – 'pillars' to create a sequential model. These pillars, starting with the most basic, describe the ability to:

1. distinguish ways in which the information 'gap' may be addressed;
2. construct strategies for locating information;
3. locate and access information;
4. compare and evaluate information gained from different sources;
5. organize, apply and communicate information in ways appropriate to the situation;
6. synthesize and build upon existing information, contributing to the creation of new knowledge.

Since the turn of the century fresh definitions of the concept have tended to include reference to increasingly ambitious hopes that information literacy cannot merely help individuals learn more effectively at university and hence do their jobs more efficiently, but also facilitate active participation in society, engender transformative change, and generally foster 'an enlightened and less fearful world' (Bundy 2004). Such an ambition was reflected in UNESCO's contribution to the information literacy-defining project, through the so-called Prague Declaration of 2003, which claimed:

> Information literacy encompasses knowledge of one's own information concerns and needs, and the ability to identify, locate, evaluate, organize and effectively create, use and communicate information to address issues and problems at hand; it is a prerequisite for participating effectively in the Information Society, and is part of the basic human right of lifelong learning. (Prague Declaration 2003)

President Obama has also contributed to the promotion of information literacy, proclaiming October 2009 to be Information Literacy Awareness Month, and declaring: 'Rather than merely possessing data, we must also learn the skills necessary to acquire, collate, and evaluate information for any situation'. He added that an 'informed and educated citizenry is essential to the functioning of our modern democratic society, and I encourage educational and community institutions across the country to help find and evaluate the information they seek, in all its forms' (Obama 2009).

Despite such high-profile support, it is worth noting that as information literacy has become increasingly ubiquitous, so criticism about the concept's utility has grown. For example, a number of scholars – particularly those with a background in critical theory – hold that those involved in the teaching of information literacy have often failed to pay enough heed to issues of power, and need to do more to develop critical consciousness in their students (Kapitzke 2003; Elmborg 2006; Lloyd 2010). Indeed, for some, traditional information literacy is a poison rather than a cure – the product of a system warped by often-disguised power relations, with librarians cast in the role of unwitting lackeys of existing power structures, with the profession itself apparently 'trapped within its own discursive formation' (Lloyd 2010, p. 245). As a result, for critical theorists such as Whitworth, it is important to recognize the presence of two different types of information literacy: the traditional skills-based variety and an explicitly critical form, of the sort that encourages people to examine closely these power relations and the role that the presentation of information plays in their maintenance (Whitworth 2009, p. 118).

EXAMPLES OF WHAT CAN BE DONE

Despite conceptual wrangling – and competition from newer concepts such as digital literacy, media literacy and, most recently, 'information fluency' (Mackey and Jacobson 2011, p. 66) – information literacy remains the label most associated with measures designed to assist individuals find suitable information, consider carefully its credibility and provenance, and then to use that information wisely and ethically. It is also noteworthy that information literacy is formally recognized as a necessary attribute by various accreditation agencies, such as, in the USA, the Middle States Commission on Higher Education (2003), and that information literacy frameworks have been created at a national level to inform education at all levels (e.g. see the Information Literacy Framework for Wales 2011). Furthermore, despite enjoying a reputation as something of a disciplinary laggard in terms of explicitly incorporating elements of information literacy into the political science curriculum, there does appear to be 'a logical fit and affinity' between the discipline and the contested concept (Williams and Evans 2008, p. 117). Therefore the remainder of this chapter will highlight some of the most interesting efforts made to integrate aspects of information literacy into the political science curriculum.

One of the earliest recorded attempts at a political science/information literacy 'marriage' was also one of the most ambitious. It took place at the University of West Georgia, USA, and – in common with many other such ventures – was a 'teaching alliance' between a librarian, Christy Stevens, and a political scientist, Patricia Campbell (Stevens and Campbell 2006, p. 543). The first step was to design a new course, Introduction to Global Studies, and the three goals guiding the development of the syllabus, assignments and other teaching and learning opportunities were the advancement of students' information literacy competencies, the encouragement of students' sense of themselves as global citizens, and the fostering of 'students' awareness of the connections among lifelong learning, global citizenship, and information literacy' (Stevens and Campbell 2006, p. 543).

Of particular note was a series of scaffolded assignments that Stevens and Campbell carefully designed together. These included the construction of a research proposal, to be focused on a particular global commodity that has caused conflict, such as oil, diamonds or drugs, with one learning outcome students' improved awareness of the nature and extent of the information needed for such a task. More explicitly information-literacy-driven was a second assignment to construct an annotated bibliography from 'five reputable and appropriate sources (a political magazine, a newspaper, a scholarly journal, a monograph, and an article from an international organization) that explicitly focused on their conflict' (Stevens and Campbell 2006, p. 547). This assignment was specifically designed to bolster students' ability to evaluate information; to identify and summarize the argument in each source; to assess a piece for evidence of bias and determine whether a source is authoritative, or not; and to reflect upon how the text might inform their own work. Tests Stevens and Campbell carried out throughout their project suggested success in both 'enhancing students' IL competences and heightening their awareness of the potential roles they can play as global citizens' (ibid., p. 553). Emboldened, the pair later extended the project to include three political science courses, each at a different level, with equally positive results (Stevens and Campbell 2007).

A more recent example of librarian/academic collaboration was that of the aforementioned Cope and Flanagan – a librarian and academic respectively based at the College of Staten Island and The City University of New York. Their work is particularly significant as it explicitly addresses some of the criticisms critical theorists made of traditional information literacy, in particular that it struggles to accommodate a new media environment that includes bloggers, the mass use of Facebook and Twitter and the like, and Internet media aggregators such as *The Huffington Post*. Indeed, as this particular teaching alliance notes:

> In this context it becomes necessary to think about IL more as a group of methods for thinking about and analysing the claims made by variegated information sources than as a set of skills that can be taught divorced from a disciplinary engagement with the information content. Simply instructing students to consult 'reliable sources' for many of their research projects

is no longer sufficient. Students now filter information from the variety of news sources that inform their engagement with the course material and the world of politics . . . [M]any of the traditional distinctions based on the type of source no longer hold. (Cope and Flanagan 2013, pp. 5–6)

To assist their students in the task of negotiating this new media landscape, Cope and Flanagan have adapted teaching and assessment on an existing course on the US Presidency and Congress, one element of which involves students monitoring and reporting on developments in particular congressional campaigns. In response to the upsurge in the use of new media as part of these campaigns, analysis focuses on a wide variety of sources explicitly including blogs and social media sites. This approach deliberately exposes students to a wider and more explicitly partisan range of sources than usual, and offers students 'a critically focused way to examine some of the more theatrical aspects of contemporary American politics while providing an analytical frame through which to understand the serious implications of the media under examination' (Cope and Flanagan 2013, p. 10). Early results of this approach have proved intriguing, with, as noted earlier, the main discovery being that the proportion of students able to navigate all types of information sources and appraise effectively the veracity of truth claims was disappointingly small. Nevertheless, Cope and Flanagan are justifiably optimistic that – with some revision – this approach offers a fruitful way of developing a class brimming with engaged political science majors and 'budding Discerning Analysts' (ibid., p. 21).

A further case study to be highlighted here is one that does not involve the traditional political scientist/librarian team approach. Rather, in one of the more imaginative responses to the challenge of providing a stimulating politically engaged approach to information literacy, Robert Detmering – a humanities librarian based at the University of Louisville – has proposed using popular film as a means of 'vividly contextualizing the access, use and interpretation of information in various settings' and, in so doing, exposing students to 'a broader, more critical conception of information literacy in an accessible but powerful manner' (Detmering 2010, p. 266). To support his proposal, Detmering identifies three films with a strong political dimension that can encourage information literacy of the variety favored by critical theorists. These are Jason Reitman's *Thank You for Smoking* (2006), Joel and Ethan Coen's *Burn after Reading* (2008) and Oliver Stone's *W.* (2008). Using the first of these films as an example, Detmering suggests that *Thank You for Smoking* – a satirical comedy based on a manipulative tobacco lobbyist's attempts to re-popularize tobacco products in the USA – can be a very effective means of 'teaching students that all information is subject to bias and ambiguity, promoting, albeit in an ironic manner, critical engagement with information' (Detmering 2010, p. 270). In addition, and of particular value for students of political science and international relations, Detmering also claims that the setting of the film 'provides a political context for information literacy and intimates that, in the absence of critical inquiry, people become the victims of forces that seek to manipulate and control them through rhetoric and the dissemination of questionable "facts"' (ibid.). Detmering appears not to have used the films for political science classes, but there does seem to be scope for adaption of his proposition for such a learning environment, particularly in light of the welcome appearance of such courses as Melinda Tarsi's 'American politics through film' (UMassAmherst 2013).

> **BOX 11.1 POLITICS RESEARCH TRAIL**
>
> Choose from *one* of these questions:
>
> 1) Is deliberative democracy preferable to representative democracy?
> 2) Is politics a virtuous activity?
> 3) Is globalization beneficial?
> 4) What is the primary purpose of the European Union?
> 5) What is the primary purpose of the United Nations?
> 6) What is the primary purpose of Political Science?
>
> Then, for your main text:
>
> **A**
> i) Locate a section in a **textbook** that is relevant to your topic, and start of your written work with a **full reference** for this section (i.e. how it would generally appear in a bibliography), using the Harvard referencing system.
> ii) Summarize the main points and arguments about your chosen topic made in this text.
>
> **B**
> i) Locate an article from a **reputable journal** that is relevant to your topic (please note that it should *not* be an article on your reading list), and provide a full reference for this article using the Harvard referencing system.
> ii) Explain why this source of information is reputable, backing responses with evidence.
> iii) Summarize the main points and arguments made in this article.
>
> **C**
> i) Locate a piece from a **reputable online website (that is *not* a journal article)** that is relevant to your topic (again, it should not be from your reading list) and provide a full reference for this piece using the Harvard referencing system.
> ii) Explain why this source of information is reputable, backing responses with evidence.
> iii) Summarize the main points and arguments made in this piece.
>
> **D**
> i) Make a case to support what you consider to be the most convincing argument made in the sources you have reviewed. This case should include *evidence*, elements of *comparison* and *references* – and from more than just three sources you have already highlighted.
>
> **E**
> i) Finally, create a **bibliography** of *all* the sources you have used.

The final case is a more self-reflective exercise, looking back at my own attempts to foster a more sophisticated treatment of information among students in various politics classes at Cardiff University, UK. Since an early pilot scheme in 2005, and in partnership with number of information specialists[1] (Thornton 2006, 2008, 2010, 2012; Thornton and Haerkoenen 2009), a number of learning experiences have been devised to foster information literacy. One of the most enduring of these is a research trail, an assignment that has similarities with Stevens and Campbell's annotated bibliography. The most recent iteration of this particular assignment can be seen in Box 11.1, and was designed to encourage and test information literacy across all students taking first-year political science, political thought and international relations modules. When creating the assessment, care was taken to make sure the expected learning objectives matched a number of necessary attributes outlined in the UK's Quality Assurance Agency for Higher

Education subject statement for politics and international relations. These include the abilities to: 'gather, organize and deploy evidence, data and information from a variety of secondary and some primary sources'; 'construct reasoned argument, synthesize relevant information and exercise critical judgement'; and 'recognise the importance of explicit referencing and the ethical requirements of study which requires critical and reflective use of information' (Quality Assurance Agency for Higher Education 2007, p. 7). There was also use of a diagnostic questionnaire to examine new students' information literacy levels, and tasks were adapted to emphasize particular features that the questionnaire results suggested were creating particular difficulties for students.

The assignment was supported by lectures and workshops, run by both the academic and librarian involved, where various attempts were made to tackle interestingly issues such as the importance of referencing, to explain the prominence afforded to peer-reviewed journal articles in the discipline, and to provide tips on where best to find authoritative articles and relevant websites. Issues of bias and trustworthiness were discussed, and there were exercises to illustrate that the line between trustworthiness and untrustworthiness is far from clear-cut, being largely a matter of judgment and context (for an example of such an exercise, see Box 11.2). The research trail itself was marked

---

BOX 11.2   INFORMATION LITERACY WORKSHOP

Here are seven sources of information (note, these references are not set out 'correctly'):

Gervais and Morris, Reading the tea leaves: Understanding tea party caucus membership in the US house of representatives, *PS – Political Science & Politics*, 45(2), pp. 245–250.

Peter Montgomery 2010. Taking the Tea Party seriously. *Right Wing Watch* [Online].

Tanner, Michael, 'Shaping a New Conservative Agenda' in Aberbach, J. D. and Peele, G. eds., *Crisis of conservatism?: The republican party, the conservative movement, and American politics after Bush*. Oxford University Press, 2011.

The Economist. 2012. The tea party strikes: Another moderate shown the door

The Tea Party movement on Wikipedia

David A. Weaver and Joshua M. Scacco, *"Tea for Three: Revisiting the Protest Paradigm and Media Coverage of the Tea Party Movement by Cable Outlet"*, 9th Annual APSA Pre-Conference on Political Communication Wednesday, August 31, 2011 University of Washington.
www.teaparty.org.

You have five tasks:

1. You must locate all these sources of information (in each case you will be able to access the full text through the Cardiff University library website).
2. Decide which of these sources you would be confident to use when writing an academic essay entitled: 'Explain the significance of the American Tea Party movement'.
3. Following the Harvard system, correctly reference each source that you would be prepared to use (as it would appear in a bibliography).
4. List the factors you have taken into account to make the decision whether a piece of information is sufficiently reputable.
5. Find one more sufficiently relevant and reputable (a) book, (b) journal article and (c) website.

and treated like any other form of assessment (being worth a proportion of the overall mark for each module), in keeping with Sheila Webber's advice that 'unless the information literacy is tied in with a credit-bearing class, the students may not be obliged to undertake any assessment at all, and may not take their information literacy seriously' (Webber 2001, p. 548).

Though some students have bemoaned the perhaps sometimes too heavily skills-based approach taken, feedback from most has been positive, particularly from students not familiar with the UK education system; and evidence – albeit limited – has been produced to indicate improvement in aspects of students' information literacy following the workshop and assessment, and, consequently, improved academic work more generally. These advances include greater student awareness of the information resources available, increased consciousness of the need to assess the trustworthiness of that information, and superior referencing skills (Thornton 2008; Thornton and Haerkoenen 2009).

Reflecting on these projects, and indeed the earlier ones mentioned, probably the most important feature that runs through most of them is the positive partnership between the academic and information specialist. Indeed, it would be difficult to argue against the claim made by Trudi Jacobson and Thomas Mackey that 'collaboration is an essential dynamic in preparing students to become information literate' (2007, p. xvii). Roles do overlap, but personal experience suggests that information specialists are best able to demonstrate the crucial skills-based aspects of information literacy, not least guidance about the most useful and up-to-date sources of information to access and how best to manipulate databases and search engines. Academics are best able to use disciplinary knowledge to make links to topics studied and to amplify the critical dimension, leading discussion on issues such as the nature of bias, most obviously evidenced in the materials produced by political parties and think tanks, but also by media organizations that claim neutrality, such as the BBC, and, indeed, by academics themselves. Experience has also indicated that information specialists tend to be enthusiastic when asked to participate in such ventures, not least because, as Head and Eisenberg (2009, pp. 34–5) have discovered, librarians and other information specialists are a resource that has traditionally been underutilized by students, and collaborations of this type vividly demonstrate to students that librarians possess perhaps unexpected skills that can directly help with their own projects.

CONCLUSION

The aim of this chapter was to highlight that, despite the existence of much 'digital native' rhetoric, today's students are often as bewildered as the rest of us by the vast array of information sources currently available. Indeed studies such as those conducted by Head and Eisenberg clearly indicate that many students are suffering from symptoms of, to use Whitworth's term, information obesity. Students of political science and international relations have displayed no evidence of being immune to this affliction. Though showing some signs of wear and tear, information literacy is still regarded as the concept best able to provide some protection from this malady. The literature suggests that a fully integrated approach, in which information literacy informs the creation of an entire political science curriculum, creating – to use John Biggs's term (1996) – a suitably 'constructively aligned' program, is the most fruitful method for fostering information literacy. However, as the cases highlighted earlier demonstrate, there are many ways to help prepare our students to survive in an increasingly wild, densely populated and often treacherous information environment, with no doubt some of the most exciting and valuable yet to appear. The common theme at the heart of most successful strategies is collaboration between the discipline-based academic and the information specialist, so the primary lesson for all political science and international relations academics keen to encourage a critical approach to information among their students is, in the first instance, to make friends with a librarian. Then again, this information could be biased; after all, I'm married to one.

NOTE

1. I would like to acknowledge the invaluable, and remarkably patient, contribution of the following information specialists: Tom Dawkes, Cathie Jackson, Sonja Haerkoenen, Rebecca Mogg, Ruth Thornton and Luisa Tramontini.

REFERENCES

ALA (1989), *Presidential Committee on Information Literacy: Final Report*, Chicago, IL: American Library Association, available at http://www.ala.org/ala/mgrps/divs/acrl/publications/whitepapers/presidential.cfm (accessed 13 November 2010).

Biggs, John (1996), 'Enhancing teaching through constructive alignment', *Higher Education*, **32**, 347–64.

Brabazon, Tara (2007), *The University of Google: Education in the (Post) Information Age*, Aldershot, UK: Ashgate.

Bundy, Alan (2004), 'Zeitgeist: information literacy and educational change', paper presented at the 4th Frankfurt Scientific Symposium, Germany, 4 October 2004, available at http://www.library.unisa.edu.au/about/papers/abpapers.asp (accessed 29 June 2006).

Cope, Jonathan and Richard Flanagan (2013), 'Information literacy in the study of American politics: using new media to teach information literacy in the political science classroom', *Behavioral & Social Sciences Librarian*, **32** (1), 3–23.

Detmering, Robert (2010), 'Exploring the political dimensions of information literacy through popular film', *portal: Libraries and the Academy*, **10** (3), 265–82.

Elmborg, James (2006), 'Critical information literacy', *The Journal of Academic Librarianship*, **32** (2), 192–9.

Head, Alison and Michael Eisenberg (2009), *Lessons Learned: How College Students Seek Information in the Digital Age*, Project Information Literacy Report, University of Washington, available at http://projectinfolit.org/pdfs/PIL_Fall2009_Year1Report_12_2009.pdf (accessed 8 March 2010).

Head, Alison and Michael Eisenberg (2011), 'How college students use the Web to conduct everyday life research', *First Monday*, **16** (4), available at http://firstmonday.org/article/view/3484/2857 (accessed 30 May 2013).

Herring, Susan (2008), 'Questioning the generational divide: technological exoticism and adult construction of online youth identity', in David Buckingham (ed.), *Youth, Identity, and Digital Media*, Cambridge, MA: MIT Press, pp. 71–94.

Information Literacy Framework for Wales (2011), 'Finding and using information in 21st century Wales', available at http://librarywales.org/uploads/media/Information_Literacy_Framework_Wales.pdf (accessed 16 January 2014).

Jacobson, Trudi and Thomas Mackey (eds) (2007), *Information Literacy Collaborations that Work*, New York: Neal-Schuman.

Kapitzke, Cushla (2003), '*In*formation literacy: a positivist epistemology and a politics of *out*formation', *Educational Theory*, **53** (1), 37–53.

Lloyd, Annemaree (2010), 'Framing information literacy as information practice: site ontology and practice theory', *Journal of Documentation*, **66** (2), 245–58.

Mackey, Thomas and Trudi Jacobson (2011), 'Reframing information literacy as a metaliteracy', *College & Research Libraries*, **72** (1), 62–78.

Middle States Commission on Higher Education (2003), *Developing Research and Communication Skills: Guidelines for Information Literacy in the Curriculum*, Philadelphia, PA: Middle States Commission on Higher Education.

Obama, Barack (2009), 'Presidential Proclamation of National Information Awareness Month', available at http://www.whitehouse.gov/the_press_office/Presidential-Proclamation-National-Information-Literacy-Awareness-Month (accessed 30 May 2013).

Prague Declaration (2003), 'Towards an information literate society', available at http://www.infolit.org/2003.htmlb (accessed 2 February 2011).

Prensky, Marc (2001), 'Digital natives, digital immigrants', *On the Horizon*, **9** (5), available at http://www.marcprensky.com/writing/prensky%20-%20digital%20natives,%20digital%20immigrants%20-%20part1.pdf (accessed 30 May 2013).

Quality Assurance Agency for Higher Education (2007), 'Politics and international relations', available at http://www.qaa.ac.uk (accessed 29 September 2009).

Ruggiero, Vincent R. (2011), *Becoming a Critical Thinker*, 7th edn, Belmont, CA: Wadsworth.

SCONUL (1999), 'Information skills in higher education: a SCONUL position paper prepared by the Information Skills Task Force, on behalf of SCONUL', available at http://www.sconul.ac.uk/groups/information_literacy/seven_pillars.html (accessed 13 November 2010).

Stevens, Christy and Patricia Campbell (2006), 'Collaborating to connect global citizenship, information literacy, and lifelong learning in the global studies classroom', *References Services Review*, **34** (4), 536–56.

Stevens, Christy and Patricia Campbell (2007), 'The politics of information literacy: integrating information literacy into the political science curriculum', in Thomas Jacobson and Trudi Mackey (eds), *Information Literacy Collaborations that Work*, New York: Neal-Schuman, pp. 123–46.

Thornton, Stephen (2006), 'Information literacy and the teaching of politics', *LATISS: Learning and Teaching in the Social Sciences*, **3** (1), 29–45.

Thornton, Stephen (2008), 'Pedagogy, politics, and information literacy', *Politics*, **28** (1), 50–56.

Thornton, Stephen (2010), 'From "scuba diving" to "jet ski-ing"? Information behavior, political science, and the Google generation', *Journal of Political Science Education*, **6** (4), 353–68.

Thornton, Stephen (2012), 'Trying to learn (politics) in a data-drenched society: can information literacy save us?', *European Political Science*, **11** (2), 213–23.

Thornton, Stephen and Sonja Haerkoenen (2009), 'Attempting to bridge the barrier between academic study and research skills training: early student responses to a fully integrated academic/skills-based method of assessment', paper presented at the Annual Political Studies Association Conference, Manchester University, UK, 8 April 2009.

UMassAmherst (2013), 'American politics through film', available at http://polsci.umass.edu/undergraduate/courses/courseguide/201_Tarsi (accessed 19 June 2013).

Webber, Sheila (2001), 'Myths and opportunities', *Library Association Record*, **103** (9), 548–9.

Whitworth, Andrew (2009), *Information Obesity*, Oxford, UK: Chandos.

Williams, Michelle and Jocelyn Evans (2008), 'Factors in information literacy', *Journal of Political Science Education*, **4** (1), 116–30.

12. Internationalization of the curriculum (Bologna Process)
Erkki Berndtson

> We, the Ministers responsible for higher education in the countries participating in the Bologna Process, met in Budapest and Vienna on March 11 and 12, 2010 to launch the European Higher Education Area (EHEA), as envisaged in the Bologna Declaration of 1999.
> (Budapest-Vienna Declaration 2010)

The number of students in higher education has been rapidly increasing in the world. In 1995, there were some 80 million students worldwide. In 2003, Marijk C. van der Wende (2003, pp. 193–4) forecast that the number will reach over 150 million by 2025. However, the development has been even faster, as recently it has been estimated that by that time the number actually will be around 262 million (Maslen 2012). Most of the growth will take place in the developing world, especially in China and India, with new universities being established to satisfy the growing demand. Many world-leading universities are also setting up branch campuses in foreign countries, at the same time as new types of providers, such as virtual universities, have emerged. A further indicator of the internationalization process is an increasing growth of cross-border education. All this has changed the global landscape of higher education. American, Asian and European universities compete with each other for the best students and scholars actively market their academic programs (e.g. Reinalda and Kulesza 2006, pp. 11–15).

In order to face the global challenge, European countries have launched an ambitious project to reform their higher education institutions, known as the Bologna Process. It aims to harmonize the European higher education systems in order to promote European citizens' employability and the international competitiveness of European universities (Bologna Declaration 1999). This is a huge project, as there are some 4000 higher education institutions in Europe, representing a wide variety of academic cultures and institutional structures. This chapter summarizes the Bologna Process, explains reasons for its development and discusses how the Process affects political science as a discipline.

THE BOLOGNA PROCESS: INSTITUTIONAL SETTING

In June 1999, 29 European Ministers of Education met in Bologna, Italy, to discuss the future of European higher education. After the meeting, they published a joint declaration (Bologna Declaration 1999), which has been seen as a beginning of the curriculum reform to construct the European Higher Education Area (EHEA). However, the Process had already begun, a year earlier. In May 1998, the Ministers of Education of France, Germany, Italy and the United Kingdom had met in Paris, to commemorate the 800th anniversary of the University of Paris. After the meeting, they gave out a joint declaration on 'Harmonisation of the Architecture of the European Higher Education

System' (Sorbonne Declaration 1998) and asked other European countries to join them in this endeavor. The Bologna Conference was an outcome of this call. It was attended by all the members of the European Union (EU) at that time (15 countries), countries soon to become members (11) and three countries outside the EU (Iceland, Norway and Switzerland).

However, the Bologna Process is not an EU project (although the European Commission is a full member) but a pan-European one (on the Bologna structure, see EHEA 2013). The number of participating countries has risen now to 47, ranging from Andorra to Kazakhstan. All countries that are party to the European Cultural Convention can become members, if they are willing to pursue and implement Process objectives in their own systems of higher education (Berlin Communiqué 2003). The only European countries that are not members at the time of writing are Belarus, Monaco and San Marino. On the other hand, there are three participant countries that are not strictly speaking European countries (Armenia, Azerbaijan and Kazakhstan).

As the Process has evolved, it has built its own bureaucracy. Every two or three years there are Ministerial Conferences to evaluate the progress within the EHEA. These Bologna Follow-up Conferences have been arranged thus far in Prague in 2001, Berlin in 2003, Bergen in 2005, London in 2007, Leuven/Louvain-la-Neuve in 2009 and Bucharest in 2012. In 2010 there was a special ten-year anniversary Conference held jointly in Budapest and Vienna. The next Ministerial Conference is scheduled to take place in Yerevan, Armenia in 2015. After each Follow-up Conference, the Ministers have given out a Communiqué to set up actions to be taken before the next Conference.

Between the Follow-up Conferences, the Process is guided by the Bologna Follow-up Group (BFUG), which consists of the representatives of the member countries and the European Commission. There are also eight consultative members: the Council of Europe, UNESCO's European Centre for Higher Education, the European University Association (EUA), the European Students' Union (ESU), the European Association of Institutions in Higher Education (EURASHE), the European Association for Quality Assurance in Higher Education (ENQA), Education International Pan-European Structure and BUSINESSEUROPE. The BFUG has a Board and a Secretariat. The Board is co-chaired by the country holding the EU presidency and one non-EU country. The Secretariat is located in the country arranging the next Ministerial Conference.

In addition, there are several working groups and networks monitoring the implementation of the reforms. Three organizations, Eurostat, Eurostudent and Eurydice, provide much of the data for planning. There are also national follow-up organizations in each participating country. Furthermore, the consultative members often organize their own conferences. As Bob Reinalda (2008, pp. 387–90) has argued, the Bologna Process has become a permanent intergovernmental organization. In 15 years, it has evolved into a complex policy-making arena. It is also an example of a multi-governance regime with different partners having their own interests and agendas.

THE OBJECTIVES OF THE BOLOGNA PROCESS

One of the problems with analyzing the Bologna Process is that the emphases of its objectives have changed from one communiqué to another (EACEA 2012, p. 15). In addition, the objectives have been constantly reformulated and reinterpreted. The changing economic and political context has also influenced the Bologna agenda. In spite of that, the main policy objectives outlined in the Bologna Communiqués form the basis of the Process. The 1999 Bologna Declaration set as 'short term objectives':

> Adoption of a system of **easily readable and comparable degrees**, also through the implementation of the Diploma Supplement, in order to promote European citizens employability and the international competitiveness of the European higher education system.
>
> Adoption of a system essentially based on **two main cycles**,[1] undergraduate and graduate. Access to the second cycle shall require successful completion of first cycle studies, lasting a minimum of three years. The degree awarded after the first cycle shall also be relevant to the European labour market as an appropriate level of qualification. The second cycle should lead to the master and/or doctorate degree as in many European countries.
>
> Establishment of a **system of credits** – such as in the ECTS system[2] – as a proper means of promoting the most widespread student mobility. Credits could also be acquired in non-higher education contexts, including lifelong learning, provided they are recognised by receiving Universities concerned.
>
> Promotion of **mobility** by overcoming obstacles to the effective exercise of free movement with particular attention to:
>
> - for students, access to study and training opportunities and to related services
> - for teachers, researchers and administrative staff, recognition and valorisation of periods spent in a European context researching, teaching and training, without prejudicing their statutory rights.
>
> Promotion of **European co-operation in quality assurance** with a view to developing comparable criteria and methodologies.
>
> Promotion of the **necessary European dimensions in higher education**, particularly with regards to curricular development, interinstitutional co-operation, mobility schemes and integrated programmes of study, training and research. (Bologna Declaration 1998)

In the 2001 Prague Conference, three new objectives were added:

> **Lifelong learning** is an essential element of the European Higher Education Area. In the future Europe, built upon a knowledge-based society and economy, lifelong learning strategies are necessary to face the competitiveness and the use of new technologies and to improve social cohesion, equal opportunities and the quality of life . . .
>
> Ministers stressed that **the involvement of universities and other higher education institutions and of students** as competent, active and constructive partners in the establishment and shaping of a European Higher Education Area is needed and welcomed . . . Ministers affirmed that students should participate in and influence the organisation and content of education at universities and other higher education institutions . . .
>
> Ministers agreed on the importance of **enhancing attractiveness of European higher education** to students from Europe and other parts of the world . . . Ministers particularly stressed that the quality of higher education and research is and should be an important determinant of Europe's international attractiveness and competitiveness. (Prague Communiqué 2001; emphasis added)

Finally, in the 2003 Berlin Conference, the tenth objective (or action line, as the objectives are also called) was added:

> Conscious of the need to promote **closer links between the EHEA and the ERA** [European Research Area] in a Europe of Knowledge, and of the importance of research as an integral part

of higher education across Europe, Ministers consider it necessary to go beyond the present focus on two main cycles of higher education to include the doctoral level as the third cycle in the Bologna Process. They emphasise the importance of research and research training and the promotion of interdisciplinarity in maintaining and improving the quality of higher education and in enhancing the competitiveness of European higher education more generally. (Berlin Communiqué 2003; emphasis added)

After 2003, no new action lines have been introduced. However, one new objective has emerged in the Communiqués, which could be taken as the eleventh action line: **social dimension**. It has never been defined as such, but it has become one in practice. The term was mentioned for the first time in the 2001 Prague Communiqué, but at the time it referred only to students' equal opportunity to participate in international mobility. In the Berlin 2003 Conference, social dimension was linked to the economic background of students as well as to gender inequalities. In 2005, it was made one of the priorities of the Process; and in the London 2007 Conference, it was defined by the policy goal that 'the student body entering, participating in and completing higher education at all levels should reflect the diversity of our populations' (London Communiqué 2007; EACEA 2012, p. 71).

Most objectives express strategic goals (easily readable and comparable degrees, European dimensions in teaching, lifelong learning, involving higher education institutions and students in the process, promoting the worldwide attractiveness of the EHEA, linking education and research together, social dimension). For that reason they are open to different interpretations. However, the strategic goals have given birth to a number of strictly defined structural reforms, such as the introduction of the three cycle degree system, the system of credits (ECTS), the implementation of the Diploma Supplement and the establishment of joint degrees. They have also aimed to renew teaching practices (e.g. demands for student-centered learning). However, teaching and learning reforms cannot be defined exactly, as they can be applied in multiple ways and their implementation is dependent on universities rather than on governmental authorities.

Finally, there are two objectives, quality assurance and mobility, that have become the overarching objectives of the Process. The Bergen 2005 Conference adopted 'Standards and Guidelines for Quality Assurance in the European Higher Education Area' (ESG), which had been prepared by the European Association for Quality Assurance in Higher Education (ENQA 2005). The guidelines offer detailed standards for evaluating quality, from the review of programs to the assessment of students. They require higher education institutions, among other things, to monitor student progress, to have published criteria and procedures for the assessment of students, to have feedback from employers and labor market representatives, to measure students' satisfaction with their studies, as well as to pay careful attention to curriculum and program design and content. As European higher education institutions are expected to aim for high quality in teaching and research (EACEA 2012, p. 15), quality assurance is seen to enhance trust among different partners and to be a condition for the EHEA having worldwide attractiveness (Leuven/Louvain-la-Neuve Communiqué 2009). Quality assurance as an overarching tool of the Process has another function. Defining quality with its own objectives, the Bologna Process makes quality assurance a self-controlling mechanism of reforms.

In harmony with this, there has been an increasing emphasis on teaching methods in recent years. These were discussed earlier mainly in the context of lifelong learning

(EACEA 2012, p. 15). However, flexible (see Berlin Communiqué 2003) and individually tailored learning paths (see Leuven/Louvain-la-Neuve Communiqué 2009) and a demand to move from teacher-driven teaching to student-centered learning (see London Communiqué 2007) have become more and more important in recent documents. In the 2012 Bucharest Conference, Ministers even decided that student-centered learning and innovative teaching methods will be one of the priorities for the 2012–15 period (Bucharest Communiqué 2012).

The other overarching objective, mobility, on the other hand, is closely linked to the European Commission's Erasmus program,[3] which started in 1987. Today it involves 33 European countries, over 2000 institutions and some 250 000 students annually. At the beginning, the program's aim was to build up European identity among students (European Commission 2000), but in recent years, the needs of the labor market have become more visible in the official documents (EACEA 2012, p. 151). The Bucharest 2012 Follow-up Conference adopted a separate addendum, 'Mobility for Better Learning: Mobility Strategy 2020 for the European Higher Education Area', to its Communiqué, as '[l]earning mobility is essential to ensure the quality of higher education, enhance students' employability and expand cross-border collaboration within the EHEA and beyond' (Mobility for Better Learning 2012).

THE BOLOGNA PROCESS – ACHIEVEMENTS AND PROBLEMS

The Bologna Process contains many positive objectives (Reinalda 2013, p. 409). Mobility and education based on research are two of the most obvious ones. There is nothing wrong with readable and comparable degrees or a system of credits either. It is also natural to strive for high quality. However, while structural reforms have been a success, the same cannot be said of the other objectives. One of the reasons for this is the general nature of many of them, which offers actors a chance to interpret them in their own way. Consequently, the implementation of the Bologna objectives has varied in different countries (Ravinet 2008, p. 355). Higher education policy makers have used the Process to advance their own national agendas (Veiga and Amaral 2006). All this has made the Process a complex and inherently contradictory undertaking (Kehm 2010, pp. 529–30).

Furthermore, although the Bologna documents are full of references to academic values, including academic autonomy and academic freedom, there remains an underlying tension between top-down political reforms and academic values. One of the reasons for this is that academic staff have been neglected as a partner until very recently (Sin 2012, p. 392). Scholars have been represented by the corporative interests of universities and labor unions. Even students and other stakeholders have been better represented. The increasing bureaucratization of the Process has produced decisions that have often been far from the realities of scholarly work. It is no wonder that academics have reacted to Bologna from different perspectives. As universities are autonomous institutions, this has led to the situation that national adoption of the Bologna objectives and their realization by higher education institutions do not always correspond with each other (Sin 2012, pp. 392–400).

The tension between top-down political reforms and academic values has been heightened by the increasing involvement of the European Commission in the Process.

The Bologna Process did not begin from scratch. In fact, it is very much based on the European Commission's policies in the field of education (on the Union's role, see Corbett 2006; Pépin 2007). An important breakthrough for the development of the European Community education policy was a 1985 decision by the European Court of Justice to interpret vocational training to include higher education (Pépin 2007, p. 122). This allowed the Commission to launch several programs in the field of education (e.g. Erasmus). Furthermore, the 1992 Maastricht Treaty recognized education as part of the Union's competences, which allowed the Commission further to develop its agenda on lifelong learning and a knowledge-based society (a Europe of Knowledge). When the Bologna Process was launched, all these objectives became accepted as part of the Bologna agenda.

The launching of the Union's Lisbon Strategy (now the Europe 2020 Strategy) in 2000, has further increased the Commission's role. The Strategy sees higher education as a vital mechanism in making Europe 'the most competitive and dynamic knowledge-based economy in the world' (European Council 2000). In order to achieve its goals, the Lisbon Strategy has included demands for governance and funding reforms in European higher education institutions. European countries should focus on 'three aspects of university reform: improve the universities' quality and make them more attractive, improve their governance, and increase and diversify their funding with or without major contributions from students' (European Commission 2013). As a result, the Bologna Process and the Lisbon Strategy have converged in many issues.

Mobility as an objective is a good example of the tension between top-down reforms and academic values. Mobility is an important academic value, which universities and scholars have always emphasized in their activity (MCU 1988). However, it should be executed well. For instance, with regard to doctoral studies it has been argued that 'sometimes the means become more important than the ends and transform good ideas into wrong practices', as 'too much mobility entails huge costs of transaction' (Mény 2010, p. 16). Doctoral students need a stable environment, where they can benefit from a dedicated supervisor, rather than constantly changing environments.

In many ways, the Commission's own policies and political goals have undermined the academic success of the Erasmus program. When the program began in 1987, it was carried out by Inter-University Cooperation Programs (ICPs), networks of departments that held joint meetings with each other. In the meetings, representatives of departments were able to meet colleagues, discuss common problems, develop joint courses and learn about other departments (Bergström 2005, p. 46). However, in 1995, the Commission decided to reorganize the program and the governance of exchanges was placed in the hands of central administrative units in higher education institutions. This has made it increasingly difficult to organize student exchange so that studies in a foreign university would contribute to studies in a home university in any systematic way. There are still many differences among European universities with regard to study requirements: course workloads for nominally equal courses vary, grading systems are far from uniform and grading 'cultures' diverge from each other (Van Cranenburgh 2005). European universities even seem to have different attitudes towards student exchange, as not all universities accept credits taken by their students in a foreign university. Besides, many departments are reluctant to send their students abroad during bachelor programs, as their curricula often do not provide space for mobility. There seems to be no common policy with regard to exchange studies. The result has been that student exchange does not work well from an academic perspective (Berndtson 2005).

As the national systems of education have been based on different intellectual traditions, organizational structures and academic practices, there remain many obstacles to realizing a unified European Higher Education Area. It is still difficult even to get information about some countries in order to compare the systems (see the scorecards in EACEA 2012). The official launching of the European Higher Education Area in 2010 has been more a myth than a reality. Some countries are even losing interest in it, while others struggle to understand its policy goals and structures (Corbett and Henkel 2013, p. 5).

However, despite its problems, the Process has become a common denominator in European higher education. It has now reached the stage when 'it is no longer possible to create national higher education policies that are anti-Bologna' (Ravinet 2008, p. 354). Given that the Communiqués have no binding authority and the participants engage in the Process voluntarily, this in itself is an achievement. The outcome is often attributed to the 'Open Method of Coordination' and its peer pressure (Lažetić 2010, pp. 556–8; Veiga and Amaral 2006, pp. 284–5). In addition, the Process can be interpreted as an example of overdetermination. In the 1990s, many European governments tried to reform their higher education institutions, but they often faced strong opposition in their home countries. The Bologna Process has given governments a possibility to use pan-European agreements as leverage in national reforms.

THE BOLOGNA PROCESS AND ACADEMIC VALUES: THE CASE OF POLITICAL SCIENCE

The Bologna Process is more problematic in the social sciences and humanities than in many other fields. One of the reasons for this is that the social sciences and humanities do not have any strong core curriculum. Political science is a good example of this.

The attitude of political scientists towards the Bologna Process has been cautious. Some have thought that reforms will endanger the status of political science as a discipline and weaken its coherence (e.g. Reinalda 2013, p. 412). A German political scientist, Suzanne Schüttemeyer, has also worried about the consequences of the Bologna reforms for the identity of the discipline:

> A particular difficulty that political science departments face in the course of adopting the new degree structure is that of teaching capacity. At a good number of universities, the discipline is represented by only two or three (full) professors and a small number of assistants . . . small departments cannot afford to build BA or MA courses in political science alone . . . In order to survive the reform, they had to throw in their lot with other departments and come up with sometimes fanciful new courses whose labels indicate only a remote resemblance with political science. It would be exaggerated to call this the end of the discipline, but it should not be overlooked as a possible danger to its identity. (Schüttemeyer 2007, pp. 166–7)

Others have acknowledged the danger, but have seen the new situation also as an opportunity:

> We have . . . to some extent to defend ourselves against potential and real threats resulting from the radical changes in Higher Education now sweeping across Europe . . . in this process of

reform we have the opportunity to promote political science as a discipline, indeed I would say as one of the three core social science disciplines. (Furlong 2007, p. 402)

One of the responses of European political scientists has been to try to formulate the core curriculum for European political science. The idea was first discussed in 2003 among a few political scientists in the unofficial meetings of the national political science associations in Europe (European Conference of National Political Science Associations, ECNPSA) and in the Council of the European Political Science Network (epsNet).[4] The result of these discussions was a statement, which was sent to participants in the Berlin Conference. In the document (ECNPSA 2003), it was proposed that the amount of political science studies in the BA degree, having political science as a major, should be at least half. Furthermore, studies in political science should consist of the core subject areas of:

1. political theory/history of political ideas
2. methodology (including statistics)
3. political system of one's own country and of the European Union
4. comparative politics
5. international relations
6. public administration and policy analysis
7. political economy/political sociology.

In the cover letter, it was announced that the proposed common core syllabus had been prepared as part of political scientists' response to 'the gathering momentum of the Bologna Process' and in the hope that political scientists 'can contribute to the further development of the European Higher Education Area'. Furthermore, it was believed that the 'document represents a valuable and significant first step in ensuring that the objectives of the Bologna Process can be implemented in our discipline' (ECNPSA 2003, pp. 223–4). In the document itself, it was added that, '[a]chieving the minimum requirements would help to achieve a system of easily readable and comparable degrees and would help to define the European dimension in teaching. It would also help in transferring credits from one university to another due to increasing student mobility' (ECNPSA 2003, p. 225).

Some European political scientists have tried to keep the idea of the core curriculum alive, as the German Political Science Association has adopted it as a recommendation to German political science departments. The German association has also tried to get other European associations to follow its example. Although some European departments outside Germany have done that, the idea of the core curriculum has not advanced very much. Although most departments teach courses that the core curriculum includes, it is very difficult to adopt it, as political science programs vary from each other considerably around Europe.

One crucial question is the relationship between political science and international relations. Are they understood as parts of the same discipline, or are they separated into two independent departments? The same can be asked also with regard to public administration. Furthermore, different cultural and intellectual traditions vary around Europe. In some countries, political science is still closely linked to law and/or history. There are also departments that emphasize political science as political sociology, while in some other departments the discipline is more policy oriented. European political science programs also display a wide variety of methodological orientations: some focus mainly on quantitative research, while others emphasize qualitative and philosophical approaches.

Furthermore, the ECNPSA recommendations have not met any response among the political and administrative echelons of the Bologna Process. The core curriculum is based on disciplinary knowledge, but the ideology of the Process is based on the assumption that the existing disciplinary system is not capable of meeting today's challenges. In that sense, the purpose of the core curriculum, to defend political science as a discipline, does not have much support among political decision-makers. Instead, the Bologna documents are full of demands, such as, '[w]e urge universities to ensure that their doctoral programmes promote interdisciplinary training and the development of transferable skills, thus meeting the needs of the wider employment market' (Bergen Communiqué 2005).

According to the Bologna documents, the employability of graduates, as well as maintaining and renewing a skilled workforce, should be achieved 'by improving cooperation between employers, students and higher education institutions, especially in the development of study programmes that help increase the innovation, entrepreneurial and research potential of graduates' (Bucharest Communiqué 2012), and higher education institutions 'should be more responsive to employers needs' (Leuven/Louvain-la-Neuve Communiqué 2009).

However, who are employers in the case of political science? The needs of the labor market are so varied that it would be difficult to base any systematic curriculum on them (Quinlan and Berndtson 2012, p. 137). Besides, a close co-operation with employers (public and private) would be problematic to political science as a discipline, as one of its tasks is to speak truth to power. There seems to be no room for critical social science in the new academia. This aspect of the discipline has been denied completely by the Bologna Process.

Bologna has become very much an economic process aiming to offer students new competencies in the global marketplace. Paradoxically, this means a devaluation of higher education degrees in the social sciences and humanities. As Richard Münch (2013, p. 428) has argued, bachelor graduates will acquire only some basic competences and they will be educated 'on the job', as many jobs in today's labor market 'require little substantial knowledge, but far more social competences and personal skills', such as self-presentation skills and international experience. One has to be able to sell oneself to employers. At the same time, Master's degrees are becoming more specialized 'to the demand by interested students who want to acquire an additional qualification for certain fields of activity' (Münch 2013, p. 427). The goal of the Bologna Process is not to develop academic curriculum; it is to change the curriculum to adapt it to the requirements of the global labor market.

As these examples show, many of the Bologna reforms are problematic for political science and other social sciences. A demand for interdisciplinarity endangers the identity and coherence of the discipline. A strong emphasis on the needs of the labor market endangers the critical role of political science as the study of power in society. A poor realization of important academic practices, as in the case of mobility, devalues their merits. Quality assurance focusing on quality using the objectives of the Process itself as the evaluation criteria standardizes education and research. All these trends point towards narrower and more one-sided knowledge.

However, the employability of graduates and academic values would not have to be opposing goals. The Bologna Process could enhance scientific objectives by trusting that academic disciplines are able to conduct innovative research and educate students for the labor market in their own terms. The question, however, is whether it is possible in today's academia to fulfill the principles of the *Magna Charta Universitatum*,[5] '[t]o meet the needs of the world around it . . . research and teaching must be morally and intellectually independent of all political authority and economic power' (MCU 1988, p. 113).

A CONCLUDING NOTE

The internationalization of universities has led European higher education authorities to emphasize the need to compete with American and Asian universities for the best students and scholars. In order to do this, Europeans like to present the Bologna Process as a model for universities in the other world regions. However, enhancing the global attractiveness of European higher education is more difficult than Bologna participants often present (Brunner 2009; Chao 2011). The main problem is that Bologna is an Europeanization project, which makes it a top-down bureaucratic process with hegemonic intentions (Hartmann 2008).

This also has implications for teaching and learning in political science and international relations. Although teaching methods have become a matter of some concern in recent Bologna documents, the main interest of the member countries and other stakeholders has been in changing the structures and conditions of teaching and learning. The impact of the Bologna Process on teaching has been an indirect one. However, this hides an important problem. The Process has not paid very much attention to differences between and within academic disciplines. There are theoretical, methodological and substantial variations in the study of politics around the world. If these variations are not taken into account, teaching and research on politics will often be based on hegemonic discourses within the discipline.

NOTES

1. In the 2003 Berlin Conference, doctoral studies were added as the third cycle.
2. In the ECTS system, students are expected to take 60 credits per year. How the credits are counted varies, but usually one credit equals 25–30 hours of work for students (EACEA 2012, pp. 46–9).
3. From the beginning of 2014, the Erasmus program for higher education has been part of Erasmus+, the new EU program for Education, Training, Youth and Sport for 2014–2020, which integrates seven existing programs into one single program.
4. The ECNPSA has now become the ECPSA (the European Confederation of Political Science Associations), which as a formal association was founded in 2007. In 2009, epsNet became a network within the ECPR (European Consortium for Political Research), but it has not been active since then.
5. The *Magna Charta Universitatum* was signed by the rectors of European universities in Bologna in 1988. It laid out 'the fundamental principles which must, now and always, support the vocation of universities' (MCU 1988, p. 113).

REFERENCES

'Bergen Communiqué. The European Higher Education Area – Achieving the Goals' (2005), *Bologna Process – European Higher Education Area website*, available at http://www.ehea.info/Uploads/Declarations/Bergen_Communique1.pdf (accessed 1 April 2014).

Bergström, Tomas (2005), 'ERASMUS – the Swedish experience: from imbalance to imbalance', in Erkki Berndtson (ed.), *Mobile Europe: Improving Faculty and Student Mobility Conditions in Europe*, Paris: epsNet Reports #9, pp. 43–6.

'Berlin Communiqué. Realising the European Higher Education Area' (2003), *Bologna Process – European Higher Education Area website*, available at http://www.ehea.info/Uploads/Declarations/Berlin_Communique1.pdf (accessed 1 April 2014).

Berndtson, Erkki (ed.) (2005), *Mobile Europe: Improving Faculty and Student Mobility Conditions in Europe*, Paris: epsNet Reports #9.

'Bologna Declaration of 19 June 1999: Joint Declaration of the European Ministers of Education' (1999), *Bologna Process – European Higher Education Area website*, available at http://www.ehea.info/Uploads/Declarations/BOLOGNA_DECLARATION1.pdf (accessed 1 April 2014).

Brunner, José Joaquín (2009), 'The Bologna Process from a Latin American perspective', *Journal of Studies in International Education*, **4** (13), 417–38.

'Bucharest Communiqué. Making the Most of Our Potential: Consolidating the European Higher Education Area' (2012), *Bologna Process – European Higher Education Area website*, available at http://www.ehea.info/Uploads/%281%29/Bucharest%20Communique%202012%281%29.pdf (accessed 1 April 2014).

'Budapest-Vienna Declaration on the European Higher Education Area' (2010), *Bologna Process – European Higher Education Area website*, available at http://www.ehea.info/Uploads/Declarations/Budapest-Vienna_Declaration.pdf (accessed 1 April 2014).

Chao Jr., Roger Y. (2011), 'Reflections on the Bologna Process: the making of an Asia Pacific higher education area', *European Journal of Higher Education*, **2–3** (1), 102–18.

Corbett, Anne (2006), 'Higher education as a form of European integration: how novel is the Bologna Process?', Working Paper No. 15, ARENA Centre for European Studies, University of Oslo.

Corbett, Anne and Mary Henkel (2013), 'The Bologna dynamic: strengths and weaknesses of the Europeanisation of higher education', *European Political Science*, **12** (4), 415–26, doi: 10.1057/eps.2013.21.

EACEA (2012), *The European Higher Education Area in 2012: Bologna Process Implementation Report*, Brussels: Eurydice.

ECNPSA (2003), *The Bologna declaration and the basic requirements of a Bachelor of Arts (BA) in political science in Europe: Recommendations from the European conference of national political science associations*, reprinted in Bob Reinalda and Ewa Kulesza (2006), *The Bologna Process – Harmonizing Europe's Higher Education*, second revised edition, Opladen and Farmington Hills, MI: Barbara Budrich Publishers, pp. 223–5.

EHEA (2013), *The EHEA Official Website*, available at http://www.ehea.info/ (accessed 22 June 2013).

ENQA (2005), *Standards and Guidelines for Quality Assurance in the European Higher Education Area*, available at http://www.enqa.eu/pubs_esg.lasso (accessed 22 June 2013).

European Commission (2000), *Final Commission Report on the Implementation of the Socrates Programme 1995–1999*, Brussels: European Commission.

European Commission (2013), *Reform of the Universities in the Framework of the Lisbon Strategy*, available at http://europa.eu/legislation_summaries/education_training_youth/lifelong_learning/c11078_en.htm (accessed 22 June 2013).

European Council (2000), 'Lisbon European Council 23 and 24 March: presidency conclusions', available at http://www.europarl.europa.eu/summits/lis1_en.htm (accessed 22 June 2013).

Furlong, Paul (2007), 'The European conference of national political science associations: problems and possibilities of co-operation', in Hans-Dieter Klingemann (ed.), *The State of Political Science in Western Europe*, Opladen and Farmington Hills, MI: Barbara Budrich Publishers, pp. 401–7.

Hartmann, Eva (2008), 'Bologna goes global: a new imperialism in the making?', *Globalisation, Societies and Education*, **3** (6), 207–20.

Kehm, Barbara M. (2010), 'The future of the Bologna Process – the Bologna Process of the future', *European Journal of Education*, **4** (45), 529–34.

Lažetić, Predrag (2010), 'Managing the Bologna Process at the European level: institution and actor dynamics', *European Journal of Education*, **4** (45), 549–62.

'Leuven/Louvain-la-Neuve Communiqué. The Bologna Process 2020 – The European Higher Education Area in the New Decade' (2009), *Bologna Process – European Higher Education Area website*, available at http://www.ehea.info/Uploads/Declarations/Leuven_Louvain-la-Neuve_Communiqu%C3%A9_April_2009.pdf (accessed 1 April 2014).

'London Communiqué. Towards the European Higher Education Area: Responding to Challenges in a

Globalised World' (2007), *Bologna Process – European Higher Education Area website*, http://www.ehea.info/Uploads/Declarations/London_Communique18May2007.pdf (accessed 1 April 2014).

Maslen, Geoff (2012), 'Worldwide student numbers forecast to double by 2025', *University World News*, **209** (19 February 2012).

'MCU – Magna Charta Universitatum' (1988), reprinted in Bob Reinalda and Ewa Kulesza (2006), *The Bologna Process – Harmonizing Europe's Higher Education*, second revised edition, Opladen and Farmington Hills, MI: Barbara Budrich Publishers, pp. 113–14.

Mény, Yves (2010), 'Political Science as a profession', *European Political Science*, **9**, 11–21.

'Mobility for Better Learning: Mobility Strategy 2020 for the European Higher Education Area' (2012), *Bologna Process – European Higher Education Area website*, available at http://www.ehea.info/Uploads/%281%29/2012%20EHEA%20Mobility%20Strategy.pdf (accessed 1 April 2014).

Münch, Richard (2013), 'The Bologna Process in the German system of higher education: from occupational monopolies to the global struggle for educational prestige', *European Political Science*, **12** (4), 424–31, doi:10.1057/eps.2013.22.

Pépin, Luce (2007), 'The history of EU cooperation in the field of education and training: how lifelong learning became a strategic objective', *European Journal of Education*, **1** (42), 121–32.

'Prague Communiqué. Towards the European Higher Education Area' (2001), *Bologna Process – European Higher Education Area website*, available at http://www.ehea.info/Uploads/Declarations/PRAGUE_COMMUNIQUE.pdf (accessed 1 April 2014).

Quinlan, Kathleen M. and Erkki Berndtson (2013), 'The emerging European higher education area: implications for instructional development', in Eszter Simon and Gabriela Pleschová (eds), *Teacher Development in Higher Education: Existing Programs, Program Impact, and Future Trends*, New York: Routledge, pp. 129–50.

Ravinet, Pauline (2008), 'From voluntary participation to monitored coordination: why European countries feel increasingly bound by their commitment to the Bologna Process', *European Journal of Education*, **3** (43), 353–67.

Reinalda, Bob (2008), 'The ongoing Bologna Process and political science', *European Political Science*, **3** (7), 382–93.

Reinalda, Bob (2013), 'Introduction: how does European harmonization affect political science?', *European Political Science*, **12** (4), 409–14, doi: 10.1057/eps.2013.20.

Reinalda, Bob and Ewa Kulesza (2006), *The Bologna Process – Harmonizing Europe's Higher Education*, second revised edition, Opladen and Farmington Hills, MI: Barbara Budrich Publishers.

Schüttemeyer, Suzanne S. (2007), 'The current state of political science in Germany', in Hans-Dieter Klingemann (ed.), *The State of Political Science in Western Europe*, Opladen and Farmington Hills, MI: Barbara Budrich Publishers, pp. 163–86.

Sin, Cristina (2012), 'Academic understandings and responses to Bologna: a three-country perspective', *European Journal of Education*, **3** (47), 392–404.

'Sorbonne Declaration. Joint Declaration on Harmonisation of the Architecture of the European Higher Education System' (1998), *Bologna Process – European Higher Education Area website*, available at: http://www.ehea.info/Uploads/Declarations/SORBONNE_DECLARATION1.pdf (accessed 1 April 2014).

Van Cranenburgh, Oda (2005), 'The BA–MA structure and mobility of students in European political science', in Erkki Berndtson (ed.), *Mobile Europe: Improving Faculty and Student Mobility Conditions in Europe*, Paris: epsNet Reports #9, pp. 55–61.

Van der Wende, Marijk C. (2003), 'Globalisation and access to higher education', *Journal of Studies in International Education*, **2** (7), 193–206.

Veiga, Amélia and Alberto Amaral (2006), 'The open method of coordination and the implementation of the Bologna Process', *Tertiary Education and Management*, **4** (12), 283–95.

13. Promoting employability and jobs skills via the political science curriculum*
Simon Lightfoot

The most frustrating question a student in the UK can be asked when they tell people they are studying political science at any level of study is, 'What are you going to do with that degree, then – become a Member of Parliament?' Given that there are 650 Members of Parliament (MPs) in the UK system and that each year over 200 students graduate from my university alone with a political science or international relations degree, that career path would seem to be a very crowded one! The question, though, is symptomatic of a broader issue for political science – what jobs does a political science degree prepare you for and what skills does a political science degree give you? The question of what a political science degree prepares you for is often at the forefront of students' minds when they are studying the subject (Holmes and Miller 2000). Consequently, the pressure is increasing on disciplines such as political science and international relations that have no clearly defined route, to prepare their students for the future. Therefore the chapter utilizes debates about employability as shorthand to encompass the variety of issues associated with this topic.

This chapter outlines how various employability skills are embedded into the political science undergraduate curriculum and how the task of university staff is to ensure that students are aware of these skills, can articulate them and can map their development over time. The focus is on the undergraduate experience, but clearly employability is important for both Masters and Research degrees in political science and international relations.[1] The chapter draws a distinction between those careers that can be seen as politics related (civil service; local government; the European Commission; working with an elected politician, a political party, political lobbyist, pressure group or think tank) and other careers. It shows how placements/internships can be used to provide work experience for students in a variety of settings. It also argues that the key skills employers seek in graduates can be found in political science degree courses and that the role of faculty is to ensure the students are aware of this fact. Students need to be able to reflect on what they have learnt and how they can apply it to the labor market. In particular, the chapter highlights that careful use of assessment tasks to mimic 'real' world activities can be a helpful way of making the links explicit. It focuses heavily on the experience of UK and US universities, although it is clear that 'graduate attributes' and the debates around them are common in many different countries (see Hager and Holland 2006 for an overview), especially in light of the Bologna Process within the European Union (Reinalda 2013).

CONTEXT

Definitions of employability abound and are not without controversy (see e.g. Ashe 2012; Arora 2013). A widely accepted definition of employability is: 'a set of achievements – skills, understandings and personal attributes – that make graduates more likely to gain employment and be successful in their chosen occupations, which benefits themselves, the workforce, the community and the economy' (Yorke 2006, p. 8). Employability is increasingly central to the higher education world. Within the US system there is growing evidence from parents and politicians that pressure is increasing for students to study career-related majors. This is linked to a belief that the purpose of university is to ensure students graduate with a good job (Budryk 2013). In the US, there is a specific issue in relation to students choosing majors that are perceived to be more employer friendly, thereby moving away from political science and international relations (Bobic 2005). Within the UK there is a heated debate as to whether the introduction of the higher tuition fees has led to a drop in admissions for the so-called non-vocational degree subjects (Matthews 2014). The European Higher Education Area (EHEA), which developed from the Bologna Process, has long identified employability as a priority for European HE. In April 2012 in Bucharest, education ministers committed 'to enhance the employability and personal and professional development of graduates throughout their careers "to serve Europe's needs"'. They explicitly link subject and generic skills when they argue that, 'at the end of a course, students will thus have an in-depth knowledge of their subject as well as generic employability skills' (Bucharest Communiqué 2012).

EMPLOYABILITY AND POLITICAL SCIENCE/ INTERNATIONAL RELATIONS

Given this context, the focus on employability (if not the term itself) is common across all degree programs in the UK and across the world. This raises the question as to whether the pressures raised by the employability agenda on political science as a discipline have some special features. Does studying for a political science/international relations degree offer particular advantages in the job market or does it have features that make political science/international relations graduates less employable than contemporaries with different degrees?

This section highlights two particular issues: to what extent do political science/international relations degrees prepare students for political careers (Niemann and Heister 2010) and to what extent do they prepare students for non-political careers? A glance at the careers section of the American Political Science Association (APSA) website highlights that a bachelor's degree in political science can lead to exciting careers and that 'political science majors gain analytical skills, administrative competence and communication abilities that are valued in a wide spectrum of potential career areas' (APSA, n.d.). It then lists a sample of careers that range from 'Activist, Advocate/Organizer' through 'CIA Analyst or Agent', 'Free-lance writer' to 'Web Content Editor'. The Political Studies Association (PSA) in the UK makes a similar point: 'a degree in politics does not exclude you from pursuing a career that is not directly related to what you have studied. Politics allows you to acquire a range of key skills and attributes that will be highly prized by employers in management, marketing, public relations, retail, accountancy, and banking' (PSA n.d., p. 11). It is evident that many employers do not hold any preferences with regard to degree discipline from their candidates and instead focus on the skills that graduates can articulate and demonstrate. As Richard Lambert, the then Director-General of the Confederation of British Industry (CBI), argued, 'Most employers are less interested in the precise details of what graduates have studied than in what the experience has taught them ... What matters is that graduates have the framework which allows them to keep on learning' (Treherne and Rowson 2011, p. 19). In 2014, the only vocational degrees are those in medical sciences/healthcare and perhaps engineering. A law degree is not needed for a career in law; indeed most of the big law firms take on 50/50 law/non-law candidates. The only non-vocational careers political science/international relations students would not be able to get into are those that specify or have a high degree of scientific or mathematical content. Yet, even then, if the student is comfortable with numbers, then careers in technology, accounting etc. can be successfully applied for.

However, this breadth of career choice can be confusing for students, as shown by studies in Sweden and Poland (Johansson, Kopciwicz and Dahlgren 2008). Nyström, Dahlgren and Dahlgren (2008, p. 223) talk about students 'searching for a professional field' because a degree in political science is broad and without a clear identified profession. Part of the issue can be linked to a level of ignorance on the part of faculty around what careers their students go into. What do political science/international relations tutors think their students go on to do? Evidence from biological sciences suggests that faculty mistakenly think that their students go on to become biological scientists/researchers, when in fact the majority do not.[2]

The recent focus on employability promotes a range of reactions from faculty. For many academics, the nature of a university education should be about enquiry and discovery and a love of a subject. Political science and international relations academics are no different, arguing that the central canon of the discipline should be taught and learnt, which leaves little room for employability aspects. Some faculty and students would have an issue with the neo-liberal aspects of the employability agenda and the idea that political science should 'give businesses what they need' (Zebich-Knos 1992). The work of many academics actively and critically engages with concepts such as employability and flexibility in the employment market and these academics would feel challenged by the need to promote them in the classroom (Ashe 2012). There is also the fear that the employability agenda is trying to turn faculty into careers advisors. In this context, perhaps the role of faculty should be to encourage students to think about their choices, such as their choice of major or the extra courses they study (a personal note here is that a number of students in Leeds express a desire to travel or work in Latin America yet haven't used their course choices to include learning Spanish).

A specific tension for social sciences is whether disciplines such as political science and international relations teach the 'wrong' skills, such as critical thinking (Lee 2013). If we ask students to question the world around them, what happens when they gain employment and perhaps start questioning the power relations within the firm? This point perhaps reflects the current debate around the future of work. Creativity is increasingly being seen in the same way as literacy – an essential element for all employees. Cliché expressions such as being able to 'think outside the box' do reflect the reality within specific sectors of the employment market, sectors that incidentally seem to be those that are recruiting graduates in large numbers. Wetherly and Barnett (2005) highlight the need for business students to be given a political awareness, whilst feedback from some employers is that they want critical thinking and challenges to perceived orthodoxy.

THE REALITY OF EMPLOYABILITY IN POLITICAL SCIENCE

Despite the increasing focus on developing employability skills in higher education in politics departments across the UK, subject-specific knowledge continues to drive curricula. How do we embed employability in the political science/international relations curriculum? Historically, in the UK at least, the commonest mode of delivering employability skills has tended to be the 'bolt on' to the existing curriculum (Craig 2010). Yet the evidence suggests that, for it to be effective, employability must be embedded into the curriculum (Maurer and Mawdsley 2013). The evidence from skills development studies is that skills development in a disciplinary context is more efficient than without that context (Jones 2009), whilst Leston-Bandeira (2013) highlights the benefits of teaching research methods in a disciplinary context; the same applies for political science/international relations and employability. Curtis (2013) therefore indicates four key areas where employability can be embedded into the curriculum:

1. at course or program level
2. in the study of the subject
3. in learning and teaching and assessment strategies, for better learning
4. through placement learning.[3]

As faculty, we need to consider to what extent employability skills are embedded at course or program level – or are they embedded in the study of the subject per se? Research suggests that skills can be embedded in a higher education curriculum (Breuning, Parker and Ishiyama 2001), although, if we focus on employability skills, research from the UK has found that these skills are often only implicitly ingrained in the curriculum (Lee 2013). There are clearly generic employability skills that all students obtain. However, if we are looking to embed skills in courses or programs, it would be useful to assess what skills employers seek.

The ten key competences that UK employers look for in graduates are (as outlined in Table 13.1): communication skills; team-working skills; integrity; intellectual ability;

Table 13.1   Graduate skills sought by UK employers (in %)

	Total number of employees			Grand Total
	1–99	100–999	1000+	
Communication skills	88	86	82	86
Team-working skills	85	84	84	85
Integrity	81	86	82	83
Intellectual ability	81	84	78	81
Confidence	80	81	78	81
Character/personality	81	79	60	75
Planning and organizational skills	74	72	75	74
Literacy (good writing skills)	68	72	75	71
Numeracy (good with numbers)	68	67	69	68
Analysis and decision-making skills	64	67	73	67

Source: The Council for Industry and Higher Education (CIHE) 2008.

confidence; character/personality; planning and organizational skills; literacy (good writing skills); numeracy (good with numbers); analysis and decision-making skills' (for a European Survey, see Eurobarometer 2010). Evidence from the US also supports this: nearly all the employers surveyed (93 percent) say that 'a demonstrated capacity to think critically, communicate clearly, and solve complex problems is more important than [a candidate's] undergraduate major' (Hart Research Associates 2013). These surveys are often generic, so it is therefore important for political science/international relations faculty to ensure employers understand what they get from political science/international relations graduates. For example, sports science had a particular perception issue whereby some employers thought their students played football and netball all day and did not appreciate the scientific basis of the degree.

THE SKILLS PRESENT IN A POLITICAL SCIENCE/ INTERNATIONAL RELATIONS DEGREE

Studying political science or international relations teaches you 'to rigorously analyse problems and to understand the big picture but not lose focus of the small details' (Karan Chadda, Client Development Manager, Populus in PSA, n.d.). The UK PSA (n.d., p. 10) identifies a number of key skills, in particular analysis/critical awareness: 'politics is about the analysis of complex and often contradictory data and being able to construct and defend arguments derived from such data. You will be able to articulate and defend your arguments in the face of criticism'. These skills are increasingly sought by employers and are basically what are tested via the application process/assessment centers as they are part and parcel of most graduate roles.

The UK PSA also highlights communication as a key element of a political science or international relations degree. They argue, 'you will be able to communicate effectively in writing and verbally as the result of studying politics. You will be required to write essays and reports and to make class presentations and contribute to discussions. You will become more confident in your ability to communicate by studying politics' (PSA n.d., p. 10). This conclusion is supported by a report in the UK by the National Union of Students and the Confederation of British Industry (NUS/CBI 2011). Communication is therefore clearly embedded in the majority of the political science/international relations curriculum in the UK, with essay writing the most common form of assessment (Blair and McGinty 2012). Essay writing allows students to demonstrate a wide range of competences, from the way the essay is written to the depth of analysis in the content. Every essay that is produced during a political science or international relations degree will require research, innovation, creativity and problem solving, written communication and critical analysis.

One issue with this discussion is that skills are seen as embedded in courses or programs, rather than as an explicit element of the discipline. The general political science or international relations degree is not likely to become vocational and nor should it. However, we can identify specific areas where employability becomes more explicitly embedded in the subject matter. Craig (2010) highlights the development of practitioner-focused degrees while Wyman, Lees-Marshment and Herbert (2012) outline the development of specific courses that explore the practice of politics and prepare students more explicitly for working in a political environment.

Finally, we need to consider whether employability is embedded through placement learning and the benefits and drawbacks of this approach. The opportunity to undertake an internship or work placement is a common aspect of many political science courses. The time allocated to placement learning can range from a whole academic year through to short placements of a few days. Some placements are an integral part of the student's program, whilst many others are co-curricular. The traditional placement in the UK tends to be the year-long placement, the so-called sandwich degree (employment is sandwiched in between study). In politics the common model is a year-long placement in Westminster working for an MP or a committee clerk (Curtis and Blair 2010). In the US, we find a similar model, with many universities offering internship opportunities in either Washington (Frantzich and Mann 1997) or state capitals (Jensen and Hunt 2007). The benefits of these programs are said to be increased self-confidence, deeper knowledge of the subject and a greater range of skills. There is also a sense that these students increase their employability by their 'insider' knowledge of the system. However, the programs are resource heavy and potentially take up a disproportionate amount of staff and student time.

There is some evidence that undertaking an internship increases future academic performance (Lowenthal and Sosland 2007). Whether this is because of the fact that, in order to obtain placements in the first place, students usually have to be highly motivated and engaged, or whether it is as a result of the time-management skills students learn on placement (it is a cliché, but students who take part in an internship often maintain 'normal' working hours on their return to university study), is hard to identify. What is clear is that there is a concern that placements are too narrow in terms of the students they recruit, and potentially the barriers to participation are high – access to opportunities can be a case of 'who you know' and the financial costs of moving to London or Washington can be prohibitive for some groups of students (Curtis and Blair 2010). Given that a third of graduate positions are expected to be filled by students who have already worked for the organizations they are applying to, this has issues for widening participation (High Fliers 2013). Shorter, more flexible placements are also required in political science and international relations to ensure the benefits of placement learning are not confined to one socio-economic group (Curtis et al. 2009; Curtis 2012). Placements with different types of organizations are therefore important. Local government, NGOs and think tanks are obvious alternative placement providers, but attention needs to be paid to the wider opportunities offered to political science and international relations students.

This links back to a distinction between careers that can be seen as politics related (civil service; local government; the European Commission; working with an elected politician, a political party, political lobbyist, pressure group or think tank) and other careers. Whilst discipline-related placements are clearly beneficial for students, any work experience is seen as important. Two thirds of graduate recruiters stress the need for work experience for receiving a job offer (High Fliers 2013). Some students are aware of this distinction, as one of my work placement students argued:

> Whilst I enjoy the politics I study in my degree, I feel that the real skills I will leave university with are good presentation skills, analytical skills and the ability to conduct independent research as part of a project. All of these skills are highly relevant to my internship with L'Oréal

and will allow me to develop them further. As a result I feel this opportunity will make me stronger in all areas for my final university year, as well as making me more employable in the future. I have never had a desire to use my politics degree to be a politician, but to use it to help me further my career in a more business based organization, such as L'Oréal. For these reasons I feel my placement is relevant to my degree and I will be using and improving the skills gained during my politics degree.

The focus on placements within political science is clearly a major plus for the discipline. However, more work needs to be done, as Curtis (2013) asserts. He stresses that more work is needed on assessment: are we assessing learning or the development of competencies? This is a serious issue, as it involves ensuring the placements remain academically rigorous whilst continuing to be relevant to both the student and the employer. Curtis also highlights the individualistic nature of placements, which sounds odd given that individuals rather than groups tend to get jobs, but his argument is that more can be done to support students on placement so that they feel part of a cohort. He also cautions that placements are not a silver-bullet option to solve all problems and warns that, unless they are carefully monitored, placements could signal a return of exclusion.

It is also worth noting the benefits of study abroad or a junior year abroad. Drake (2013) highlights the benefits of the ERASMUS study abroad scheme in the UK. She notes that the students 'valued the scheme . . . for its "employability" potential' (Drake 2013, p. 20). The benefits of study abroad are that employers see students who undertake such an experience as potentially more flexible, more adaptable, more open to new ideas, more able to handle a challenge and more resourceful. Study abroad can also offer a way for students to distinguish their academic career from other suitably qualified applicants. These were all benefits of the study abroad scheme as articulated by the students in Drake's research: study abroad would be 'a unique point to put on a CV' and 'it is important to employers to look like you are willing to try new places and travel' (Drake 2013, p. 20). Experience in a different country can also bring benefits in terms of language learning, which can be an advantage especially in the European context.

Getting core skills such as time management or task prioritization is extremely useful. 'The fact is that managing time, prioritizing and deciding how best to allocate your energies are central to effectiveness at work. Your course gives you an ideal opportunity in those self-management skills' (NUS/CBI 2011). Can we integrate more employability experiences into the classroom? Simulations offer an excellent opportunity for students to gain key employability experiences whilst also demonstrating depth of academic knowledge (Usherwood 2009). One often overlooked skill is the art of learning to deal with setbacks and losing out in arguments, something simulations allow students to experience in safety (Sasley 2010). Dealing with setbacks is a key life skill that is often at odds with pressures on modern universities to ensure good grades and good student retention.[4]

It has been shown that students often fail to connect skills development from one course to another (Jenkins and Walker 2013), whilst Robinson (2013) highlights evidence from Canada demonstrating that students tend to perceive a range of skills being developed through their co-curricular activities rather than their degree. Therefore communication skills are perceived to be developed through working in a bar or restaurant and talking to customers rather than giving presentations or discussing ideas in seminars.

Another issue appears to be that students are not able to articulate the skills they obtain as part of their political science/international relations degree. At Leeds we have adopted a Decide, Plan and Compete strategy for employability, in response to the challenge of ensuring students can articulate the skills they have acquired. Ashe's (2012, p. 135) study shows that the majority of her students 'struggled to relate the subject-specific content of their politics degree to graduate employment'. The specific call from Curtis (2013) for political science is to make the tacit explicit. To do that, we need to 'foster a culture in which the wider picture in relation to graduate skills is clear' (Pegg et al. 2012, p. 30). Utilizing alumni and practitioners to offer advice to students is invaluable. Messages that seem remote delivered by a 40-year-old member of faculty somehow translate to an undergraduate audience when delivered by a 22-year-old graduate with the sort of job the audience aspires to (Curtis 2012).

One option is to make employability a key element of the learning outcomes, exercises and assessment of a course or program. Evidence gained from working in the UK system is that a minority of students perceive assessment as the judgment of worth for any activity – the 'is this going to be in the test?' mentality. For Curtis (2013), it is crucial that we think about how we embed these skills in learning and teaching and assessment strategies, for better learning. We therefore find excellent examples, such as the Policy Brief (see Boys and Keating 2009; Pennock 2011; Trueb 2013). This assessment, which can be used across a range of political science and international relations courses, encourages the students to write a policy brief around a specific topic. For example, in an EU course at Leeds, students wrote a short assignment exploring the journey of a specific piece of legislation. Supporters of this method argue that it encourages students to develop 'real world' skills (very few jobs require the employee to regularly write 3000 words; most tend to need short, persuasive briefs) whilst also demonstrating academic knowledge (Moody and Bobic 2011). Grossmann (2011) highlights how online publishing can be utilized both to assess student knowledge and to promote wider civic engagement, whilst Clark (2011) shows that a political science research methods course can be used to embed transferable skills, especially analysis of statistical data. Curtis (2013) highlights a course that teaches speaking in the UK, which obviously transfers to politics given the subject's reliance on rhetoric and debate, but also to nearly all jobs, whilst Holmes and Miller (2000) highlight a course where politics students organized a conference for credit.

Not only are these types of assessment tasks useful in bringing the real world into the classroom and offering students alternative assessment tasks, but these types of skills are increasingly being used by employers at the selection stage. 'Four-fifths of employers evaluated applicants through group exercises and two-thirds used presentations. Other popular elements were written exercises, case studies and role plays' (High Fliers 2013, p. 8). Therefore, to ensure graduates in political science or international relations are able to compete in the job market, the discipline needs to provide them with the skills to do so as an integrated part of their program. It is one thing not to get a job because other people were better qualified; it is quite another thing not to get the job because you did not know the rules of the game. Lee (2013) defines this knowledge as empowerment-based employability skills.

CONCLUSION

Political science and international relations degrees provide students with a range of highly marketable skills that allow graduates in these disciplines to remain highly employable. As much as anything, it's about making prospective students and their parents as well as employers aware of these skills to change perceptions when the question is asked, 'What can you do with a political science/international relations degree?' There is also a fear that we need to be careful about raising expectations in the students that are unrealistic. Can every student get a graduate-level job? In the same way that not everyone who plays hockey gets to play in the NHL or every talented band gets a record deal, in the midst of a global recession jobs are scarce. On average, Britain's top employers received 46 applications for every vacancy in 2013, compared with 51 in 2012. Increasingly, faculty are realizing that 'a degree is no longer a meal ticket to your future but merely a license to hunt' (Hawkins and Gilleard n.d., p. 8). It is no longer enough just having a good degree from a good university.

Much useful work has been undertaken concerning employability within political science,[5] but there is more that can be done. Whatever we do, the crucial element is that we ensure political science and international relations degrees remain relevant, despite increasing evidence suggesting that a degree is not enough in itself for employment (see Tomlinson 2008). However, we must remain mindful of the fact that, as Tymon (2013) argues, for many students employability is a turn-off. The pressure on students to get the best degree possible can leave little time for co-curricular activities or just enjoying university life. Taking this on board, we must ensure that all political science/international relations students have the opportunity to access advice about careers and most importantly skills development. We need to make sure that we take employability seriously and show our students that they can have the 'last laugh' (Breuning, Parker and Ishiyama 2001) in a highly competitive job market.

NOTES

* I would like to thank three undergraduate students from the University of Leeds (Jess Douglas, Ryan Tilley and Kerry Jackson) for their research support and the University of Leeds TESS fund for providing funding for the project 'Research-led employability'. I also want to acknowledge the helpful suggestions for improvements and comments offered by Steve Carter, Eszter Simon and Charlotte Wakeling.
1. Perhaps the big issue in terms of research degrees is, if we are training the next generation of academics, do the jobs for them exist?
2. Interview with careers consultant, 9 July 2013.
3. Placement learning is a model whereby students undertake a placement in a work environment as part of their degree program. It is similar to internships for credit schemes run in many US universities.
4. Whilst the focus of this chapter is on employability, it is worth pointing out that student-centeredness and individual work may also foster this resilience, as long as students are not left alone when they fail.
5. The International Political Education Database (IPED) highlights the wealth of articles written on employability: https://sites.google.com/site/psatlg/Home/resources/journal-articles/iped---employability (accessed 7 November 2013).

REFERENCES

APSA (n.d.), *Careers in Political Science*, available at http://www.apsanet.org/content_6457.cfm (accessed 3 February 2014).
Arora, B. (2013), 'A Gramscian analysis of the employability agenda', *British Journal of Sociology of Education*, 1–14, online first, doi: 10.1080/01425692.2013.838415.
Ashe, F. (2012), 'Harnessing political theory to facilitate students' engagement with graduate "employability": a critical pyramid approach', *Politics*, **32** (2), 129–37.
Blair, Alasdair and Sam McGinty (2012), 'Developing assessment practices in politics', in Cathy Gormley-Heenan and Simon Lightfoot (eds), *Teaching Politics and IR*, Basingstoke, UK: Palgrave, pp. 105–22.
Bobic, M. (2005), '"Do you want fries with that?" A review of the bachelor's program in political science', *Politics & Policy*, **33** (2), 349–70.
Boys, J.D. and M. Keating (2009), 'The Policy Brief: building practical and academic skills in international relations and political science', *Politics*, **29** (3), 201–8.
Breuning, M., P. Parker and J. Ishiyama (2001), 'The last laugh: skill building through a liberal arts political science curriculum', *PS: Political Science & Politics*, **34** (3), 657–61.
'Bucharest Communiqué. Making the Most of Our Potential: Consolidating the European Higher Education Area' (2012), *Bologna Process – European Higher Education Area website*, available at http://www.ehea.info/Uploads/%281%29/Bucharest%202012%281%29.pdf (accessed 1 April 2014).
Budryk, Z. (2013), 'More than a major', *Inside Higher Education*, 10 April, available at http://www.insidehighered.com/news/2013/04/10/survey-finds-business-executives-arent-focused-majors-those-they-hire#ixzz2Toyec1wy (accessed 10 March 2014).
Clark, A. (2011), 'Embedding transferable skills and enhancing student learning in a political science research methods module: evidence from the United Kingdom', *PS: Political Science & Politics*, **44** (1), 135–9.
Craig, J. (2010), 'Practitioner-focused degrees in politics', *Journal of Political Science Education*, **6** (4), 391–404.
Curtis, S. (2012), 'Politics placements and employability: a new approach', *European Political Science*, **11** (2), 153–63.
Curtis, S. and A. Blair (2010), 'Experiencing politics in action: widening participation in placement learning and politics as a vocation', *Journal of Political Science Education*, **6** (4), 369–90.
Curtis, S., B. Axford, A. Blair, C. Gibson, R. Huggins and P. Sherrington (2009), 'Making short politics placements work', *Politics*, **29** (1), 62–70.
Curtis, Steven (2013), 'Employability and the Politics Curriculum', paper presented at the HEA Seminar on Employability, 24 April 2013, UEA.
Drake, H. (2013), 'Learning from peers: the role of the student advisor in internationalising the European Studies curriculum', *European Political Science*, **13**, 12–22.
Eurobarometer (2010), *Employers' Perceptions of Graduate Employability*, European Commission, Brussels, available at http://ec.europa.eu/public_opinion/flash/fl_304_sum_en.pdf (accessed 1 June 2012).
Frantzich, Stephen and Sheilah Mann (1997), 'Experiencing government: political science internships', in Richard Battistoni and William E. Hudson (eds), *Experiencing Citizenship: Concepts and Models for Service Learning in Political Science*, Washington, DC: American Association for Higher Education, pp. 193–202.
Grossmann, M. (2011), 'Online student publishing in the classroom: the experience of the Michigan Policy Network', *PS: Political Science & Politics*, **44** (3), 634–40.
Hager, Paul and Susan Holland (2006), *Graduate Attributes, Learning and Employability*, Dordrecht: Springer.
Hart Research Associates (2013), 'It Takes More than a Major: Employer Priorities for College Learning and Student Success. An Online Survey among Employers', available at https://www.aacu.org/leap/presidentstrust/compact/2013SurveySummary.cfm (accessed 3 February 2014).
Hawkins, Peter and Carl Gilleard (n.d.), 'If Only I'd Known – Making the Cost of Higher Education: A Guide for Parents', UK: Association of Graduate Recruiters, available at http://www.qualityresearchinternational.com/esecttools/esectpubs/agrif.pdf (accessed 14 January 2014).
High Fliers (2013), *Report into Graduate Market 2013*, available at http://www.highfliers.co.uk/download/GMReport13.pdf (accessed 14 January 2014).
Holmes, A. and S. Miller (2000), 'A case for advanced skills and employability in higher education', *Journal of Vocational Education & Training*, **52** (4), 653–64.
Jenkins, Alan and Lawrie Walker (2013), 'Introduction', in Alan Jenkins and Lawrie Walker (eds), *Developing Student Capability through Modular Course*, Abingdon, UK: Routledge, pp. 19–24.
Jensen, J. and L. Hunt (2007), 'College in the state capital: does it increase the civic engagement of political science undergraduate majors?' *PS: Political Science & Politics*, **40** (3), 563–9.
Johansson, K., L. Kopciwicz and L. Dahlgren (2008), 'Learning for an unknown context: a comparative case study on some Swedish and Polish Political Science students' experiences of the transition from university to working life', *Compare: A Journal of Comparative and International Education*, **38** (2), 219–31.

Jones, A. (2009), 'Redisciplining generic attributes: the disciplinary context in focus', *Studies in Higher Education*, **34** (1), 85–100.
Lee, Donna (2013), 'Responding to the Employability Agenda: Developments in the Politics and International Relations Curriculum', paper presented at the HEA Seminar on Employability, 24 April, UEA.
Leston-Bandeira, C. (2013), 'Methods teaching through a discipline research-oriented approach', *Politics*, **33** (3), 207–19.
Lowenthal, D. and J. Sosland (2007), 'Making the grade: how a semester in Washington may influence future academic performance', *Journal of Political Science Education*, **3** (2), 143–60.
Matthews, D. (2014), 'Analysis: the subjects favoured and forsaken by students over 15 years', *Times Higher Education Supplement*, 16 January.
Maurer, H. and J. Mawdsley (2013), 'Students & skills, employability and the teaching of European studies: challenges and opportunities', *European Political Science*, **13**, 32–42.
Moody, R. and M. Bobic (2011), 'Teaching the net generation without leaving the rest of us behind: how technology in the classroom influences student composition', *Politics & Policy*, **39** (2), 169–94.
Niemann, A. and S. Heister (2010), 'Scientific political consulting and university education in Germany: demand and supply patterns in the context of the Bologna Process', *European Political Science*, **9** (3), 398–416.
NUS/CBI (2011), *Working Towards Your Future: Making the Most of Your Time in Higher Education*, London: NUS/CBI.
Nyström, S., M. Abrandt Dahlgren and L. Dahlgren (2008), 'A winding road – professional trajectories from higher education to working life: a case study of political science and psychology graduates', *Studies in Continuing Education*, **30** (3), 215–29.
Pegg, Ann, Jeff Waldock, Sonia Hendy-Isaac and Ruth Lawton (2012), *Pedagogy for Employability*, Heslington, York, UK: Higher Education Academy.
Pennock, A. (2011), 'The case for using policy writing in undergraduate political science courses', *PS: Political Science & Politics*, **44** (1), 141–6.
PSA (n.d.), *Study Politics: A Short Guide to Studying Politics at University in the UK*, available at http://www.psa.ac.uk/sites/default/files/12552_PSA_SP_20pp%20v3.pdf (accessed 3 February 2014).
Reinalda, B. (2013), 'Introduction: how does European harmonisation affect political science', *European Political Science*, **12** (4), 409–14.
Robinson, A. (2013), 'The workplace relevance of the liberal arts political science BA and how it might be enhanced: reflections on an exploratory survey of the NGO sector', *PS: Political Science & Politics*, **46**, 147–53.
Sasley, B.E. (2010), 'Teaching students how to fail: simulations as tools of explanation', *International Studies Perspectives*, **11** (1), 61–74.
The Council for Industry and Higher Education (CIHE) (2008), *Graduate Employability: What do Employers Think and Want?*, London: CIHE.
Tomlinson, M. (2008), '"The degree is not enough": students' perceptions of the role of higher education credentials for graduate work and employability', *British Journal of Sociology of Education*, **29** (1), 49–61.
Treherne, M. and A. Rowson (2011), 'Students, Research and Employability in the Faculty of Arts', *University of Leeds*, available at http://www.sddu.leeds.ac.uk/uploaded/StudentsResearchAndEmployabilityInArts.docx (accessed 19 April 2014).
Trueb, B. (2013), 'Teaching students to write for "real life": policy paper writing in the classroom', *PS: Political Science & Politics*, **46** (1), 137–41.
Tymon, A. (2013), 'The student perspective on employability', *Studies in Higher Education*, **38** (6), 841–56.
Usherwood, S. (2009), 'Grounding simulations in reality: a case study from an undergraduate politics degree', *On the Horizon*, **17** (4), 296–302.
Wetherly, P. and N. Barnett (2005), 'What has politics got to do with business?', *European Political Science*, **4** (3), 358–70.
Wyman, Matthew, Jennifer Lees-Marshment and Jon Herbert (2012), 'From politics past to politics future: addressing the employability agenda through a professional politics curriculum', in Cathy Gormley-Heenan and Simon Lightfoot (eds), *Teaching Politics and IR*, Basingstoke: Palgrave, pp. 236–54.
Yorke, Mantz (2006), *Employability in Higher Education: What It Is – What It Is Not*, Heslington, York, UK: Higher Education Academy.
Zebich-Knos, M. (1992), 'Giving businesses what they need', *PS: Political Science & Politics*, **25** (4), 727–33.

PART II

TEACHING SUBJECT AREAS

14. After the apocalypse: a simulation for Introduction to Politics classes
Wendy L. Watson, Jesse Hamner, Elizabeth A. Oldmixon and Kimi King

INTRODUCTION

Several years ago a student who had previously been enrolled in one of the authors' introductory classes asked for a letter of recommendation to law school. This was a good but unremarkable student. He came to class, but he did not appear to take notes. He participated minimally, and he earned a low B for the semester. When the student provided a draft of his statement of purpose and an unofficial transcript, the instructor was pleasantly surprised to learn that this student had an excellent academic record and a real passion for speech and hearing sciences. His performance in class did not reflect his overall level of achievement and potential; political science just was not his thing. This is the challenge of teaching introductory courses, but it is especially important for political science courses. The students are not necessarily there because of a burning desire to learn about political culture and the importance of institutional rules (like we surely were when we were undergraduates). Rather, they are likely registered in order to fulfill a general education or social sciences requirement. As political scientists we may love the study of politics, and our majors may be deeply engaged, but Introduction to Politics students are just as likely disgruntled music, math or philosophy majors, successful and bright in their chosen field, but not the least bit interested in politics. However, as luck would have it, teaching is not like preaching to a choir, and as a result we have all faced the sea of blank, polite faces and wondered how we would ever manage to get them to learn what we have to offer.

While many of our students may not be positively inclined toward the class, it is important to engage them in the material for several reasons. First, many of us have written statements of teaching philosophy wherein we un-ironically argue the value of fostering critical thinking and instilling the norms and skill sets that facilitate good democratic citizenship. It might be more challenging, but it is *at least* as important that we fulfill this obligation vis-à-vis the larger student population as it is with political science majors. Introduction to Politics, after all, will likely be the only rigorous treatment of political science to which non-majors are exposed. Second, this class gives departments an opportunity to recruit. As public universities receive less and less funding from the states, and as the academy more generally is facing profound financial stress, growing the number of majors may be positively related to securing resources, such as faculty lines, from upper-level administrators. Third, the more students are engaged, the more enjoyable the class is for students and faculty alike. Fifteen weeks is an awfully long time to be miserable. An engaging class, on the other hand, can be energizing, intellectually stimulating and (practically speaking) may yield higher teaching evaluations.

In this chapter, we provide an example of an active learning technique that effectively conveys important course concepts, and does so in such a way that majors and non-majors alike are drawn in and develop greater agency over the learning process. Rather than face-to-face lectures where students passively receive information, active learning 'encourages students to participate in the learning process through techniques such as simulations, structured debates and the case method' (Archer and Miller 2011, p. 429). We each employed a constitution-writing simulation in different sections of our department's gateway class. Each of us tweaked the format and the rules, but the scenario was the same: imagine the class comprises human survivors of a zombie apocalypse. Society has been transformed, and the institutions of government have fallen—the United States is no more. The class is tasked with writing a new constitution for the emerging society.

WHY ACTIVE LEARNING?

The strength of active learning techniques is that they give students *experience* with what we want them to learn. Any of us could deliver a lecture on the intricacies of how a bill becomes a law or could put students in the position of having to shepherd their own bill through the legislative process. Both approaches can be effective teaching techniques, but the goal is that with experience students will internalize the material to a greater degree. Indeed, several studies document that active learning enhances student success. Citing Stice (1987), Baranowski (2006, p. 33) notes that, 'while students retain only about 10% of what they read and 20% of what they hear, they retain up to 90% of what they do and say'. Moreover, it appeals to different learning preferences and styles among students (Brock and Cameron 1999). The academy is increasingly open to active learning techniques. It is no surprise, then, that a robust literature on this topic generally (Meyers and Jones 1993) and regarding political science more specifically (Glazier 2011; Huerta 2007; Mariani 2007; Kathlene and Choate 1999, for just a few examples) has developed in recent years. As Glazier (2011) notes, moreover, the American Political Science Association's Teaching and Learning Conference routinely organizes a 'track' on active learning techniques.

We think the simulation described below is especially well suited to the material in Introduction to Politics classes. It puts students in a position to grapple for themselves with questions such as: What values inform the choices that we are making? What institutional arrangements make the most sense, given our values and context? What will the effect be of the rules and institutions we choose? When is it okay to compromise? It also gives students experience with deliberation and provides the opportunity to apply empirical theories that are central to political science, such as social choice theory, principal-agent theory and game theory. Rather than describe democratization, the simulation puts students in a position to decide whether democracy makes sense in the first place. The result is that abstractions make much more sense because they are addressed within an experiential activity.

THE SIMULATION

In the most basic terms, the simulation requires students, working in groups, to recreate institutions of government in the wake of a zombie apocalypse. The simulation is set at some point in the future. In the set-up material (an example of one class is provided in Appendix 14.1 and other examples are available from the other authors), students are informed that an outbreak of a virus has created a zombie horde—individuals who lack higher cognitive function and are driven by a desire to kill other humans. While some infected individuals now exhibit a less-dangerous form of the virus, the 'full-blown' zombies remain a threat to the healthy population. The plague has also ravaged the countryside. While there are remnants of state governments, the institutions of the national government have all been destroyed. It is now up to the survivors to rebuild a state structure. In a sense, the hypothetical circumstances of the simulation place students in a state of nature, where they are asked to forge a new social contract. All things are possible because students are not required to design a democracy.

The simulation was originally used in Dr. Watson's relatively small class (49 students). Work was assessed in three ways. First, each group used a wiki feature of our university's learning management system (Blackboard) to draft their new constitution; the group constitutions were graded for coherence, thoroughness, creativity and the students' justifications for their choices. Students were given time in class to work on the project, but use of the wiki feature allowed them to coordinate outside of class more easily. Second, each group presented a short argument (5–7 minutes) aimed at persuading their classmates that their constitution created the best system of government. The presentations involved an audio-visual component that allowed students significant room for creativity, and they were graded for that creativity, in addition to clarity and persuasiveness. Finally, each individual student wrote a short reflective essay about how and why they changed the original constitution and which of those changes they would like to see in the current U.S. Constitution. By way of example, Dr. Hamner's directions for the paper and the rubric he used for grading it can be found in Appendix 14.3.

Dr. King utilized the simulation in a 'super-mass' class (roughly 320 students), who were placed into teams of 16 persons, forming 20 different 'regions' that formed after the apocalypse. The assessment was based on the discussion-board participation, blogs and wiki document created by the student teams. Students were given time in class to divide up the different sections that each team must consider (although not necessarily adopt). Student grades were based 75 percent on the group grade for the wiki (which can be adjusted up or down on the rubric by the teaching assistants, depending on an individual's contributions) and 25 percent on a peer rubric (which students are required to fill out in class) (see Appendix 14.4).

Faculty can adjust the assignment to require certain key components to be included or considered to vary the assignments by semester (helping to avoid academic integrity issues that can arise). For example, an instructor could require articles linking the states or regions to a federal government or might order mandates for certain institutions of government or provide a bill of rights for states/regions to consider adopting. Faculty can also vary key points in the simulation to emphasize topic areas (health care, stem cell research, immigration, etc).

These variations result in different conclusions by different groups. For example, some groups opted to move particular amendments—most notably the Bill of Rights—into the main body of the constitution. Others added additional fundamental rights or altered the structures of government (e.g. having a unicameral legislature or giving the president greater national security powers) to better respond to crises. Most groups struggled with the issue of constraints on 'zombie-Americans'. Most strikingly, almost all of the groups opted unequivocally for security over liberty, choosing to quarantine or kill anyone infected with the virus. In sum, the goal of the simulation was to have students think critically about the constitution, drawing on both its strengths and weaknesses to create a new United States government, and the work product of our students strongly indicates that the goal was met.

A THEME AND VARIATIONS

All educators, and especially those teaching university political science courses, face dilemmas dealing with constructivist learning (Windschitl 2002). Using 'zombies' creates a neutral space for students, as individuals and groups to debate 'rights' versus 'liberties' and remove the negative connotations that can occur if the out-groups or minorities (however defined) are the focus (e.g. ethnic, racial or religious minorities). We also think that the simulation and variations present unique pedagogical opportunities to examine intersectionalities premised on underlying theories regarding marginalized groups and controversial topics. As such, we also think the simulation (and its variations) might be ripe for consideration in pedagogical research (Rasmussen 2014).

All of us used the same basic outline for the simulation, but we each tweaked the simulation to suit our course needs, to implement institutional and individual student learning objectives and to enhance the semester-long structure of the course. Instructors might decide to employ one or more of these variations to make the simulation work better for their class needs.

Constitutional Convention

Drs. Oldmixon and Hamner also set aside additional days for the simulation requiring the groups to work together to create a single document on which they could all agree. This variation drives home the idea that government institutions are the product of compromise and that compromise does not always result in the most efficient solution. Time allowing, a convention would be an appropriate and dynamic addition to any type of introductory class. Oldmixon and Hamner considered having a larger constitutional convention wherein both classes could meet together and deliberate over their two documents. While this was not feasible at the time, it is something to consider if multiple sections of the same class are being taught.

Think Locally and Contextually

King gave each of the 20 teams a regional territory with a specific profile that distinguished it from the other groups (regions), and teams were even assigned spatially in the classroom seating assignments to represent the geographic layout of the U.S.A. She provided each group with a portfolio for their territory that included racial, religious, cultural, geographic and economic indicators including a scaled number indicating its percent chance of a continuing zombie security threat. Specifically, King used Elazar's (1972) state culture model to give students a deeper sense of context in constructing their own constitutions. This variation helped students understand that government is not one size fits all but, rather, must be considered in light of key contextual and structural factors. It is striking to note that student teams—without any prompting from the teaching personnel—regularly decided on their own to form regional compacts with other neighboring teams to cement alliances for resources and security.

Debate

If your class size allows it, the simulation could form the basis for in-class debate about fundamental powers of the state or sensitive policy areas. One controversial approach to the debate would be to assume that zombies infected with the lesser strain of the virus have a chance of giving birth to children infected with the more serious strain of the virus. This assumption raises the question of whether everyone infected with any form of the virus should be forcibly sterilized. Another topic would be to question whether the state should attempt to annihilate or to contain the zombies infected with the stronger strain of the virus. As noted above, our students generally opted to eliminate the zombie threat, so this debate topic might require the instructor to assign positions on either side of the debate to specific teams. While these topics seem somewhat fanciful, they raise genuine issues of the proper scope of state authority and the balance of that authority with individual rights.

Similarly, in a budget simulation portion of King's simulation, students debated the merits of stem cell research and sex education programs for zombies. While such topics can be difficult to get students to discuss, the assignment prompted lively debates about not only the assigned topics but also other policy-relevant topics such as marriage, birth control, sterilization, physician-assisted suicide and abortion. In the end, when students went back to assign their budget priorities, they also had to evaluate those priorities in light of constitutional prohibitions, rights and liberties.

Finally, King required students to debate the issues of the death penalty and abortion by requiring students to address these two issues in their bills of rights.

Downsizing

We opted for long-form simulations that we could utilize throughout the semester, and we all varied how we used the zombie apocalypse and constitution in other exercises. Shorter simulations, however, are also pedagogically useful (Baranowski 2006; Glazier 2011), and the simulation is fairly adaptable. If using for only one class period, students could debate and draft a single element of a constitution, such as a preamble or an article on judicial power or civil right provisions. Students could also be broken down into small groups to reflect on and discuss how and what they think the effect of various institutional choices might be as the new country develops.

In addition to writing the full constitution, King used the simulation in the second half of the course to do a budget simulation where there is a 'zombie threat' requiring students to allocate monies for both social welfare or national security programs—thus forcing students into making a tradeoff between domestic and international funding. In other words, there is room to adjust this simulation from a single semester-long simulation to one or a series of shorter simulations. In all the simulations, students are required to think about the strengths and weaknesses of their original constitution and how it limits their future options and behavior as a governmental entity.

Broader Introduction to Politics Classes

As noted above, the simulation was created for use in an introduction to American politics course, but it is applicable in other introductory politics courses. Those faculty teaching comparative and international courses would most likely place the simulation in the context of a newly emerging democracy or transitional government emerging from a post-conflict society to allow the students to think about the critical components of institutions and behaviors that would be most relevant to the constructs and subjects of their organized courses. We suspect students would be less likely to default to the American model in such courses given that the content is generally more global in nature. Instead of regions in the U.S.A., students could be assigned the task of developing a constitution for a particular country or proposing a constitution for an international federation (such as the African Union). Indeed, in a comparative politics course, students could be tasked with researching their assigned countries and developing the nation's descriptive portfolio as an additional graded component of the assignment. Similarly, international relations faculty might want to use the metaphor of the zombies to emphasize issues relating to ethnic cleansing, enemy combatant status, human rights, war crimes or other aspects of conflict studies and peace science.

Carrots and Sticks

Given that simulations almost never have substantive 'skin in the game', it can be difficult to motivate students to engage fully in the exercise. The element of creativity and fun of this simulation certainly helps, but a carrot-and-stick approach can further motivate students to participate in the simulation and take away the concepts and skills the simulation is intended to provide. Hamner developed several tactics for encouraging more significant involvement in the group project.

One powerful 'carrot' is the prospect of grade enhancement. In a class using pop quizzes, 'replacing' the pop-quiz grades can provide some motivation to simulation participants, as can 'extra credit' on an exam. In addition, Hamner provided a carrot connected to the in-class convention that gave groups an incentive to fight for the provisions of their own constitution: the group whose draft constitution is most strongly reflected in the class constitution earned a bump in their group grade (see Appendix 14.2 for more information here).

On the 'stick' side of the equation, Hamner's convention rules provided that, at the end of the three class periods, if the class conceded it cannot create a complete document because of unwillingness to compromise, every group's grade will be reduced by one letter grade. The combination of 'carrot' and 'stick' encourages debate, compromise and communication, among groups both during and outside of class, and encourages groups to develop strategies for the convention in advance. To that end, the carrots and sticks proved very effective. One group sponsored an open Google+ Hangout—as a result, the final day of the convention went smoothly. In a different, larger, class, one group used the 'last minute' to force much of its agenda through, unmodified.

Both of these tactics were successful, in that the class completed a constitution; the spirit of collaboration was more present in the first, while self-interest dominated in the second. As part of the group grade is based on how much of a group's draft constitution made it into the class constitution, the 'last-minute-pressure' group received the highest grade in the class. The other groups did not recognize until it was too late that they would have to align against the 'last-minute-pressure' group. In both cases, the classes took correct lessons from these individual incidents in the simulation, although the lessons in the larger class were somewhat more cynical and cold than the collaborative victory in the smaller class.

CONCLUSION

Increasingly, higher-education administrators, parents and students are demanding classes that develop practical skills—real-time problem solving, interactive communications and teamwork. We, as instructors, tend to focus our innovative energy on our upper-division classes, seeing those advanced courses as the best forum for inculcating higher-order skills. Yet it is crucial to engage students at an early point in their academic careers, and that means stretching our understanding of the role of introductory classes.

The simulation (and variations) described here give instructors of introductory political science classes—regardless of focus, size or length—an opportunity to employ an experiential learning activity. This particular simulation provides a platform for students to learn about the nuts and bolts of government institutions; the extent to which those institutions are shaped by cultural and historic conditions; and the nature of compromise, strategy and cooperation. Moreover, the simulation gives students the opportunity to write, to present and to persuade. Ultimately, the goal is to engage students where they are in terms of their different world-views, cultural experiences and levels of academic preparedness. The authors hope that the materials provided will form a basis for experiential learning in colleges and universities of all types, but we also encourage instructors to adapt the simulation to their own unique circumstances.

REFERENCES

Archer, Candice C. and Milissa K. Miller (2011), 'Prioritizing Active Learning: An Exploration of Gateway Courses in Political Science', *PS: Political Science & Politics*, **44** (2), 429–34.

Baranowski, Michael W. (2006), 'Single Session Simulations: The Effectiveness of Short Congressional Simulations in Introductory American Government Classes', *Journal of Political Science Education*, **2**, 33–49.

Brock, Kathy L. and Beverly J. Cameron (1999), 'Enlivening Political Science Courses with Kolb's Learning Preference Model', *PS: Political Science & Politics*, **32**, 251–6.

Elazar, Daniel J. (1972), *American Federalism: A View From the States*, second edition, New York: Thomas Y. Crowell.

Glazier, Rebecca A. (2011), 'Running Simulations without Ruining Your Life: Simple Ways to Incorporate Active Learning into Your Teaching', *Journal of Political Science Education*, **7**, 375–93.

Huerta, Juan Carlos (2007), 'Getting Active in the Large Lecture', *Journal of Political Science Education*, **3**, 237–49.
Kathlene, Lyn and Judd Choate (1999), 'Running for Elected Office: A Ten-Week Political Campaign Simulation for Upper-Division Courses', *PS: Political Science & Politics*, **32**, 69–76.
Mariani, Mack D. (2007), 'Connecting Students to Politics through a Multi-Class Campaign Simulation', *PS: Political Science & Politics*, **40**, 789–94.
Meyers, Chet and Thomas B. Jones (1993), *Promoting Active Learning: Strategies for the College Classroom*, San Francisco, CA: Jossey-Bass.
Rasmussen, Amy Cabrera (2014), 'Toward an Intersectional Political Science Pedagogy', *Journal of Political Science Education*, **10** (1), 102–16.
Stice, James E. (1987), 'Using Kolb's Learning Cycle to Improve Student Learning', *Engineering Education*, **77**, 291–6.
Windschitl, Mark (2002), 'Framing Constructivism in Practice as the Negotiation of Dilemmas: An Analysis of the Conceptual, Pedagogical, Cultural, and Political Challenges Facing Teachers', *Review of Educational Research*, **72** (2), 131–75.

APPENDIX 14.1: ORIGINAL SIMULATION

The year is 2114, and a zombie apocalypse has wiped out a considerable portion of the population of the United States and led to the disintegration of our national political institutions. While the apocalypse took a heavy social toll, it left many of our resources (notably, communication, transportation and manufacturing facilities) intact. We have adequate food, water and power; but (like today) we are aware that these resources are finite.

The zombies themselves are still around, though their number has diminished and the threat level from the zombies has declined in most regions. The virus that caused the outbreak, a mutation of the bat-borne Duvenhage virus, has mutated during the outbreak. Infected persons exhibit distinct characteristics (a shuffling gait, extreme pallor, slurred speech due to partial paralysis of the vocal cords, intense cravings for iron-rich foods). However, cognitive impairment and uncontrollable cravings for human brains exhibit in only about 10 percent of the infected population. Despite the possibility of reintegration of the zombie population into the uninfected human population, many uninfected humans consider the zombies to be no longer human and show an intense distrust and dislike of the population.

On the political front, individual states have survived the outbreak, and are now seeking to join forces for protection against the growing threat of a Canadian invasion. Moreover, the states desire greater bargaining power (with respect to both trade and diplomatic relations) they will have if united. In short, the time has come to rebuild the United States and that means drafting a new governing document. . . a new constitution.

You will, over the course of the semester, develop a governing document for this new, modern U.S.A. You may use concepts and elements from our original constitution, but you should update them by putting them into language that a typical citizen could understand. You are also free, of course, to change features of the constitution. Perhaps your group believes that a unicameral (not bicameral) legislature would be better suited in today's society, or perhaps you do not believe a legislature makes sense at all. Use the comment feature of the wiki to explain the rationale behind your decisions.

While you are free to add to the constitution, there are a few items your constitution MUST address:

1. the key principles guiding the creation of your constitution (in the form of a preamble);
2. the mechanism for adopting and modifying the constitution;
3. the role of the state governments;
4. the structure, powers and selection mechanism for the national legislature;
5. the structure, powers and selection mechanism for the national executive;
6. the structure, powers and selection mechanism for the national judiciary;
7. limitations on the powers and decisions of the national government (both internal and external); and
8. fundamental rights of citizens (including defining citizens).

You should organize your constitution around 'Articles' (parts), with each Article getting its own page on the wiki. Your 'main page' of your wiki should include the preamble for your constitution (the set of guiding principles).

APPENDIX 14.2: CONSTITUTIONAL CONVENTION GUIDELINES

1. Plan

One plan will be selected by your professor as the best of the un-modified constitutions. The class, however, will develop a hybrid/negotiated constitution, just as the Virginia Plan and the New Jersey Plan were ultimately merged—among other ideas—to form the 1789 U.S. Constitution.

2. The Objective (for the Class)

To see how difficult it is to synthesize and compromise to create a complete plan for a government; to create a new constitution you all think is worthy of running a country well.

3. The Objective (for You and Your Group)

For you to get the 'finished' constitution to most closely resemble your group's proposal. Notably, it will be practically impossible for you to meet your group objective(s) without a coalition of support. It is prudent that the individual groups attempt to form group coalitions around issues and article sections on which they already agree *prior to the constitutional convention* (will there be three branches of government?, etc.). This early coalition building may be done in person or online (i.e. Google+ Hangout, Facebook group, Blackboard discussion boards, etc.), but the purpose is for students to understand how goals are achieved outside of active sessions in class. Should a coalition reach the size of a supermajority, the in-class vote will not be taken on the issue at hand. Despite this formality, remember that the point of the convention is to get as much of your group's constitution into the class constitution, so it would be unwise to simply agree to whatever other groups have proposed (remember logrolling: 'I'll vote for yours if you vote for mine').

4. The Goodies

Each group will get '100 percent on a pop quiz' cards sufficient for each group member to get one card. There will also be one *extra card*, per group, allotted. These cards are tradable and can be used to influence negotiations. These cards will allow the bearer to replace one quiz grade with a 100 percent. If you already have 100 percent on all the quizzes, these cards will be used to boost your quiz average *over* 100 percent.

Cards are indivisible. Cards may be destroyed by the group currently possessing the card.

The group must agree on the distribution of quiz-grade cards. However, you may not use external inducements ('I need a ride to the airport for Thanksgiving . . .' or 'Do you like Sam Adams' Octoberfest?') to achieve this distribution. You may trade cards within or among groups, in addition to 'logrolling' and rhetorical (appeals to logic; appeals to morality; appeals to popularity) negotiation.

It is possible for a group to take the quiz grades and then effectively disengage from the constitutional convention, with only the internal group politics of the extra quiz bonus card to handle. Your professor reserves the right to reduce the value of the quiz cards, if a group is not participating.

Cogent, articulate discussion favoring or against a given addition or change can be rewarded with Extra Credit Cards, though sparingly. Dr. Hamner will have some cards with a face value of one point on the final exam. These cards, too, are tradable and indivisible.

5. The Gotcha

If you cannot form a constitution you can all agree upon by the end of the last class period allotted to creating a unified constitution, all groups lose one letter grade on their projects. I am not joking. It's impressive how motivating it can be, but also, an unwillingness to compromise is not the hallmark of a well-played negotiation.

I would not expect a group to hold the grades hostage (think: suicide bomber), but a group whose members are confident enough that they can earn a final class grade that they want—with a maximum of a 'B' on the project—would be impressive negotiators indeed.

6. How We Will Work Together

For ease of reference, we will refer to the new, synthesized/agreed-upon constitution as 'the Class Constitution' and we will order the articles, as much as practicable, according to the 'old' U.S. Constitution. You all more or less stuck to that format anyway.

The new constitution starts as a nearly blank sheet of paper, with only placeholders for the articles, tentatively set along the same lines as the U.S. Constitution, for ease of use. In other words, Article III will deal with the court system, and Article I will deal with the legislature. Any article beyond Article VII (modification of the constitution) will be set up in the order in which the request to add such an article was received. You're free to argue about the Preamble, too. The Bill of Rights, originally an add-on, may be integrated into the constitution or not, at your discretion.

- The groups may decide, up front, how much of a majority they want to have as a requirement for successful inclusion into the constitution. How much veto power should any one or two groups have?
- Each group is to appoint one delegate per section. The speaker may be the same for all sections or may change per floor issue depending on expertise, etc.
- Each group is allotted one vote per issue with the criteria for each vote being determined within the group (i.e. unanimity, majority, plurality) and set forth by the delegate in the convention. (Abstention is permitted but frowned upon in terms of grading.)
- Each article/section of the constitution will be proposed by the first group to volunteer, the motion must then be seconded by a different group and the issue will then be on the floor for debate.

- If the motion is carried by the majority of groups that you have requested, the section will be included without debate or a floor vote.
- At the end of debate (one pro argument and one con argument, or as dictated by the moderator), the section will be put to a class vote with each delegate casting yay or nay, as dictated by the group, for the proposed section.
- Five yay votes, by group, for a section constitutes a supermajority and the section will be included in the class constitution (hence the value of coalitions).
- Once an issue has been approved for inclusion, it may not be retracted. Amendments may later change the articles, but only after the constitution is otherwise complete.
- The constitutional convention will be closed when the delegation is satisfied with the class constitution (it behooves your group to have a secretary or note taker of some kind), and all issues as dictated by Dr. Hamner's outline have been addressed.
- Private requests may be brought, written on a slip of paper, to the referee's table at any time once the convention is convened.

7. How We Will Behave

While we will not adhere to *Robert's Rules, Mason's Manual* or Westminster Rules, you will display decorum and politeness. You will wait your turn to speak. You will treat everyone as a respected colleague. While snark and sarcasm may be permissible at some points in the discussion, you should limit their use and focus instead on cogent, clean, concise arguments for or against a given proposal.

Dr. Hamner will act as referee and traffic cop for the discussion. Two or three 50-minute classes is hardly enough time to treat all requests and proposals fairly. As such, you will do well to set up your argument quickly and not waste anyone's time. If people begin to use too much time, Dr. Hamner will cut them off.

8. You Can Set Up Rules

The class will agree to further rules the day before the convention's start. You can propose such rules as:

- Time limits for speakers—30 seconds? 2 minutes?
- Levels of agreement for inclusion in the class constitution. As noted above, must all changes be unanimous? Can 'all but one group' be enough to create a successful constitution? And: what does this decision say about minority rights in the new government?
- Other rules are encouraged.

9. Boilerplate

The moderator(s) reserve(s) the right to eject any delegate or group member for a violation of procedure or inappropriate behavior (e.g. abusive language, insults, or disruptive actions). However unlikely its use, the moderator reserves veto power over all potential legislation (as a benevolent and practical dictator).

APPENDIX 14.3: ESSAY-GRADING RUBRIC

Overall

All negotiations and plans involve tradeoffs. I'm curious what tradeoffs you made, what problems you attempted to solve and what problems you left for the fledgling government to solve. I'm curious what you think of the existing constitution, and why your group's attempt is better.

What You Included

You must, at a minimum, provide a plan for how the government is structured, how it is updated (elections, appointments, term limits, etc.), the extent of its power and how you deal with the problem of a warlike Canada and millions of slurring but mostly functional Type 2 zombie-ish humans, plus a few hundred thousand Type 1 Romero-esque (or Walking Dead-type) flesh-eating zombies, despite still being 'alive' and 'human'.

You must explain how you structured the lawmaking body/-ies, the judicial system and the executive branch, if you planned to provide one. It would be smart to include a discussion of citizen's rights, civil liberties, and how your group considers what the role and limits of government should be.

What You Left Out

The U.S. Constitution is flexible, but even it is flummoxed by certain topics. Sometimes a lack of detail is not an omission but an understanding that times change and the world keeps developing new problems that must be addressed by lawmaking, bureaucracy and other governmental action.

Some issues are so divisive at present that it might be wise, if a bit cowardly, to leave them for the new government to handle. If you choose to omit highly significant chunks of the government's structure or mission from your constitution, you must justify those choices. Leaving things out is not appropriate for many components of your project and will affect your grade if I perceive it to be evidence of your lack of effort.

What Issues Got the Most Attention

Civil rights? National defense? Care for the poor or elderly? Taxation? Term limits? There are plenty of complaints about our existing constitution. On what topics did you spend the most time wrangling with the problem of designing a government? What topics were the most divisive? Did you strategically leave issues for the newly constituted government to handle?

Table 14A.1 *Grading rubric*

Rubric for Constitution paper
Each description is *additional* to the previous column(s)

	Acceptable	Exemplary
Writing style	No spelling errors; standard English; no colloquialisms; subject-verb agreement. 3 sentences or more per paragraph. Few "passive" verbs. No flowerly language. Objective, detached tone. Limited use of "I".	Direct, condensed writing; proper but limited use of subject-specific jargon; sentences connect easily. 1 paragraph per idea. Paragraphs blend nicely (lead) into each other.
Introduction Structure	Overview of primary issues your group faced. How you ordered the Articles and themes.	Reasoning behind the ordering (emphasis or importance goes first? Most basic tenets go first?).
Civil Rights	Basic rights as a American.	Expansion & flexibility of rights.
Civil Liberties	Basic liberties as an American.	Limits of civil liberties; limits of government interference; plan for questions you haven't seen yet.
Executive	Outline the duties & powers of the Executive branch.	How the executive integrates and separates from the rest of the government.
Legislative	Composition of house(s) of the legislature; election frequency and rules how laws are passed.	Checks & balances; links to the bureaucracy; lobbying rules, if any.
Judiciary	Legal system basics; appellate courts hierarchy.	Capital punishment at the national level? Civil & criminal trial rights; Constitutional questions & judicial review.

APPENDIX 14.4: TEACHING ASSISTANT RUBRIC

Table 14A.2 Teaching assistant rubric—total across all 5 categories = 75

Points	5	10	15
Format	Constitution contains few of the required elements, or elements are largely incomplete.	Constitution contains most elements, though some may be missing or incomplete.	Constitution contains all required elements, including conflict-resolution mechanisms, protections for basic rights and structures of governments.
Knowledge	Draft constitution is unclear and/or is unrelated to whether the constitution should be passed regionally or nationally. Text is vague and poorly organized. Demonstrates minimal background knowledge of issues.	Draft constitution is clear and is related to the constitution's passage at the regional or national level. Text may be unclear or poorly organized. Demonstrates basic background knowledge of issues.	Draft constitution is clear and is related to the constitution's purpose and the goal of passage at the regional or national level. All text is organized and concise. Demonstrates extensive background knowledge issues.
Culture	Political culture of the assigned regions is inconsistent with the structure of the constitution submitted by team.	Some confusion about political culture of the assigned regions. Structure of the constitution does not demonstrate clear understanding of the region's political culture.	Political culture of the assigned region is consistent with the structure of the constitution.
Effectiveness	Constitution demonstrates superficial understanding of issues post apocalypse. It proposes a solution that is ineffective, unrealistic and/or offensive.	Constitution demonstrates a moderate level of understanding of issues post apocalypse. Constitution is an effective resolution.	Constitution demonstrates thoughtful analysis of post-apocalypse issues and is an effective resolution.
Research	Research about issues, reading the U.S. Constitution or thinking about government structures are absent or incomplete.	Research about issues, reading the U.S. Constitution or thinking about government structures are present but need further development.	Research about issues, reading the U.S. Constitution or thinking about government structures are thoroughly analyzed and developed.

Table 14A.3 Peer (student) rubric—total across all 5 categories = 25

Participation	Effort	Preparation	Knowledge of the issues	Presentation
Was the person on time and did s/he pay attention? Did they work in the group (either online or in-class)?	Did the person make an effort to find and understand the materials? Did they seek help when they were unable to understand materials? Did the person read the instructions?	Did they come to class/simulation understanding the assignment? Did they bring the materials they needed to do the project?	How well did the person understand the issues s/he was assigned? Did they seek help when they were unable to understand specific issues? How well did the person demonstrate a comprehensive understanding of the concepts involved?	Did the person do an adequate job presenting their verbal points? Did the person's arguments/questions make sense?

Note: On a scale of 1–5 for each category.

15. Teaching conflict and conflict resolution
Agnieszka Paczynska

THE CHALLENGES OF TEACHING ABOUT CONFLICT AND CONFLICT RESOLUTION

Conflict is a central feature of the human experience. Conflict can be defined as a difference or incompatibility of interests and goals or a perception that such a divergence exists. It can also be defined as a struggle for power or over allocation of resources. Conflict can result from changes in the environment or the institutional context that alters the status quo. Conflict can be interpersonal or communal. It can unfold between social groups, between and within states, and between states and non-state actors. How it manifests is equally varied and spans the gamut from verbal altercations like those that take place on a daily basis in the U.S. Congress, to mass demonstrations and clashes with police, such as those that took place in Gazi Park in Istanbul during spring 2013, to the violence that has engulfed many northern Mexican cities where drug cartels fight for control of this lucrative business, to the war in the Democratic Republic of Congo and the U.S.-led war in Afghanistan.

How an instructor decides to teach about conflict and conflict resolution depends in the first place on the course he or she is teaching. However, despite the variety of conflicts that human societies experience and the fact that teaching about conflicts will differ, often significantly, depending on whether the instructor is teaching a course on international relations, comparative politics, American politics or political theory, there are a number of challenges that all instructors face in teaching this subject. Two related challenges in particular are important to recognize and include in any course on conflict and conflict resolution. First, conflicts, even those that at first glance appear to be relatively simple, are in fact complex, multidimensional and play a variety of roles in social dynamics. For instance, often there are many parties to a conflict, each with different interests and objectives, pursuing different strategies and employing different tactics. Moreover, these interests, objectives, strategies and tactics can evolve significantly over time, just like the relationships among parties to a conflict can shift over its duration. Likewise, although particular grievances may have fueled the conflict initially, those grievances themselves can change considerably as a consequence of the conflict dynamics. Even interpersonal conflicts are embedded within a broader social, political, economic and cultural context. Second, understanding conflict dynamics and processes of conflict resolution requires drawing on multiple disciplines and reaching beyond political science theories. Insights from psychology, sociology, anthropology or communication studies prove to be essential in teaching students about conflict and conflict resolution. These challenges of teaching conflict and conflict resolution mean that active learning approaches are especially useful pedagogical tools for the instructor. This chapter will therefore discuss a variety of ways in which such active learning approaches can be brought into the classroom.

WHERE TO BEGIN?

Most students begin their study of conflict with implicit models of conflict already in mind. Most, when asked to say what comes to mind when thinking about conflict, will tend to identify its negative, destructive and violent features. Therefore, it is useful to begin by asking students more questions about the nature of conflict that allow them, on their own, to realize that their initial ideas about it did not in fact reflect the more nuanced views about conflict they have already developed based on their own life experiences. For instance: How do you view conflict: As a battle to be won? A problem to be solved? As a danger? As an opportunity? As something that depends on the context? As instructors, we should provide students with the opportunity to realize that conflicts are complex, multidimensional, and can play both a positive and a negative role in society.

This allows for the discussion to shift toward exploring the ways in which conflict can nourish social change, stimulate innovation, facilitate reconciliation, lead to better decision making and foster group solidarity, as well as the potentially devastating consequences of conflicts, including psychological trauma, negative health consequences, fracturing of social bonds, injury and death, as well as material destruction. Asking students to name particular examples of conflicts provides an opportunity for the instructor to explore with students the multidimensional nature of conflict. Depending on his or her area of expertise, the instructor can ask students to explore, for instance, the Civil Rights Movement in the United States, the Solidarity movement in Poland or the Arab Uprisings and what role these large-scale social conflicts played in their respective societies (Paczynska 2012). By drawing on examples of conflict in Darfur or Afghanistan, for instance, the students can be introduced to conflict dynamics in situations in which there are multiple parties to a conflict and in which those parties pursue strategies with an eye toward multiple audiences and constituencies. Likewise, when shifting toward discussions of conflict resolution processes, instructors also need to help students understand that the complexity of conflicts means that there are often no simple, easy solutions and that there are no conflict resolution formulas that can be readily applied across cases. The experiential learning exercises discussed later in this chapter will illustrate how an instructor can facilitate student learning about complexity.

Drawing on contemporary conflicts can be especially effective in helping students understand the complexity of conflicts, the multiple dimensions at which they play out and the challenges of effective conflict resolution. Many undergraduate students, even those majoring in political science, do not consistently follow the news. By referencing conflicts that are unfolding during the semester, the instructor can ask students to track particular conflicts in newspapers and other sources of information and reference these conflicts when teaching about particular theoretical concepts.

In spring 2013, for instance, in a course I was teaching, the first few sessions were devoted to humanitarian intervention and the responsibility to protect. As it happened, just as the semester was starting, the conflict in Mali erupted and was followed by an international military intervention. This provided an excellent opportunity for students to explore questions such as: Who decides whether another state has proven unable to exercise its sovereignty responsibly? What is the threshold of a population experiencing serious harm that the state is unable or unwilling to stop or prevent that triggers an intervention? Who intervenes and with what mandate?

Such contemporary examples also allow students to explore who the parties to a conflict are, the different levels of parties' involvement in a conflict, and the different needs and interests of these parties. Following contemporary conflicts over the semester, for instance the civil war in Syria, can also provide students with the opportunity to analyze the shifting relationships between parties to a conflict, the entrance of new actors into a conflict context and often the evolving engagement of the international community.

Drawing on personal experiences of conflict can introduce students to the different ways individuals respond to tense, contentious situations. Drawing on insights from social psychology, for example, instructors can guide students through an exploration of individual conflict styles, the typical strategies and tactics that emerge in interpersonal conflicts, and how different cultural, social and political settings shape and influence these responses to conflict. For example, conflict strategies that are common across cases are yielding, contending, avoiding and problem solving (Pruitt and Kim 2004). Students can then explore how these individual-level responses affect conflict dynamics at the community as well as international level. An effective way of allowing students to make these linkages is through active learning methods.

WHY ACTIVE LEARNING?

As Levintova et al. point out, 'research on political engagement and participation as well as scholarship on educational outcomes of general education courses converge on one point: active learning exercises, real-world problem-solving exercises and simulations' are effective pedagogical tools; 'active learning can help students care about subject matter, can develop deeper learning and other essential skills' (2011, p. 247). Extant literature largely demonstrates that active learning has a positive impact on student learning, engagement and interest in the subject being taught. The research my colleagues at George Mason University and I have undertaken over three and a half years as part of the Undergraduate Experiential Learning Project (UELP) indicates that experiential learning activities help students grasp material better, allow them to more effectively apply theories in practice and develop their sense of empathy.[1]

Active learning approaches lend themselves especially well to teaching about conflict and conflict resolution. In order for students to grasp the complexity of conflicts, their multidimensional nature and the challenges involved in conflict resolution, 'the most effective way of accomplishing these goals, is the use of active and engaged teaching methods, including case studies, simulations, role plays, games, virtual history and service learning' (Paczynska 2012, p. 524). Experiential learning approaches facilitate deepening students' engagement with the material and they provide an opportunity for students to more easily grasp complex theories as well as to connect how theoretical and conceptual frameworks can be applied in practice. Students learning about conflict and conflict resolution can greatly benefit from this type of pedagogical approach. It not only helps them grasp difficult theoretical concepts, but it also provides them with the opportunity to experience the complexity of conflicts first hand. Additionally, it helps them not only to appreciate the intellectual challenges of analyzing conflicts but to experience their emotional aspects as well.

At the same time, however, before moving forward with utilizing different types of experiential learning activities, instructors should first evaluate what their learning objectives are in a particular class meeting and then decide whether an active learning approach will be an effective way to accomplish those objectives – and if so, what kind of active learning activity they should choose. Here I will briefly discuss a number of exercises my colleagues and I have developed and extensively tested as part of the UELP.

ACTIVE LEARNING IN THE CLASSROOM

For many instructors, moving away from a lecture format can seem daunting. Many have never experienced active learning as students and are at a loss as to how to incorporate such techniques into their own classrooms. Designing role-plays and simulations appears especially time consuming and, often, quite mysterious. It is therefore important to be aware of the many resources available publicly that can help instructors in developing their own experiential learning exercises and in providing ready-made models of particular exercises. Journals such as *Journal of Political Science Education*, *Simulations and Gaming* and *Journal of Peace Education* feature articles that explore how to teach about conflict. Other journals, such as *PS: Political Science & Politics*, *International Studies Perspectives* and *Conflict Resolution Quarterly* also regularly feature articles that discuss active learning approaches. Since 2012, the American Political Science Association (APSA)'s Teaching and Learning Conference has added a new track, Conflict and Conflict Resolution. Papers from this track, available through the APSA website, are another useful source of ideas. There are also ready-made simulations that are available publicly, for instance at the websites of the United States Institute of Peace and the George Mason University School for Conflict Analysis and Resolution's UELP. At the same time, while some experiential learning activities are complex, require multiple class meetings and take time to develop, other active learning activities can be both shorter and simpler to develop and implement. Glazier, for instance, recommends running what she refers to as low-intensity simulations, which require less preparation by the instructor and use less technology than more elaborate simulations (Glazier 2011).

In addition to role-plays and simulations, examples of which will be discussed later in this chapter, there are other types of active learning exercises that can be effectively utilized when teaching about conflict and conflict resolution. Some can be done during class meetings. Others can involve activities outside of the classroom. The latter category can be an especially useful way to expose students to real-world conflict dynamics. Here instructors can utilize whatever their particular community has to offer and draw on current events, whether international, national or local. For instance, students can be asked to attend a city council or town hall meeting on a contentious local issue, to attend a demonstration or a protest (such as the ones that were staged across many American cities following the non-guilty verdict in the Zimmerman murder trial) or to listen to a lecture whether at the college or in the community. Following the event, students write an analysis of the conflict they observed and discuss how the theories they had studied in the classroom helped them better understand these social dynamics.

Group projects in which students are asked to analyze a particular conflict, a particular party to a conflict or a conflict resolution intervention and then present the findings to the whole class are also an effective means to develop students' critical and analytical thinking skills, oral presentation skills as well as how to work in groups. Although instructors are sometimes distressed by conflicts that can emerge among students during group work, such tensions can also be an opportunity for students to draw on the theories they study in class to whatever problems develop in a group. Instructors can encourage and support students as they act as facilitators in resolving their own conflicts.

USING FILMS

When introducing undergraduate students to such conflict topics as the diffusion of social movements, uprisings, civil wars as well as post-conflict reconstruction and peace-building, showing short video clips or documentaries can be a very useful teaching tool since it brings into the classroom what often is a very alien reality. For instance, short documentaries like *The Wajir Story*, which depicts grassroots peacebuilding efforts in the Wajir District in Kenya, are an effective way to begin discussions of what reconciliation following a conflict entails and the role of local efforts and outside third-party mediators and facilitators in conflict resolution. Other documentaries, such as *Goodbye Mubarak*, which depicts social mobilization by various opposition actors in Egypt in the year leading up the January 2011 revolution, can serve as a starting point for discussion of how grievances are translated into collective action; the role of fear in constraining and/or facilitating collective action; how collective action problems can be overcome; how people who feel powerless become empowered; and what strategies work more and less effectively in organizing collective action. The wide variety of available documentaries allows the instructor to tailor the specific film to the learning objectives of the course.

In addition to documentaries, using films can be an effective way for students to explore complex conflict dynamics. In my classes, for instance, I have used the film *Matewan* on a regular basis. This 1987 drama depicts coal miners' strikes that took place in 1920 in a West Virginia town. Because the conflict involves multiple parties, including the coal mining company, the white striking miners, African–American and Italian immigrants who are brought in by the company as replacement workers but who later join forces with the white miners, as well as union organizers from outside the community, it provides students with the opportunity to observe dynamics of conflict escalation and de-escalation, the formation and shifting of conflict groups, as well as the root causes of conflict.

After watching the film, each student was asked to write a paper that analyzed the conflict, using the following questions as a guide: What were the main issues at stake in the conflict? Did the nature of the issues change over time – and if so, why? Who were the parties? What were the relationships among the parties? How was power distributed among the parties? Did the relationship among the parties change over the course of the conflict – and if so, how? What was the context in which the conflict unfolded? What conflict regulating mechanisms (institutions, norms) exist and how did they influence the course of the conflict? What conditions led to the formation of conflict groups? What strategies and tactics were pursued? What were the conflict dynamics? Did the conflict escalate, reach a stalemate or de-escalate at given points – and if so, why? Were there any types of interventions tried – and if so, what types? Were important third parties involved – and if so, what was their impact? What was the outcome of the conflict? Did one party lose and one party win? Did the outcome serve as the basis for another conflict or for sustainable reconciliation between the parties?

Alternatively, students can be provided these questions in class, divided into small groups of about six students each and asked to jointly write down responses to these questions. Once these responses are completed, each group presents their conclusions to the class.

With more advanced students, the analysis of a film and application of theory to the analysis can be expanded. For instance, students can first be introduced to different analytical models for examining conflicts, each emphasizing a different aspect of conflict. Because these models can be quite complex, students often have difficulty in applying these models to actual conflict situations. One way to facilitate this learning is to show students a film and provide them with questions they can consider while viewing the film that push them to think about who the parties to conflict are, the tactics they are using and the conflict dynamics that unfold. Following the screening, students work in groups and apply one of the conflict models they were introduced to earlier to the conflict they saw in the film. After each group presents their findings to the class, everyone is able to jointly explore the differences among the analytic models and the consequences of using different models for how the conflict is understood (Finley, Hirsch and Nalbo 2013). Students are often surprised by how the application of different models generates different perspectives and understandings of the same conflict.

Using films and video clips can be especially useful in large courses where the number of students makes it challenging to run role-plays or simulations. Furthermore, even in a large class, students can be divided into smaller groups and asked to discuss these issues together and then have each group report back to the whole class the key points that emerged from these discussions. This is useful for students who might be reluctant to speak up in a large lecture setting, while such joint discussion encourages them to develop critical thinking skills.

EXAMPLES OF ROLE-PLAYS AND SIMULATIONS

Role-plays and simulations are an effective way to teach students about the complexity of conflict and conflict resolution. Although the two terms are often used interchangeably, simulations tend to place students in familiar or realistic situations and do not necessarily ask them to take on a role of a particular person. On the other hand, in role-plays students are asked to take on a particular role and are provided with information about that person's identity, thoughts, interests and sometimes feelings as well as the context in which the conflict they will be role-playing unfolds. Role-plays are especially effective pedagogical tools for giving students a sense of the many complex and sometimes contradictory emotions of people involved in a conflict.

However, it is important for instructors to remember that different exercises will achieve different learning objectives and it is therefore essential to match appropriately the exercise used in the classroom with the goals that the instructor hopes to achieve. At the same time, it is important to remember that some role-plays can be very simple while others are quite complex. Likewise, simulations vary greatly. Some can be done during one class meeting, while others require multiple sessions and extensive student preparation. Simulations and role-plays can be an effective tool in teaching students about negotiations, strategic decision making, appreciating multiple perspectives and interests in conflict situations, the complex emotions that conflicts generate among participants, and the difficulties involved in making potentially life-and-death decisions when information is incomplete and/or ambiguous.

Running role-plays and simulations can be challenging for those teaching large survey courses or when the curriculum does not make it possible to run an exercise over multiple sessions. However, there are ways of addressing these challenges. One is to conduct the exercise virtually, outside of the classroom (Bridge and Radford 2013). As more and more universities are shifting toward online courses, the platforms that are available to instructors to run simulations virtually become more readily available. Second, it is possible to divide large classes into smaller groups of students, with each group doing the same simulation or role-play at the same time. Third, many simulations can be low intensity and possible to implement in one class meeting (Glazier 2011).

As part of the UELP project, a team of faculty and graduate students at the School for Conflict Analysis and Resolution, George Mason University has developed a variety of simulations and role-plays. Each one is designed to achieve particular learning objectives. For instance, *Can We Drink the Water? Simulating Conflict Dynamics in an Appalachian Mining Community* aims, through a simulation of a community meeting 'held in response to the discovery of contaminated water in an elementary school', to give students first-hand experience of the intractable nature of a conflict and of working to address even one dimension of a conflict; and to gain awareness of interpersonal and group dynamics of a contentious group meeting (Hirsch, Cerasani and Romano 2013).

Another, very different simulation, *Adding Fuel to the Fire: Energy Resources and International Negotiation in the Eastern Mediterranean* is a multi-session international negotiation simulation exercise, set up as a United Nations summit that seeks to prevent the eruption of an interstate conflict over the control of gas and oil resources discovered in the Eastern Mediterranean. This exercise 'aims to provide students with an opportunity to enhance their understanding of the complex dynamics of conflict, negotiations at the interstate, regional and international levels and the roles of identity, interests and international law as potential drivers of escalation or resolution' (Lazarus, Mescioglu-Gur and Gatsias 2013).

Here I will focus in particular on two exercises that I developed and that have been extensively tested in the classroom as part of the UELP: *Community at Odds in Voinjama, Liberia: An Introduction to Conflict Mapping* and *Community at Odds in Voinjama, Liberia: An Introduction to Conflict Intervention*. These two experiential learning activities can either be done together or run as stand-alone exercises. The first allows students to explore the complexities of doing even a very rudimentary conflict analysis or conflict mapping. The second provides students with the opportunity to think about the processes of designing conflict resolution intervention strategies. Both exercises are set in the Liberian city of Voinjama, Lofa County, shortly after deadly clashes in February 2010 strained community relations and destroyed some of the city's infrastructure. The first exercise, in particular, draws on an actual experience of a conflict assessment team that conducted interviews in Voinjama, Liberia in spring 2010.

Both exercises' learning goals include facilitating students' ability to link theory with practice. As a recent report has argued, many employers find that students graduating from undergraduate programs often have difficulty in applying theoretical concepts in real-life situations (Zelizer and Johnston 2005). For students interested in conflict and conflict resolution, developing these analytical and critical learning skills is essential.

Conflict analysis has now become a standard component of intervention and program planning for government donors, international organizations, international NGOs, as well as local NGOs and organizations. The conflict assessment frameworks employed by these actors differ somewhat from one another because of the different objectives, goals and positions vis-à-vis the communities in which assessments are conducted. They all, however, share the principle that designing an effective intervention is predicated on a good understanding of conflict dynamics. There is a general consensus within the development, humanitarian assistance and peacebuilding communities that, in order to design and implement an effective intervention, it is essential to have a good understanding of the context and to diagnose the conflict dynamics as accurately as possible. Any intervention, whether explicitly aimed at conflict transformation or not, affects social dynamics and therefore may contribute either to deepening tensions within a community or to reducing these tensions. In other words, what is essential in analyzing conflict dynamics is the recognition that conflicts are multidimensional and complex, and therefore no single cause can be found that explains what either puts a society at a greater risk of experiencing violent conflict or understanding why violent conflict had occurred. Conflict sensitive programming has now become the standard approach to intervention.

When conducting conflict assessments, as in other qualitative research, researchers often commit a number of sampling biases. One is omission bias. Here the researcher does not interview a particular group of people – for instance, an ethnic minority. In this case, a particular set of views and perceptions might be omitted from analysis. The other is inclusive bias. Here the sample is chosen based on convenience. For instance, in a particular locale, men dominate in the public sphere and interviews are therefore conducted only with men, omitting the views of women in the community. The problem arises if the data collected from the men are then extrapolated to represent the views of the entire community. However, gathering data, understanding the multiple perspectives of those involved in and affected by conflict, and assessing and evaluating data can be challenging. The *Community at Odds in Voinjama, Liberia: An Introduction to Conflict Mapping* exercise allows students to experience first hand the challenges in conducting a conflict assessment as well as the potential biases in data collection and analysis that researchers in the field often encounter.

In this exercise, students are divided into four groups and are asked to conduct a basic conflict assessment in the town of Voinjama, Liberia. Each group receives a packet of information that includes newspaper accounts of what happened in Voinjama, interviews with different town residents, as well as maps of the area and photographs of the town. Students were asked to develop a very basic conflict assessment and answer the following questions: 1) Who were the parties to the conflict? 2) What were the parties' interests? 3) What were the parties' grievances? 4) What were the trigger events? 5) What were the root causes of the conflict?

The students are not aware that each group is given slightly different information as a basis for conducting their conflict assessment. In addition to one newspaper account that favors a particular explanation of the conflict, each group receives a different set of interviews. The first has mostly interviews with religious leaders in the town; the second has interviews primarily with tribal elders; the third has interviews primarily with security personnel (UN peacekeepers, police); the fourth has interviews with various local government officials and civic leaders. All groups share some interviews, for instance, with market women. In other words, each group receives information that pushes them toward a particular analysis of the conflict. Consequently, the groups present analysis that argues that the conflict was between religious communities (Christian, Muslim); that it was an ethnic conflict (Loma, Mandingo); that it was caused by disgruntled former combatants who remain largely unemployed and are looking for a fight; and finally that it occurred between those who wield political and economic power in the community and those who are marginalized.

Once each group completes its map and presents its analysis to the class, differences in each group's assessments become apparent. The realization that each group has produced a very different map of the conflict is disconcerting for the students and pushes them to ask questions about and reflect on the process of data collection and analysis. During the discussion that follows group presentations, the students explore the complexity of conflict, the process of data gathering and evaluation, and how the data gathered shapes the assessment of a conflict. This first-hand experience shows students how incomplete and insufficient information can push an analyst toward making assumptions about a particular conflict that are, in fact, wrong. With the instructor's encouragement, the students explore the processes of data collection and analysis by asking questions such as: How did you evaluate the information? How did you assess the importance of the information provided in the newspaper accounts and/or the interviewees' statements? Did you discard any information – and if so, why? Did you think you had sufficient information to map the conflict? If not, why did you think there were gaps in your knowledge? What kind of gaps did you identify? What kind of information would you need to collect to fill in these knowledge gaps? If you had sufficient information, what made you confident that you did? How did the information you had shape the map that your group produced? How might your map shape your analysis of the conflict or your decision about how to intervene to promote conflict transformation? Now that you have seen every group's map, what do you think about the process of gathering information needed to map a conflict (Paczynska 2013)?

The exercise also helps students to recognize that often there is not one view of a particular conflict and that different actors, whether those directly involved in a conflict or those who are affected by the conflict, often have very different understandings of what triggered the conflict, what the causes of the conflict were and even who are the parties to the conflict. These differences in perceptions are shaped by people's position vis-à-vis the conflict, their personal histories, experiences and background as well as their own biases and interests. Students are able to recognize how the process of collecting data can significantly affect our understanding of a conflict and lead to developing an inaccurate conflict assessment or a conflict map. It also highlights the importance of including as many different perspectives as possible during the process of data collection to ensure that vital voices and perspectives are not ignored in preparing the conflict analysis while at the same time making students aware that the data collected are never perfect or comprehensive. It provides them with the opportunity to, on their own, arrive at the conclusion that conflicts are multidimensional and complex, and therefore the causes of any conflict are likely to be varied and impossible to reduce to a single variable. This alerts them to the challenges that those seeking to intervene in a conflict with the goal of facilitating its resolution face a difficult terrain.

A companion experiential learning activity, *Community at Odds in Voinjama, Liberia: An Introduction to Conflict Intervention* picks up where the first one leaves off and asks students to step into the role of one of four organizations tasked with developing intervention strategies to facilitate conflict resolution in the town of Voinjama following the February 2010 clashes. This exercise can be done following the completion of the conflict mapping exercise or it can be done as a stand-alone activity. If done as a stand-alone activity, students should be provided with a conflict assessment document that reflects the complexity of the social, political and economic dynamics in Voinjama. During this exercise, students are again divided into four groups. Each group is assigned the role of a particular group. The four groups are an international conflict resolution NGO, an international service oriented organization focusing primarily on education and health issues, a local Lofa County Interfaith Council and a national Liberian National Commission on Human Rights and Reconciliation.

Along with their group assignment, each student also receives a description of the organization they will be representing. While all four are fictitious organizations, all are based on existing entities. The international conflict resolution NGO, for instance, is modeled on the NGO Search for Common Ground, while the international service organization is modeled on the Peace Corps. Initially, I piloted the exercises using real organizations. However, I found that this presented some challenges. Because students receive their group assignments and group descriptions prior to class so that they have time to think about the role they will be playing, they inevitably attempted to research their organizations on the Internet. However, although students who were assigned the role of the Search for Common Ground or the Peace Corps were able to readily find these organizations' websites, those assigned the Lofa County Interfaith Council were not since this was a fairly informal group lacking access to technology and with no web presence.

These differences in students' ability to access additional information created tensions within the classroom as some students felt they were at a disadvantage due to their particular group assignment. These are common tradeoffs when designing experiential learning activities: To what extent is the exercise based on 'real' events? To what extent is the exercise based on stylized facts? To what extent does the exercise simplify what is inevitably a complex social, political and economic reality? Depending on the learning objectives of a particular activity, the answers to these questions are likely to differ.

Once the students were assigned the role of a particular organization, they were asked to think about a number of related questions concerning the process of designing an intervention with the goal of addressing the causes of conflict. Some of the key objectives of this exercise are for students to better understand how to link the diagnosis of conflict dynamics with intervention strategies; consider how third-party goals for intervention align, or not, with local community goals and explore the ethical implications of such interventions; think about the possible collaborations and tensions that arise when a variety of third-party actors, often with very different mandates, interests and resources, intervene in the same environment; and learn to recognize the realistic parameters of an intervention. Many students interested in studying conflict resolution tend to be idealistic and want to step in and solve all problems that lead to the conflict. This exercise helps them think through the limits of what it is that they can and cannot do.

As in the conflict mapping exercise, students are pushed to consider the complexity of the environment in which they are trying to intervene, exploring how different groups' positions vis-à-vis the conflict (international versus community based, for instance) shape intervention strategies and how these interventions might be viewed by the community, as well as the limits of what a third-party intervention can and cannot achieve. The exercise also raises questions that are central to conflict sensitive humanitarian, development and conflict resolution programming. Most importantly, it asks students to consider: How do you ensure that the intervention that you are designing does not make the conflict worse rather than facilitating its resolution? What kind of ground knowledge would you need to design an effective intervention? How would you go about ensuring that what the community wanted and saw as desirable was what you provided? How would you determine what outcomes parties want from the intervention? And finally, what are the ethical implications of third-party intervention?

In courses that focus on development assistance and post-conflict reconstruction, this type of exercise also provides the instructor with the opportunity to encourage students to think about how third-party interventions interact with the ideas about the need for local ownership of projects, and local input into decisions about activities that affect the community. Although much of the recent literature notes the importance of local participation, this idea has proven to be difficult to implement in practice and those on the receiving end of international aid often feel very disenfranchised and disillusioned by how external assistance is provided even while remaining appreciative that the world cares enough to provide that assistance in the first place (Anderson, Brown and Jean 2012).

CONCLUSION

Teaching about conflict and conflict resolution presents particular challenges, especially conveying to students the complex and multidimensional nature of conflicts. Many of the conflicts students are likely to encounter in political science and international relations courses, such as wars, civil wars or revolutions, can seem very alien from their everyday lives. On the other hand, the omnipresence of conflicts in all societies means that students can draw on their own life experiences when introduced to the subject in class. Instructors can further help students better understand conflict analysis and resolution by drawing on contemporary conflicts, whether those that are unfolding in their own communities, nationally or internationally, and relying on active learning approaches to facilitate students' understanding of the complexity of conflict dynamics.

NOTE

1. The Undergraduate Experiential Learning Project has been made possible by the Fund for Improvement of Post-Secondary Education (FIPSE) grant from the U.S. Department of Education. All exercises discussed here are available on the project's website at http://scar.gmu.edu/experientiallearningproject/home.

REFERENCES

Anderson, M.B., D. Brown and I. Jean (2012), *Time to listen: Hearing people on the receiving end of international aid*, Cambridge, MA: CDA Collaborative Learning Project.

Bridge, D. and S. Radford (2013), 'Teaching diplomacy by other means: Using an outside of class simulation to teach international relations theory', paper presented at the American Political Science Association's Teaching and Learning Conference, 8–10 February, Long Beach, CA.

Finley, E., S. Hirsch and D. Nalbo (2013), 'Analyzing conflict through film: Applying analytic models', Undergraduate Experiential Learning Project, available at: http://scar.gmu.edu/experientiallearningproject/home.

Glazier, R.A. (2011), 'Running simulations without ruining your life: Simple ways to incorporate active learning into your teaching', *Journal of Political Science Education*, **7** (4), 375–93.

Hirsch, S., G. Cerasani and A. Romano (2013), 'Can we drink the water? Simulating conflict dynamics in an Appalachian mining community', Undergraduate Experiential Learning Project, available at: http://scar.gmu.edu/experientiallearningproject/home.

Lazarus, N., G. Mescioglu-Gur and T. Gatsias (2013), 'Adding fuel to the fire: Energy resources and international negotiation in the eastern Mediterranean', Undergraduate Experiential Learning Project, available at: http://scar.gmu.edu/experientiallearningproject/home.

Levintova, E., T. Johnson, D. Scheberle and K. Vonk (2011), 'Global citizens are made, not born: Multiclass role-playing simulation of global decision making', *Journal of Political Science Education*, **7** (3), 245–74.

Paczynska, A. (2013), 'Community at odds in Voinjama, Liberia: An introduction to conflict mapping', Undergraduate Experiential Learning Project, available at: http://scar.gmu.edu/experientiallearningproject/home.

Paczynska, A. (2012), 'Conflict and conflict resolution track summary', *PS: Political Science & Politics*, **45** (3), 524–6.

Pruitt, D.G. and S.H. Kim (2004), *Social conflict: Escalation, stalemate, and settlement*, third edition, New York: McGraw-Hill.

Zelizer, C. and L. Johnston (2005), *Skills, networks and knowledge: Developing a career in international peace and conflict resolution*, Washington, DC: Alliance for Peacebuilding.

16. Teaching about diversity issues
Boris E. Ricks

INTRODUCTION

The increasing demographic diversity in the U.S. population begun in the past century continues into this century. Projections based on the 2010 Census indicate that the U.S.A. will soon become a plurality nation where no one single group represents a majority. As America becomes more racially and ethnically diverse, millennials[1] will command a broader awareness and deeper understanding of diversity, global significance and cross-cultural perspectives. The nation's minority population is steadily rising and now makes up roughly 40 percent of the United States, advancing an unmistakable trend that could make minorities the new American majority by midcentury. In the decades to come, students from diverse backgrounds will constitute a substantial portion of higher education coeds.

These demographic shifts present both perils and prospects for college and university faculty in general and political science faculty in particular. Should the discipline and/or those who study political science take the lead in teaching, fostering and infusing diversity? The political science curriculum, which ignores, oversimplifies and/or marginalizes the experiences of those who are an integral part of society, not only undervalues but constitutes a disservice to higher education and the discipline in general.

The purpose of this chapter is to discuss the importance and significance of expanding and enhancing political science education to be more inclusive of diverse pedagogical approaches, curricula, textbooks, instruction and various identities. Diversity[2] infusion should be at the core of teaching and learning in political science. Political science curricula, teaching and instruction are enhanced and broadened by diverse pedagogies, methods, perspectives, approaches and educational experiences. Studies indicate that diversity of thought, perspective and background enhances performance (Gurin 1999; Alger 1997; Knowles and Harleston 1997; Milem 2003; Liu 1998). This chapter seeks to address the issues and/or challenges in integrating diversity into political science education. First, we look at higher education and the rapidly changing demographics of student populations. Second, we look at diversity and what diversity means to political science teaching and learning. Third, we look at textbooks, curricula and instruction in political science education. Fourth, we look at a theoretical framework for infusing diversity into political science teaching and learning. Finally, we offer recommendations to infuse diversity into political science teaching and learning.

HIGHER EDUCATION AND STUDENT DEMOGRAPHICS

America's colleges and universities are different in many ways. Some are public, others are private, some are large urban universities, some are small rural campuses, others are two-year community colleges. Some offer graduate and professional programs, others focus primarily on undergraduate liberal arts education. One of the many challenges facing American higher education is the freedom to determine who shall teach and be taught (and to a lesser extent, what they shall be taught). Addressing this challenge has been celebrated in some places and criticized in others. As a result, some schools have experienced contraction in the hiring, retention, tenure and promotion of faculty of color; precipitous declines in the enrollment of students of color (reversing decades of progress in the effort to assure that all groups have an equal opportunity for access to higher education); resistance to diverse curricular offerings; opposition towards student-centered approaches to teaching and learning; and issues concerning campus climate.[3]

In a world preoccupied with outward appearances and organized hypocrisy, it is truly no surprise that we have experienced the demise of diversity, multicultural education and affirmative action programs within higher education in general and political science teaching and learning in particular. Recent attacks and conservative political pursuits have caused many institutions in the academy to pause and ponder just how far they are willing to go to diversify textbooks, curricula and instructional approaches. Some institutions have even eliminated outreach efforts to diversify the student body, faculty and staff, while others have become baffled as to how to proceed. Some institutions of higher learning have even challenged the curriculum and supplemental resources used by new and experienced faculty alike.

Major demographic shifts, increasing interracial tensions concerning resources and the increasing percentage of students who speak a first language other than English render 'diversity infusion' an invaluable resource in the 21st-century classroom. Radical shifts in the racial and ethnic population within the U.S.A. from 1970 to 2010 along with projections to 2050 have far-reaching consequences for political science teaching and learning. For example, in 1970, whites accounted for about 83.2 percent of the U.S. population; as of 2010, whites accounted for about 63.7 percent of the population (about a 20 percent drop). Furthermore, it is projected that, by 2040, whites will account for about 50 percent of the U.S. population. By 2050, whites will likely be a plurality at about 46.3 percent (almost a 40 percent drop since 1970). These shifts in the U.S. population are driven primarily by dramatic growth among Latinos (Hispanics). Latinos accounted for about 4.5 percent of the population in 1970; by 2010, Latinos accounted for about 16.3 percent (a growth rate of just over 360 percent).

Similarly, the Asian–American population has grown substantially since 1970, when Asians accounted for only about 0.8 percent of the U.S. population; Asians now account for about 4.8 percent of the population. Furthermore, Asians are projected to account for as much as 7.6 percent of the U.S. population in 2050. By contrast, African Americans accounted for about 11.1 percent of the nation's population in 1970 and have only grown slightly since then, to about 12.6 percent in 2010. Estimates suggest African Americans will remain relatively stable at between 11 and 12 percent through 2050. American Indians and Alaska Natives are projected to remain under 1 percent of the U.S. population through 2050.

Persons of two or more races were 1.7 percent of the national population in 2000, the first year the U.S. Census Bureau gathered these data, and this number is estimated to be as much as 3 percent in 2050. In other words, it is now projected that the United States is likely to be a country equally comprised of whites and people of color by 2040, and it is very likely to be a 'majority-minority' nation by 2050. So, what does all this mean for political science? What impact does this have upon political science teaching and learning? Are political science faculty prepared to 'infuse' their curriculum and integrate shifting demographics, growing multicultural diversity and ever-widening economic disparities into teaching and learning approaches? Political science, as a scholarly disciplinary, is well positioned to offer a conceptual framework (interdisciplinary in nature) to address race, ethnicity, gender, poverty, inequality and other issues that enhance diversity.

Therefore, one goal of political science education is to help students identify important socio-political practices, analyze extreme demographic shifts, develop cutting-edge research, embrace innovative teaching pedagogy and interpret extreme demographic shifts. The U.S. Census Bureau estimates that people of color made up about 39 percent of the nation's population in 2010 and predicts that they will make up about 49 percent in 2025 and about 60 percent in 2050. About 50 percent of the students enrolled in the nation's schools in 2010 were students of color. On the other hand, in 2003, 42 percent of white students, 32 percent of black students, and 23 percent of Latino students aged 18 to 24 years old were enrolled in college, according to the National Center for Education Statistics. Rapid demographic change and population shifts have significantly altered the current and future higher education landscape.

For example, in California, the racial and ethnic make-up of public school students looks like what public schools in the United States will look like in the very near future. In some of the nation's largest cities and metropolitan areas, such as New York, Los Angeles, Chicago, Houston, San Francisco, Washington, D.C. and Seattle, half or more of the public school students are students of color. During the 1998–1999 school year, students of color made up 67.1 percent of the student population in the public schools of California, the nation's most populous state.

DIVERSITY IN POLITICAL SCIENCE EDUCATION

The American Political Science Association (APSA), founded in 1903, is the leading professional organization for the study of political science. APSA serves more than 15,000 members in over 80 countries and brings together political scientists from all fields of inquiry, regions and occupational endeavors to expand the understanding of government and politics. Therefore, the impetus for integrating and infusing diversity within political science teaching and learning emanates from APSA and its members.

The task of diversifying curricula, instruction, textbooks and resources to reflect societal realities is underscored and supported by APSA. Yet, more association members must follow the lead of APSA and embrace one of many opportunities to infuse diversity. Political science, the study of governments, public policies and political processes, is the appropriate discipline to incorporate diversity into relevant curricula and course content. Political scientists use both humanistic and scientific perspectives as well as a variety of methodological approaches to examine processes, systems and political dynamics.

For example, the APSA Teaching and Learning Conference is a distinctive meeting in which APSA strives to promote greater understanding of diversity, cutting-edge approaches, techniques and methodologies for the political science classroom. The conference provides a forum for scholars to share effective and innovative teaching and learning models and to discuss broad themes and values of political science education. Teaching and learning about diversity in the United States is an intellectually, emotionally and politically challenging undertaking, complicated by the shortage of supportive spaces to think and talk about the -isms[4] in diverse groups. It is made even more difficult because of the racial divide in knowledge about and experience with racism (Bell 2003). For many faculty who were taught and teach from a monocultural perspective reflecting a single norm of thought and knowledge base, the prospect of a curriculum infusion or pedagogical immersion can be somewhat disturbing.

Although diversity is not new to the academy and its benefits are increasingly accepted, research (Hurtado 2001; Ofori-Dankwa and Lane 2000) has identified an imbalance with regard to institutional and faculty involvement in diversity curriculum initiatives. For the purpose of this work, diversity infusion is defined as including issues of race, ethnicity, gender, lifestyle preference and inequality (see earlier definition). The term 'curriculum' refers to the structure and/or content of courses and/or programs; the term 'instruction' refers to the methods, strategies or techniques used in teaching. While research is emerging on curriculum development, innovative pedagogy and cutting-edge scholarship, too little research has been conducted specifically on the process of diversity infusion as faculty members themselves move to makeover the curriculum.

What influences faculty to makeover their courses by infusing diversity into the curriculum (i.e., teaching and learning methods)? What are the barriers faculty face to makeover their courses? What are the consequences of this type of participation/non-participation?

TEXTBOOKS

In political science, as in other social science disciplines, there is a need to improve the textbooks used by faculty to instruct undergraduates. Political science textbooks are usually the primary resource tool used to expose students to American government and politics. However, a vast majority of political science textbooks oversimplifies and underexamines the politics surrounding the intersection(s) of race, ethnicity, gender, class and lifestyle preference in political discourse. The omission of relevant discourse undermines the roles people of color, women and other minorities played in the United States.

The politics of race, ethnicity, gender and equality require political science textbooks to be modified and/or revised to document the freedom struggles of all people. For example, African Americans, most of whom as legal citizens of this country were originally excluded from participation in the political process. In addition, the discussion of Latinos/-as is very limited in political science textbooks and often directly associated with narrow immigration discussions. The political contributions of U.S. and foreign-born Latinos is largely ignored. According to Monforti and McGlynn (2010), the discussion of Latinos in political science textbooks is incredibly brief and often limited to civil rights chapters. Furthermore, Latinos are primarily mentioned in the discussion of immigration, while their overall contribution to the political development of the United States is largely ignored.

Finally, the coverage of Asian Pacific Americans, if any, tends to be confined to the civil rights chapters, leaving many with the impression that Asian Pacific Americans played little to no role in American political discourse. The absence of people of color aside from piecemeal images underscores the need to modify and revise introductory textbooks in American government to reflect the past and present roles that people of color, women and other minorities played and continue to play in American government.

The vast majority of political science textbooks often employ an institutional or behavioral approach to teaching and learning. Unfortunately, this approach usually lacks diversity in content, context, consequence and contribution. Often, the institutional or behavioral approach examines political institutions and processes from a majority white perspective, with emphasis placed on the political actors who dominate these institutions, yet they lack the broader and deeper perspective on U.S. institutions and culture. This approach also oversimplifies the role of race, ethnicity, gender and sexual preference(s) in the adjudication of power and resource allocation. According to Wallace and Allen (2008), more research is needed to find ways to teach students how to critically examine images in textbooks, primary sources and other supplemental resources to help them develop more complex and sophisticated understandings of groups around them.

However, American government and politics textbooks must begin to address and create new frames of reference to more proactively utilize the lens of race, ethnicity and cultural competence to interpret politics. Furthermore, the conception, creation and publication of American government textbooks should not proceed without conscientious scholars for various culturally competent backgrounds. It is long overdue for publishers to publish political science textbooks that accurately depict American historical, economic and political developments.

CURRICULUM

The political science curriculum must be modified to effectively integrate diversity, globalization and inclusiveness into the coursework. It is important for students from various communities and backgrounds to see themselves reflected in the political science curriculum. Internationalizing the political science curriculum is an approach to increase cross-cultural awareness, globalization and study-abroad opportunities. The political science curriculum must better prepare undergraduates to address the demands of the global context. Internationalization often implies increased contact and exchange with other countries and institutions. With these exchanges, political science faculty must do a better job incorporating students from all backgrounds into coursework and selections.

A deeper value and appreciation for international issues, cultural competence and critical thinking should be infused into the political science curriculum. Curricular modifications inclusive of diversity issues are strongly encouraged. Political science faculty must better understand students, curricula, current events and the intersection thereof to meet the current teaching and learning demands. Diversity infusion, global perspectives and curricular modifications add nuance to pedagogical approaches, which develop an increasing awareness among all students of the world's complexity and interdependence.

It is important that political science faculty encourage a curriculum that moves students beyond their comfort zones and challenges them to see things from different perspectives. Educational technology and multimedia resources can effectively and purposefully improve students' knowledge of world news and global affairs. The urgent need for political science students to better understand the cultural, economic, social, political and environmental challenges of our time from more than one perspective is the challenge of the discipline.

INSTRUCTION

Political science instruction is rooted in the traditional approach, which has been employed by faculty for decades. The long-established reliance on lectures, tutorials and private study make up the foundation for the traditional approach to teaching political science. Although this approach has its merits, it also has its limitations. Nevertheless, there are many factors at play when discussing teaching style with political science faculty. One widely agreed-upon instructional role for political science faculty is to help students develop critical thinking and analytical reasoning skills. Critical thinking, a common theme across the social sciences, allows for students to engage with a body of knowledge, rather than being trained in a specific area.

Political science faculty also acknowledge the importance of civic engagement as an instructional approach with practical benefits. Although political science is an academic discipline geared towards professional training, there is no single career path for students of the discipline. Political science education equips students with a wide variety of transferable skill sets that are negotiable in the global marketplace.

Political science instruction varies from university to university, college to college and department to department. However, many political science departments focus instruction around student learning objectives (SLOs). These are measurable instructional goals established for a specific group of students over a set period of time. SLOs serve as one of the assessment measures for political science teaching and learning. For example, at California State University, Northridge the SLOs are as follows:

  I. **Professional Interaction and Effective Communication** – Students should demonstrate persuasive and rhetorical communication skills for strong oral and written communication in small and large groups.
 II. **Develop a Global Perspective** – Students should demonstrate knowledge and theories relevant to global politics and policies. This includes knowledge of Western and non-Western political systems, processes, values and models of politics and patterns of interaction among them. Students should demonstrate an understanding and respect for economic, socio-cultural, political and environmental interaction of global life.
III. **Active Citizenship and Civic Engagement** – Students should demonstrate a knowledge and awareness of contemporary issues, political institutions and problems in the community and their historical contexts. Students should demonstrate an understanding of the importance of community involvement and leadership.
IV. **Critical Thinking** – Students should demonstrate increasingly sophisticated skills in reading primary sources critically. Students should be able to research and evaluate the

models, methods and analyses of others in the field of Political Science, and critically integrate and evaluate others' work.
V. **Political Decision Making** – Students should demonstrate an in-depth understanding and knowledge of the political institutions through which public policies are formulated, modified and implemented.
VI. **Political Analytical Skills** – Students should demonstrate a working knowledge of research designs, hypothesis formulation, measurement of variables, data collection and analysis.

If we look closely at SLOs II and III, we find an infusion of diversity that permits faculty to focus on the critical areas discussed thus far.

The rapid growth in student enrollment has resulted in more lecture-based teaching and reduced small-group teaching. Growth in student numbers without parallel growth in faculty has decreased the capacity of departments to provide seminars and smaller class sizes. An increasing engagement and awareness of the issues around teaching and learning is likely to further develop and improve traditional teaching practices. The discipline has witnessed greater diversity in relation to forms of assessment and the effective use of information technology. Many of these developments have been a consequence of engagement with other disciplines. However, this engagement is limited in its impact, allowing political science to maintain a signature pedagogy that has evolved yet remains distinct and effective.

THEORETICAL FRAMEWORK FOR DIVERSITY INFUSION

Diverse teaching and learning environments help to prepare students to succeed in our increasingly diverse nation. The future workforce of America must be able to transcend the boundaries of race, gender, lifestyle preferences, language, culture and more as our economy becomes more globally interconnected. In this context, diversity aims to broaden and deepen both the educational experience and the scholarly environment, as students and political science faculty learn to interact effectively with each other, preparing them to participate in an increasingly complex and pluralistic society.

If we examine the configuration of public education and the history since *Brown v. Board* (1954),[5] it is probable that critical race theory (CRT) has the capacity to serve as an adequate explanatory approach to explain the sustained inequity that people of color experience in higher education. CRT, as a diversity infusion approach, views political science curricula as a culturally specific project designed to maintain an exclusive (rather than inclusive) society. Adopting and adapting CRT as a framework to address issues of diversity and equity means that college faculty will have to expose racism in political science education and propose radical solutions for addressing it. CRT is a school of sociological thought that emphasizes the socially constructed nature of race, racism and power. CRT considers legal cases to be the result of the workings of power and opposes the continuation of racial subjugation and subordination (Lopez 2000).

CRT involves a collection of activists and scholars interested in studying and transforming the relationship among race, racism and power. The movement considers many of the same issues that conventional civil rights and ethnic studies discourses take up, but it places them in a broader perspective that includes politics, economics, history, context, and group- and self-interest (Delgado and Stefancic 2001). Critical race theory first emerged as a counter-legal scholarship to the positivist and liberal legal discourse of civil rights. This scholarly tradition argues against the slow pace of racial reform in the U.S.A. Critical race theory begins with the notion that racism is normal in American society. It departs from mainstream legal scholarship by sometimes employing storytelling. It critiques liberalism and argues that whites have been the primary beneficiaries of civil rights legislation. Since schooling in the U.S.A. purports to prepare citizens, CRT looks at how citizenship and race might interact (Ladson-Billings 2010).

According to Delgado (1995, p. xiii), 'Critical Race Theory sprang up in the mid-1970s with the early work of Derrick Bell and Alan Freeman, both of whom were deeply distressed over the slow pace of racial reform in the United States. They argued that the traditional approaches of filing *amicus* briefs, conducting protests and marches, and appealing to the moral sensibilities of decent citizens produced smaller and fewer gains than in previous times. Before long they were being joined by other legal scholars who shared their frustration with traditional civil rights strategies.'

Critical race theory is, thus, both an outgrowth of and a separate entity from an earlier legal movement called critical legal studies (CLS). Critical legal studies is a leftist legal movement that challenged the traditional legal scholarship that focused on doctrinal and policy analysis (Gordon 1990) in favor of a form of law that spoke to the specificity of individuals and groups in social and cultural contexts. Critical legal studies scholars also challenged the notion that 'the civil rights struggle represents a long, steady, march toward social transformation' (Crenshaw 1988, p. 1334). The primary goal of this project is to increase teaching effectiveness and learning satisfaction among political science faculty who choose to makeover (transform) their courses, by incorporating issues of diversity into the curriculum and pedagogical approach. To align with this goal, there is a focus on infusing diversity into political science teaching and learning.

Therefore, the opportunity for political science faculty to develop the skill set and competency for infusing diversity into their curriculum requires both theoretical and practical tasks. Participating faculty members will require guidance, resources, interdisciplinary support networks and peer assistance in order to successfully infuse diversity into the curriculum and pedagogical approach. In addition, there is an expectation that participating faculty will achieve a series of outcomes through their participations. First, faculty should gain a greater understanding of the social construction of race. Further, they should begin to understand how individuals internalize and respond to racism and privilege (conscious and unconscious levels). Third, they should increase awareness of individual, institutional and societal manifestations of racism. Lastly, they should feel capable and motivated to work with others to achieve social justice in higher education.

IMPLICATIONS FOR PSE

Helping faculty develop a pedagogy that makes the most of the diverse perspectives and student backgrounds in their classrooms can foster active thinking, intellectual engagement and democratic participation. A diverse student body, faculty, staff and curriculum are important resources that can enhance the teaching and learning environment. Diversity infusion is transformative and can benefit higher education in numerous ways. First and foremost, diversity enriches the educational experience. We learn from those whose experiences, beliefs and perspectives are different from our own, and these lessons can be taught best in a richly diverse intellectual and social environment. Further, diversity promotes personal growth—and a healthy society. Diversity challenges stereotyped preconceptions; it encourages critical thinking; and it helps students learn to communicate effectively with people of varied backgrounds. It strengthens communities and the workplace. Education within a diverse setting prepares students to become good citizens in an increasingly complex, pluralistic society; it fosters mutual respect and teamwork; and it helps build communities whose members are judged by the quality of their character and their contributions.

PROPOSED PLAN OF ACTION

In order to help faculty feel more prepared to infuse diversity into their classrooms, administrators should take a series of actions to facilitate growth. Immediately, faculty should be provided with education and training about diversity infusion methods and approaches, beginning with a clear discussion of why diversity is important and relevant for higher education. By clearly delineating the need for paying attention to diversity, faculty will hopefully be more willing to embrace the presentation of methods and approaches. To help facilitate faculty growth, administrators should create faculty-learning communities that help to stimulate intellectual challenge concerning diversity infusion methods and approaches. Through these communities, faculty will be able to learn from each other and find support while embracing the pedagogical paradigm shift.

An institution can benefit from incentivizing diversity infusion research, writing and scholarly activities. At a bare minimum, access to such materials should be increased. Establishing a research center for the development and maintenance of diversity infusion efforts can help demonstrate to faculty the breadth and depth of options available. Promoting faculty efforts by offering institutional grants for diversity infusion can also increase participation in the effort. At the institutional level, administrators and faculty together should establish benchmarks and develop plans to hold everyone accountable for implementing recommendations. In the early phases, outside experts may be necessary to help facilitate discussions and oversee initial implementation.

SUMMARY AND CONCLUSION

Careful planning and deliberate facilitation can create a safe environment to incorporate curriculum diversity in ways that encourage participation and enable people from all groups to develop the capacity for tolerance and understanding. Diverse curricula and pedagogical approaches contribute to the student's academic development, satisfaction with college, level of cultural awareness, and commitment to promoting racial and social justice. This project seeks to document how, why and to what extent faculty get involved in diversity infusion efforts and underscores the need to examine faculty involvement to increase participation in diversity efforts. A clearer understanding of faculty motivations will help college officials, administrators and trustees to implement programs and policies that define diversity infusion as an essential and core component of higher education.

Expanding and enhancing political science teaching and learning rests upon culturally competent and globally relevant pedagogy; placing more emphasis on student learning outcomes; inspiring students with active learning strategies and practices; motivating and energizing faculty with incentive awards; building community among students, faculty and staff; and understanding and addressing campus climate issues when and where possible.

NOTES

1. Millennials (1980–1995) are the demographic cohort born following Generation X (1965–1980), a cohort more racially diverse, politically progressive, economically stressed, social media connected and independent than earlier cohorts (Pew Research Center 2014).
2. Diversity is designed to increase educational equity for all students. In this context, diversity is a commitment to recognizing and appreciating the variety of characteristics that make individuals unique in an atmosphere that promotes and celebrates individual and collective achievement. Examples of these characteristics are: age; cognitive style; culture; disability (mental, learning, physical); economic background; education; ethnicity; gender identity; geographic background; language(s) spoken; marital/partnered status; physical appearance; political affiliation; race; religious beliefs; and sexual orientation.
3. Pennsylvania State University Professor Susan Rankin defines *campus climate* as 'the current attitudes, behaviors and standards of faculty, staff, administrators and students concerning the level of respect for individual needs, abilities and potential'. See http://campusclimate.ucop.edu/what-is-campus-climate/index.html (accessed 2 December 2014). Diversity and inclusion are extremely important aspects of campus climate. Numerous studies have concluded that how students experience their campus environment influences both learning and developmental outcomes (Rankin 2004a, 2004b, 2005a, 2005b; Rankin and Reason 2005; Rankin and Russell 2005). Basically, discriminatory environments have a negative effect on student learning.
4. Racism, Sexism, Classism, Ableism, Anti-Semitism, Ageism and Heterosexism.
5. *Brown v. Board of Education of Topeka*, 347 U.S. 483 (1954), was a landmark decision of the United States Supreme Court, which overturned earlier rulings going back to *Plessy v. Ferguson* in 1896, by declaring that state laws that established separate public schools for black and white students denied black children equal educational opportunities. Handed down on 17 May 1954, the Warren Court's unanimous (9–0) decision stated that 'separate educational facilities are inherently unequal'. As a result, de jure racial segregation was ruled a violation of the Equal Protection Clause of the Fourteenth Amendment of the United States Constitution.

REFERENCES

Alger, Jonathan R. (1997), 'The Educational Value of Diversity', *Academe*, **80** (1), 20–23.
Bell, Lee Anne (2003), 'Telling Tales: What Stories Can Teach Us About Racism', *Race Ethnicity and Education*, **6** (1), 8–25.
Crenshaw, Kimberle W. (1988), 'Race, Reform, and Retrenchment: Transformation and Legitimation in Anti-Discrimination Law', *Harvard Law Review*, **101** (7), 1331–87.
Delgado, Richard (ed.) (1995), *Critical Race Theory: The Cutting Edge*, Philadelphia, PA: Temple University Press.
Delgado, Richard and Jean Stefancic (2001), *Critical Race Theory: An Introduction*, New York: NYU Press.
Gordon, Robert (1990), 'New Developments in Legal Theory', in D. Kairys (ed.), *The Politics of Law: A Progressive Critique*, New York: Pantheon Books, pp. 413–25.
Gurin, Patricia (1999), 'Expert Report of Patricia Gurin', in *The Compelling Need for Diversity in Higher Education*, Ann Arbor, MI: University of Michigan Press.

Hurtado, Sylvia (2001), 'Linking Diversity and Educational Purpose: How Diversity Affects the Classroom Environment and Student Development', in G. Orfield (ed.), *Diversity Challenged: Evidence on the Impact of Affirmative Action*, Cambridge, MA: Harvard Educational Publishing Group, pp. 187–203.

Knowles, Marjorie F. and Bernard W. Harleston (1997), *Achieving Diversity in the Professoriate: Challenges and Opportunities*, Washington, D.C.: American Council on Education.

Ladson-Billings, Gloria (1998), 'Just What Is Critical Race Theory and What's It Doing in a Nice Field like Education?', *International Journal of Qualitative Studies in Education*, **11** (1), 7–24.

Liu, Goodwin (1998), 'Affirmative Action in Higher Education: The Diversity Rationale and the Compelling Interest Test', *Harvard Civil Rights-Civil Liberties Law Review*, **33**, 381–442.

Lopez, Ian F. Haney (2000), 'Institutional Racism: Judicial Conduct and a New Theory of Racial Discrimination', *Yale Law Journal*, **109** (8), 1717.

Milem, J.F. (2003), 'The Educational Benefits of Diversity: Evidence from Multiple Sectors', in M.J. Chang, D. Witt, J. Jones and K. Hakuta (eds.), *Compelling Interest: Examining the Evidence on Racial Dynamics in Colleges and Universities*, Palo Alto, CA: Stanford University Press, pp. 126–69.

Monforti, Jessica Lavariega and Adam McGlynn (2010), 'Aqui Estamos? A Survey of Latino Portrayal in Introductory U.S. Government and Politics Textbooks', *PS: Political Science & Politics*, **43** (2), 309–16.

Ofori-Dankwa, J. and R.W. Lane (2000), 'Four Approaches to Cultural Diversity: Implications for Teaching at Institutions of Higher Education', *Teaching in Higher Education*, **5** (4), 493–9.

Pew Research Center (2014), 'Millennials in Adulthood Report', available at: http://www.pewsocialtrends.org/2014/03/07/millennials-in-adulthood/ (accessed 7 March 2014).

Rankin, S. (2004a), 'Campus Climate for Lesbian, Gay, Bisexual & Transgender People', *The Diversity Factor*, **12** (1).

Rankin, S. (2004b), 'College/University Climate for Sexual Minorities', in J. Buck (ed.), *Student Characteristics Matter*, University Park, PA: Undergraduate Education and International Programs, Pennsylvania State University, pp. 75–85.

Rankin, S. (2005a), 'Climate for LGBT College Youth', in J. Sears (ed.), *Encyclopedia of Sexualities, Youth & Education*, Westport, CT: Greenwood Publishing Company.

Rankin, S. (2005b), 'Slow but Steady: Administrators Taking Heart to GBT Safety, Services', *GLBT Campus Matters: Guidance for Higher Education* 1(1), Madison, WI: Magna Publications.

Rankin, S. and R. Reason (2005), 'Differing Perceptions: How Students of Color and White Students Perceive Campus Climate for Underrepresented Groups', *Journal of Student College Development*, **46** (1), 43–61.

Rankin, S. and S. Russell (2005), 'Secondary School Climate for Sexual Minority Students', in J. Sears (ed.), *Encyclopedia of Sexualities, Youth & Education*, Westport, CT: Greenwood Publishing Company.

Wallace, Sherri L. and Marcus D. Allen (2008), 'Survey of African American Portrayal in Introductory Textbooks in American Government/Politics: A Report of the APSA Standing Committee on the Status of Blacks in the Profession', *PS: Political Science & Politics*, **41** (1), 153–9.

17. Teaching gender politics
Fiona Buckley

GENDER POLITICS

The concept of gender is continually experiencing a 'process of definition refinement and theory production' (Lovenduski 1998, p. 337). Nicholson (1994, p. 79 cited in Lovenduski 1998) notes that, while gender was developed as a contrasting term to sex 'to depict that which is socially constructed as opposed to that which is biologically given', the term is often used to refer 'to any social construction' to do with 'the male/female distinction'. In many respects this 'theoretical conundrum' (Lovenduski 1998, p. 337) has generated an ongoing search for conceptual definition, the result of which is that the study of gender politics has changed significantly during the past 40 years.

Early studies of gender and politics were primarily concerned with examining women in politics reducing research to what Ritter (2007, p. 389) describes as exercises in counting: how many women vote, are elected, are appointed ministers, are supporters of one party or another, etc. The continuing absence of women from centers of political power dictates that a focus on women remains necessary. However, in recent years the study of gender and politics has developed to conceptualize gender in a variety of ways. Ritter (2007, p. 389) observes, 'political scientists appear to be learning from gender studies scholars in other disciplines (as well as from feminist theorists in their own discipline), in ways that promote a richer understanding of gender as a social category that helps to organize political life at all levels'. Such developments have served to expand our knowledge and understanding of the various ways in which gender manifests itself in the 'political' and impacts upon the actors, institutions, interactions, political power and policy outputs of the political process.

Krook (2009, p. 24) notes that, as the study of gender politics has evolved, it has contributed to expanding the definition of 'politics', moving the focus away from simply examining 'formal' processes and institutions such as elections and government, to one that encompasses and embraces the 'informal' such as non-State actors (e.g. social movements), the power dynamics of everyday life and gender relations. Duerst-Lahti and Kelly (1995) proffer the concept of 'gender power', arguing that gender is an attribute of power and in certain settings, masculinity is dominant and privileged. This is particularly relevant in the study of politics as political institutions and political processes have been predominantly populated by those of a masculine gender, thus conferring advantages on these political actors.

However, as Krook (2009, p. 24) advises, gender politics is committed to 'political change' and research in this area 'should contribute to some type of positive transformation, whether this entails the broad empowerment of women as a group or the deconstruction of gendered categories in politics and public policy'. Such obligation has seen, for example, a large body of work emerge in recent years concerned with identifying and examining mechanisms to increase the presence of women in politics (e.g. gender quotas). Thus gender politics research presents a challenge to students of political science to rethink and reformulate their political analysis techniques. It bestows an opportunity on teachers of gender politics, usually feminist scholars but not exclusively so, to devise 'innovative techniques' (Krook 2009, p. 23) to share and illustrate gender politics material.

This chapter presents some practical advice and useful strategies for the teaching of an introductory gender politics class. It draws from the literature on 'Teaching Gender Politics', primarily the work of Janet Lee (1993) and Mona Lena Krook (2009), to identify the goals of gender politics and feminist education, and discusses issues of course design, course pedagogy and questions of power, respect and trust in the gender politics classroom. The chapter concludes with a list of useful resources for teachers of gender politics.

FEMINIST EDUCATION

While the focus in gender politics courses is on 'gender' rather than on 'women', the fact that women remain the under-represented sex in most political arenas means that the aims of feminist education remain relevant, and the focus on women remains necessary. Janet Lee's 'Teaching Gender Politics' (1993, p. 27) advises that feminist education encourages women to 'make sense of their lives' by questioning how 'systems of oppression' affect their life experiences. She suggests that feminist education should have the following aims:

> to improve women's status in society and to foster community and empowerment in the classroom (Rich 1985). Feminist teachers ... help students to develop skills in feminist process – that is, they teach specific skills and encourage experience in communication and group process, cooperation, and networking – as well as the ability to integrate theories of women's lives with practical strategies for personal and societal change. The goal is a joining of affect and intellect where personal experience becomes the site for intellectual investigation and inquiry (Schneiderwind 1983; Shrewsbury 1987). The hope is to facilitate active learning where knowledge is relevant and useful, where classroom work is connected to the everyday experiences of students' lives, and where students are engaged and moving the learning process forward.

From Lee's work we see that feminist education has four central tenets: 1) consciousness raising, 2) encouraging reflective practice, 3) engendering change and empowerment, and 4) promoting feminist activism.

Consciousness raising in feminism has traditionally been concerned with increasing social consciousness of sexism and female oppression in society. In feminist education, consciousness raising is about prioritizing the personal experience and highlighting personal feelings as a way of challenging predominantly held beliefs, knowledge and truths. To facilitate personal narratives and an exchange of personal experiences, Lee (1993) encourages the practice of self-reflection, individually and within groups. She asks her students to highlight and share their experiences of oppression, gender related or otherwise, to enable them to gain a general understanding of the privileges that some in society enjoy but that simultaneously disadvantage others. Thus, feminist education challenges students to bring to light cases of social, economic and political inequalities between women and men.

Engendering change and personal empowerment as well as promoting feminist activity are key components of feminist education. Linked to this is what Campbell and Childs (2013, p. 186) describe as 'a feminist imperative' in feminist political science:

> The feminist imperative is derived from the fact that feminist researchers are precisely motivated to undertake dissemination, engagement and impact activities *because* of their feminism. Feminist political scientists, *because they are feminists*, want to change, as well as observe, the world. Many of the women who report on our research, elicit our views and receive our evidence are 'sisters' in the feminist sense of the word too. A shared political project which, at the minimum, values the presence of women and women's perspectives in politics facilitates cooperation. The *feminist imperative* requires action within and without the academy.

Thus, providing students with the knowledge and skills to conduct 'good' gender analysis is a core ambition of gender politics courses.

As action is central to feminism, many gender politics courses devote time to learning about the history, impact, types as well as the tools of feminist activism. Lee (1993, p. 28) advises 'integrating activism directly into the curriculum can be effective for facilitating experiential learning. "Activism" must be defined broadly as pertaining to issues of personal growth and individual change as well as to social change'. The type of feminist activism engaged in is often determined by how one conceptualizes feminism. The role of the gender politics teacher is to outline the various feminist perspectives, namely liberal feminism, radical feminism, socialist feminism and the feminism of difference. Each perspective has its own political goals and, as Krook (2009, p. 24) advises, poses a challenge to existing modes of political analysis. However, this has led to charges 'against feminist scholarship on the grounds that it fails to be "objective", as such motives interfere with the discovery of "truth"' (Krook 2009, p. 25). In response, feminist researchers have queried the 'situated and partial nature of all knowledge claims' (Krook 2009, p. 25).

There are ongoing debates too about whether specific feminist research methods exist. Krook (2009, p. 25) highlights the work of scholars such as Reinharz (1992) and Ramazanoglu with Holland (2002) who argue that no specific feminist research methods exist; rather, there is one feminist methodology that is 'distinctive to the extent that it is shaped by feminist theory, politics and ethics and is grounded in women's experience' (Ramazanoglu with Holland 2002, p. 16). In 'Teaching Gender and Politics: Feminist Methods in Political Science', Krook (2009, p. 25) identifies four main goals to which feminist method texts attend, namely 'paying attention to "gender," challenging norms of objectivity and incorporating subjectivity into research, trying to avoid exploiting women as subjects and objects of knowledge and empowering women in various ways through research'. With such broad-reaching aims, Krook argues that feminist scholars, similar to other researchers, employ a variety of research methods in their quest for evidence. However, what makes the work of feminist scholars distinctive is their effort 'to adapt many of the same methods as other researchers in ways that make them more consistent with feminist concerns' (Krook 2009, p. 25). Thus, the challenge for gender politics teachers is to highlight feminist concerns and provide students with the tools to conduct gender analysis.

The next two sections discuss course design and pedagogy for an introductory gender politics course. These sections are partly informed by personal experience of designing and delivering a course in gender politics but primarily by the aforementioned work of Janet Lee (1993), whose article 'Teaching Gender Politics' reflects upon her experiences of teaching gender politics to a group of sociology students, and Mona Lena Krook (2009), whose article 'Teaching Gender and Politics: Feminist Methods in Political Science' surveyed course content and teaching methods in a variety of 'gender politics' and 'women and politics' courses in Europe and the United States between 2002 and 2008. As a relatively new teacher of gender politics, I have found these articles particularly useful as I have set about designing my own course.

COURSE DESIGN

A shared goal of all teachers of gender politics and courses examining women in politics is to expand students' knowledge of political science. Consistent with the goals of feminist political science more generally, Krook's (2009, p. 26) survey of gender politics courses reveals that such courses aim to 1) 'familiarize students with the concept of "gender"', 2) 'enlarge the scope of what is considered to be "political"', and 3) 'offer insights into possible strategies for political "change"'.

Familiarizing Students with the Concept of Gender

To enable students to analyze politics through a gendered and/or feminist lens, one needs to introduce students to the concept of gender. Gender politics courses usually begin with a section on gender theory where gender is conceptualized as a social construct. The theoretical discussion is expanded to describe gender as a property of an individual or institution and the concept of gendered institutions may be introduced at this stage to analyze the gendered nature of political institutions. Gender may also be conceptualized as a set of norms of appropriate behavior that emerge from specific gendered social or institutional settings and it will be noted that gender is something that people can perform. The discussion of gender theory will illustrate that, because political institutions have traditionally been dominated by men, these institutions are gendered to appropriate masculinity as the norm, thus conferring political advantages on masculine actors.[1] The theoretical section of the course will also include a discussion of the various forms of feminism, a history of feminist activism and a description of the modes of action undertaken by feminist actors. To make this discussion relevant and accessible to students, case studies and examples from the women's movement and feminist activism can be introduced. Students never tire of learning of the campaigns undertaken during the various waves of feminist activism. Many courses will then move on to explore the androcentric nature of politics, exposing the 'gender blindness' of political concepts and institutions and the limitations of existing political science literature for gender politics research. This usually entails a focus on women as political actors and the differential impacts of the outputs of political processes – public policy – on women and men. The historic and continuing absence of women from political arenas will be examined to understand why women are under-represented in political institutions. Mechanisms to increase women's political participation will be explored. Krook (2009, p. 26) advises 'the intent in all instances is to analyze how gender operates in the political realm and, as a consequence, rethink and re-conceptualize political concepts through a feminist lens'.

Enlarging the Scope of What is Considered to be Political

As well as discussing formal political institutions such as executives, parliaments, parties and elections, Krook (2009) advises that many gender politics courses will extend the site of enquiry to include social movements, civil society, the judiciary, the media, and international and transnational organizations in recognition of the importance of such locations as places of women's political agency. By doing so, the gender politics teacher draws 'attention to the partial nature of how "politics" has been studied' (Krook 2009, p. 26). Additionally, Krook (2009, p. 26) notes that many gender politics courses will include a section examining issues that are often associated with women but not generally studied in political science, such as reproductive rights, domestic violence, women's roles in conflict and peace resolution, and equality law. Again this serves to expand students' understanding and knowledge of the 'political'.

Strategies for Political Change

Gender politics courses will usually include discussions of efforts to promote political change. In her survey of gender politics courses, Krook (2009, p. 26) highlights one gender politics course advising that its aim is not only to 'expose the limits of conventional modes of political analysis, but also to move from describing the world to thinking about how to reconstitute these realities'. Krook goes on to advise that the majority of courses focus on politics in a single country, but many also include some degree of cross-national comparison as a means to:

> (1) raise students' awareness of distinct trends elsewhere and (2) explore why change has occurred in some countries but not in others. While crucial for improved knowledge of political processes, exposure to such information is also intended to foster the ability to imagine an alternative to the status quo. (Krook 2009, p. 26)

For the most part, the gender politics courses surveyed by Krook include sections on gender quotas, gender mainstreaming and gender proofing (in particular the gender proofing of state or national budgets) to illustrate and examine the impact of change strategies on women's access to politics and on public policymaking.

COURSE PEDAGOGY

While gender politics courses tend to make use of standard teaching methods, such as lectures, seminars, invited guest speakers, and the showing of films and internet clips, and the assessment techniques are similar to those found elsewhere in political science, notably essay assignments, research papers, oral presentations, end-of-term exams and book or article reviews, the teaching and learning of gender politics differs from other political science courses in terms of its commitment to the four central tenets of feminist education which were noted earlier as 1) consciousness raising, 2) encouraging reflective practice, 3) engendering change and empowerment, and 4) promoting feminist activism. This section outlines a variety of teaching methods and strategies that can be incorporated into gender politics courses to accommodate these broad principles.

Consciousness Raising and Reflective Practice

Consciousness raising and reflective practice are discussed together as to set in motion consciousness raising one must be able to reflect upon and draw from one's personal experiences. Many gender politics courses will begin by encouraging students to locate gender analysis in their everyday lives. What may sound like a lofty aim can be achieved through short exercises such as asking students to contemplate the following questions:

- 'Look around your college campus or local town; how many buildings, streets, bridges, etc. are named after a woman?'
- 'Why is it that male sports stars enjoy greater access to greater rewards (fame, advertisement endorsements, big money contracts) than female sports stars?'
- When you were growing up, who did most of the housework in your home – female or male relations?'
- 'Why are the aisles of major toy stores stocked with pink toys for girls and blue toys for boys?'

Through these questions, students' awareness of the differential roles, treatment and privileges of women and men in society is heightened. More structured questions can alert students' awareness to what Janet Lee (1993) describes as connections between institutional and interpersonal issues. In her classes, Janet Lee (p. 28) asks students to discuss, 'how is societal male privilege acted out in our personal relationships?', which she advises is an effective question for making students conscious of the gender processes of their everyday lives and can contribute to an examination of 'privilege and choice, constraint and oppression'. Very importantly, Lee (1993, p. 28) notes:

> Central in making these institutional–interpersonal connections is the need to encourage men to recognize their gender privileges as men. A dialogue encouraging students to name these privileges can develop through discussions of men's everyday experiences, as opposed to women's, in a variety of settings. These settings might include ... the media and their representation of women; and privileges that are experienced personally, such as jogging after dark, removing one's shirt on a hot day ... and the matter of domestic labor – who does what in the home and who benefits.

She advises that the issue of privilege should not stop with a discussion of gender and encourages the use of similar exercises to 'help white students to understand issues of race privilege, young people to understand ageism and middle-class students to understand economic inequities' (Lee 1993, p. 28).

To facilitate reflection and consciousness raising of issues such as gender analysis, privilege and institutional–interpersonal linkages, Lee has found that reflective journals and group discussions are effective methods through which students can engage with such issues. She notes that reflective journals can be a useful tool in providing students with the space and safety to make connections between academic coursework and personal experiences. Students can reflect upon assigned readings and classroom activities, evaluate classes, and 'record and reflect upon personal growth in the issue of gender politics' (Lee 1993, p. 27). Lee does caution about the drawbacks associated with using reflective journals, in particular the difficulties of assessing 'students' writings comparatively'. To overcome this, she advises that it is important to clearly articulate the criteria by which the journal will be evaluated and recommends that students are presented with a detailed handout outlining the criteria of the assessment, including advice and examples on how course readings are to be integrated into their reflective journals. The assessment handout should offer guidance to students on how to demonstrate evidence of self-assessment of learning and personal growth. Again, written examples of this can be a useful tool to steer students through the self-reflection process. In terms of grading, Lee (1993, p. 27) suggests that students must show 'familiarity with and integration or synthesis of key concepts' to achieve high grades.

Small group discussions with structured questions are useful for encouraging students to engage in a gender analysis of their everyday lives. To ensure a good group discussion takes place and students stay on track, Lee (1993, p. 28) advises that 'students play assigned roles such as facilitator, timekeeper, or note-taker' and be required to hand something in at the end of the exercise. Also, time for group 'reporting back' should be scheduled as it helps 'the less vocal students to speak up' – sometimes 'it's easier to report the group's ideas than one's personal thoughts' (Lee 1993, p. 28).

Distributing newspaper reports in class about current political figures and asking students to examine and discuss the differential treatment of male and female politicians in the press will always generate a lively discussion. Such an exercise not only allows students to sharpen their gender analysis skills, but it also allows them to take their first tentative steps into discourse and content analysis. Other group exercises such as introducing students to government or state archival material can unearth historic examples that clearly demonstrate the privileges accorded to men on the basis of their biological sex. For example, the National Archives of Ireland (n.d.) dedicates a section to sources on women's history. Similarly, distributing accessible but thought-provoking newspaper articles in class, such as one that appeared in the *Galway Advertiser* highlighting 'Ten things an Irish woman could not do in 1970' ('Ten things' 2012) provides students with an understanding of the social conservatism that predominated Irish society up to the 1980s and the 'patriarchal dividend' (Connell 1996) of material, status and power advantages that men in Ireland enjoyed during this time.

Finally, Lee (1993, p. 28) advises that techniques such as storytelling, oral histories and ethnography are helpful to engage students in gender analysis, as such exercises encourage students 'to remember' and 'to feel' and facilitate connections 'on an emotional level' with life experiences. In this regard, Lee recommends using the following questions: 'Remember back in your childhood when you first became aware of sexism. What was the situation? How did you feel? What are the politics involved here?' Oral history assignments, whereby students interview their mothers or an older woman about the changing role of women in their lifetime, and ethnographic or observation studies, whereby students go outside the classroom and observe the gendered dynamics, roles and stereotypes at play in places such as supermarkets, restaurants, hospitals, the toy shop and university campuses, provide useful sources for learning about gender politics, according to Lee (1993, p. 28).

Engendering Change and Empowerment

Incorporating the feminist concern of change and empowerment into gender politics courses can take several formats. In her review of gender politics courses in the U.S.A. and Europe, Krook (2009, pp. 27–8) observes three main trends in this regard: 1) connecting classroom material to the 'real world', 2) providing students with opportunities to cultivate 'new skills' and encourage 'personal transformation', and 3) identifying female political role models.

Many gender politics courses provide students with opportunities 'to literally go outside the classroom' (Krook 2009, p. 27). Activities may include watching politics 'in action' by attending a parliamentary or local government meeting, meeting and interviewing women politicians or interning in a political, government or advocacy agency. Courses may also bring 'the outside world into the classroom' (Krook 2009, p. 27) by inviting political women in to discuss their experiences, campaign work and, if an elected official, their pathways to political office. The aforementioned techniques can be time intensive to arrange but are endeavors appreciated by students. If it is not possible to arrange study trips to a parliament or have political actors attend the classroom, Krook (2009, p. 27) advises that requesting students to bring in newspaper articles for class discussion is a very useful technique for linking current events with 'the theories and concepts introduced in class to help students better understand and analyze recent political developments'.

Cultivating new skills and encouraging personal transformation can be accomplished through a range of activities, as Krook (2009, pp. 27–8) identifies in her study of gender politics courses. Firstly, she notes that many courses offer advice to students on how to become politically active. This may entail offering training sessions on 'how to run for elected office' or inviting guest speakers into class to advise on how to 'get involved in politics as activists, campaign workers and candidates'. Secondly, Krook highlights that, in many courses, students are encouraged to learn specific political skills, for example 'doing background research, preparing speeches, making presentations, training in giving television and radio interviews, writing op-ed pieces and blog entries and engaging in effective networking' (Krook 2009, p. 28). Thirdly, Krook notes that some courses focus on improving students' oral communication skills 'by scheduling tasks that require them to synthesize and articulate arguments related to gender and politics' (Krook 2009, p. 28). This can take the format of in-class debates, leading a class seminar or, as Krook notes, the more daunting task of making a speech to the class on 'the importance of women's political participation, representation and leadership' (Krook 2009, p. 28). Finally, she advises that students can be introduced to new written genres, ones that are particularly useful in activist politics, for example writing 'a short advocacy paper making a case for a specific government policy on an issue affecting women' (Krook 2009, p. 28) or authoring an opinion piece or letter to a newspaper editor on an issue of the students' choice but 'with the intent to influence policy-making' (Krook 2009, p. 28).

Identifying a female political role model or an example of a woman in politics is a popular choice of coursework assigned in many of the gender politics courses surveyed by Krook. She found that in many gender politics classes, students are asked to profile an individual woman politician, living or dead, discussing her upbringing, professional background, her rise to power, policy priorities, parliamentary experience, committee and/or ministerial responsibilities, and key policy decisions made throughout her career. In such assignments, 'students are obliged to draw explicit links between these findings and various themes introduced in the course' (Krook 2009, p. 28). In some courses, students are requested to conduct an interview with a woman politician, in particular a woman who has been associated with introducing a public policy change that has impacted positively upon women's lives. The assignment allows students to hone their elite interviewing skills, but it also helps students to 'understand how policymaking works' and identify the 'constraints and opportunities' present for women 'to act on behalf of women as a group' (Krook 2009, p. 28). Another type of project that Krook identifies are assignments that request students to interview separately a female and a male politician and ask students to write a paper reflecting on if and how women and men lead differently in these positions:

> By making the question of 'difference' an empirical question, rather than a theoretical given, this assignment encourages students to grapple with the concept of 'gender' in a real world laboratory, pushing them to consider when and where it may be relevant – or not. (Krook 2009, p. 28)

Activism

As noted earlier, activism is a central component of many gender politics courses. Many courses will discuss the various waves of feminist movement and activity throughout history, detailing the aims of each campaign, the types of activist tools involved and the legislative changes achieved. Lee (1993, p. 28) advises that integrating activism into gender politics courses can be an effective method 'for facilitating experiential learning'. Examples of the types of activism in which Lee's students have been engaged include planning or helping with a campus, community or national campaign; writing to politicians and the letter pages of newspapers; and volunteering and/or interning at social agencies, community organizations and campaign groups. Other forms of activism include engaging students in service learning by, for example, empowering women through voter education projects. Lee advises that inviting activists into the classroom is also important, as such talks can help students to 'work through feelings of despair or helplessness' that they may feel about a particular issue, thus facilitating the channeling of 'anger in positive ways that can effect change' (Lee 1993, p. 28).

CLASSROOM ENVIRONMENT

A respectful and trustful environment is essential for fostering student engagement and discussion of the various topics addressed in a gender politics course. Lee (1993) outlines five useful strategies that may be employed to ensure a comfortable classroom for all.

Firstly, Lee (1993, pp. 30–32) advises that raising awareness of issues of *power* in the classroom is useful in facilitating 'openness and honesty'. She suggests that having a class discussion on the privileges of teachers in comparison to those of students and vice-versa is an effective way of displaying how power and privileges can 'create different dynamics and subjectivities in the classroom'. More generally, such a discussion is a useful starting point for exploring the differential power arrangements that exist in society, which is a good preempt for a discussion on the various gender power arrangements that exist in politics.

Secondly, Lee instructs that teachers must be attentive to how issues of *diversity* affect students' participation in class. 'Being "different" from the majority in race, age, class or gender can be silencing' (Lee 1993, p. 30), resulting in students being less willing to participate. Lee advises that combining an 'unlearning component' that addresses 'all systems of oppression' tends to create 'more comfortable places for those in the targeted or discriminated-against group'. She also warns not to marginalize lesbians and gay men by assuming that all your students are heterosexual.

Thirdly, Lee highlights that *men* are usually in the minority in gender politics courses. 'These men either act out a perceived unique and special role as "nice" men who deserve special praise, encouragement, nurturance, and caretaking from the women in the class, or display increasing fear and defensiveness' (Lee 1993, p. 30). In the latter case, Lee notes that male defensiveness can 'polarize' a class, encouraging some students to feel that feminist classrooms are 'men-hating'. She outlines a number of classroom techniques to overcome such situations:

> I tell my male students that I want them to experience the feeling of being 'off-center' and to allow someone else's experience to define reality. I also encourage men to talk to each other in the classroom and not to rely on women to take care of them and do emotional work. For that reason I segregate men into all-male groups for some discussion sessions and encourage them to disclose to and connect with each other. This arrangement also preserves a safe space for women, which is especially important for certain topics such as violence and sexuality. (Lee 1993, pp. 30–31)

Of course, separating male students into men-only groups should not always be the default option. In my teaching, I have found mixed-group discussion a useful mechanism for male and female students to share and discuss a wide variety of opinions on which there is agreement and disagreement. Agreement and disagreement does not necessarily follow along expected gender lines, providing an interesting discussion point in itself.

Fourthly, to ensure *respect and trust* in the classroom, Lee advises teachers to be as respectful toward their students as they might like their students to be toward them. To encourage openness and disclosure amongst students, she suggests that that 'appropriate self-disclosure by the teacher and the sharing of emotions such as anger, sadness, or enthusiasm go a long way in helping to humanize the classroom' (Lee 1993, p. 31). Group work may also assist in this regard as when students have had the opportunity to get to know one other, trust is fostered, which usually contributes to improved classroom discussion (Lee 1993). Finally, Lee notes that *democratic classroom structures* encourage active learning of gender politics:

> Try working with students on syllabus construction; at least encourage negotiation and be flexible in order to take into account students' interests and changes as the term progresses. (1993, p. 31)

CONCLUSION

The teaching of gender politics broadens students' knowledge of politics, widening their understanding of where and how politics takes place. Challenging existing political knowledge and beliefs through a gendered analysis can be empowering for students but also revelatory of the gendered privileges that exist in society. Increasing awareness of 'real-world' politics and 'real-world' gender dynamics by connecting the classroom with the outside world is a key aim of many gender politics courses. Gender politics teachers employ a variety of techniques to make this connection, reflecting the various goals and approaches of feminist education, feminism and feminist political science. Thus, with its wealth of pedagogical experience, emphasizing active, experiential and reflective learning, the teaching and learning of gender politics can offer much to the rest of political science. Leaving the last word to Mona Lena Krook (2009, p. 28), 'Features of feminist ... teaching might thus be understood as a model of "good practice," instructive for many other courses offered in political science.'

SOME USEFUL RESOURCES FOR TEACHERS OF GENDER POLITICS

- For a syllabus archive on gender and politics, see the website of the 'Gender and Politics Standing Group' of the European Consortium for Political Research (ECPR) http://www.ecpg.eu/syllabus-bank.html (accessed 30 November 2014).
- For general information on Gender and Education, see http://www.genderandeducation.com/ (accessed 5 July 2014).
- For a gendered analysis of political science concepts, see Amy Mazur and Gary Goertz (eds) (2008), *Politics, Gender and Concepts: Theory and Methodology*, Cambridge: Cambridge University Press.
- For critical perspectives on the teaching of gender and politics, see the journal *Politics and Gender*, **9** (2), June 2013.
- For a guide on feminist readings for students and teachers, see Susan M. Shaw and Janet Lee (eds) (2011), *Women's Voices, Feminist Visions: Classic and Contemporary Readings*, New York: McGraw-Hill.
- For an overview of key concepts and theories in the study of gender politics, see Rosie Campbell and Sarah Childs (eds) (2014), *Deeds and Words: Gendering Politics after Joni Lovenduski*, Essex: ECPR Press.

NOTE

1. For a more detailed discussion on gender as a category, as a set of practices, as a property and as a performance, please see Duerst-Lahti and Kelly (1995) and Butler (1990). For a more detailed discussion of gendered institutions see Lovenduski (1998), Escobar-Lemmon and Taylor Robinson (2005 and 2009) and Chappell (2006).

REFERENCES

Butler, J. (1990), *Gender Trouble*, New York: Routledge.
Campbell, R. and S. Childs (2013), 'The Impact Imperative: Here Come the Women:-)', *Political Studies Review*, **11**, 182–9.
Chappell, L. (2006), 'Comparing Political Institutions: Revealing the Gendered "Logic of Appropriateness"', *Politics and Gender*, **2** (2), 223–35.
Connell, R.W. (1996), 'Politics of Changing Men', *Australian Humanities Review*, available at http://www.australianhumanitiesreview.org/archive/Issue-Dec-1996/connell.html (accessed 15 January 2014).
Duerst-Lahti, G. and R.M. Kelly (eds) (1995), *Gender Power, Leadership and Governance*, Ann Arbor, MI: University of Michigan Press.
Escobar-Lemmon, M. and M.M. Taylor-Robinson (2005), 'Women Ministers in Latin American Government: When, Where, and Why?', *American Journal of Political Science*, **49** (4), 829–44.
Escobar-Lemmon, M. and M.M. Taylor-Robinson (2009), 'Getting to the Top: Career Paths of Women in Latin American Cabinets', *Political Research Quarterly*, **62** (4), 685–99.
Krook, M.L. (2009), 'Teaching Gender and Politics: Feminist Methods in Political Science', *Qualitative & Multi-Method Research*, **7** (1), 23–9.
Lee, J. (1993), 'Teaching Gender Politics', *Teaching Sociology*, **21** (1), 26–32.
Lovenduski, J. (1998), 'Gendering Research in Political Science', *Annual Review of Political Science*, **1**, 333–56.
National Archives of Ireland (n.d.), 'Research Guides and Articles: Guide to Sources on Women's History', available at http://www.nationalarchives.ie/research/research-guides-and-articles/guide-to-sources-on-womens-history/ (accessed 1 March 2014).
Nicholson, L. (1994), 'Interpreting Gender', *Signs*, **20**, 79–105.
Ramazanoglu, C. with J. Holland (2002), *Feminist Methodology: Challenges and Choices*, Thousand Oaks, CA: Sage.
Reinharz, S. (1992), *Feminist Methods in Social Research*, New York: Oxford University Press.
Rich, A. (1985), 'Taking Women Students Seriously', in C. Bunch and S. Pollack (eds), *Gendered Subjects*, Boston, MA: Routledge, pp. 21–8.
Ritter, G. (2007), 'Gender and Politics over Time', *Politics and Gender*, **3** (3), 386–97.
Schneiderwind, N. (1983), 'Feminist Values: Guidelines for a Teaching Methodology in Women's Studies', in C. Bunch and S. Pollack (eds), *Learning Our Way*, Trumansburg, NY: Crossing Press, pp. 261–71.
Shrewsbury, C. (1987), 'What is Feminist Pedagogy?', *Women's Studies Quarterly*, **15** (3–4), 6–14.
'Ten Things an Irish Woman Could Not Do in 1970' (2012), *Galway Advertiser*, 13 December, available at http://www.advertiser.ie/galway/article/57301/ten-things-an-irish-woman-could-not-do-in-1970-and-be-prepared-to-cringe (accessed 1 March 2014).

18. Teaching graduate research methods
Mitchell Brown*

In fundamental ways, research methods courses and training in graduate programs are the critical lynchpin of a student's education. At the doctoral level, the yardstick used to measure an academic's success is his or her ability to engage in enduring and current substantive debates and add to these through the production of new knowledge in the field. Doing so is impossible without quality methods education of some sort, and is therefore essential for the future of any discipline. Methods training is equally, albeit differently, important in master's level graduate courses. Particularly in terminal degree programs like a Master of Public Administration (MPA), students seek to obtain transferable skills that they can then utilize in applied settings. In addition, there is at least anecdotal evidence about how strong methods education travels beyond the search for a tenure track job. Murakami (2012) writes, 'the research skills I had accrued as a graduate student were much rarer and more difficult to acquire' than other skills that non-academics have competing for jobs outside academia (p. 813). Various industries are putting greater emphasis on these transferable skills, with pressure coming from both employers and governments (Clark 2011).

One of the greatest challenges in discussing graduate methods education is determining what this encompasses, as there are myriad approaches to teaching graduate research methods. For example, see the divergent opinions in graduate curricular development discussed by Schwartz-Shea and Bennett (2003) in the PS Symposium on methodological pluralism in journals and graduate education. Typically, what comes to mind is training in quantitative analytic techniques, followed by qualitative analysis. However, there is a range of approaches across institutions that include survey classes on scope and methods, design, rational choice, and formal theory and critical analysis. Some programs also offer specialized courses on different forms of data collection, from field research techniques to in-depth training in survey design. Regionally we also see differences. Though the quantitative/qualitative divide is shrinking, US research methods courses rely on more sophisticated modeling, while European institutions offer simpler quantitative as well as interpretive analysis courses (Rihoux, Kittel and Moses 2008).

In this chapter, I examine the state of graduate research methods education and training. A review of the literature, focusing on department level approaches as well as best practice techniques to approaching different components of research methods, introduces the chapter. I then turn to a contemporary examination of methods education, laying out departmental requirements and the substance of courses, and tie those to the success of graduates. I differentiate between types of degrees and levels of degrees, and look at other non-degree opportunities for methods training. Finally, I make recommendations for programs, courses and pedagogy research.

STATE OF THE LITERATURE

Reviewing best practices in political science research methods education is challenging. While, presumably, most faculty who teach methods are quality methodologists themselves, very few systematic studies of best practices exist in the field. This is exemplified by attending the 'Teaching Research Methods' section at the annual Teaching and Learning Conference (TLC) hosted by the American Political Science Association (APSA). Faculty presentations of 'what works' often provide great ideas about ways to approach methods education, but they very rarely present well-designed evaluations of those techniques. In their defense, instructors are often able to tell intuitively when students 'get it' and what happened in the classroom to produce that result. But what methodologists also know is that anecdotal evidence is not the same thing as systematic evidence. If we are trying to establish best practices to enable replication, systematic examination of our pedagogical approaches with control groups across multiple contexts is required.

There have been marked increases in publications pertaining to the scholarship of teaching and learning generally since 1996 (Kehl 2002). However, less systematic scholarship exists about the best ways to approach methods education generally, and even less about graduate methods education specifically. While models for studying this part of our work certainly exist (see for example Deardorff, Hamann and Ishiyama 2009), and there are increasing numbers of presentation and publication venues for this type of research, most notably the decade-old APSA Teaching and Learning Conference and the *Journal of Political Science Education*, very few scholars devote their considerable talent to the systematic study of how best to teach research methods. The field is in part to blame for this: few departments exist that simultaneously teach adequate numbers of graduate students for systematic study; and, more importantly, most departments do not 'count' this type of work as scholarly productivity.

One of the greatest challenges discussing graduate methods education is determining what it encompasses. There is an array of approaches from design to analysis with differing emphasis or weighting placed on each type. Over a decade ago in a review of US doctoral level programs, Schwartz-Shea (2003) found a heavy emphasis on quantitative requirements (66 percent of departments surveyed) over qualitative requirements (9 percent of departments surveyed), and departments evenly split on whether or not they require coursework in philosophy of science and/or scope and history of the discipline. In the same study, she shows a range in course requirements from no methods courses (30 percent of departments) to as many as 4–6 courses (12 percent of departments).

The obvious normative question is what *ought* to be taught in the graduate curriculum, and the answer is either a) everything, or b) it depends. If we take the position that students are fundamentally intelligent and capable of self-learning, then we are left with the 'everything' answer. In this scenario, departments should provide a general overview of the possible methodological approaches, their uses, and their strengths and weaknesses, and (good) students will either refine their skills in these areas through outside reading and practical use or through additional training from outside, specialized programs. The best approach to graduate methods education in this model would be a general course in research design that begins with philosophy of science and discussions of meta-theory, grand theory and middle-range theories, followed by a more in-depth perusal of design approaches and their attendant strengths and weaknesses as well as approaches to sampling and case selection. Ideally, a course like this would be followed by a basic introduction to statistics course to ensure that students have the basic knowledge needed both to engage with the literature and to serve as a base for developing subsequent skills. All of these skills should then be further honed in additional courses with integration across the curriculum where possible.

However, another argument contends that departments do and ought to specialize in certain methodological approaches, and students ought to know and understand this as both a limitation and an opportunity upon matriculating and accept that their skills development will be targeted in a particular way by their choice of graduate program. Evidence suggests that we have some of each approach across the discipline. Programs that take this approach tend to have methods-heavy curricula focused around their particular methodological orientation.

Approaches

Graduate methods education is a cornerstone of graduate students' potential success in the academic job market, later as they work to earn tenure, or as a practitioner in many fields. Poor methods training stifles students' abilities to be successful in these endeavors, though what is less clear is the best ways to use methods training to prosper in these areas. Departments are faced with two major considerations when approaching the development of graduate methods curriculum. First, do they integrate methods instruction across their curriculum, or do they deliver this material in specific courses only? Do they integrate opportunities outside of the classroom to enhance student skills? Second, what software do they use for data analysis? Can alternative technologies be used for delivery of material?

A critical component of research methods education comes from not just specific methods courses but integrating methods education across the curriculum. There are two main ways to approach the integration of methods training. In the first, programs have a standard set of methods courses that all students complete, and the skills taught in these courses are reinforced across the substantive courses through assignments in which students practice using their methods training. In the second, departments identify a set of benchmark skills that students need to have mastered by graduation, and responsibility for teaching and reinforcing these methods skills is then spread across the faculty through the intentional inclusion of methods training in the relevant substantive courses (Centellas 2011). A common approach taken by most departments is to require some formal training in the classroom, and then to provide other avenues for feedback through more informal, usually 'brown bag', research presentations to faculty and sometimes to other students (see for example the MOPS approach used by the University of Colorado described in Fugate, Jaramillo and Preuhs 2001).

The second major consideration for departments in how to provide methods training concerns the use of technology. While previous literature on methods training and technology was concerned with how much technology is too cumbersome (see for example Rodgers and Manrique 1992), technology in the classroom is now ubiquitous. The contemporary technology debate has two different components: what software to use and how to deliver degree programs. With respect to software, university resources often drive these decisions. In wealthier universities, an array of software choices is available. However, in many colleges and universities decisions made at the administrative level concerning which programs to buy licenses for, for computer labs, proscribe what software can be used.

From a teaching perspective, software is often an issue of preference of the instructor more than anything else is. However, to the extent that instructors have decision-making authority about software they should take into consideration the needs, current and future, of students. Doctoral students pursuing only introductory statistics education will likely need only minimal knowledge of statistical software, so programs like SPSS with drop down menus are adequate. Doctoral students pursuing more advanced training, particularly through outside training programs, need to learn programs like Stata and R. However, master's level students pursuing degrees for practical application are not likely to work in environments that can afford these programs. Instead, they should be taught introductory statistics skills in more widely available programs like Excel. While not designed for more advanced analysis, basic statistics can be computed with this type of software, and these types of students are best served by being trained using this type of software.

An emerging concern is the use of distance learning techniques for graduate education. Traditional universities are slowly moving towards more on-line and distance methods courses and programs. Examples like the University of South Dakota's hybrid learning program are emerging (for more discussion, see Nordyke et al. 2011). What is unclear is the relative efficacy of distance and/or hybrid learning courses compared to traditional modes of methods education specifically. These types of programs may take a blended approach in which intensive, once monthly in-person instruction sessions are followed by asynchronous practice of skills, question and answer sessions, and feedback. Methods instructors taking this approach would need to break out topics and skills by major approaches and types for each month's focus. For example, in a four-month course on introduction to statistics Month 1 may cover descriptive statistics, Month 2 probability, Month 3 bivariate analysis and Month 4 basics of multivariate analysis. Alternatively, an on-line only approach to the development of an on-line only research methods course syllabus might be structured like the more traditional weekly in-person format, but with delivery of lectures based around each specific skill set using lecture capture and screen capture technology in concert. The limitation of both of these approaches is the important information teaching and learning that is done in the traditional methods course among the students in peer-based study groups.

Best Practice Techniques

The instructor level questions when teaching research methods concern what material to cover, how to deliver that material, which texts to purchase, and assessment measures and techniques. The literature about these curriculum design issues specific to graduate research methods is scant; what does exist revolves around two major topics—delivery techniques and methods anxiety.

We have some evidence that active learning techniques in methods education enhances student learning (Currin-Percival and Johnson 2010). An active learning approach considered extremely effective is engaging the student in an original research project.

Another active approach is working students through the entire research process that research active faculty use to produce research articles, starting with the development of a question, then building a literature review, developing a research design and implementing at least a portion of that design by collecting some simple data on the topic and analyzing them (McBride 1994). While seemingly ideal, these are often difficult to accomplish in one semester. Some departments choose to engage in this process over a series of related courses. In the absence of the ability to change the curriculum to develop multi-semester methods instruction, instructors should consider parallel projects within one course. In the first, students could develop a research proposal around their area of interest over the course of the semester. Simultaneously, students could work in groups on data collection, analysis and presentation projects that are highly structured by the instructor, thus allowing students to gain hands-on experience within the limited timeframe of one semester.

Research about math aversion and how to combat it comprises the second significant area of the research methods literature, and rightly so as this topic comes up in many, if not most, discussions held when research methods teachers come together. Even at the graduate level, we have students who experience methods anxiety, though at this level the problem is often easier to handle than at the undergraduate level. A doctoral student either learns the skills required to produce original research or s/he does not succeed, thus confronting methods anxiety is primarily the responsibility of the student. That said, there are some approaches to alleviating anxiety that, at least anecdotally, mitigate it. Bernstein and Allen (2013) suggest engaging students in long-term projects on one specific topic that is then analyzed using first a qualitative and then a quantitative approach. Some posit that the problem with math aversion in learning research methods is a function of never having been taught how to learn math (Buchler 2009). Thus, part of the challenge is conveying different techniques for learning course materials from those utilized in the classroom concerned with substantive as opposed to procedural materials. Finally, graduate methods instruction is typically math-lite after the first introduction to statistics course, and the focus of the instructor is on teaching students which tools to use given different research questions and available data, how to use those tools, and how to interpret the results from the subsequent analysis.

STATE OF THE DISCIPLINE

I now turn to an examination of the contemporary state of the discipline today. In the first part, I look at graduate methods requirements outside and inside the USA. In the second, I analyze 20 typical methods syllabi at the master's and doctoral levels. In the third, I attempt to measure the efficacy of methods instruction by looking at the productivity and attainment of tenure track jobs for current and recent doctoral students. In summary, while there is an array of requirements, there continues to be an overwhelming emphasis on empirical investigation through quantitative analysis. Further, this works: methods education is related to publishing and attaining tenure track jobs.

Requirements

I examined 16 major political science, international relations, policy and public administration graduate programs outside the USA, including programs in Australia, Canada, China, Japan, New Zealand and the UK. Most of these grant master's level degrees and have a range of methods requirements for students, though typically only one course is required and completion is expected during the first year of study. At the low end of the spectrum, three of the programs have no methods requirements; at the high end, one of the programs requires five courses in addition to a research paper.

Within the US context, I reviewed 198 graduate programs in political science, international relations, policy and public administration.[1] Among these, 120 offered an MPA, 42 an MA or MS in political science, and 115 a PhD. The average (median and mode) methods hours requirement for MPA programs was three (or the equivalent of one required methods course) with a range of 0–9 hours. For MA programs in political science, this was also 3 hours (or the equivalent of one required methods course) with a range of 0–9 hours. For PhD programs, the average is 6 hours (or the equivalent of two required methods courses) with a range of 0–20 hours.

Looking across all of the programs, the median is 3 hours, and the range is 0–9 hours. The median required hours for quantitative analysis is three with a range of 0–15 hours, and the qualitative analysis course median is 0 hours with a range of 0–4. There is no variance in these averages across degree type. Across all 198 of these programs, only one has required methods courses that are not campus based (meaning on-line only or hybrid courses), suggesting that, while there are ongoing conversations about delivery of graduate research methods courses, almost no institutions have yet moved to this model.

I also looked across the US schools to determine if there was a difference in methods requirements with respect to region. Among MPA programs, schools in the Midwest and South require significantly more hours than schools in other regions ($\chi^2 = 41.153$, significant at $p<.05$). There were no regional differences for MA/MS and PhD program requirements.

Substance of Courses

To examine the substance of courses, I pulled syllabi from 20 different courses from graduate programs across the USA and from all of the different types of degree programs examined above. These are summarized in Table 18.1. In short, a range of topics is covered in the classes, but some clear patterns and trends emerge across degree level. Across all levels, there were no examples of qualitative data analysis techniques in these courses. Further, there were no common methods texts used within or across the degree types. The only texts used by more than one class included Pollock's *The Essentials of Political Analysis*, Gujarati and Porter's *Basic Econometrics*, King, Keohane and Verba's *Designing Social Inquiry* and Faraway's *Extending the Linear Model with R*. Frequently the instructors assigned illustrative journal articles to accompany the topics covered in each class, particularly for the combined master's/PhD courses.

In terms of substance, master's level courses tend to focus on the research process and design, with significant attention paid to design type, potential for error and bias, data collection techniques and basic quantitative data analysis techniques. In these courses,

Table 18.1 Substance of courses across degree levels

	Master's Level	Joint MA/PhD Level	PhD Level
Substance in Course			
Epistemology	●	●	
Asking good questions	●		
Developing theory/literature use	●●	●	●
Hypotheses	●●●	●●●	●●
Operationalization/measurement	●	●●	●
Sampling		●	●
Research design	●●	●	●
Data collection	●●●	●	
Qualitative analysis			
Univariate statistics	●●●	●●●	●
Bivariate statistics	●●●	●●●	●●
OLS		●●	●●●
OLS assumptions			●●●
OLS violations			●●●
MLE/logit/probit etc.			●●●
Time series			●●
Factor analysis			●
Structural equation modeling			●
Probability theory		●●●	●
Bayesianism	●	●	
Presenting data		●	
Assignment Types			
Homework/problems	●●●	●●●	●●●
Small group work	●		
Case studies	●		
Papers	●●●	●●●	●●●
Presentations	●		
Exams	●●●	●●●	●●●
Software			
Excel		●	
SPSS	●●	●	
Stata		●	●●●
R			●●●

Note: ● mentioned in one syllabus; ●● mentioned in 2–3 syllabi; ●●● mentioned in >3 syllabi.

there is a wide array of assessment approaches, much more so than in the other types of degree programs examined and reflecting many of the suggestions in the literature about the utility of active learning approaches. This may have to do with the applied nature of these programs, as well as the accreditation process that these programs undergo, which focuses on improving student learning outcomes. These classes universally used SPSS (where mentioned in the syllabi).

Twenty percent of the courses we examined are combination courses for masters and doctoral students. In none of these syllabi are there differences in requirements for course completion or grading. These classes tend to merge a focus on design issues with more in-depth quantitative analysis than the master's level only courses, but none move beyond OLS regression. Assessment in these courses always combines homework/problem sets, exams and some type of paper. These courses use an array of data analysis software, including Excel.

The doctoral only courses focus primarily on quantitative statistical analysis, with a split between two types of courses. In the first, the courses start with a quick review of univariate and bivariate analysis, and then focus on OLS regression, assumptions of OLS, types of violations and a brief introduction to 'fixes' for violations of those assumptions. The other major type of doctoral course focuses in depth on extensions to OLS and other types of quantitative analysis approaches, particularly MLE and followed by time series analysis. In the case of the latter, these departments usually offer a series of methods courses that culminate in the more in-depth analytic techniques. Assessment in these courses typically involves either homework/problem sets combined with exams or homework/problem sets combined with papers. Data analysis software in these courses includes Stata alone, Stata and R (most common), or R alone.

Sophistication of Graduates

The ultimate measures of the utility of methods courses is whether or not there is a relationship to adding to the body of knowledge through attaining a tenure track job and whether there is a relationship to publications. To examine this, I used information from the websites of all of the doctoral programs included in the above analysis, specifically listings of their current and recent graduates over the past five years (2009–2013). When available, CVs were pulled. Across these institutions, 823 individual students were coded for year graduated, single and co-authored articles, single and co-authored books, and placement in a tenure track job.[2]

The graduates and current students examined were primarily in US schools, with only 40 (or 4.8 percent) at non-US institutions. These students represented three types of degrees: international relations (4.3 percent), political science, including IR as a major area of concentration (94 percent), and public administration (1.7 percent). Almost half of these people coded were still working on their dissertations at the time data were collected. Of the rest, about 6 percent were in a lecturer or instructor position, 16 percent were working in a research, applied, or post-doc position, and slightly over 26 percent had a tenure track job.

At the time we coded the data, 26.6 percent of the graduates had landed tenure track jobs. The first analysis conducted was the most obvious—what is the relationship between articles and book chapters published and having a tenure track job? As should be expected, the more articles and book chapters a candidate has, the more likely she or he is to get a tenure track job ($\chi^2 = 147.538$, significant at $p<.000$).[3] Given that, a quarter of the current and former students examined have jobs. I then examined the spread of the data to determine at what point (in terms of numbers of articles) individuals reached that 3:1 job threshold—it is between two and three articles, a manageable threshold for students if they are given proper time before going on the market and supportive mentoring while in school. This type of mentorship ought to especially focus on opportunities for

Table 18.2 Journal articles (single and co-authored) by current and recent doctoral students

Number of Articles	Count of Students per Publication Amounts: All Articles and Book Chapters	Count of Students per Publication Amounts: Top Journals
0	236	705
1	151	86
2	120	25
3	91	5
4	58	1
5	44	1
6	37	0
7	23	0
8	16	0
9	12	0
10+	35	0

co-authorship, as there was no discernable difference between landing a tenure track job and having single-authored versus multiple-authored articles and book chapters (χ^2 = 87.999, significant at p<.000 and χ^2 = 97.052, significant at p<.000 respectively). The same relationships do NOT exist for publication of books.

I also wanted to determine whether there was a difference between what are often referred to as top journals versus any journals in terms of holding a tenure track job.[4] While there is a difference in the range of publications (0–6 for top journals per individuals versus 0–24 for all articles and book chapters; see Table 18.2), there is also a relationship between having any articles and having them in top journals (χ^2 = 570.699, significant at p<.000 and pairwise correlation =.368, significant at p<.000). The point at which students with top journals overtake those without top journal articles in attaining tenure track jobs is one article. The message in both of these analyses is clear: if we want graduate students to get tenure track job offers, they need to be published, and the choice departments and advisors need to make is between quantity and quality.

All of this begs the question about the relationship between methods courses and publishing to attaining tenure track jobs. The data show a clear relationship between methods hours and tenure track jobs (χ^2 = 40.192, significant at p<.000), though this is not as strong as that between publishing and tenure track jobs. The tipping point for translating methods training into jobs is at 9 credit hours, and at 12 credit hours the candidates have a higher likelihood of getting a tenure track job than not. The weakest relationship is directly between required methods hours and publishing journal articles and book chapters, though it is still positive and significant (pairwise correlation is .088, significant at p<.05). In a simple multivariate analysis, both publishing journal articles and book chapters and methods hours maintain significance in predicting whether or not students attain tenure track positions, but the marginal impact of publishing is about seven times higher than formal methods training through required courses.

Outside Resources

While many programs face limitations in the training they can offer, there are myriad programs that allow for additional methods training for graduate students. In the USA, most typically accomplish this by supporting student travel to attend the ICPSR program housed at the University of Michigan. In addition, several other methods training programs have popped up in recent years. Among these are the Consortium on Qualitative Research Methods housed at the Maxwell School at Syracuse University and the summer institutes put on by EITM (Empirical Investigations of Theoretical Models). Outside of the USA, the European Consortium for Political Research (ECPR) holds a Summer School in Methods and Techniques (SSMT) and a Winter School in Methods and Techniques (WSMT) that provide a range of courses in both quantitative and qualitative methods as well as training for use of various types of software.

Several associations have also taken on extensions of methods training at their meetings, like the Western Political Science Association and the American Political Science Association through the use of 'methods cafes' in which participants go from table to table in a large room with an expert in a different methodological approach at each table to answer questions about the method (Yanow and Schwartz-Shea 2007). In addition, the advent of short courses held the day before the APSA conference has broadened avenues for methods training for graduate students.

RECOMMENDATIONS

When considering how to approach graduate research methods instruction, there are several levels of decision making. Graduate programs must determine 'methods to what ends', and when that question has been answered structure their course and extra-curricular offerings to achieve those goals. All of this presupposes a thoughtful approach to curriculum development and faculty buy-in, conditions that, in some departments, are difficult to achieve.

The answer to 'methods to what ends' will necessarily depend on the type of degree program. For master's level programs, especially those offering an MPA or MPP degree, the focus should be on concrete, transferable skills. In programs in which only one methods course can be required because of other demands on course time for mandatory course offerings, the curriculum should provide a basic overview and training in the introductory methods course, and then systematically incorporate each of the methods skills that the faculty as a whole deem important for students to master across substantive courses to best reinforce student learning.

For doctoral level programs, the approach to methods education is usually, and ought to be, different. The professional goal for students is typically to place them in the most appropriate tenure track job for their skills and interests. Placement is also related to publishing. Thus, departments ought to structure methods training in such a way that doctoral students have a strong grasp of the skills needed for research and publication in their subfields, whether this be quantitative, qualitative or some type of formal modeling. Simultaneously, departments need to develop mechanisms for encouraging student participation in research and publication, either through working with each other or serving as research assistants with professors, through research 'brown bags', and through participation in outside methods training programs. An integral part of this must include departmental support for faculty to write and publish with their students. Such support might include ensuring that co-authored pieces with students are fully 'counted' towards productivity, both in terms of research and teaching, as well as ensuring that students are funded adequately so that they can stay in programs long enough to finish coursework, pass comprehensive exams, write dissertations and simultaneously publish their work.

In addition, a greater emphasis on systematic research about teaching research methods would benefit the field. Top quality pedagogy research about graduate research methods education is possible only if two conditions are met. First, departments must start recognizing pedagogy research when weighing faculty research productivity. Second, because of the size of our graduate programs and the (in)frequency with which some courses are taught, faculty who teach graduate research methods ought to do a better job of working together across institutions to pool their courses for pedagogy experiments.

Finally, a critical but missing component in much of graduate methods education is the exploration of ethics in the research process. Calls for more emphasis on ethics include a greater emphasis on understanding the ethical implications across all types of data, as well as shifting the focus on understanding ethics as a discrete event (getting approval from Institutional Review Boards (IRBs) before collecting data) to a process that should be built into every stage of the research experience (Fujii 2012). In all of the material I examined, there was not a single mention of research ethics, despite the growing (and sometimes overly cumbersome) role of IRBs in all of our primary, and sometimes even secondary, research.

NOTES

* I would like to thank my research assistants Dillon Rheuby and Will McManus for their invaluable help in pulling together literature, course syllabi and CVs for this chapter. I would also like to thank Bob Smith for his helpful suggestions and review of early drafts of this chapter.
1. This includes graduate programs in Alabama (3), Alaska (1), Arizona (3), Arkansas (1), California (17), Colorado (3), Connecticut (3), Delaware (1), the District of Columbia (5), Florida (9), Georgia (4), Hawaii (1), Idaho (2), Illinois (12), Indiana (6), Iowa (2), Kansas (2), Kentucky (3), Louisiana (4), Massachusetts (8), Michigan (6), Minnesota (1), Mississippi (6), Missouri (5), Montana (1), Nebraska (2), Nevada (2), New Hampshire (1), New Jersey (3), New Mexico (1), New York (16), North Carolina (4), North Dakota (1), Ohio (8), Oklahoma (3), Oregon (2), Pennsylvania (7), Rhode Island (2), South Carolina (1), South Dakota (2), Tennessee (3), Texas (16), Utah (2), Vermont (1), Virginia (5), Washington (2), West Virginia (1), Wisconsin (2), Wyoming (1) and on-line only (1).
2. Gender was also coded. While men comprised 67 percent of the graduate students and recent graduates examined, this was not significant in any of the analyses.
3. A major caveat to this is for students from Ivy League schools—pedigree matters more than other factors in this case.
4. The journals coded as the 'top' journals include *American Political Science Review*, *American Journal of Political Science*, *Journal of Politics*, *International Organization*, *Journal of Conflict Resolution*, *Comparative Politics*, *Journal of Public Administration Research and Theory*, and *Public Administration Review*.

BIBLIOGRAPHY

Bernstein, Jeffrey and Brooke Allen (2013), 'Overcoming Methods Anxiety: Qualitative First, Quantitative Next, Frequent Feedback along the Way', *Journal of Political Science Education*, **9**, 1–15.
Buchler, Justin (2009), 'Teaching Quantitative Methodology to the Math Averse', *PS: Political Science & Politics*, **42**, 527–30.
Buehler, Melissa and Anthony Marcum (2007), 'Looking into the Teaching Crystal: Graduate Teaching and the Future of Political Science', *Journal of Political Science Education*, **3**, 21–38.
Centellas, Miguel (2011), 'Preaching What We Practice: Bringing Scope and Methods "Back In"', *PS: Political Science & Politics*, **44**, 817–22.
Clark, Alistair (2011), 'Embedding Transferable Skills and Enhancing Student Learning in a Political Science Research Methods Module: Evidence from the United Kingdom', *PS: Political Science & Politics*, **44**, 135–9.
Cohen, David (2002), 'Surviving the Ph.D.: Hints for Navigating the Sometimes Stormy Seas of Graduate Education in Political Science', *PS: Political Science & Politics*, **35**, 585–8.
Craig, John (2010), 'Practitioner-Focused Degrees in Politics', *Journal of Political Science Education*, **6**, 391–404.
Currin-Percival, Mary and Martin Johnson (2010), 'Understanding Sample Surveys: Selective Learning about Social Science Research Methods', *PS: Political Science & Politics*, **43**, 533–40.
Damron, Danny and Jonathan Mott (2005), 'Creating an Interactive Classroom: Enhancing Student Engagement and Learning in Political Science Courses', *Journal of Political Science Education*, **1**, 367–83.
Deardorff, Michelle and Paul Folger (2005), 'Assessment that Matters: Integrating the "Chore" Department-Based Assessment with Real Improvements in Political Science Education', *Journal of Political Science Education*, **1**, 277–87.
Deardorff, Michelle, Kerstin Hamann and John Ishiyama (2009), *Assessment in Political Science*, Washington, DC: American Political Science Association.
Dolowitz, David (2007), 'The Big E: How Electronic Information Can Be Fitted Into the Academic Process', *Journal of Political Science Education*, **3**, 177–90.
Fitzgerald, Jennifer and Vanessa Baird (2011), 'Taking a Step Back: Teaching Critical Thinking by Distinguishing Appropriate Types of Evidence', *PS: Political Science & Politics*, **44**, 619–24.
Florez-Morris, Mauricio and Irene Tafur (2010), 'Using Video Production in Political Science Courses as an Instructional Strategy for Engaging Students in Active Learning', *Journal of Political Science Education*, **6**, 315–19.
Fugate, Gregory, Patricia Jaramillo and Robert Preuhs (2001), 'Graduate Students Mentoring Graduate Students: A Model for Professional Development', *PS: Political Science & Politics*, **34**, 132–3.
Fujii, Lee Ann (2012), 'Research Ethics 101: Dilemmas and Responsibilities', *PS: Political Science & Politics*, **45**, 717–23.
Gershkoff, Amy (2005), 'Multiple Methods, More Success: How to Help Students of All Learning Styles Succeed in Quantitative Political Analysis Courses', *PS: Political Science & Politics*, **38**, 299–304.
Goss, Kristin, David Gastwirth and Seema Parkash (2010), 'Research Service-Learning: Making the Academy Relevant Again', *Journal of Political Science Education*, **6**, 117–41.
Hartlaub, Stephen and Frank Lancaster (2008), 'Teacher Characteristics and Pedagogy in Political Science', *Journal of Political Science Education*, **4**, 377–93.
Herrnson, Paul (1995), 'Replication, Verification, Secondary Analysis, and Data Collection in Political Science', *PS: Political Science & Politics*, **28**, 452–5.
Hubbell, Larry (1994), 'Teaching Research Methods: An Experiential and Heterodoxical Approach', *PS: Political Science & Politics*, **27**, 60–64.
Ishiyama, John, Tom Miles and Christine Balarezo (2010), 'Training the Next Generation of Teaching Professors: A Comparative Study of PhD Programs in Political Science', *PS: Political Science & Politics*, **43**, 515–22.
Jansson, Maria, Maria Wendt and Cecilia Ase (2009), 'Teaching Political Science through Memory Work', *Journal of Political Science Education*, **5**, 179–97.
Kehl, Jenny (2002), 'Indicators of the Increase of Political Science Scholarship on Teaching and Learning in Political Science', *PS: Political Science & Politics*, **35**, 229–32.
Knotts, Gibbs and Eleanor Main (1999), 'Teaching Ph.D. Students to Teach Political Science: The Emory TATTO Program', *PS: Political Science & Politics*, **32**, 607–10.
Latimer, Christopher and Karen Hempson (2012), 'Using Deliberation in the Classroom: A Teaching Pedagogy to Enhance Student Knowledge, Opinion Formation, and Civic Engagement', *Journal of Political Science Education*, **8**, 372–88.
McBride, Allan (1994), 'Teaching Research Methods Using Appropriate Technology', *PS: Political Science & Politics*, **27**, 553–7.

Murakami, Michael (2012), 'The Broad Value of a PhD in Political Science', *PS: Political Science & Politics*, **45**, 812–14.

Nordyke, Shane, Daniel Palmer, William Anderson, Rich Braunstein and Matt Fairholm (2011), 'A Nontraditional PhD Program in a Traditional World: A Story of Blended Strategies and Students', *Journal of Political Science Education*, **7**, 275–94.

Quinn, John (2009), 'When You Can't Find the Perfect Match: Using the Accumulated Most Similar Design in Case Studies', *Journal of Political Science Education*, **5**, 250–67.

Rihoux, Benoit, Bernhard Kittel and Jonathon Moses (2008), 'Political Science Methodology: Opening Windows across Europe . . . and the Atlantic', *PS: Political Science & Politics*, **41**, 255–8.

Rodgers, Pamela and Cecilia Manrique (1992), 'The Dilemma of Teaching Political Science Research Methods: How Much Computers? How Much Statistics? How Much Methods?', *PS: Political Science & Politics*, **25**, 234–7.

Rudder, Catherine (1983), 'The Quality of Graduate Education in Political Science: A Report on the New Rankings', *PS: Political Science & Politics*, **16**, 48–53.

Schmidt, Benjamin and Matthew Chingos (2007), 'Ranking Doctoral Programs by Placement: A New Method', *PS: Political Science & Politics*, **40**, 523–9.

Schwartz-Shea, Peregrine (2003), 'Is This the Curriculum We Want? Doctoral Requirements and Offerings in Methods and Methodology', *PS: Political Science & Politics*, **36**, 379–86.

Schwartz-Shea, Peregrine and Andre Bennett (2003), 'Introduction: Methodological Pluralism in Journals and Graduate Education? Commentaries on New Evidence', *PS: Political Science & Politics*, **36**, 371–2.

Wolfe, Angela (2012), 'Implementing Collaborative Learning Methods in the Political Science Classroom', *Journal of Political Science Education*, **8**, 420–32.

Yanow, Dvora and Peregrine Schwartz-Shea (2007), 'The Methods Cafe: An Innovative Idea for Methods Teaching at Conference Meetings', *PS: Political Science & Politics*, **40**, 383–6.

19. Teaching undergraduate research methods
Cristina Leston-Bandeira

Teaching research methods is like no other subject area in politics and international relations – those who teach it are often the unlucky ones who 'can' do it, not necessarily those with a research expertise in the area. These are courses often labeled as difficult, boring, unnecessary and irrelevant, and yet compulsory – in short, courses with all of the ingredients to make them strong contenders for the most unpopular course award. And yet, all of the successful strategies that work in the teaching of other subject areas should also work for methods teaching. What is more, as a key employability skill and as one of the principle foundations of our discipline, research methods should be an essential area of investment from departments, in particular at undergraduate level. Getting undergraduate methods teaching right has exponential benefits to our student population, as it supports students to then develop and apply methods skills to their other degree modules and, in some cases, develop them further for stronger postgraduate study, at the same time as developing a better understanding of the real world of politics.

The chapter reviews key challenges in the teaching of undergraduate research methods, then reflects on what makes for successful undergraduate research methods teaching. With the support of existing examples of methods teaching, the chapter explores ten recommendations that aim to develop a more engaging and effective teaching of methods to undergraduates. It shows that undergraduate research methods can be engaging if focused on the discipline, the research process, application and the student. It also shows the value of shaping the teaching to the audience and not expecting an unrealistic level of skills, demystifying the complexity associated with research, designing creative assessment methods and adopting a blended learning approach to ensure extensive support. Finally the value of peer support networks and individual tutor support to students should not be underestimated.

UNDERGRADUATE METHODS TEACHING AND ITS CHALLENGES

Whilst in other social sciences disciplines the teaching of research methods has become well established at undergraduate level, the picture is much more patchy within the discipline of politics and international relations. In the UK, for instance, methods courses are still not compulsory in all undergraduate politics and international relations degrees, despite the fact that students are usually expected to develop a final degree project or dissertation. What's more, where research methods are taught, it is largely quantitative, with few institutions covering qualitative research in any great detail (Turner and Thies 2009). The main challenge is its seemingly overwhelming unpopularity with students and – to some extent – lecturers. Methods modules are considered to be 'dull' (Hosticka 1980, p. 213; Owens 1983, p. 100). This applies in particular to the statistics or quantitative elements of courses. Studies have found a 'terror of math[s]' amongst social science students (Bos and Schneider 2009, p. 379) and this can mean that students are often fearful or anxious about methods modules. Anxiety is not limited to quantitative research, though. There is evidence of high student anxiety over other areas, such as the originality of research questions and the trustworthiness of sources (Bos and Schneider, 2009, p. 378). These anxieties can be a barrier to teaching, meaning that these modules are often 'dreaded' by lecturers too (Young and Perlman 1984, p. 63).

The aura of negativity associated with methods learning is in fact one of the key challenges that lecturers often have to face – negative perceptions from students, but often also from colleagues, who as a consequence may not want to be involved. Ryan et al. summarize well the general malaise towards methods teaching, concluding that, 'while it might be a stretch to say that teaching a research methods module is actively avoided by many, and it is of course a passion for some, it is however a struggle for many' (2014, p. 86). Methods teaching is branded as a difficult and unpopular subject to teach, before anyone even steps into the classroom. As shown below, the perceived complexity associated to methods is a key challenge that lecturers need to address before even getting started on the content delivery. This is exacerbated in the case of quantitative methods by the varied levels of prior experience from students. Whilst in some countries students will have taken mathematics until the end of their secondary studies, in others, such as the UK, they stop at the age of 16. Besides this, students choosing to take politics and international relations degrees are often those who lack confidence in numeracy skills.

DEVELOPING SUCCESSFUL UNDERGRADUATE METHODS COURSES

The teaching of undergraduate methods therefore faces considerable challenges. It is, however, also a very rich area, which benefits from many publicly available resources, and one where good practice can easily be shared. It is also an area that has attracted considerable public investment in recent years. Ten recommendations are explored below to support the development of successful undergraduate research methods teaching – summarized in Table 19.1.

Table 19.1   Ten recommendations for successful undergraduate methods teaching

1. Focus on the discipline
2. Focus on the process
3. Focus on application
4. Focus on the student
5. Shape it to your audience
6. De-mystify it
7. Design creative assessment methods
8. Utilize a blended learning approach
9. Enable support networks between students
10. Enable individual support from tutor to student

1. Focus on the Discipline

Students are unlikely to be interested in methods per se. If they are doing a degree in politics and international studies, they are likely to be interested in politics and international studies. Focusing on the actual discipline is therefore an approach that is far more likely to engage students into the content being delivered: the discipline is a key mediator in making students understand the role played by research (Healey 2005, p. 186). As far as possible, research methods should therefore be taught through its application in the discipline of politics and international relations.

There are a number of ways in which this can be applied. Firstly, students learn better if they are able to relate theories and methodologies to 'substantive examples in which they are interested' (Janda 2001 quoted in Adeney and Carey 2009, p. 196); if they are able to see the benefits of the 'quantification of politics in everyday life' (p. 196), they will have a greater appreciation for social science research. Thus simply demonstrating our reliance on data can highlight their importance to the subject. This can be done by asking other academics from the department to talk to students about their research, focusing on the type of data they analyze, or simply reviewing a policy report from a specific government department. Adeney and Carey (2009, p. 196) took this one step further, inviting speakers from a range of organizations, such as Ipsos MORI, to speak to students and highlight the importance of quantitative research to their future careers.

Secondly, publically available data can be used as a teaching tool. This could consist of providing a simple demonstration in a lecture. Material should be connected to the real world 'wherever possible' (Carlson 2009, p. 208). Alternatively, freely available or open source data can provide data-sets for a class project or other student assessment. Examples include National Election Studies and surveys (Wald 1981, p. 224), the Interactive Data Library (Hewitt 2001) and the British Social Attitudes Survey (Daddow 2010, p. 22). Open Educational Resources now also help to disseminate this type of data, with many focusing specifically on research methods.

Any of the above can be easily integrated into the teaching on research methods: in the actual classroom, in the material being used to support the teaching; in material made available through a virtual learning environment (VLE); through any material being made available to students; by constituting part of an actual lecture or indeed being integrated into an assessment task. All of the above can also simply be integrated throughout a degree program, rather than isolated in a single module on methods.

Another way to focus on the discipline is by students defining themselves their own methods tools (Leston-Bandeira 2013). This approach works if combined with support facilitated by a VLE and the provision for one-to-one support from tutors. In that case study, students develop a research project on a topic that they choose, having to define their own research question and design, then implement the project and finally analyze the results. The ability of choosing their own research topic is the key factor explaining the very positive feedback for this module, showing that 'embedding the teaching of methods in the discipline of politics – and in the students' own individual interest in politics – is a crucial element in engaging students in this learning process' (Leston-Bandeira 2013, p. 215). This is a holistic approach that integrates the whole of the teaching into the discipline, but the same approach can be adopted on a much smaller scale, such as asking students to define a questionnaire on a topic they are interested in or to identify data in a subject area they are interested in. Through this approach, students develop their understanding of the research methods and engage in this process, because they are exploring an issue of interest.

2. Focus on the Process

Before being able to understand specific methods, students need to develop an appreciation of the research process, in particular at undergraduate level. Too often we jump into teaching research techniques that are far too specialized, before ensuring that students have an appreciation of the process of undertaking research. The value of making students conceptualize their own research question, plan its associated research design and then apply the project, should therefore not be disregarded. An understanding of the process is crucial as a first step towards subsequently developing expertise on any research method. Focusing on the process also has the advantage of being more inclusive of all methods, without a divide between qualitative and quantitative. Developing an understanding of the variety of methods employed in politics and international relations is of particular value for our graduates' future professional careers (Thies and Hogan 2005, p. 293).

This has implications for the design of a methods course. Classes need to be taught following the path of a research process and the sequence associated between lectures needs to be clearly signposted to students at every class. Assessment can also incorporate elements demonstrating understanding of the whole process. A simple way of doing this is through a Reflective Statement, where students reflect on the process of undertaking their research project or activity, having to explain the decisions taken during that task. Another simple method is by introducing small Q&A exercises in lectures, at various points of the course curriculum, where students explore the consequences for decisions taken in research in different scenarios.

Research methods modules are designed to enable students to develop independent learning of the highest levels to produce high quality work, ultimately primary and original work; the independent element is therefore particularly important. In order to develop that sense of independent initiative, it is crucial that students understand what decisions need to be taken, at what point and their consequences; that is, students need to have an appreciation of the whole of the research process. Their lack of previous experience with independent research means that students frequently have very little understanding of the actual process of planning, implementing, analysing and evaluating research projects. Students therefore do not automatically 'think like social scientists' (Dickovick 2009, p. 148). For instance, when asked what they are expecting from a comparative politics module, most students will highlight individual countries of interest to them rather than anything to do with methodology or the comparison of different countries (Dickovick 2009, p. 139). They wish to learn rather than analyse politics, and thus in constructing a research project they are venturing into the unknown. Students need, therefore, to be expected to engage with the research process directly, for example by establishing a research question and identifying relevant sources of data. This works well as a peer support type of activity, whereby students question each other's decisions and develop an understanding of possible solutions together.

Focusing on the process of conducting research ensures that students 'appreciate the wider issues of research design' (Adeney and Carey 2009, p. 196). They are able to learn the tools of the trade. Hewitt (2001, p. 371) likens this to a carpenter who would need to know how to use a hammer in order to adequately complete his work. In this way, 'specific [research] tools have specific purposes and, if one is to employ them correctly, one must first understand what they mean, what they are meant to do and how and when to use them' (Grix 2002, p. 176). Focusing on the process of conducting research gives students the overall picture of where each method fits. Having an understanding of the process should be a requisite before developing any more specialized learning on specific epistemology or methods and/or embarking on a project such as a dissertation.

3. Focus on Application

Methods are exciting when they let us develop our own knowledge and understanding; that is, when we apply them and feed on the findings. The best way to convey this to students is therefore to make them apply the methods. It is the application of methods that conveys the pains, challenges and successes of undertaking research.

The tendency of departments to begin with an 'abstract discussion of the philosophy of science often obscures the basic issues' that students need to understand to be able to embark on a process of independent research (Powner 2006, p. 521). Actively engaging students in the application and implementation of research methods can therefore be a more effective means of teaching (Doherty 2011, p. 164; Hosticka 1980), allowing students to experience the process first hand and familiarizing them with 'the nuts and bolts of how the scientific method can be applied in empirical social research' (Doherty 2011, p. 164). It is only by going through the process of actually interviewing someone, for example as part of their assessment, that students are able to appreciate the subtleties of asking non-biased questions and the frustrations of actually booking an interview. A workshop practical activity can also be developed where students practice interviewing each other or their lecturer, who can play the role of the awkward interviewee misinterpreting questions. Carlson (2009) gives another practical example: as an introduction to a research methods module, students had to collect data about the clothes in their own wardrobe and complete a database listing the various countries their clothes had originated from. This is a practical, innovative, simple but engaging manner to make students experience a specific methodological process.

It may be that different activities are used in each teaching session or 'intertwined throughout an academic term' (Dickovick 2009, p. 138) as a way of demonstrating the application of research. Leston-Bandeira's example utilizes a holistic approach where the whole module is built around the idea of applying a research project from the conceptualization of a research question to analysis of results (2013, p. 210). Or one theme may be used for the teaching of an entire methods course. Buchler believes that this allows students to 'see how each technique fits into a narrative and shows the full process of social science' (2009, p. 530). Feedback from students who have experienced this form of teaching has been very positive. The use of class polling projects has been reported to enhance student enjoyment and understanding of the subject (Berry and Robinson 2012; Cole 2003 quoted in Currin-Percival and Johnson 2010) – and as a result, students put in a great deal of effort. Focusing on application makes research methods more tangible:

it enables students to better engage with the methods and understand why they are relevant, both of which lead to deeper learning.

4. Focus on the Student

As with any good pedagogic example, student centered techniques work best for methods teaching, in particular at undergraduate level. The teaching should be developed around the student, rather than expecting the student to be a passive listener to the lecturer. This can include any of the following and more: interactivity in lectures, use of clickers to clarify concepts, student led seminars, individual student projects. If the student is the focus of the teaching activity, they are more likely to become engaged and to reflect on the issues at stake. Focusing on the student and involving them in research 'will bring to life a subject that is often seen as dull' (Hosticka 1980, p. 217). Active learning techniques work particularly well with methods teaching, as they focus on the student and usually involve some form of application.

As Carlson reminds us, 'methods should not be taught through lectures alone' (2009, p. 206); in fact many now experiment with no lecture delivery, developing the teaching around workshops, seminars and online platforms. Where lectures play an important role in conveying information, then these should include some form of student participation, through active learning techniques such as the use of interactive response systems (clickers). But the literature reports extensively on more creative examples of student centered learning. Centellas (2011, p. 821) outlines examples of simple exercises that can be conducted in class. They include asking students to outline the concepts and variables used in a textbook, article or film, and to initiate a debate between class members about how the key concept has been measured. Stover suggests asking students to code data from videos of news broadcasts (1979, p. 35), whilst Wald (1981, p. 224) suggests an interesting means by which to teach variables and cross-tabulations to students. Students are lined up in a column on one side of the room and told that their desks are coded information based on a set of personal characteristics and other variables in a set of data. They are then asked to sort themselves by gender, thus forming two columns on different sides of the room. Asking them to sort each of their columns again (in this case their intended vote in a forthcoming election) creates a 2×2 cross table similar to that which would be created by data analysis software and which enhanced the students' understanding of data manipulation (Wald 1981, p. 224).

Another simple way of focusing the teaching on the student is by involving them in taking decisions about research. Allowing students to choose their own questions and to form their own hypotheses ensures that they 'own the data and the results' (Adeney and Carey 2009, p. 196). Students can experience this ownership of the learning process by defining their own research question, design and application, therefore shaping their learning to their own interests (Leston-Bandeira 2013, p. 214). This is an approach that can be very successful, as long as support is provided to cover a very wide range of types of methodologies. Focusing on the student is not just about engagement, though. Involving students in making research decisions gives them 'an appreciation of the choices that must be made and a sensitivity to considerations involved in making those choices' (Hosticka 1980, p. 210).

5. Shape it to your Audience

One of the key problems in student engagement with methods learning is the mismatch between the prior skills expected to take a methods course, and the actual skills undergraduates have. This can become a problem particularly in the case of quantitative methods. If the students are unlikely to have done math since they were 16, one should not expect them to have sound or even competent numerical skills. Instead, this should be addressed and teaching should start with basics, building up on these progressively towards more complex topics. Undergraduate methods teaching needs to be different from postgraduate methods teaching. If the material being taught is made too complex by the tutor, then students will often 'automatically resign themselves to never understanding the information' (Hy and Hughes 1988, p. 61). Adopting a gradual approach, which allows the student to build on concepts and understanding, is therefore essential for a successful undergraduate methods course.

Today's undergraduate students have a very varied experience of mathematics and statistical analysis (Andersen and Harsell 2005, p. 20; Rodgers and Manrique 2002). Whilst some students will want to be taught advanced statistical modeling, others will have had no previous exposure to quantitative research or even very simple mathematics (Young and Perlman 1984, p. 63). This can be turned to the lecturer's own advantage. As an introduction to the module and to empirical research, the lecturer could explicitly find out more about the students' background in methods skills. This can be done through, for example, a questionnaire. Depending on each situation, this can be a larger or smaller activity and it may involve students to a greater or lesser degree. Students may be involved in defining the questions or in analyzing the results. It can take place within one class or over some weeks through, for instance, the utilization of a VLE. Besides providing for a practical application of research skills, this gives the lecturer valuable information about the students they are about to teach.

When teaching quantitative methods, it is not sufficient to assume that students have understood what has been taught. Students are often 'reluctant to say when they don't understand something math related', which has been presented in a lecture (Buchler 2009, p. 528). This is where interactive response systems can be very useful to ascertain levels of comprehension amongst students, before moving on to the next concept. Through the use of clickers, lecturers can test their students' understanding halfway through a lecture, by directly enquiring about how comfortable they feel with a specific concept, or simply by asking a question related to the concept being taught. As clickers allow for anonymous voting, they are very useful to quickly ascertain genuine levels of understanding.

6. De-mystify it

Associated with some of the points above, a key barrier in teaching methods, in particular at undergraduate level, is the complexity and level of difficulty associated with it. This is such a key barrier to engagement with methods that it needs addressing directly as a specific issue. As mentioned above, even before starting a methods course, most students' perceptions are that this is a very difficult and complex subject area. The ability to develop research is perceived as something that only professionals can do, with an aura of specialization, which makes it seem the realm of the few rather than an opportunity for the many. Just as one would not expect an undergraduate student to write an essay with the quality of an academic journal article, one would not expect undergraduate students to develop research at that level. And yet, we often forget about this. More importantly, students do not necessarily see this difference and the wide range of levels of complexity within research. This has many consequences to the way we engage students with methods, but particularly to the assessment criteria. These need to recognize the value of demonstrating competence in undertaking specific research tasks, rather than only focus on more intellectually based skills such as analysis.

Considerable care needs therefore to be put into demonstrating to students that anyone can develop primary research, and that developing research is ultimately about common sense, rigor and clarity, with principles and specific techniques helping the researcher along the way. This can of course expand considerably in complexity, but ultimately those foundations can be developed by anyone through many different paths. A child investigating the different shapes of shells on a beach, then bringing a selection of these to class and explaining what this shows about shells, may be a very basic form of research, but it is research nonetheless, to include investigative skills and conclusions based on evidence. De-complexifying the process of undertaking research is partly about identifying the different elements that compose research (epistemology, sample, evidence, etc.) and about demonstrating the diversity that research methods can assume, depending on the topic or the approach chosen; in short, de-complexifying research is also about explaining what research means.

De-complexifying research can take many forms. It can consist of showing previous students' work, discussing research ideas between students or involving students in explaining and demonstrating research. If students can relate to research, they are less likely to think it is too clever and complex for them. Showing previous students' assignments is a simple but effective way to convey to undergraduate students that it is perfectly in their reach to produce research, but it demonstrates also what research looks like at a simpler level. The type of research outputs students come across at university are very likely to be highly specialized and complex, not something they are necessarily able to relate to. Showcasing research methods assignments done by previous students is one way of demonstrating what research is about, at a simpler level. For instance, browsing through previous students' research proposals can be a key defining moment when everything falls into place and students understand what is required of them (Leston-Bandeira 2013, p. 213); it is a foundational step to then developing their own proposal.

Another method of de-complexifying research is involving students in discussing methods' concepts, experiences and approaches. This leads students to explain research in their own terms, which helps further to relate to the topic. By having to express their own experiences with carrying out research, students are naturally developing a sense of ownership of research and demonstrating that fellow students can also do it. It also helps to develop deeper learning. As Hewitt states, 'in the process of gathering new information and explaining it to other group members, students internalize knowledge more completely' (2001, p. 379). This works particularly well to teach concepts. Because of the nature of concepts, academics often convey these in a highly abstract manner; asking students to explain a specific concept is often a far more effective way of communicating its meaning.

7. Design Creative Assessment Methods

Following the principles explored above that students engage best if teaching is learner centered and through application, assessment should be designed to enable students to develop their own interests – for example, to develop their own mini-project, questionnaire experiment, content analysis or whatever it may be. As Healey demonstrated, 'getting [students] to do research themselves through undertaking some or all of the stages involved in carrying out a research project' (2005, p. 187) is the most effective way to engage students with this process.

There are a variety of ways in which students can be assessed during research methods modules. The most common assessment methods are research projects or reports, which often then progress into student dissertations. These projects can be individual (Centellas 2011, p. 821; Cole 2003 quoted in Currin-Percival and Johnson 2010), in small groups (Stover 1979; Clark 2011, p. 136) or a single project completed by the whole class (Stover 1979). These projects can be tutor or student initiated, or can even be commissioned by outside bodies and organizations (Owens 1983); although problems can arise from imposing research projects on students, with some often not fully understanding what the aims of the research are (Hosticka 1980, pp. 212–13). As Bos and Schneider suggest, 'creating assignments that have natural steps to achieving a larger methods goal can be very helpful' (2009, p. 382). Thus, some modules include a series of individual (and progressively more complex) assignments rather than one report. However, Ryan et al. report on negative feedback from students when faced with (too) many different forms of assessment (2014, p. 92) and there is value in not assessing all techniques being taught (Acton and McCreight 2013).

Other assessment methods include the production of individual student research journals and the use of memoranda written by students and subsequently graded by their peers in class (Hy and Hughes 1988, p. 63). Set as learning contracts, memoranda can be very effective because they force students to reflect about what they propose to work on and be realistic about establishing targets. A memorandum could be established, for example, around specific criteria to assess the effectiveness of survey data analysis. Evidence suggests that students evaluate their participation in such projects very highly. Cole for instance notes that as a result students 'felt they understood both the substance of the course they were enrolled in and survey research methods better' (Cole 2003 quoted in Currin-Percival and Johnson 2010, p. 535).

8. Utilize a Blended Learning Approach

Complementing face-to-face teaching with an effective use of a virtual platform (Blackboard, Moodle, other VLEs or even social media) enables lecturers to extend engagement and support much further. It provides another channel to give access to wider resources, but also for communication and discussion. This is particularly useful for large modules and for courses focusing on the students' individual choices for research, where the VLE can play 'a central role in providing not only information but also active support and communication' (Leston-Bandeira, 2013, p. 211).

Daddow notes that it is useful to 'generate data from students through surveys completed in VLEs' (2010, p. 22), whilst Roberts (2008) discusses the podcasting of methods lectures and the uploading of what he describes as 'fireside chats' on specific research issues that are available to students online at any point throughout the course. This enables students to listen again to lectures on issues as and when they arise during their research. VLEs can be used even more extensively not only to provide access to a wide range of material but also to facilitate discussions online. For example, they can be used to support the development of research questions through a forum, whereby students post their research ideas, which are then discussed online by tutors and students (Leston-Bandeira 2013, p. 213). A blended learning approach helps therefore to provide students with a wider net of support and extend the value of face-to-face teaching. This is particularly useful to engage those students who do less well in methods courses.

9. Enable Support Networks between Students

As highlighted above, there is great value in promoting the discussion of methods and research amongst students, particularly at undergraduate level. This not only enables better engagement but also serves to make research seem less complicated. By translating methods concepts into their own language, and slowly appropriating the methods language and embedding it with meaning, discussion amongst students has considerable power in making methods more tangible.

Discussion of research amongst students – particularly during individual research projects – is an effective means of making the process of conducting research less daunting. Students can find it particularly difficult to establish a research question and class discussions can help with this. Centellas notes that 'at least one class period' is set aside for peer review (2011, p. 821) in which students can gain insights from others in their group. Individual mentoring can also be useful, with Rodgers and Manrique proposing that a good strategy is 'to allow the more skilled students to mentor their fellow students who are at a lower skill level' (1992, p. 234). Networks between students can therefore play an important role in peer support. These networks can be promoted in many ways, such as through informal online discussions, through workshops where students present progress or through peer assisted study sessions. Centellas (2011, p. 821), for instance, sets aside one week in which students deliver short presentations and receive comments on their individual research projects. Hy and Hughes (1988, p. 63) made use of memoranda to other students through which they were able to critically appraise each other's written work.

10. Enable Individual Support from Tutor to Student

For as simple as we may make it, methods can be very complex and difficult. Individual support through drop-in workshop sessions, for instance, is a good way to provide support outside the complexity of lectures.

It is generally acknowledged in the literature that research methods modules often require a disproportionate amount of tutor input, particularly when compared to similar level modules. A number of case studies report on having to dedicate considerably more time to a course on methods compared to other modules (Acton and McCreight, 2013; Hosticka 1980; Leston-Bandeira 2013). This raises questions at a more strategic level. If universities are serious in recognizing the importance of research methods, not only as a key employability skill but also in its exponential positive effect on students' performance across their degrees, there needs to be a recognition that teaching methods successfully at undergraduate level requires considerable time and care.

CONCLUSION

Teaching research methods to undergraduate students needs to be different to teaching postgraduate students. If done properly, it can provide for a sound foundation upon which to develop the more specialized postgraduate research methods teaching. Whilst our politics and international relations students may have a natural suspicion towards the idea of taking research methods, this can in fact result in a very positive and altogether revealing experience. Successful methods teaching needs to engage students through their interest in the discipline. It needs also to focus on the process of undertaking research, prior to developing actual techniques in much more depth. And it is the application of these methods that will best convey to students the pains and pleasures of undertaking research; it is through the application of a method that students will internalize its understanding. Then, other than following simple good teaching principles such as enabling support networks, the use of blended learning and learner centered approaches, it is important to de-mystify research and shape the teaching to the audience. In order to engage students in the journey of undertaking primary research, lecturers need to address the task of de-constructing the negative perceptions towards methods – and part of this is about showing that anyone can do research; it is simply a matter of varying levels of complexity.

REFERENCES

Acton, C. and B. McCreight (2013), 'Engaging Sociology Students in Quantitative Methods: An Evaluation of Assessment for Learning in Research Methods Teaching', *HEA Social Sciences Annual Conference*, Liverpool, 23–24 May, abstract available at: www.heacademy.ac.uk/resources/detail/disciplines/Soc_Sci/Conf2013/Assessment (accessed 17 June 2013).

Adeney, K. and S. Carey (2009), 'Contextualising the Teaching of Statistics in Political Science', *Politics*, **29** (3), 193–200.

Andersen, K. and D.M. Harsell (2005), 'Assessing the Impact of a Quantitative Skills Course for Undergraduates', *Journal of Political Science Education*, **1** (1), 17–27.

Berry, M. and T. Robinson (2012), 'An Entrance to Exit Polling: Strategies for Using Exit Polls as Experiential Learning Projects', *PS: Political Science & Politics*, **45** (3), 501–5.

Bos, A. and M. Schneider (2009), 'Stepping Around the Brick Wall: Overcoming Student Obstacles in Methods Courses', *PS: Political Science & Politics*, **42** (2), 375–83.

Buchler, J. (2009), 'Teaching Quantitative Methodology to the Math Averse', *PS: Political Science & Politics*, **42** (3), 527–30.

Carlson, J. (2009), '"Who Are You Wearing?" Using the Red Carpet Question Pedagogically', *International Studies Perspectives*, **10** (2), 198–215.

Centellas, M. (2011), 'Preaching What We Practice: Bringing Scope and Methods "Back In"', *PS: Political Science & Politics*, **44** (4), 817–22.

Clark, A. (2011), 'Embedding Transferable Skills and Enhancing Student Learning in a Political Science Research Methods Module: Evidence from the United Kingdom', *PS: Political Science & Politics*, **44** (1), 135–9.

Cole, Alexandra (2003), 'To Survey or Not to Survey: The Use of Exit Polling as a Teaching Tool', *PS: Political Science & Politics*, **36** (2), 245–52.

Currin-Percival, M. and M. Johnson (2010), 'Understanding Sample Surveys: Selective Learning about Social Science Research Methods', *PS: Political Science & Politics*, **43** (3), 533–40.
Daddow, O. (2010), '"I Didn't Take a Politics Degree to Study Maths": Teaching Quantitative Methods in a Qualitative Discipline', *MSOR Connections*, **10** (1), 21–4.
Dickovick, J. (2009), 'Methods in the Madness: Integrative Approaches to Methodology in Introductory Comparative Politics', *Journal of Political Science Education*, **5** (2), 138–53.
Doherty, D. (2011), 'Teaching Experimental Methods: A Framework for Hands-On Modules', *Journal of Political Science Education*, **7** (2), 163–72.
Grix, J. (2002), 'Introducing Students to the Generic Terminology of Social Research', *Politics*, **22** (3), 175–86.
Healey, M. (2005), 'Linking Research and Teaching to Benefit Student Learning', *Journal of Geography in Higher Education*, **29** (2), 183–201.
Hewitt, J. (2001), 'Engaging International Data in the Classroom: Using the ICB Interactive Data Library to Teach Conflict and Crisis Analysis', *International Studies Perspectives*, **2** (4), 371–83.
Hosticka, C. (1980), 'Teaching Applied Research Methods: "The Use of Real Projects"', *Teaching Political Science*, **7** (2), 209–18.
Hy, R. and L. Hughes (1988), 'Activating Public Administration Students in a Statistics Course: A Team-Teaching Approach', *Teaching Political Science*, **15** (2), 60–64.
Janda, K. (2001), 'Teaching Research Methods: The Best Job in the Department', *The Political Methodologist*, **10** (1), 6–7.
Leston-Bandeira, C. (2013), 'Methods Teaching through a Discipline Research-Oriented Approach', *Politics*, **33** (3), 207–19.
Owens, W. (1983), 'Teaching Methodology through Community Surveys', *Teaching Political Science*, **10** (2), 100–105.
Powner, L. (2006), 'Teaching the Scientific Method in the Active Learning Classroom', *PS: Political Science & Politics*, **39** (3), 521–4.
Roberts, M. (2008), 'Adventures in Podcasting', *PS: Political Science & Politics*, **41** (3), 585–93.
Rodgers, P. and C. Manrique (1992), 'The Dilemma of Teaching Political Science Research Methods: How Much Computers? How Much Statistics? How Much Methods?', *PS: Political Science & Politics*, **25** (2), 234–7.
Ryan, M., C. Saunders, E. Rainsford and E. Thompson (2014), 'Improving Research Methods Teaching and Learning in Politics and International Relations: A "Reality Show" Approach', *Politics*, **34** (1), 85–97.
Stover, W. (1979), 'Learning through Doing: "Undergraduate Political Science Education and Social Science Research"', *Teaching Political Science*, **7** (1), 33–50.
Thies, C. and R. Hogan (2005), 'The State of Undergraduate Research Methods Training in Political Science', *PS: Political Science & Politics*, **38** (2), 293–7.
Turner, C. and C. Thies (2009), 'What We Mean by Scope and Methods: A Survey of Undergraduate Scope and Methods Courses', *PS: Political Science & Politics*, **42** (2), 367–73.
Wald, K. (1981), 'How to Cross-Tabulate Your Students', *Teaching Political Science*, **8** (2), 223–6.
Young, T. and B. Perlman (1984), 'Teaching Research Methodology in Public Administration', *Teaching Political Science*, **11** (2), 63–9.

20. Teaching political theory
Matthew J. Moore

Not everyone has an opinion about calculus, chemistry or even Congress, but everyone has an opinion about the purpose of human life, whether anyone has a right to rule over others (and why), and the proper distribution of the benefits and burdens of social cooperation. Because your students will have opinions about those things, it will be possible to draw them into political theory, and their engagement will make the class fun, for them and for you. But first, you have to know *how* to draw them in, which is what this chapter focuses on.

Because of the history of the discipline of political science, both the definition of political theory and the question of its role in political science are issues we need to address briefly before talking about teaching. What political theory consists of is the source of much debate in the profession. First we need to distinguish between what is often called formal political theory, which involves making mathematical models of political systems, and political theory (also commonly referred to as political philosophy), which concerns texts and arguments that make normative proposals about how government and society should be run. This chapter deals only with the second type of political theory, sometimes called normative political theory. Even within that narrower category, there is significant disagreement about what political theory is and does, with some scholars emphasizing making and analyzing normative claims, others focusing on intellectual history and yet others using political theory as a subject for various kinds of critical analysis (such as deconstruction, feminist analysis and so on). For undergraduate courses, the distinctions probably will not matter much, but for graduate-level courses you may want to teach the debate itself as part of the course, as part of the process of socializing new political scientists into the profession.

A related question is whether political theory is properly part of political science (or belongs in another discipline, such as philosophy or history).[1] The basic conflict here is between people who see political science as being primarily about developing testable empirical explanations, and thus see political theory as being perhaps intrinsically valuable but not properly part of political science, and others who see political science as inescapably having both descriptive and normative aspects, and thus see political theory as essential to the discipline (see Rehfeld 2010). Here, too, for undergraduate courses this debate probably is not that important, but a graduate class might want to introduce students to the issue and some of the major literature.

One final preliminary question is why we teach political theory. Political theorist Wendy Brown once quipped that political theory is 'the intellectual practice of teachers who are besotted with 24 books—give or take another couple of dozen' (Ryan 2004, p. 13), and on that view we teach political theory because we love it and find it intrinsically valuable. More concretely, Joel Kassiola identifies a handful of goals that seem to capture many people's intuitions about this question: to expose students to a tradition of thought, to show them the basic questions that structure and animate that tradition, to improve students' reading and writing skills, and finally to help them to become better critical thinkers (Kassiola 2007, p. 783).

READINGS AND ASSIGNMENTS

A successful course starts with a good syllabus (see more in Chapter 24 of this book). To put together a good syllabus, there are a few preliminary questions you'll need to answer. First, where does this course fit in the overall curriculum? In particular, you will need to know 1) whether this course is an overview or if it is focused on a particular aspect of political theory, 2) if the course has to cover particular texts, thinkers, issues or eras—if so, you also need to know how much flexibility you have to choose the particular texts or thinkers, and finally 3) at what level the course is being offered—is it a graduate or undergraduate course, and if the latter, is it an introductory, intermediate or advanced course? For planning purposes, the major difference between undergraduate and graduate is that undergraduate courses typically focus on primary literature, with relatively modest examinations of major secondary literature and little to no emphasis on internal debates about the nature of political theory as a scholarly discipline, whereas graduate courses typically put more emphasis on secondary literature and internal debates within the field.

Depending on your answers to those preliminary questions, you are likely to choose one of the two main approaches to teaching political theory—using a textbook that provides an overview of the field (usually with excerpts from primary sources), or using primary texts. Survey data of political theorists suggest that using primary texts is much more common than using textbooks, and that even faculty who assign textbooks frequently supplement them with additional primary sources (see Moore 2011). Both approaches have pros and cons. Using a textbook ensures broad coverage of the field and provides helpful background and contextual information (which may otherwise go by the wayside), while using primary sources exposes students directly to the issues and arguments that have been influential historically and that animate and excite political thinkers today.

If you choose to use a textbook, there are many available—some online sleuthing can reveal the current options. Be sure to look at some syllabi online, too, since they can reveal which textbooks people are actually using. If you choose to use primary sources, there are several types to choose from—monographs, anthologies and online/public domain texts in a variety of formats.[2] It is worth looking around before you settle on an edition—undergraduates will not care whether you are using the latest or most heavily footnoted edition, but they will be grateful if the version you choose is inexpensive (or free online). You might also consider using a secondary text aimed at helping students make sense of the primary texts, or at introducing them to some particular aspect of the field (methods of interpretation, critical perspectives, historical context and so on).

As you are selecting texts, keep in mind the question of how much reading it is reasonable to assign. In general, textbooks will be set up so that it is appropriate to assign either a chapter per week or a chapter per class meeting. For primary texts, the number of pages that it is reasonable to assign varies widely, depending on the texts themselves and the structure of the course. For the U.S.A. and similar systems, where undergraduate courses typically meet for 3–4 hours per week over 10–15 weeks, and where students are typically taking three to five such courses simultaneously, here are my personal rules of thumb: introductory courses, 50 pages/week; intermediate courses, 50–100 pages/week; advanced courses, 100–125 pages/week; graduate courses, a book per week, with the assumption that not everyone will read everything every week. In contrast, many European courses meet once a week for 1–2 hours, and in that setting a smaller reading load would be appropriate. Your best guide on this question is to ask your colleagues how much they assign in similar classes.

There are some good empirical data available about what texts and thinkers political theorists regularly teach (Moore 2011). Assuming that you have some choice about what you assign, here are some principles for choosing:

- *Classics*: are there some texts that you think anyone who has taken a political theory class should have read? If so, include some of them.
- *Conflict*: it is not going to be any fun if all of the texts agree with each other (seven flavors of libertarianism!). Choose texts to introduce at least a little conflict.
- *Comparative*: students respond well to reading things they have never read or (better) have never even heard of. Consider including some texts from non-Western thinkers or traditions, which are likely to be unfamiliar (see Moore 2011; Leslie 2007).
- *Unique*: avoid texts that are covered in other classes your students are likely to have taken (an Introduction to Politics class, a General Education philosophy class).
- *Diversity*: students vary in gender, race/ethnicity, religion, ideology and so on. If at least one text in your class speaks to an aspect of a student's identity (as they understand it), that student is more likely to identify and engage with the class.
- *Controversy*: include at least one text that will be sure to incite controversy, to keep the students engaged.
- *Burnout*: if you have time to do the prep, choose a text that you have never read/taught, so that you avoid boredom and burnout.
- *Beyond the obvious*: do not forget that many different kinds of texts and media may be appropriate—literature (Cowell-Meyers 2006), science fiction (Haddad 2005), pop culture (Centellas 2010), films, websites, music and so on.

In addition to reading and in-class activities, you will want students to complete some assignments. The nature and extent of course assignments vary tremendously, depending on the institution, the course level, your own teaching load, student culture and so on. A good general strategy is to try to structure the course assignments so that students have a graded opportunity to practice the skills and demonstrate the knowledge that you think someone who has completed your class should possess. For example, your assignments might focus on expository writing skills (papers), oral presentation skills (both solo and group presentations, debates), critical thinking (papers, presentations and tests), demonstrating an appropriate level of knowledge of the course material (papers, presentations, tests), the ability to read and analyze novel texts and so on. For activities other than lecture and discussion, one challenge is getting the students to pay attention and engage. For example, students are often tempted to ignore other students' oral presentations. A general strategy to deal with this is to make paying attention part of each student's grade. In my classes, students grade each other's oral presentations, and part of each student's grade is based on whether they complete an evaluation form for each other student's presentation.

In my ten-week, introductory-level, undergraduate classes, I usually require one diagram/outline of an argument, one 2–3-page reading summary, an 8–10-page compare-and-contrast paper and an essay exam. My intermediate-level classes require four to six reading summaries, a 15–20-page research paper and an essay exam. Finally, advanced courses require six to eight reading summaries, an essay exam and a longer (20–25 pages), more complex research paper. In my own experience, graduate-level courses typically require fewer but more substantial assignments, such as one large research paper (though experience indicates that graduate students could also use practice on some basic skills that could be covered in other assignments, such as preparing a literature review).

Finally, you will do better if you recognize that, while the best students will do the work you assign out of love of the material or intellectual curiosity, the vast majority are only taking your class because they have to, and those students need a reason to do the work you want them to do. Do not expect them to do their best work on ungraded assignments or activities. If the work is important, make it count towards their grade in some way.

PEDAGOGY: PRINCIPLES AND TECHNIQUES

Many aspects of pedagogy are covered elsewhere in this book, so here I just touch on four general pedagogical concerns and techniques, before moving on to issues specific to political theory. First, as you have no doubt heard before, there is good evidence that students learn more if they are actively engaged in the learning process rather than passively receiving information (Omelicheva and Avdeyeva 2008). Second, to keep yourself focused on active learning, it is helpful to think of the course as learning driven rather than teaching driven. In other words, the class will be successful only if the students actually learn what you want them to learn, not if you merely show up and teach the required number of class meetings. Third, anecdotal evidence suggests that students do better in courses in which the professor knows their name and calls on them by name. Obviously it is not always possible to achieve that, for example in very large lecture courses, but even under those circumstances, you could approximate the best practice, for example by learning as many names as possible or by calling on people by name from a seating chart or roster. Finally, in addition to learning about political theory, your students also need to be taught general intellectual skills—how to argue, how to write an expository paper, how to read difficult texts, how to quote and cite quotes properly, and so on. If you want your students to have those skills, plan to spend some time teaching them. It does not do any good merely to be appalled that they do not have the skills already or to assume that they will learn those skills in some other class.

Issues Specific to Political Theory

In addition to the general pedagogical concerns discussed above, there are a number of issues that are specific (if not unique) to teaching political theory. Very roughly, these issues fall into two groups: navigating what the students already believe, and ensuring that they learn what you want them to learn. The first issue—navigating what students already believe—comes up in a number of different ways in the classroom. One version that you're probably already aware of is the issue of (perceptions of) bias. Some students feel that their political views are underrepresented and/or disrespected in the academy generally. In the context of a course that specifically addresses and evaluates various political ideas, such students are likely to be very aware of (perhaps even paranoid about) what they perceive to be bias on the part of the professor (Kelly-Woessner and Woessner 2006; Woessner and Kelly-Woessner 2009). Ultimately, of course, it is up to you how you want to approach this issue. Personally, I like to take a two-pronged approach. The first prong is reminding myself that students are unlikely to learn much from me if they feel disrespected or dismissed. That leads me to include a range of political views in my syllabi, in the hope of having at least one reading that each student can relate to. The second prong is trying to behave the way I want my students to behave; if they see me dismissing ideas and theories without considering them seriously and evaluating their arguments, then they will do the same with the course readings, and they will learn nothing.

A second pedagogical issue concerning students' existing beliefs is simply getting them to talk about what they believe in public. Both because of the widespread cultural taboo against arguing about politics in a group of strangers, and because of fear of being criticized or exposing one's ignorance, apathy, unpopular opinions or naïveté, many students are hesitant to reveal their political and philosophical views in class. There are two basic strategies for overcoming this problem—give them many opportunities to talk about their ideas and beliefs in small doses when the stakes are low, and create a classroom culture in which everyone's views are listened to and considered respectfully. An example of the first strategy is asking students brief questions about particular aspects of their beliefs by way of illustrating a point in a reading. If the reading touches on the question of the meaning of human life, ask a few students (or ask for volunteers) to quickly state their own idea about the meaning of life. An example of how to create a tolerant classroom culture is for you to model it, by taking what students say seriously and treating their views as valid.[3]

The last two pedagogical issues related to what students already believe are closely related to each other. One is getting students past what I call 'easy and obvious'—the belief that the answers to the questions posed by political theory are easy and obvious, and that they all boil down to power, self-interest, domination, patriarchy, hierarchy, gender, race, colonization, capitalism, conspiracies, UFOs or whatever their preferred all-purpose conversation-ender is. The second, related, problem is getting students to take a fresh look at issues they think they already understand, like the history of slavery and race relations in the U.S.A., the status of gender relations today, the question of whether socialism is a viable socio-political system, whether supply-side economics is valuable or true and so on. At root, both of these issues have to do with students preferring to hold on to their existing view of the world and resisting being challenged. In my own experience, struggling against these tendencies is a perpetual battle in the political theory classroom. I have found two approaches especially helpful: 1) trying to get the students to see that the theories we study are based on plausible, even compelling, assumptions about and interpretations of the world; 2) directly addressing the problem and asking students to adopt a variant of the Principle of Charity when reading: if smart people have been debating this issue for hundreds of years, it is a good bet that it is actually complicated and hard to resolve.

The other set of pedagogical issues specific to political theory has to do with making sure that the students learn what you want them to learn from the course. One variant of that is the task of striking the right balance between advocacy and criticism. In simple terms, will your course be about why each theory is right or why each theory is wrong? In practice, of course, it will be a bit of both, but deciding where to strike the balance is important. Personally I prefer to make my courses about why the theories are right, because I think that's the most effective way to get the students past their tendency to hold onto their existing beliefs and not take the course readings seriously. Of course I do talk about the problems and criticisms of each theory, but I'd rather that the students be unable to choose among so many compelling options than that they leave my course thinking that every theory is so flawed that none of them is worth the trouble.

The final pedagogical issue, also related to what you want students to learn, is striking the right balances between primary sources and background material, between theory and metatheory (discussing Locke versus discussing theories of how to read Locke), between the content of the texts and the debates within the profession about where the texts fit and what to do with them and so on. Deciding where to strike those balances depends on what role your course plays in the broader curriculum, whether it is an undergraduate or graduate course, and your own personality and intellectual bent. Personally, in my undergraduate courses I lean heavily towards getting the students involved directly with the texts and arguments, relegating most background information to the syllabus and bringing up broader intellectual debates as illustrations or asides, rather than as central concerns of the course.

Techniques

Now that you know what to do, you need to figure out how to do it. Which techniques will be useful or even possible depends on many factors, especially how big your class is and how comfortable you are letting go of control of the classroom. The techniques discussed below can work in classes ranging from seminars to multi-hundred-person lectures, though they may need to be tweaked or applied in a limited setting, such as a discussion section. Experimentation is the name of the game here (and it will also keep you from getting bored with your course). The same is true of letting go of control of the classroom. Active learning requires students to have some ownership and control of their learning experience, and that requires you to step back to some degree. How much you can (and should) step back, given your personality and teaching style, the demands of the curriculum, and the ability of students to take control effectively and productively, can only be determined through trial and error.

Political theorists use a variety of techniques in the classroom, but discussion and lecturing are by far the most common (Moore 2011, p. 114). A good lecture should be well organized, clear and thorough. In my own opinion, it should also be brief, or at least broken up with other kinds of activities. A good discussion takes a great deal of work to achieve, along with some luck, and also a willingness to let a thriving discussion go off topic for a while, if that keeps the energy high and the students engaged—they'll learn more overall because they're actively paying attention. Consider using a variety of discussion techniques, including Socratic or semi-Socratic method (you asking the students questions to explicate the reading), small group discussions (perhaps just to get the students started thinking or perhaps to generate brief presentations) (Pollock, Hamann and Wilson 2011), debates, simulations (Gorton and Havercroft 2012; Wedig 2010; Glazier 2011), role-playing (Schaap 2005) and so on. The goal is to get them engaged and actively learning. For more on classroom discussions, see Chapter 37 of this book.

The basic principle behind using discussions in class is to get students actively engaged in learning, and to give them a venue to ask questions and/or offer tentative answers with relatively little riding on whether they are getting the course material 'right'. A number of other classroom techniques aim at those same goals, such as using games and puzzles. For example, I often create crossword puzzles about course readings, and have students complete them during class.[4] The puzzles force the students to think actively about the reading we are discussing, while also providing them with a study guide. Most importantly, they are something different from our usual routine of lecture and discussion. There are also free online resources to make trivia-style games like *Jeopardy*, word searches and many other types of games.

Other active-learning techniques include having students create and/or perform dramas (Lukes 1981), songs or movies (Freie 1997; Woodcock 2012). In my introductory-level course, I have students make a movie explaining one of our course readings to the average college student. They have to figure out by themselves what the reading said, then either shoot and edit live video (very easy to do with cellphones and YouTube) or make animated movies (easy to do through many free online services).

My favorite active-learning technique is what I call political theory speed dating. The students sit in two rows that face each other. When the timer goes off, one side has 2 minutes to explain their political philosophy to the person sitting across from them, who must listen without responding. After 2 minutes, everyone gets up and moves one seat to the left (the people on the ends move to the opposite row). Then it is the opposite side's turn to talk for 2 minutes. Repeat for as long as you want to spend on the activity (I usually do it for one class period). The goal is to have everyone talk and listen to everyone, but also to discourage dialogue, which may inhibit students or make them feel judged or criticized (that's why the students move after each turn, so that they do not hear from the person they just talked to). I also sometimes use a modified (and shorter) version of this to have students talk over a particular issue or set of issues, or to have a series of mini-debates. This is a great activity to keep up your sleeve for a week in which you cover the assigned material more quickly than you expected, and end up with some time to fill.

In-class writing can also be an effective way to break up lecture and discussion periods, and to get/require the students to engage more actively. Writing activities can be done by individuals, small groups or the entire class. They can focus on creating outlines or diagrams of arguments, making study guides for course material, eliciting students' personal responses (Mott 2008) to the material and/or issues, and so on.

Yet another approach is using media and the visual arts (Miller 2000; see also Chapter 33, which discusses using film and media). Personally, I think that using media can be a risky strategy. Sometimes it adds a dimension to a discussion that cannot be achieved any other way. For example, I show excerpts of Adolf Eichmann's trial when I teach Hannah Arendt's *Eichmann in Jerusalem*. Hearing and seeing Eichmann's testimony is more immediate and affecting than only reading Arendt's recounting of it. However, sometimes using media just creates a different kind of passive-learning experience for the students and does not add anything of value. You have to experiment to see what works for you, and of course what works with one group of students may fail miserably with another. The same goes for presentation software like PowerPoint. Used well, it can add to the class and make it more engaging, but used badly it just becomes a flashier lecture for students to ignore.

The question of using media naturally leads to the broader question of teaching with technology, which may include a course website, wikis, podcasts (Roberts 2008; Taylor 2009), online testing/submission of assignments/grading, computer or online simulations, online discussions (Williams and Lahman 2011), audience-response clickers (Ulbig and Notman 2012; see also Chapter 25 of this book), blogs (Lawrence and Dion 2010) and so on. Many of these can be helpful by simplifying workflow, adding depth to the course material, giving students a break from lecture and discussion, and prodding students to be active learners, but all of them can also be either a waste of time or a distraction from the central concerns of the course. The trick is to strike the right balance and to keep experimenting.

Although this chapter assumes that your course will be delivered either entirely or mostly face to face, online and hybrid courses are increasingly popular, so your course may be delivered either partially or completely online (Dolan 2008). Although the methods differ from those used in traditional courses, the goals of online courses are the same: get the students to do the reading, provide help for them to understand the reading (lectures, online notes/whiteboards/discussions, student presentations/media projects), get the students to engage actively with the material (using many of the techniques already discussed) and evaluate the students' work to see whether they have developed the skills and knowledge you think they should have.

Both service learning and civic education have been popular within political science generally over the past couple of decades, but political theorists seem not to have adopted these techniques to any great degree (Moore 2011, p. 114). However, that is no reason not to use them, if they meet your substantive and pedagogical goals. An example of a service-learning activity in political theory might be having students teach a theory text to high-school students, to the general public, as part of a prison-education program or in some other non-traditional setting.

Learning Styles, Universal Design and Assessment

As you may already know, there is evidence that students have a variety of learning styles, which disposes them to approaching their classes and assignments in varying ways (Driver, Jette and Lira 2008; Leithner 2011). There are many different taxonomies of learning styles, distinguishing between abstract and concrete approaches to learning (Brock and Cameron 1999) and among visual, auditory, kinesthetic learners and so on. Appealing to different learning styles does not need to be burdensome. For example, you could post your lecture notes on the course website, thus making the material accessible to both auditory and visual learners. To engage kinesthetic learners you could have students come up to the board to make lists of terms, lead class discussions, make presentations and so on. (Even for non-kinesthetic learners, getting out of their seats occasionally is both welcome and helpful.) Similarly, you can appeal to both concrete and abstract learners by explaining the course readings in abstract terms (here's what Rawls says about distributive justice), while also illustrating with concrete examples (how, if at all, does access to college reflect Rawls's views?).

A related issue concerns universal design—that is, ensuring that the whole course is accessible to all students, regardless of disabilities, varying learning styles and so on. The issues of accommodating students with disabilities and appealing to different learning styles overlap, since a sighted auditory learner might listen to a machine-read text rather than reading it. Ideally, universal design is genuinely universal, allowing all students to engage with the course materials on their own terms (Ernst and Ernst 2005). In many countries, legislation requires that class materials be made accessible to students with disabilities—be sure to check with your institution about such local requirements.

Finally, there is the issue of assessment: figuring out whether the students have learned what you wanted them to learn. In essence, there are two reasons to assess student learning—to make sure that you are teaching the best course that you can teach, and to demonstrate to interested stakeholders (the students, parents, administrators, state legislatures, accreditation bodies) that your institution's graduates have the skills and knowledge that they should have. It helps to bear two general points in mind: 1) grades are not adequate assessment measures, because they capture too many different qualities of student work all at once (substantive quality, spelling and other technical issues, whether it was turned in on time or late, and so on); 2) assessment does not have to be burdensome or a great deal of extra work; it can be as modest as grading student work using a rubric that disaggregates several dimensions of achievement, and then recording and analyzing those data (for more information on assessment, see Chapter 9 of this book).

CONCLUSION

Now that you know what to do and how to do it, we come to the question we so often ask our students: So what? What's the point of teaching political theory? When it comes to graduate students, the answer is easy: you are training the next generation of political theorists (and other political scientists). But the question is harder when it comes to undergraduates (who inevitably make up the vast majority of students you will teach). Only a tiny fraction of undergraduates will love political theory so much that they become political theorists. In contrast, nearly all will take only one theory class (yours), because they are required to for one reason or another, and within just a few months or years they will forget most of what they learned. Off the cuff, those observations might appear depressing, possibly even evidence of the futility of teaching theory in the first place. But those would be seriously mistaken conclusions. Your job is not to ensure that each of your students remembers unto death every detail of Locke's theory of property or Rousseau's concept of civil religion. Rather, your job is to show students that political theory addresses questions that are of interest and relevance to them, to help them learn some of those theories and their answers to those questions and to help them develop a series of skills and habits of thought that are conducive both to political theory and to leading a critical and informed life. With any luck the skills and dispositions will stick, the recognition of the purview and value of political theory will remain, and the door will stay open for them to come back to theory when circumstances permit or require.

NOTES

1. This issue resurfaces in the profession every few years. For a thorough examination of the history of the debate, and the underlying issues, see the work of John Gunnell, especially Gunnell 1993 and 2011.
2. I curate a website (politicaltheorytexts.org) that collects public domain texts in political theory that are suitable for classroom use (because they have page, section or line numbers).
3. Of course there can be extreme cases where a student's views or responses to others' views cannot be harmonized with a tolerant classroom culture. For more on how to respond to such unusual cases, see Chapter 35 of this book.
4. There are a number of free crossword-creating websites and programs available online.

BIBLIOGRAPHY

Brock, Kathy L. and Beverly J. Cameron (1999), 'Enlivening Political Science Courses with Kolb's Learning Preference Model', *PS: Political Science & Politics*, **32** (2), 251–6.
Centellas, Miguel (2010), 'Pop Culture in the Classroom: American Idol, Karl Marx, and Alexis De Tocqueville', *PS: Political Science & Politics*, **43** (3), 561–5.
Cowell-Meyers, Kimberly (2006), 'Teaching Politics Using Antigone', *PS: Political Science & Politics*, **39** (2), 347–9.
Dolan, Kathleen (2008), 'Comparing Modes of Instruction: The Relative Efficacy of On-Line and In-Person Teaching for Student Learning', *PS: Political Science & Politics*, **41** (2), 387–91.
Driver, Darrell, Kyle Jette and Leonard Lira (2008), 'Student Learning Identities: Developing a Learning Taxonomy for the Political Science Classroom', *Journal of Political Science Education*, **4** (1), 61–85.
Ernst, Howard R. and Tracey L. Ernst (2005), 'The Promise and Pitfalls of Differentiated Instruction for Undergraduate Political Science Courses: Student and Instructor Impressions of an Unconventional Teaching Strategy', *Journal of Political Science Education*, **1** (1), 39–59.
Freie, John F. (1997), 'A Dramaturgical Approach to Teaching Political Science', *PS: Political Science & Politics*, **30** (4), 728–32.
Glazier, Rebecca A. (2011), 'Running Simulations without Ruining Your Life: Simple Ways to Incorporate Active Learning into Your Teaching', *Journal of Political Science Education*, **7** (4), 375–93.
Gorton, William and Jonathan Havercroft (2012), 'Using Historical Simulations to Teach Political Theory', *Journal of Political Science Education*, **8** (1), 50–68.
Gunnell, John G. (1993), *The Descent of Political Theory: The Genealogy of an American Vocation*, Chicago, IL: University of Chicago Press.
Gunnell, John G. (2011), *Political Theory and Social Science: Cutting against the Grain*, first edition, New York: Palgrave Macmillan.
Haddad, Khristina (2005), 'What Do You Desire? What Do You Fear? Theorize It! Teaching Political Theory through Utopian Writing', *PS: Political Science & Politics*, **38** (3), 399–405.
Kassiola, Joel (2007), 'Effective Teaching and Learning in Introductory Political Theory: It All Starts with Challenging and Engaging Assigned Readings', *PS: Political Science & Politics*, **40** (4), 783–7.
Kelly-Woessner, April and Matthew Woessner (2006), 'My Professor is a Partisan Hack: How Perceptions of a Professor's Political Views Affect Student Course Evaluations', *PS: Political Science & Politics*, **39** (3), 495–501.
Lawrence, Christopher N. and Michelle L. Dion (2010), 'Blogging in the Political Science Classroom', *PS: Political Science & Politics*, **43** (1), 151–6.
Leithner, Anika (2011), 'Do Student Learning Styles Translate to Different "Testing Styles"?', *Journal of Political Science Education*, **7** (4), 416–33.
Leslie, Isis (2007), 'Internationalizing Political Theory Courses', *PS: Political Science & Politics*, **40** (1), 108–10.
Lukes, Timothy J. (1981), 'Play Therapy in Political Theory: Machiavelli's "Mandragola"', *Teaching Political Science*, **9** (1), 35–8.
March, Andrew F. (2009), 'What Is Comparative Political Theory?', *The Review of Politics*, **71** (4), 531–65.
Miller, Char R. (2000), 'Drawing out Theory: Art and the Teaching of Political Theory', *PS: Political Science & Politics*, **33** (2), 213–18.

Moore, Matthew J. (2011), 'How (and What) Political Theorists Teach: Results of a National Survey', *Journal of Political Science Education*, **7** (1), 95–128.
Mott, Margaret (2008), 'Passing Our Lives through the Fire of Thought: The Personal Essay in the Political Theory Classroom', *PS: Political Science & Politics*, **41** (1), 207–11.
Omelicheva, Mariya Y. and Olga Avdeyeva (2008), 'Teaching with Lecture or Debate? Testing the Effectiveness of Traditional Versus Active Learning Methods of Instruction', *PS: Political Science & Politics*, **41** (3), 603–7.
Pollock, Philip H., Kerstin Hamann and Bruce M. Wilson (2011), 'Learning through Discussions: Comparing the Benefits of Small-Group and Large-Class Settings', *Journal of Political Science Education*, **7** (1), 48–64.
Rehfeld, Andrew (2010), 'Offensive Political Theory', *Perspectives on Politics*, **8** (2), 465–86.
Roberts, Matthew (2008), 'Adventures in Podcasting', *PS: Political Science & Politics*, **41** (3), 585–93.
Ryan, Alan (2004), 'Intellectual Courage', *Social Research*, **71** (1), 13–28.
Schaap, Andrew (2005), 'Learning Political Theory by Role Playing', *Politics*, **25** (1), 46–52.
Taylor, Mark Zachary (2009), 'Podcast Lectures as a Primary Teaching Technology: Results of a One-Year Trial', *Journal of Political Science Education*, **5** (2), 119–37.
Ulbig, Stacy G. and Fondren Notman (2012), 'Is Class Appreciation Just a Click Away?: Using Student Response System Technology to Enhance Shy Students' Introductory American Government Experience', *Journal of Political Science Education*, **8** (4), 352–71.
Wedig, Timothy (2010), 'Getting the Most from Classroom Simulations: Strategies for Maximizing Learning Outcomes', *PS: Political Science & Politics*, **43** (3), 547–55.
Williams, Leonard and Mary Lahman (2011), 'Online Discussion, Student Engagement, and Critical Thinking', *Journal of Political Science Education*, **7** (2), 143–62.
Woessner, Matthew and April Kelly-Woessner (2009), 'I Think My Professor is a Democrat: Considering Whether Students Recognize and React to Faculty Politics', *PS: Political Science & Politics*, **42** (2), 343–52.
Woodcock, Pete (2012), 'Bravery, Technological Literacy and Political Philosophy: Replacing Oral Presentations with Student-Created Video Presentations', *Enhancing Learning in the Social Sciences*, **4** (2), available at http://journals.heacademy.ac.uk/doi/abs/10.11120/elss.2012.04020006 (accessed 17 November 2014).

21. Teaching controversial topics
David Malet

It is never good when a student stands up and starts screaming that you are trying to brainwash the class – or is it? The student was objecting to a video depicting poor labor conditions in factories in developing nations, the first result pulled from a Google Videos search for 'sweatshops'. On the one hand, this student soon found himself involved in frank debate with classmates about government intervention in markets, including the provenance of the public university in which this exchange was taking place. On the other hand, being challenged by his peers did not calm the situation, and the student created a disruptive atmosphere by attempting to shout over the instructor with accusations that the object of the class was socialist indoctrination.

How about when the impending end of the United States military's ban on gay service members leads one student in uniform to declare that if another man made a pass at him he would 'kick his teeth in'? This statement produced laughter from several classmates, but these caused an offended gay student to demand an apology. Should the instructor take sides in the dispute, or leave the students to work it out themselves?

Or what about when different words commonly used as racial epithets are casually tossed into discussions of anti-immigration measures (in two different countries) by students who argue that they are common-use terms with no offensive connotation? If there are gasps but no students actually speak out, is the instructor obligated to intervene? Or when a (blue-eyed blonde) student declares her support for racial profiling in airports, because she is sure that she would 'not need to worry about a blue-eyed blond' being a terrorist?

As a rule, instructors are responsible for creating an open environment for discussion in which no student believes that she or he is experiencing intimidation or discrimination. In practice, this often means overtly taking sides in heated debates over current events, and even noting inappropriate language signals a position and can produce charges of bias by students who believe that you have sided against them. Given these difficulties, and the near inevitability of some students believing that either their own political views or individual characteristics have been attacked, is it not simply better to steer away from controversial issues to avoid these pitfalls and maintain peace in the classroom?

I would argue instead that political controversies in domestic politics and international relations should be embraced, so long as a safe environment for debate has been established, as the best way to demonstrate to students the importance of key concepts and the relevance of theories. Teaching about politics can be uniquely rewarding because it provides the opportunity to engage students with the key issues of the times, presumably the very controversies that sparked both their interest in taking a political science course and your interest in teaching one. Indeed, most undergraduates who take classes in either domestic or international politics are probably there to learn more about, or debate, the issues that they see covered in the media – in other words, real world rather than theoretical concerns of literature to which they have not yet been exposed. It is no coincidence that enrollments in American Politics courses increase during presidential election years (Jagoda 2008).

However, engaging in a discussion of any contested issue also invites the potential for controversy in the classroom in a way that is unique to political science as well. Hedley and Markowitz (2001, p. 196) observe that students do not challenge the validity of the information presented to them, or the motives or legitimacy of the instructor, in natural science classes the way that some do in the social sciences. Hare (1973, p. 52), also notes that students do not typically get emotionally worked up over the 'great debates' appearing in scholarly journals. Do you remember when, in your first-year international relations discussion section, two classmates began yelling at each other about the case for structure over agency? Neither do I.

My own experience has been that, when you tell people that you are a professor of political science, many of them feel comfortable responding, 'Oh, I can tell you about politics!' As I muse to my students, I do not think that biologists are confronted with, 'Oh, I can tell you about photosynthesis!' It goes much better when I say that I am a professor of international relations: apparently fewer people feel confident expressing views on global issues and most simply say, 'Oh... that is really important these days.' Sure, only lately.

These exchanges are indicative of the likelihood that, to most students uninitiated in concepts of rational choice, collective action and post-positivism, enrollment in a class about politics means discussing opinions about issues. It probably means conflicting, or at least contrasting, views of the kind that they see in pundit shows and during candidate debates. It is rare in such programming to see one view discredited on the basis of faulty data or to see a winner proclaimed based on the preponderance of evidence. The motto of one news channel, 'We report, you decide', offers the rhetorical shelter of the primacy of opinions.

So, while not every political science major will be keen to speak in public or to debate issues in front of their peers, most will likely expect controversies to at least be discussed. But many of these students will also expect that their views will be respected, not just their freedom to hold their own views. The notion, attributed to Daniel Patrick Moynihan, that everyone is entitled to their own opinion, but not to their own facts, seems unfamiliar and unwelcome to many students who offer opinions about current controversial issues. It is these students who pose the greatest challenge in attempting to teach using controversial cases.

This chapter examines the challenges and potential benefits of teaching about politics using material related to controversial issues and cases. Although instructors must take some caution to avoid offending students, and occasionally other interests within or outside the institution, the benefits to the students and their increased investment in the class greatly outweigh the minor additional risks. Students get to apply their learning by connecting theoretical material to current events, making the material appear particularly timely and relevant. Engaging students in controversial debates with their peers also teaches them that arguments are won by evidence and effective presentation, a skill useful in drafting essays and memos. Despite the challenges, then, coverage of controversial issues benefits students and creates a more engaging learning and teaching experience.

WHY TEACH CONTROVERSIAL ISSUES?

The first controversy that must be addressed is what precisely makes an issue a controversial one. A number of educators have used Fraser's (1964, p. 153) definition that

> A controversial issue involves a problem about which different individuals and groups urge conflicting courses of action. It is an issue for which society has not found a solution that can be universally or almost universally accepted. It is an issue of sufficient significance that each of the proposed ways of dealing with it is objectionable to some section of the community and arouses protest ... when a course of action is formulated that virtually all sectors of society accept, the issue is no longer controversial. (In Hare 1973, pp. 51–2; McKernan 1982, p. 58).

Of course, this standard itself is open to challenge because it is difficult to imagine many issues on which there is complete public unanimity, and the threshold for what constitutes protest is undefined. For the purposes of higher education, is a controversial issue one that is likely to generate spontaneous dissent from students? Or one that will only produce division if you ask for dissenters? If there is one strong and vociferous dissenter in a class of 50, is there really a controversy when 95 percent of the room is apparently in agreement?

Controversial issues seem to follow the standard for pornography set by a United States Supreme Court justice in a famous case: you simply know it when you see it. Except, when it comes to controversial political issues, the teacher might not recognize having raised one until a student protests. For example, in the instance I cited at the beginning of this chapter, it did not occur to me that a student would deny the existence of sweatshops in the world and allege that any attempt to discuss them in an international relations class amounted to a surreptitious attempt to impose socialist political dogma. This particular student obviously felt strongly enough about it to yell at the instructor and challenge his legitimacy. Whether this was a normal reaction or not is another matter; in fact I subsequently learned that this particular student had a history of violent altercations. I was frankly relieved that he only came back to class one more time, during which he stood in the doorway and refused briefly to enter the room, before disappearing.

Fortunately, the fear that students will respond in threatening ways if their political views are challenged is not a typical reason to rely on caution in using controversial topics, but teachers should always be aware of the potential for unforeseen responses to even seemingly non-controversial subjects. Establishing ground rules for debate at the beginning of the semester will be useful for avoiding charges of selective enforcement of the rules, and it is probably best to step in when voices become raised. An unruly atmosphere tends to discourage serious participation and is not in itself why most students want controversial material in the classroom.

Some authors who have described or advocated for the use of controversial topics in curricular material claim that it is necessary to do so because the number of controversies being debated by the public is increasing, so contentious issues of public concern are becoming unavoidable. However, educators have been making this claim for decades (Fredericks and Miller 1993; Lusk and Weinberg 1994; Keezer 1940). There is nothing novel, edgy or unique about building discussions, activities or simulations around current controversies, and there is a long record in the pedagogy of doing so. It is only the particular current issues themselves that generate passions and objections.

Greenan (1933, p. 99) argued that adaptation to societal change is necessary to prevent disorder and revolution. It is therefore necessary for educators to equip students to make decisions approximating the dilemmas that they would actually face as citizens. Additionally, acquiring these analytic and critical thinking skills aids students in developing processes of reasoning and recognizing that assertion alone does not provide compelling reasons or evidence (Martens 2007, pp. 4–6).

One method of determining the utility of employing contentious subjects is to ask the students themselves whether the material was controversial and what value they derived from studying it. Harris (1940, pp. 49–51) surveyed 535 secondary students who had been enrolled in a social science curriculum that expressly included current events in politics. All respondents indicated that they had studied controversial subjects and 95 percent reported finding them interesting. Reported open-ended responses included expressions of the value of becoming active and informed citizens and of understanding other points of view.

INTERNAL AND EXTERNAL CHALLENGES

It is impossible to determine whether Harris's students had been prompted in any way that affected their answers, but the article did report that approximately half of the respondents felt that the instructor had directly expressed his own views during debates. About 60 percent stated that they could discern the instructor's opinions through nonverbal cues such as body language, inflection of voice or the nature of the questions posed to students or the inclusion of what they perceived to be left-leaning memes or talking points (Harris 1940, pp. 52–3).

Whether it is beneficial for instructors to attempt to influence how students view controversial – or any political – issues is a matter for debate in itself. The traditional view has been that it is acceptable for teachers to make their own views known, so long as they distinguish 'editorial' from 'journalistic' content (Adams et al. 1948). Others have gone further, arguing that 'honest' educators must report facts as they understand them with the benefit of their expertise and greater knowledge of historical and issue contexts, and that students would in fact be shortchanged by being left to judge between competing claims without full background knowledge (Mitchell 1940, pp. 339–40).

More recently, the post-positivist turn in social science has led educators to advocate for the value of allowing students to find their own truths through a rigorously developed analytic framework that gives them the tools to evaluate both evidence received in the course and the impact of their own biases in how they process it. Fredericks and Miller (1993, pp. 160–64) note that the dilemma of incommensurability provides untrained students with a genuine problem in attempting to evaluate the validity of such controversial claims as denial of the Holocaust, the vastly different age of the earth proposed by creationists and race-based eugenic pseudoscience. The potential danger that students will be confronted with claims that they cannot refute or adjudicate requires that they essentially receive methods training before controversial subjects could be taught responsibly, with the recommended remedy being the teaching of critical tests of sufficient evidence.

In teaching critical theories of politics, common in courses that include any Marxian-influenced perspectives of the study of social structures or of identity norms to maintain elite economic or political power, it is nearly impossible to avoid competing perspectives because either course texts or class discussions inevitably turn to the existence and validity of these approaches. Even if the instructor does not openly support, for example, feminist claims that expectations of duties performed by the wives of soldiers and diplomats have been gendered as women's work so that there is no obligation to pay for services rendered, students will likely take the mere inclusion of such perspectives as an endorsement – legitimation by inclusion.

Hedley and Markowitz (2001, p. 195) add that, when teaching about sociological topics related to exploitation through social structures, it is not uncommon to get 'students [who] resist by challenging our knowledge claims as professors, challenging the knowledge claims of our textbooks and other course materials, morally legitimating the current system of power, and morally delegitimizing alternatives'. They argue that this occurs precisely because students are socialized to believe that their society is equal and fair, and also that they are individual decision-makers and so they reject explanations of structural constraints that predispose their opinions. These students will often impose normative interpretations on causal statements, believing that questions about why inequalities exist are tantamount to assigning blame. In order to avoid making these students feel a moral obligation to defend social order, the authors also propose methodological pre-training, providing students with exercises that encourage them to recognize and sociologically explain their dichotomous beliefs of norm/other (Hedley and Markowitz 2001, pp. 195–9).

Impressions of instructor bias can also be accentuated if the professor is seen to have a personal or ideological stake in persuading students to adopt a particular viewpoint. A critical or 'radical' position taken by a white male is more likely to be regarded by students as examining all sides, not as advancing an agenda for social change (Lusk and Weinberg 1994, p. 302). The difficulty is particularly acute for graduate teaching assistants in the discussion sections of large introductory courses – exactly the kind of classes that professors want to use to hook uncommitted first-year students with engaging material – because these class leaders are regarded as just students without the gravitas or presumed impartiality of learned professors. Their presumed views (based on material covered) are open to challenge as being no more valid than those of the students who view them as more akin to peers, with the challenge for female and minority teachers amplified (Wahl et al. 2000, p. 317).

Skeptical students may continually scrutinize instructor behavior as well as course content to glean some hint of bias, but there is generally no reason to be concerned about being tagged, fairly or not, as including a particular ideological bent in your material. Teachers in higher education enjoy advantages that those in secondary education do not: professors are accorded academic freedom to challenge conventional assumptions in the name of advancing their fields of study. It is also rare to confront parental or political opprobrium for expressing controversial views, let alone introducing controversial topics for debate. Perhaps the best evidence from this comes from a study of teachers in Northern Ireland who taught about current societal issues but ranked reprisal by paramilitary factions lowest among their concerns about teaching subjects (McKernan 1982, pp. 58–69).

However, it would be naïve to imagine that the active citizenry that professors of politics hope to create takes no interest in the instructors or curricula shaping the next generation of voters. For example, one study (Lehman 1955) found that, in the state of Pennsylvania, 45 interest groups were able to influence 76 different state curriculum prescriptions over a 12-year period. In the twenty-first century, activists have led social media protest campaigns against academics who express views that are objectionable to them. One high-profile instance involved a politically active leftist professor who published an essay on 9/11 arguing that the United States was reaping the hostility due as a result of its policies (Morson 2007). In this case, the subsequent investigations that led to his ouster focused on academic misconduct, but all faculty, and particularly those untenured at the junior rank, should consider whether they are prepared to defend any and all remarks, even those intended only to stimulate debate.

Similarly, while professors generally enjoy license to use strong or profane language with impunity, it is another matter entirely when they use terms that students perceive to be disparaging or stereotyping of an individual's or a group's characteristics. These slights may occur even without the awareness of the professor, as depicted in Roth's 2000 novel *The Human Stain*. All instructors should take care to avoid derogatory language or the employment of gender or ethnic stereotyping, and to keep current in their argot as previously acceptable or non-connotative terms become objectionable. Some 'controversies', even if unintentional, will not enjoy the support of the teaching institution in the name of academic freedom. For this reason, I also weigh in if no student does when epithets are used in the classroom: the perpetrator is usually genuinely unaware that they have used offensive language, but you risk the appearance of indifference or worse to students who may be afraid to speak out. A verified complaint by a single student may be sufficient for dismissal (Dent 2012).

Some conservative scholars claim that they have been denied career advancement by a liberal academy that does not support their views, leading some to avoid careers in academia (Gross 2013). Indeed, the canon of literature on teaching controversies is rife with normative claims about the benefits of reducing conservatism (Keezer 1940, p. 116) and the value of university pedagogy in eliminating moral reductionism (Perry 1970 in Hedley and Markowitz 2001, p. 200). Conversely, political interest groups and media on the right have also attacked or even tried to oust scholars whom they believe to be promoting a progressive bias through their research or teaching (Krugman 2011).

Even seemingly non-ideological issues such as climate change have become political footballs and led to external attacks against academics. It should not be surprising when these issues involve any policies that affect political and financial interests, as Ibsen's 1882 play *An Enemy of the People* attests. Again, beyond considering how to incorporate deliberately controversial material in teaching, especially in the era of camera phones and instant uploads to social media, the savvy professor must consider the potential for anything they teach to be regarded as controversial by their students and disseminated widely.

STRATEGIES FOR TEACHING CONTROVERSIAL SUBJECTS

With an awareness of the potential pitfalls, teaching using intentionally controversial material offers the opportunity for lively and enlightening classes on politics. I therefore offer a few tips for how to incorporate controversial subjects effectively, followed by some examples of teaching controversies in practice.

The first rule for success is that, to generate interest in the class, the topic has to be controversial to the students, and not necessarily to the instructor. As noted, undergraduates are not likely to be invested in, or even familiar with, the major theoretical or methodological controversies of political science and international relations, and most will be unlikely to find them engaging. Likewise, even debates over current affairs will only hold significance for students with some investment in or emotional connection to the topic. The implementation of a particularly objectionable regulation by the Federal government or the plight of a particularly mistreated minority group in a distant country may not stir passions among students who are unfamiliar with the players and the ramifications of their actions.

However, it can also be difficult to foment a debate about what the instructor believes is a controversial issue because students do not find it interesting. It may be that a stalwart old controversy is not particularly contested among the students' age or regional demographic. If an issue fails to draw heat, then it is probably best to cut your losses, explain the logic of each opposing side, and move on if you are losing the room.

Some instructors use texts created for the purpose of familiarizing students with current controversies and highlighting the legitimate divisions that exist between the opposing views, such as the *Taking Sides* series (Payne and Gainey 2003, p. 57). My preferred way to familiarize students with a new issue, and to create an emotional connection to the topic, is to have them learn about it through a video such as a news report that brings an abstract controversy to life by introducing the people affected by it. Short videos of a couple of minutes in length can be shown in class if you have a 'smart room' with internet access and projection, otherwise you can assign clips for viewing prior to class.

The next element required for the effective incorporation of controversial subjects is the establishment of an environment in which students feel safe to express their views freely. The instructor needs to establish that there is a genuine debate over the topic, and perhaps even offer the main arguments on both sides if they are not forthcoming from the students themselves. Although many academics may take free and open debate as a given, many students will begin the semester believing that they might be penalized for disagreeing with the instructor, not least because some of them will believe that this has already happened to them in other political science courses that they have taken. Instructors, particularly if teaching a class with a large cohort of international students or when working in another country themselves, should be aware of differing cultural norms about the importance of consensus, and challenging peers or authority figures. Likewise, students who have lived in more authoritarian political systems may not be accustomed to giving their opinion without some form of reprisal.

Lusk and Weinberg (1994, p. 302) argue that professors should recognize that the principal inhibitor of student participation is their fear of opprobrium not from the instructor but from their classmates. College students have interactions with each other, and reputations to consider, outside of the classroom as well. Creation of a safe space for debate helps to ameliorate, but does not eliminate, reluctance to speak about controversial issues and risk unpopularity, beyond the usual fear of appearing ignorant or simply speaking publicly at all. Further, studies have indicated that members of the preponderant student demographics in a class tend to feel more secure in staking positions on controversial issues because they expect to enjoy the support of most of the room.

Payne and Gainey (2003, pp. 52, 55–6) suggest five potential techniques for engaging greater numbers of students in discussions to prevent having a minority, and possibly one unrepresentative of the diversity of the classroom, control the discussion. These include calling on students, by name if known, or at random from the roster or by demographic profile if balancing is the object, and encouraging participation through eye contact, physically moving closer to students, and showing emotional enthusiasm yourself.

The authors also suggest employing an 'uncomfortable silence' that prompts individual students to continue speaking when you stare at them expectantly after they conclude their point. They differentiate it from the awkward silence that follows a question that no student volunteers to answer. My own experience has been that an uncomfortable silence works well when directed at the entire class. If you ask a question and no one answers, there is nothing wrong with a minute of silence and chirping crickets. The students need time to process new and sometimes difficult information, and they feel awkward with you staring at them as well. Wait a reasonable amount of time and you will almost always have one of your regular active participants attempt a response or at least ask for additional clarification. As long as you have previously demonstrated a commitment to openness, students will be willing to go out on a limb to offer views.

And that is why the third strategy for encouraging engagement with controversial topics is to let students know early in the course that in most – but not all – cases the questions that come up in class will not have 'the answer', one indisputably correct solution to a policy or theoretical dispute that has bedeviled more learned and invested people than themselves for a long time. When one student asked me to 'just give us the truth' about a particular foreign policy problem that was provoking an (in my view wonderfully) unresolvable debate in class, my response was that if we knew 'the truth' then we would not need to have elections. And I appropriated the line from *Indiana Jones and the Last Crusade* about how our course was concerned with facts while my philosophy colleague down the hall hunted for truth.

I further encourage students to examine the complexity of controversial issues, both current and historical, by assigning case studies to analyze, exercises intended to build skills in applying knowledge to particular problems and not to demonstrate that there is a single approach that is best suited for success. The use of case studies or narratives about a significant event (Muth, Polizzi and Glenn 2007, p. 16), which was originally popularized by the Harvard Business School, helps to make the point that all political and policy decisions involve degrees of controversy, at least for the participants involved, and illustrate difficulties in developing collective action.

I let students know that the evaluative tools that I prefer to employ, case studies and policy memos, provide training for a range of careers in the public, private and non-profit sectors, and that policymaking often means determining the least-worst outcome given the complexities involved rather than an optimal solution. Other possibilities for using the course assessments to foster a willingness to explore controversial topics include requiring students to keep journals critically analyzing texts or asking them to present the evidence for all sides in a debate and then requiring them to identify what evidence would be necessary to make a determination. They might also play devil's advocate and make the case for the opposing side on a divisive issue, giving them a richer knowledge and requiring them to defend their own assumptions (Hedley and Markowitz 2001, pp. 201–202). Hillary Clinton (2003, p. 24) credits a high school social science teacher's devil's advocate assignment for causing her to shift her ideological and party alignments.

Having students analyze case studies and then prepare policy memos for final exams is a form of assessment that is particularly well suited for teaching controversial topics, because students are required to present all sides, take a position, and explain why they are supporting their preferred option as opposed to others. When students ask if it is necessary to present the other side, I tell them that their case will be more persuasive when they demonstrate that the opposing argument is not as convincing as the position that they adopt. I ask them to imagine themselves to be lawyers in courtroom drama making a presentation to the jury. The side with the best argument, using the evidence as support, wins. Simply ignoring the strong points that the other side makes and leaving it to the audience to decide is a recipe for defeat. In this sense, students are given the opposite task of the teacher – to make an evaluation and a compelling argument once they have sorted through the information presented by all the parties to controversies rather than attempting to present the arguments for all sides equitably.

Using controversial topics to stimulate classroom participation and improve student awareness of current events and critical thinking skills usually produces a win for all involved. However, it does take additional time and effort to consider which issues are appropriate and how to best convey the challenges of decision-making. I often begin classes with a slide taken from a news item that has appeared since the previous class, just to remind students that what we are covering is a living issue, whether conflicts over immigration or international conferences on climate change. Sometimes I have to dig deep in the web to find a relevant story, but usually the world obliges readily. However, it is usually not the 'ripped from the headlines' topics, which students have not read or processed, that most engage them, but rather perennial debates and typically those with a social policy dimension. It took almost the entire semester of using headline items to lead the lecture for an international relations theory class before I was able to prompt a genuinely contentious exchange between students using the hoary old issue of border security.

I use familiar or accessible controversies in the first week of each class (e.g. which of these individuals in the news today we should label terrorists in a terrorism class, or why Israelis get an army but Palestinians do not to introduce the concept of sovereignty when teaching international relations) to get students comfortable talking in class at the outset.

I let students know that there are competing theories that apply to these issues, but I have found with undergraduates that stressing the application of the concepts to current events makes a theory class palatable when it otherwise would not be. When you inform students that people are willing to kill for and to die for theories such as Marxism and liberal democracy, they cease to be abstract and demand that the student evaluates them. Huntington's *Clash of Civilizations* was a notable and provocative work of scholarship first published before most of the undergraduates studying today were born. When you tell them that Osama bin Laden used it as one of his justifications for al-Qaeda's major terrorist attacks, it is no longer a purely hypothetical exercise to students and becomes another controversy that requires analysis.

I will often use short articles or opinion pieces as objects in case studies to spark discussions as well. I have had success with material ranging from a rant about American race relations by comedian David Spade to a column by foreign policy analyst Robert Kagan arguing that the Obama and Bush foreign policies would be indistinguishable. It is convenient to use them to fill time on the first day of class and as starting points for discussion, but I find that students are not actually prepared at that early juncture to debate the merits of the arguments and instead most offer what they expect I want, their agreement with the author.

One additional technique that I have found to be effective, but which carries some risk, is to have students role-play when studying the motives of violent political actors and their supporters. This includes in-class group exercises in which students assume particular demographic profiles and then determine whether they would support fascist parties, analyzing events surrounding World War II from an Axis perspective, and having graduate students assume the role of publicity-seeking terrorists and identify strategic targets. In all of these instances, the goal is to deepen student understanding of the political goals of antagonistic actors who are often caricatured as one-dimensional villains. I am always careful to explain in advance the learning outcomes of such activities, and have yet to receive any complaints. Some accept my explanation that it is essential to understand what terrorists actually want if you want to know whether you are preventing them from attaining their objectives, and others just seem to enjoy playing the bad guys. In either case, the result of engaged students figuring out how to apply theory to empirical cases is a win for all involved.

Professors teaching controversial topics need to take care to avoid personalizing debates or raising potentially offensive topics without elucidating a clear and justifiable pedagogical reason for doing so. And it is unfortunately a necessary element of classroom management to be on guard for students who seem to be getting too wrapped up in conflict or are behaving in any way that is threatening to the instructor or other students.

However, there has been little in 15 years of teaching in this fashion that has made the potential risks appear to outweigh the evident benefits of doing so. When controversies arise organically, students are more prepared to have a healthy debate. By mid-semester their classmates will ask them to provide a more compelling case than 'I just don't believe the science' when discussing climate change and appropriate responses. In short, I find no controversy in propounding the use of intentionally controversial subjects and current issues.

REFERENCES

Adams, Ruth, Myrtle Rodgers, Avery F. Olney and J.N. Smelser (1948), 'Rules for Controversial Issues', *The Clearing House*, **22** (7), 412.
Clinton, Hillary Rodham (2003), *Living History*, New York: Simon and Schuster.
Dent, Julia (2012), 'Funny Story: Conservative Prof Fired for Telling Joke', *The College Fix*, January 18.
Fraser, Dorothy (1964), *Deciding What to Teach*, Washington, D.C.: National Education Association, United States of America.

Fredericks, Marcel and Steven I. Miller (1993), 'Truth in Packaging: Teaching Controversial Topics to Undergraduates in the Human Sciences', *Teaching Sociology*, **21** (2), 160–65.
Greenan, John (1933), 'Controversial Subjects in the Curriculum', *Junior-Senior High School Clearing House*, **8** (2), 98–101.
Gross, Neil (2013), *Why Are Professors Liberal and Why Do Conservatives Care?*, Boston, MA: Harvard University Press.
Hare, William (1973), 'Controversial Issues and the Teacher', *The High School Journal*, **57** (2), 51–60.
Harris, John (1940), 'Controversial Questions in One High School', *The School Review*, **48** (1), 49–54.
Hedley, Mark and Linda Markowitz (2001), 'Avoiding Moral Dichotomies: Teaching Controversial Topics to Resistant Students', *Teaching Sociology*, **29** (2), 195–208.
Jagoda, Naomi (2008), 'Political Science Classes Fill Up in Election Season', *The Daily Pennsylvanian*, September 11.
Keezer, Dexter Merriam (1940), 'The Problem of Handling Controversial Issues', *The Journal of Higher Education*, **11** (3), 115–24.
Krugman, Paul (2011), 'American Thought Police', *The New York Times*, March 27.
Lehman, D. (1955), *Legislative Control of Secondary School Curriculum*, Unpublished EdD thesis, University of Pittsburgh.
Lusk, Amy B. and Adam S. Weinberg (1994), 'Discussing Controversial Topics in the Classroom: Creating a Context for Learning', *Teaching Sociology*, **22** (4), 301–8.
Martens, Elizabeth A. (2007), 'The Instructional Use of Argument across the Curriculum', *Middle School Journal*, **38** (5), 4–13.
McKernan, James (1982), 'Constraints on the Handling of Controversial Issues in Northern Ireland Post-Primary Schools', *British Educational Research Journal*, **8** (1), 57–71.
Mitchell, Broadus (1940), 'Treatment of Controversial Questions in the Teaching of Political Economy', *The American Economic Review*, **30** (2), 339–43.
Morson, Berny (2007), 'CU Regents Fire Ward Churchill', *Rocky Mountain News*, July 25.
Muth, K. Denise, Nicholas C. Polizzi and Shawn M. Glynn (2007), 'Case-based Teacher Preparation for Teaching Controversial Topics in Middle School', *Middle School Journal*, **38** (5), 14–19.
Payne, Brian K. and Randy R. Gainey (2003), 'Understanding and Developing Controversial Issues in College Courses', *College Teaching*, **51** (2), 52–8.
Perry, W.G. (1970), *Forms of Intellectual and Ethical Development in the College Years*, New York: Holt, Rinehart and Winston.
Wahl, Anna-Maria, Eduardo T. Perez, Mary Jo Deegan, Thomas W. Sanchez and Cheryl Applegate (2000), 'The Controversial Classroom: Institutional Resources and Pedagogical Strategies for a Race Relations Course', *Teaching Sociology*, **28** (4), 316–32.

22. Teaching at the community college: faculty role, responsibilities and pedagogical techniques
Erin Richards

Teaching jobs at community colleges currently constitute approximately 40 percent of all academic jobs available in the U.S.A. (Jenkins 2011). Further, as many community colleges experience turnover as faculty hired at the peak of community college openings in the 1960s and 1970s retire, and as more students choose to begin their college education at community colleges,[1] two-year schools will continue to provide a significant number of the jobs available to political scientists for the foreseeable future. However, the community college environment is a distinctly different environment from that found at four-year schools—private or public—and requires a different approach to applying for the job, teaching, collegiality, service and even professional development.

This chapter will address each of these elements in greater detail with the goal of giving the reader an overview of life as a faculty member at a community college. There are many similarities in the pedagogical strategies that are most effective in the community college classroom, but a faculty member's teaching load, administrative responsibilities and other duties will vary from institution to institution and from state to state depending on the purpose and type of two-year system a state has created. In addition, while this chapter will address briefly some of the different pedagogical strategies that are effective for the diverse environment found in a community college classroom, it seeks to give a more holistic review of what it means to be a faculty member at a community college. One other caveat: as good political scientists, we all know the impact that federalism can have on institutions at the state level and particularly on educational institutions that are often the sole purview of state government. As such, the discussions in this chapter will be focused on generalizations of community colleges nationwide and my own experience with community colleges in Washington State, but any person interested in pursuing a career at a community college should be sure to do an in-depth investigation into the system and institutions in whatever state they wish to teach.

GETTING THE JOB: APPLYING TO A COMMUNITY COLLEGE

The key to any successful job hunt is highlighting the applicant's qualifications to meet the needs of the employer. This approach is no different in the community college environment where the primary responsibility of any faculty member is teaching. As such, when applying for community college faculty positions, it is critical to highlight in the vitae and especially in the cover letter the applicant's teaching experience including classes taught, innovative teaching approaches used in the classroom, curriculum development experience, teaching philosophy and any professional development centered on teaching. Further, because research is not generally a part of the job of a community college faculty member, research interests, projects and publications should be secondary on the curriculum vitae. This is not to say that publications and research are not important. As more and more institutions seek to hire PhDs for faculty positions, publications—especially those that are centered on teaching and pedagogy—can help to set an applicant apart. However, to many hiring committees, an application centered on a research agenda is one that suggests either that the applicant is not aware of what community colleges do or that the applicant is not really interested in the teaching centered nature of the community college—both of which are reasons that the applicant will not make it past the screening phase.

Further, because the emphasis of community colleges is on teaching, many community colleges incorporate a teaching demonstration as part of the interview process. However, it is important to structure this demonstration to be consistent with the mission of the community college. Many community colleges now embrace the student centered, active learning[2] model of education and expect their faculty to use this approach in their teaching. Faculty in the community college environment are expected to be 'the guide on the side' rather than the 'sage on the stage' (King 1993). As such, a job candidate should choose their teaching demonstration strategically to meet the teaching philosophy employed by the institution where they are interviewing. However, this teaching approach should also be authentic to the applicant, otherwise a discord between the applicant and the institution's philosophy will be apparent—and, like all jobs, part of the interview is about finding a fit between an applicant and an institution. Remember to not be afraid of taking a new or innovative approach to the teaching demonstration. Because of their focus on teaching, community colleges are often at the forefront of new ways to teach old material, and innovation and creativity in teaching are appreciated, especially when it comes to crafting strategies to connect with the diverse student body of a community college classroom.

THE COMMUNITY COLLEGE JOB

One of the most significant differences between a position at a four-year institution and at a community college is the responsibilities of a faculty member. While most political scientists expect research to be part of their professional career, in general, the expectation that a faculty member engages in research and publication is non-existent at a community college primarily because the job of a faculty member at this type of institution is to teach. As such, the teaching loads of faculty members at community colleges may be much heavier than the load for a faculty member at a four-year school.

In addition to teaching, a community college faculty member can expect that their job description will include service, professional development and, in some cases, advising responsibilities. Because these responsibilities will vary so significantly from institution to institution, this is something that an applicant should be sure to address during the interview process. Service requirements may be divided between service to the institution and service to peers and/or community, and the amount of time expected for a faculty member to devote to these commitments may depend on whether the faculty member is in an adjunct position, is in the tenure process or is a tenured faculty member. Service can also range from serving on committees to do the work of the institution, to engaging in program, degree or curriculum review for accreditation purposes, to institutional curriculum development, among other opportunities. A wise faculty member will make choices to fulfill their service requirements by pursuing opportunities that also allow them to delve further into their own interests, and potentially combine professional development as an academic and teacher with service. The good news is that, at most institutions, what constitutes service, advising and professional development is broadly defined so the faculty member has a great deal of leeway in determining what he or she will do to meet the other responsibilities associated with their position.

Further, given the significant time demands on faculty for teaching, and the time required to fulfill other obligations associated with the position, there is often very little time left for research and it is rare for a community college faculty member to be granted time within their working day to engage in research. This is just one reason, among many, that many two-year faculty do not engage in research—and if they do, that research is often directly related to their teaching and professional development responsibilities. On a positive note, with the increasing number of publication outlets focused on teaching and pedagogically-centered research, there are opportunities for those faculty who do wish to maintain a research agenda centered on pedagogy to do so, but realistically, it is quite difficult during the school year to find time to engage in this type of research.

The most significant part of the community college faculty's job is to teach introductory level courses. It is not uncommon for two-year schools on the semester system to ask their faculty to teach five to six classes per term while faculty at a school on the quarter system will teach three courses per term. Furthermore, it is common for faculty to have multiple sections of one course each term and/or to teach the same courses repetitively throughout the year. Most institutions offer similar introductory level courses including Introduction to American Government, International Relations, Comparative Government, State and Local Government, and Introduction to Political Thought or Theory. At most schools, there is usually fairly high and perpetual demand for these courses so it is not uncommon for community college faculty to teach these introductory courses—and these introductory courses only—from term to term. Further, most community colleges have a relatively small number of political science faculty so it is unusual for a faculty member at a two-year school to be able to teach only courses in the areas in which they specialized in graduate school. Community college faculty members are expected to be a 'jack of all trades' because of their need to teach introductory courses in all subfields on a regular basis, and a community college faculty member should not expect to be able to specialize in one subfield or another but should expect to teach across the entire discipline on a regular basis.

The repetitive nature of a faculty member's teaching load presents several challenges. The first is keeping up with the research for all of the different fields in which a faculty member teaches. The role of the introductory course is to give students an overview of the entire field of political science in each of the major areas of study; however, the heavy teaching load at the community college leaves little time for a faculty member to engage in a great deal of research into the current state of the discipline in all subfields. Further, because community colleges may have only a few political scientists on faculty, it is unlikely that a faculty member will have a colleague who specializes in a particular subfield to act as the local expert. Needless to say, it can be challenging to keep completely up to date with all the developments in the field—this is not typically a challenge faced by faculty at four-year institutions, where they are able to specialize and are not often asked to teach outside their area of expertise. However, this is a challenge that can be met through the professional development requirements that are part of most community college faculty job descriptions. In particular, this challenge can be addressed by prioritizing attendance at professional conferences. Regional or national political science conferences allow a faculty member to keep up to date with all of the latest research and to form connections with scholars specializing in those fields who can become a 'go-to' person in the future, when they need further information on particular topics.

However, conference attendance should not be limited to those conferences with a substantive political science focus, as attending conferences focused on pedagogy and effective teaching can also be beneficial. The American Political Science Association (APSA) Teaching and Learning Conference is one such conference that addresses the pedagogy side of the political science discipline. This conference focuses on subjects such as strategies for engaging students with material in new ways and new approaches to teaching standard courses that can be useful for faculty as they work to revamp classes to help keep them fresh, as well as addressing the learning needs of the wide variety of students found in a community college classroom. However, it is also beneficial to consider attending teaching focused conferences for a wide variety of disciplines as strategies discussed in other fields can also be beneficial in the political science classroom.

Another strategy for compensating for the wide breadth required of community college faculty is to develop a professional network or de facto department using resources outside of the institution. Because political science departments may be small or even non-existent at community colleges as many political scientists are the only ones on faculty, community college faculty must often get creative in finding colleagues. Faculty who live in metropolitan areas or other areas with a large number of colleges and universities—two- or four-year—can reach out to political science colleagues to develop regional connections. For example, about half of the state's community colleges are found in the metropolitan area where this author lives. The political scientists at these schools connect and meet quarterly to discuss curriculum and pedagogy, creating a de facto department and one of the greatest sources of ideas for teaching and curriculum development.

Another approach to overcoming the challenge of small departments and the requirement that faculty at community college become generalists is to think in interdisciplinary terms. One of the advantages of having only a few faculty in any given department at a community college is that the opportunities to work with colleagues in other disciplines are plentiful. Indeed, some of the best pedagogical ideas I have gotten are from colleagues who teach in other disciplines. Many of the strategies discussed later in this chapter for how to address the diversity in a community college classroom are those that have been adapted from colleagues in other disciplines, such as developmental English where pedagogy has been front and center for quite some time. Not only do political scientists have a lot to learn in terms of subject content from colleagues in other disciplines, but there is also a lot to learn from them in pedagogical approaches, creating a richer and more comprehensive educational experience for students.

A second challenge associated with the teaching responsibilities of a faculty member at the community college is staying interested in courses that the faculty member teaches multiple sections of every single term. This is indeed a challenge, because if a faculty member is bored with a course or not interested in the subject matter, students will know and it will be hard to keep students engaged in the course. One solution is to find ways to 'get a break' from teaching the same courses over and over by investigating what other courses—perhaps related to your own interests—might also meet the needs of students seeking to fulfill college general education requirements or students preparing for transfer and developing those courses to expand course offerings at an institution. A note of caution: remember that the job of the community college is to teach introductory courses, so it is critical when developing new courses to be sure that the courses will transfer to four-year schools. It is not uncommon for advisors to steer budget- and time-conscious students away from classes that may pose problems for transfer, so any step a faculty member can take to ensure that their class does not fall into this category will only benefit them in the long run.

Further, many states, including Texas,[3] Missouri, Virginia and California,[4] now have very specific requirements either for the types of classes to be taught or the curriculum that must be covered in those classes, and many states also have common core courses[5] that are taught statewide that must meet particular curriculum standards in order to ensure continuity and transferability. Thus, when developing a new course be sure to pay attention to the requirements present in the state to ensure the new course meets all of the requirements established. While finding that perfect fit can be challenging, the benefits to both the student and faculty member certainly outweigh the challenges in the long run.

Faculty members also should not be afraid to try new and creative approaches to teaching old material. Indeed, innovative teaching approaches are often encouraged at community colleges. For example, how might one be able to teach political science topics through films? Is there a way to introduce service learning into the curriculum? Or might there be a quarter-long project that can be incorporated into the class to allow students to master course material? What creative final projects or other non-traditional means of teaching or assessment can be incorporated into the course?[6] Is there another class in another discipline whose content might complement or supplement the information being taught in the faculty member's political science course that would allow the topic to be addressed in a cross-disciplinary fashion? There is a plethora of ways in which courses or units within a course or even just an assignment can be redesigned to make them more active in their learning approach and which have the side effect of being more interesting for faculty members. In many ways, given the civic engagement nature of the political science curriculum, political science is particularly suited to creative approaches to teaching and faculty members should take advantage of those opportunities! While students may move on to other courses, faculty members will continue to teach the same courses over and over, so it is vital to find ways to keep the material and courses interesting and relevant while still ensuring students get the content they need in order to be prepared for their next academic steps.

TEACHING IN THE COMMUNITY COLLEGE CLASSROOM

Because the mission of community colleges is to provide educational access to the entire community resulting in open admission policies at most two-year schools, the community college classroom is often composed of a very diverse mix of students. Students can range from high school students enrolled in dual credit programs that allow them to earn both high school and college credit,[7] to the traditionally aged college student attending the community college to save money on college expenses or starting their higher education career at the two-year school because of the inability to gain admittance into a four-year university, to the non-traditionally aged college student who is returning to school for the first time or for retraining, to the senior citizen taking advantage of a college course in their community purely for their own enrichment.

Further, students in a community college classroom are as diverse in their reasons for taking classes as they are in age. There will be students who are in a course to meet requirements for completing their desired associate's degree, who are there purely because of interest in the topic, or who are there because they intend to become a political science major, although this type of student is usually few and far between. The diversity of students in a community college classroom will also apply to responsibilities students have outside of the classroom. There will likely be many students who work outside of school, have families, and who must deal with housing, transportation and financial issues in addition to their educational responsibilities.

It is important to note that these responsibilities will have an impact on teaching strategies and the ability to engage students inside and outside the classroom, thus the type of diversity typical of a community college classroom affects the classroom dynamic both in positive and not so positive ways, and this dynamic creates some interesting challenges for a community college professor in how they approach their pedagogy. One thing is for certain: each class will have its own dynamic depending on the make-up of the students in the course, and the prudent community college faculty will quickly learn how to read their classroom and adapt both their teaching and assessment styles to suit the class they face.

However, there are some common challenges that will most likely be present in any community college classroom including varied levels of student preparation, basic academic skill development, interest in the subject matter and motivation depending on the purpose for which the student is taking the course. Thus, in discussing 'how to teach at the community college', this part of the chapter will offer things to think about when approaching pedagogy, as well as ideas and suggestions for how to address the significant levels of diversity and academic preparation that one faces in a community college classroom.

The Challenge of a Diverse Classroom: Meeting Students Where They Are

Perhaps one of the most discussed and substantial challenges a community college faculty member faces is the wide spectrum of preparation and basic college level skills students possess. While many four-year schools are able to exert some level of selectivity in the composition of their student body, most community colleges operate an open admissions policies allowing anyone who wishes to enroll to matriculate. As a result, community college faculty must accommodate students who range in skill levels from no or minimal college level skills to those students who are quite sophisticated in their writing, critical thinking and reading abilities. It is not uncommon for a community college classroom to have students in it who do not possess the ability to read or write at the college level, which can present a challenge in something as simple as selecting a textbook that will be accessible to a student who is not yet 'college ready'.

However, part of the job of a community college faculty member is to help students who do not yet have college level skills develop those skills in order to be successful in a college classroom. There are, of course, many schools of thought on how to approach this issue, from 'dumbing it down' to ensure that all students are able to meet expectations, to setting the bar high and leaving those students who are not able to meet requirements to make the extra effort and choices to 'come up to snuff', to a compromise somewhere in the middle.

Multiple factors will drive the decision a faculty member makes about how to address the diversity of skill levels in the classroom, but the type of additional academic support such as writing centers, peer tutoring or supplemental instruction available to students should factor into the pedagogical decisions a faculty member makes. Faculty may also find that they have to spend more time and effort on encouraging underprepared students to take advantage of the services that are available to help them succeed academically. As noted earlier in this chapter, many students in the community college environment have a multitude of responsibilities outside of the classroom; for many students, their role as college student is a second job, and sometimes, second priority. Thus, they may not have a lot of the extra time that is required for them to get the help they need. Conversations about time management, effective study strategies, and tips and tricks for understanding course material may be the most helpful conversations a faculty member can have with students who are struggling academically. In other words, much of what a faculty member does to help students has nothing to do with the actual subject matter of the course, but rather is more focused on life skills to help students balance their many competing responsibilities.

Engaging students who already have college level skills in addition to helping students without those skills come up to college level standards is also a challenge for faculty at a community college. However, here too there are strategies a faculty member can employ to keep the bright students engaged in the classroom. For example, faculty can engage those students who are at a college level as leaders in the classroom through active learning techniques such as the flipped classroom and team based learning. Depending on the project, the point in the term and the personality of the students involved, the brighter students can either be in groups with those who may be struggling, allowing these students who 'get it' to further develop and master their knowledge by teaching their classmates, or faculty can put the brighter students into one or two groups, allowing that group to move at a faster pace or engage with the material at a different level. Faculty can also create assignments that allow bright students to explore concepts in greater detail while also not punishing lesser prepared students. For example, creative assignments can give flexibility to bright students to push the boundaries but also provide a way for lesser prepared students to be successful. In my state and local government class, the students have a project that requires them to teach someone else about a concept they learned in the course. Students have complete flexibility to choose the method they wish to use to teach this concept and there have been some wonderful projects as a result from both my bright students as well as those students who struggle. The goal in teaching in a community college classroom is to be creative to help meet students where they are to help them succeed, thus meeting the primary mission of the community college.

There are other strategies that can be used to deal with the diverse levels of preparation in the classroom. First, it is essential to be absolutely explicit with students about topics such as the expectations of students in the college environment, both in the classroom and the institution; what resources—both institutional and otherwise—are available to students to help them succeed; what types of skills are needed to be successful in college; and how a student can go about developing those skills. It is important to remember that many students at a community college may be first generation college students who have no point of reference or support at home for what is involved in a college education. Thus, as a faculty member, you are not only teaching your subject matter to the students, but you are also teaching them how to be college students and you cannot assume that students will just 'know' what is expected of them in the college classroom.

Teaching Writing in the Community College Classroom

One of the most frequently heard complaints about students in the community college classroom is the lack of the ability to write at a college level. However, this can be because no one has ever communicated to students what constitutes college level writing or given the students information on what is expected in college level papers. Luckily, this is a pretty easy topic to address in the classroom by incorporating discussions about what constitutes good writing throughout the term, and, if appropriate, making writing a learning outcome for the course. Conversations about writing do not need to be something that takes a long time; they can be infused in small pieces throughout the curriculum. For example, at the beginning of the quarter, I talk with my students about the steps involved in the writing process (draft, revise, publish) as a means of reminding them that any written work they turn in needs to have some degree of editing done. This discussion also serves the purpose of clearly setting expectations for students, as well as giving me the opportunity to discuss the resources available on campus to help students engage in these important steps of the writing process. These discussions also serve as a reminder about the resources they have such as spell check and peer review to help them turn in the best quality written work possible. I find that a very simple five-minute discussion in addition to quick and gentle reminders throughout the term as due dates for written work approach tend to decrease the number of typos in the work I receive from students and, in many cases, increases the quality of the assignments I receive.

Scaffolding Assignments: Intentionality in Skill Building

Another critical element to teaching in the community college given the diverse levels of student preparation is scaffolding. Widely used in other disciplines such as developmental math and English and in foreign languages, the idea that assignments and concepts build on one another—scaffolding—is also applicable to the political science classroom. While most instructors know intuitively that skills build on one another, and most of us do structure our assignments to reflect this principle, the idea that students are building skills throughout a term that they are expected to use on subsequent assignments is not something that is necessarily obvious to students, and especially to those students who are struggling to achieve college level standards. Thus, it is again imperative that faculty members be explicit in showing students that they do possess the skills required to complete assignments and that they structure their teaching and assignments to help with this.

For example, at the end of the quarter in one of my courses I require students to turn in a policy brief in which they are required to use various topics studied throughout the quarter to analyze a policy area of their choice. However, before they turn that brief in, they practice skills they will need to be successful on that assignment in smaller, lower stakes assignments assigned earlier in the quarter. In the final policy brief, students are required to analyze a public opinion poll; however, they first practice that poll analysis through an assignment earlier in the quarter on which they receive my feedback on how well they were able to apply the concepts to the polls given. They are then explicitly given instructions to take that feedback and apply it to the policy brief they turn in at the end of the quarter. This way, the first time students practice a skill is not on a high stakes assignment at the end of the quarter and they have feedback from earlier in the quarter that will hopefully allow them to be more successful on that higher point assignment. This not only serves the purpose of students turning in higher quality work, but it also allows students the opportunity to build confidence, which also helps with turning in better quality work. If a student believes they possess the skills necessary to be successful, they are more likely to be successful and it is our job as community college faculty members to help students build up that confidence.

Scaffolding need not be something that is incredibly time consuming, but taking smaller steps earlier in the quarter and giving students feedback has the effect of 1) allowing the instructor to get an 'early warning' about whether students are grasping concepts being presented, 2) allowing students to build confidence in their ability to master skills as they get feedback and have the opportunity to again practice those skills using that feedback and 3) reducing instructor frustration at the end of the quarter when assignments are turned in. Further, given the student population that instructors often work with in the community college setting, giving students the opportunity to be successful can significantly increase retention for at-risk students—a population that the community college often serves in large numbers.

The strategies listed here are by no means the be all and end all of effective teaching strategies that a faculty member can use to help students in their classroom. Indeed, these are merely jumping-off points for a new community college faculty member to begin their teaching in an environment that is most likely fundamentally different from the one they encountered in graduate school. The truly successful community college member will be one who is open to new ideas, creativity and innovation in the classroom and who is willing to seek out and experiment with what may seem like new and crazy ideas in order to connect with their students and help them to be successful.

CONCLUSION

There are many challenges associated with teaching at a community college, but there are also many rewards. There is nothing more rewarding than watching a student who came in struggling find their purpose and walk across the stage for their associate degree two, three or four years later triumphant. Or have a student who at first was not sure that they would ever be able to pass a college course come and tell you that they have been accepted to the university of their choice. There is also nothing more rewarding than watching students transform their lives and the lives of their family because they now have more education. Any day I wonder about what my purpose in academia is, all I have to do is think about the number of students whose lives I have had the opportunity to touch and transform and I am reinvigorated to continue to pursue new and creative ways to connect with my students.

Community colleges are in a unique position in higher education particularly with regards to teaching. Because our sole job is to teach, community college faculty have the opportunity to lead the field in new and innovative pedagogy to transform political science education for the future. The community college environment is one that invites creativity and innovation, and is where we may find the future of our discipline.

NOTES

1. In the 2009–2010 school year, approximately 40 percent of the nation's undergraduates were enrolled in community colleges (Knapp et al. 2011).
2. Active learning is technically defined as a pedagogical model that uses strategies other than students passively listening to the professor as a means for learning material. The active learning approach gives faculty a great deal of freedom, flexibility and the ability to be creative in conveying concepts to students and measuring their learning.
3. Texas requires all students to complete a two-course sequence in American, state and local politics.
4. For example, S.B. 1440 in California requires that a student completing approved courses at Californian community colleges must be guaranteed admission to an institution within the California State University at junior standing (S.B. 440). This has impacts for curriculum at the community college level that may constrain faculty course development.
5. To ensure transferability, states may designate particular courses as 'common' among all institutions and the assumption is that the curriculum covered in those courses is 'common' as well.
6. I encourage readers to search the archives of the American Political Science Association Teaching and Learning Conference papers, as there is a plethora of really good ideas on how to teach political science concepts in new and interesting ways. There is also a wonderful discussion of assessment that should guide a faculty member as they consider new assignments or significant course revisions.
7. A 2013 report documented that 82 percent of high schools nationwide reported students enrolled in a dual credit or dual enrollment course (Thomas et al. 2013).

BIBLIOGRAPHY

California Community College Chancellor's Office & California State University (2013), 'SB 1440 – Associate Degrees for Transfer', available at http://www.sb1440.org/ (accessed 20 August 2013).
ETR Associates (2013), 'What is Service Learning?', available at http://www.servicelearning.org/what-is-service-learning (accessed 20 August 2013).
Jenkins, R. (2011), 'Advice on Starting a Career in Community Colleges', available at http://www.communitycollegetimes.com/Pages/Campus-Issues/Advice-on-starting-a-career-in-community-colleges.aspx (accessed 20 August 2013).
King, A. (1993), 'From Sage on the Stage to Guide on the Side', *College Teaching*, **41** (1), 30–35.
Knapp, L., J. Kelly-Reid and S. Ginder (2011), 'Enrollment in Postsecondary Institutions, Fall 2009: Graduation Rates, 2003 & 2006 Cohorts; and Financial Statistics, Fiscal Year 2009', available at http://nces.ed.gov/pubs2011/2011230.pdf (accessed 7 August 2013).
McCartney, A., E. Bennion and D. Simpson (eds) (2013), *Teaching Civic Engagement: From Student to Active Citizen*, Washington D.C.: American Political Science Association.
Thomas, N., S. Marken, L. Gray, L. Lewis and J. Ralph (2013), 'Dual Credit and Exam-Based Courses in U.S. Public High Schools: 2010–2011', available at http://nces.ed.gov/pubs2013/2013001.pdf (accessed 7 August 2013).

23. Teaching international relations
Rebecca Glazier

In recent years, the calls to internationalize the curriculum and to prepare our students to be global citizens have grown ever louder (e.g. Barber et al. 2007; Breuning and Ishiyama 2007; Rajaee 2005). The demand comes from university administration, government and industry, but also from the students themselves. Global intelligence is seen as increasingly important in terms of career and life preparedness.

In the face of these demands, the question of how best to teach international relations becomes ever more important. This chapter outlines some best practices for teaching international relations (IR), drawn from research in the field, peer-reviewed publications and my own experience. The diverse ideas presented here are by no means exhaustive. Instead, the purposes of this chapter are twofold. First, because learning happens best when students are interested in what they are studying (Colby et al. 2003), I present the case for making student engagement a central teaching goal. Second, I provide readers with a variety of proven teaching strategies to help reach that goal.

MOVING BEYOND LECTURE

If we really want learning to happen, we have to go beyond the surface of communicating facts and figures and get students to connect with the material—by making it engaging and accessible. This is easier in international relations classes than in many other courses. In a globalizing world, the things that we are teaching our students in IR are increasingly part of their lives. Students experience and contribute to globalization as they simultaneously learn about it (Amoore and Langley 2001; Darling and Foster 2012). Research tells us that students remember information when they need it (Burch 2000) and when they see its applicability in the real world (Asal and Kratoville 2013). Thus, one key to engaging students is meeting them where they are (Cox 2003). IR instructors can use the relevance of international issues to teach important IR concepts to students in an engaging way that makes sense to them.

Getting students engaged in IR takes more than just talking at them. Interestingly, the specific non-lecture teaching strategy one chooses is not all that important. Much more important is simply moving from solely passive learning to incorporate some active learning techniques (Taylor 2013). As Powner and Allendoerfer (2008) conclude, all forms of active learning, whether simulations, discussion, role-play or beyond, are 'equally good for improving learning'; it is engagement itself that 'increases student performance above lecture-only' instruction (p. 85). Thus, no instructors—not even instructors of very large introductory courses (De Matos-Ala and Hornsby 2013)—should feel that engaging students is out of their reach.

The techniques described here can help students move from a simple interest in international politics to a deep understanding (Taylor 2013). Of course, the pragmatic question of exactly *how* to do that takes some time to answer. And there is no one answer; the specifics will depend on the instructor's goals and teaching style. Let us turn now to the nuts and bolts of making engagement happen.

STRATEGIES FOR ENGAGING STUDENTS

Once you have decided to get beyond lecture and engage students in learning about international relations, the choices for how to do so are vast. Here, I highlight a few options that have pedagogical and empirical support.

For those venturing out of the safe harbor of lecture-only teaching for the first time, the waters may be a bit daunting. Instead of becoming overwhelmed by the multitude of choices, a good strategy may be to select one of the suggested options and try it out in a class. In the face of so many new ideas, it may be tempting to force a teaching technique that you are not comfortable with. Don't. As Baum (2002) cautions, adopting a teaching style that is not natural for you will probably be counterproductive. Instead, consider the advice of other instructors and then innovate within the framework of your own personal teaching style. If you are excited about your teaching, the students will be, too. If you are skeptical about a strategy, the students will not buy in to it. Find something that you can get behind and embrace it.

One additional cautionary note, especially for junior faculty: be careful to maintain balance. What that balance—among teaching, research, service, family, and life in general—will look like depends on your personal preferences and the incentive structure at your institution. Some departments and universities are more supportive of teaching innovation than others are. Know where yours stands—and what your own priorities are—before making significant investments in major teaching overhauls. There are many suggestions in this chapter, but do not be limited by them. We are part of an incredibly diverse and surprisingly creative field. Perusing past issues of teaching journals will reveal articles on teaching IR using zombies (Blanton 2013; Hall 2011), *The Lord of the Rings* (Ruane and James 2008) and *Harry Potter* (Nexon and Neumann 2006). Although the options may be nearly limitless, I recommend a pragmatic approach to teaching innovation: limit yourself to one new teaching technique each time you teach a class. This approach is also better for assessment, as it means limiting the number of new variables introduced.

Speaking of assessment, if you want to know if your departure from lecture-only teaching is working as you intend, collect data (Raymond and Usherwood 2013)! What happens to test scores, to student engagement, to retention, to your own evaluations? My advice to those teaching IR is to read carefully the following suggestions (or search the literature for ones you like better), pick one to try, and start assessing its effectiveness in your courses. Chapter 36 has some great advice on how to get started in the scholarship of teaching and learning.

Simulations

From war games in the 1950s (Guetzkow et al. 1963) to diplomatic training in the 1970s to complex computer-based models today (ICONS 2013; Statecraft 2013), simulations have a long history in IR, both inside and outside of the classroom. Although the use of simulations for research has declined over time, the use of simulations for teaching has greatly increased (Starkey and Blake 2001). Today, simulations are one of the most widely used and written about methods for actively teaching IR.

There is some controversy over how much simulations may or may not improve learning (e.g. Christopher 1999; Ellington, Gordon and Fowlie 1998; Raymond 2010); however, many studies support the use of simulations, demonstrating improvements in student engagement (Hess 1999; Wolfe and Crooktall 1998; Ruben 1999; Brown and King 2000; Smith and Boyer 1996), content knowledge (Krain and Shadle 2006; Asal 2005), retention (Shellman and Turan 2006; Krain and Lantis 2006), complex and abstract thinking (Starkey and Blake 2001; McIntosh 2001) and empathy (Stover 2005). A more complete discussion of simulations and how to design them is available in Chapter 26. I have personally found simulations to be a great way of engaging students in learning about IR. Of course, there are also drawbacks to using simulations, mainly in terms of the time and effort required to carry them out (McIntosh 2001; Asal and Blake 2006; Glazier 2011; Haack 2008; Rivera and Simons 2008).

If you decide to try simulations, there is no cookie cutter approach (Wedig 2010; Asal 2005; Asal and Blake 2006). Simulations range from the highly formal and structured—for instance, models of important decision making bodies like the United Nations (Taylor 2013; McCartney 2006; McIntosh 2001), the North Atlantic Treaty Organization (Meleshevich and Tamashiro 2008) or the UN Security Council (DiCicco 2013)—to the comparatively simple and informal (Asal 2005; Glazier 2011). No matter the simulation, there are some best practices to keep in mind (Asal and Kratoville 2013).

Think carefully before you begin
The most important part of a simulation happens before class (Asal and Blake 2006; Shellman and Turan 2006; Youde 2008; Raymond 2010; Wedig 2010). Simulations should make reaching course learning goals easier. Keep those goals in mind when considering which type of simulation to use, the method of delivery, the length and the assessment mechanism. Adding a simulation to a course for its own sake risks doing more harm than good (Wedig 2010). There are a few key articles that can help first time or experienced simulation users think through some of these central decisions (Asal and Blake 2006; Wedig 2010; Asal and Kratoville 2013; Schnurr, De Santo and Craig 2013).

Connect the simulation to the class
Make the connection of the simulation to the core concepts of the class central throughout. It should be clear to the students how the simulation is related to the materials they are learning in the class. Talk about theory before, during and after the simulation (Asal and Kratoville 2013) and 'debrief' after the simulation is over (Asal 2005; Asal and Blake 2006; Shellman and Turan 2006; Wedig 2010; Van Dyke, DeClair and Loedel 2000; Youde 2008; Lederman 1984).

Start out simple
Particularly for those instructors who are new to using simulations, it is okay to start slow. Teaching and learning journals are filled with simulations that can be easily

adapted. Some of these are simple activities that will take no more than a portion of a class period, like Asal's (2005) Classical Realism game or Powner and Croco's (2005) Prisoner's Dilemma reenactments. Others may take a single class period to implement, like the simple simulations Glazier (2011) recommends or Thomas' (2002) Isle of Ted simulation. Still others require much more class time, but they also come with a significant amount of technical support and material preparation (for a small fee), like the ICONS simulation (Brown and King 2000; Starkey and Blake 2001; ICONS 2013) or Statecraft simulation (Statecraft 2013). Instructors could even consider giving up a large amount of the control and allowing the students to design (Frombgen et al. 2013) or run the simulation (Raymond 2010).

Civic Engagement and Service Learning

Another area where teaching and learning scholarship is on the rise, and where some best practices for teaching IR can be found, is in civic engagement and service learning. Courses that are designed to incorporate civic engagement and/or service learning are great at engaging students—taking them beyond learning facts to participating in informed advocacy. Although most of the research has been done on engagement in the American political system, civic engagement is much more than that (McDonald 2012; McCartney 2006). As civic engagement and internationalizing the curriculum both garner increasing attention as educational goals, more instructors are combining the two in an effort at international civic engagement. Although often resource intensive, engaging students globally provides a unique experience that students are likely to appreciate, value and learn from (Lorenzini 2010; Marlin-Bennett 2002), in addition to preparing students for success in an increasingly globalized world (McCartney 2006) and preparing them to make valuable contributions to their communities (Jacoby and Brown 2009).

When it comes to fostering civic engagement at the global level, there are four different approaches identified in the literature (Lorenzini 2010). First is international service learning. These courses involve traveling abroad with students to participate in a community service project and are challenging to teach for a number of reasons, including costs and logistics. Despite these challenges, international service learning experiences can truly be transformative for students, instilling in them a deeper understanding of the world and even a greater sense of justice (Grusky 2000; Monard-Weissman 2003; McKay, Gaffoglio and Esquibel 2008; Brunell 2013).

Second is transborder service learning. For this type of global civic engagement, students in one country participate in service learning in another country, but without the time and expense of a traditional study abroad experience. One transborder service learning experience, in which students conducted a food drive and delivered the donated food to poor children in Nogales, Mexico, is described by Cabrera and Anastasi (2008). McDonald (2012) provides another example: an innovative microfinance project that takes advantage of technology to help students have a truly international service learning experience without traveling abroad at all.

Third are placebound interactions, where students stay in their country of origin. Koulish (1998) describes a service learning course in which students assist immigrants with learning English and US history in preparation to become citizens. Dicklitch (2003) similarly has students work with non-US citizens, helping prepare cases of asylum seekers. Another example comes from Patterson (2000), whose service learning course involves students in the work of an NGO dedicated to refugee resettlement. Although certainly resource intensive, these kinds of global civic engagement experiences can really bring home to students the reality of international issues. Topics like human rights become much more real when students work with international human rights advocates (Marlin-Bennett 2002), participate in the asylum-seeking process (Dicklitch 2003) and begin to understand what life might be like for victims of human rights abuses (Krain and Nurse 2004).

Finally, there are international civic engagement projects, where the focus is less on the international component and more on the civic engagement element. One great example of this kind of global civic engagement is the high school Model United Nations conference McCartney's (2006) students hosted. Another example comes from a marketing professor, whose capstone students operated a collegiate chapter of a non-profit engaged in international community service (Metcalf 2010). In these classes, students are working on international issues—and teaching others about them—right in their own backyards. This combination of global focus and local action is a perfect way to foster civic skills and engagement.

I have had success teaching courses on international organizations with an international civic engagement component. In one of my courses, students participated in a regional Model Arab League simulation and helped host a Model Arab League simulation for local high school students. The depth of knowledge about international organizations and processes that comes from participating in intensive simulations like these is hard to replicate in a traditional classroom. In addition to content knowledge, the benefits of engagement with global issues and civic efficacy that often accompany these and other international civic engagement opportunities provide clear reasons for trying these teaching techniques.

Technology and Media

Taking the material to where students are today invariably means using technology, and media and technology are a great way to get students engaged in IR. Research indicates that using multimedia forms of instruction makes the presentation of material clearer and engages students—increasing both their attention and their motivation (Bartlett and Strough 2003; Seaman 1998; Ulbig 2009). And it is not surprising that improvements in learning are seen as well (Frey 1994; Mayer 1997; McNeil and Nelson 1991; Sekuler 1996; Smith and Woody 2000; Welsh and Null 1991), including improvements in test scores (Bartlett and Strough 2003; Erwin and Rieppi 1999; Smith and Woody 2000) and even civic engagement (Ulbig 2009). Learning happens best when students are interested in what they are studying (Colby et al. 2003). Using technology and media also helps prepare students for success in an increasingly plugged-in world.

With research demonstrating that multimedia instruction significantly improves learning, instructors have a number of options to choose from when it comes to incorporating media and technology into their teaching. One of the most popular, although admittedly not all that high-tech, is using film. Film is a particularly useful way to engage students, to provide them the foundation to move on to more complex topics (Valeriano 2013; Swimelar 2013; Waalkes 2003; Engert and Spencer 2009), and to improve their retention and cognition (Kuzma and Haney 2001; Pollard 2002). In one way, film can be thought of as leveling the playing field for students. Students come to a class with different levels of preparedness; a movie can provide a common background and a springboard for discussion (Krain 2010; Valeriano 2013; Kuzma and Haney 2001; Boyer et al. 2002).

Although some are concerned about the academic seriousness of film (Broughton 2008; Sealey 2008), there are strong reasons to believe that it can be a useful teaching tool. Success depends in large part on thoughtful film selection (Boyer et al. 2002). Tangentially related films or those introduced only superficially may end up confusing students more than helping them (Swimelar 2013). Engert and Spencer (2009) identify four main ways of utilizing film in the IR classroom: to teach events, issues, cultural identities and theories. Instructors interested in using film should think carefully about the desired learning goals first and then begin selecting movies. There is a long tradition of using movies to teach about war in IR (Lieberfeld 2007), although scholars have found that it is also very useful for teaching IR theory (Simpson and Kaussler 2009), or specific concepts like the state (Waalkes 2003) or human rights (Swimelar 2013). Robert Gregg, one of the central scholars in the field of IR and film, even curated a list of the ten best films for IR (Gregg 1999).

These are all excellent starting points for instructors interested in incorporating film into their teaching, but selecting the film is not the end of the road. Instructors must decide when to screen it, how much class time to devote to discussion and what, if any, assignments to tie to the film. If time is an issue in a shorter class period, students can be assigned to watch a film outside of class. I have used *Ghosts of Rwanda*, an excellent documentary available for streaming from PBS, to teach my IR students about genocide, humanitarian intervention and the responsibility to protect. I have found that a few thoughtful discussion questions, together with some direct links to course concepts from the instructor, are usually all it takes to get students thinking critically about a film and using it to understand IR. I am always impressed with how many students end up referencing a film in their research papers or final exam essays.

Beyond the movies, there are many additional media and technological resources to improve teaching and learning. Increasingly, the Internet is changing the way we teach and the way we research (Carpenter and Drezner 2010). As Darling and Foster (2012) argue, today's global policy debates take place online. Getting students engaged in IR by getting them online not only exposes them to current international developments, but also provides them the opportunities to develop the kind of communication skills and visual literacy they will need to be relevant in the 21st century (Selcher 2005; Felten 2008; Sealey 2008; Swimelar 2013). Although some may fear the future of teaching with technology, IR scholar/teachers are increasingly encouraging their peers to embrace the potential benefits. As Brunell (2013) recommends, "rather than thinking of technology as alienating and causing students to become more socially isolated and political disengaged, we need to start thinking of technology as a means to increase their global interest and political engagement" (p. 18). Take, for instance, videoconferencing, a technology that makes it possible to bring globalization into the classroom like never before (Martin 2007). Instructors are also beginning to take advantage of the benefits of technology to incorporate simulations into online or hybrid classes (Parmentier 2013; Schnurr, De Santo and Craig 2013).

When it comes to using media and technology, a word of caution is appropriate: do not go overboard. It is possible to get too much of a good thing. For instance, while images are helpful (Ulbig 2009), animation is not shown to add any additional gains in learning or engagement (ChanLin 1998), and too much busyness in a presentation or the superficial introduction of multimedia materials may end up as a distraction that could even hinder learning (Hashemzadeh and Wilson 2007; Mayer et al. 1996; Swimelar 2013).

Current Events

While some of the previous suggestions may call for major course overhauls, other strategies are more easily implemented. For instance, one simple and effective way to engage students in learning about IR is through the use of current events. The fascinating daily developments in global affairs are one of the reasons why students are drawn to our field in the first place. Instructors can take advantage of this interest by connecting concepts and theories to the 'real world' of IR. Many instructors do this almost intuitively—having newspapers as required readings, taking a few minutes to discuss current events at the beginning of every class, or bringing up recent developments to illustrate a concept (Kahne, Sporte and De la Torre 2006; Niemi and Junn 2005; Levine 2007). Using current events more systematically is one change almost any instructor could make with relatively little upfront cost.

Almost as easily, instructors can put a twist on current events that students are sure to love by incorporating satire into their IR courses (Glazier 2014). Using editorial cartoons to illustrate political problems or critiques is a classic teaching tool in the field of political science (Hammett and Mather 2010; Stark 2003; Baumgartner 2008). More recently, satirical sources like The Onion, *The Daily Show* and *The Colbert Report* have expanded the world of satire that instructors can draw on and that students are regularly exposed to (Beavers 2011; Baumgartner and Morris 2008). Far from feeling guilty about 'wasting' class time on clips from *Saturday Night Live*, instructors should embrace the pedagogical benefits of satire. Studies show that viewers of late night satire are more informed about politics (Young 2004; Pew Research Center 2008), more confident about their ability to understand politics (Baumgartner and Morris 2006) and more likely to be politically active (Moy, Xenos and Hess 2005; Cao and Brewer 2008). If you want to try some satire in your IR class, Rebecca Glazier curates a Satirical Resource Repository online (http://www.rebeccaglazier.net/satirical-resource-repository/), where you can browse satire specific to the field of IR, or search for satire by keyword (e.g., war, realism, democracy, etc.). I have found that assigning students to identify and critically analyze satire themselves leads to even greater engagement (Glazier 2014).

CONCLUSION

In addition to the ideas presented here, there are many other ways to engage students in learning about international relations. Instructors should not feel limited by the teaching strategies in this chapter or compelled to undertake major course overhauls. Find an idea that draws you in and make it your own. Instructors could even consider combining some of the strategies discussed here. For instance, using movies to provide background information for a simulation (Simpson and Kaussler 2009), using the teaching structure of simulations to teach with film more actively (Sunderland, Rothermel and Lusk 2009), using technology to get students civically engaged (Bers and Chau 2010) or infusing simulations with a civic engagement component (Bernstein 2008). These creative combinations are likely to find success, as fostering student engagement through multiple means is a best practice for teaching in the IR classroom and beyond (Krain 2010).

Engaging students in IR can be a rewarding experience for the instructor and for the students. When students care about the material, they are more likely to learn it and retain it (Colby et al. 2003). Whether engaged through the best practices discussed here or through other teaching strategies, students are better learners when the material matters to them. For instructors, engaging students in learning about IR is a goal that is both laudable and achievable.

REFERENCES

Amoore, L. and P. Langley (2001), 'Experiencing globalization: Active teaching and learning in international political economy', *International Studies Perspectives*, **2** (1), 15–32.

Asal, V. (2005), 'Playing games with international relations', *International Studies Perspectives*, **6** (3), 359–73.

Asal, V. and E.L. Blake (2006), 'Creating simulations for political science education', *Journal of Political Science Education*, **2** (1), 1–18.

Asal, V. and J. Kratoville (2013), 'Constructing international relations simulations: Examining the pedagogy of IR simulations through a constructivist learning theory lens', *Journal of Political Science Education*, **9** (2), 132–43.

Barber, B.R., M. Cassell, I. Leslie, D.E. Ward, S.L. Lamy, P.L. Martin and C. Ingebritsen (2007), 'Internationalizing the undergraduate curriculum', *PS: Political Science & Politics*, **40** (1), 105–20.

Bartlett, R.M. and J. Strough (2003), 'Multimedia versus traditional course instruction in introductory social psychology', *Teaching of Psychology*, **30** (4), 335–8.

Baum, L. (2002), 'Enthusiasm in teaching', *PS: Political Science & Politics*, **35** (1), 87–90.

Baumgartner, J.C. (2008), 'Polls and elections: Editorial cartoons 2.0: The effects of digital political satire on presidential candidate evaluations', *Presidential Studies Quarterly*, **38** (4), 735–58.

Baumgartner, J.C. and J.S. Morris (2006), 'The Daily Show effect', *American Politics Research*, **34** (3), 341–67.

Baumgartner, J.C. and J.S. Morris (2008), 'One "nation", under Stephen? The effects of *The Colbert Report* on American youth', *Journal of Broadcasting & Electronic Media*, **52** (4), 622–43.

Beavers, S.L. (2011), 'Getting political science in on the joke: Using *The Daily Show* and other comedy to teach politics', *PS: Political Science & Politics*, **44** (2), 415–19.

Bernstein, J.L. (2008), 'Cultivating civic competence: Simulations and skill-building in an introductory government class', *Journal of Political Science Education*, **4** (1), 1–20.

Bers, M. and C. Chau (2010), 'The virtual campus of the future: Stimulating and simulating civic actions in a virtual world', *Journal of Computing in Higher Education*, **22** (1), 1–23.

Blanton, R.G. (2013), 'Zombies and international relations: A simple guide for bringing the undead into your classroom', *International Studies Perspectives*, **14** (1), 1–13.

Boyer, M.A., V.K. Pollard, L.M. Kuzma and P.J. Haney (2002), 'At the movies: A continuing dialogue on the challenges of teaching with film', *International Studies Perspectives*, **3** (1), 89–94.

Breuning, M. and J. Ishiyama (2007), 'Marketing the international studies major: Claims and content of programs at primarily undergraduate institutions in the Midwest', *International Studies Perspectives*, **8** (1), 121–33.

Broughton, J. (2008), 'Inconvenient feet: How youth and popular culture meet resistance in education', in Kelvin S. Sealey (ed.), *Film, politics, and education*, New York: Peter Lang, pp. 17–42.

Brown, S.W. and F.B. King (2000), 'Constructivist pedagogy and how we learn: Educational psychology meets international studies', *International Studies Perspectives*, **1** (3), 245–54.

Brunell, L.A. (2013), 'Building global citizenship: Engaging global issues, practicing civic skills', *Journal of Political Science Education*, **9** (1), 16–33.

Burch, K. (2000), 'A primer on problem-based learning for international relations courses', *International Studies Perspectives*, **1** (1), 31–44.

Cabrera, L. and J. Anastasi (2008), 'Transborder service learning: New fronteras in civic engagement', *PS: Political Science & Politics*, **41** (2), 393–9.
Cao, X. and P.R. Brewer (2008), 'Political comedy shows and public participation in politics', *International Journal of Public Opinion Research*, **20** (1), 90–99.
Carpenter, C. and D.W. Drezner (2010), 'International relations 2.0: The implications of new media for an old professional', *International Studies Perspectives*, **11** (3), 255–72.
ChanLin, L.J. (1998), 'Animation to teach students of different knowledge levels', *Journal of Instructional Psychology*, **5** (3), 166–75.
Christopher, E.M. (1999), 'Simulations and games as subversive activities', *Simulation and Gaming*, **30** (4), 441–56.
Colby, A., T. Ehrlich, E. Beaumont and J. Stephens (2003), *Educating citizens: Preparing America's undergraduates for lives of moral and civic responsibility*, New York: John Wiley and Sons.
Cox, S.M. (2003), 'In the pits: Teaching from the bottom up', *PS: Political Science & Politics*, **36** (1), 75–6.
Darling, J. and M. Foster (2012), 'Preparing students to join the global public sphere', *International Studies Perspectives*, **13** (4), 423–36.
De Matos-Ala, J. and D.J. Hornsby (2013), 'Introducing International Studies: Student engagement in large classes', *International Studies Perspectives*, doi: 10.1111/insp.12036.
DiCicco, J.M. (2013), 'National Security Council: Simulating decision-making dilemmas in real time', *International Studies Perspectives*, **15** (4), 438–58.
Dicklitch, S. (2003), 'Real service=real learning: Making political science relevant through service-learning', *PS: Political Science & Politics*, **36** (4), 773–6.
Ellington, H., M. Gordon and J. Fowlie (1998), *Using games and simulations in the classroom*, London: Kogan Page.
Engert, S. and A. Spencer (2009), 'International relations at the movies: Teaching and learning about international politics through film', *Perspectives: Central European Review of International Affairs*, **17** (1), 83–103.
Erwin, T.D. and R. Rieppi (1999), 'Comparing multimedia and traditional approaches in undergraduate psychology classes', *Teaching of Psychology*, **26** (1), 58–61.
Felten, P. (2008), 'Visual literacy', *Change: The Magazine of Higher Learning*, **40** (6), 60–64.
Frey, D.K. (1994), 'Analysis of students' perceptual styles and their use of multimedia', *Perceptual and Motor Skills*, **79** (1), 643–9.
Frombgen, E., D. Babalola, A. Beye, S. Boyce, T. Flint, L. Mancini and K. Van Eaton (2013), 'Giving up control in the classroom: having students create and carry out simulations in IR courses', *PS: Political Science & Politics*, **46** (2), 395–9.
Glazier, R.A. (2011), 'Running simulations without ruining your life: Simple ways to incorporate active learning into your teaching', *Journal of Political Science Education*, **7** (4), 375–93.
Glazier, R.A. (2014), 'Satire and political efficacy in the political science classroom', *PS: Political Science & Politics*, **47** (4), 867–72.
Gregg, R.W. (1999), 'The ten best films about international relations', *World Policy Journal*, **16** (2), 129–34.
Grusky, S. (2000), 'International service learning: A critical guide from an impassioned advocate', *American Behavioral Scientist*, **43** (5), 858–67.
Guetzkow, H.S., C.F. Alger, R.A. Brody, R.C. Noel and R.C. Snyder (1963), *Simulation in international relations: Developments for research and teaching*, Englewood Cliffs, NJ: Prentice-Hall.
Haack, K. (2008), 'UN studies and the curriculum as active learning tool', *International Studies Perspectives*, **9** (4), 395–410.
Hall, D. (2011), 'Varieties of zombieism: Approaching Comparative Political Economy through *28 Days Later* and *Wild Zero*', *International Studies Perspectives*, **12** (1), 1–17.
Hammett, D. and C. Mather (2010), 'Beyond decoding: Political cartoons in the classroom', *Journal of Geography in Higher Education*, **35** (1), 103–19.
Hashemzadeh, N. and L. Wilson (2007), 'Teaching with the lights out: What do we really know about the impact of technology intensive instruction?', *College Student Journal*, **41** (3), 601–12.
Hess, F.M. (1999), *Bringing the social sciences alive*, Needham Heights, MA: Allyn and Bacon.
ICONS (2013), *ICONS Project*, available at http://www.icons.umd.edu/ (accessed 4 March 2014).
Jacoby, B. and N.C. Brown (2009), 'Preparing students for global civic engagement', in Barbara Jacoby and Associates (eds.), *Civic engagement in higher education: Concepts and practices*, San Francisco, CA: Jossey-Bass, pp. 213–26.
Kahne, J.E., S.E. Sporte and M. De la Torre (2006), 'Small high schools on a larger scale', Consortium on Chicago School Research, University of Chicago, available at http://files.eric.ed.gov/fulltext/ED498333.pdf (accessed 4 March 2014).
Koulish, R. (1998), 'Citizenship service learning: Becoming citizens by assisting immigrants', *PS: Political Science & Politics*, **31** (3), 562–7.

Krain, M. (2010), 'The effects of different types of case learning on student engagement', *International Studies Perspectives*, **11** (3), 291–308.
Krain, M. and J.S. Lantis (2006), 'Building knowledge? Evaluating the effectiveness of the global problems summit simulation', *International Studies Perspectives*, **7** (4), 395–407.
Krain, M. and A. Nurse (2004), 'Teaching human rights through service learning', *Human Rights Quarterly*, **26** (1), 189–207.
Krain, M. and C.J. Shadle (2006), 'Starving for knowledge: An active learning approach to teaching about world hunger', *International Studies Perspectives*, **7** (1), 51–66.
Kuzma, L.M. and P.J. Haney (2001), 'And . . . action! Using film to learn about foreign policy', *International Studies Perspectives*, **2** (1), 33–50.
Lederman, L.C. (1984), 'Debriefing: A critical reexamination of the postexperience analytic process with implications for its effective use', *Simulation & Games*, **15** (4), 415–31.
Levine, P. (2007), *The future of democracy: Developing the next generation of America citizens*, Lebanon, NH: University Press of New England.
Lieberfeld, D. (2007), 'Teaching about war through film and literature', *PS: Political Science & Politics*, **40** (03), 571–4.
Lorenzini, M. (2010), 'From global knowledge to global civic engagement', paper presented at APSA 2010 Teaching & Learning Conference, Washington DC.
Marlin-Bennett, R. (2002), 'Linking experiential and classroom education: Lessons learned from the American University–Amnesty International USA summer institute on human rights', *International Studies Perspectives*, **3** (4), 384–95.
Martin, P.L. (2007), 'Global videoconferencing as a tool for internationalizing our classrooms', *PS: Political Science & Politics*, **40** (1), 116–17.
Mayer, R.E. (1997), 'Multimedia learning: Are we asking the right questions?', *Educational Psychologist*, **32** (1), 1–19.
Mayer, R.E., W. Bove, A. Bryman, R. Mars and L. Tapangco (1996), 'When less is more: Meaningful learning from visual and verbal summaries of science textbook lessons', *Journal of Educational Psychology*, **88** (1), 64–73.
McCartney, A.R.M. (2006), 'Making the world real: Using a civic engagement course to bring home our global connections', *Journal of Political Science Education*, **2** (1), 113–28.
McDonald, M. (2012), 'Civic engagement with an international focus: The Western Carolina Microfinance Project', paper presented at APSA 2012 Teaching & Learning Conference, Washington DC.
McIntosh, D. (2001), 'The uses and limits of the model United Nations in an international relations classroom', *International Studies Perspectives*, **2** (3), 269–80.
McKay, V.C., N. Gaffoglio and E. Esquibel (2008), 'Sociocultural and transformational experiences in Cambodia', *Teaching and Learning: International Best Practice*, **8**, 245–65.
McNeil, B.J. and K.R. Nelson (1991), 'Meta-analysis of interactive video instruction: A 10 year review of achievement effects', *Journal of Computer-Based Instruction*, **18** (1), 1–6.
Meleshevich, A.A. and H. Tamashiro (2008), 'Learning to learn; learning to win: How to succeed in the simulated world of model NATO', *PS: Political Science & Politics*, **41** (4), 865–9.
Metcalf, L.E. (2010), 'Creating international community service learning experiences in a capstone marketing-projects course', *Journal of Marketing Education*, **32** (2), 155–71.
Monard-Weissman, K. (2003), 'Fostering a sense of justice through international service-learning', *Academic Exchange Quarterly*, **7** (2), 164–9.
Moy, P., M.A. Xenos and V.K. Hess (2005), 'Communication and citizenship: Mapping the political effects of infotainment', *Mass Communication and Society*, **8** (2), 111–31.
Nexon, D.H. and I.B. Neumann (2006), *Harry Potter and international relations*, Lanham, MD: Rowman & Littlefield.
Niemi, R.G. and J. Junn. (2005), *Civic education: What makes students learn*, New Haven, CT: Yale University Press.
Parmentier, M.J.C. (2013), 'Simulating in cyberspace: Designing and assessing simple role playing activities for online regional studies courses', *International Studies Perspectives*, **14** (2), 121–33.
Patterson, A.S. (2000), 'It's a small world: Incorporating service learning into international relations courses', *PS: Political Science & Politics*, **33** (4), 817–22.
Pew Research Center (2008), 'Journalism, satire or just laughs? "The Daily Show with Jon Stewart" examined', *Pew Research Journalism Project*, available at http://www.journalism.org/2008/05/08/journalism-satire-or-just-laughs-the-daily-show-with-jon-stewart-examined/ (accessed 4 March 2014).
Pollard, V.K. (2002), 'Cognitive leverage of film in international studies classrooms', *International Studies Quarterly*, **3** (1), 89–92.
Powner, L.C. and M.G. Allendoerfer (2008), 'Evaluating hypotheses about active learning', *International Studies Perspectives*, **9** (1), 75–89.

Powner, L.C. and S.E. Croco (2005), 'Making formal models freshman friendly', paper presented at the Annual Meeting of the International Studies Association, Honolulu, Hawaii.

Rajaee, B. (2005), 'Update on international programs and activities in 2004', *PS: Political Science & Politics*, **38** (1), 159.

Raymond, C. (2010), 'Do role-playing simulations generate measurable and meaningful outcomes? A simulation's effect on exam scores and teaching evaluations', *International Studies Perspectives*, **11** (1), 51–60.

Raymond, C. and S. Usherwood (2013), 'Assessment in simulations', *Journal of Political Science Education*, **9** (2), 157–67.

Rivera, S.W. and J.T. Simons (2008), 'Engaging students through extended simulations', *Journal of Political Science Education*, **4** (3), 298–316.

Ruane, A.E. and P. James (2008), 'The international relations of Middle-earth: Learning from *The Lord of the Rings*', *International Studies Perspectives*, **9** (4), 377–94.

Ruben, B.D. (1999), 'Simulation, games, and experience-based learning: The quest for a new paradigm for teaching and learning', *Simulation and Gaming*, **30** (4), 498–506.

Schnurr, M.A., E. De Santo and R. Craig (2013), 'Using a blended learning approach to simulate the negotiation of a multilateral environmental agreement', *International Studies Perspectives*, **14** (2), 109–20.

Sealey, K.S. (ed.) (2008), *Film, politics, and education: Cinematic pedagogy across the disciplines*, New York: Peter Lang.

Seaman, M.A. (1998), 'Developing visual displays for lecture-based courses', *Teaching of Psychology*, **25** (2), 141–5.

Sekuler, R. (1996), 'Teaching sensory processes with multimedia: One of my teaching assistants is a mouse', *Behavior Research Methods, Instruments, & Computers*, **28** (2), 282–5.

Selcher, W.A. (2005), 'Use of internet sources in international studies teaching and research', *International Studies Perspectives*, **6** (2), 174–89.

Shellman, S.M. and K. Turan (2006), 'Do simulations enhance student learning? An empirical evaluation of an IR simulation', *Journal of Political Science Education*, **2** (1), 19–32.

Simpson, A.W. and B. Kaussler (2009), 'IR teaching reloaded: Using films and simulations in the teaching of international relations', *International Studies Perspectives*, **10** (4), 413–27.

Smith, E.T. and M.A. Boyer (1996), 'Designing in-class simulations', *PS: Political Science & Politics*, **29** (4), 690–94.

Smith, S.M. and P.C. Woody (2000), 'Interactive effect of multimedia instruction and learning styles', *Teaching of Psychology*, **27** (3), 220–23.

Stark, C. (2003), '"What, me worry?": Teaching media literacy through satire and *Mad* magazine', *The Clearing House: A Journal of Educational Strategies, Issues and Ideas*, **76** (6), 305–9.

Starkey, B.A. and E.L. Blake (2001), 'Simulation in international relations education', *Simulation and Gaming*, **32** (4), 537–53.

Statecraft (2013), *Statecraft: An International Relations Simulation*, available at http://www.statecraftsim.com/ (accessed 4 March 2014).

Stover, W.J. (2005), 'Teaching and learning empathy: An interactive, online diplomatic simulation of Middle East conflict', *Journal of Political Science Education*, **1** (2), 207–19.

Sunderland, S., J.C. Rothermel and A. Lusk (2009), 'Making movies active: Lessons from simulations', *PS: Political Science & Politics*, **42** (3), 543–7.

Swimelar, S. (2013), 'Visualizing international relations: Assessing student learning through film', *International Studies Perspectives*, **14** (1), 14–38.

Taylor, K. (2013), 'Simulations inside and outside the IR classroom: A comparative analysis', *International Studies Perspectives*, **14** (2), 134–49.

Thomas, G.D. (2002), 'The Isle of Ted Simulation: Teaching collective action in international relations and organization', *PS: Political Science & Politics*, **35** (3), 555–9.

Ulbig, S. (2009), 'Engaging the unengaged: Using visual images to enhance students' "Poli Sci 101" experience', *PS: Political Science & Politics*, **42** (2), 385–91.

Valeriano, B. (2013), 'Teaching introduction to international politics with film', *Journal of Political Science Education*, **9** (1), 52–72.

Van Dyke, G.J., E.G. DeClair and P.H. Loedel (2000), 'Stimulating simulations: making the European Union a classroom reality', *International Studies Perspectives*, **1** (2), 145–59.

Waalkes, S. (2003), 'Using film clips as cases to teach the rise and "decline" of the state', *International Studies Perspectives*, **4** (2), 156–74.

Wedig, T. (2010), 'Getting the most from classroom simulations: Strategies for maximizing learning outcomes', *PS: Political Science & Politics*, **43** (3), 547–55.

Welsh, J.A and C.H. Null (1991), 'The effects of computer-based instruction on college students' comprehension of classic research', *Behavior Research Methods, Instruments, & Computers*, **23** (2), 301–5.

Wolfe, J. and D. Crooktall (1998), 'Developing a scientific knowledge of simulation/gaming', *Simulation and Gaming*, **29** (1), 7–20.
Youde, J. (2008), 'Crushing their dreams? Simulations and student idealism', *International Studies Perspectives*, **9** (3), 348–56.
Young, D.G. (2004), 'Daily Show viewers knowledgeable about presidential campaign, National Annenberg Election Survey shows', available at http://www.annenbergpublicpolicycenter.org/downloads/political_communication/naes/2004_03_late-night-knowledge-2_9-21_pr.pdf (accessed 26 November 2014).

PART III

IN-CLASS TEACHING TECHNIQUES

24. Effective syllabus design
John Ishiyama and Robert G. Rodriguez

In this chapter we focus on some of the basic elements of syllabus design and some of the more often mentioned best practices in constructing a syllabus, particularly those practices based on the existing empirical literature (Slattery and Carlson 2005; Albers 2003). Syllabus design is one of the most important, but most often overlooked, aspects of conducting a course, and is certainly one of the more challenging activities facing new instructors. Syllabi serve several important purposes, the most basic of which is to communicate the instructor's course design (e.g. goals, organization, policies, expectations and requirements) to the students in the class. In addition, syllabi can be used to convey the instructor's enthusiasm for the topic and the expectations for the course, as well as to establish a 'contract' with students by publicly stating policies, requirements and procedures. Course syllabi may also relay information about resources such as the location of a writing center, services for students with disabilities or relevant sections of the student code of conduct. Further, the syllabus can also be used to communicate course goals and content to colleagues and other faculty members.

In this chapter we first examine some of the literature that identifies the primary purposes of syllabi, and the effects syllabi have on student performance and perceptions of the instructor. Second, we outline some basic guidelines in syllabus design. Finally, we provide a set of suggestions regarding the structure of a syllabus and issues to keep in mind when designing a syllabus by offering a concrete template/example.

LITERATURE ON PURPOSE AND EFFECTS OF SYLLABI

Syllabi are a central part of teaching for a number of reasons (Duffy and Jones 1995). Syllabi can improve communication between instructors and students, and clarify course expectations (Behnke and Miller 1989; Smith and Razzouk 1993). Indeed, the syllabus is 'a formal statement of what the course is about, what students will be asked to do, and how their performance will be evaluated. Unlike the comments an instructor makes in class, it is a lasting statement to which students can refer again and again' (chapter 3 of Teaching Handbook, The Ohio State University, Office of Faculty and TA Development cited in Ishiyama and Hartlaub 2002, p.567; see also Altman 1989; Danielson 1995; Matejka and Kurke 1994). In a sense, the syllabus serves as a 'road map' for students to refer to as they wind their way through the course.

As such, as many have noted (see e.g. Ishiyama and Hartlaub 2002; Duffy and Jones 1995; Danielson 1995), well-constructed course syllabi serve several important purposes. These include communicating the basic design of the course, particularly the learning objectives or goals, the organization of the course, the instructors' and the university's policies, as well as course expectations and requirements (Albers 2003).

However, the syllabus also conveys more intangible messages, such as the degree to which the instructor appears to be 'welcoming' and approachable (Ishiyama and Hartlaub 2002). The syllabus also contributes to classroom socialization (Duffy and Jones 1995). For example, Danielson (1995) argues that the syllabus can contribute to the classroom socialization process by serving as a contract (analogous to the psychological contract operating in organizations) and by reducing classroom uncertainties, and clarifying any ambiguities in how grades will be calculated. Robles (1993) has investigated the empirical link between the content of the syllabus and how it affects student expectations about the course (see also Becker and Calhoon 1999).

Others have argued that the syllabus plays an important role in improving student performance. Kern (1990) finds that creating a competency based syllabus, in which student competencies required for the course, as well as competencies to be developed during the course, were outlined and explained, results in increased student performance. Serafin (1990) also finds that changes introduced to the course syllabus that listed learning objectives positively affected the final grade performance of students. Indeed, she finds that the more explicit is the course syllabus in terms of number of objectives, content, instructional resources and grading components, the better the performance of college students (see also Harris 1993; Schlesinger 1987).

A study conducted by Perrine, Lisle and Tucker (1995) focused on another effect of syllabi—student perceptions of instructors. In this study the authors found evidence to suggest that the syllabus can affect a student's willingness to seek help from college instructors. They tested the student's willingness to seek help as a function of student age, class size, and whether an explicit supportive statement is placed on the syllabus. Students in select classes (N=104) were read brief syllabi of two courses in which class size and an offer of outside-of-class help from the instructor were manipulated. The study's results suggested that students were more likely to express willingness to seek help from an instructor when the offer of outside help explicitly appeared on the syllabus. In addition, there was a significant effect for age on support seeking. These findings suggest that instructors might be able to encourage more students to seek outside-of-class help by placing supportive statements on a class syllabus.

A study by John Ishiyama and Stephen Hartlaub (2002) examined how the way in which a syllabus was worded also affected student perceptions of a course. However, their concern was focused more on how requirements expressed on a syllabus, or the way in which a syllabus was worded, impacted the perceptions of the instructor. In particular they examined the impact of the use of 'rewarding' versus 'punishing' language.

Indeed, there has been consistent, though limited, interest in the different effects of the language of inducements. Baldwin (1971a, 1971b) explored the impact of positive versus negative sanctions in international bargaining. Tjosvold (1995) examined the relationship between rewards and punishments and the perceptions of those affected. In general, those who were rewarded thought power was used more fairly, and had more positive attitudes towards those in power. On the other hand, those who were punished had negative attitudes regarding those in power. In a similar way, Ishiyama and Hartlaub (2002) found that teachers who phrase their syllabi in rewarding versus punishing language affect student evaluations of instructors. Indeed, the same requirements, expressed differently, may lead to very different student evaluations of the faculty member.

In the Ishiyama and Hartlaub (2002) study, two groups of students in general education introduction to political science classes were asked to read two syllabi (one per group). The syllabi were identical except for how requirements for the hypothetical course were stated. In one syllabus phrases were used such as 'students *should* complete all readings', versus 'students *must* complete all readings' in the other syllabus. Further, the two syllabi had identical requirements, but they varied slightly in the language used to describe these requirements. For example, the punishing syllabus read, 'If for some substantial reason you cannot turn in your papers or take an exam at the scheduled time you must contact me *prior* to the due date, or test date, or you will be graded down 20%', whereas the rewarding syllabus read, 'If for some substantial reason you cannot turn in your papers or take an exam at the scheduled time you should contact me *prior* to the due date, or test date, or you will only be eligible for 80% of the total points'. Ishiyama and Hartlaub (2002) found that syllabi that used rewarding language were more likely to have freshmen and sophomore students view the instructor as more open and approachable (although this did not have the same effect for upper class students).

In sum, the literature has pointed to the important role syllabi play in clarifying course objectives and affecting student expectations for the course, as well as perceptions of the instructor. In the following section we offer a set of guidelines on syllabus construction that highlight some considerations when designing a syllabus.

WHAT TO CONSIDER IN SYLLABUS DESIGN

When putting together a syllabus, there are some general principles to keep in mind. First, even though students do not necessarily need to be made aware of this, the principle of 'constructive alignment' should guide syllabus development. Constructive alignment requires that instructors harmonize course goals (or learning outcomes), activities and assessment methods. This contributes to making students learn in a deep rather than a surface way, because it allows students to engage in activities that they need to complete to attain learning outcomes. It is also fair to students, as well-aligned courses only assess knowledge and skills that students had an opportunity to learn and/or improve during the course (Biggs 1999).

Second, it is worthwhile mentioning, although it seems obvious, that it is important to keep in mind the audience for which the syllabus is written. Many times novice instructors write syllabi that resemble the syllabi they remember in graduate school—this strategy does not often work well, as they are designing a syllabus for an introductory level class. Students in their first year of college are often still transitioning to the adult world and are not yet familiar with what syllabi are, much less how important it is to familiarize themselves with the information syllabi contain.

Third, decide what the courses objectives are for the class, and make them very explicit in the beginning of the syllabus. What is it that you want your students to learn? Are these objectives consistent with the mission of the department or unit in which you are teaching? The latter is often not always clear to new instructors, so it is important to share your syllabus with your colleagues and ask them to review it. Also, make sure that learning objectives are consistent with any government or university mandated requirements at your institution.

Fourth, it is important that you make very explicit the expectations and policies of the course. Often we assume that students will understand the ways of the profession and how we generally communicate as professionals and scholars—they don't. Never assume anything, particularly with freshman and sophomores in today's collegiate world. Students have changed in profound ways since you were an undergraduate. Their popular culture and historical reference points may be completely different from your own. Read the 'Mindset List' produced each year by Beloit College for further information on this point, at www.beloit.edu/mindset/.

Fifth, it is important to recognize that students do not often read the syllabus (and longer syllabi are less likely to be read than shorter syllabi). It might be useful to consider providing incentives to students in order to get them to read the syllabus. One technique is to conduct a 'syllabus quiz', which tests early in the term whether the students have read through the syllabus. Another tactic may be to have a detachable sheet stapled to the back of a syllabus where a student affirms that she/he has read the syllabus in its entirety and agrees to be bound by the terms contained therein. This heightens the sense among students that the syllabus is indeed a contract and that they should probably read the document before they sign off on it.

WHAT SHOULD BE IN A SYLLABUS?

In the following section, we outline some of the basic components of a syllabus. To be sure, the actual design of an instructor's syllabus will depend upon the individual instructor—there is no 'one size fits all' when it comes to syllabus design. Generally speaking, however, a syllabus will include the following components:

1) First, there are some obvious things to include, such as a title of the course and the instructor's information, semester and year, number of units, meeting times and location, instructor and Teaching Assistant (TA) information (e.g. name, office, office hours, contact information). See Box 24.1 for an example.
2) In addition there should be a description of the course that identifies its scope and purposes, as well as the learning objectives. Box 24.2 contains an example, from one of the author's Introduction to American Politics courses.
3) Further there should be a section that includes required and/or optional materials (e.g. books, reserve readings, software and supplies, with authors and editions if necessary). This section of the syllabus should be very specific, indicating the desired editions of the texts, ISBN numbers, and whether electronic versions or previous versions of the texts are acceptable. Contemporary instructors should realize that today students have a wealth of options in purchasing or renting books beyond the college bookstore, and as consumers many take the time to find their books elsewhere. If the instructor chooses not to allow electronic devices in the classroom, it is essential to convey that electronic resources are not acceptable. In addition, there should be a section on course requirements, or what students will have to do in terms of assignment for the course such as homework, examinations, projects, attendance, class discussion and presentation, etc. This section should describe the nature and format of assignments and the expected length of written work, and provide due dates for these assignments and the scheduled dates for examinations.

BOX 24.1 EXAMPLE OF BASIC INFORMATION TO BE INCLUDED IN THE SYLLABUS

Political Science (PSCI) class number and section, term
Course name
Class location, days, hours

Instructor:
Instructor name
Office: Office location
Office Hours: Days and hours (and by appointment if you prefer)
Office Phone: Phone number
E-mail: email@unt.edu

	TA1 Name	TA2 Name	TA3 Name
Office Location:			
Office Phone:			
Office Hours:	Wednesday, 10:00am–1:00pm	Tuesday and Thursday, 10:00am–12:00pm	Wednesday, 11:00pm–12:30pm Thursday, 12:30pm–2:00pm
E-mail:			

BOX 24.2 EXAMPLE OF COURSE DESCRIPTION

I. Course Goals: This is an introductory American government course designed to examine the development of the institutional structures of the US and Texas political systems. To be able to analyze the US political system, we will be adopting an explicitly **Comparative Perspective, i.e. how does the US political system compare with the political system of other countries?** There are two reasons for this. First, being able to understand the development and operation of the political systems of other countries helps us understand why the American political system developed in the way it did. Further, comparison offers potential alternatives to consider if one were interested in effecting improvement in the US system. The second is more practical: the instructor is primarily trained as a comparative political scientist and has extensive experience studying other political systems, particularly in Europe, the former Soviet Union, and Africa. Thus, every effort will be made to understand the US political system in comparison with other political systems.

By the end of the semester, students will be able to identify, analyze and evaluate the national institutions of government-Congress, the Presidency, the Bureaucracy, the Judiciary and related state level institutions. Student learning objectives include:

1.1 Demonstrating the ability to identify and explain constitutionalism.
1.2 Comprehending the principles of Federalism.
1.3 Synthesizing the roles of the executive, legislative and judicial branches of government.
2.1 Demonstrating an awareness and recognition of the scope of democratic theory.
2.2 Differentiating between civil rights and civil liberties.

This course satisfies state mandated requirements for a course emphasizing the US and Texas constitutions.

> **BOX 24.3 EXAMPLE OF RESOURCES TO BE INCLUDED IN THE SYLLABUS**
>
> ASSIGNMENTS AND LEARNING
>
> The assignments for the course will together add up to your grade for the course. However, they are also targeted to achieve specific learning outcomes. Here's what each type of assignment is designed to do:
>
> The *map exercises* develop and/or enhance geographic literacy. The exercises include tasks both to help you learn where countries are located relative to one another and asking you to research other questions related to culture, history and geography. Note that the assignments will be made available through the BlackboardLearn system, but they are due in class.
>
> The *online quizzes* test learning through reading. You will take five online quizzes through the BlackboardLearn system, within the windows of availability noted in the syllabus. Each quiz tests what you have learnt from a small group of chapters. The emphasis will be on conceptual learning. The quizzes are an opportunity not only to earn points but also to identify areas of strength and weakness in your grasp of the material. Make sure to discuss any identified weaknesses with your instructor and/or assistant to help you prepare for the two examinations.
>
> The *book review paper* represents an opportunity to seriously consider the impact of socio-cultural values on perception and behavior, and to see the world from a very different perspective. A set of questions will guide your evaluation of the book's contents. As you formulate your evaluation of the book, the paper also provides an opportunity to sharpen skills in critical thinking and analysis, as well as practice in formulating your thoughts and assessments in writing. The assignment for the book review paper will be posted on BlackboardLearn.
>
> The in-class *examinations* encourage you to attain command of the material presented in the course beyond memorization. The examinations will use an essay format and will go beyond testing your knowledge of course concepts, theories and facts. The examinations will ask you to apply and/or critically evaluate theories and concepts in light of historical and contemporary facts. A study guide for each examination will be released approximately one week prior to each examination and will be posted on BlackboardLearn.
>
> *Class attendance and participation* is encouraged and rewarded. You will also earn a small proportion of your grade just by showing up. Attendance is rewarded to help you cultivate a positive habit: showing up matters and contributes to success.

It is also useful to identify how individual assignments may be connected to the learning objectives you have enumerated in your syllabus. Thus Box 24.3 outlines an example of how a set of assignments might be linked with a set of learning objectives.

4) It is important also to be very clear about the evaluation and grading policy. What will the final grade or evaluation of the students be based upon? For transparency, provide a breakdown of components and an explanation of the grading policies or the course (such as weights for the individual assignment grades, curves, extra-credit options, potentially dropping the lowest grade, etc.). In addition, you can include a description of course policies regarding attendance, tardiness, academic integrity, missing homework and examinations, recording classroom activities, food in class, laptop use, etc. Precision is important to contemporary college stu-

dents. Clearly state your grading scale on your syllabus, particularly if your institution allows for +/− grades. For example, is 89.9 percent in the course an 'A', a 'B' or a 'B+'?

5) It is also useful to have some statement of a student code of conduct. If your institution has an official statement, this can be included. Generally, however, you want to describe expectations regarding student behavior in the classroom, particularly emphasizing mutual respect of classmates, open mindedness and classroom decorum.

6) The use (and inevitably, misuse) of electronic devices such as cell phones and laptops has become rampant in recent years. In particular, texting on a cell phone or updating Facebook statuses or checking email on laptops/tablets during class have unfortunately become commonplace. Depending upon the instructor's personal preferences, a statement on the allowable use of electronic devices should be included in the syllabus. Any potential rewards for not misusing electronic devices (or consequences for doing so) should be clearly stated. One successful tactic that has all but eradicated misuse of electronic devices in the classroom has been utilized for years by the co-author of this chapter from A&M–Commerce. The premise is quite simple and extraordinarily effective. The instructor bans the use of all electronic devices, and states this on the syllabus. This eliminates any laptop/tablet use immediately, since those objects are fairly large and obvious to the naked eye. However, to eliminate cell phone use, the instructor builds in a few percentage points for 'quizzes' into the course grade. The reward for no one using an electronic device in class is that everyone in the class receives the maximum percentage points offered for quizzes. However, if someone is found to be using an electronic device such as texting on a small cell phone, then the entire class must take a quiz on the spot. Since students realize that they will probably not perform well on a pop quiz, the peer pressure not to cause the entire class to have a quiz is enormous, and acts as a major deterrent. Over the past eight years of utilizing this tactic, cell phone use in classes ranging up to 55 students has been reduced to 0–2 incidents per semester in each course.

7) There should also be some type of class calendar or schedule. Give students a sense of what to expect on a daily basis (or at the very least on a weekly basis). What can be expected in terms of topics covered and the types of assignments (assigned readings, homework, project due dates and exam dates)? Also make sure to be clear as to what students can expect in terms of availability concerning office hours, email communication, etc.

8) Academic dishonesty regrettably continues to be a problem in the contemporary classroom, particularly with the accessibility of information on virtually any topic via the internet. A statement on the university, departmental and class procedures on how academic dishonesty is addressed should be in the syllabus. Importantly, a statement on how to *avoid* academic dishonesty is perhaps equally as important.

Box 24.4 provides the first two pages of an example syllabus for illustrative purposes.

BOX 24.4   SAMPLE SYLLABUS

Political Science (PSCI) 3600.001
Comparative Politics

Dr. John Ishiyama
Office:
Office Hours: 1:30 pm–3:00 pm Mondays and Thursdays and by appointment
Office Phone:
Email:

Graduate Teaching Assistant:
Office: Wooten Hall 136
Office Hours: 11:00 am–12:00 pm Tuesdays and Thursdays
Office Phone:
Email:

I. Goals and Objectives of the Course: This course is designed as a general overview of the subfield of comparative politics. This is not a current events course, although certainly current events affect the substance of what we study. This course is primarily designed to provide both a broad overview of major theoretical approaches to the study of comparative politics, the method by which comparativists compare political phenomenon across nation-states, and the application of these approaches and methods of comparison to the study of political development and comparative political systems. Thus, the readings illustrate both the variety of theoretical perspectives and methodological approaches to studying comparative political development.

One of the primary goals of this course is to promote the analytical skills of the student. This involves not only knowing some basic facts about the world (such as where countries are located) and exposure to the practice of conducting critical analysis (such as what appears in a typical political science journal article) but also the ability to apply academic learning to real-world problems. To help cultivate such skills this course will be centered on a 'problem solving' exercise—how to build democracy in countries that are currently not democratic. During the course of the term we will be investigating some of the basic factors that affect democratic development. These include the relationship between economics, culture, institutions and democracy.

To promote such problem-solving skills you will take a map quiz, review a classic article in comparative politics, and design a constitutional arrangement for a country that is currently authoritarian. In this project, students will be asked to formulate a constitutional design that would be most appropriate for this country, if it were to democratize. This constitutional design will include the design of executive power, the structure of the legislature, the electoral system, the territorial division of power and the design of the judiciary (more on this later in the term). These constitutional designs will be due Monday March 7 by 5:00 pm.

II. Texts: There are two required texts for this course:

III. University of North Texas—Policy on Cheating and Plagiarism:
Academic Integrity. (See UNT Policy 18.1.16 at http://www.unt.edu/policy/UNT Policy/volume3/18_1_16.pdf)
Categories of Academic Dishonesty.

Cheating. The use of unauthorized assistance in an academic exercise, including but not limited to:

- use of any unauthorized assistance to take exams, tests, quizzes or other assessments;
- dependence upon the aid of sources beyond those authorized by the instructor in writing papers, preparing reports, solving problems or carrying out other assignments;
- acquisition, without permission, of tests, notes or other academic materials belonging to a faculty or staff member of the university;

- dual submission of a paper or project, or re-submission of a paper or project to a different class without express permission from the instructor;
- any other act designed to give a student an unfair advantage on an academic assignment.

Plagiarism. Use of another's thoughts or words without proper attribution in any academic exercise, regardless of the student's intent, including but not limited to:

- the knowing or negligent use by paraphrase or direct quotation of the published or unpublished work of another person without full and clear acknowledgement or citation;
- the knowing or negligent unacknowledged use of materials prepared by another person or by an agency engaged in selling term papers or other academic materials.

Forgery. Altering a score, grade or official academic university record or forging the signature of an instructor or other student.

Fabrication. Falsifying or inventing any information, data or research as part of an academic exercise.

Facilitating Academic Dishonesty. Helping or assisting another in the commission of academic dishonesty.

Sabotage. Acting to prevent others from completing their work or willfully disrupting the academic work of others.

Available Academic Penalties.
The following academic penalties may be assessed at the instructor's discretion upon determination that academic dishonesty has occurred. Admonitions and educational assignments are not appealable.

Admonition. The student may be issued a verbal or written warning.

Assignment of Educational Coursework. The student may be required to perform additional coursework not required of other students in the specific course.

Partial or No Credit for an Assignment or Assessment. The instructor may award partial or no credit for the assignment or assessment on which the student engaged in academic dishonesty, to be calculated into the final course grade.

Department of Political Science POLICY ON ACADEMIC INTEGRITY
The Political Science Department adheres to and enforces the university's policy on academic integrity (cheating, plagiarism, forgery, fabrication, facilitating academic dishonesty and sabotage). Students in this class should review the policy, which may be located at _____. Violations of academic integrity in this course will be addressed in compliance with the penalties and procedures laid out in this policy.

IV. University of North Texas—Statement of ADA Compliance:
The Political Science Department cooperates with the Office of Disability Accommodation to make reasonable accommodations for qualified students with disabilities. Please present your written accommodation request on or before the sixth class day (beginning of the second week of classes).

V. Course Requirements
a) **There will be three exams scheduled for this term**
  Two In-Class Major Exams = 200 pts (100 pts each exam) (February 16 and March 29)
  A comprehensive major final examination = 125 pts (May 10)
b) **One Map Quiz** (on January 31) = 30 pts
c) **Article Review Paper** (due February 9, 5–7 pages) = 50pts
d) **One Constitution Paper** (May 7, 10–12 pages) = 75 pts
The total number of points for this class = 480 pts

VI. Policy on Attendance: I do not take regular attendance—however, I will take 'spot attendance'. Thus, if you are not in class consistently I will know and this will affect my evaluation of your performance. Also, since much of the exam material is based on class lectures, it would be in your best interest to attend regularly.

VII. Schedule of Lecture Topics and Readings:
January 17: Introduction to the course (What is this course about?)
    No readings
January 19–24: **The origins of Comparative Politics and structural functionalism**
    Readings:
January 26–31: **Modernization and the political consequences of economic development**
    Readings:
    MAP QUIZ January 31
February 2–7: **Culture and Ethnic Politics**
    Readings:
February 9–14: **Social Structure and Politics**
    Readings:
    First article review due by beginning of period on February 9

FEBRUARY 16—FIRST EXAMINATION

[rest of syllabus redacted]

OTHER GENERAL ADVICE ON WRITING A SYLLABUS

We have offered above some guidelines for writing a basic syllabus. However, there are also a number of general things to keep in mind.

In terms of timing, it is a good idea to write your syllabus fairly late in the process, after you have essentially laid out the plan for your course but well before the first day of class. Although we have provided an example syllabus above, one generally good piece of advice is to confer with a colleague and take a look at that colleague's syllabus, particularly if you are new to teaching. Find a colleague who is known as an excellent instructor and take a look at his/her syllabus. Syllabi vary by discipline and department and it is a very good idea to see what the norm is in your academic unit. The instructor must ensure that her/his syllabus includes any state or university mandated requirements/statements. A syllabus designed by a valued colleague provides a good model to emulate.

Also keep in mind that students think of the syllabus as a type of 'contract' and that it should give some predictability to the class. Based upon these expectations, students can have some of their questions addressed. Indeed, there are a number of questions when reading a syllabus, which you may want to consider. These include: Will I be able to work during the semester? How do I budget my time and can I handle the amount of work required? Is it possible for me to get a good grade for the course? Do I need to have prerequisite skills and knowledge to do well in this course? Where do I get help if I need it? If you anticipate these questions when writing up your syllabus this will provide students with a sense of your priorities, and provides them with information that can help them decide whether to continue with the course.

The 'contractual' aspect of the syllabus will also serve to protect the instructor in the inevitable circumstance that a dispute should arise with a student. The instructor can rely on the syllabus as a documented notification of classroom policies and procedures. Furthermore, it is essential to include a statement to the effect that 'this syllabus is subject to change' in the event that changes are necessitated during the semester—otherwise, a student could also reasonably claim that, if the syllabus is a 'contract', then you, as the instructor, are not living up to your end of it.

It is important either to distribute or to make available via a course site (such as Blackboard or some other system) a copy of the syllabus and go over the syllabus in class. It is important that the requirements of the course are made clear, as well as what your expectations are as an instructor. As mentioned above, it might be useful to provide an incentive for students to actually read the syllabus, by conducting a syllabus quiz or by having students sign a statement that they have read and are bound by the terms of the syllabus.

Occasionally it will be necessary to make changes in the schedule and adapt the syllabus. Sometimes, and this is true for many new instructors, you might find that your original design had learning goals and objectives that were far too ambitious and that you may have to alter requirements and course expectations. Other times you may miss a class due to illness, or perhaps you may suddenly be called out of town—or you might fall behind (perhaps because you underestimated the amount of time you spend on particular topics). Be sure that you build in to the syllabus some room to adapt your syllabus to deal with these issues. However, if you do have to alter the syllabus and the schedule, make sure that you inform the students in advance (or as much in advance as possible). If you make changes, do not significantly increase the amount of work (you can of course reduce it). Remember, students think of the syllabus as a contract, and thus do not generally look very favorably upon sudden or extreme changes in the schedule or the requirements. If a situation arises where you must miss class and have time to announce it, one option is to use modern technology to your advantage. Given college students' nearly universal accessibility to the internet, assigning students to watch a YouTube video on a relevant topic and writing a short essay about it in lieu of attending the class session(s) you have to miss may be an effective solution.

CONCLUSIONS

In this chapter we emphasized the importance of careful syllabus design, in as much as syllabi affect student performance and perceptions of the instructor. In addition, we provided some basic guidelines regarding the basic structure of the syllabus and posited some questions that the instructor should consider when designing a course syllabus.

However, it is important to emphasize that one size does not fit all, and the effectiveness of a syllabus varies according both to context and to disciplinary, institutional, departmental, and possibly government directed departmental norms. Instructors should be creative—the syllabus says something about you as an instructor. Have fun designing the syllabus—it is after all a reflection of you as a person as well.

REFERENCES

Albers, C. (2003), 'Using the Syllabus to Document the Scholarship of Teaching', *Teaching Sociology*, **31** (1), 60–72.
Altman, H.B. (1989), 'Syllabus Shares "What the Teacher Wants"', *The Teaching Professor*, **3** (May), 1–2.
Baldwin, David (1971a), 'The Power of Positive Sanctions', *World Politics*, **24** (January), 19–38.
Baldwin, David (1971b), 'Thinking about Threats', *Journal of Conflict Resolution*, **15**, 71–8.
Becker, Angela H. and Sharon K. Calhoon (1999), 'What Introductory Psychology Students Attend to on a Course Syllabus', *Teaching of Psychology*, **26**, 6–11.
Behnke, R. and P. Miller (1989), 'Information in Class Syllabus May Build Student Interest', *Journalism Educator*, **44**, 45–57.
Biggs, John (1999), *Teaching for Quality Learning at University*, Buckingham, UK: SRHE and Open University Press.
Danielson, Mary Ann (1995), 'The Role of the Course Syllabi in Classroom Socialization', Bloomington, IN: Indiana University, ERIC Clearinghouse for Social Studies/Social Science Education, ERIC: ED387845.
Duffy, Donna Killian and Janet Wright Jones (1995), *Teaching within the Rhythms of the Semester*, San Francisco, CA: Jossey-Bass.
Harris, Mary McDonald (1993), 'Motivating with the Course Syllabus', *The National Teaching and Learning Forum*, **3** (1), 1–3.
Ishiyama, John and Stephen Hartlaub (2002), 'Does the Wording of Syllabi Affect Student Course Assessment in Introductory Political Science Classes?', *PS: Political Science & Politics*, **35**, 567–70.
Kern, R. (1990), 'Use of Competency-Based Course Syllabus and Its Effects on Student Performance in Introductory Computer Courses', *Community/Junior College Quarterly of Research and Practice*, **14**, 115–22.
Matejka, Ken and Lance B. Kurke (1994), 'Designing a Great Syllabus', *College Teaching*, **42**, 115–19.
Perrine, Rose M., James Lisle and Debbie L. Tucker (1995), 'Effects of a Syllabus Offer of Help, Student Age, and Class Size on College Students' Willingness to Seek Support from Faculty', *The Journal of Experimental Education*, **64**, 41–52.
Robles, Alfredo (1993), 'How "International" are International Relations Syllabi?', *PS: Political Science & Politics*, **26**, 526–8.
Schlesinger, A.B. (1987), 'One Syllabus that Encourages Thinking, Not Just Learning', *The Teaching Professor*, (August), 8.
Serafin, Ana Gil (1990), 'Course Syllabi and Their Effects on Students' Final Grade Performance', Bloomington, IN: Indiana University, ERIC Clearinghouse for Social Studies/Social Science Education, ERIC: ED328202.
Slattery, J. and J. Carlson (2005), 'Preparing an Effective Syllabus: College Teaching', **53** (4), 159–64.
Smith, R. and N. Razzouk (1993), 'Improving Classroom Communication: The Case of the Course Syllabus', *Journal of Education for Business*, **68**, 215–22.
Tjosvold, Dean (1995), 'Effects of Power to Reward and Punish in Cooperative and Competitive Contexts', *Journal of Social Psychology*, **135**, 723–36.

25. Integrating technology into the classroom
Gabriela Pleschová*

Recent advancements in information technologies (ITs) have made their use very popular in a variety of arenas, and higher education is no exception. Whereas two decades ago only a few devices counted as 'information technology', namely the overhead projector, television, video and computer, today it is possible to identify a large variety of technologies that people use in their daily lives and that can become helpful for learning too. Some examples of these are online discussion forums, podcasting, audience response systems, online blogs, social bookmarking, wikis, Facebook, Twitter and multimedia CDs.

The popularity of information technologies as learning tools stems from the fact that ITs can bring a number of benefits for university learners and teachers. Previous studies have found that technologies stimulate interactivity, facilitate peer learning and improve feedback, which is especially valuable in large classes. Also, IT was reported to enhance learning in courses with rapidly changing content (Pleschová 2010).

For political science classes in particular, the employment of IT has brought a number of specific advantages. Students of politics often learn about issues that change from week to week and sometimes even on a daily basis, like elections, political campaigns or international conflicts. Also, in some higher education systems, as for example in the USA, studying politics moreover entails helping learners to become active citizens (Craig 2012, pp. 29–30). Information technologies thus allow political science students to follow current events, learn about various perspectives to explain these events, as well as react to the world around them, which is so essential for the discipline.

However, IT – as any other learning tool – also raises a number of challenges. For example, technologies may be introduced with the motivation of reducing the costs of providing education, rather than because they can make learning more effective (Middleton 2010, p. 11). Additionally, the fact that IT allows students to access an enormous quantity of information may create a scenario of information overload, which can hamper learning unless students are trained in how to deal with such vast information supply (Thornton 2012, p. 97). Further issues include the cost of new technologies for universities as well as for individual students, demands on time and effort from users initially less skilled in working with IT, as well as student attitudes (likes and dislikes) towards IT introduced into their courses.

This chapter explores three examples of information technologies that have recently become popular learning tools in the political science classroom: online discussion forums, podcasting and an audience response system (ARS). These three tools have been chosen as they are reported to facilitate student learning in a variety of ways. They can enhance student preparation and engagement, further improve student argumentation and writing skills, and make feedback to student work more efficient, among other outcomes. Based on the number of publications in contemporary political science education literature, online forums, podcasting and ARSs are the most widely used IT tools in political science classes today.[1]

This chapter presents examples of how to introduce each of these IT tools into the classroom, and discusses their costs and efficiency, student perceptions and effects on student learning. The chapter critically reviews findings from existing studies into the use of these three tools in political science classes, suggesting how to use them effectively. The chapter concludes with general recommendations on how to employ information technologies to enhance learning.

ONLINE DISCUSSION FORUMS

In order to stimulate student thinking and discussion beyond the classroom, teachers may invite students to contribute to an online discussion forum. This is a web-based platform that stores and displays written postings and allows reaction to them. Sometimes, this forum is called a 'discussion board'. When used for educational purposes, participation in a discussion forum is mostly restricted to the class members, but it is also possible to allow other people to read and comment on the postings.

Examples of How to Design a Forum

Discussion forums can be a useful tool to encourage students to think about the assigned readings in an introductory political science class. For each class, students can be pre-assigned a thought question and required to post an answer online, perhaps around a half page in length. For example, students can be asked to watch a political speech and discuss the speakers' political orientation, connect the content of a reading to their own experience, or explain what they considered most unclear in an assigned text. Using the forum, students can also react to other classmates' postings. Based on the student contributions, the teacher can design learning activities in a way that addresses the issues that were most unclear to the students or where students demonstrated misunderstanding (Trudeau 2005).

Alternatively, the teacher can use discussion forums to assign students questions reflecting the course topics. For example, in a course on Irish politics, students can be asked questions like, 'Does Ireland need an Office of President? Why? Why not? If you could reform the Office, what changes would you make?' Each forum can be open for a set period of time (e.g. two weeks), after which student postings in the forum are reviewed in class. While participation in the forum may be voluntary, responding to questions may help students to prepare for the final exam (Buckley 2011).

Another option can be asking students to post drafts of their assignments on the forum, allowing their classmates to comment on them. This way, students can improve their works before they are presented in class (Schattschneider 2010).

Cost and Efficiency

Teachers typically use discussion forums that are supported by the university's Virtual Learning Environment (VLE)[2] and have no additional cost to set up. Teachers at schools where online platforms are not available could use free tools such as Facebook groups as a substitute for this forum. Still, using a forum can demand a significant amount of the teacher's time, even if it is well designed and free. Buckley (2011, p. 413) reports spending an hour per day – altogether about five hours per week – reviewing postings. In some educational contexts, this may be too much. Therefore, it can be advised that teachers set some limits on the length and number of student contributions and reactions. Sometimes, the VLE allows the teacher to print out all postings as a single document, which can be very convenient (Trudeau 2005).

Student Perceptions of Online Forums

Student reactions to this learning tool are of two types. When student contribution to the forum is optional, often only a handful of students make postings while the majority prefer to lurk or not to contribute at all. In these cases, students do not consider the forum a driver for increased interaction and only some would recommend using it in future classes (Buckley 2011, see also Schattschneider 2010). However, when the postings contribute to students' grades, a large majority of students consider the forum important for their learning (Trudeau 2005, p. 297). Also, students from classes where contributions to the forum were not assessed wished that their online activity would be graded (Buckley 2011).

Although teachers may not sympathize with similar calls, it is important to remember that, by concentrating on those tasks that count towards their grade, students are simply acting rationally. Experience, moreover, shows that assessment helps to encourage well-thought-out postings (Trudeau 2005, p. 295). If the online forum is new for the teacher, and/or for the students, and the teacher does not wish to make students suffer from being subjects of an experiment, he or she can make the task only a small component of the students' grade (5 or 10 percent). Or, students can be awarded points for any reasonable answer, with excellent postings being awarded extra points (Trudeau 2005, p. 293). The teacher can even introduce a special competition to encourage quality contributions – for example, that the best titles on a posting will receive a special prize (Trudeau 2005, p. 322). This does not necessarily need to be a mark.

Some teachers using forums recommend that issues discussed online should be congruent with what is discussed in class (Trudeau 2005, p. 300). However, students sometimes feel that there is little sense in discussing the same issues both online and later in class, and these perceptions are especially typical for small classes (Schattschneider 2010; Buckley 2011, p. 409). Students may be right: repetitiveness leads to boredom, which decreases student engagement. Therefore, when using the forum, it should bring an added value for students beyond the in-class discussion. For example, the teacher can use the summary from the online discussion as a stepping stone for a further activity completed in class.

Impact on Student Learning

If students regularly contribute to the forum, it can have a positive effect on their learning, although the evidence is inconclusive. Trudeau (2005) observed that classes were much more productive after a discussion forum was used than before. Students felt free to pose questions, and the assignment helped the teacher to better prepare for classes, as he already knew what students thought about some major issues from the topic. Buckley

(2011) also was satisfied with the student argumentation, critical thinking and presentation of opinion demonstrated in the online postings.

The challenging facet of using the forum appears to be encouraging students to post messages rather than solely view what others have written. Thurston's (2005, p. 363) research showed that only 3 percent of student activity in an online forum was contributing, while the rest of the 'hits' involved reading messages. This was similar to Buckley's (2011) experience. While one study concluded that the more students 'read' other students' postings, the higher grade they achieved (Hamann, Pollock and Wilson 2009), the authors could not ascertain how many contributions were truly read and therefore they counted as 'read' all postings students clicked on. This does not seem a viable approach because previous research has uncovered a profound difference in learning outcomes between students who read materials in a deep way and those who read them in a surface way (Marton and Säljö 1976).

According to Buckley, students are more likely to be active online contributors if they are used to weekly assignments. If students are used to assessment based on a few term assignments with the majority of marks resting on a final exam, it takes them some time to change their study habits. Additionally, when the class is small enough that everyone knows each other, students are more comfortable discussing online. In bigger classes, some students prefer not to contribute to the forum because of shyness and a fear of being bullied for expressing their opinion, even where there is no evidence of bullying on the forum (Buckley 2011).

While students from both of Buckley's classes who had contributed to the forum achieved high grades in their final exam, whereas those who failed had not participated, the teacher could not demonstrate that the discussion forum alone contributed to student learning outcomes. It was often the case that the good students to begin with were the only students to contribute to the forum (Buckley 2011).

To conclude, the most challenging aspect of using the internet discussion forums remains the same as in the traditional classroom: to make students discuss, rather than solely answer the teacher's questions. Probably because none of the teachers in the abovementioned studies awarded grades for comments on earlier postings, all three concluded that the students had discussed among each other very little. This goes against the main purpose of using the online discussion forum.

Using the Forum More Effectively

In order to make the forums a better driver of student learning, several recommendations can be made. First, many students tend to compose their contributions to a forum in a similar way as when communicating online with their friends. Therefore, students need guidelines on how an 'academic' contribution should look and what makes an 'academic' posting in a particular course an excellent one. Also, it can be useful to discuss with students some rules for contributing so that students do not feel intimidated to honestly express their opinion.

Aside from this, for discussion forums, well-constructed prompts lie at the heart of the assignment design. In order to stimulate students to develop their higher-order thinking, the assigned questions should be well crafted, preferably asking students to analyze, compare, critique or similar, rather than to recall facts (Trudeau 2005, pp. 294–5). To support active learning, students should be engaged in designing some questions too.

Additionally, to encourage quality postings, student contributions should be assessed. If the teacher wants students to comment on contributions from their classmates rather than solely post individual contributions, students need further incentives to do this. For example, the teacher can require each student to comment on a certain number of postings during semester, making it clear how those comments should look. Alternatively, for each forum, students can be divided into two groups: those who make individual postings and those who comment on them.

PODCASTING

Another way teachers can use IT to facilitate learning is using podcasts. A podcast is an audio or video file that can be downloaded from the internet and listened to or watched on a computer or MP3 player (Taylor 2009, p. 121). Using a Really Simple Syndication (RSS) feed, any podcast can be automatically downloaded to an IT device right after it is uploaded to a website, which can be very convenient for users (Ralph, Head and Lightfoot 2010, p. 14).

Examples of Using Podcasts

One way of using podcasts is making them a replacement for lectures. For example, students can be asked to listen to audio lectures outside of class, while face-to-face classes focus on interactive learning activities (Taylor 2009). Or, teachers can make short audio summaries of the key points from the lectures, including advice for further reading/listening (Ralph, Head and Lightfoot 2010). This use of podcasts, however, may encourage the undesired expectation that students should just passively watch or listen to podcasts and remember information from them.

A different method, which requires more engagement from students, is assigning a worksheet to accompany the podcast. This worksheet may, for example, start with relatively simple issues and continue with more sophisticated problems (Woodcock and Duckworth 2010). Other alternatives include asking students themselves to prepare podcasts, for example summaries of seminar discussions (Ralph, Head and Lightfoot 2010), or asking students to create audio presentations instead of physically presenting in class. Teachers can also use podcasts as a form of audio feedback to student work or as recordings from research seminars in order to encourage more students to attend these seminars (Lightfoot 2010).

Cost and Efficiency

As many computers and mobile phones now have a recording function, short podcasts can be created quite easily and with no extra costs. Also, because many students today own personal computers, smart phones and MP3 players, podcasts usually do not require any additional costs from the students. Nevertheless, to make longer recordings, as for example from the lecture, specialized equipment may be necessary (Lightfoot 2010, p. 23).

When podcasts are used to give feedback on student work, teachers can save time, and some also consider it less stressful than preparing written feedback (Lightfoot 2010, p. 22). On the other hand, creating podcast summaries from lectures is usually time-consuming as it first requires a careful script (Lightfoot 2010, p. 23). Also, preparing podcasts that record entire lectures may require a significant amount of work or become unfeasible unless a VLE or a webpage allows large files to be stored and rapidly downloaded (Ralph, Head and Lightfoot 2010, p. 19). Aside from this, editing a podcast is more time-consuming than editing a text (Taylor 2009, p. 132); therefore, using podcasts instead of assigned readings may require more from the teacher.

Student Perceptions of Podcasts

Initially, the proponents of podcasts argued that listening to audio files could be beneficial to students who learn best through listening, as well as appealing to modern students who are accustomed to using information technologies in their daily lives (Ralph, Head and Lightfoot 2010, pp. 14–15). However, research on learning styles that was popular mainly in the 1980s (see for example Kolb 1984) could not come up with credible explanations of how people learn. Also, it was uncovered that student appreciation of IT in their personal lives does not automatically translate into their learning. Therefore, feedback from students was sought to shed more light on student attitudes to the use of podcasts.

These surveys of student opinion brought some surprising results. First, although teachers initially expected students to listen to podcasts on their MP3 players, it has been found that students prefer to use their personal computers, perhaps because they do not wish to mix their study with private lives (Woodcock and Duckworth 2010, p. 31; Ralph, Head and Lightfoot 2010, p. 19; Taylor 2009, p. 124). Also, students reject the idea of listening to podcasts in place of attending lectures (Ralph, Head and Lightfoot 2010, p. 11). Further, when podcasts have replaced their lectures, students are much more supportive of the interactive learning activities that are done during the lecture time than of the mere use of podcasts (Taylor 2009). Students do not even appreciate when teachers prepare podcasts with enthusiasm and solely for the purpose of listening to them outside the class rather than as recordings of lectures (Taylor 2009, p. 122; Roscoe 2012, p. 9).

When podcasts are used as study materials, students call for shorter recordings between 5 and 15 minutes, though they also welcome audio material from the entire lecture (Lightfoot 2010, p. 21). On the other hand, students tend to ignore the worksheets accompanying the podcast lectures (Woodcock and Duckworth 2010, p. 26) unless the worksheets are an assessed learning task. Lightfoot (2010, p. 23) reports another interesting finding from student feedback: once students have podcasts available in one course, they demand them in other courses as well, which, as he believes, may be contrary to some staff expertise or may not even fit the expected course outcomes.

Impact on Student Learning

The desired effects of podcasts on student learning still need to be proven. Ralph, Head and Lightfoot (2010) could not find enough evidence that student engagement with podcasts influenced their study results. Only a minority of students produced podcasts that were of sufficient quality, even if podcasts demonstrated students' creativity. Also, Taylor (2009, p. 126) could not establish any relationship between student views on podcasts and their course grade. Assumed outcomes that require further empirical evidence include that podcasting can be useful for students who may have difficulty processing information the first time (Lightfoot 2010, p. 19), including those who are studying in their second language (Ralph, Head and Lightfoot 2010, p. 16).

What is important is that, when podcasts are used as a passive learning activity, such as when podcasts replace frontal lecturing, they probably cannot have positive effects on student learning. For example, the aspect students found most helpful about the podcast lectures were the transcripts that accompanied the podcasts, and typically they listened to podcasts while also reading the transcripts (Taylor 2009, pp. 120, 124). Similarly to this, students in another study mainly considered podcasts as useful when recapping lectures (Woodcock and Duckworth 2010, p. 31). This suggests that students may tend to use podcast lectures simply to more easily memorize for the exam. This must concern all teachers who introduce podcasts so that they help students to achieve more complex learning outcomes than remembering facts.

Using Podcasts More Effectively

In order to make podcasts more useful for enhancing student learning, teachers should avoid using podcasts merely as a replacement for lectures. Students need to actively engage with the podcasts, either by completing a set of tasks after listening to a podcast or by creating podcasts themselves. Because preparing podcasts can be a new task for many students, students should be given examples of how a quality podcast sounds. Ideally, students should be presented with a variety of examples in order to encourage them to think about different ways to approach the task, rather than copying a single pattern.

Using platforms such as iTunes to host podcasts, and YouTube for recordings with video, may make manipulation with the files easy for those who are used to these applications in their private lives. Nevertheless, it is important to double check with students to ensure that everyone is familiar with these platforms and that their computers and other devices are compatible with them.

AUDIENCE RESPONSE SYSTEMS

An audience response system (ARS) is a set of IT devices that enables students to respond to closed questions by choosing one of the given responses. These responses are then almost immediately collated and presented so that everyone can view them. Some people may know this technology from television shows such as *Who Wants to Be a Millionaire?* and a number of different synonyms exist for it, including 'clickers', 'handheld transmitters' or 'Personal Response Systems' (PRSs). Usually, this system is employed in large classes where counting student 'votes' would be impractical or pedagogically undesirable. Student responses can either be anonymous or the teacher can attach a name to each device to track individual responses (Damron and Mott 2005, p. 375).

Examples of Using ARSs

ARSs can be used effectively in large introductory classes, even in those with over a hundred students. Students can use the ARS to answer various types of questions, including, for example: 'How well do you understand author's main findings?' or 'Where would you place George W. Bush on the issue of abortion?' (Kam and Sommer 2006, p. 113). Posing these types of questions, the teacher can get immediate feedback from every student in class and find out which issues require further elaboration. This can help to make instruction more student centered, rather than keeping it focused on the teacher's intentions. Alternatively, the teacher can ask questions which do not have any 'right answer', as for example 'Do you think the media has more or less impact today compared with the author's time?' (Kam and Sommer 2006, p. 113). This way, the teacher can stimulate debate and engage students more with the topic. Also, students themselves can be engaged in designing the questions.

Using the ARS, the class can, for example, start with a short presentation by the teacher, which is followed by students responding to questions with the ARS, which they then discuss in groups (Gormley-Heenan and McCartan 2009). Alternatively, students can use the ARS only in some classes that are a part of a larger learning project. For example, students can first prepare questions for an opinion poll designed to provide information for their simulation of a presidential campaign. Then, students can play the role of the mock electorate by voting through the ARS. Data from the poll can later be analyzed to prepare the campaign strategies for different political parties. Several groups of students can be assigned various roles in this process (Kam and Sommer 2006).

Another alternative of using the ARS is allowing students to try methods of experimental research. This way, students can better understand and appreciate the nature of scholarly research. Moreover, it can help them to more easily understand topics such as persuasion and framing (Kam and Sommer 2006).

Cost and Efficiency

Teachers who think of introducing an ARS need to carefully plan which system to choose, as there are large differences in usage and quality and therefore in cost. For example, Kam and Sommer (2006, p. 117) report paying $3,200 for the whole system, although they admit that, to decrease the costs for the institution, students could be asked to buy their own transmitters for $35 each. Damron purchased the system for $750, plus the transmitters for each student for about $20 each. Because students of his colleague Mott bought their own devices for $20 each, the teacher received the technology for free from the publisher of the textbook they used (Damron and Mott 2005, p. 373).

Fortunately, this technology is becoming cheaper with time and because of its increasing popularity. Also, many alternatives to the ARS exist, which can be used with laptops or mobiles and can be free of cost, such as Google Forms, PollDaddy, Pinnion, Piazza or SoapBox (see Brady 2012 for an overview). However, their functionalities are typically not entirely the same as those of an ARS: for example, some allow synchronous and others asynchronous polling. Also, students and teachers may feel reluctant to learn working with just another type of software.

One of the greatest assets of the ARS is that it enables the teacher to see immediate feedback from the students. However, while the ARS saves some time it also requires some effort. Before using the ARS, handheld transmitters need to be distributed to students and then also collected back. For a large class of over a hundred students, this may take up to 30 minutes, including troubleshooting the equipment (Damron and Mott 2005, p. 378). Therefore, it can be efficient to make students purchase their own devices or to let students keep the transmitters for a number of classes. Students then need to be repeatedly reminded not to forget to bring their device to class. This need not happen if the teacher decides to replace the ARS with a combination of student mobile phones/ laptops and free software, as previously mentioned.

Student Perceptions of ARSs

Students typically demonstrate great enthusiasm for using ARSs. It is not unusual to find that 98 percent of students like using the system and almost everyone recommends introducing it into other courses too (Kam and Sommer 2006, p. 114; Damron and Mott 2006, p. 380). Students appreciate that anonymous responding through the ARS encourages everyone to contribute and to honestly say what they think. Thanks to this, as perceived by the students, the ARS helps to increase in-class interaction (Damron and Mott 2005, p. 375; Gormley-Heenan and McCartan 2009, p. 386).

Moreover, students value that, thanks to the ARS, they can discuss controversial topics more easily (Kam and Sommer 2006, p. 114), as well as build up their self-confidence because technology allows them to self-reflect without fellow students knowing their responses (Gormley-Heenan and McCartan 2009, pp. 386, 388). Students also welcome that technology makes classes more efficient. For example, before using the ARS, students complained that 'voting' during the simulation had taken too much time and was inaccurate (Damron and Mott 2005, p. 382).

However, students are not entirely positive about ARSs. One study (Ulbig and Notman 2012, p. 358) reported that about 5 percent of the class complained that it was not fair to require students to purchase the clickers and about one fifth of students did not consider the price–benefit ratio appropriate.

Impact on Student Learning

Studies evaluating the effects of ARSs on political science students are mainly based on teacher observations and feedback from students, with teachers' observations confirming mostly positive student perceptions. Using the ARS, teachers could see students becoming more self-confident about posing questions, as well as contributing to livelier and more meaningful in-class discussions (Kam and Sommer 2006, pp. 115–16; Gormley-Heenan and McCartan 2009; Damron and Mott 2005, p. 377). Once students could discuss anonymous responses in small groups, they became more courageous about defending their personal opinions and supporting them with arguments. This was particularly important in a class with most students coming from a divided society – as for example Northern Ireland is – where people tend to keep their political opinions to themselves (Gormley-Heenan and McCartan 2009, p. 389).

Similar benefits were also reported when students could not discuss but only view the results from 'voting' on the screen. In that case, more students were willing to express their opinion – probably because they could see more colleagues sharing their opinion. This way minority views received more attention in class and the discussions were no longer dominated by a single opinion (Damron and Mott 2005, p. 377). Using the ARS, students were also found to be better aware of classmates' opinions on issues discussed in class (Kam and Sommer 2006).

Aside from this, shy students were found to particularly benefit from using the ARS. Ulbig and Notman (2012) employed an ARS in an introductory American government course with about 90 students. One class (the experimental class) regularly responded to in-class quiz questions using the ARS. The other class (the control class) answered the same questions using a paper answer sheet. Measured by a factual knowledge test, both shyer and less shy students in the control group gained similar knowledge at the end of semester. As opposed to this, shyer students from the experimental class made evidently bigger gains than their less shy classmates. Moreover, shyer students from the experimental group improved their attitudes towards the course more than their less shy classmates. Because comparisons based on the final exam and grade could not support the results from the test (Ulbig and Notman 2012, p. 364), more research is still needed on what type of students may benefit most from using an ARS. Additionally, it remains unclear whether the ARS can help shyer students to develop skills other than fact-remembering.

Using the ARS More Effectively

For stimulating desired learning with an ARS, question design appears to be the key, as it is when using online forums. While formulating questions, teachers should align them with the intended outcomes of the class. Initially, the teacher may start with relatively simple questions in order to increase student engagement. Later, the problems should increase in sophistication in order to develop students' higher-order thinking skills. Aside from this, it seems useful to combine voting in class with other activities, such as small group discussions, simulations, writing reflective papers, etc. Using clickers this way, students can discuss the arguments that support their votes, as well as the arguments that support alternative responses, instead of just pushing the button for their vote. Also, engaging students in question design seems useful, as students can learn to differentiate between various types of questions and see the connections between the formulations of questions and their answers.

CONCLUSION: GENERAL GUIDELINES ON HOW TO USE INFORMATION TECHNOLOGIES EFFECTIVELY

This chapter has discussed three examples of information technologies increasingly used in political science education: online discussion forums, podcasting and audience response systems. Existing evidence suggests that, when used in a pedagogically sound way, they have the potential to enhance student learning. This is similar to introducing other types of IT, as for example those mentioned at the beginning of this chapter. Some general principles for effective use of technology can be summarized as follows.

Consulting with Colleagues and Literature

Before introducing technology into a course, it is advisable to read several studies from teachers who have recently taught with that technology, ideally in similar courses. These studies can be easily located through the International Political Education Database. Also, it is recommended to observe classes that employ a particular type of IT. Learning from others may help to reduce future pitfalls significantly.

Piloting

Using technology for learning may be new for students, even if they are familiar with it in their daily lives. Also, student expectations, experience and attitudes towards IT may differ widely. The challenges of using IT, as well as student reactions, thus cannot be totally foreseen. It is therefore recommended that teachers first pilot the introduction of new technology in one – perhaps smaller – class, and use the results to inform more ambitious innovations in the future.

Supporting Peer Learning

Information technologies can improve student engagement and active learning through peer learning. However, to benefit from peer learning, students may first need to gain an appreciation for it. Therefore, if, for example, students are asked to create podcast summaries from seminar discussions for their classmates, the teacher should first discuss with students how learning from each other can be valuable (Lightfoot 2010, p. 25). Students also need guidelines and encouragement so that they can produce high-quality summaries that are helpful for learning. This is similar when using online forums and ARSs.

Providing Feedback to Students

When students engage in learning online, they should receive feedback on how well they completed the task; otherwise, they may replicate their mistakes in future assignments or be unsure if the way they approached the task is the correct one. For example, if students are asked to fill in worksheets that accompany podcasts, later in the seminar the teacher should discuss the answers with students (Woodcock and Duckworth 2010, p. 32).

Constructive Alignment

Innovation of teaching and learning with new technology can be considered successful if it helps students to better achieve the course's learning outcomes. Therefore, teachers should seek evidence on how technology impacts student learning using assessment as one source of this evidence (Biggs and Tang 2007). Moreover, assessing what students learn with technology gives students a stake in engaging with the tasks. Previous studies showed that students invested little into a learning activity (whether supported with IT or not) if it was not assessed.

Engaging with Novelty

Although students largely appreciate learning with IT, they may consider technology attractive mainly because it is something new. Therefore, even if students call for introducing the technology to other courses, this may not result in the desired effects. For example, it may seem efficient to allow students who have already bought clickers for one class to also use them in other classes. However, students may soon grow to dislike the system when it becomes a norm across the school and therefore boring. Additionally, it is important that, when teachers require that students invest in purchasing clickers, they frame their reasoning in terms of the ARS's benefits for improving student learning, rather than in terms of technology being appealing to their generation.

NOTES

* I would like to thank John Craig, Fiona Buckley and Simon Lightfoot for their useful comments on the earlier versions of this chapter.
1. This judgment was based on the number of studies included in the International Political Education Database in February 2013.
2. A Virtual Learning Environment is a web system with many functions that support teaching and learning, including communication between teachers and students and among students, learning activities, assessment tasks, delivery of learning materials, etc. Typically, students and teachers can access the VLE at any time both on and off campus.

REFERENCES

Biggs, John B. and Catherine S. Tang (2007), *Teaching for Quality Learning at University: What the Student Does*, third edition, Maidenhead, UK: McGraw-Hill/Society for Research into Higher Education/Open University Press.
Brady, A. (2012), 'Alternatives to Physical Clickers in the Classroom', available at http://blogs.princeton.edu/etc/2012/04/10/alternatives-to-physical-clickers-in-the-classroom/ (accessed 14 March 2014).
Buckley, F. (2011), 'Online discussion forums', *European Political Science*, **10** (3), 402–415.
Craig, J. (2012), 'What (if anything) is different about teaching and learning in politics?', in Cathy Gormley-Heenan and Simon Lightfoot (eds.), *Teaching Politics and International Relations*, Basingstoke, UK: Palgrave Macmillan, pp. 22–37.
Damron, D. and J. Mott (2005), 'Creating an interactive classroom: Enhancing student engagement and learning in political science courses', *Journal of Political Science Education*, **1** (3), 367–83.
Gormley-Heenan, C. and K. McCartan (2009), 'Making it matter: Teaching and learning in political science using an audience response system', *European Political Science*, **8** (3), 379–91.
Hamann, K., P.H. Pollock and B.M. Wilson (2009), 'Learning from "listening" to peers in online Political Science classes', *Journal of Political Science Education*, **5** (1), 1–11.
International Political Education Database (IPED), available at https://sites.google.com/site/psatlg/Home/resources/journal-articles (accessed 15 February 2014).
Kam, C.D. and B. Sommer (2006), 'Real-time polling technology in a Public Opinion course', *PS: Political Science & Politics*, **39** (1), 113–17.
Kolb, David A. (1984), *Experiential Learning: Experience as the Source of Learning and Development*, Englewood Cliffs, NJ: Prentice Hall.
Lightfoot, S. (2010), 'Recent innovations in learning and teaching in Politics and IR: Can podcasts enhance the student experience?', in Gabriela Pleschová (ed.), *IT in Action: Stimulating Quality Learning at Undergraduate Students*, Opladen and Farmington Hills, MI: Budrich UniPress, pp. 17–27.
Marton, F. and R. Säljö (1976), 'On qualitative differences in learning: Outcome and process', *British Journal of Educational Psychology*, **46**, pp. 4–11.
Middleton, D. (2010), 'Putting the learning into e-learning', *European Political Science*, **9**, 5–12.

Pleschová, Gabriela (ed.) (2010), *IT in Action: Stimulating Quality Learning at Undergraduate Students*, Opladen and Farmington Hills, MI: Budrich UniPress.

Ralph, J., N. Head and S. Lightfoot (2010), 'Pol-casting: The use of podcasting in the teaching and learning of Politics and International Relations', *European Political Science*, 9, 13–24.

Roscoe, D.D. (2012), 'Comparing student outcomes in blended and face-to-face courses', *Journal of Political Science Education*, 8 (1), 1–19.

Schattschneider, J. (2010), 'Forum and blog: Enriching civic education teacher training with ICT', in Gabriela Pleschová (ed.), *IT in Action: Stimulating Quality Learning at Undergraduate Students*, Opladen and Farmington Hills, MI: Budrich UniPress, pp. 59–79.

Taylor, M.Z. (2009), 'Podcast lectures as a primary teaching technology: Results of a one-year trial', *Journal of Political Science Education*, 5 (2), 119–37.

Thornton, S. (2012), 'Issues and controversies associated with the use of new technologies', in Cathy Gormley-Heenan and Simon Lightfoot (eds.), *Teaching Politics and International Relations*, Basingstoke, UK: Palgrave Macmillan, pp. 91–104.

Thurston, A. (2005), 'Building online learning communities', *Technology, Pedagogy and Education*, 14 (3), 353–69.

Trudeau, R.H. (2005), 'Get them to read, get them to talk: Using discussion forums to enhance student learning', *Journal of Political Science Education*, 1 (3), 289–322.

Ulbig, S.G. and F. Notman (2012), 'Is class appreciation just a click away? Using Student Response System technology to enhance shy students' introductory American Government experience', *Journal of Political Science Education*, 8 (4), 352–71.

Woodcock, P. and G. Duckworth (2010), 'iPod therefore I am: Using PC videos to aid the teaching of the history of political philosophy', *European Political Science*, 9 (1), 25–33.

26. War, peace and everything in between: simulations in international relations
Victor Asal, Chad Raymond and Simon Usherwood

INTRODUCTION

Have you ever had a student get so passionate about a theoretical argument in a class that they appeared to be willing to take the argument outside? All three of us have seen this kind of passion in our students when they have participated in classroom International Relations (IR) simulations. There is something rewarding about watching a student spell out in painful detail how he doesn't want to lie but – having read Machiavelli or Morgenthau and being surrounded by a 'million other countries who are all looking to conquer me' when playing the game Diplomacy – he understands that lying is the smart thing to do and regular morality can be chucked out the window. That sense of having accomplished something significant as a teacher only increases when other students in the classroom, including those that had been lied to, nod in agreement and point out how events in the game directly demonstrate aspects of various IR theories (Asal 2005).

Over the last 20 years a growing literature has argued that involving students in these kinds of experiences is an effective tool in teaching IR (Asal 2005; Krain and Lantis 2006; Raymond and Sorensen 2008; Usherwood 2009). In our experience as teachers we have found that simulations allow students to become 'lab rats in their own experiments' (Asal et al. 2014, p. 347), a process in which they can comprehend the theoretical material that they are learning in a way that is much more meaningful to them than when they get the same information solely out of a book. With simulations, they establish ownership of their own 'histories' by interrogating the actors in those histories as they are being created.

This chapter is meant to be an introductory primer on starting to use simulations in the IR classroom. To that end we first discuss in more detail why and how simulations can be useful in the classroom, and describe two simple simulations that have proven effective in our teaching. We discuss briefly how one might go about building one's own pedagogical simulations, and finally we close the chapter with a list of resources for educators who want to use these simulations.

WHY SIMULATIONS ARE USEFUL

The utility of simulations lies principally in their adaptability. By building on some simple assumptions about the world, they open up a vast range of possibilities for both student and instructor to explore.

The argument in favor of using simulations starts with the assertion that active learning is more valuable than passive learning. A simulation offers the opportunity to 'live the world' of the phenomenon that we are studying, and it is in this 'living' that learning occurs in a profound way that engages students by requiring them to develop a personal model of that 'world' and how to engage with it: if I have to pretend to be the head of the French Defense Ministry unit responsible for sub-Saharan policy, and I have to then engage in a simulated interaction with officials from NATO, then I can get a much more nuanced understanding of the international response to Mali than I can from a lecture on the same subject.

However, simulations go beyond the active-learning assumption, embodying two core ideas. The first of these is the notion that the world can be modeled, by which we understand that a set of relatively simple rules can encapsulate the fundamentals of a given situation. Those rules might take the form of some kind of decision-making architecture, or of personal or institutional characteristics, or indeed of random events (e.g. using dice to generate chaotic situations). Thus, a simulation does not have to specify every possible aspect of the matter in hand, but only the fundamentals, which are then brought to life by students.

This 'bringing to life' leads directly to the final assumption, namely that the world is complex, by which we understand that, despite such simple rules, the results are intrinsically uncertain and non-linear, because of the chaotic nature of human interaction. Put differently, when we run a simulation, then we do so in the knowledge that both the process and the outcome will vary from iteration to iteration, and indeed it is precisely that uncertainty that we wish to convey to students. Even when the same students have played the game more than once, they have ended up with very different experiences each time.

Taken together, the assumptions of simulations allow us to access deeper engagement and reflection with the world that surrounds us. Moreover, the use of an active pedagogy enables students to participate in that process in a way that generates a number of different benefits.

Firstly, simulations allow students to explore and understand substantive issues. This includes both the subject under discussion and the materials that are drawn into that discussion. Simulations allow participants to integrate a wide range of source materials into a more coherent whole, discuss and debate it, and then to reflect on the dimensions and interactions which that whole contains. Thus we might run a simulation on a foreign-policy decision, to allow participants to see how hard and soft elements of policy can work together in strengthening a particular policy position. Likewise, we might use a two-level game to highlight the interplay of domestic and international factors in creating foreign policy. Simulations thus enable students to efficiently match 'theoretical concepts with empirical, accessible behavior' (Enterline and Jepsen 2009, p. 58). Traditional pedagogies, in contrast, require that students passively receive information from the instructor, work to understand it and then, after some delay, attempt to apply it. When such a delay exists, the content being learned becomes less relevant to students, resulting in decreased interest and less learning (Dorn 1989, p. 6).

Secondly, simulations allow us to consider the dynamics of negotiation and institutional dynamics more generally (Lantis 1998). Here, the focus rests on skills development, as participants come to appreciate the role of research and preparation, presentation, rhetoric and consensus-building as fundamental parts of the institutional life that they are recreating. The utility is specific, but also general. This is a very common feature of simulations of international organization, where the specific institutional practices contained within rules of procedure and the varied structural power of different actors can be more meaningfully communicated to participants than in a passive-learning environment: instructors might get participants to compare the institutional logics of the Council and the European Parliament, for example, as a way into understanding the operation of the European Union.

Finally, and more rarely, simulations allow for the creation or enhancement of a group identity. Simulations offer excellent ice-breaking functions, through their requirement of purposive interaction, just as they also offer a means to introduce problem-solving techniques to students who might not have encountered them before. Certainly, this is rarely the primary motivation, and the boundary to games in the broader sense becomes less clear, but undoubtedly within higher education and other educational environments, we can observe the development of group affiliation through the shared experience (Schick 2008).

Typically, these multiple purposes are not explicitly articulated by simulation designers, who rather have a more nebulous objective of improving participant understanding. However, as we will discuss below, having a clear and focused purpose is a common issue for simulations; designers and instructors would do well to reflect on how these potential purposes relate to their simulation. This is particularly true when considering the overlap between substance, process and group-building, and potential for reinforcement between them. By presenting knowledge to students in a way that heightens their interest in understanding, student motivation to learn is heightened. Simulations enhance both extrinsic (reward-driven) and intrinsic (satisfaction-driven) motivation because they present challenging but achievable goals in situations possessing uncertain outcomes, provide students with prompt feedback on the effects of their decisions, and generate feelings of autonomy, accomplishment, relevance and relatedness to others (Carnes 2011; Koh et al. 2010; de Freitas 2006; Mitchell and Savill-Smith 2004). While some students might be averse to the competitive, group-oriented or role-play aspects of some simulations, these potentially harmful effects can be mitigated by careful simulation design.

The active-learning environment and improvements in motivation suggest that students who participate in simulations will acquire greater amounts of both content and affective knowledge than they do from other instructional methods. However, ensuring that these gains occur requires that the instructor has a clear understanding of what the simulation is intended to achieve and that the simulation be integrated with a valid system of assessment (see Facer et al. 2004; Egenfeldt-Nielsen 2005). If this integration is absent, 'simulations are not effective in achieving their broader learning outcomes regardless of how motivated the learners are during game-play' (de Freitas 2006, p. 350).

ASSESSMENT: GETTING THE MOST OUT OF A SIMULATION

Any instructor contemplating a simulation for instructional use therefore must first identify the specific learning outcomes that are to be achieved, be they the acquisition of more substantive knowledge, the development of skills, or deeper awareness among students of their own or others' values and emotions. Probably the worst mistake an instructor can make in this regard is to employ a simulation without consideration of the specific reasons for doing so. The second worst mistake is to not incorporate an assessment regime that effectively measures whether the desired learning outcomes are being achieved.

A first step is to consider how we can assess the utility of using simulations. Because of cognitive biases, individuals are remarkably bad at gauging what and how they have learned (Wilson and Nesbitt 1978; Brademeier and Greenblat 1981; Nestler and von Collani 2008; Maznick and Zimmerman 2009). They also tend not to recognize what forms of learning are the most beneficial and are often reluctant to learn whatever is new and unfamiliar (Kirschner and Merrienboer 2013, pp. 177–8). As a result, student self-reporting about what they think they have learned from participating in a simulation is generally not a valid method of assessing its efficacy. A better approach is to employ pre-test/post-test instruments to measure changes in domain knowledge or attitudinal indicators that may be associated with students' participation in a simulation.

Meaningful assessment includes the use of experimental treatment and control groups. As with a pre-test, a control group allows an instructor to establish a baseline for identifying a simulation's effects on learning. A control group can be created by running a simulation in some rather than all sections of a course, or making a simulation an optional experience for students in a single section. Regardless of format, conditions for treatment and control groups should be as similar as possible with participation in the simulation being the only meaningful variation – a situation that is often difficult to achieve given the institutional constraints that most instructors face.

With this in mind, we can then focus on specific assessment strategies for students participating in the simulations. If the simulation is only part of a course, then conventional mechanisms, such as term papers or final exams, might be used, albeit with the caveat that this will tend to focus attention on substantive knowledge aspects. If there is a need to focus student learning on skills development then some more nuanced approaches are required.

The key difficulty is one of observation of performative elements within a simulation. It is impossible for an individual instructor to closely observe any more than a handful of people for a couple of hours. If assessment is to be of 'how did students do?', then that requires not only a set of standards against which to judge performance but also the means to be able to make that judgment. Thus if either the number or time constraint is breached, then the instructor needs either other observers or other recording sessions. However this is arranged, care is needed, given the subjective nature of the process, as well as the potential for missing aspects of the action.

One solution to this is to move evaluation onto the students, by asking them to produce papers where they make judgments about their performance, allowing them to contextualize what they have done, as well as to connect it to substantive aspects. Thus, they might be required to consider the verisimilitude of the simulation in relation to real-world events, reflect on how theoretical approaches have played out in practice or discuss the impact of various skills on the progress of events.

Whatever the choices made, the assessment needs to be flagged from the start and to be reinforced by both the gameplay in the simulation and the debriefing afterwards. Simulations are not exercises in self-teaching. They require students to explicitly recall, discuss and analyze their actions and motivations. Debriefing surveys and writing assignments are thus highly useful assessment tools, because they allow students to compare their experiences in the simulation to the predictions of academic literature. The format of and instructions for such assignments should explicitly relate to the learning outcomes that a simulation is intended to affect. Lamy's DEPPP (Describe, Explain, Predict, Prescribe, Participate) approach lays out how one can elicit constructive feedback from students in an ordered and useful fashion (Cusimano 2000).

Any instructor who is considering using a simulation in the classroom should consider how the simulation might negatively affect student performance. Simulations are unusual events for most students, and students can find them to be, especially in their initial phases, confusing, awkward and emotionally intense. Debriefing serves as an opportunity both for students to process what they have experienced and for the instructor to gather useful data (Petranek, Corey and Black 1992). While some students might be, as described by Lantis (1998, p. 49), 'comfortable with the rules of [a simulation's] procedure from the outset and [are] ready to use them to their own advantage', others can be hesitant to act. Such problems can be addressed through assessing students' interpretations of the simulation and their agency within it, rather than assessing them solely on the results of a competition that produces winners and losers. To derive the greatest benefits from a simulation, students might need instruction that is complementary to the content of the simulation itself. Simulations can also consume students' time and energy outside of class in ways that are not conducive for learning (O'Toole and Absalom 2003, p. 185; Rivera and Simons 2008, p. 301). Decreasing the amount of time outside of class that is devoted to a simulation might result in a more equitable learning opportunity for students. Rivera and Simons (2008, p. 302) recommend that simulations be designed to include the assessment of both individual efforts and group results in order to minimize the effects of free riders.

REVIEW OF EXISTING SIMULATIONS

If we reviewed all of the useful existing IR simulations out there today, it would potentially fill up the entire chapter – and conceivably the entire volume. Because of this, we focus on a select few that we have had positive experiences with ourselves and direct readers to resources for using these simulations that describe how to use them at greater length (see Glazier 2011). The first simulation we recommend is the game Diplomacy (Calhamer 1993). This game of international diplomacy created during the Cold War recreates the international situation that existed in Europe before the outbreak of World War I with seven international powers competing for control of the continent. When students play Diplomacy, they become involved with a game that is almost a direct translation into gameplay of realism and balance of power theory (Van Belle 1998). The goal of the game is to conquer Europe, but no power is strong enough to do it by themselves, which means alliances are necessary yet trust is a rare commodity. All gameplay is simultaneous and luck plays no part, except in the initial allocation of countries, with some being much more vulnerable than others. Negotiation becomes a key part of gameplay and there is no rule against lying or deception. We have used the game with each country being played by teams of up to three players as well as running two games in the same class – both of these have been effective means of running the game in class. The simulation is very effective in terms of teaching realist theories and perspectives of IR, but it does demand at least 4–6 hours of gameplay to be effective although part of that gameplay can take place outside of class. For more detail on using the simulation in class see Asal (2005), while Bridge and Radford (2014) offer a very effective overview in how to use the simulation in its online format.

A game that also captures aspects of realism in a more abstract fashion than Diplomacy is the Classical Realism Game (often called the Hobbes Game), which we have played with groups ranging from 15 to 250 students. While Diplomacy is grounded in a specific place and time, the Hobbes Game is much more abstract. Students are given minimal instructions:

> To play the game ... the instructor should be equipped with ... decks of cards and ... students ... use 'rock–paper–scissors' to determine their fate ... Each student is given a card and a die. You should say to the students ... 'The object of this game is to survive. If your card is taken from you, you die. You can take someone's cards by challenging them to a duel. A duel is carried out by each student throwing their die (high roll wins) or playing a round of rock–paper–scissors. The loser dies and the winner gets his/her cards. If someone challenges you, you must fight. Until the deck runs out, I will give one card to anyone who has died to bring him or her back to life. Once the cards have all been distributed, if you are killed, you stay dead. Go to it.' (Asal 2005, p. 366)

When playing the Hobbes Game, it is very important to make clear to the students that they *do not* need to challenge people but they must fight if someone challenges them. The game is specifically set up so that if everyone cooperates everyone can get the bonus on the quiz – but that is rarely what happens. Hobbes would be delighted how many students see everyone else as an enemy and proceed to slay each other due to 'first, competition; secondly, diffidence; thirdly, glory' (Hobbes 1996, p. 220). Students are able to wrestle with Hobbes' dim view of human nature in a very useful way after witnessing a (simulated) brutal version of anarchy.

A game that captures Liberalism in a fashion similar to how the Hobbes Game captures Realism is the Prisoner's Dilemma to the Nth Degree game which we have played with groups again ranging from 15 to 250 students. While the game Diplomacy is grounded in a specific place and time the Prisoner's Dilemma to the Nth Degree game is much more abstract. Students are asked to play one round of the famous Prisoner's Dilemma, then an iterated version with a set stopping point and then play again with no set stopping point to the game (Asal 2005, p. 368). Finally, students are placed into teams where they can all collaborate or students can defect – but the defecting students can be thrown off the team. Suddenly the concept of cooperation under anarchy (Oye 1986) becomes crystal clear. We should note also that Jackson (2013) details a useful version of the Prisoner's Dilemma that exploits the ubiquitous Excel spreadsheet software for gameplay.

Another useful simulation created by Ambrosio (2004) helps students understand the dynamics of ethnic conflict and the important international dimension of such conflicts. Called the Dacia Simulation, it has the students divided up into different actors who have been invited to a constitutional convention for the fictional country of Dacia. Representatives include neighboring countries, superpowers, as well as parties representing the minority and majority ethnic groups in Dacia. Using this simulation, we have found that students get a much better sense of both the internal dynamics of ethnic competition and conflict, and the important international dimensions of ethnic conflict.

HOW DO YOU BUILD THESE THINGS?

As noted above, simulations can be organized in so many different ways that it might be seen as counter-productive to suggest a single model for so doing. However, it is still useful and pertinent to observe that, whatever approach one takes to building and running a simulation, three core requirements have to be satisfied as a precondition to a successful outcome.

The first core requirement is that the learning objectives must be clear to all participants. This is as true for the simulation designer and leader as it is for students participating in the simulation (Gredler 1992). When this does not happen, then simulations become little more than diversions, without real pedagogic value. The simulation designer needs to have a well-defined set of learning objectives in order to create a simulation that speaks to them, as well as a sense of what else it might be conveying to participants: given the multi-faceted nature of simulations, this means accepting that any given scenario will necessarily do several things simultaneously. Likewise, for participants, there is the need to set out in explicit terms the objective of the task, the nature and degree of support and/or preparation that is available and allowed, as well as the nature of any assessment attached to the exercise.

The learning objectives can most obviously be related back to the three categories of purpose identified above: decision outcomes/substantive knowledge, negotiation dynamics/skills development or group socialization. Their overlapping nature makes clarity of purpose all the more important. The articulation of these objectives helps to guide everyone involved, especially in larger simulations. As the simulation designer gains in confidence and tries more ambitious scenarios, so they tend to become less well bounded and participants might be asked to create or modify the basic rules, all of which makes clarity of purpose even more important.

This leads into the second key requirement that the learning objectives have to be aligned with the gameplay and with any assessment. Alignment is essential in all pedagogies (Biggs 1996, 2003), but particularly in the case of simulations, where the flexibility that draws us to their use also raises issues of ensuring that it is followed through. Once the simulation designer is able to describe the objectives in clear terms, then it becomes much simpler to see whether the gameplay allows the participants to focus on the objectives and whether the assessment tests the achievement of them. From the perspective of the participant, clear alignment of the elements reduces the potential for dislocation, improves immersion into the simulated environment and ultimately creates the opportunity for a much fuller learning experience.

Thus, a simulation that wants to build understanding of the internal institutional dynamics of the UN Security Council would be advised to recreate the structures surrounding the Council itself and make use of the full rules of procedure, while a simulation that was more interested in the tensions between members in producing policy might run on simplified rules but allow for iterated decision-making in a crisis scenario. Likewise, UN General Assembly games might organize states into undifferentiated groups or just provide for a reduced membership, depending upon the purpose the designer has in mind. At the level of assessment, if the focus is on negotiation dynamics, then it is possible to assess on the basis of a reflective piece by each participant that stresses such elements in their experience, while a simulation that wants to develop abilities in substantive policy might tie the gameplay to real-world decisions in the same field to explore similarities and contrasts.

Underpinning these two elements is the final one of a meaningful system of feedback to participants. Without feedback, simulations cannot be easily brought back into the rest of the students' learning experience, even if the experience at the time feels worthwhile. Of all the three points set out here, this is the one that is most overlooked and the most consequential. Newmann and Twigg (2000) provide a rare example of how this can be done. The substance of feedback can be focused on processes, actors or outputs within the simulation: again, the emphasis would logically follow from the learning objectives, but where these are multiple in nature then it would be advisable to look at all three, since they form the basic units of any simulated interaction.

This feedback can take place at any point in the proceedings. Usually, it would come immediately after the main gameplay, since this is the point where participants are best able to recall detail and connect it to their wider learning. But it can also take place at other points. If there is any substantial preparation required prior to the main gameplay, then feedback can be provided on negotiating briefs or positions, in order to ensure participants enter with a more fully prepared approach. Likewise, it is possible to design interim feedback for longer simulations, although this needs to be done with care, in order not to disrupt proceedings too much from their natural flow. One way of achieving this is to create a two-level game, with the simulation leader acting as national governments or parties, requiring participants to report back periodically on their progress.

Whenever feedback occurs and regardless of what the focus is meant to be, the process is most usefully driven by the participants themselves, be that through verbal or written contributions. As the participants in the simulation, they have insights into their actions and outputs that might have not been noticed by the game leader or other observers; by giving primacy to their thoughts and reflections, we can strengthen their confidence in self-evaluation and self-criticism. This participant-led feedback can then be supplemented by inputs from observers, documentary evidence, as well as reflection on the simulation *qua* simulation, this last being instructive in promoting discussion on how the scenario differs from the real-world situation.

Taken together, these three elements of clear objectives, alignment and feedback offer a backbone to the process of creating a simulation. But that then needs to be fleshed out into a practical set of documentation that can be used. One good way to go about this is to consider what others have done before, and we discuss some examples later in this chapter: these can stimulate reflection and adaptation to local needs. However, it is also instructive to provide some steps in building a simulation from scratch.

The starting point always has to be a clear idea about what is to be captured by the simulation. This might be as specific as, 'Why did the US invade Grenada in 1982?', or as general as, 'Is collective action possible in international fora?' This is perhaps the hardest part of the process, since it requires the designer to consider what they actually want to achieve. As a general rule, changing focus – by moving closer to, or further from, the topic – is a productive way of scoping issues, dimensions and possible ways in.

This then feeds into a second step, namely of devising a gameplay mechanism that allows for that topic to be simulated. This might be a formal meeting or an informal discussion; it might require the production of a collaborative text or a public debate – typically, the topic will lend itself to one of these rather obviously. Recreations of formal meetings can draw on both materials and rules of procedure, but they might be more constraining in the range of options open to students.

With these aspects in place, then attention can turn to more practical matters. This includes the number of students needed to run the simulation, the amount of time and space available, and the amount of assessment linked to the simulation. These are often not in the control of the simulation designer, so the 'ideal-world' version initially developed will need to be adjusted to fit the situation in hand.

On the number of players, roles can be combined or dropped, if there are few, or subdivided and added to, if there are many. It is relatively simple to switch representation of an organization from one individual into a team, just as additional organizations can be cut. The key consideration is whether such changes fundamentally affect the nature of the game: Cold War rivalry can be played out between two players or one hundred, but each option will stress different aspects.

Likewise, constraints on timetables and teaching spaces might mean that there is only a short slot of an hour rather than months of contact time, or that a raked lecture theatre is the only space available for small-group negotiations. Longer simulations allow for more immersion into the subject matter, but they are also more likely to cause disruption to other teaching, especially if long blocks of time are needed. Options to consider include the use of asynchronous or online debate, the division of a big topic into a series of smaller, shorter exercises or the use of crisis scenarios to unexpectedly change the tempo of the simulation. However, the primary concern has to be whether the time allows for students to reasonably expect to be able to achieve the objectives of the simulation.

With regard to assessment, there is little consensus as to how far this is needed at all and, if it is, what should be assessed. The easiest way to approach this is to relate it back to the benefits outlined earlier in the chapter, namely the development of substantive knowledge and the development of skills. On the one hand, simulations build a much deeper engagement with the material, but on the other, this is often a largely implicit process, so the necessity of feedback becomes even clearer in allowing students to recognize what they have done. While this can cause some issues in designing an assessment that fits what has happened in the simulation, it needs to be balanced against the higher likelihood of students engaging with the simulation because it is assessed.

Put together, these steps should allow for the designer to create the documentation needed to run a game. To check whether it is actually sufficient and appropriate, the following questions should be posed. Firstly, is the central objective of the simulation still clearly in focus? Secondly, can the gameplay be explained to students in simple-to-understand terms? Thirdly, is the volume of work placed on students reasonable and proportionate to the objectives and their other commitments? Fourthly, what is the worst that could happen and are there any failsafes?

Discussion with colleagues is a key part of this design process, to explore the different aspects involved. Even where this is possible, the normal recommendation to a new user of simulations is to start with something basic and then build out from it, ideally over a series of iterations of use, so that the interplay of elements is more readily apparent and the scope for adaptation is clearer.

RESOURCES

In this final section we list several key sources for educators who would like to use simulations in the teaching of IR. These are websites where educators can find simulations and discussions on how to use them:

- *International Political Education Database (IPED)*: http://bit.ly/IPEDatabase
- *The Active Learning in Political Science (ALPS) blog*: http://bit.ly/ALPSblogging
- *How To Do Simulation Games*: http://bit.ly/SimGuide
- *PAXsims blog*: http://paxsims.wordpress.com/

REFERENCES

Ambrosio, Thomas (2004), 'Bringing Ethnic Conflict into the Classroom: A Student-Centered Simulation of Multiethnic Politics', *PS-WASHINGTON*, **37** (2), 285–90.

Asal, V., S.S. Sin, N.P. Fahrenkopf and X. She (2014), 'The Comparative Politics Game Show: Using Games to Teach Comparative Politics Theories', *International Studies Perspectives*, **15** (3), 347–58.

Asal, Victor (2005), 'Playing Games with International Relations', *International Studies Perspectives*, **6** (3), 359–73.

Biggs, John (1996), 'Enhancing Teaching through Constructive Alignment', *Higher Education*, **32** (3), 347–64.

Biggs, John (2003), *Teaching for Quality Learning at University*, Buckingham: Open University Press.

Brademeier, Mary E. and Cathy Stein Greenblat (1981), 'The Educational Effectiveness of Simulation Games', *Simulation & Games*, **12** (3), 307–32.

Bridge, David and Simon Radford (2014), 'Teaching Diplomacy by Other Means: Using an Outside-of Class Simulation to Teach International Relations Theory', *International Studies Perspectives*, **15** (4), 423–37.

Calhamer, A.B. (1993), 'The Invention of Diplomacy', in Martin Rex (ed.), *The Gamer's Guide to Diplomacy*, Baltimore, MD: The Avalon Hill Game Company, p. 27.

Carnes, M.C. (2011), 'Setting Students' Minds on Fire', *The Chronicle of Higher Education*, **57** (27), A72.

Cusimano, M. (2000), 'Case Teaching Without Cases', in J.S. Lantis, L.M. Kuzma and J. Boehrer (eds), *The New International Studies Classroom: Active Teaching, Active Learning*, Boulder, CO: Lynne Rienner Publishers, pp. 77–94.

Dorn, Dean S. (1989), 'Simulation Games: One More Tool on the Pedagogical Shelf', *Teaching Sociology*, **17** (1), 1–18.

Egenfeldt-Nielsen, Simon (2005), *Beyond Edutainment: Exploring the Educational Potential of Computer Games*, Copenhagen: University of Copenhagen.

Enterline, Andrew J. and Eric M. Jepsen (2009), 'Chinazambia and Boliviafranca: A Simulation of Domestic Politics and Foreign Policy', *International Studies Perspectives*, **10**, 49–59.

Facer, K., R. Joiner, D. Stanton, J. Reid, R. Hull and D. Kirk (2004), 'Savannah: Mobile Gaming and Learning?', *Journal of Computer Assisted Learning*, **20** (6), 399–409.

Freitas, Sara I. de (2006), 'Using Games and Simulations for Supporting Learning', *Learning, Media and Technology*, **31** (4), 343–58.

Glazier, Rebecca A. (2011), 'Running Simulations without Ruining Your Life: Simple Ways to Incorporate Active Learning into Your Teaching', *Journal of Political Science Education*, **7** (4), 375–93.

Gredler, Margaret (1992), *Designing and Evaluating Games and Simulations: A Process Approach*, London: Kogan Page.

Hobbes, T. (1996), 'Of the Natural Condition of Mankind as Concerning their Felicity and Misery', in J. Vasquez (ed.), *Classics of International Relations*, Englewood Cliffs, NJ: Prentice-Hall, pp. 219–21.

Jackson, Steven F. (2013), 'Political Simulations Using Excel', *Journal of Political Science Education*, **9** (2), 209–21.

Kirschner, Paul A. and Jeroen J.G. van Merrienboer (2013), 'Do Learners Really Know Best? Urban Legends in Education', *Educational Psychologist*, **48** (3), 169–83.

Koh, Caroline, Hock Soon Tan, Kim Cheng Tan, Linda Fang, Fook Meng Fong, Dominic Kan, Sau Lin Lye and May Lin Wee (2010), 'Investigating the Effect of 3D Simulation-Based Learning on the Motivation and Performance of Engineering Students', *Journal of Engineering Education*, **99** (3), 237–51.

Krain, Matthew and Jeffrey S. Lantis (2006), 'Building Knowledge? Evaluating the Effectiveness of the Global Problems Summit Simulation', *International Studies Perspectives*, **7** (4), 395–407.

Lantis, Jeffrey S. (1998), 'Simulations and Experiential Learning in the International Relations Classroom', *International Negotiation*, **3**, 39–57.

Maznick, Amy M. and Corinne Zimmerman (2009), 'Evaluating Scientific Research in the Context of Prior Belief: Hindsight Bias or Confirmation Bias?', *Journal of Psychology of Science and Technology*, **2** (1), 29–36.

Mitchell, Alice and Carol Savill-Smith (2004), *The Use of Computer and Video Games for Learning: A Review of the Literature*, London: Learning and Skills Development Agency.

Nestler, Steffen and Gernot von Collani (2008), 'Hindsight Bias, Conjunctive Explanations, and Causal Attribution', *Social Cognition*, **26** (4), 482–93.

Newmann, William and Judyth Twigg (2000), 'Active Engagement of the Intro IR Student: A Simulation Approach', *PS: Political Science & Politics*, **33** (4), 835–42.

O'Toole, J. Mitchell and Douglas J. Absalom (2003), 'The Impact of Blended Learning on Student Outcomes: Is There Room on the Horse for Two?', *Journal of Educational Media*, **28** (2–3), 179–90.

Oye, Kenneth (ed.) (1986), *Cooperation Under Anarchy*, Princeton, NJ: Princeton University Press.

Petranek, Charles, Susan Corey and Rebecca Black (1992), 'Three Levels of Learning in Simulations: Participating, Debriefing, and Journal Writing', *Simulation and Gaming*, **23** (2), 174–85.

Raymond, Chad and Kerstin Sorensen (2008), 'The Use of a Middle East Crisis Simulation in an International Relations Course', *PS: Political Science & Politics*, **41** (1), 179–82.

Rivera, Sharon Werning and Janet Thomas Simons (2008), 'Engaging Students through Extended Simulations', *Journal of Political Science Education*, **4** (2), 298–316.

Schick, Laurie (2008), 'Breaking Frame in a Role-Play Simulation: A Language Socialization Perspective', *Simulation and Gaming*, **39** (2), 184–97.

Usherwood, S. (2009), 'Enhancing Student Immersion in Negotiation-Based Learning Environments', *International Journal of Learning*, **16** (7), 607–14.

Van Belle, D.A. (1998), 'Balance of Power and System Stability: Simulating Complex Anarchical Environments over the Internet', *Political Research Quarterly*, **51** (1), 265–82.

Wilson, Timothy de Camp and Richard E. Nisbett (1978), 'The Accuracy of Verbal Reports about the Effects of Stimuli on Evaluations and Behavior', *Social Psychology*, **41** (2), 118–31.

27. Developing your own in-class simulations: design advice and a 'commons' simulation example
Mark A. Boyer and Elizabeth T. Smith

Simulations have long been part of scientific research methods. Meteorologists use computer simulations to help predict the path of weather fronts; economists use them to make economic forecasts for an economy; military strategists use simulations to conjecture about the course of events during military campaigns; and the list could go on. Less traditional, however, is the use of simulation as a teaching tool.

Sometimes viewed by one's colleagues as merely 'playing games' in the classroom, simulation has been perceived in some teaching environments as diverting faculty and student attention away from the main goal: absorbing the lessons. But even when teachers are sympathetic to an active learning approach, the use of simulation in the classroom is often hindered by a lack of available and applicable simulations on relevant topics. Thus, the two current authors have often settled on creating their games specific to their goals and approach in the classroom. As such, this chapter seeks to provide some on-the-ground criteria for others to use in developing their own simulation.

Before moving onto the primary tasks of this chapter, it is also worth noting the degree to which the dearth of published simulation pedagogy in political science has been addressed in the past decade or so. Prior to 2000, *PS* was one of the very few quarterly journals that regularly published work on the pedagogy, even if only a small percentage of that work centered on simulation methods. Since that time, *International Studies Perspectives* and the *Journal of Political Science Education* have both emerged as additional outlets for high-quality, peer-reviewed work on pedagogy generally and simulation more specifically. The emergence of more outlets for work on pedagogy, we think, has helped elevate the status of scholarly work in the area and also encouraged more of us to devote time and energy to developing innovative approaches to classroom teaching.

SIMULATIONS AND ACTIVE LEARNING

Simulations have the power to recreate complex, dynamic political processes in the classroom, allowing students to examine the motivations, behavioral constraints, resources and interactions among institutional actors. Woodworth and Gump argue that simulations are 'the nearest thing we have to a laboratory' as social scientists (Woodworth and Gump 2001, p. 92); indeed they do provide such laboratories, even if imperfect ones. Nonetheless, through simulations, students gain a deeper understanding of institutions (their successes and challenges), processes and the often unpredictable variable of human behavior.

At the simplest level, using simulations in the classroom is one way of encouraging student participation. Other types of active learning approaches include case teaching, discussion teaching more generally or even the use of problem-based learning exercises. Active learning approaches:

1. seek to give students a deeper level of insight into the political process;
2. encourage students to be more attentive and more active in the learning process;
3. help students retain information for longer periods of time;
4. develop critical thinking and analytical skills through collaborative efforts;
5. enable students to develop speaking and presentation skills, simultaneously building their confidence.[1]

Simulations also seek to mirror real-world situations. Students can therefore experience many of the same constraints and motivations for action (or inaction) experienced by the real players. This is not to say that simulation is a perfect model of reality, but it gives students an understanding of political processes short of actually being directly involved. Our experience with simulation even suggests that it motivates students to become involved in the real processes that our simulations seek to emulate. It is therefore important for faculty to help students differentiate the simulated process from the real-world process during a debriefing period after the simulation, but this does not mean that the simulation diverges far from the real process.

The principal disadvantage of using simulation is that the teacher must sacrifice a degree of substantive coverage in return for a deeper level of student understanding on what might be a narrower range of topics. In many ways, however, this disadvantage is negligible, especially when considering the increase in retention levels. One study has found that students retain 10 percent of what they read, 20 percent of what they hear, 30 percent of what they see, 50 percent of what they see and hear, 70 percent of what they say, and 90 percent of what they do and say together (Stice 1987, p. 293). Even if these figures are only approximate, they indicate that broad knowledge obtained through passive approaches to learning will not be retained over the long term. This implies that, though some course material must be foregone in the short term, there is likely a gain in longer term knowledge and skills through active learning experiences.

As we know, simulations come in many varieties. One broad type is machine simulation, like those used by economists to model and forecast economic phenomena. Another is man-machine or computer-assisted simulations that employ a mix of computer technology and human input. The role of the computer can vary in this type of simulation. In the ICONS simulations based at the University of Maryland (www.icons.umd.edu) or the GlobalEd simulations based at the University of Connecticut (www.globaled.uconn.edu), the Internet is employed to create an interface system that allows many students to negotiate international problems from geographically distant locations (see e.g. Crookall and Wilkenfeld 1985; Boyer et al. 2009). Another man-machine simulation (see Boyer 1999) designed by one of the authors of this chapter uses a PC to generate payoff structures for a coalitional bargaining game based on a formal theoretical chapter from Howard Raiffa's *The Art and Science of Negotiation* (1982). The computer in this simulation acts primarily as a calculator generating payoffs for coalition formation while the students negotiate and control the actual outcomes of the exercise.

The last type of simulation is role-playing simulations, in which students are assigned roles within a socio-political process and then asked to act like real political actors.

> **BOX 27.1 SUMMARY OF SIMULATION DEVELOPMENT REQUIREMENTS**
>
> **Define Teaching Goals**
> The first step in designing a simulation is to define your goals.
>
> **Simulation Construction**
>
> 1. Identify the major actors in the process and create role statements for each that focus on interests and motivations.
> 2. Establish realistic structural or power relationships among the actors.
> 3. Write a scenario or problem statement for actors to resolve.
> 4. Assemble necessary data or resources.
> 5. Create specific ground rules for students (e.g. length of simulation, permitted interactions, restrictions).
>
> **Running the Simulation**
> You must have everything prepared before the start of the simulation, and you must be prepared to answer student questions about rules, scenario or other game elements; otherwise, the simulation will take on a life of its own and not serve your teaching goals.
>
> **Debriefing**
> Develop a series of questions that place the simulation into the context of the course. This includes examining differences between simulation and reality; actors and their constraints; and the reasons for specific outcomes. Your questions should be tied directly to your teaching goals.

Computers are generally not involved in such simulations, but might play a peripheral role. This type of simulation and its design are the primary focus of this chapter.

SIMULATION DESIGN

In an effort to provide the reader with the primary components of simulation development, the following sections focus on: 1) the identification of your teaching goals; 2) simulation construction; 3) the actual running of the simulation; and 4) the debriefing. These components are summarized briefly in Box 27.1. We do not focus on assessment directly here, as that has been well covered in Chapter 26 and at other places as well.

Teaching Goals

The first step in developing a simulation is defining the goals you wish to achieve in your classroom relative to the simulation exercise. Defining goals clearly is essential to determining the structure and methods of your simulation. It is also essential to be realistic about what you want to achieve. That is, focus on only a small number of significant concepts/goals rather than trying to create the simulation to end all simulations. In most instances, simple is better than complex, especially if you want and need your students to get engaged quickly.

For instance, if you are teaching a course on American politics and want to illustrate the Congressional committee process, you must design a simulation that allows one

Table 27.1 A non-random sampling of some recently published simulations

Title	Author(s)	Citation
Simulating two-level negotiations	Young	(2006) *International Studies Perspectives*, **7** (1), 77–82.
The Meyerhoff incident: simulating bioterrorism in a national security class	Franke	(2006) *PS: Political Science & Politics*, **39** (1), 153–156.
Simulating the free trade area of the Americas	Switky and Avilés	(2007) *PS: Political Science & Politics*, **40** (2), 399–405.
War and peace: simulating security decision making in the classroom	Kanner	(2007) *PS: Political Science & Politics*, **40** (4), 795–800.
Experiential learning in an arms control simulation	Kelle	(2008) *PS: Political Science & Politics*, **41** (2), 379–385.
Chinazambia and Boliviafranca: a simulation of domestic politics and foreign policy	Enterline and Jepsen	(2009) *International Studies Perspectives*, **10** (1), 49–59.
Representation and the rules of the game: an electoral simulation	Hoffman	(2009) *PS: Political Science & Politics*, **42** (3), 531–535.
Beyond model UN: simulating multi-level, multi-actor diplomacy using the millennium development goals	Crossley-Frolick	(2010) *International Studies Perspectives*, **11** (2), 184–201.
Peacekeeping the game	Goon	(2011) *International Studies Perspectives*, **12** (3), 250–272.
Simulating city councils: increasing student awareness and involvement	Rinfret	(2012) *PS: Political Science & Politics*, **45** (3), 513–515.
Teaching diplomacy by other means: using an outside-of-class simulation to teach international relations theory	Bridge and Radford	(2013) *International Studies Perspectives*, online first, doi: 10.1111/insp.12017.
The comparative politics game show: using games to teach comparative politics theories	Asal, Sin, Fahrenkopf and She	(2013), *International Studies Perspectives*, online first, doi: 10.1111/insp.12010.
The drama of international relations: a South China Sea simulation	Kempston and Thomas	(2013) *International Studies Perspectives*, online first, doi: 10.1111/insp.12045.
The settlement game: a simulation teaching institutional theories of public law	Bridge	(2013) *PS: Political Science & Politics*, **46** (4), 813–817.

party to dominate and also incorporates parliamentary procedure. If you are teaching a course on comparative politics and wish to illustrate how different political systems produce different types of policies, you might develop a simulation that focuses on a set of bilateral negotiations between an authoritarian political system and an open political system. Please see Table 27.1 for a non-scientific sampling of the diversity of recent published simulations.

It is very helpful to put your goals down in writing before beginning. By doing this, you can keep them handy as you create the structures of the exercise. When the simulation is over, you will need to return to these goals as you construct your debriefing questions and summary.

Simulation Construction

The second step in creating a simulation is to identify the major actors in the particular process to be studied. If the goal is to study policy development, who are the real players in the process? Think about all the possible influences on the process and include as many of them as can realistically be simulated in the time you have available and given the size of your class. For instance, in an American politics context, you would want to include interest groups, congressional subcommittees, agency directors, party leadership and so on. In the Congressional committee example from above, this would include the committee chair, the various members of both political parties, the structures of the subcommittees, relevant members of the bureaucracy, lobbyists, and even staff members.

A 'role sheet' should be constructed for each player or group of players. Role sheets explain the institutional position of the player (e.g. White House Press Secretary), his or her major goals and motivations (e.g. primary concern about the President's public image and reelection fortunes), and the constraints and resources involved with the role. If appropriate and useful, these role sheets may suggest how a player might further his or her goals. For the White House Press Secretary, this might include manipulation of the media or the use of leaks of crucial information to others in the simulation.

Role statements should also reflect the structural or power relationships that exist in the real-world environment and how they should manifest themselves in the simulation. In a simulation focused on bilateral trade negotiations, this might entail giving export and import figures that show the degree of trade dependence or independence possessed by either party. In a Congressional committee simulation, this would mean explaining the gate-keeping function of the committee chair and the varying powers and resources of the majority and minority parties.

In some simulation contexts, like the example included at the end of this chapter, specific roles may be less important. As we will see in the Commons Simulation, the only role that really matters is the role represented by the power ranking among the actors in the simulation. In this case, students latch on to the power dynamic in the game quite quickly and need little guidance about what that means for the negotiations engendered in the simulation.

The next task is the creation of a simulation scenario that presents a compelling issue or problem requiring thought and action on students' part. Scenarios do not need to be complex and many can be as short as a few sentences or even a page in most instances. The main requirement is that the students recognize that they are required to act and resolve the problem at hand. In this way, simulation use is well grounded in the pedagogy of problem based learning (Burch 2000; Brown et al. 2013). Students must analyze the problem, collect data and develop a solution to the problem as presented, placing them directly in the context of real-world decision-makers.

Newspapers are often a good source of scenario ideas. If the process to be studied is policy development, find an article about a specific policy currently under debate and use it as the basis of the simulation. Using current topics also has the advantage of emphasizing the complexity of current events and the decisions that surround them. As we all know as scholar–teachers, teaching complexity is no simple task, but this method can help drive the point home to students.

Simulations require that specific tasks be assigned to specific players. Each task should be modeled after a real-world task. Examples could include designing a budget, reaching a consensus on the resolution of a problem, resolving a foreign policy crisis in a way acceptable at both domestic and international levels, creating public policy or, in the case of the example included below, devising a system to avoid the depletion of fisheries in international waters. This full-simulation example is included in Box 27.2 and provides all the materials needed to run the exercise in a single class period.

You can also help focus on the degree to which seemingly mundane problems are embedded with political issues. A simulation created by one of the authors of this chapter involved a local community's problems in dealing with extraordinary snowfall. This problem focused on an overextended snow removal budget and how community might grapple with that challenge. The simulation therefore involved a decision-making body (like a town council) conducting a public hearing, a council debate and finally a vote on the transfer of funds across budgetary categories to cover the public works shortfall. Issues of school budget constraints and other concerns were high on the list of tradeoffs that had to be balanced in the local political setting.

Some scenarios play out better if a series of tasks are proposed. For instance, in a simulation designed to emulate the formation of foreign policy priorities, students meet to prioritize foreign policy problems, first, in homogenous intra-agency groups, and, later, in heterogeneous interagency groups with representatives of all relevant foreign policy agencies. If bureaucratic politics analyses are truly simulated, the interagency portion of the simulation should prove much more difficult because each agency group defends its own programs and advocates policies designed to enhance its standing. A simulation of negotiations with terrorist organizations might include a series of decision points involving terrorist demands.

The major difficulty of multi-task simulations is for the teacher who must be prepared to let students make their own decisions. The teacher must also be prepared to adapt the parameters of the simulation to fit with student decisions. In a terrorist negotiation simulation, this might mean evaluating the effectiveness of the use of force or reporting on the number of hostages killed in response to a decision made by students. In very direct ways, the teacher must be willing to adapt on the fly and adjust some aspects of the pedagogy as the process develops. This is difficult for many of us 'control-freaks', who insist on classroom predictability. But the value of ceding some authority to the students outweighs the uncertainty of the developing classroom process.

Finally, it is essential to provide any data or resources necessary for completing the assigned task. Newspaper articles, budgets and assigned readings can provide necessary background. Inventories of military capabilities, budgetary allotments, the 'nuts and bolts' of initial bargaining proposals – these are often crucial for realistic decision-making. Such data can be provided through lectures, presented in hard copy at the start of the simulation, or the teacher might even require students to conduct research in advance. The greatest advantage of this last alternative is that it requires students to think about the simulation before it actually begins.

In the Commons Simulation below, a conscious decision was made to allow the teams to define 'power' as they saw fit in the context of the game. This makes for some uncertainty in the way the game plays out, but it also drives home the point that power in global politics is not a one-dimensional, static concept. Thus, the decision to allow ambiguity in the student instructions actually leads to a worthwhile discussion about

BOX 27.2 A COMMONS SIMULATION: INTERNATIONAL FISHERY MANAGEMENT

Simulation Title
Protecting or Dividing the Commons? A Simple Simulation of International Fishery Management

Course Application
Upper division undergraduate class in Global Environmental Politics.

Teaching Goals
The goal is to illustrate the tension between self-interest and collective interest in a commons situation. This simulation was designed for use *before* the introduction of theoretical material on common pool resources and public goods theory more generally. Students gain an appreciation for mixed-motive situations in managing environmental resources.

Simulation Construction
The construction of this simulation is quite simple, as it is designed for delivery during a single class period. Students are presented with the following sheet of materials and little else. Given the distribution of technology personally and in the classroom, access to the Wikipedia page referenced below has never been an issue in implementation. But if Internet access is not available, copies of the Wikipedia page could be printed for distribution.

STUDENT SHEET
Primary Goals for Your Country

- In an effort to serve its economic goals, each country tries to maximize its potential revenue (sale of the fish) from fishing in the Great Sea.
- The whole community of countries needs to ensure that the resource is not depleted to the point where fish stocks diminish over time.

Guides for Interaction

1. Ten countries ranging in 'power' from 1 to 10 (as designated by the country number), with 10 the most powerful and 1 the least powerful.
2. Useful resource page: http://en.wikipedia.org/wiki/Overfishing#Acceptable_levels.
3. There are 1000 fishing units in this fishery. Only 25 percent of those units can be safely harvested each year for the fish population to replenish annually to approximately 1000 units.

Required *Group* Output: a plan to divide fishing rights to ensure 'fair' access to fish and a sustainable catch long term. That is, efforts should be made to preserve the 1000 units over time. This should include specific catch targets for each country.
Required *Country* Output: a statement of what your country's catch target will be. Provide a brief explanation of the rationale for your target.

Running the Simulation
Students should be handed out the student instruction sheet. You then need to divide the class into ten teams of approximately equal size. One helpful hint is to scatter the order of teams around the room. That is, it is best not to have all the 'powerful' teams physically located in one area of the room. It just makes for better interaction as the interaction develops. There may be a period of ambiguity at the start, but try to resist stepping in too quickly. Eventually (usually only about 5 minutes) some type of leadership will emerge. And sometimes that organic leadership leads to very interesting dynamics that are worth exploring in the debriefing.

Debriefing
As the primary goal was to illustrate the tension between self- (or national) interest vs. collective interest in resource use issues, this simulation lends itself well to discussion of realism from the start

> of the debriefing. It is also worth exploring the issue of 'what is fair' and 'how is or should power be defined'. These types of normative discussion raise an array of valuable teaching moments. In addition, in this teaching application, running this simulation as a 'primer' for the theoretical discussion makes the theory more real and concrete for students. As public goods theory is often an abstract set of concepts for students to absorb, the concrete-ness of this simulation provides real-world examples from the start.

power among students during the exercise and also during the debriefing once the game is concluded.

Running the Simulation

Organization is the key to running successful simulations. For more complex simulations, the scenario and role assignments should be handed out well before the start of the exercise. It is then helpful to solicit questions from the students. This will allow the pace of the simulation to move quickly. The more complex the simulation, the more important it is to distribute roles well in advance, so that players have an opportunity to research their roles and think about strategy. Depending on the amount of time you have set aside for the exercise, you may also encourage students to work in groups before the simulation so they can formulate collective strategies.

Roles should be assigned according to your teaching goals. If you are unconcerned with the conflict between personal values and bureaucratic position, then you may allow students to choose their own roles. If you wish to emphasize the 'where you stand depends on where you sit' dictum, you might want to be more careful. For example, in a bureaucratic politics simulation conducted by one of the authors, students completed an attitudinal survey that focused on their reactions to Russia and the use of force in foreign policy. 'Hawks' were then assigned to the human rights bureau of the State Department and the 'doves' were placed in the Pentagon. The role assignment procedure depends on what you hope to accomplish in the simulation.

It is useful to post task assignments in advance along with a timeline for the completion of each task. Name tags facilitate interaction among the students during the simulation. Information about all the assigned roles should be distributed without giving away the secret motivations indicated in individual role assignments.

Finally, it is important to announce basic ground rules at the outset. In general, whatever would be allowed in the context of the real situation should be allowed in the simulation: alliances, spying, leaks of information, use of parliamentary procedure to block proposed actions by adversaries, party caucuses, etc. Announcing ground rules may also inspire creative strategy ideas by outlining what is permissible in the game. For instance, in a Congressional politics simulation, students might find they are having difficulty in resolving an issue because of the dynamics between representatives of opposing political parties assembled in the room. The majority party might then decide to caucus and remove the minority party from the room for a period of time in order to solidify internal support. The minority, then, can use the media players to publicize and to criticize the secrecy and lack of open policy-making exhibited by the majority party.

When given a role and a task to perform, students generally respond quite well. Do not be worried if the simulation starts a bit slowly. Even with the increasing use of active learning approaches in the college classroom, this may still be the first experience that many students have in this type of learning environment and it may take them a few minutes to feel at home in the simulated world. Because of the complexity involved, players may at times lose track of the task, the scenario or the time. Careful monitoring, judicious coaching (be careful not to coach too much) and even intervention keeps the simulation moving. Be available to respond to student questions on all aspects of the simulation. Rotate among the groups to be sure participants are playing out their roles appropriately. Remember that some coaching of key players may be necessary, for few students have been placed in such a decision-making environment prior to this experience. Give plenty of warning about time deadlines. But also remember that the problem of missing deadlines can be a learning experience. You know something has been accomplished when a student remarks, 'It's amazing how much like the U.S. Congress this class has become – a day late and a few billion dollars short.'

Debriefing

Much of the value of simulations is contained in the subsequent debriefing and summary time. If the simulation has gone well, students are emotionally involved, very invested in the task at hand and probably still arguing many of the aspects of the simulation experience. At the end of one international development simulation conducted by one of the authors, one student exclaimed, 'But I was just about ready to develop!' In order to capitalize on this enthusiasm, it is often helpful to ask participants to remain in their groups during debriefing so you can put the simulation back into the substantive context of the course through your questions and comments. The following are some suggested approaches to debriefing questions:

1. Open-ended questions that identify processes, goals, motivations, constraints and resources.
   - What happened?
   - Why was no consensus achieved?
   - If we did not develop the best policy, why not?
   - Is there a right answer?
   - Who were the winners and losers?
   - What angered you about this simulation? Why?
   - What were the substantive issues? Were they the same for all players?

   Such questions allow students to explain in their own words the political and institutional forces behind their behavior. You will also need to tease out deeper knowledge from their answers, as we'll discuss briefly below.

2. Interview the major players about their goals, motivations and frustrations. This allows students to explain in their own words the political and institutional forces behind their behavior.
   - 'Mr. President, what exactly were you trying to accomplish and what prevented you from doing it?'
   - 'Mr. Speaker, the President claims that the majority party was obstructionist. Are you guilty of causing gridlock?'

- 'Madam Chairman, you are a presidential appointee yet you quietly made a decision of which the President would not approve. What makes you so independent? How far would you go if you were really pushed?'
3. Queries about communication: such questions can uncover patterns and de facto norms that may have developed implicitly during the game.
    - To whom did you talk? Why?
    - To whom did not you talk? Why?
    - What impact did incomplete information have on your strategy?
    - Whom did you trust? Why?
    - Why did not you talk to the President?
4. Questions about the reality of the game. This type of question helps students recognize the degree to which the simulation mirrored real-world situations.
    - In what ways did the simulation diverge from reality and in what ways was it similar to the real world?

    Asking about the reality of the game allows you and your students to focus on the limits of your simulation model and whether or not those limitations would matter in the real world.

It is also worth noting that the questions laid out above are what might be called 'structural' questions that provide the basic organization for your debriefing. As you do more of this type of classroom work, however, you will find that you become better at injecting 'facilitating' questions that keep the debriefing moving into deeper levels of learning and critical thinking. Facilitating questions are perhaps the most important aspect of the debriefing as they push students to explore their feelings and get to more complex aspects of the observed behavior. Examples of such questions inside the 'structural' form of the debriefing include:

- Tell me more.
- Unpack that idea more. Explain why you did what you did.
- Do others agree with that statement? Why or why not?

Additionally, sometimes it is very helpful to facilitate the discussion by queuing off of the body language and unspoken expressions by students. Some students will not talk unless asked to do so, but their body language will sometimes give the instructor an opening. For instance, the instructor might say: 'Okay, you are smiling at what she just said. Why?' Or: 'Clearly, you do not agree or you would not be shaking your head. What's the problem here?' Capitalizing on such opportunities to draw in students who are reticent to speak is important for engagement and the overall success of the learning construct. To ease the tension produced by 'cold-calling' students in class, it is helpful to warn students that you may draw them into the discussion with 'warm-calls' of this sort.

Once debriefing questions are completed, it is also worth spending some time summarizing the major points and how they relate to the subject under study. You may relate the simulation to relevant conceptual and theoretical frameworks, and you may find it useful to refer back to the simulation during subsequent lectures and discussions. Summarizing the material covered during the simulation is helpful for students who take careful notes and feel they must walk away from the experience with something tangible on paper.

EVALUATING THE TEACHING RESULTS

The greatest unknown in using simulations is the impact of the method on student learning. Both of the authors of this chapter have accumulated large amounts of anecdotal evidence supporting the idea that simulation promotes greater depth of understanding and higher levels of retention while promoting the development of stronger critical thinking and analytical skills and generating enthusiasm for learning. Unfortunately, none of this evidence has been collected, standardized or quantified in any sort of systematic way. Indeed, many of our colleagues still believe we receive large teaching enrollments and solid teaching evaluations because the students enjoy playing games rather than sitting through the more traditional, lecture style course. But we conclude otherwise.

That said, there are ways to uncover how students learn from the simulation. One way is to ask students to answer three simple questions at the end of the simulation.

1. What are the advantages/disadvantages of using simulation in class?
2. What did you learn from the simulation?
3. How does this class differ from other classes you have taken?

By using these three questions and reviewing student responses, you can begin to analyze the impact that simulation techniques have on students. You can also weigh the value of using the technique in the future. For those wishing a more rigorous and systematic approach to evaluation, you might begin by reading Fratantuono (1994) or delve into the wealth of work in educational psychology on the value of problem based learning generally and simulation more specifically. A couple of good starting points might be Lawless et al. (2010) and Johnson et al. (2011).

In sum, simulations are powerful pedagogical tools for understanding complex interactions. They can provide insights into why political actors make choices that seem unreasonable or irrational. Simulations uncover the real motivational forces intrinsic to players as they struggle with their choices. As with any teaching method, simulation demands a great attention to detail.[2] Developing simulations may seem complex, but the payoffs are high, as you can tailor the exercise for your own exact class application.

NOTES

1. For further development of these teaching assumptions, please see John Boehrer and Martin Linsky's (1990) discussion of eight categories of teaching objectives and Nathaniel Cantor's (1953, pp. 59–71, 286–310) discussion of the differences between 'orthodox teaching' and 'modern learning'.
2. This is adapted from a method developed by a number of colleagues in the Pew Faculty Fellowship in International Affairs to evaluate the impact of case method teaching.

REFERENCES

Boehrer, John and Martin Linsky (1990), 'Teaching with Cases: Learning to Question', *New Directions for Teaching and Learning*, **42** (Summer), 41–57.
Boyer, M.A. (1999), 'Coalitions, Motives, and Payoffs: A Classroom Simulation of Mixed Motive Negotiations', *Social Science Computer Review*, **17** (3), 305–12.
Boyer, M.A., B. Urlacher, N.B. Hudson, A. Niv-Solomon, L. Janik, M.J. Butle, S.W. Brown and A. Ioannou (2009), 'Gender and Negotiation: Some Experimental Findings from an International Studies Simulation', *International Studies Quarterly*, **53**, 23–47.
Brown, S.W., K.A. Lawless and M.A. Boyer (2013), 'Promoting Positive Academic Dispositions Using a Web-Based PBL Environment: The GlobalEd 2 Project', *Interdisciplinary Journal of Problem-Based Learning*, **7** (1), 67–90.
Burch, Kurt (2000), 'A Primer on Problem-Based Learning for International Relations Courses', *International Studies Perspectives*, **1** (1), 31–44.
Cantor, Nathaniel (1953), *The Teaching–Learning Process*, New York: Holt, Rinehart and Winston.
Crookall, David and Jonathan Wilkenfeld (1985), 'ICONS: Communications Technologies and International Relations', *System*, **13** (3), 253–8.
Fratantuono, Michael J. (1994), 'Evaluating the Case Method', *International Studies Notes*, **19** (2), 34–44.
Johnson, Paula R., Mark A. Boyer and Scott W. Brown (2011), 'Vital Interests: Cultivating Global Competence in the International Studies Classroom', *Globalisation, Societies and Education*, **9** (3–4), 503–19.
Lawless, K.A., S.W. Brown, M.A. Boyer, K. Brodowinska, D. O'Brien, G. Khodos, A.B. Cutter, M.F. Enriquez, G. Mullin, N. Powell and G. Williams (2010), 'GlobalEd 2: Learning and Applying Science Outside of the Laboratory through Interdisciplinary, Technology-Based Simulations', in J. Sanchez and K. Zhang (eds.), *Proceedings of World Conference on E-Learning in Corporate, Government, Healthcare, and Higher Education 2010*, Chesapeake, VA: AACE, pp. 1939–43.
Raiffa, Howard (1982), *The Art and Science of Negotiation*, Cambridge, MA: Harvard University Press.
Stice, James E. (1987), 'Using Kolb's Learning Cycle to Improve Student Learning', *Engineering Education*, **77** (5), 291–6.
Woodworth, James R. and W. Robert Gump (2001), *Camelot: A Role Playing Simulation for Political Decision Making*, fourth edition, Belmont, CA: Wadsworth Publishing.

28. Group work in political science: how to get collaboration into the classroom
Bobbi Gentry

When we consider the variety of tools in the pedagogical toolbox, as faculty we often consider group work with both excitement and hesitation. Students consider group work a mixed bag depending on which group they are a part of, and faculty worry about conflicts that may arise as a result of group assignments. Successful group work assignments highlight collaboration, set expectations, build on the strengths of students, provide opportunities for every student to contribute and encourage interpersonal skills that students will use in their future. Group work requires some careful consideration on the part of faculty to attempt to address biases that students might have coming into the work. Successful group work assignments will encourage students to collaborate, communicate and engage in higher order thinking. Group work in the political science classroom is an opportunity to create an active learning environment and encourages the development of collaborative skills. Faculty should carefully construct assignments that are meant for a group and consider discovery or problem based assignments to make group work a success.

Group work is essential to political science education because politics depends on group work: as Robert Swansbrough asserts, 'politics . . . depends upon leaders who can attract, motivate, and coordinate teams to win electoral victories, organize government, and develop public policies that benefit the nation' (2003, p. 769). Consider the classroom a collaborative learning environment, much like a collaborative game. In many collaborative games, we focus on the competition while working in teams against an opponent (consider sports teams) or against game mechanics (consider some board games such as *Pandemic*). Sports teams would not function without the different strengths, creativities and energies of the multiple members of the team. While working with others can be frustrating, the collaboration and successful results are shared experiences and achievements as a group. For example, model simulations of legislative bodies offer frustration when the many interests of actors are competing, but the final product of legislation or resolution is a shared experience of success.

Consider three major ideas when making successful group work assignments: collaboration, cooperation and contribution. Collaboration must occur; students should not just be off on their own working on separate parts. Collaboration means students working together, challenging one another and creating a final product of mutual contribution. Students within group work projects often do not know how to cooperate with one another. Cooperation is a necessary prerequisite to a successful group project and is a skill that students need to hone for their future careers. Cooperation means that students discuss differences, come to conclusions and resolve disputes within the group. Contribution means that the student provides individual effort that makes the entire project bigger than the sum of its parts. Each student's contribution is essential for the final product, but the sum result is greater than each individual's contribution.

Group work needs to be carefully constructed or else the common pitfalls of the assignment will be evident. Frequently the dislike of a group work project has to do with creating a lot more work for the hard working people in the group and letting the other students slack. Part of the reason that good students tend to dislike group work is because it is not collaborative but a piecemeal split of responsibility without clear reasoning and thought as to why. Another reason is also how individual students will be assessed for their final grade because the responsibility for the grade includes others in the group. For group work to be inherently collaborative, faculty must purposefully create assignments, clarify expectations, consider role assignment and encourage interdependency. In poorly structured assignments, everyone is dependent on the group's most valuable players (MVPs) or hard workers rather than an exchange of effort, thoughts and work of all group members. For students to learn the collaborative skills that are necessary to their careers, they need practice and feedback. Faculty should consider what makes collaboration possible in the real world and apply it in the classroom. Perhaps one of the most important distinctions for group work is to discuss division of labor versus collaboration.

REASONS FOR GROUP WORK

Faculty members choose to do group work because it encourages active learning with student interaction. Group work offers opportunities for students to hone their interpersonal skills, work on larger projects and build on the strengths of the members. Group work requires that students contribute and become a part of a functioning group, which requires problem solving and mediation when challenges arise. Faculty can ask more of their students in a group work project and can ask students to identify their contribution. Good group projects should be challenging and engage multiple parties to be successful. Students should be able to contribute in a number of ways such as brainstorming, posing questions, identifying weaknesses, making connections, offering advice, tutoring each other on challenging concepts and applications, and encouraging one another. Well thought out group work assignments have collaboration at their core and are meant for students to challenge one another in a cooperative environment where students may compete as groups.

When we rethink the classroom as a collaborative environment versus a competitive environment, then we open opportunities to engage in creative endeavors that are larger than ourselves, meaning a project that is bigger than any one individual student's capacity. Collaboration and cooperation are key to creating successful group work. Input from multiple actors is essential. If one student does the assignment while the others do not participate, then that is not group work. Dividing the labor does not always equate to a successful group work project; students must be collaborating, meaning they need to encourage, engage and question one another to challenge each other to create a better project. Group work succeeds when our students are learning in a social context, they become a part of something larger than themselves and they have a responsibility to others. The assignment is no longer about one student working by themselves to write, create or research; it becomes an opportunity for students to create something bigger and better.

From collaboration, students learn both concepts and interpersonal skills. The content of our political science courses can be difficult and dense, but as experts within the field we often overlook our curse of knowledge. The understanding of political science concepts, contexts and methods is easier for faculty because of how much time we have spent in this subject area; consequently, we forget what it is like being a student seeing the subject for the first time. Students explaining the concepts to other students can greatly increase understanding and retention of material (Centellas and Love 2012). Often students can learn more by teaching others. We choose group work in our classrooms because it prepares our students with skills useful to their future career, promotes an active classroom community and encourages peer tutoring. Social skills are necessary for careers and life; knowing that our students need help with these collaborative skills should encourage us to provide classroom environments and expectations to improve these skills.

TYPES OF GROUP WORK

Collaborative assignments are projects where students work together to achieve a common goal. Within the literature of cooperative learning, Johnson, Johnson and Smith (1998) identify three distinct types of cooperation. First, formal cooperative learning asks students to work together to achieve shared learning goals, such as a single group presentation. Second, in informal cooperative learning ad hoc groups form as the professor asks students to discuss a question posted, provide a hypothesis or summarize the material just discussed. An example of ad hoc groups includes peer tutoring or pair, share exercises, where students discuss with each other problems and solutions, such as Feeley's (2013) peer instruction method where students address problems together, explain to each other and work to solve larger political issues. Lastly, in cooperative base groups, the groups 'are longer term with stable membership whose primary responsibility is to provide each student the support and encouragement he or she needs to make academic progress and complete the course successfully' (Johnson, Johnson and Smith 1998, pp. 10–11). A long-term group that is established early in the semester might be a debate team or Model United Nations pair that works together in the same committee to promote their country's interests. The length and depth of collaboration distinguishes each cooperative learning type, and offers faculty a wide variety of possible collaborative assignments.

Another type of collaborative learning environment in political science is simulations, which are approximations of reality where students play roles to simulate interactions among individuals, countries or institutions and learn about differing views, competing values, interactions and consequences (Dorn 1989). Wedig (2010) suggests careful consideration of a type of simulation to use in the classroom and suggests several categories to find the right simulation. At the very core, the simulation should connect and support the course content and have clear learning outcomes. Wedig (2010) identifies three stages of simulation development: how to design the simulation, how the instructor chooses to act during the simulation and how to debrief the exercise. When considering simulation design, Wedig (2010, pp. 549–51) considers delivery method (face to face or online), participants (single class or distributed), interaction style (synchronous or asynchronous) and role assignment (teams or individual). During a simulation, faculty also have to decide what role they will play in the simulation: observer, control group or facilitator. A faculty member can choose to be the observer whose only role is to record the interactions of students and how they collaborate together. Another alternative could be that the faculty member could be a control group such as Germany in a World War II simulation. Lastly, faculty could choose the role of facilitator such as the chair of a committee or the mediator in any disputes of the group. Faculty who do not carefully consider their role within group work run the risk of being too passive or too involved. The right simulation for a classroom can depend on resources, faculty time and student involvement. But in the end, Wedig asserts, 'effective simulations should be driven by students rather than the instructor' (2010, p. 552).

With a wide variety of simulations, faculty consider classroom versus competition style simulations. Swansbrough (2003) found that breaking students up into committee teams to simulate Congress works to eliminate the lack of student engagement because students are assigned a specific representative and have to actively work to put forward their representative's position. The upfront preparation needed by each student can make or break the success of the committee and therefore team effectiveness. Students determine the effectiveness of the simulation based on how individuals are motivated, prepared and contributing (p. 771). Students tend to have higher expectations of each other in the classroom when the simulation encourages preparation and contribution.

Successful collaboration can also include outside actors; for example, Public Achievement, a program for collaboration of undergraduates and children in primary or secondary school to solve school and community problems, offers opportunities for civic engagement with students of all ages. Hildreth (2000) finds that undergraduates in experiential civic engagement are successful in their collaboration with young people in primary and secondary education. When undergraduates act as coaches, the collaboration is about guidance rather than directing. The success of such programs works because undergraduates can reflect on and evaluate their place in the world. Public Achievement is another example of a nontraditional setting where collaboration includes many different actors, not just undergraduates and faculty members. Group work can be a way to connect undergraduates with their college community and promote positive community collaboration to solve political and societal issues.

Finally, another type of group work is the assignment of think, pair, share, where students reflect on a problem posed in class, group up to discuss alternatives and share their solutions with the group (Millis and Cottell 1998). To encourage active participation of all group members, they use talking chips where each student who makes a contribution then surrenders their chip to the group; as a consequence, this activity requires equal participation where students are encouraged to speak up and talkative students are encouraged to listen to others before speaking again. In these problem solving assignments, students theorize, discuss their method of thought and explain their solutions. Within the groups, students can contribute by asking probing questions and learn through teaching others. The benefit of think, pair, share is for students working with one another to explain, debate, discuss and grapple with the concepts, theories and application of the material. Students are better able to explain the concepts in terms of their own understanding, and to build on a base knowledge that they already have. Faculty can also use this time to move through groups to see where students need more clarification.

DISADVANTAGES AND PROBLEMS OF GROUP WORK AND HOW TO AVOID THEM

Hesitations about group work come from many different sources, including faculty, administrators and students. Some faculty hesitate with group work because they believe less content will be covered, students will have serious group dynamic problems and final group work may not be completed or meet expectations (Formicola and Taylor 2013). Some students hate group work because they do not expect other students to take the group work seriously and therefore do not expect other students to come in prepared (Galatas 2006). While hesitations come from faculty and students, faculty who employ group work in their classroom have developed specific solutions.

Faculty often shy away from group work because it will take away too much class time or the budgeted amount of time is shorter than the time that is actually needed to complete the assignment. Still others believe that group work will take away class time needed to cover the necessary material. The challenge for faculty is to integrate the group work to facilitate learning, not take away from it. Faculty who use collaborative learning in their classrooms find that they cover material better, with more student understanding and with more depth (Feeley 2013). Group work must be purposefully built into the learning goals of the course; therefore, time must be allocated to discuss skills, provide content knowledge necessary and provide assessment. The group work literature suggests students learn the content with more depth and develop necessary skills to succeed in the workplace. Group work has some sacrifice of time, but the benefits for quality student learning of the content and skills outweigh the sacrifice.

In any group work situation, the challenge can often be the effect of Free Riders. As Mancur Olson (1965) tells us, free riders are those who benefit even though others are doing the work. A decision that a faculty member must make is to intervene in group dynamics or to let them play out where students work to solve the problems. One suggestion is to employ the Knickrehm method, which suggests grading the group project and then students evaluate others based on shares, i.e. contribution cubes that symbolize each group member's assessed work toward the final product by other group members (Maranto and Gresham 1998). Just like in the World Series where players divide the money based on shares allocated among the players, students are given shares such as nine shares in a five-person group. On average students should receive two cubes, with one cube left over to give to an outstanding member. Students can give more or fewer cubes based on others' contributions. There can be an MVP, who receives a maximum of four cubes.

Faculty also hesitate to have group work assignments because students may evaluate the faculty member on the success of the group work assignment in student evaluations. While the faculty member is the architect of the assignment, personal dynamics within the group can also play a role in the success of the group. Successful group work often boosts faculty evaluation scores, creates a community of learning in the class and encourages collaboration outside of class. Unsuccessful group work can often be detrimental to faculty evaluations, unless there is an evaluation about the group work that is separate from the course and faculty member. Again, the solution comes back to the careful consideration of the assignment and the purpose of the group work in the class. Early on in the course, faculty need to discuss the expectations of group work and encourage students to discuss what their expectations of others in the group might be. During the evaluation period, faculty should provide class specific assessment of the group work and discuss how that assessment is different from course and faculty evaluation.

How professors assess students on their contribution to the group work is another challenge. Questions sometimes arise and students contest grades based on group work assignments. King and Behnke (2005) discuss challenges for administrators when students contest grades that are based on group work. They recommend avoiding assigning a single grade to all students of a group and instead having a discussion within the group about expectations of group members. The challenge of assessment of individual work within a group project continues to be a discussion in the literature, but three different methods of assessment have been devised to address this challenge. These methods of assessment include individual (how each person contributed to the project), peer and self (how well did I contribute). Millis and Cottell (1998) offer several different types of assessment that promote learning about the content and how to work successfully in groups. One method is to have a group score that is then modified based on contribution (p. 191). Utilizing peer evaluation that has been carefully described in the assignment and syllabus can be helpful if it utilizes concrete criteria (p. 194). The most popular method of assessment is the Knickrehm method, which incorporates peer evaluation based on shares as discussed above. In the end, faculty must be clear about their grading practices and evaluation methods for group work.

For students, opinions are mixed; while many students have positive feelings towards group work, they are hesitant or neutral towards group work assessment (White et al. 2005, p. 620). Students can also be hesitant with group work, but as Johnson and Johnson (2006) note, students need group work skills for their careers. Faculty have a responsibility to develop and encourage skill development in their students. Students commonly hesitate because they lack trust in their peers to do the work (Galatas 2006), to evaluate each individual's contribution fairly (Maranto and Gresham 1998) and to be as prepared as they are (Galatas 2006). Formicola and Taylor found 'interpersonal skills and team collaboration provided the greatest obstacles for the successful completion of the semester long project' (2013, p. 5). In their study, the challenges of student disengagement included members not attending meetings, half-completed assignments and individual assignments rather than a complete whole work. However, they observed that the projects did come together at the end of the semester. Good group work assignments encourage better group cohesion because they remind students intrinsically that they are interdependent.

ADVANTAGES

Cooperative learning became more popular as a result of major changes in education that included encouraging more active participation of students than passive participation like taking notes and regurgitating the information from the faculty lecture. One of the major transitions to a more active style of learning was to rethink knowledge. As Cross notes, knowledge is 'something that teachers and students work interdependently to develop' (1998, p. 5), and how we conceptualize that within disciplines can include negotiating meaning among 'communities of knowledgeable peers' (Bruffe quoted in Cross 1998, p. 5). Rethinking knowledge also requires rethinking the role of the professor; a common analogy identifies passive learning as the sage on the stage versus the guide on the side. Cooperative learning considers the interdependence of learning communities and the collaboration of professors, students and groups.

Michaelson, Knight and Fink (2002) argue that the success of group collaboration and cohesiveness all depends on the assignment; therefore, successful group work is based on well thought out assignments. Problems often arise in group dynamics if the assignment can be completed by 'completely independent, individual work' (p. 54), involves problems that are too easy or has too much writing. They pose five questions for a successful assignment:

1. Does it promote a high level of individual accountability for team members?
2. Does it bring members into close physical proximity?
3. Does it motivate a great deal of discussion among team members?
4. Does it ensure that members receive immediate, unambiguous and meaningful feedback (preferably involving direct comparisons with the performance outputs from other teams)?
5. Does it provide explicit rewards for team performance?

The three-phase model of group assignments consists of individual preparation, group application, and individual and group assessment. Using this model, teams outperform the highest individual score over 90 percent of the time (Michaelson, Knight and Fink 2002, p. 21). An example of this three-phase model is individual reading of a unit, then individual assessment usually through multiple choice tests, then students getting together in teams to discuss the test and retake the test as a team. A different model of team based learning includes a problem where groups must make a specific choice and defend it. Within this problem based team learning, Michaelson, Knight and Fink (2002) suggest focusing on three elements: every group has the same problem that has a specific choice, and groups report their choice simultaneously (pp. 62–3). For example, if groups were asked to evaluate the Voting Rights Act of 1965 as effective or ineffective, then students would break into groups, make a specific choice, and then report simultaneously by writing their choice on the board and identifying the most important factor influencing their position.

One recent work in political science based on peer teaching and learning is Feeley's (2013) work on student collaboration in small groups to discuss a problem. The professor posts a question that could be open ended or multiple choice, then students write their answer down along with an explanation. Feeley's think, group, share and decide model works to encourage discussion, collaboration and defending arguments. Students as a result see the value in alternative points of view, address probing questions and come to more varied conclusions than they would have originally. Another example of students learning from one another is an activity I call quote, concept and idea. The class begins with the faculty member at the back of the classroom, therefore changing the focus to students as teachers. On the board are reading titles such as chapters four and five or Birkland, Wildavsky and Lippmann; students write on the board a quote, concept or idea from the reading. We then go around the class explaining the ideas to one another in terms of student understanding. The faculty member can prompt students to explain more, but in essence students are putting the information into language that they understand and will remember by creating cognitive connections for each other.

One major aspect of group work that is overlooked is small group discussions. Often in our classes, faculty encourage some sort of participation and assume that almost everyone will participate. Faculty should consider participation requirements, be clear about expectations and set up a code of conduct. One example of group discussions includes a fish bowl discussion, where students are seated in two concentric circles with a larger outer circle where most students are sitting and a smaller circle with four chairs in the middle, which comprises the fish bowl, where the interaction of four students at a time is being observed by the rest of the class. Students must take turns engaging in the fish bowl discussion by joining the center circle and then by explaining, asking questions or disagreeing. The benefits of this type of group discussion include exchanging different points of view, encouraging participation of students who are typically quiet and engaging in a dialogue about a problem. Group discussions can be open ended and allow students to see the academic engagement of ideas as a dialogue and development of arguments (Bean 2013). Bean suggests one way to improve student knowledge is to encourage teaching that supports inquiry and challenges students' assumptions, beliefs and arguments about the world.

Another advantage of group work is to address a common problem of young people today. The problem is that they do not possess the social skills necessary to establish and maintain positive relationships with their peers (Johnson, Johnson and Smith 2006). Differentiating between task work as the academic subject matter and teamwork as the interpersonal skills needed to succeed in groups, Johnson, Johnson and Smith (2006) have identified four levels of cooperative skills that students can learn from group work. First, the forming of groups sets expectations and norms of appropriate behavior. This is the period where students are getting to know one another and their expectations, limitations and possible contributions. The second level is group functioning, where the group begins to communicate through sharing ideas, asking for facts and reasoning, giving direction, encouraging everyone to participate, asking for help and clarification, and expressing support and acceptance. An example of functioning is during group work sessions where students are discussing a possible United Nations resolution and ask how this resolution might affect their country. Third, group formulating is the processing as a group through summarizing, seeking accuracy, seeking elaboration and checking for understanding. In small groups, students may want to clarify what is in the resolution, what it limits, what it allows and how it could be implemented. Lastly, fermenting allows the group to come to conclusions both as individuals and as a group through criticizing ideas without criticizing people, differentiating ideas and reasoning of group members, integrating ideas into a single position and asking for justification. At a model simulation, the fermenting is often the floor debate, where different perspectives become articulated. Identifying specific cooperative skills throughout the group work process allows faculty to introduce the relevance of the skills and allows students to practice the skills in a classroom environment.

WHAT GOOD GROUP WORK ENTAILS: AN EXAMPLE MODEL

Make the Project so that a Student Cannot Do It Alone

The first key aspect to creating successful group work assignments is to create an assignment that is too big for a single person to do. The project must be large enough that the overachieving student who does not want to work with others will be overwhelmed. Faculty should expect different outcomes from a group work assignment, such as a presentation including all members. Taking an example from State and Local Government, where students are learning policymaking, problem solving and policy analysis at the community level, students are broken up into groups of three as a community board. The learning goals of this group are to collaborate on identifying a community problem, identifying actors involved, examining the history of the subject and making proposals. The assignments are problem definition, historical and organizational impact, and policy proposal. For this assignment to be bigger, the community board should identify at least five problems in the community. This group work can happen in a few sessions of class or can take place throughout the entire semester.

Expectations Must Be Clear

Deadlines, multiple roles and outcomes must be clear to students. Faculty should consider whether they should set up the expectations or whether their students should set up expectations of each other. Making this decision could be based on lower versus upper division courses. Informing students that portions of the course grade are group work assignments up front allows students to opt out of the course and gives fair warning as to the expectations of collaboration. The first assignment that students do in their new community board group is to identify expectations of one another and write these into a contract. One helpful way to break expectations down is into academic, professional and personal expectations of the members of the group. For the faculty member, they can explain the point value for the group work assignments and how collaboration will be evaluated both by peers and the faculty member.

Accountability is the Immediate Follow-up to Expectations

There should be consequences both positive and negative to the successful completion of expectations and not meeting expectations. Centellas and Love suggest both collective and individual assessment is necessary to encourage cooperation and provides a disincentive to be free riders (2012, p. 507). After the contract is signed by all members of the community board, each member is now accountable to the other members of the board for attendance, participation, out of class meetings and other expectations. From my experience, students perform when they are held accountable both by the grade and in the contract. One example of grade accountability could be a group grade for a presentation and an individual grade for contribution measured by individual contribution.

Allow for Creativity

Students should be able to be creative in the group work assignment. Finding creative ways to engage the material, determine group dynamics and create outcomes is important for group work assignments. Group work should encourage the creativity of all members of the group and allow members to challenge each other to think outside the box. Group work assignments should inspire creativity in problem solving, alternatives and defining the context. For the community board, the faculty member could either identify the problem or allow the board to. From my work, students are often terrified to begin the process, but will come up with clear problems in their community. Creativity in defining the problem and coming up with multiple solutions lets students take ownership of the problem definition and solution. Creativity, in my experience, enables students to have more control, more voice, and as a result feel more empowered to make changes.

Provide Frequent Feedback

Students need feedback throughout the group work process. Students should be able to provide feedback to each other, while the faculty member should provide feedback about skills and knowledge. Early intervention in a problem of group dynamics may be necessary to have a successful finale to the project. With the community board example, faculty should provide time at the end of the class session, or as an assignment to bring into the next class, to allow students to communicate what worked well in the group, what did not work and what can be improved for next time. Faculty members should provide group feedback and individual feedback about how the process is working, including addressing the challenges of group work and consensus building.

Consider How You Will Incorporate Introverts and Extroverts into the Project

As we know from class, there are students who enjoy collaboration and feed on interactions with others. On the other hand, we also have students who enjoy working alone and who do not speak up as much because they are considering the evidence at hand. For this second group, working in a group can be taxing both emotionally and mentally. Considering that group work engages extroverts who enjoy the energy of others, consider how introverts might be better incorporated into the project. In Centellas and Love's research, students who were more comfortable with social interactions were more satisfied with the group's product (2012, p. 510). While our typical classroom format of the lecture is conducive to introvert learning, we need to make room for extroverts to express themselves and encourage introverts to work with others to produce collaborative work. With the community board, students share the role of board leader, where they make the decisions for the day. Switching the lead role allows students to experience multiple leadership styles and shifts contributions of each student.

Consider What Role the Faculty Will Play in the Collaborative Process

Faculty must consider how hands on they will be in the process. Identifying the faculty's role in the group work is important. The role of the faculty might expand from the typical evaluator for a grade. Do you believe it is the faculty's role to resolve conflicts within groups? Assist in idea creation? Add challenges or roadblocks throughout the group work? Before the group work even begins, the expectations of the faculty throughout the process must be clear for both faculty and students. With the community board, the faculty member is the guide on the side who aids students through challenges, addresses feedback as a group and individually, and provides rubrics for expectations on the assignments. The faculty member in this example does not write the contract, decide the problems or propose the solutions. Involvement in the board is only to facilitate the interaction of the students to identify and solve community problems.

Consider What Roles Students Have in the Collaborative Process

Faculty should consider whether they are assigning roles or whether students self-assign. There is some disagreement in the literature; group work assignments can have specific roles such as committee chair or minority and majority spokesperson. Some collaborative learning faculty consider roles as creating a hierarchy rather than creating equality within the group. For functionality, other faculty consider it necessary to have a leader, timekeeper and reporter. Depending on the amount of collaboration and the purpose of the group work in the course, faculty should determine what makes sense for their group work. Again, the changing role of community board leader produces changes in contribution and the learning of collaboration as a skill.

Assign Readings along with Collaborative Assignments

To achieve both content and skill learning, assign specific and focused reading assignments along with the group work (Centellas and Love 2012, p. 510). As Wedig (2010) suggests, the group work should be purposeful in achieving the learning outcomes of the course. Not every course is suitable to have a group work assignment. Some courses are easier to adapt to a group work assignment, such as model simulation courses that are inherently collaborative. When faculty are clear that their group work is a collaborative activity that encourages students learning from one another, then they can carefully build into the course a group work assignment. Other faculty suggest a complete rethinking of the course to include collaboration and content. Regardless, context and content are necessary preparation for students coming into a group work assignment. For the community board assignment, watching local televised council meetings, reading policy briefs and discussing the processes of policymaking all inform students about the content and process of solving community problems.

Allow Time for Reflection and Debriefing

Johnson, Johnson and Smith (1998) suggest that students need to process as a group the successes and challenges that occurred while in the group, including discussing group dynamics, the interpersonal skills needed to succeed, and the actions of individuals and the group. Group work can at times be emotionally charged and students need room to decompress and discuss. Reflection allows students to take a step back, look more objectively at the situation, and discuss how success and failure contributed to their learning. Consider using individual reflection with a take home assignment and group reflection written in class. Debriefing of group work can take many forms including discussion, individual assignments, and connections between the class readings and the group work (Wedig 2010). Students need room to vent about their emotions in the group exercise and to discuss the application of theory from the class to the interactions in the group work. Reflection on the success and challenges of working with others can better inform students as to the skills they need to hone for the workplace. At the end of the community board, students present their problems and solutions to the entire class. A short reflection paper about the experience including the successes, challenges and surprises can generate new insights into how to make a better group work project next time. Students feel listened to when faculty engage them in debriefing about what worked well and what they might change about the assignments next time.

CONCLUSION

As an alternative to traditional lectures and individual assignments, group work offers the chance for students to achieve more together and to build skills useful for the job market. For faculty, group work provides a way to have a community of learners who succeed together and an environment of discovery. There are many different types of group work, but at the center of this pedagogy are collaboration, cooperation and contribution. While the hesitations of faculty, administrators and students may challenge the prospect of group work, successful group work addresses the hesitations and builds assessment carefully into the project. Every good group work assignment is a purposeful blend of content and skills to achieve specific learning outcomes. The mechanics of group work allow for a variety of assignments and some contemplation about the assignment. Group work within political science promotes active learning, peer instruction and skills development. As our students prepare for the job market, companies are looking for individuals who can collaborate, problem solve, manage disagreements and contribute within groups. Group work offers opportunities to ask more of students, develop a community of learning, and promote alternatives to the traditional classroom, lecture and assignments.

BIBLIOGRAPHY

Bean, John C. (2011), *Engaging Ideas: The Professor's Guide to Integrating Writing, Critical Thinking, and Active Learning in the Classroom*, Hoboken, NJ: John Wiley & Sons.
Centellas, Miguel and Gregory Love (2012), 'We're Off to Replace the Wizard: Lessons from a Collaborative Group Project Assignment', *PS: Political Science & Politics*, **45** (3), 506–12.
Cross, K. Patricia (1998), 'Why Learning Communities? Why Now?', *About Campus*, (July/August), 4–11.
Dorn, D.S. (1989), 'Simulation Games: One More Tool On the Pedagogical Shelf', *Teaching Sociology*, **17**, 1–18.
Feeley, Maureen (2013), 'The Impact of Peer Instruction Pedagogy on Student Learning, Attitudes toward Learning and Student Engagement: Evidence from a Large Enrollment Political Science Course', paper presented at the American Political Science Association's Teaching and Learning Conference, Long Beach, California.
Formicola, Jo Renee and Michael Taylor (2013), 'Technology, Politics, and Campaign Management: A

Comparative Pedagogical Paradigm', paper presented at the Midwestern Political Science Association Conference, Chicago, Illinois.

Galatas, Steven E. (2006), 'A Simulation of the Council of the European Union: Assessment of the Impact on Student Learning', *PS: Political Science & Politics*, **39** (1), 147–51.

Hildreth, R.W. (2000), 'Theorizing Citizenship and Evaluating Public Achievement', *PS: Political Science & Politics*, **33** (3), 627–32.

Johnson, D. and F.P. Johnson (2006), *Joining Together: Group Theory and Group Skills*, Boston, MA: Allyn & Bacon.

Johnson, D., R. Johnson and K. Smith (1998), 'Cooperative Learning Returns to College: What Evidence is there that it Works?', *Change*, **30** (4), 26–35.

Johnson, D., R. Johnson and K. Smith (2006), *Active Learning: Cooperation in the College Classroom*, second edition, Edina, MN: Interaction Book Co.

King, Paul E. and Ralph R. Behnke (2005), 'Problems Associated with Evaluating Student Performance in Groups', *College Teaching*, **53** (2), 57–61.

Maranto, Robert and April Gresham (1998), '"World Series Shares" to Fight Free Riding in Group Projects', *PS: Political Science & Politics*, **31** (4), 789–91.

Michaelson, L.K., A.B. Knight and L.D. Fink (eds), (2002), *Team-Based Learning: A Transformative Use of Small Groups*, Westport, CT: Praeger.

Millis, Barbara J. and Phillip G. Cottell (1998), *Cooperative Learning for Higher Education Faculty*, Phoenix, AZ: American Council on Education and Oryx Press.

Occhipinti, John D. (2003), 'Active and Accountable: Teaching Comparative Politics Using Cooperative Team Learning', *PS: Political Science & Politics*, **36** (1), 69–74.

Olson Jr., Mancur (1965), *Logic of Collective Action: Public Goods and the Theory of Groups*, Harvard Economic Studies, Cambridge, MA: Harvard University Press.

Swansbrough, Robert H. (2003), 'Familiarity Breeds Respect toward Congress: Teams in the Classroom and Workplace', *PS: Political Science & Politics*, **36** (4), 769–72.

Wedig, Timothy (2010), 'Getting the Most from Classroom Simulations: Strategies for Maximizing Learning Outcomes', *PS: Political Science & Politics*, **43** (3), 547–55.

White, Fiona, Hilary Lloyd, Geoff Kennedy and Chris Stewart (2005), 'An Investigation of Undergraduate Students' Feelings and Attitudes towards Group Work and Group Assessment', *Research and Development in Higher Education*, **28**, 618–23.

29. Designing team-based learning activities
Andreas Broscheid

Group activities such as discussions or simulations have been common features of political science education for a long time—not surprisingly, considering the fact that politics is a social endeavor. Group learning is difficult, though, as students often resist cooperation as they compete for grades or find it difficult to schedule meetings for groups. As a result, group work often dissolves into individual work by a group of students and the potential of cooperative education—students learning from each other and developing knowledge on their own—remains untapped.

Team-Based Learning (TBL) is an educational approach that attempts to overcome the difficulties of group learning. Developed since the 1980s by Larry Michaelsen, then a professor of management at the University of Oklahoma, TBL lets students acquire foundational knowledge on their own before class and uses class time for highly structured group activities and discussions that help students apply the material to important problems (Michaelsen, Knight and Fink 2004; Sweet and Michaelsen 2012a). A system of graded individual and group assignments provides incentives for students to work individually and in their groups. The term 'team' instead of 'group' indicates that students are expected to be responsible not only for their own learning but also for the learning of their teammates, with whom they collaborate throughout the entire semester.

TBL has been used extensively in business and the health professions, but its application has been spreading to other disciplines, including the social sciences and humanities (Sweet and Michaelsen 2012b). A professional organization dedicated to TBL organizes yearly conferences on the topic, implementation fidelity guidelines have been developed (Haidet et al. 2012) and the term 'Team-Based Learning' has been trademarked.

In this chapter, I first provide a brief introduction into the main elements of TBL, followed by an example of using TBL in an undergraduate research methods course. I close with suggestions for implementation.

THE MAIN ELEMENTS OF TEAM-BASED LEARNING

TBL is defined by three elements: the use of student teams for most class activities, the Readiness Assurance Process and class discussion centered on *4S* application activities. I describe each of these elements in turn. If not otherwise noted, the description is based on the chapters in Part I of Michaelsen, Knight and Fink (2004) and on Sweet and Michaelsen (2012a).

Permanent Student Teams

Most in-class learning activities in TBL take place in student teams. The use of the term *team* instead of *group* among TBL practitioners indicates an emphasis on group cohesion as one of the conditions of effective learning, as team members become responsible for each other's learning. In TBL lingo, student teams are expected to *gel* after a few weeks of classes. To achieve this, TBL practitioners do the following. Instructors form student teams of six to eight students according to explicit criteria that they communicate to the students. The two main criteria are meaningful heterogeneity and avoidance of subgroup formation. The purpose of heterogeneous groups is to enable students to learn from each other. As a result, the type of student heterogeneity that is meaningful is frequently related to existing skills, but it can also be based on personal interests of students, their academic majors, professional goals and the like. To avoid subgroup formation, instructors typically try to identify students who are friends or family or room or athletic team or fraternity/sorority mates and divide them among teams.

One distinction between TBL and other cooperative learning approaches is the fact that teams are fairly large. The rationale for the team size is to assure sufficient group heterogeneity and to provide teams with the resources needed to solve challenging applied questions. TBL counters the danger of subgroup formation through careful group selection as well as the use of activities that focus the teams on common tasks. In addition, student peer evaluations can be used to provide incentives for students to participate in their teams.

While team sizes of six to eight students are the norm in TBL, I have been able to implement the approach with team sizes as low as four to six students. While smaller teams generally did well, some suffered more strongly from attendance problems than the larger teams: in large classes that I taught with TBL, on occasion only one team member was left when the other three were absent.

Another difference to other cooperative learning approaches is the fact that TBL does not require the instructor to explicitly teach teamwork, for example by assigning team roles. But it is possible to do so. For example, I have found it useful, particularly in large classes with many teams, to assign team facilitators on a rotating basis, who are responsible for reporting and recording their teams' discussions and conclusions. This can be combined with instruction on how to be a successful facilitator and peer-review and self-reflection exercises to reinforce the instruction.

Readiness Assurance Process (RAP)

As the name suggests, the Readiness Assurance Process (RAP) intends to make sure that students are prepared for the application exercises that form the center of a TBL course. One of the advantages of the RAP is that it can be used not just to prepare students for applied activities but also to provide coverage of the course material, while application activities provide in-depth discussion of select questions. As a result, TBL manages to combine opportunities for active learning and fairly broad coverage of course material.

The RAP is the first part of every course unit, which can be one or more weeks in length. Michaelsen (2004) suggests that a semester-length course should contain five to seven units, which means that each unit is two to three weeks in length. In my own courses, I generally employ a larger number of shorter units, of one week in length, since there is an external expectation that the courses cover different topics each week and since this permits me to spread out the course readings. Michaelsen's argument against shorter course units is that students get tired of weekly RAPs. In my experience, this is not the case: students consistently report that they enjoy the weekly RAPs. Michaelsen's experiences indicate that students at different institutions and in different disciplines may respond differently; as a result, I recommend that instructors using TBL pay attention to potential RAP fatigue and adjust their courses accordingly.

The first two stages of the RAP are based on individual student work. First, students read the texts assigned for the course unit. These texts should be chosen so that they provide the information students need to successfully solve applied problems later in the unit. Second, each student takes an individual Readiness Assurance Test (iRAT). A typical iRAT consists of a set of multiple-choice questions that test whether students have understood and can use the central points in the readings.

While the RAP has to prepare students for the succeeding applied activities, I also use it to make sure students are aware of, and have thought about, those points in the readings that I want them generally to remember and understand. The size of the iRAT varies from course to course—I typically use 10–15 questions per iRAT. While several of those questions are simple comprehension questions, a considerable number of them should target higher-level learning objectives (Krathwohl 2002).

In the textbook version of TBL, students take the iRAT in class at the beginning of the first class meeting of a course unit. Following the iRAT, the student teams immediately retake the same test, this time as a team Readiness Assurance Test (tRAT). If the test contains sufficient numbers of higher-level questions, the tRAT process will provoke the first student discussion of parts of the readings.

After the student teams have taken the tRATs, the correct test answers are revealed and the tests are scored. This can be done in several ways: When portable Scantron scorers were more common, it was feasible to let students record their answers on Scantron sheets that the instructor would immediately send through the machine. Nowadays, it is more convenient to use electronic response systems such as Clickers to record student responses and automatically score them. For tRATs, so-called IF-AT (Immediate Feedback Assessment Technique) forms are quite popular. These are scratch-off cards on which students have a choice of four scratch-off fields per question; if they choose the field that corresponds to the correct answer, the answer is immediately revealed and the students can record a point. If the instructor is so inclined, students who choose the wrong answer may be permitted to try another answer for partial credit.

Both the iRAT and tRAT scores contribute to a portion of students' course grades. This is motivated by a desire to provide individual as well as team accountability for learning. If the RAT questions are sufficiently challenging, students experience a learning and grade benefit from engaging in their teams and pooling the intellectual resources and perspectives that the individual members bring.

One of the potential problems of grading team activities is that some students may free-ride on the effort and engagement of their fellow team members. One way to counter student complaints about this problem is to let students determine the relative weights of iRAT and tRAT scores at the beginning of the semester. Students who fear that other team members will take advantage of them can opt to weigh their iRAT scores more highly. I have found that most students assume (correctly) that they will do better on the tRATs than the iRATs and opt for the highest permissible tRAT weight. As a result, I usually fix iRAT scores at 10–15 percent of the overall course grade and tRAT scores at 5–10 percent.

A strategy to avoid student free-riding is to let students evaluate their fellow team members at the end of the semester and to lower the tRAT scores of those students who are found to slack off in team activities, who are regularly too late and/or who miss many classes. An informational mid-semester peer evaluation exercise can be used to warn students who are potentially at risk of bad peer evaluations and to create an opportunity for intra-team conversations about participation.

After students have received their iRAT and tRAT scores, teams can appeal tRAT answers that they got wrong but that they believe are at least as correct as the answer that the instructor provided. Such appeals must be done in writing and be based on a close discussion of the class readings and the question wording. To win an appeal, it is not enough to show that the team's chosen answer option could also be correct; the appeal has to document that the instructor's choice was mistaken or that the team's answer was at least as good as the instructor's. The instructor reads the appeal and grants or denies the appealed point within one week. If the appeal is granted, both the appealing team's tRAT score and the iRAT scores of members giving the same answer are raised by a point.

According to the textbook version of TBL, only teams, not individual students, are allowed to submit appeals to reinforce team learning and team cohesion. Individual appeals carry the risk of burdening the instructor with too much work. In my own classes, I have permitted individual appeals with the argument that, if an appeal is right, then it would be unfair to keep individual students from submitting it. Since each individual RAT question counts for only a small portion of the course grade, I have found that I am not overwhelmed with appeals. One positive aspect of individual appeals, particularly in large classes, is that they have led to conversations with struggling students about the class material.

The last stage of the RAP is instructor feedback on iRAT/tRAT questions that students find difficult or unclear. Topics for such feedback can be gathered by the instructor by listening in on student conversations during the tRAT and appeal phases. Alternatively, the instructor may choose to engage students in a *muddiest point* exercise in which they identify issues in the readings that are least clear to them.

The RAP can easily take up a whole 50-minute class period: 10–15 minutes for the iRAT, 10–15 minutes for the tRAT, 5 minutes to score the tests, 5–10 minutes to write appeals and the remainder for short feedback lectures. To save some class time, I have given the iRATs as open-book online quizzes that students have to complete before the first class meeting of a unit. The advantage of this procedure is that slower students can take as much time as they want for the iRAT (I do not time the online quizzes), without letting quicker students wait. In addition, the online iRATs easily accommodate students with disability-based access plans that require extended times for in-class assignments.

Online iRATs create two types of problems. First, if they contain mainly low-level questions whose answers can be looked up in the readings, students may decide not to do the readings before taking the iRATs and to simply look up the answers to the questions once they see them. To counter this challenge, online iRATs have to contain questions that target broader points of the readings and higher-level learning objectives.

The second problem of online iRATs is that they require instructors to delay revealing correct answers to students. If the iRAT takes place in the classroom, students learn which of their answers are correct immediately after taking the tRATs. Such immediate feedback is an important component (not only) of TBL: It exploits students' temporary investment in an activity by providing feedback when the memory of the activity is still fresh and students are willing to react to the feedback. If instructors provided immediate feedback for online iRATs before students take the tRAT, then students would know (some of) the answers to the tRAT as well and fail to engage in the team discussions on the RAT questions. In my experience, it is not too harmful to delay feedback on online iRATs until after the in-class tRATs. Taking the tRATs re-engages students in the questions, and they tend to remember what answers they gave.

'4S' Applied Activities

The majority of TBL class time is spent on activities that let students apply the knowledge tested by the RAP to important questions of the discipline. The activity typically starts in the student teams, followed by a plenary discussion in which teams compare and analyze their respective output. To assure that all students focus on the same applied questions and are easily able to communicate and compare their conclusions, the applied activities follow the so-called *4S* format: all teams deal with the same significant question whose answer can be simultaneously reported as a simple choice.

Probably the most important characteristic of the applied activities is that they are 'significant'. One way to gauge what questions are significant is to ask: What do we want students to be able to do with the course content in, say, five years? What are the central questions that political scientists try to answer in the subfield covered by the course? What are the central political science questions that we want students to think deeply and competently about? What are the most important skills that we want students to acquire as a habit? Answers to these and similar questions help identify class activities that engage students and do not waste their time.

The remaining three S's are more technical: they require that activities force student teams to work on the same problem and that their answers be reported simultaneously as a specific choice. For example, a course on the judicial process could ask teams to decide whether the federal government should impose caps on medical malpractice awards. The question is the same for all teams, the team answers constitute a specific simple choice (yes/no) and the answers can be reported simultaneously, using various technologies described below.

The medical malpractice activity also illustrates that *4S* questions, despite the fact that they often have multiple-choice character, can require complex debates from the students: the example involves questions of federalism, civil process, economics and more. In fact, the question is probably too complex for novice students. It may be useful as a capstone question at the end of a class unit on civil cases, for example, preceded by a series of simpler questions, such as whether students think that medical malpractice suits increase or decrease the costs of medicine.

The process of applied activities is as follows. The instructor introduces the question and presents the choice to the students; student teams deliberate for the necessary time period and present their choices. The instructor then asks individual teams to justify their choices before the class, ask questions of teams who made a different choice and react to each other's explanations. After this plenary discussion, the instructor should provide an opportunity for students to take stock of what they learned in the activity. This can be done through a brief summary lecture of main points learned through the activity, a short writing exercise in which students write two or three sentences about what they learned, or the like.

Technologically, there are several ways for teams to communicate their choices. In a large class, the perfect response system is a Clickers-style electronic response system: student teams make their choices without knowing what other teams decided (and are therefore less subject to peer pressure) and the instructor can easily identify which team made which choice and ask for an explanation. A technologically simpler but similarly effective reporting mechanism in a smaller class is to have students write their answers on a sheet of paper and to deliver the answer to the instructor. In a large class, it is also viable to identify answer options with different colors and to distribute notecards or post-it notes with the different colors to the student teams. To give their response, students simply hold up their chosen notecard or stick the chosen post-it on a wall.

The beauty of the *4S* structure is that it focuses the whole class on a common choice or problem. Since the activity involves a single choice, it is impossible for teams to split up the task and transform the team experience into coordinated individual work. As a result, Michaelsen and Bauman Knight (2004) emphasize that instructors should avoid activities that can be easily divided among participants, such as making lists or writing team papers.

My own experiences tend to confirm Michaelsen and Bauman Knight's preference for *4S* activities. Particularly at the beginning of the semester, I have found it important to make sure students are focused on a common task. Once teams have gotten used to working with each other and team members have formed attachments to each other, it is possible to introduce more open-ended activities. For example, in a fairly small (about thirty students, four teams) class, I asked teams to create concept maps of certain topics and then to compare and contrast the different teams' maps. All team members seemed to be engaged in creating the maps.

EXAMPLE: TBL IN A POLITICAL SCIENCE RESEARCH METHODS COURSE

I decided to employ TBL in an undergraduate political research class for several reasons. First, the course was expected to provide coverage of a number of discrete topics, such as formulating testable research questions, identifying and reviewing scholarly literature, evaluating quantitative data, and employing various quantitative statistical tools to evaluate hypotheses. At the same time, students were expected to learn how to apply these topics to their own research (and at the end of the semester they had to produce an original research paper). TBL's emphasis on applied learning in combination with coverage through the RAP was a promising approach to such a course.

Second, I hoped that working with other students in class would provoke more students to actively engage the class material. Instead of listening to my explanations, they would first ask their fellow students to answer their questions about points they did not understand. More students would be forced to use the class material to solve research-related problems in class. The experience of solving research problems in class would give students confidence that they could handle the tasks involved in a research project. At the same time, solving those problems in a group would remove some of the pressure that students might experience when they tried to do research on their own. Finally, I hoped that regular interaction with other students in class would make learning more fun and would increase class attendance.

The first research methods class in which I used TBL had a 23-student enrollment. The class met three times per week for 50 minutes each for class activities and spent an additional 50 minutes in a computer lab. I employed TBL in the three weekly 'regular' class meetings but not in the computer lab meetings, since the lab setup made it impossible to maintain the teams used in the regular classroom.

I followed the Michaelsen model of TBL fairly closely: During the first week of classes, I formed three teams of seven to eight students each. I asked students whether they were friends (or family members) of other students in the class and placed those who were in different teams. Then I asked who had enjoyed or hated the statistics course that was a prerequisite for research methods; to the extent possible, each team received students who liked statistics as well as students who disliked it. I made sure every team had at least one student with a laptop and one student who enjoyed writing. To the extent possible, I also mixed student seniority (the class contained mainly juniors and seniors).

I then explained why I had formed the groups and used the criteria that I had used. I introduced the TBL approach and the reasons for why I was using it. Most importantly, I explained the RAP, the use of applied activities in the class and the advantages of TBL over lecture-based teaching.

RAPs took place during the first class meetings of each week. Each team received a folder with iRAT and tRAT forms as well as appeals forms. Students completed the iRATs on paper in class, and then the teams did the same with the tRATs. Once all teams were done, I displayed a slide with the correct answers and asked all students to score their quizzes. Students then put their scored quizzes back into the folders, which I collected at the end of the class meeting. After the RATs, I gave students a few minutes to write appeals, answered questions and gave short lectures on topics that students had been struggling with in the RATs or that I found particularly important. I gave students 10 minutes each for the iRATs and tRATs, extending the time if several teams needed it and moving on earlier if everybody was done before time was up. On the whole, the RAP took about 30–40 minutes, leaving no time for application activities on the same day.

For the application activities, I did not always strictly follow Michaelsen's *4S* model of application activities. For example, one activity that I used to reinforce the identification of scholarly literature was to provide students with several scholarly and non-scholarly sources and ask the teams to classify them and to explain to the class which ones they thought were scholarly and why. While all teams got the same sources, they had to make several choices and did not report simultaneously. In another exercise, teams received a series of research questions and had to classify them as normative or non-normative, general or specific, empirical or non-empirical and so on. Again, the result was a list of answers, which according to Michaelsen could induce students to split up the work— luckily, though, this did not actually happen. In another example that diverges from Michaelsen's model of team activities, I asked teams to create several survey questions measuring a particular concept; I then distributed all questions to all teams and had them select the four best questions, based on criteria for good questions discussed in the readings.

I decided to use such non-TBL activities for two reasons. First, most of the activities, while not necessarily focusing on a single choice, still forced teams to make common choices that could be compared across teams. I did not find that teams split up the tasks. Second, I used more frequent RATs than what the TBL literature recommends. Michaelsen (2004) argues that RATs should not be employed more frequently than about every three weeks, to avoid student boredom. In that case, it makes sense to use team activities that force students to make a single, simple choice, since this strengthens cooperation in the team. Since I used weekly RATs, though, I expected that teams would quickly gel even without 4S activities (though this was only partly happening, as I note below).

Taken together, iRATs and tRATs accounted for 20 percent of the course grade. At the beginning of the semester, teams could choose the precise balance with which the iRAT and tRAT scores would affect the RAT portion of the course grade, within boundaries that I set (e.g. tRATs could not count more than the iRATs). All teams decided that tRATs should account for as much as I would permit—that is, for half of the 20 percent portion determined by the RATs. Besides the iRAT and tRAT scores, students' grades were composed of their performance on midterm and final exams, homework assignments, and the final research paper. As a result, only 10 percent of the grade was due to team activities.

To counter potential free-riding in the teams, students were asked to conduct confidential peer evaluations at the end of the semester. If a team member decided to free-ride, the other students could let me know and I would lower the tRAT portion of the free-rider's grade. If other students contributed extraordinarily to their team, their fellows could also acknowledge this and I would raise their tRAT grade.

The outcomes of this first TBL class were decidedly mixed. I had the general impression that students were doing better: they did get higher grades on average than students in previous classes; they also generally seemed to have a better grasp on exam questions that past students had struggled with. Several students seemed to like the group work. But I did not conduct systematic measurements to confirm these impressions more reliably.

More importantly, there were indications that TBL did not work as well as I would have wished. First of all, there were indications that not every student fully participated in team activities. While one team (the smallest of the three) seemed to work well, individual students in the other teams did not participate in group activities, played with their cell phones or chatted with other students not engaged in team activities. Attendance was as spotty as in previous semesters. Evidently, neither the expectation of peer evaluations nor the activities focusing on a common task were enough to induce all students to participate actively. The end-of-semester anonymous student teaching evaluations were the lowest I had received up to that point.

What had gone wrong? The open-ended responses on the student teaching evaluations suggested two problems. First, students expressed anxiety that the separate applied class activities, while useful in themselves, did not provide them with the skills to conduct their own research project. Several students argued that they felt the bigger picture was missing—how different steps of the research process contribute to the whole research process. Second, the evaluations suggested that I had not succeeded in getting buy-in from many students with respect to TBL—several students expressed skepticism as to its effectiveness. In addition, it seemed that the comparatively large team sizes, even though they were consistent with the team size recommended in the literature, hindered student collaboration in teams, as it was too easy for individual students to drift away from teamwork.

Based on these experiences and observations, I redesigned the research methods class for the following semester. Class size and meeting times were similar to the previous semester. I kept the overall TBL structure but made a number of changes to how I used TBL.

First, I put more emphasis on selling TBL to students at the beginning of the semester. While I had explained the rationale at the beginning of the previous class as well, I now took more time to explain the drawbacks of passive and lecture-based learning and provided more information on research that documented the benefits of active learning. I also used humorous and emotional images for the introductory sell and used the opportunity to provide some background information about myself and my own education.

Second, I reduced the team size, forming four teams of five to six students each instead of the larger teams. As I noted above, the downside of smaller team sizes is that student absences have a stronger effect on the ability to work in teams. While occasionally only two members of a team actually attended class, absences were not a huge problem throughout the semester.

Third, I put more emphasis on short lectures that presented the big-picture view of the research process and explained where the day's activities fitted in. For that purpose, I created a Prezi slide that displayed a flow chart of the research process as a cycle. The slide allowed me to zoom in on more detailed explanations of class topics and activities in the context of specific stages of the research process. It helped me make sure students did not get lost in the application activities and kept track of the larger class focus to which they were connected.

I investigated student learning of course content in this second TBL semester with a ten-question multiple-choice quiz that I gave students during the first week of classes and then again at the end of the semester. The James Madison University Institutional Review Board approved the data collection. While this assessment clearly did not cover many of the learning objectives of the class, it captured a range of topics discussed in class and included questions that in my experience distinguish successful from less-successful students. The results of the pretest in the first week of classes confirmed that it covered material that the students did not know: 15 of the 19 students taking the test gave fewer than six correct answers (corresponding to an 'F'), and a further three students gave only six correct answers (corresponding to a 'D'). In other words, the D+F rate of the pretest was about 95 percent, with an average score of 4.26 correct answers.

Due to logistical reasons, I was not able to conduct the pretest in a comparison non-TBL research methods class taught by a colleague. However, for the post-test, I was able to run the knowledge test in the comparison class. In the post-test, only two of 14 students in the TBL section gave fewer than six correct answers and all other students gave seven or more correct answers. This corresponds to a 14 percent D+F rate. The average number of correct answers was 7.64. In the non-TBL section, the D+F rate was 40 percent, with an average score of 6.6 correct answers (n=20). While the small number of observations suggests caution with the comparison, the control group numbers are roughly in line with my own experiences teaching research methods before switching to TBL. Based on these numbers, it appears that students in the TBL section were more successful learning the course material; in particular, the data suggest that the TBL section may have helped students who otherwise would have been at risk of failing.

In addition to the ten-question knowledge test, I asked students in the TBL section a series of questions about whether they found TBL useful. Overwhelming majorities of students stated that it was mostly or completely true for them that the team activities helped them learn (78.4 percent), prepared them for exams (85.8 percent) and helped them do better in class (71.4 percent). Exactly half thought it was mostly or completely true that they were getting better at teamwork, which indicates that students felt that TBL developed their teamwork skills. Clear majorities of students enjoyed the class format: all students stated that it was mostly or completely true that they got along with their team members and 85.7 percent stated that it was mostly or completely true that they enjoyed working in their teams. Not everybody preferred the TBL format to other pedagogies, though. While more than half (57.1 percent) clearly stated that they did not prefer another class format, three students (21.4 percent) thought it was mostly or completely true for them that they preferred another format.

These results confirmed my intuitive sense that TBL was successful the second time around. The emotional chemistry among students and between students and instructor was better than in the previous semester, fewer students missed class, and student course evaluations were at the high end for a research methods class.

CONCLUSIONS

I have found that Team-Based Learning can be an effective approach to increase student engagement and to help students learn more and have more fun in their classes. TBL helps switch the focus of learning from catalogues of factual and conceptual information to applying this content to important questions that we want students to think deeply about. The approach is scalable to larger classes: I have used TBL successfully in classes of up to 185 students.

However, making TBL work is not always easy. It is important to provide the incentives for students to engage in their teams and to work on their common tasks. Writing higher-level RAT questions and effective *4S* application activities takes time and experience. Beginning as well as advanced practitioners therefore benefit from collaboration with experienced TBLers, either in person or through participation on the listserv of the Team-Based Learning collaborative (http://www.teambasedlearning.org/).

Finally, for TBL to be effective, instructors have to make an effort to sell the approach to students by explaining its rationale, by providing evidence for its effectiveness, and by providing feedback on learning objectives and outcomes throughout the course. I have found that it is important to pay attention to student responses throughout the semester, for example by employing a formative mid-semester course evaluation or asking students for regular feedback. TBL conflicts with many students' expectations of how class meetings should be run and knowing their reactions is essential to addressing their concerns and convincing them to engage in their learning.

REFERENCES

Haidet, P., R.E. Levine, D.X. Parmelee, S. Crow, F. Kennedy, P.A. Kelly, L. Perkowski, L. Michaelsen and B.F. Richards (2012), 'Perspective: Guidelines for Reporting Team-Based Learning Activities in the Medical and Health Sciences Education Literature', *Academic Medicine: Journal of the Association of American Medical Colleges*, **87** (3), 292–9.

Krathwohl, D.R. (2002), 'A Revision of Bloom's Taxonomy: An Overview', *Theory Into Practice*, **41** (4), 212–18.

Michaelsen, L.K. (2004), 'Getting Started with Team-Based Learning', in Larry K. Michaelsen, Arletta Bauman Knight and L. Dee Fink (eds), *Team-Based Learning: A Transformative Use of Small Groups in College Teaching*, Sterling, VA: Stylus, pp. 27–50.

Michaelsen, L.K. and A.B. Knight (2004), 'Creating Effective Assignments: A Key Component of Team-Based Learning', in Larry K. Michaelsen, Arletta Bauman Knight and L. Dee Fink (eds), *Team-Based Learning: A Transformative Use of Small Groups in College Teaching*, Sterling, VA: Stylus, pp. 51–72.

Michaelsen, L.K., A.B. Knight and L.D. Fink (2004), *Team-Based Learning: A Transformative Use of Small Groups in College Teaching*, Sterling, VA: Stylus.

Sweet, M. and L.K. Michaelsen (2012a), 'Critical Thinking and Engagement: Creating Cognitive Apprenticeships with Team-Based Learning', in Michael Sweet and Larry K. Michaelsen (eds), *Team-Based Learning in the Social Sciences and Humanities*, Sterling, VA: Stylus, pp. 5–32.

Sweet, M. and L.K. Michaelsen (2012b), *Team-Based Learning in the Social Sciences and Humanities*, Sterling, VA: Stylus.

30. Experiential education in political science and international relations
Elizabeth A. Bennion

Experiential education is based on the belief that optimal learning occurs through experience. Students learn best when participating actively in hands-on opportunities that connect content to *application* in the real world. Experiential education is an approach to learning in which educators 'purposefully engage with learners in direct experience and focused reflection in order to increase knowledge, develop skills, clarify values and develop people's capacity to contribute to their communities'.[1]

Educators' desire to enhance student learning through high-impact teaching practices is bringing experiential learning into (physical and virtual) classrooms. Experiential learning is no longer relegated to non-academic internships, work and community service; experiential education, as a philosophy of learning, requires that experience be combined with critical reflection to promote learning. Experiential education promotes student engagement and furthers defined learning objectives through active 'hands-on' learning inside and outside of the classroom.

Experiential learning is divided into two major categories: field-based experiences and classroom-based learning. Field-based learning, integrated into higher education in the 1930s, is the oldest and most established form of experiential learning. Field-based learning includes internships, practicums, cooperative education[2] and service learning (Lewis and Williams 1994). Classroom-based experiential learning takes many forms, including role-playing, games, case studies, simulations, presentations and various types of group work in which students are required to *use* the skills the course seeks to develop. Experiential learning in the classroom has been growing in breadth and depth since Chickering and Gamson recommended 'active learning' as one of the seven '"principles of good practice" for excellence in undergraduate education' in 1987 (Lewis and Williams 1994, p. 8). The recent increase in online courses means such 'classroom-based' experiential learning increasingly is taking place outside of the classroom in an online 'virtual classroom' environment.

Grounded in well-established theories and findings about how students learn, experiential learning[3] can achieve desired learning outcomes in both large and small classes through classroom, community, workplace and/or online engagement. If designed properly, experiential approaches to student learning maintain high academic standards while promoting *academic* engagement through critical reflection linking theory and practice. Through a combination of concrete experience and critical reflection, students can make new discoveries, take responsibility for their learning, give and receive constructive feedback, and understand why specific lessons are beneficial to their personal and professional lives.

This chapter focuses on 'fruitful and creative'[4] experiences that promote learning in the fields of political science and international relations. It highlights best practices in experiential education, providing a list of best practices and specific examples of experiential education models across a range of subfields. The goal of this chapter is to encourage teachers worldwide to offer their students high-impact experiential learning opportunities that develop the knowledge, skills and motivations needed to produce lifelong learners who make a positive difference in their communities.[5]

EXPERIENTIAL EDUCATION: LEARNING BY DOING – LESSONS FROM JOHN DEWEY

The concept of experiential learning is not new – cooperative learning programs took place before the 1930s. Many histories of experiential education highlight the work of American philosopher, psychologist and educational reformer John Dewey (1859–1952). Dewey's work provides four central lessons: 1) there is a connection between experience and learning, 2) education should focus on developing habits of mind, rather than memorization of facts, 3) individual learning outcomes and outlooks will vary based on diverse backgrounds and experiences of learners, and 4) not all experiences are equally educational.

Lesson 1: Experience Fosters Learning

Dewey highlighted the connection between experience and learning. Dewey originally wrote about the benefits of experiential education in 1938, explaining, 'there is an intimate and necessary relation between the processes of actual experience and education' (Dewey 1997 [1938], p. 20). Dewey believed that the teaching (and testing) of 'facts' often occurs at the expense of learning and understanding. He supported 'progressive' education, embracing the idea that we should teach people how to think.[6] Progressive educators value habits of mind over memorization of facts and reject the idea that tests, alone, can measure whether a person is educated.

Recent research supports Dewey's views regarding the importance of experience in the learning process. Extensive research exists into how young adults learn and develop as well as how educators can have a long-term impact on students' understandings of the world.[7] The conceptual model of the brain as fixed has been replaced by new evidence that the architecture of the brain is flexible and is constantly shaped by experience (Zull 2004 cited in Bowen 2012, p. 76). If a neuron fires often, it grows and extends out toward other neurons, connects with them and sends signals back and forth through synapses. Synapses convert the isolated neurons into a network of neurons. At the molecular level, changes in the connections that make up these networks define learning. Two things cause networks to form: practice and emotion. When learners practice, the brain grows (Dragnski et al. 2004 cited in Bowen 2012, p. 77). Research suggests that lasting learning is motivated by emotion and solidified by practice (Damasio 1994 cited in Bowen 2012, p. 78). A lecture can motivate students and stimulate emotion, but it does not give them much practice at forming their own explanations and networks (Bowen 2012, p. 78). Students may learn enough facts and definitions in a class to pass exams, but lecture-based pedagogy does not always succeed in teaching students to think critically, analytically or evaluatively (Damron and Mott 2005). Learning requires more than just new facts; it is motivated by 'forcing students to confront, analyze and articulate compelling discrepancies that require change in what they believe' (Bowen 2012, p. 80). Mental models change slowly because pre-existing beliefs are difficult to change. Testing these beliefs through experience is one way to learn that these beliefs do not 'work' in the real world. Recent neurological research supports Dewey's contentions about the central role of experience in promoting learning and comprehension.

Lesson 2: Academic Engagement Promotes Learning

A second lesson from Dewey's writing is the importance of developing habits of mind, rather than merely encouraging memorization of facts. Dewey argues that, by focusing only on content, the teacher eliminates the opportunity for students to develop their own opinions of concepts based on interaction with the information. Dewey rejects a passive role for students, arguing that learning does not take place by absorbing information but, rather, when the learner transforms this information into new forms, images and symbols that fit with their own development and interests. Accordingly, students' progress in learning is not about completing a succession of studies but, rather, about developing new attitudes toward, and interests in, the world around them.

Recent research supports Dewey's emphasis on the importance of active learning in which students are required to create meaning and test theories rather than memorizing established facts. A metacognitive approach that combines factual knowledge with an emphasis on conceptual frameworks, applications and student control over learning fosters deep and lasting learning (Bain 2004; Bowen 2012).

Students learn best through active learning that requires them to make discoveries and create meaning. Neuroscience suggests that the positive emotions in learning are generated in the parts of the brains that are used most heavily when students develop their own ideas. Recent scholarship demonstrates that the frontal cortex and pleasure centers deep in the brain are stimulated by independent thinking, rather than by explanations (Zull 2004 cited in Bowen 2012). For this reason, both experience and experimentation foster long-term learning outcomes.

To foster lasting learning, educators should 'engage the whole brain: Instructors should provide experiences and assignments that engage all aspects of the cerebral cortex: sensory cortex (getting information), integrative cortex (making meaning of information), integrative cortex (creating new ideas from these meanings) and motor cortex (acting on those ideas)' (Zull 2004, p. 71 cited in Bowen 2012, p. 89). Simply lecturing to students is less effective than active learning in developing high-order cognitive skills. Delivering content alone has virtually no effect on students' beliefs about the world (Bowen 2012). Student motivation and preconceptions are important. If students learn new information for the purpose of a test, they quickly revert to their old ways of thinking (Bransford and Brown 2000 cited in Bowen 2012). Students can memorize data that conflict with their beliefs, but without active engagement with the new material, in the form of discussions, writing, debates, projects and hands-on applications, students really do not consider the implications of the new content for their existing understandings, beliefs and worldview (Bransford and Brown 2000, p. 92 cited in Bowen 2012). Such research supports Dewey's contentions about the importance of active engagement and experimentation throughout the learning process.

Lesson 3: There is No Single, Uniform Learning Experience

Each student's experience will be individualized based on past experiences, and not all students will take away the same outlook of a concept. Recent research confirms the importance of past experiences in processing and interpreting new experiences. The brain is not a blank slate waiting to be written upon or an empty bowl waiting to be filled. Contexts for learning include student apathy or interest, religious and political beliefs, educational background, psychological development and underlying worldview.

The experiential learning classroom mimics society, where all people have different views of topics and information. Experiential education both recognizes the importance of past experience in shaping people's understandings of the world and provides an opportunity for new experiences to challenge existing assumptions about the way the world works. People have a difficult time learning things that contradict their current understanding of the world; most of us believe that new information we receive confirms our earlier beliefs, theories, interpretations and arguments.[8] Often we seek out information that confirms these beliefs, while overlooking or avoiding contradictory views and data. When confronted with information that seems contradictory to what we believe, we perform 'all kinds of mental gymnastics to avoid confronting and revising fundamental underlying principles' (Bain 2004, p. 23). And yet, to learn and grow, we must confront competing theories and evidence. To teach effectively, and promote student learning, we must encourage our students to do so, too. Ultimately, learners must discover how the theories, facts, skills and dispositions they are learning are applicable to their own lives. Past experiences will shape current (and future) understandings of complex or contested concepts. Even the same experience may be interpreted in different, yet equally valid, ways by people from different backgrounds. As Dewey recognized, learners have diverse experiences that shape the ways they interpret their experiences as they learn and grow.

Lesson 4: Quality Matters

Finally, a fourth lesson from Dewey's early writing is that not all experiences 'are genuinely or equally educative' (Dewey 1977 [1938], p. 13). The quality of the experience is essential. Dewey maintained that, in order for education to be progressive, there must be a solid philosophy that privileges experiences that are 'fruitful and creative' (Dewey 1977 [1938], p. 17) and that enhance subsequent learning experiences.

MODERN EXPERIENTIAL LEARNING THEORY: BLOOM'S TAXONOMY AND KOLB'S LEARNING CYCLE

All of the research cited above is consistent with Bloom's (1956) taxonomy of education objectives, and Krathwohl's (2002) revision of the taxonomy into the form most widely used today. By classifying cognitive skills into six levels of increasing complexity, educators are reminded that the goal is not simply to test students on their ability to *remember*, retrieve, recognize or recall relevant facts but, rather, to produce students who *understand* key concepts, *apply* knowledge to solve new problems, *analyze* data, structures or situations, *evaluate* programs, policies and practices, and *create* new knowledge – generating

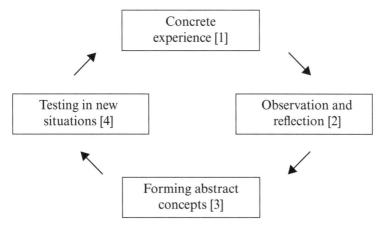

Figure 30.1   Kolb's experiential learning cycle

new ideas, planning new programs or producing new organizations that reflect their working knowledge and beliefs about politics, public policy and the public good.

In 1975, Kolb and Roger Fry developed the 'Experiential Learning Cycle' (see Figure 30.1). According to this model, experiential learning occurs in a four-stage cycle whereby 'immediate or concrete experiences are the basis for observations and reflections. These reflections are assimilated and distilled into abstract concepts from which new implications for action can be drawn' (Kolb, Boyatzis and Charalampos 1999, online p. 3). Importantly, experiential learning involves direct experience with the concept being studied rather than just thought about the concept or discussion about possible experience with the concept (Borzak 1981). Experiential learning theory can be distinguished from cognitive and behavioral learning theories in that it privileges affect (i.e. feelings and emotions) and allows subjective experience in the learning process (Kolb, Boyatzis and Charalampos 1999). The process is cyclical: new inferences and understandings and theories are repeatedly tested and become a guide for creating fresh experiences. When designing experiential learning opportunities for students, it is important to keep in mind some common traits, possible formats and best practices.

Experiential Education Basics: Common Traits

Most experiential education programs have several qualities in common. These qualities include (but are not limited to):

- emphasis on learning by doing – hands-on projects
- emphasis on problem solving and critical thinking
- emphasis on understanding and action as the goals of learning
- de-emphasis on rote memorization
- group work and development of team work/social skills
- collaborative and cooperative learning projects
- integration of community service and service learning projects

- de-emphasis on textbooks in favor of varied learning resources
- emphasis on lifelong learning
- personalized education accounting for each individual's personal goals
- assessment by evaluation of student's projects and productions
- selection of subject content based on what skills will be needed in future society
- education for social responsibility and democracy.

Each of the above pedagogical approaches promotes 'learning by doing' with a goal of developing the skills, knowledge and dispositions required for lifelong learning and engagement.

Experiential Education Basics: Best Practices

In addition to shared traits, successful approaches to experiential learning follow a set of best practices before, during and after the learning experience. The National Society for Experiential Education lists 'Eight Principals of Good Practice for All Experiential Learning Activities'.[9] These include (in abridged format):

- *Intention*: All parties must be clear from the outset why experience is the chosen approach to the learning that is to take place and to the knowledge that will be demonstrated, applied or result from it.
- *Preparedness and planning*: Participants must ensure that they enter the experience with sufficient foundation to support a successful experience.
- *Authenticity*: The experience must have a real-world context and/or be useful and meaningful in reference to an applied setting or situation.
- *Reflection*: For knowledge to be discovered and internalized the learner must test assumptions and hypotheses about the outcomes of decisions and actions taken, then weigh the outcomes against past learning and future implications.
- *Orientation and training*: For the full value of the experience to be accessible to both the learner and the learning facilitator(s), and to any involved organizational partners, it is essential that they be prepared with important background information about each other and about the context and environment in which the experience will operate.
- *Monitoring and continuous improvement*: Any learning activity will be dynamic and changing, and the parties involved all bear responsibility for ensuring that the experience, as it is in process, continues to provide the richest learning possible, while affirming the learner.
- *Assessment and evaluation*: Outcomes and processes should be systematically documented with regard to initial intentions and quality outcomes. Assessment is a means to develop and refine the specific learning goals and quality objectives identified during the planning stages of the experience, while evaluation provides comprehensive data about the experiential process as a whole and whether it has met the intentions which suggested it.
- *Acknowledgment*: Recognition of learning and impact occur throughout the experience by way of the reflective and monitoring processes and through reporting, documentation and sharing of accomplishments.

These best practices insure that students are adequately prepared to *engage in* and *reflect upon* a meaningful experience and that instructors are able to assess learning outcomes and evaluate the quality of the experience in ways that foster continuous improvement and opportunities for future students.[10] Table 30.1 includes an example of how these principles can be put into practice in the political science classroom.

Experiential Education Basics: Common Formats

Experiential learning takes on a wide variety of formats while maintaining underlying principles including: intentionality, engagement, reflection and (re)iteration. Regardless of the format, experiential learning requires that experience be designed as a deliberate means to advance specific learning objectives. The learning must be active, not passive, requiring students to actively explore new ideas rather than merely memorizing facts. Activities must be linked to reflection. 'Learning by doing' is not automatic; reflection designed to promote deeper understanding and inform subsequent action must be integrated into the learning experience. Finally, experiential learning is most effective when there are multiple opportunities (iterations) to apply what has been learned. Ideally, experiential learning experiences are not isolated activities but, instead, are integral to a student's education (at the departmental and university levels) rather than an occasional add-on. No single activity or course will achieve all the long-term benefits of experiential learning, but there are a variety of formats that can be used to further both short- and long-term learning objectives of a specific program or course. For this reason, it is ideal to plan curricula and course content on the basis of an experiential learning philosophy; course content should be coordinated among faculty within a department, college or campus to maximize learning opportunities and to create a scaffolded learning environment in which later classes build upon knowledge and skills acquired earlier in the curriculum. Additionally, extracurricular activities provide an opportunity to supplement curricular approaches.

Earlier in this chapter, experiential learning was divided into two main categories: classroom-based and field-based experiential learning. Learning can take place within a (physical or online) classroom or out in the community – in partnership with civic associations, government offices and agencies, non-profit organizations and/or for-profit businesses. Some campuses conceive of this division in a different way, especially when considering the respective roles of academic affairs, student affairs or career services in promoting experiential learning. In this framework, experiential learning activities are defined as course centered, program centered or workplace centered.[11] Course-centered approaches to experiential learning include: field courses (or field work), international courses, community service learning, studios, independent study, laboratories, theses, capstones, simulations, problem-based learning, external projects/contracts, productions/exhibitions and workshops. Program-centered activities include: student exchanges, student conferences, student competitions, artistic productions and exhibitions, tutoring and peer support, charettes,[12] involvement in faculty research and voluntary activities (if academically related). Finally, workplace-centered activities include: co-ops, internships, practicums, placements and work-study. See Table 30.2 for a chart of learning activity by learning site. See Table 30.3 for definitions of common experiential learning activities.[13] Students' exposure to multiple classroom and community-based experiences will enhance desired learning outcomes.

Table 30.1 Eight principles of good practice – an example (professor: Elizabeth Bennion, Indiana University South Bend; courses: American Politics, Elections and Voting Behavior)

Principle	Example	Application
Intention	Students will gain a better understanding of the techniques, dynamics and challenges of voter mobilization campaigns.	Stated in the syllabus. Restated, in writing, on the assignment and training materials. Reinforced, verbally, during multiple class sessions.
Preparedness and planning	Students will be taught applicable election laws, voter mobilization techniques, and strategies for maximizing the quantity and quality of voter contacts.	Covered in multiple class sessions by instructor and professional campaign consultant. Reinforced at a 4-hour Sunday training session including role-playing and hands-on use of canvassing materials.
Authenticity	Students will learn about voter mobilization campaigns in a real-world context by participating in an actual door-to-door campaign.	Students partnered up and participated in a non-partisan, ten-precinct, voter mobilization campaign, using walklists, pre-rehearsed talking points, and instructor-prepared handouts.
Reflection	Students will test assumptions and hypotheses about voter attitudes and the usefulness of door-to-door contacts for increasing voter interest and turnout.	Students were each required to complete a survey and write a two-page reflection paper describing the best and worst part of their experiences and reflecting on three lessons they learned in the field, comparing their understandings of key concepts before and after the field experience.
Orientation and training	Students will familiarize themselves with the neighborhoods to be canvassed and the persons supervising their work.	Student met the precinct captains, talked with the precinct captains about project expectations, reviewed their walk routes and drove the routes during the training sessions.
Monitoring and continuous improvement	The mobilization campaign will provide a rich learning experience and will continually evolve based on student feedback.	Precinct captains debriefed the instructor and one another after each shift and made changes based on student/canvasser feedback. The instructor surveyed all students (anonymously) and used feedback to improve the experience for future classes.
Assessment and evaluation	Outcomes will be systematically documented. The experience will be evaluated using comprehensive data. Assessment will be used to develop and refine learning goals.	The instructor required student reflection papers, anonymous surveys and precinct captain debriefings, all of which provided detailed information about student learning experiences. All voter contacts were (scientifically) randomized, tracked and compared with county voter files to measure the effect of the students' mobilization campaign on local voters.
Acknowledgment	Student learning outcomes will be monitored and reported in ways that celebrate accomplishment and encourage future accomplishment.	Results of the campaign on students and voters were published in the *Journal of Political Science Education* and the *Annals of the American Academy of Social Sciences*. Copies were shared with student canvassers and university stakeholders.

Table 30.2 Categorization of experiential learning activities

Course centered	Program centered	Workplace centered
field courses	student exchanges	co-ops
international courses	student conferences	internships
community service learning	student competitions	practicums
studios	artistic productions and exhibitions	placements
independent studies	tutoring and peer support	work-study
laboratories	charettes (or like activities)	
theses	involvement in faculty research	
capstones	voluntary activity (if academically related)	
simulations		
problem-based learning		
external projects/contracts		
productions/exhibitions		
workshops		

EXPERIENTIAL EDUCATION IN POLITICAL SCIENCE AND INTERNATIONAL RELATIONS

Teacher–scholars in the fields of political science and international relations have used many different formats to promote student learning and engagement. Experiential learning has been integrated across subfields and institution types. The most common approaches to experiential learning in political science and international relations courses include simulations, problem-based learning, service learning and community-based research.

Simulations

Simulations are activities designed to imitate the operation of a real-world process or system over time. Simulations are used in political science and international relations courses to illustrate political processes. They may take many forms. In civics simulations, participants assume roles in a simulated society. In simulations of government organizations, participants take on roles of elected or appointed officials, government staff and other stakeholders (e.g. political lobbyists) trying to create effective policy while constrained by institutional rules, informal norms, laws, culture and/or public opinion. In international relations simulations, participants engage in negotiations, alliance formation, trade, diplomacy and the use of force, while keeping in mind constraints imposed by country conditions, rules of engagement, economic power and cultural norms. Such simulations might be based either on fictitious political systems or on current or historical events. Sometimes simulations take the form of games, especially in the online environment. Often, simulations involve role play. *Role-playing* is designed primarily to build first-person experience in a safe and supportive environment. Students take on the identities of various political actors requiring intensive research and developing a personal stake in the proceedings. Role play is effective in both face-to-face and online environments.

Table 30.3 Definitions of experiential learning activities

Capstone	An entire course or a portion of a course expected at or near the end of a student's academic career. The course usually requires students to demonstrate all or a portion of the skills/knowledge they have acquired as a part of their degree.
Case study	A written description of a problem or situation. A case study does not include analysis or conclusions but only the facts arranged in a chronological sequence. The purpose of a case study is to place participants in the role of decision-makers, asking them to distinguish pertinent from peripheral facts, to identify central alternatives among several issues competing for attention, and to formulate strategies and policy recommendations. Most case studies depict real situations. In some instances, the data are disguised; infrequently, the case may be fictional.
Charette	An interdisciplinary event where a specific task/problem/issue has to be creatively addressed under a short deadline, presented to experts and critiqued.
Clinical placement	Students attend a different workplace setting from their job in order to complete a practice course in their discipline. Students are expected to accumulate a specific number of hours of work over the semester to put toward the course. The course syllabus and assignments are identical regardless of the work-study setting.
Competition	Students, usually a part of local or national teams, are introduced to real-world situations. Competitions allow students to apply the theories and information they have learned in the classroom to real organizations.
Conference	An opportunity for students to manage and showcase their knowledge and skills and to interact with people and organizations within their discipline.
Co-op	Cooperative education links an academic program with progressive discipline-related work experience and brings substantial, unique benefits to students, employers and the university. Students obtain valuable and paid work experience in steps throughout their course of study that directly relates their classroom learning to relevant employer needs and practices.
Creative practice	Creative practice, supported by communication, analysis and organization, allows intellectual, technical and creative activity to occur.
Debate	An argument, or discussion, usually in an ordered or formal setting, often with more than two people, generally ending with a vote or other decision.
Exhibition	A creative large-scale public display of art, products, skills and/or activities that relates to a student's discipline.
External project	Involvement of external organizations in classroom projects/research related to the discipline.
Field camp; field experience; field study; field trip	Field education provides opportunities for students to apply theory learned in their classroom courses within authentic workplace settings. Field courses clearly link theory and practice and can have a varying timespan, depending on the program.

Independent study	Independent study is a student-initiated experience planned to allow students the opportunity to pursue an area of interest in their field with the faculty guidance.
International (study-abroad) course	A full or partial course that takes place at an international location.
Internship	An internship is an opportunity to integrate career-related experience into a student's education by participating in planned, supervised work.
Laboratory	A place for practice, observation or testing under controlled conditions.
Placement	Students gain discipline-related work experience as a partial component of their program, often one day per week over a semester or in blocks.
Practicum	Learners focus on the syntheses and application of advanced practice knowledge within a practice setting related to their field of study.
Problem-based learning	An instructional method that challenges students to 'learn to learn', working cooperatively in groups to seek solutions to real-world problems. These problems are used to engage students' curiosity and initiate learning the subject matter. Problem-based learning prepares students to think critically and analytically and to find and use appropriate resources.
Production	A large-scale undertaking highlighting creative expression that relates to a student's discipline.
Research project	Projects and research undertaken by students as a component of a course or as research assistants.
Service learning	Service learning is a type of experiential learning that engages students in volunteer service within the community as an integrated aspect of a course. The service is linked both to community-identified needs and to course objectives.
Simulation	Using role-playing, practicum simulation or other methods to represent a potential or real situation.
Simulation (computer)	Software used in experimental testing or to imitate or represent a potential or real situation.
Simulation (performance-based)	Performance-based methods are used to enhance interpersonal communication and to teach, evaluate and challenge. Simulation protocols are designed to simulate 'real-life' situations.
Student exchange	Student exchange programs help students broaden their cultural and professional outlook and knowledge through exchanges at universities around the world, often for a period of one semester.
Studio	Studios provide an opportunity to put theoretical ideas and concepts into practice under the guidance of faculty members.
Thesis	A thesis course allows students – typically seniors – to produce scholarly work under faculty supervision appropriate to the discipline.
Work-study	A government program that helps students to meet their education costs by working part time during the year; the government pays a portion of student wages.
Workshop	An educational gathering or seminar emphasizing interaction and exchange of information. It usually involves problem-solving and hands-on training and requires the active involvement of the participants.

Problem-Based Learning

Problem-Based Learning (PBL) is a student-centered pedagogy in which students learn about a subject by solving a problem. PBL is designed to help students develop flexible knowledge, collaboration skills and effective problem-solving skills through self-directed learning that increases intrinsic motivation to learn (Hmelo-Silver 2004). Like simulations, PBL problems place students in situations that mimic real-life problems faced by individuals in the political world. What differs from many standard political science simulations is the level of detail that students receive for the steps they must take from that point forward; simulations typically provide specific instructions and steps to guide students, while PBL instructions are brief and do not give specifics on how to solve the problem. PBL scenarios emphasize the importance of the process of *finding* a solution as much as the solution itself. PBL assignments do not have a simple right answer nor should the assignments provide all of the needed information. 'As with real problems, students will have to work with imperfect and incomplete information' (High-Pippert 2003, p. 21).

While the phrase 'problem-based learning' is a twentieth-century invention, the pedagogy behind it is similar to the Socratic method of teaching students to learn the value of developing questions (Easley 2007). Students must determine what questions to ask and what information is required to solve the problem. Working in groups, students identify what they already know, what they need to know and what new information is needed to resolve the problem. This approach is particularly applicable to political science: political problems usually have indeterminate 'solutions'. Solutions are always political, drawn from asserted premises and consequent conflict or debate. PBL provides a way to prepare students to analyze, to interpret or to integrate new situations or information.[14] Instructors take on the role of facilitator ('tutor') rather than expert. The tutor becomes a resource rather than a focus point of learning. The role of the tutor is to offer support and guidance, building students' confidence while challenging them in ways that promote deeper understanding and learning.

Service Learning

Service learning combines experiential learning and community service. This form of learning is designed to emphasize critical thinking and personal reflection while encouraging a heightened sense of community, civic engagement and personal responsibility. Participants learn and develop through active participation in thoughtfully organized service that is conducted in the community and meets a community-defined need. The experience is coordinated through cooperation between an institution of higher education or community service program and key community stakeholders.

In order to further learning outcomes, service must be integrated into and enhance the academic curriculum of the students, or the educational components of the community service program in which the participants are enrolled. To facilitate learning, instructors and other supervisors must provide structured time for participants to reflect on the service experience. Instructors can help students to develop links between the theories and research findings discussed in class and the real-world experiences students are having in the community. Political science and international relations instructors must be particularly careful not to reinforce stereotypes or attitudes of benevolence. Critics of early service learning efforts pointed out that the experiences were no different from volunteering and failed to get students to think through the institutional and political factors creating the social problems requiring amelioration through volunteer services.[15] To move away from the 'volunteerism trap', and to enhance the value of the students' learning experience through the development and utilization of additional skills, instructors are increasingly working with community partners to create research-based service opportunities for their students.

Community-based Research

Community-based research, also called community-based participatory research (CBPR) is 'a collaborative effort between academic researchers and non-academy based community members that aims to generate social action and positive social change through the use of multiple knowledge sources and research methods'.[16] Ideally, the research questions originate from off-campus communities and the process involves meaningful participation by all partners in every stage of the research. The 'community' is often self-defined and might include a geographic community, community of individuals with a common problem or issue, or a community of individuals with a common interest or goal. The partnership approach to research involves community members, organizational representatives and researchers in all aspects of the research process; all partners contribute expertise and share decision-making and ownership of the project. CBPR is designed to increase knowledge and understanding of a given phenomenon in order to improve the health and quality of life of a community and its members.

PUTTING IT ALL TOGETHER: COMBINING APPROACHES TO EXPERIENTIAL EDUCATION

Although I have discussed various approaches to experiential learning separately, it is often most effective to combine these approaches in ways that promote student learning and community development.

Problem-Based Learning Using IR Simulations

Problem-Based Learning is often introduced in the form of case studies or real-world challenges. Problems can also be posed in the context of complex simulations that require students to solve real-world problems with limited information and within cultural and institutional constraints. For example, Model United Nations programs provide a diverse group of informed college/university students and faculty from all over the world a forum for addressing global concerns in a real-world context (http://www.nmun.org/).

Instructors can also build their own campus-wide program or take advantage of regional programs (e.g. the Midwest Model UN in the United States, http://mmun.org/). International relations instructors also can get their college students involved in offering model UN opportunities to local low-middle-income high school students who cannot afford to participate in international, national or regional Model UN programs, as Alison McCartney did at Towson University in Maryland.[17]

Similarly, European Union (EU) simulations that assign students to national teams and as part of EU institutions provide an example of PBL through role play and simulation. Model EU, like Model UN, can be done within a class, campus or region or on a national and international scale (see e.g. http://meu-strasbourg.org/). More information about PBL is discussed in Chapter 29 of this book, while examples of high impact simulations are found in chapters 26 and 27.

IR Service Learning Using Community-based Research

Travel abroad is only one way to introduce real-world, meaningful experiential learning opportunities for students in international and comparative politics courses. Community-based research and service learning projects that require students to think globally and act locally provide another opportunity for experiential learning. Government professor Susan Dicklitch, Director of the Ware Institute for Civic Engagement at Franklin & Marshall College in Lancaster, Pennsylvania, provides an example of a successful effort. Dicklitch combines service learning and community-based student research in her human rights course, allowing students to use their research skills while promoting high-level cognitive learning, high-level affective learning and effective community service. Students in her Human Rights – Human Wrongs course, a senior-level, international/comparative political science seminar, supplement reading and theoretical discussions about human rights with hands-on field work interviewing refugees applying for political asylum.

The course begins with a general introduction to international human rights law and then moves on to intensive training in U.S. asylum law, appropriate techniques for interviewing survivors of torture, and legal research and writing. Specialists are brought in to speak to the class, including a clinical psychologist, an immigration judge and an asylee (someone who has won asylum). In addition, students take a tour of the prison and attend an asylum hearing. Usually, one class period is devoted to each of these activities. Students sign a confidentiality agreement as well as a memorandum of understanding (vetted by the college's attorney) with community partners, including the Pennsylvania Immigration Resource Center (PIRC), which provides a five-hour legal seminar early in the semester. Students essentially serve as paralegals to PIRC and other local attorneys and work under the direct supervision of an attorney. Students help structure their detainees' affidavits of persecution, compile relevant country-specific human rights-conditions research and write legal briefs or memos.

As they compile documentation, students learn about the law of asylum and international human rights, but also about their *application* to individuals. Students learn first hand about the human rights conditions in other countries and what effects these conditions have on people in those countries. They learn to discern a strong case from a weak case, think critically about the evidence and hone their research skills as they progress through the stages of Bloom's taxonomy, including knowledge, comprehension, application, analysis, synthesis and evaluation (Dicklitch 2013). Students gain knowledge, develop skills, and organize and internalize values as they participate in this experiential learning course.

LOCAL POLITICS EXAMPLES: COMMUNITY-BASED RESEARCH AND ENGAGEMENT

As demonstrated above, *problem-based learning* can be combined with *service learning* by working with community agencies or groups to define the problems to be solved. *Service learning* in the field can then be combined with *community-based research* to propose solutions to these problems. Thomas Ehrlich, for example, used PBL in his (U.S.-based) civic engagement and public policy course. Ehrlich developed a forum of civic leaders to meet with students about housing and welfare rules and how new federal and state legislation had impacted public benefits. After the forum, students spent at least five hours per week in a service agency that helped welfare recipients; the students also did field projects in neighborhoods that had high populations of welfare recipients. From these field projects, each student group prepared a 'Neighborhood Study on the Impact of Welfare Reform' (Ehrlich 1999). Similarly, students in Shannon Jenkins's urban politics course worked with local government to develop a sustainable master plan for the city of New Bedford, Massachusetts, an urban area that had experienced population and economic decline. Through this experience, students developed a greater understanding of the actors and institution of city government in an urban setting, the process of urban policy development, the policy problems faced by contemporary U.S. cities, potential solutions to these problems and the limits on urban actors' abilities to solve the problems (Jenkins 2008). In addition, the course enhanced students' commitment to civic engagement and provided information useful to the community. This blending of PBL and service learning gave students in Erlich's and Jenkins's classes an opportunity to work on a 'real-world' problem while also experiencing the importance of civic-mindedness, thereby furthering the primary goal of much experiential education in the fields of political science and international relations – developing the knowledge, skills and dispositions required for students to make a meaningful difference in the world.

A QUICK WORD ABOUT ASSESSING EXPERIENTIAL EDUCATION OUTCOMES

Experiential learning focuses on *how* and *how well* students are learning, rather than focusing on *what* or *how much* students learn (Macdonald 2005). For this reason, experiential learning can create assessment challenges. With exams and traditional term papers, the professor can more clearly judge student *content mastery* than with the byproducts or final products of experiential learning projects that have no 'right' answer. Rubrics designed to assess learning outcomes demonstrated through project portfolios, oral presentations, reflective essays and reciprocal peer reviews are all appropriate forms of assessment (Macdonald 2005). As with all effective assessment, the effective assessment of experiential learning outcomes requires three things: 1) a clear understanding on the part of the instructor about what the experiential learning experiences are intended to achieve, 2) learning experiences that are aligned to the assessment regime, and 3) a strong element of debriefing and feedback (Raymond and Rosen 2013). Oral debriefing and written reflection are required for students to move from experience to learning; these reflections, if properly designed, provide important assessment data, allowing instructors to know what went well and what needs to be improved to enhance future learning experiences. Well-designed assessment instruments may also be used to produce high-quality, publishable SoTL research. See, for example, the project described in Table 30.1.[18] Whether using assessment for grading, course revisions, departmental evaluation, or publication, students must know that any grades attached to their reflections will not be based on being 'right' or 'wrong' but will, instead, be based on the thoughtfulness of students' reflections, including their metacognitive analysis about the content, process and significance of their learning experiences.[19]

NOTES

1. Association for Experiential Education, http://www.aee.org/what-is-ee (accessed 24 November 2014).
2. Cooperative education is a structured method of combining classroom-based education with practical (usually paid) work experience. For more information about the roots of this movement see Grubb and Villeneuve (1995).
3. Experiential learning focuses on the learning process for the individual. It is often used synonymously with the phrase experiential education; however, while experiential learning considers the individual learning process, experiential education refers to a broader philosophy of education. As such, it is concerned with issues such as the nature of the student–teacher relationship, the structure of educational classrooms, curricula and school systems, and the purpose – and intended learning outcomes – of the educational process. For a broader discussion of experiential education as a philosophy, see Itin 1999.
4. John Dewey, whose learning philosophy is discussed in the next paragraph, encouraged 'fruitful and creative' experiences to promote and deepen learning.
5. The author thanks the Indiana University South Bend Research and Development Committee for providing the grant that supported this project.
6. The term 'progressive' was used to distinguish this education from the traditional curriculum of the nineteenth century, which was rooted in classical preparation for the university and strongly differentiated by socioeconomic level.
7. For a good review of this literature see Bowen (2012).
8. For a detailed discussion of this problem see Bain 2004 and Bowen 2012.
9. See http://www.nsee.org/standards-and-practice (accessed 17 November 2014).
10. For more information about how to assess civic learning outcomes see chapters 25–27 in McCartney, Bennion and Simpson (2013c).
11. This framework was created by Ron Goldsmith of Ryerson University in Toronto, Ontario. See http://www.ryerson.ca/content/dam/provost/planning/archives/experiential.pdf (accessed 17 November 2014).
12. A charette is an interdisciplinary event where a specific task, problem or issue has to be creatively addressed within a short deadline, presented to experts and critiqued.
13. Both tables are based on documents produced by Ryerson University, a 'career-focused' urban university in Toronto, Ontario (Canada). Ryerson is focused on 'innovation and entrepreneurship', with an explicit mission to serve societal needs and a long-standing commitment to engaging its community. See http://www.ryerson.ca/experiential (accessed 17 November 2014).
14. For more information on the PBL approach to student learning see Chapter 31 of this book, as well as Savin-Baden (2000). For a practical guide to PBL see Duch, Groh and Allen (2001).
15. To learn more about how service learning has evolved in response to early criticisms, see McCartney (2013a).
16. See http://socialconcerns.nd.edu/faculty/cbr.shtml (accessed 17 November 2014).
17. Alison Rios Millett McCartney designed a Model UN program in which college students coach high school students after completing an international relations course. See chapter 17 of McCartney, Bennion and Simpson (2013c) for more information about this project, including college student learning outcomes. See also http://community.apsanet.org/TeachingCivicEngagement/Home/ (accessed 17 November 2014).
18. Well-designed assessment instruments may also be used to produce high-quality, publishable SoTL research. See, for example, the project described in Table 30.1. This resulted in two publications: one about the effectiveness of the student-based voter mobilization campaign (Bennion 2005) and the other about the learning outcomes of the voter registration drives on the student fieldworkers (Bennion 2006).
19. For more information about assessing experiential learning in the areas of civic, political and

international education, see McCartney, Bennion and Simpson (2013c): in chapter 25. Bennion offers an assessment toolkit providing a full range of quantitative, qualitative and mixed-methods options for assessing civic and political engagement activities. In chapter 26, Bennion and Dill provide an overview of current assessment techniques in the discipline of political science. In chapter 27, Bennion suggests ways to move forward with the rigorous assessment of experienced-based civic engagement pedagogies.

BIBLIOGRAPHY

Bain, Ken (2004), *What the Best College Teachers Do*, Cambridge, MA: Harvard University Press.
Bennion, Elizabeth A. (2005), 'Caught in the Ground Wars: Mobilizing Voters during a Competitive Congressional Campaign', *The Annals of the American Academy of Political and Social Science*, **601** (1), 123–41.
Bennion, Elizabeth A. (2006), 'Civic Education and Citizen Engagement: Mobilizing Voters as a Required Field Experiment', *Journal of Political Science Education*, **2** (2), 205–27.
Bloom, Benjamin Samuel (ed.) (1956), *Taxonomy of Educational Objectives. The Classification of Education Goals – Handbook 1: Cognitive Domain*, New York: David McKay.
Borzak, Lenore (ed.) (1981), *Field Study: A Source Book for Experiential Learning*, Beverly Hills, CA: Sage Publications.
Bowen, Jose Antonio (2012), *Teaching Naked: How Moving Technology Out of Your College Classroom will Improve Student Learning*, San Francisco, CA: Jossey-Bass.
Bransford, John D. and Ann L. Brown (2000), *How People Learn: Brain, Mind, Experience, and School* (exp. ed.), Washington, DC: National Research Council, Committee on Learning Research and Educational Practice.
Chickering, Arthur W. and Zelda F. Gamson (1987), 'Seven Principles for Good Practice in Undergraduate Education', *American Association of Higher Education Bulletin*, **39** (7), 3–7.
Damasio, Antonio R. (1994), *Descartes' Error: Emotion, Reason, and the Human Brain*, New York: Avon Books.
Damron, Danny and Jonathan Mott (2005), 'Creating an Interactive Classroom: Enhancing Student Engagement and Learning in Political Science Courses', *Journal of Political Science Education*, **1** (3), 367–83.
Dewey, John (1997 [1938]), *Experience and Education*, New York: Macmillan.
Dicklitch, Susan (2013), 'Blending Cognitive, Affective, and Effective Learning in Civic Engagement Courses: The Case of Human Rights–Human Wrongs', in Alison Rios Millett McCartney, Elizabeth A. Bennion and Dick Simpson (eds.), *Teaching Civic Engagement: From Student to Active Citizen*, Washington, DC: American Political Science Association, pp. 247–58.
Dragnski, B., C. Baser, V. Busch, G. Schuierer, U. Bogdahn and A. May (2004), 'Neuro-plasticity: Changes in Grey Matter Induced by Training', *Nature*, **427** (6972), 311–12.
Duch, Barbara J., Susan E. Groh and Deborah E. Allen (eds.) (2001), *The Power of Problem-Based Learning: A Practical 'How To' for Teaching Undergraduate Courses in Any Discipline*, Sterling, VA: Stylus Publishing.
Easley, Shawn L. (2007), 'Problem-Based Learning: An Interactive Approach to the Teaching of American Government', Paper presented at the Annual APSA Teaching and Learning Conference, 9–11 February, Charlotte, NC.
Ehrlich, Thomas (1999), 'Civic Education: Lessons Learned', *PS: Political Science & Politics*, **32** (2), 245–50.
Grubb, W. Norton and Jennifer Curry Villeneuve (1995), *Co-operative Education in Cincinnati*, Berkeley, CA: National Center for Research in Vocational Education.
High-Pippert, Angela (2003), 'Problem-Based Learning in Political Science: An Invitation', Paper presented at the Annual Meeting of the American Political Science Association, 28–31 August, Philadelphia, PA.
Hmelo-Silver, Cindy E. (2004), 'Problem-Based Learning: What and How Do Students Learn?', *Educational Psychology Review*, **16** (4), 235–66.
Itin, Christian M. (1999), 'Reasserting the Philosophy of Experiential Education as a Vehicle for Change in the 21st Century', *The Journal of Experiential Education*, **22** (2), 91–8.
Jenkins, Shannon (2008), 'Sustainable Master Planning in Urban Politics and Policy: A Service-Learning Project', *Journal of Political Science Education*, **4** (3), 357–69.
Kaunert, Christian (2009), 'The European Union Simulation: From Problem-Based Learning (PBL) to Student Interest', *European Political Science*, **8** (2), 254–65.
Kolb, David A. and Roger Fry (1975), 'Toward an Applied Theory of Experiential Learning', in C. Cooper (ed.), *Theories of Group Processes*, London: John Wiley, pp. 33–58.
Kolb, David A., Richard E. Boyatzis and Mainemelis Charalampos (1999), 'Experiential Learning Theory: Previous Research and New Directions', in Robert J. Sternberg and Li-fang Zhang (eds.), *Perspectives on*

Cognitive, Learning, and Thinking Styles, Mahwah, NJ: Lawrence Erlbaum, pp. 193–210; available at http://www.d.umn.edu/~kgilbert/educ5165-731/Readings/experiential-learning-theory.pdf (accessed 24 November 2014).

Krathwohl, David R. (2002), 'A Revision of Bloom's Taxonomy: An Overview', *Theory Into Practice*, **41** (4), 212–18.

Lewis, Linda H. and Carol J. Williams (1994), 'Experiential Learning: Past and Present. New Directions for Adult and Continuing Education', in Lewis Jackson and Rosemary S. Caffarella (eds.), *Experiential Learning: A New Approach*, San Francisco, CA: Jossey-Bass, pp. 5–16.

Macdonald, Ronald (2005), 'Assessment Strategies for Enquiry and Problem-Based Learning', in Terry Barrett, Iain Mac Labhrainn and Helen Fallon (eds.), *Handbook of Enquiry and Problem Based Learning*, Galway, Ireland: CELT, pp. 85–93.

McCartney, Alison Rios Millett (2013a), 'Teaching Civic Engagement: Debates, Definitions, Benefits, and Challenges', in Alison Rios Millett McCartney, Elizabeth A. Bennion and Dick Simpson (eds.), *Teaching Civic Engagement: From Student to Active Citizen*, Washington, DC: American Political Science Association, pp. 9–20.

McCartney, Alison Rios Millett (2013b), 'Bringing the World Home: Effectively Connecting Civic Engagement and International Relations', in Alison Rios Millett McCartney, Elizabeth A. Bennion and Dick Simpson (eds.), *Teaching Civic Engagement: From Student to Active Citizen*, Washington, DC: American Political Science Association, pp. 259–78.

McCartney, Alison Rios Millett, Elizabeth A. Bennion and Dick Simpson (eds.) (2013c), *Teaching Civic Engagement: From Student to Active Citizen*, Washington, DC: American Political Science Association.

Raymond, Chad and Amanda M. Rosen (2013), 'Simulations as Active Assessment?: Typologizing by Purpose and Source', *Journal of Political Science Education*, **9** (2), 144–56.

Savin-Baden, Maggi (2000), *Problem-Based Learning in Higher Education: Untold Stories*, first edition, Buckingham, UK: SRHE and Open University Press.

Williamson, Jonathan and Alison S. Gregory (2010), 'Problem-Based Learning in Introductory American Politics Classes', *Journal of Political Science Education*, **6** (3), 274–96.

Zull, James E. (2004), 'The Art of Changing the Brain', *Educational Leadership*, **62** (1), 68–72.

31. Best practices in Problem-Based Learning
Heidi Maurer

WHAT IS PROBLEM-BASED LEARNING?

Problem-Based Learning (PBL) emphasizes the interactive and comprehensive nature of learning. As a pedagogical approach, PBL was first developed in medical studies in the late 1960s (Albanese and Mitchell 1993, p. 52). In contrast to traditional lecture-based methods of instruction, PBL follows the underlying constructivist rationale that knowledge is context dependent and should be constructed; instead of 'just' transferring knowledge passively from professor to student in a lecture, students in a PBL setting are *actively* involved in constructing knowledge (for an overview of active learning techniques, see Ishiyama 2012).

PBL is said to lead to deep learning because students actively engage in knowledge construction by deciding independently about the relevant questions in order to solve the identified puzzle, i.e. learners mimic time and again a normal research process. Because of its collaborative setting, PBL also exposes learners to team and communication skills. The PBL set-up, furthermore, puts special emphasis on learning strategies ('learning how to learn'), as over time learners train to reflect independently on the success and shortcomings of their learning processes—guiding them to become independent and self-sustained learners (see e.g., Moust, Bouhuijs and Schmidt 2007, p. 12).

This chapter provides a first introduction to what it means to use PBL in teaching and learning activities; but, even more importantly, it discusses what kinds of aspects need to be considered when adapting PBL to harness its full potential. It first discusses the main rationales of PBL, while the second part shares best practices on two key aspects of PBL implementation: the design of appropriate assignments as a starting point and the adaptation of roles for academic staff and students. The chapter shows that PBL is a flexible tool that needs to be adapted to the learners and situation. Faculty, however, need to constantly check to what extent the underlying logic is met, so that the active, constructed and collaborative elements of learning with PBL are effectively utilized.

WHY USE PBL: ITS RATIONALE AND UNDERLYING LOGIC

PBL is a learner-centered and interactive way of learning. It is 'learning through discussion, problem solving, and study with peers' (Hmelo-Silver 2004, cited in Hmelo-Silver and Barrows 2006, p. 24). In the PBL setting, as used at Maastricht University, students are working together with their peers in small groups of up to fifteen students ('tutorials') under the guidance of an academic staff member ('tutor'). The number of lectures is restricted to one per week, while the starting point for the learning process consists of a short task, puzzle or problem descriptions ('assignments') that have been designed by the academic staff member responsible for the content of the course ('course coordinator').

Prior to consulting the materials for a specific topic, students are given the assignment and use this to collectively agree on specific questions ('learning objectives') that guide their research process of the topic at hand.

Generally, PBL is based on three core principles for successful and comprehensive learning (see Gijselaers 1996; Schmidt et al. 2009; Barrows 1996). Learning in a PBL setting: 1) follows a problem-based process of knowledge construction; 2) is learner centered; and 3) is collaborative. In the practical implementation of PBL, the three elements are often emphasized to different degrees. The chapter now turns to examining the three features in more detail, as their presence is a necessary condition to fully harness the added benefit that PBL can provide.

PBL is a Problem-based Process of Knowledge Construction

A central element of PBL is that students do not just passively receive knowledge from the instructor, but instead they are actively involved in constructing knowledge (Gijselaers 1996, p. 13; Glaser 1991). In a PBL setting, 'students learn through solving problems and reflecting on their experience' (Barrows and Tamblyn 1980, cited in Hmelo-Silver and Barrows 2006, p. 21). Two reasons identified by pedagogical research make active learning more favorable than passive knowledge transfer.

First, learning is treated as 'sense-making activity' (Hmelo-Silver and Barrows 2006, p. 34). Students do not just grab what is identified as knowledge by academic authority and memorize it, but they give meaning to facts and construct knowledge to solve a puzzle. Knowledge is thus not an abstract and objective aim for knowledge's sake, but factual knowledge becomes an instrument required to solve a task. This rationale of PBL relates smoothly to Bloom's taxonomy (Huitt 2011) about different levels of educational objectives, which starts from the idea of knowledge transfer before building up to more complex objectives, including comprehension, application, analysis, synthesis and evaluation.

Secondly, knowledge is context dependent, and learning needs to be contextualized as well. Assignments and PBL tasks often ask students to apply academic knowledge to practical ('real-world') situations. By doing so, learners establish relevance for their research steps before consulting the suggested material. More importantly, this setting helps learners to understand what the gained knowledge is applicable for. Consequently, learning in a PBL setting is ideally situating knowledge construction in contexts where academic knowledge can be used and applied.

PBL is Learner Centered

PBL is often superficially portrayed as little more than small-group teaching. And indeed, PBL as an interactive learning activity works best in groups of around twelve students. Yet, it is not only the size but also rather the quality of interaction within this small group that makes the PBL experience different.

First, *learners* (not the instructors) *identify the content* of the respective PBL cycle based on prior knowledge, interest and relevance identified by the tutorial group. The coordinator defines topics and designs assignments that trigger interest, but the tutorial group in a consensus-seeking process defines the precise learning objectives for each session. Involving learners *before* the start of the learning activity makes PBL differ considerably from other forms of active learning, in which students, for example, are asked to be in charge of implementing a task given by the instructor (e.g., preparing a presentation about some topic). In a PBL setting, students are not only active in implementing the given task, but during the pre-discussion they actively define their exact approach to the assignment. This set-up supports deep learning because learners are able to research what they are specifically interested in; learners define the relevance of and give meaning to the identified puzzle; and learners link the new topic to existing knowledge and familiar interpretations (Glaser 1991, pp. 132–3). Additionally, in discussing possible learning objectives, the group members exchange individually existing knowledge. According to neurological research, this favors deep learning again as new information is linked to previously acquired and familiar knowledge.

Secondly, in PBL, learners are not only central in defining the content of learning, but they also actively shape the *process* of learning. Students are dynamically in charge of their learning process by fulfilling the roles of chair, secretary (or whiteboard worker) and active participants during the tutorials. In the most ideal case, students run the tutorials themselves, without any intervention of the tutor: the student 'chair' runs the meeting, moderates the discussion, and ensures an efficient and engaging exchange between group members. The 'secretary' takes minutes and supports the group discussion by visualizing and making notes on the whiteboard. Yet, it is the responsibility of all group members to participate actively and make their meeting work.

By engaging in this learning process, learners mimic every time a small-scale research process (see Figure 31.1): from identifying the questions, engaging with the literature, looking for empirical evidence, formulating arguments, to presenting individual research findings to colleagues in subsequent meetings. Next to the interactive element in the small-group setting, the ample scheduled self-study time plays a major role in a PBL

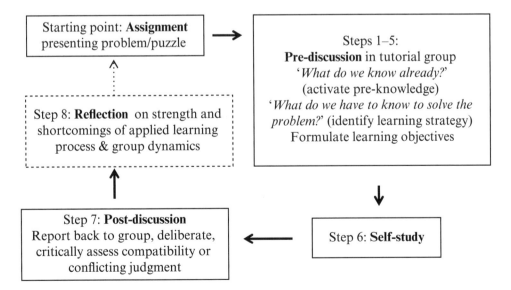

Figure 31.1   The PBL cycle

environment. Students need to extensively engage with the defined learning goals individually before then comparing and contrasting their research findings during the post-discussion. A large part of the work during the learning process therefore takes place outside of the classroom during the self-study. The pre- and post-discussions are possibilities for checking one's own understanding and deliberating among members of the team. At the end of the PBL cycle after each post-discussion, it is highly recommended to integrate a reflection moment, during which the group assesses its learning process, discusses shortcomings and agrees on potential adaptations for the next learning cycle.

Learner centeredness in PBL thus refers to two dimensions: it is the learner who defines the exact learning objectives and the strategy of how to research the posed questions in terms of content ('what is learned'). In addition, it is the learner who reflects on the chosen process and considers potential adaptations for the future to overcome experienced shortcomings ('how it is learned').

PBL is Collaborative Learning

Finally yet importantly, PBL builds upon collaborative learning by assuming that deliberation and discussion advance knowledge and understanding. During the post-discussion tutorial, members elaborate on the information that they collected, deliberate with peers, exchange views and train argumentation. Additionally, learners not only reformulate acquired knowledge in their own words and thus memorize and retain information, but they are confronted with different perceptions and lines of argument. This collaborative learning trains students in judging information provided by others, in relating arguments to their own learning and in critically assessing compatible or conflicting judgments. Hmelo-Silver and Barrows emphasize the importance of the collaborative element of PBL, as 'learning occurs as knowledge is negotiated among learners, [and] students co-construct knowledge through productive discourse practices' (Hmelo-Silver and Barrows 2006, pp. 23–4). Savery and Duffy also confirm this:

> Since understanding is an individual construction, we cannot share understandings but rather we can test the degree to which our individual understandings are compatible. [. . .] Knowledge evolved through social negotiation and through the evaluation of the viability of individual understanding. (Savery and Duffy 1995, pp. 1–2)

Because of the constant collaboration with peers and the tutor, learners become socialized to working in a group, and they train their communication skills as a result.

HOW TO USE PBL

The chapter has discussed the main rationale of PBL as a learner-centered and interactive way of learning on a conceptual level so far. While those three rationales are easy to explain, their implementation and application in practice is more challenging as they always need to be aligned with the needs, the students' background and the institutional setting. In the following sections, the chapter illustrates PBL in action as implemented in the social sciences at Maastricht University in various forms. First-year students use more structured and pre-cooked PBL materials and their learning is facilitated by the seven-step approach. With advanced students, there is more room for flexibility in design. Generally, courses run for four to eight weeks, with two tutorial meetings and one lecture per week. Each tutorial is scheduled for two hours, of which 40–50 minutes are allocated for the pre-discussion, 10 minutes for a short break and 60–70 minutes for the post-discussion. In the time between tutorials, students are expected to engage in their self-study for 10–12 hours.

The following pages illustrate in a practical manner the elements considered most crucial in the academic literature for making PBL work: appropriate assignments, adapted role conceptions of students and academic staff, and a heightened emphasis on group dynamics and skills.

DESIGNING ASSIGNMENTS THAT PUZZLE, GUIDE AND PROVIDE SPACE

Assignments provide the starting point for the tutorial group members to engage with a specific topic before they participate in the individual research process. Assignments are meant to engage with the learner, raise curiosity, link to previous knowledge of learners and guide the group in their learning process while allowing them enough space to define the relevance and questions according to their own interests and backgrounds. Assignments need to be authentic in representing a real-life scenario (Hmelo-Silver 2012, p. 10). In very practical terms, they should allow the group to be able to come to a definable puzzle and a few learning objectives to guide the self-study and to allow for a post-discussion within 50–70 minutes.

Designing assignments is a creative and enjoyable task, but even the best are rarely able to write a perfect assignment right from the start. Rather, on the contrary, revisions occur over multiple years with feedback from colleagues and students helping to gradually improve assignments. It also proved useful to involve various faculty members in the process of assignment design and to provide possibilities for exchange and training on how to write assignments for different student groups.

The process of constructing an assignment combines two different aspects: the problem generation and the structuring of the problem. While the former is about the content of the task (i.e. what is the problem presented?), the latter focuses on how the problem is presented towards the learner in the assignment. Because PBL is learner centered, the design and set-up of each assignment generally needs to be adapted to the respective student body. As with many educational activities, but even more so for PBL, the assignment designer should know as much as possible about students' backgrounds and their specific knowledge and skills levels. Overall, requirements for 'good' assignments can be summarized with three main characteristics: 1) allow deliberation (instead of just description); 2) guide the tutorial group; and 3) include a certain amount of scaffolding. At the same time, successful assignments should provide space for the learners to define their own interests and establish relevance. These three characteristics of a good PBL assignment are illustrated in more detail below.

First, the overall objective of a PBL assignment should be deliberation about an authentic real-life scenario not description. It should not only ask students to describe a certain situation or gather factual knowledge, but it should provide opportunity for

> **BOX 31.1   PBL ASSIGNMENT EXAMPLE: LEARNING ABOUT DECISION-MAKING IN A POLITICS COURSE**
>
> Your company heard a rumor that there is a new law under consideration that would considerably affect your production process. Thus, you are tasked to devise a strategy to ensure that the concerns of your company are heard: when are you going to talk to whom? Explain your choices.

> **BOX 31.2   PBL ASSIGNMENT EXAMPLE 2: LEARNING ABOUT BASICS OF INTERNATIONAL LAW IN AN INTERNATIONAL RELATIONS COURSE**
>
> Kosovo just declared independence. You are tasked by your foreign ministry to write a position paper about how to react to this unilateral declaration of independence. What recommendation will you give to your foreign minister, and what arguments will you prepare for her that she can then put forward during the planned press conference?

the multi-dimensional exploration of a puzzle (Jonassen and Hung 2008, p. 16; Hmelo-Silver and Barrows 2006, p. 24). More generally speaking, good assignments do not push learners to one perfect answer but instead allow them to experience different lines of arguments with varying conceptual and empirical emphasis. Additionally, assignments should be authentic in their contextualization while linking to students' pre-knowledge and the realities of potential future workplaces (Jonassen and Hung 2008, pp. 16–21).

The following example is taken from a politics course. The topic at hand is decision-making, and students are being asked to learn about a specific legislative procedure because of how often it is used. Yet, in an active learning logic, the understanding about this procedure could be used to solve a task, for example as shown in Box 31.1.

A second example is taken from an international relations course. You are discussing the principles of international law. Yet instead of just letting students learn the definitions, you confront them with a specific case (e.g., see the Kosovo independence declaration in Box 31.2).

In both cases, there is not one perfect answer and merely describing the concepts is not sufficient. Instead, students have to develop a line of argumentation where they use the knowledge gained as evidence to support their main claim.

Secondly, good assignments guide learners, integrate scaffolding techniques, and vary in their approach and set-up. The rule of thumb is that assignments should be as unstructured as possible, and the openness of assignments in terms of providing guidance in a specific direction needs to be adapted to the level of the learners' PBL experience. Assignments for learners who are new to active learning or to the specific disciplinary domain should provide more guidance and structure. Over time, this supportive measure can be reduced (McCaughan 2013) and assignments for experienced learners can give more freedom in defining how to solve the puzzle at hand (Hmelo-Silver 2012, pp. 11–12). This can also be used in order to vary the type of assignments that learners encounter, to scaffold the learning process and to prevent boring students with the same style of assignment repeatedly.

Schmidt and Moust (2000, p. 68) distinguish four different types of assignments based on the kind of knowledge that learners have to use in order to solve the task. Explanation problems are the least complex, where learners are asked to explain a certain situation. Fact-finding problems step one level higher in complexity as learners have to apply descriptive knowledge. Strategy problems build on those two abilities of learners, additionally asking learners to apply their knowledge and show procedural knowledge. Lastly, in moral dilemma resolution problems learners have to normatively discuss certain situations based on the knowledge they have gained. In relating those last three categories, Jonassen and Hung (2008) provide a three-dimensional categorization by distinguishing between diagnosis-solution problems, decision-making problems and situated cases that present policy problems. Policy problems provide the most openness and do not pre-define the exact puzzle at hand. In these, learners are tasked to relate the practical challenge described to an academic puzzle that they need to solve in order to come up with a practical solution (for a more detailed elaboration on types of assignments see Sockalingam 2010).

In PBL assignments, it is, however, not only the approach to the content that needs scaffolding but also the skills that will be developed through the completion of the assignment. The difficulty of skills can be increased steadily with variation, allowing all involved to focus on the training of specific academic and professional skills throughout a course. Assignments for first-year students, for example, provide the required literature, while assignments for second-year students give some tips, but students have to identify relevant readings themselves to train their ability to find and check sources for their reliability, suitability and appropriateness.

By scaffolding the complexity of the knowledge learned and skills required, we again find direct correlates with Bloom's taxonomy. In a first assignment, learners comprehend certain processes and facts. In a next step, they apply that now familiar knowledge to solve a task and/or analyze a more complex problem. At the highest level, learners have to synthesize knowledge gained from different previous assignments and evaluate the applicability of former discussed issues.

As an example, a scaffolding assignment from an EU politics course is used. A central element of EU politics courses is to teach students about various institutions that compose European governance: students learn about one institution after the other—its structure, its competences and its internal decision-making structures. This is a traditional set-up, although in reality it does not really create enthusiasm with students or provide motivation for deep learning. Yet, one can also try a more active learning appropriate approach: in a first introductory assignment, students become familiarized with the existence of different institutions, and they are pushed to think about the use and relevance of institutions more generally (see Box 31.3).

The assignment provides a quote from the treaty outlining the institutions, then a reference describing that often created institutions follow their own mind. The assignment ends with a quote explaining why a member state representative still argued for the creation of a supranational institution despite the perceived challenge of limited control. The objective of this assignment is that students question the set-up of common institutions and think about the concepts of delegation and control. In their learning objectives, students learn about the institutions and check what the objective and control mechanisms are. Once students have established this starting point, they follow up with two

> **BOX 31.3   ASSIGNMENT EXAMPLE: 'WHY INSTITUTIONS'**
>
> '1. The Union shall have an institutional framework which shall aim to promote its values, advance its objectives, serve its interests, those of its citizens and those of the Member States, and ensure the consistency, effectiveness and continuity of its policies and actions. [...]
> 2. Each institution shall act within the limits of the powers conferred on it in the Treaties, and in conformity with the procedures, conditions and objectives set out in them. The institutions shall practice mutual sincere cooperation.'
>
> Art. 13, Treaty on European Union
>
> The European Commission is often portrayed as the most 'supranational' actor, representing the European interest and being considered as the 'technical expert' of policy drafts.
> The Commission consists of different layers and levels, and critical voices warn to ignore the political impact of the European Commission, as the following quote by former Commissioner Verheugen demonstrates:
>
> 'Too much is being decided by civil servants,' said Günter Verheugen, Vice President of the European Commission in charge of Enterprise and Industry, in a frank interview on Thursday with the *Süddeutsche Zeitung*. He said commissioners sitting in Brussels had to be careful not to allow decisions on important questions fall under the control of bureaucrats with no democratic mandate. 'The whole development in the last ten years has brought the civil servants such power that in the meantime the most important political task of the 25 commissioners is controlling this apparatus. There is a permanent power struggle between commissioners and high ranking bureaucrats. Some of them think: the commissioner is gone after five years and so is just a squatter, but I'm sticking around,' he continued.
>
> EU Observer on 5 October 2006, 'Commission bureaucrats are getting too powerful', retrieved on 3 October 2011 from http://euobserver.com/?aid=22572
>
> This situation poses a traditional principal-agent dilemma for the member states. The EU institutional framework over years developed into a carefully balanced system of checks and balances that allows member states control to a certain degree, while at the same time still allowing for the benefits of installing a supranational actor.

assignments that are more complex, where they have to build on their knowledge and apply it (see example in Box 31.4). The idea is that they compare the role, competences and decision-making of institutions in different ways, rather than just describing the institutions. Since such a task would overwhelm students right at the start, we gradually build up towards more complex assignment objectives. Also, it showed that it is more conducive for PBL to build assignments upon concepts rather than descriptive and factual knowledge.

Third, successful assignments provide enough space for learners to define the learning objectives according to their pre-knowledge and their own defined relevance. Inexperienced, but also experienced, assignment designers might fall into the trap of constructing assignments that just hide the questions that they want students to ask. Box 31.5 shows what such an unsuccessful assignment might look like.

This assignment about the Maastricht Treaty describes the pillar structure, how the negotiations had been difficult and that involved parties did not agree. Assessed at a superficial level, the assignment works well as students very quickly come up with questions in a short pre-discussion. However, the problem is that they only engage with the presented material on a superficial level and can easily deconstruct what was hidden in

> **BOX 31.4   ASSIGNMENT EXAMPLE: 'EU INSTITUTIONS'**
>
> You and some of your friends are fed up with politicians and the political mood in your country and in Europe more generally. After giving it some thought you decide that you want to get involved in EU politics yourself.
>
> You think it would be most appropriate to become an MEP in the next European Parliament elections, while your friends argue that it is comparably easier to become a Commissioner. On the other hand, they claim that as MEP you can have more influence and shape policies more easily than as Commissioner. You are just not really convinced by their arguments, and therefore ask for postponing your discussion until you have had time for some background research.
>
> You consult another friend of yours who works in Brussels as an MEP's assistant. She is quite skeptical about your plans. It might not be as easy to run for MEP as you thought, while on the other hand you might have got the wrong idea about the level of discretion MEPs have in terms of representing and pushing for their own ideas and convictions. Your friend also suggests that, in case you really make it to become an MEP, you should carefully lobby and select the different posts that are available in the EP, as some are more lucrative in terms of influence than others. Yet, she also tells you that she heard from colleagues that Commissioners cannot just do and decide whatever they want, but that they are also constrained in different ways. You thank her for her insights, and prepare for the meeting with your friends to discuss if Commissioner or MEP is the right way to go. What arguments do you prepare to convince your friends? Or maybe you even changed your opinion?

the text instead of engaging with the stimulus provided and asking their own questions. This considerably hampers any positive effects of PBL.

This rather descriptive and unsuccessful assignment has subsequently been revised to become the task that is shown in Box 31.6. This revised version provides enough room for students to brainstorm and formulate their own questions; it does not describe to students what has happened, but it provides them with a few quotes from involved parties through which they can identify different perceptions and expectations. The main objective of the assignment is to make students understand that the awkward political structure of the European Union, as introduced by the Maastricht Treaty, was not a perfect plan but rather a compromise between different parties, different ideas and different preferences. Students read the assignment and formulate learning objectives in the prediscussion, which normally centers on the motivations of involved actors, the negotiation process and the implications of the Maastricht Treaty for the European integration process. Discovering how those discrepancies of the actors were solved engages students and makes them more likely to want to know how those different positions led to the outcome, which is visualized with the temple structure at the end of the assignment. This example shows that, while the content of the assignment has not been changed at all, the presentation made a considerable difference in how this assignment worked as an active learning tool to engage students and raise curiosity.

In terms of content coverage, the course set-up, sequence and depth of assignments has to provide enough time for learners to discover the puzzle independently while accounting for potential detours. Allowing learners to make 'wrong' decisions that are then rectified and letting learners 'fail' in order to learn how to do it in a more successful manner is a challenge when too much content is put into one assignment or into an entire course. Independent discovery by learners in a PBL environment generally needs

> **BOX 31.5 ASSIGNMENT EXAMPLE: 'MAASTRICHT TREATY' (TOO DESCRIPTIVE)**
>
> Many observers perceived the debacle of getting the Lisbon Treaty in force as a unique experience in European integration history. But considering the European integration process over time, it resembles precedent treaty changes that have occurred since the Single European Act. Changing the polity and politics of a political system is always tricky—also at national level. And the European Union is no exception in this regard, although it developed an elaborate mechanism for this kind of change.
>
> 1992 can be seen as the (satisfactory) conclusion of developments triggered by the Delors Commission and the SEA: the completion of the single market and the signing of the Treaty on European Union (TEU). While the TEU arguably signified a qualitative jump of the European integration process, ratification proved a difficult process.
>
> The 'temple structure' that the Maastricht Treaty gave to the European Union was unique and complex: the European Community pillar was based on the community method, while CFSP and JHA followed a different logic of cooperation. The Treaties of Amsterdam and Nice made only relatively marginal changes, while the Treaty of Lisbon, in contrast, altered the institutional structure profoundly:
>
>> 'Unlike the Single European Act and the Treaties of Amsterdam and Nice, the Treaty of Lisbon provides for a fundamental change of the existing treaty system. It dissolves the pillar structure of the European Union and formally confers legal personality to the Union. As regards its significance for the development of the European Union, it hence resembles the Treaty of Maastricht'.[1]
>> German Federal Constitutional Court (2009)
>
> Content-wise, the consecutive treaty revisions had allowed for an incremental progress of completing the single market, of enlarging and of deepening. Formal institutions were added, and the areas of exclusive and shared competences of the European Union increased steadily over time, among other changes.
>
> 1. German Federal Constitutional Court (30 June 2009). Act Approving the Treaty of Lisbon compatible with the Basic Law. Retrieved on 22 February 2010 from http://www.bundesverfassungsgericht.de/entscheidungen/es20090630_2bve000208en.html.

considerably more time than if learners would just be presented with what the academic staff member considers the correct answer. Thus, PBL courses have to provide enough space and time to allow the learners to discover the topics independently and without having to rush from one issue to the next. This also implies that in a PBL set-up less content can be covered than in a purely lecture-based course. Advocates, however, argue that what is lost in quantity is made up for by the considerably improved quality of the learning process, which emphasizes deep learning and understanding for the learner instead of the transfer of factual knowledge. In practice, it also proved better to cover less in an intensive manner than to rush learners from one topic to the next without them having enough time to reflect and process the actively constructed knowledge.

Another aspect needing consideration when adapting to a PBL environment is the issue of feedback and assessment. The group process of investigating puzzles needs constant feedback and reflection moments for learners to improve how they work together. Next to flexible feedback moments, two standardized reflection moments help

> BOX 31.6   ASSIGNMENT EXAMPLE: 'MAASTRICHT TREATY' (REVISED)
>
> 'We're not here just to make a single market—that doesn't interest me—but to make a political union.'
> – Jacques Delors
>
> 'Those in favour of the creation of a European state want to see all European co-operation channelled through the institutions established by the Treaty of Rome. We do not accept that model.'
> – Douglas Hurd, UK Foreign Secretary (1991)
>
> 'We now seek political unification, the construction of a United States of Europe.'
> – Helmut Kohl, German Chancellor (1991)
>
> 'The "Community" or "Union" is a phenomenon unique in history. [...] This result [the Maastricht Treaty] was not handed to us on a plate. It follows a year of intensive and difficult negotiations in which all sides demonstrated that they were prepared to move together down the road to a united Europe and to compromise where necessary in order to do so. [...] It is now fair to say that from a historical perspective Maastricht has certainly been the most important EC summit since the signing of the Treaties of Rome.'
> – Douglas Hurd (1992)
>
> 'I should like to have achieved more definite progress and to have moved now to extend the range of areas for which the Community is responsible. But we had to make a choice between conflicting claims. This was necessary and reflected our determination to achieve a result in Maastricht—which demanded compromise on all sides. [...] In Maastricht we have broken new ground in various areas. [...] We had to decide whether we were prepared to let the whole Treaty fall over this issue.'
> – Helmut Kohl (1991)
>
> 1992 can be seen as the (satisfactory?) conclusion of developments triggered by the Delors Commission and the SEA. While the TEU arguably signified a qualitative jump of the European integration process, its negotiation and especially its ratification proved a difficult process.
>
> The 'temple structure' that the Maastricht Treaty gave to the European Union was unique and complex: the European Community pillar was based on the community method, while CFSP and JHA followed a different logic of cooperation. Even nowadays, after the formal abolition of the pillar structure in the Lisbon Treaty, this approach of 'a temple proving stronger than a tree' is still considered as the main characteristic for scholars to identify the EU as a political system *sui generis*.

students to reflect on their approach to learning and researching: at the beginning of the course, students are asked for a self-evaluation in which they assess their strengths and weaknesses in terms of skills and/or content that they want to put special emphasis on. At the mid-term and/or end of the course, students repeat this exercise and can reflect on their progress in terms of tackling their weaknesses. Next to this individual assessment, regular group reflections facilitate the students' development into independent learners (but note: groups need clear instructions for reflection, e.g., 'What two aspects work really well in our group? What two aspects should we consider improving in what manner?'). Assessment in a PBL environment is a debatable issue: while the traditional literature emphasizes that progressive exams should be used, our faculty, for example, use traditional exams (papers, essays, collective exams), assuming that PBL is the method of learning but that knowledge is still the outcome of the learning process. Yet, the form of the exam questions in a PBL environment should fit the style of learning that students have engaged in.

ADAPTING TO NEW ROLES: STUDENTS LEARN ACTIVELY, TEACHER BECOMES FACILITATOR

Most of us even today—in the century of the information society—are still trained to follow the traditional way of teaching and learning: the teacher stands in front and tells the students what to learn and how to learn it. Getting suddenly acquainted to active and independent learning with 10–15 group members in an effective and pleasant manner does not just not happen by itself: it requires an adjustment period, training, repeated reflections and adjustments. Involved actors, therefore, need to adapt to their new roles in a PBL environment. This adaptation process is best facilitated by raising awareness and training exercises but most importantly by constant reflection opportunities.

New staff should receive an introductory training that familiarizes them with the underlying logic of PBL. More than just this introduction, however, staff should experience PBL themselves, for example by mimicking a PBL assignment process. For a sustainable exchange about PBL teaching experiences, voluntary workshops throughout the teaching period or other activities can be a useful means to raise awareness for the distinct aspects of teaching and learning in a PBL environment. Additionally, it can be helpful to provide group facilitation techniques and materials.

Academic staff members have to learn to switch from the idea of an intervening and controlling lecturer into the role of a questioning and guiding facilitator. Tutors have to internalize the idea that it is not about 'teaching' as in 'lecturing' but that it is about 'learning'. As such, the tutor's task is not primarily to contribute content expertise, but instead to facilitate group learning processes, group interaction and skills development. Useful facilitation strategies are to ask open-ended questions, push for explanations, help students to sum up and re-voice what was said or encourage students to generate hypotheses instead of just presenting empirical data (for an interesting overview of facilitation techniques that tutors can use in a PBL setting, see Barrows as referred to in McCaughan 2013, p. 14; Hmelo-Silver and Barrows 2006, pp. 21–32). The most difficult task of a facilitator is to judge when to intervene and how. The tutor should not immediately step in when the group goes off track or is misunderstanding an argument. Experienced tutors develop a good feeling for when to allow the group to attempt to find the right track or when it is necessary to step in to ensure that students do not go home with a wrong perception of knowledge in mind. Even more so, the way of intervening should be as subtle and as minimally invasive as possible to ensure that attention is not on the tutor (as expert) but goes back to the group effort of explaining and understanding a certain topic.

Spending some time at the beginning of each new course to get to know the group members and to engage in some group-building exercises can facilitate the working mode of tutorial groups. PBL can, for example, highlight positive and distorting behaviors of group members in a tutorial meeting. In addition, tutors need to be aware of the role-modeling effect that is often observed in PBL environments. Because of the close interaction between tutor and learners, non-verbal behavior of the tutor is observed, picked up and mimicked by learners. This can be used as a helpful tool, for example when the tutor for newcomers to PBL performs the task as chair or secretary so that learners have an example to start with and then can adapt those roles according to their own ideas. Yet, it also means that facilitators have to adhere to formal and informal group rules as well. If the group, for example, decided to sanction distracting or inappropriate behavior (e.g., arriving late, ringing of mobile phones or hiding behind a laptop screen etc.), a facilitator would need to follow the same rules.

Students also have to adapt to their new role in an active learning environment, especially if they are already socialized to a more traditional lecture-based environment. Before students even join a PBL activity, they should be made aware of this different learning approach: they have to work more independently in the self-study, they have to be actively involved in their tutorial groups and they must work closely with other group members.

In addition, in order to help students ease into the way of working actively in a group, Maastricht University developed the seven-step approach (often also called 'seven-jump') to facilitate and structure students' learning processes within the PBL framework, especially during the pre-discussion. In order to familiarize students with a process of arriving together at a few interesting and relevant learning objectives and to help students to mimic a simple research process, the seven-step approach tackles each assignment in the same manner. In the *pre-discussion* of an assignment, students follow the first five steps of the seven-step approach, followed by the self-study and the post-discussion:

1. *Clarification of terms and words*: The whole group begins at the same starting point. This can also include discussing illustrations or quotes that the assignment provides.
2. *Formulation of a problem statement*: The whole group agrees on a common problem that frames the whole assignment and provides a title for the session. Problem statements can take the form of more traditional titles, but sometimes they are also formulated as broader research questions or provoking statements. What is important is that the problem statement captures the 'puzzle' that the group wants to solve instead of just describing the wider topic.
3. *Brainstorm*: The problem statement guides all next steps, and group members brainstorm about the problem statement. The group discusses different assumptions about the answer to our problem statement, activates prior knowledge and shares expectations with group members.
4. *Classification and structuring of brainstorm*: The group identifies common patterns and arranges the different ideas in a few categories that in the next step inform the learning objective.
5. *Formulation of learning objectives*: As the last step of the pre-discussion, students use the categories created out of the structured brainstorm to formulate common learning objectives. This way of formulating learning objectives in the ideal case reflects the different approaches to the wider topic that students have agreed to research. It is important that learning objectives are formulated clearly and are to the point, as otherwise the post-discussion in the tutorial group goes in too many different directions.
6. *Independent self-study*: Each group member answers the learning objectives independently, prepares evolving questions and produces points for discussion.
7. *Post-discussion*: This occurs in the next meeting (for more detailed elaboration on the seven-step approach, see Maurer and Neuhold 2012).

This pre-structured approach can support groups of students unfamiliar with PBL at the beginning, while more experienced students have internalized the way of working together towards the learning objectives quite quickly and are even able to adapt the process in their own way to make it work for the group.

Overall, while group interaction and peer communication are central elements of PBL in practice, they can also clearly hamper the success of a group working together. Regular reflection moments on how to improve group and communication skills are therefore central in a PBL environment. Those can be done at the end of each post-discussion, but they should especially be used when the group process during an assignment has not worked so well or group members have suggestions for improving the group work. These reflective exercises also facilitate the development of each tutorial member as a self-directed learner and train students for future teamwork situations in the professional environment.

CONCLUSION

This chapter has discussed and illustrated the main tenets of PBL learning works best if it is learner centered and collaborative and if it centers on a problem-based process of active knowledge construction. The emphasis in such a learning environment is not only on expert knowledge and the content of learning but also on skills and learning as a process. In a practical manner, the chapter has reflected on the experience of how to implement PBL by focusing on two core aspects: the design of appropriate assignments and the adaptation of roles by academic staff and students. The aim of this chapter was to raise awareness of those aspects that need to be considered when applying and implementing PBL in its various forms. The chapter has shown also that, as with most learning techniques, there is no one perfect way of using PBL, but the rationales underlying PBL can be adapted flexibly to different contexts and situations.

REFERENCES

Albanese, Mark and Susan Mitchell (1993), 'Problem-Based Learning: A Review of Literature on Its Outcomes and Implementation Issues', *Academic Medicine*, **68** (1), 52–81.

Barrows, Howard S. (1996), 'Problem-Based Learning in Medicine and Beyond: A Brief Overview', in L. Wilkerson and W.H. Gijselaers (eds.), *Bringing Problem-Based Learning to Higher Education: Theory and Practice*, San Francisco, CA: Jossey-Bass, pp. 3–11.

Gijselaers, Wim (1996), 'Connecting Problem-Based Practices with Educational Theory', in LuAnn Wilkerson and Wim H. Gijselaers (eds.), *Bringing Problem-Based Learning to Higher Education: Theory and Practice*, San Francisco, CA: Jossey-Bass, pp. 13–21.

Glaser, Robert (1991), 'The Maturing of the Relationship between the Science of Learning and Cognition and Educational Practice', *Learning and Instructions*, **1**, 129–44.

Hmelo-Silver, Cindy (2012), 'International Perspectives on Problem-Based Learning: Contexts, Cultures, Challenges, and Adaptations', *Interdisciplinary Journal of Problem-Based Learning*, **6** (1), doi: http://dx.doi.org/10.7771/1541-5015.1310.

Hmelo-Silver, Cindy and Howard Barrows (2006), 'Goals and Strategies of a Problem-Based Learning Facilitator', *Interdisciplinary Journal of Problem-Based Learning*, **1** (1), doi: http://dx.doi.org/10.7771/1541-5015.1004.

Huitt, William (2011), 'Bloom et al.'s Taxonomy of the Cognitive Domain', *Educational Psychology Interactive*, Valdosta, GA: Valdosta State University, available at http://www.edpsycinteractive.org/topics/cogsys/bloom.html (accessed 3 October 2013).

Ishiyama, John (2012), 'Frequently Used Active Learning Techniques and Their Impact: A Critical Review of Existing Journal Literature in the United States', *European Political Science*, **12**, 116–26.

Jonassen, David H. and Woei Hung (2008), 'All Problems Are Not Equal: Implications for PBL', *Interdisciplinary Journal of Problem-Based Learning*, **2** (2), doi: http://dx.doi.org/10.7771/1541-5015.1080.

Maurer, Heidi and Christine Neuhold (2012), 'Problems Everywhere? Strengths and Challenges of a Problem-Based Learning Approach in European Studies', paper prepared for the Higher Education Academy Social Science Conference, 28 and 29 May, Liverpool, available at http://www.academia.edu/attachments/30896834/download_file (accessed 3 November 2013).

McCaughan, Kareen (2013), 'Barrows' Integration of Cognitive and Clinical Psychology in PBL Tutor Guidelines', *Interdisciplinary Journal of Problem-Based Learning*, **7** (1), article 2.

Moust, Jos, Peter Bouhuijs and Henk Schmidt (2007), 'Features of Problem-Based Learning: An Introduction', in Jos Moust, Peter Bouhuijs and Henk Schmidt (eds.), *Introduction to Problem-based Learning: A Guide for Students*, Gronigen/Houten: Nordhoff Uitgevers, pp. 9–17.

Savery, John R. and Thomas T. Duffy (1995), 'Problem Based Learning: An Instructional Model and Its Constructivist Framework', *Educational Technology*, **35** (5), 31–8.

Schmidt, Henk G. and Jos H. Moust (2000), 'Towards a Taxonomy of Problems Used in Problem-Based Learning Curricula', *Journal on Excellence in College Teaching*, **11** (2), 57–72.

Schmidt, Henk G., Henk T. Van Der Molen, Wilco W.R. Te Winkel and Wynand H.F.W. Wijnen (2009), 'Constructivist, Problem-Based Learning Does Work: A Meta-Analysis of Curricular Comparisons Involving a Single Medical School', *Educational Psychologist*, **44** (4), 227–49.

Sockalingam, Nachamma (2010), *Characteristics of Problems in Problem-Based Learning*, Rotterdam: Erasmus University Rotterdam, EUR Publishing.

32. Developing student scholars: best practices in promoting undergraduate research
James M. Scott

Many factors contribute to a rich and successful academic experience for undergraduates. When carefully integrated into a sound academic foundation and program, meaningful undergraduate research experiences are a vital and valuable element that fosters creativity, intellectual curiosity and a sense of discovery (see e.g., Boyd and Wesemann 2009; Hodge, Pasquesi and Hirsch 2007; Hu et al. 2008; Hunter et al. 2008; Malachowski 2002). Undergraduate research, according to the Council on Undergraduate Research (2011), is '[a]n inquiry or investigation conducted by an undergraduate student that makes an original intellectual or creative contribution to the Discipline'. Through such research experiences, undergraduates learn in ways that both complement and supplement traditional learning in classrooms and course-work. The immersive experience, substantive specialization and application of classroom knowledge deepen learning and independent thinking (e.g., Healey 2005; Lopatto 2003). Effective research experiences extend disciplinary understanding and help to shape career goals, while building student confidence (and credentials) for future endeavors. The mentoring relationships that characterize the best undergraduate research experiences are proven to benefit both student and faculty success and satisfaction (e.g., Malachowski 1996; Osborne and Karukstis 2009).

As part of a strategy of applied and active learning, undergraduate research experiences promise significant contributions to engaged learning and student success during and after their undergraduate programs (e.g., Hunter et al. 2008; Petrella and Jung 2008). According to Beckham and Hensel (2009, p. 43) undergraduate research experiences result in more actively engaged and motivated students, contribute to more organized and creative thinking, and often lead students to pursue graduate education with better preparation for success. Their written and oral communications skills are better developed and they develop the habit of asking 'what if' and 'why' questions that serve them in many areas of their lives. Designing, establishing and implementing effective undergraduate research opportunities is therefore a worthy endeavor for faculty and administrators. What foundations, components, strategies and practices best contribute to effective undergraduate research opportunities? This chapter reviews underlying ideas, approaches and practices central to successful undergraduate research opportunities, presenting a range of options and observations for interested practitioners to consider.

FOUNDATIONS AND CONCEPTUALIZATIONS OF UNDERGRADUATE RESEARCH

A useful conceptual foundation for the role and approach to undergraduate research distinguishes between two dimensions (Healey 2005; Healey and Jenkins 2009): the role

Best practices in promoting undergraduate research 385

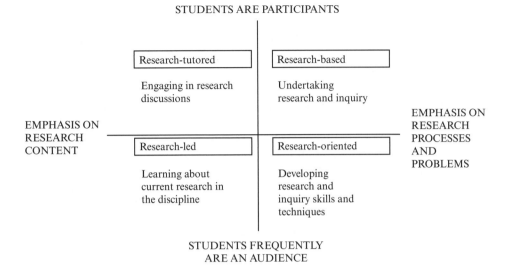

Source: Healey and Jenkins (2009).

Figure 32.1 Approaches to undergraduate research

of the student (as audience or as participant) and the research emphasis (on content or on process/problems). Combining these two dimensions produces a simple 2×2 conception of the foundations of undergraduate research and inquiry. As Figure 32.1 shows, this conceptualization yields four approaches:

- *Research led*: learning about current research in the discipline, typically by including scholarly research articles in course reading assignments.
- *Research oriented*: developing research skills and techniques, typically through an undergraduate scope and methods course, which may or may not be required of all political science students.
- *Research tutored*: engaging in research discussions, typically through small, focused seminars in which students and the faculty member(s) engage in intensive examination of a problem, research questions and scholarly work.
- *Research based*: undertaking research and inquiry, with students actively engaged in independent scholarly research projects, often in the form of a senior thesis or capstone project.

Two important observations rest on the conceptualization. First, note that the most common approaches involve classroom applications exposing students to the research of others. According to Healey and Jenkins (2009), most undergraduate research efforts involve approaches below the horizontal axis of Figure 32.1, but the *most effective* strategies and programs include elements from the upper quadrants of the figure. However, emphasizing approaches from the upper quadrants to the exclusion of the lower is undesirable and likely to be ineffective as well. Combining classroom and out-of-classroom opportunities is also preferable to classroom-only approaches.

Second, conceptualizing the foundations of undergraduate research in this way suggests the need to design experiences that incorporate activities in each quadrant. Whether constructing a suite of undergraduate research opportunities to offer to students in sequence over their 4-year career (e.g., Hodge, Pasquesi and Hirsh 2007; Karukstis and Elgren 2007), or a specific program or opportunity (e.g., a summer research program), incorporating elements of all four quadrants is essential to a successful strategy. Students should be introduced to political science research, engage in intensive discussion of research problems, receive foundational research training in the concepts, approaches and skills needed, and have independent research experiences (e.g., Boyd and Wesemann 2009; Hu et al. 2008; Lopatto 2003; Malachowski 2002). Moreover, the best approaches, whether *across* a sequence over four years or *within* a standalone program in a summer or semester, move students from the lower left to the upper right quadrants of Figure 32.1 systematically (see also Malachowski 2002, 2004). To the extent that these foundational matters are considered and addressed in the design and during the practice of undergraduate research, the resulting programs and opportunities are likely to be more effective and cohesive.

STRATEGIES AND APPROACHES

In the absence of unlimited time, resources and staff, effective strategies and approaches to undergraduate research in political science necessarily involve a variety of choices and tradeoffs, each of which brings a unique mix of benefits and costs. According to Beckham and Hensel (2009), substantial differences in the approaches to and outcomes of undergraduate research occur between and within institutions depending on the emphases placed on a variety of dimensions (see Table 32.1). Effective undergraduate research programs can be designed in a number of ways, but emphasizing one or another feature has important consequences. For example, as Beckham and Hensel (2009, p. 40) note,

Table 32.1 Issues and choices in undergraduate research programs

Student, process centred	Outcome, produce centred
Student initiated	Faculty initiated
All students	Honors students
Curriculum-based	Co-curricular fellowships
Collaborative	Individual
Original to the student	Original to the discipline
Multi- or interdisciplinary	Discipline-based
Campus/community audience	Professional audience
Starting year one	Capstone/final year
Pervades the curriculum	Focused

Source: Beckham and Hensel (2009).

To the degree that the primary purpose of undergraduate research is to foster student learning, the emphasis might be on helping students to move along a developmental trajectory in the practice of research. The developmental process might begin in the first year of college and continue until the student is capable of doing independent research under the supervision of a faculty mentor. If, however, the primary understanding of undergraduate research is the production of a sophisticated product, or to provide competent students to assist in faculty research, then only the most promising students will be invited to participate in the research project.

Hence, such choices and tradeoffs should be the subject of discussion and conscious decision, not incidental consequences.

While Table 32.1 lays out a series of interlocking dimensions along which choices and tradeoffs exist, consider just four central issues that should be addressed through discussion and design, and that have notable implications for students, resources and staffing.

- *Curricular or co-curricular programs?* Are the research opportunities intended to pervade the academic program of political science majors and thus be integrated into a sequence or series of courses, or offered as opportunities outside of the normal semester course selections?
- *All students or some students?* Is the research program or opportunity intended to achieve learning objectives for all students, or to engage the best students (particularly those interested in graduate school) in intensive experiences that challenge and development beyond the ordinary?
- *First year or last year?* Are the research opportunities best started in freshman-level experiences and developed throughout the 4-year program, or reserved for capstone projects at the end of programs?
- *Faculty projects or student projects?* Are the research opportunities targeted at independent, faculty-mentored student projects that place the student in the driver's seat, or as faculty-driven projects in which mentoring occurs as students contribute to faculty projects?

Such practices and approaches each have merit, but involve significant opportunity costs that should be recognized and embraced by design. Moreover, to be most effective the particular formulations adopted should carefully reflect and support the campus culture and institutional mission and vision. With these broad parameters in mind, let us briefly review a range of approaches to and components of undergraduate research in political science, along with some suggestions and observations about effectiveness.

Course-based Approaches

Approaches to undergraduate research may involve research opportunities within the parameters of required and/or elective course work. In general, there are at least two main avenues in which course-based approaches can be pursued. In the first, students are introduced to research principles and thought-ways early, in a freshmen research seminar that stresses research-led strategies and introduces core research methods, with a significant research project as a course assignment as a typical core course feature.

Subsequent research skills and training may be developed in a sophomore-level scope and methods course, which may be an elective, required for all students or for those in particular degree tracks. Junior- and senior-level students then typically complete course-based research paper assignments in upper-division courses and/or in capstone courses (e.g., Hodge, Pasquesi and Hirsh 2007; Karukstis and Elgren 2007). With some exceptions, this avenue stresses students and the learning process, and emphasizes the critical and analytical thinking and problem-solving skills involved in research more than the specialized training and products of research. The more such course-based strategies are required of all students, the more this tends to be true.

In the second avenue, research and inquiry are integrated into courses as a pedagogical strategy. This avenue may involve similar core courses as the first avenue, but the hallmark of this approach involves problem-based or inquiry-based learning strategies embedded in a range of substantive courses, not simply those designated as research methods or research courses.[1] Roy, Kustra and Borin (2003) provide a good description:

> Teaching through 'inquiry' involves engaging students in the research process with instructor support and coaching at a level appropriate to their starting skills ... An inquiry course:
>
> - Is question driven, rather than topic or thesis driven.
> - Begins with a general theme to act as a starting point or trigger for learning.
> - Emphasizes asking good researchable questions on the theme, and coaches students in doing this.
> - Builds library, interview and web search skills, along with the critical thinking skills necessary for thoughtful review of the information. Coaches students on how to best report their learning in oral or written form.
> - Provides some mechanism (interviews, drafts, minutes of group meetings, bench mark activities, etc.) to help students monitor their progress within the course.
> - Draws on the expertise and knowledge of the instructor to model effective inquiry and to promote reflection.

According to Healey and Jenkins (2009, pp. 21–2), summarizing the work of others, inquiry-based learning can be 'structured – where lecturers provide an issue or problem and an outline for addressing it; guided – where lecturers provide questions to stimulate inquiry, but students are self-directed as regards exploring these questions; and open – where students formulate the questions themselves as well as going through the full inquiry cycle'. Which form of inquiry-based learning is most appropriate depends in part on course-level and student starting skills.

The principal benefits of these approaches rest in the diffusion of critical, analytical and research skills, as well as creative, inquiry-oriented thinking across all students in a given program. Key challenges involve the demands of addressing and serving all students in a given class or program – despite varying career interests and academic abilities – and the resource/staffing demands inherent in organizing and structuring courses and a program around these approaches. Among the many concerns are managing class size (typically smaller) to enable the instructional time and quality needed, and the related problem of staffing sufficient courses (smaller class sizes yields the demand for more classes.

EXTRA-COURSE BASED APPROACHES

Undergraduate research programs targeted at a subset of political science students typically involve extra-course based approaches in which special opportunities are provided to select students (often through self-identification or competitive application processes). In these approaches, students work through intensive research-based experiences outside normal courses, with faculty direction and supervision.

The least formal or institutionalized of such approaches involves independent study/research opportunities for students supervised by a faculty member. Such opportunities may be quite rewarding for high-initiative students and highly engaged faculty members, but because of their informal and idiosyncratic nature both the effectiveness and value of this approach are very uneven. In the best situations, a department-wide consensus and policy for the nature, structure and process of independent study/research opportunities, as well as the requirements and conditions under which they may be offered, improves the consistency and quality of the experience. In general, however, attempting to build and maintain an undergraduate research program in such ad hoc fashion is inefficient and ineffective.

A second common avenue in this category is the use of a capstone experience for providing undergraduate research experiences. According to the Boyer Commission (1998, p. 27), in a research-based capstone experience, 'All the skills of research developed in earlier work should be marshaled in a project that demands the framing of a significant question or set of questions, the research or creative exploration to find answers and the communication skills to convey the results to audiences both expert and uninitiated in the subject matter'. Capstone experiences may be required of all students, or offered as electives to select students.

As vehicles for undergraduate research experiences, capstones can be very effective, but their success turns on their structure. In short, research capstones work best as the culmination of a sequence – not simply as an integrative experience at the end of general coursework, but as the last stage of a sequence of courses and experiences that introduce students to research, equip them with research methods skills and guide them through their projects. For example, the University of California, Berkeley describes their capstone sequence in three stages:[2]

Stage One: Exposure
In stage one, students learn to recognize a good research question and are exposed to methods of approaching the problem, including identifying, gathering, evaluating and synthesizing evidence, information and ideas ... In this stage, faculty members typically are fully responsible for structuring the research/creative problem and the approach used for investigation/creative exploration. Through engagement with exposure-level activities, students begin to gain an understanding of the process by which knowledge is created and the ability to distinguish important questions from unimportant questions in a given field of knowledge.

Stage Two: Experience
Students in this stage acquire research skills such as conducting a literature review, coding data or learning qualitative interviewing techniques, paleography or laboratory bench skills. They may have opportunities to practice structuring a research/creative problem and plan for investigation/exploration, which they execute under close faculty supervision. Or they may contribute

to the conceptual development, execution and analysis of an ongoing research/creative project that a faculty member has defined.

Stage Three: Capstone
Students undertaking a capstone project marshal the skills needed to develop their own research or creative questions and to initiate investigations and explorations the outcome of which is largely unknown . . . under the guidance of a mentor. Capstone experiences also typically include an opportunity to present the results of inquiry or creative engagement to a larger audience.

A third common approach is the use of senior or honors thesis experiences. Typically an option in many academic programs, often required of select students (e.g., participants in university or departmental honors programs), and occasionally required of all students in some institutions (e.g., Princeton University), an undergraduate thesis provides an intensive independent research experience under the guidance of a faculty mentor or faculty committee. The selective nature helps to better ensure (although not guarantee) the engagement of the students and the relevance of the experience to their professional and personal goals/development.

Undergraduate thesis programs are most effective when conducted across multiple semesters. A typical two-semester sequence provides a first-semester tutorial in which students formulate a project while participating in seminars and workshops focused on supporting and guiding the development of a viable research project. The second semester is then devoted to completing the project under the active and careful mentoring of faculty. Such a thesis sequence is best when two features are present: 1) it is embedded within course/program requirements that introduce students to research principles and approaches, provide training and experience in research methods, and include research-based learning prior to the thesis itself; 2) it rests on deep and extensive mentoring relationships and practices in which project mentors are engaged early in the first semester at the project-formation stage.

A fourth avenue is the use of special summer or academic-year programs to provide intensive research experiences to select students. These experiences may be offered through university-wide programs (e.g., the UROP – Undergraduate Research Opportunity Program – established at a great many collegiate institutions) to which students apply in a competitive process. They may be discipline- or college-specific, interdisciplinary, or open to participation by students in any discipline. Such programs typically provide some student and faculty support through fellowships, travel or research funds and/or stipends, and are themselves funded through internal and external monies. Although rare for political science, granting institutions provide support for undergraduate research in a variety of ways. For example, the Research Experience for Undergraduates program at the National Science Foundation invites site proposals for extended residential research programs, usually in the summer.

Such summer research experiences provide good opportunities for a select few students in an intensive, focused setting. Students are typically able to devote their attention to their research experience in the relative freedom of the summer – especially if the program provides significant student financial support that reduces the need for summer employment – and faculty mentors are able to provide support to student projects in the absence of normal semester teaching requirements. Programs that provide extensive mentoring, offer training and support in seminars and workshops, and foster a sense of community among students (and with faculty mentors) engaged in research efforts (in part through common training and through community-building efforts) are generally more effective than those that are more individual-based efforts.

FACULTY–STUDENT COLLABORATIVE APPROACHES

The final category of approaches in this brief review involves student research experiences within the context of faculty scholarship rather than independent student projects. In this approach, select students are enlisted in faculty-initiated research projects and engage in work to help develop and complete those projects. Three general avenues are typical. First, faculty members may recruit high-quality students to serve as undergraduate research assistants. Students work with faculty members in a variety of capacities – collecting and/or entering data, searching and reviewing literature, and so on – and learn of the research process through their involvement in the faculty project. Students receive support for their work, perhaps through individual faculty grant funds, or through department funds designated for student research assistants. Second, particularly high-quality students may be engaged as co-authors in a faculty project. They may perform many of the same tasks as a research assistant, but they may also participate in the formulation of the project and in preparation of the manuscript by contributing to the writing as well. Third, faculty members in political science departments with graduate programs may assemble faculty–graduate student–undergraduate student research teams that involve both of the preceding elements but also include three-layered mentoring: faculty to graduate student; faculty to undergraduate student; graduate student to undergraduate student.

Collaborative approaches may be richly rewarding for undergraduates. Engaging high-initiative and high-quality upper-level students in such intensive and immersive experiences working closely with a faculty member can provide insights and training uncommon in other avenues. By definition, however, such experiences are reserved for a highly select set of students and thus do not often reach the rest of the student body. This is necessary because trusting a student to contribute directly to faculty scholarship involves a level of confidence, trust and commitment that must necessarily be restricted because it involves the faculty member's own work and scholarly reputation. Moreover, to the extent that undergraduate students are involved in the early stages of the project – its conception, formulation and design – the experiences tend to be more effective and consequential for the students. Enabling and supporting students to develop their own projects related to the joint work is also an effective way to promote and support student scholarship, as students move from supportive to independent roles in the process. These approaches come with a cost, however. To be effective undergraduate research experiences, substantial mentoring, coaching, discussion and reflection must be incorporated into the opportunity. Faculty members must commit to and plan for significant time teaching, training and coaching for these experiences to be as valuable for student research training as they are for faculty productivity. Finally, such approaches are best implemented in conjunction with those offering broader participation and benefits for the students in a program.

SOME KEYS TO EFFECTIVE UNDERGRADUATE RESEARCH EXPERIENCES

Considering the foundational matters and various options and approaches, what makes for the most effective undergraduate research experiences?[3] Although a compendium of observations on this question would be extensive, drawing on two decades of personal experience in the design and implementation of undergraduate research programs in political science[4] and key insights of the scholarship on undergraduate research practices, two areas in particular may be emphasized in the context of this discussion: 1) organizing the experience; 2) effective and efficient mentoring.

Organizing for Success

Good undergraduate research programs develop by design, not happenstance. Whatever the form or approach, a number of considerations and practices improve the experience for both students and faculty. First, note two broad foundational matters of program design:

- Most broadly, undergraduate research experiences are more effective when efforts are made *to integrate the quadrants* of Figure 32.1. As noted earlier, a given opportunity, or a more general curricular system emphasizing research for undergraduates should involve elements and activities from all four quadrants systematically, with a trajectory that moves students from lower left to upper right – i.e., from research led to research based.
- Whether it is a specific research program or opportunity, or a broader research curriculum, more effective experiences *combine training and doing*. For research experiences to yield maximum benefits, undergraduate students need both process and project learning – the research skills and training gained from scope and methods course and other research skill development, and the learning derived from immersion in a project.

Second, in the context of particular research opportunities, several additional observations may be offered:

- Although easy to overlook, undergraduate political science students benefit substantially from coaching and *direction on the standard template* for an article-format scholarly manuscript. To be sure, alterations and deviations from the standard format are appropriate and necessary, but undergraduates should learn and follow the template thoroughly and well. Deviating from it comes with experience, which they do not have. For example, in the Democracy, Interdependence and World Politics Summer Research program at Texas Christian University, students have used *The Guide to Writing Graduate Political Science Projects* (http://psci.unt.edu/~aje0004/~enterline.htm) created by Dr. Andrew Enterline and shared with the program since 2005 as their template.
- As students and faculty work on the relevant research projects, the experience should *mirror the structure of the research process*. Mentoring and training should

proceed from the formulation and justification of effective research questions through the development of theory/hypotheses rooted in and building on existing scholarship to research design, evidence collection and analysis. To the extent that support and training is integrated into and parallels the project developments, students are more likely to design and complete a successful project. When possible, it is very helpful to *workshop the pieces of the project* as they develop, so that training and project development go hand in hand.

- Although student research experiences are often focused on plunging into the relevant literatures and/or collecting evidence/data, much gain occurs when substantial time is devoted to the formulation of a good, focused research question and the development of 'the story' or theory/argument of the project. *Focusing on the early steps* forces students to think about the 'how', 'why' and 'what if' of the relationship they wish to explore, contributing to better research design and results. Devoting time and resources to student efforts to 'tell the story' underlying the investigation of the relationship between A and B is essential.

- Project development and completion should be structured, with *accountability and checkpoints along the way* to ensure student progress. Such structure also provides multiple points of feedback for students. These points of structure and accountability are important throughout the experience, but they are particularly valuable during the 'grunt' phase of the project – the evidence collection phase after the initial excitement and creativity of project formulation and theorizing, and before the enthusiasm and satisfaction of results and analysis.

- Research experiences for undergraduates should *finish publicly*. There are many routes for this, including research symposia, university showcases, thesis presentations and conference presentations. Completed research projects should be both disseminated and acknowledged/celebrated.

The Importance of Mentoring

Perhaps the most essential element of effective undergraduate research experiences is the faculty mentoring on which it depends. In the absence of good mentoring, undergraduate research rarely succeeds, so maximizing the quality and impact of mentoring is critical. According to Osborne and Karukstis (2009, p. 42), mentorship 'is a serious, collaborative interaction between the faculty mentor and the student' that engages the student in inquiry, and in which the mentor 'guides the student into deeper intellectual engagement' while focusing equally on 'the student's development and on the results or product of the scholarly or creative project'. As this description suggests, the faculty mentor plays multiple roles supervising, coaching, facilitating, training, guiding and supporting the student, and mentoring involves both process and product emphases. It is both richly rewarding for students and faculty, and time-consuming (e.g., Boyd and Wesemann 2009; Childs et al. 2007; Clark 1997; Lopatto 2003; Malachowski 1996). According to many studies, 'deep engagement in undergraduate research with a faculty mentor is positively correlated with improvement in student grades, first-year to second-year retention rates, persistence to graduation, and motivation to pursue and succeed in graduate school' (Osborne and Karukstis 2009, p. 45; see also Ishiyama 2002; Ishiyama and Hopkins 2002). The benefits of good mentoring include student cognitive and behavioral development, satisfaction, learning, and personal/professional gains (e.g., Seymour et al. 2004).

Productive and effective mentoring thus requires commitment and interest on the part of the faculty member, and necessitates a 'student-first' approach to the endeavor (Malachowski 2004). Effectiveness is increased with:

- Establishment of a contract laying out roles and responsibilities for both students and faculty members. Such a contract might also outline project schedules and meeting patterns. When students are engaged in faculty projects (i.e., in collaborative approaches), such a contract should specify the extent of student use of the project data and the appropriate attributions in current and future work.
- Effective mentoring focuses on the research stages of the project, from broad formulation to completion, and involves specific and targeted guidance for and during each stage.
- Effective mentoring requires regular meetings and accountability.
- Effective mentoring requires prompt and extensive feedback, and blocks of time for face-to-face discussion.
- Effective mentoring involves both process mentoring, focused on student learning and development, and project mentoring, focused on project construction and completion.
- Effective mentoring progresses through stages, with direction and guidance more prevalent at the outset, and support and student empowerment/autonomy more prevalent later (Malachowski 1996, pp. 92–3).

OBSERVATIONS AND CONCLUSIONS

Effective undergraduate research programs and experiences need multifaceted and extensive support. This support ranges from institutional commitments to department commitments to individual faculty commitments. It involves resources, time, recognition and reward, and the achievements of both the student-scholars and the faculty mentors must be celebrated. Of course, gaining the support of the institution, department faculty and students will depend on the context of the institution, but Healey and Jenkins (2009, pp. 80–81) offer a series of suggestions for achieving support and institutionalization, as shown in Table 32.2.

There is no 'optimal' practice or set of practices for successful undergraduate research programs. Effectiveness depends on tailoring practice to the particular mix of opportunities and programs being considered or addressed. It is helpful, however, to consider undergraduate research as a part – an important one, but just one – of a complex of active and experiential learning approaches that enrich student learning and development and prepare them better for future endeavors. As Figure 32.2 suggests, viewed in this way, undergraduate research is perhaps best understood as a component of interrelated and interlocking programs that also include internships, study abroad and service learning opportunities. Thus, while some elements of undergraduate research (e.g., inquiry-based learning) may be beneficial for all students, it is not necessary for the most extensive undergraduate research experiences to be extended to every student since

Table 32.2   Strategies for support of undergraduate research

A.	Develop supportive institutional strategies and policies
1.	Embed in vision and teaching and learning and research strategies of university.
2.	Develop supportive institutional curricula frameworks and structures.
3.	Link undergraduate research and inquiry to institutional policies for employability.
4.	Link undergraduate research and inquiry to institutional policies for widening participation.
5.	Link undergraduate research and inquiry to institutional policies for civic and community engagement.
B.	Encourage and support student awareness and experience of undergraduate research and inquiry
6.	Embed undergraduate research and inquiry from day students enter university.
7.	Raise students' awareness of research.
8.	Provide opportunities for selected students to undertake undergraduate research and inquiry within and outside the curriculum.
9.	Provide opportunities for all students to undertake undergraduate research and inquiry within and outside the curriculum.
10.	Have students investigate issues that are of importance to the university or other students.
11.	Value the role that student organisations can play in supporting undergraduate research.
12.	Celebrate undergraduate research and inquiry.
13	Provide support and encouragement to students undertaking undergraduate research and inquiry.
C.	Ensure institutional practices support undergraduate research and inquiry policies
14.	Ensure quality assurance, quality enhancement and institutional assessment processes and policies support students as researchers.
15.	Ensure appropriate learning spaces are available to support undergraduate research and inquiry.
16.	Align student support from library, information and communication technology services and laboratories with needs of students undertaking undergraduate research and inquiry.
D.	Encourage academic staff awareness and support and reward engagement with undergraduate research and inquiry
17.	Increase academic staff awareness of undergraduate research and inquiry.
18.	Provide support to academic staff with regard to professional development so that they are encouraged to become engaged in undergraduate research and inquiry.
19.	Provide incentives and rewards for academic staff to support undergraduate research and inquiry, particularly through workload planning, institutional and departmental recruitment, criteria for appointment, performance review and promotion processes.

Source: Healey and Jenkins (2009).

some will benefit more from other applied/experiential learning opportunities. These approaches can be integrated for some students.

In 1998, the Boyer Commission (1998, esp. pp. 15–22, 27–8) urged the development and integration of undergraduate research into undergraduate programs. Consistent with these recommendations, the discussion in these pages suggests that an ideal framework for a well-designed undergraduate research program would involve two

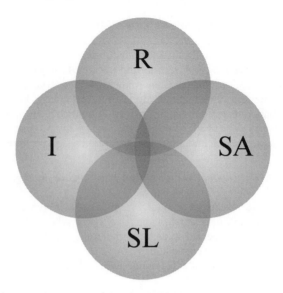

Note: I = internship; R = research; SA = study abroad; SL = service learning.

Figure 32.2 Undergraduate research in context

components: 1) structures, processes and support for extensive faculty mentoring; 2) a program designed to engage students early (in a freshman research experience or through inquiry-based courses), provide training and skills (through research methods requirements/options), and culminate in an intensive research experience (a thesis or capstone, summer program and/or faculty–student collaboration). As Osborne and Karukstis (2009) suggest, the benefits of such opportunities potentially extend to all students through the transformed coursework, to select students through the elective opportunities they can access, to faculty, and to the broader institution as well.

NOTES

1. There is an extensive literature into inquiry-based and problem-based teaching. For entry points, see Blackmore and Cousin (2003), Brew (2003, 2006), Jenkins and Healey (2009), Kreber (2006), and Spronken-Smith and Harland (2009).
2. See Preparing Students for Successful Capstone Experiences, at http://vpapf.chance.berkeley.edu/accreditation/ee_essays_1.html (accessed January 2014).
3. There is a broad literature on this question. Good entry points include Boyd and Wesemann (2009), Hodge, Pasquesi and Hirsh (2007), Hu et al. (2008), Jenkins and Healey (2007), Karukstis and Elgren (2007), Lopatto (2003), and Malachowski (2002, 2004).
4. In addition to the insights offered by the extensive scholarship on this matter, the author also relies on and incorporates observations derived from the development, implementation and maintenance of the Democracy, Interdependence and World Politics Summer Research Program, an NSF-supported Research Experience for Undergraduates (2005–present), as well as relevant undergraduate research programs at Texas Christian University (the author's current institution) and previous institutions at which the author has worked.

BIBLIOGRAPHY

Barnett, R. (ed.) (2005), *Reshaping the university: new relationships between research, scholarship and teaching*, Maidenhead, UK: McGraw-Hill/Open University Press.
Beckham, M. and N. Hensel (2009), 'Making explicit the implicit: defining undergraduate research', *CUR Quarterly*, **29** (4), 40–44.
Blackmore, P. and G. Cousin (2003), 'Linking teaching and research through research-based learning', *Educational Developments*, **4** (4), 24–7.
Boyd, M. and J. Wesemann (eds) (2009), *Broadening participation in undergraduate research: fostering excellence and enhancing the impact*, Washington, DC: Council on Undergraduate Research.
Boyer Commission on Educating Undergraduates in the Research University (1998), *Reinventing undergraduate education: a blueprint for America's research universities*, Stony Brook, NY: State University of New York at Stony Brook.
Boyer Commission on Educating Undergraduates in the Research University (2003), *Reinventing undergraduate education: three years after the Boyer Report*, Stony Brook, NY: State University of New York at Stony Brook.
Brew, A. (2003), 'Teaching and research: new relationships and their implications for inquiry-based teaching and learning in higher education', *Higher Education Research & Development*, **22** (1), 3–18.
Brew, A. (2006), *Research and teaching: beyond the divide*, London: Palgrave Macmillan.
Chang, H. (2005), 'Turning an undergraduate class into a professional research community', *Teaching in Higher Education*, **10** (3), 387–94.
Childs, P., M. Healey, K. Lynch, L. McEwen, K. Mason O'Connor, C. Roberts and C. Short (2007), *Leading, promoting and supporting undergraduate research in the new university sector*, National Teaching Fellowship Project.
Clark, B.R. (1997), 'The modern integration of research activities with teaching and learning', *Journal of Higher Education*, **68** (3), 242–55.
Council on Undergraduate Research (2011), *CUR mission statement*, available at www.cur.org/about_cur (accessed 7 June 2014).
Healey, M. (2005), 'Linking research and teaching: exploring disciplinary spaces and the role of inquiry-based learning', in R. Barnett (ed.), *Reshaping the university: new relationships between research, scholarship and teaching*, Maidenhead: McGraw-Hill/Open University Press, pp. 30–42.
Healey, M. and A. Jenkins (2006), 'Strengthening the teaching–research linkage in undergraduate courses and programmes', in C. Kreber (ed.), *Exploring research-based teaching: new directions in teaching and learning*, San Francisco, CA: Jossey-Bass/Wiley, pp. 45–55.
Healey, M. and A. Jenkins (2009), *Developing undergraduate research and inquiry*, York: The Higher Education Academy.
Hodge, D., K. Pasquesi and M. Hirsh (2007), 'From convocation to capstone: developing the student as scholar', keynote address at the Association of American Colleges and Universities Network for Academic Renewal Conference, 19–21 April, Long Beach, California, available at www.miami.muohio.edu/president/reports_and_speeches/pdfs/From_Convocation_to_Capstone.pdf (accessed 11 May 2013).
Hu, S., S. Scheuch, R. Schwartz, J. Gaston Gayles and L. Shaoqing (2008), *Reinventing undergraduate education: engaging college students in research and creative activities*, ASHE Higher Education Report, **33** (4), San Francisco, CA: Jossey-Bass.
Huber, M.T. (2006), 'Disciplines, pedagogy, and inquiry-based learning about teaching', in C. Kreber (ed.), *Exploring research-based teaching: new directions in teaching and learning*, San Francisco, CA: Jossey-Bass, pp. 69–77.
Hunter, A.-B., T.J. Weston, S.L. Laursen and H. Thiry (2008), 'URSSA: evaluating student gains from undergraduate research in the sciences', *CUR Quarterly*, **29** (3), 15–19.
Ishiyama, J. (2002), 'Does early participation in undergraduate research benefit social science and humanities students?', *Journal of College Students*, **36**, 380–86.
Ishiyama, J. and V. Hopkins (2002), 'Assessing the impact of a graduate-school preparation program on first-generation, low-income college students at a public liberal arts university', *Journal of College Student Retention*, **4**, 393–405.
Jenkins, A. and M. Healey (2007), 'Critiquing excellence: undergraduate research for all students', in A. Skelton (ed.), *International perspectives on teaching excellence in higher education*, London: Routledge, pp. 117–32.
Jenkins, A. and M. Healey (2009), 'Developing the student as a researcher through the curriculum', in C. Rust (ed.), *Improving student learning through the curriculum*, Oxford: Oxford Centre for Staff and Learning Development and Oxford Brookes University, pp. 1–21.
Karukstis, K. and T. Elgren (2007), *Developing and sustaining a research-supportive curriculum: a compendium of successful practices*, Washington, DC: Council on Undergraduate Research.

Katkin, W. (2003), 'The Boyer Commission report and its impact on undergraduate research', in J. Kinkead (ed.), *Valuing and supporting undergraduate research*, New Directions for Teaching and Learning 93, San Francisco, CA: Jossey-Bass, pp. 19–39.

Kreber, C. (ed.) (2006), *Exploring research-based teaching: new directions in teaching and learning*, San Francisco, CA: Jossey-Bass.

Lopatto, D. (2003), 'The essential features of undergraduate research', *CUR Quarterly*, **24**, 139–42.

Malachowski, M. (1996), 'The mentoring role in undergraduate research', *CUR Quarterly*, **17**, 91–106.

Malachowski, M. (2002), 'What is essential for a first-rate undergraduate research program?', President's Column, *CUR Quarterly*, **23**, 57.

Malachowski, M. (2004), 'The importance of placing students first in designing research programs at predominately undergraduate institutions', *CUR Quarterly*, **24**, 106–8.

National Conferences on Undergraduate Research and Council on Undergraduate Research (2005), *Joint statement of principles in support of undergraduate research, scholarship, and creative activities*, available at www.ncur.org/ugresearch.htm (accessed 11 May 2009).

Osborne, J. and K. Karukstis (2009), 'The benefits of undergraduate research, scholarship, and creative activity', in M. Boyd and J. Wesemann (eds), *Broadening participation in undergraduate research: fostering excellence and enhancing the impact*, Washington, DC: Council on Undergraduate Research, pp. 41–53.

Petrella, John K. and Alan Jung (2008), 'Undergraduate research: importance, benefits, and challenge', *International Journal of Exercise Science*, **1** (3), available at http://digitalcommons.wku.edu/ijes/vol1/iss3/1 (accessed 2 June 2014).

Roy, D., E. Kustra and P. Borin (2003), 'What is unique about inquiry courses?', available at http://cll.mcmaster.ca/resources/misc/whats_unique_about_inquiry.html (accessed 4 August 2013).

Seymour, E., A. Hunter, S. Laursen and T. DeAntoni (2004), 'Establishing the benefits of research experiences for undergraduates: first findings from a three-year study', *Science Education*, **88**, 493–534.

Spronken-Smith, R.A. and T. Harland (2009), 'Learning to teach with problem-based learning', *Active Learning in Higher Education*, **10** (2), 138–53.

33. Teaching international relations with film and literature: using non-traditional texts in the classroom
Jennifer K. Lobasz and Brandon Valeriano*

INTRODUCTION

Does interstellar diplomacy belong on an international relations (IR) syllabus? How about little green men? If the answer to both questions is, as we suggest, 'Yes', then will *Mars Attacks!* serve just as well as *War of the Worlds*? These questions are plausible rather than ludicrous insofar as instructors are increasingly willing to use films, television shows and novels in the university classroom. This move represents not only a pedagogical strategy but also IR scholars' growing acceptance of the use of popular culture as a resource for thinking through the discipline's central questions (Weldes 2003; Nexon and Neumann 2006; Hunt 2007; Grayson et al. 2009).

Film and literature have always had the capacity to inform and instruct as well as entertain. While Hollywood blockbusters and graphic novels surely count as non-traditional texts in IR, we hold that they can be just as useful for understanding politics today as earlier pop culture artifacts such as *Uncle Tom's Cabin*, *Birth of a Nation* and *The Jungle* were in their own time.

We also argue that courses built around popular culture texts as described in this chapter enhance student learning. As documented in Valeriano (2013), surveys and evaluations over the course of three years suggest that the film approach is at least as successful as conventional textbook-based introductions to IR. Students in the film-based classes received higher average grades than their counterparts in the traditional entry-level class, and reported higher levels of retention and satisfaction as well.

In this chapter, we assess the scholarship concerning the place of popular culture texts in teaching IR, and reflect on our own experiences in teaching film- and literature-centric courses. We conclude with lessons from the field and a list of selected works that we recommend for classroom use.

NON-TRADITIONAL TEXTS IN THE IR CLASSROOM

Teachers of introductory-level courses face a perennial dilemma: how to engage students who demonstrate varying degrees of interest in and prior exposure to the subject matter. Political science and IR majors may sit alongside those who had simply needed to fulfill an elective requirement and were attracted by the course's time-slot. Indeed, finding course material suitable for everyone from the self-taught expert in minor World War II battles to the 18-year-old with a vague grasp of history and little awareness of current events can be a challenge.

One approach to this problem is to supplement—or possibly even jettison—the traditionally assigned textbook in such courses. Even when textbooks are well written and attractively designed, they still lack the overarching dramatic narratives of novels and feature films. Thus we argue that it is the *stories*, and only incidentally the special effects or trendy genres, that make these non-traditional texts useful for teaching IR. Gregg (1998, p. 4) points to film in particular for its capacity 'to dramatize the undramatic' aspects of global politics by scaling abstract theories and concepts down to the level of individual characters and their stories. Simpson and Kaussler (2009, p. 425) concur by writing that films 'encourage interest, help research, and illustrate aspects of international politics that may not be written in books or articles'.

We contend that this process of illustration is true of both novels and films. As we discuss below, Ursula K. Le Guin's *The Left Hand of Darkness*, for instance, deftly dramatizes the often subtle intricacies of cross-cultural communication and diplomacy through its tale of interplanetary envoy Genly Ai and his mission to establish first contact with two feuding states on a distant and isolated world. Much like the *Star Trek* television and movie franchise that scholars have recognized for addressing the challenges of liberal internationalism and other relevant topics too numerous to list here (see Weldes 1999; Neumann 2001; Jackson and Nexon 2003), Le Guin's science fiction novels bring important theoretical debates to life for students who might otherwise find them irrelevant or inaccessible.

Stories, whether written in books or projected onto screens, serve as compelling points of entry to our discipline. Fiction, perversely, makes the stakes of global politics appear *real* to our students, and demonstrates why the study of IR is important and meaningful. Moreover, rather than 'dumbing down' the course or teaching to the lowest common denominator, our approach serves even those stellar students with a strong command of world history and passion for theory. In addition to drawing connections between fictional texts and the historical cases with which they are familiar, these students further benefit from being forced away from their known store of facts in order to reconsider their assumptions about how states and other international actors behave in various contexts. In the words of Nexon and Neumann (2006, p. 12), 'Popular culture thus serves as a medium for what critical analysts of science fiction call "ontological displacement"'. Such works invite us to step back from our ingrained suppositions about a certain phenomenon and our vested interests in ongoing debates to gain a different perspective upon our social world.

Do note that canonical expertise in science fiction, war movies or any other genre is not a prerequisite for success with using non-traditional texts to teach IR and related subjects. Just as students benefit from the ontological displacement referred to above, so might the instructor delving into an unfamiliar niche of film or fiction.

FILM IN THE IR CLASSROOM

George W. Bush was reportedly enamored with *High Noon* (1952), the classic Western in which a lone, formerly retired marshal must stand his ground against a band of outlaws. Media reports leading up to the U.S. invasion of Iraq in 2003 were consequently quick to portray both Bush and the country itself in the Gary Cooper role, an image seized upon by war supporters and detractors alike. As the popularity of *High Noon* metaphors for debating the scope of U.S. responsibilities to intervene across the globe illustrates, popular culture can provide a powerful medium for understanding foundational concepts and competing perspectives in world politics. This is as true in the classroom as in the Oval Office, and in this section we discuss our experiences incorporating film in particular within IR courses.

Valeriano first began teaching a film-based 'Introduction to International Relations' at the University of Illinois at Chicago, and has continued in various forms and formats for five years. Films are typically sandwiched between a half-hour pre-movie lecture and a half-hour post-movie wrap up and discussion. The pre-movie lecture is important because it allows the instructor to introduce concepts and to discuss facts about the screenwriter, director and historical context of the movie in order to prepare the viewer. Two hours are generally reserved for watching the movies during class. Time is reserved after the movie to reflect and discuss the implications of the viewing experience and the connection between the film and concept. This can either be done through normal discussion or group exercises where the students have to pick a part of the movie that illustrates a key concept. In explaining the concept to the class, the student is is able to internalize the idea.

We hold that students should be encouraged to watch assigned movies with more attention to the illustration of course concepts than to acting prowess, special effects or irrelevant plot intricacies, but this is a choice open to the instructor. The goal is not to dive into the subtext or hidden meanings of a film, but to use the film to illustrate concepts in more vivid ways than any text can. The instructor may then schedule a session for focused discussions of core concepts approximately every fourth or fifth class meeting in order to revisit and reinforce prior topics. A class such as this should focus on a dialogue between the concept and the illustration of the concept, reinforcing the understanding of abstract ideas in students who are often disconnected from history.

Generally, there are four areas to cover in a course that utilizes film to communicate lessons. The first section concerns morality, human nature and the roots of human behavior. *Lord of the Flies* (1963) famously addresses each of these topics, and provides an engaging and entertaining introduction to the course. Another useful film to examine is *The Fog of War* (2003), which covers critical lessons in the conduct of foreign policy, in addition to remorse, decision-making and the consequences of actions. Finally, this section can be wrapped up with an examination of the nature of death, killing and survival in the international system using *All Quiet on the Western Front* (1930). It is useful to the have the students remember that we are often talking about life and death, real issues of consequence on the international sphere. Academia and IR theory can feel remote from the quotidian concerns of everyday people, and *All Quiet* helps remind us of the actual human beings who affect and are affected by global politics.

The next section of the course introduces realism, liberalism and alternative approaches to the study of IR. While Gregg (1998) finds that 'the realist school has been dominant in films about international relations' (p. 10), and points to the prevalence of state-centric portraits of conflict within an anarchic global system, one can find excellent illustrations of both alternative mainstream theories and critical theoretical perspectives nevertheless. Table 33.1 lists and discusses some popular choices (as does Valeriano 2013).

Table 33.1 Films and IR

Topic	Film	Date	Issues
Realism	*300*	2006	National Interest, Power
	Casablanca	1942	Sovereignty
	The Godfather	1972	Balance of Power
	Munich	2005	Power Politics, Remorse
Liberalism	*Wilson*	1944	Democracy, Institutions
	The Quiet American	2002	Colonialism, Intervention
	Breaker Morant	1980	Law of War
Constructivism	*Judgement at Nuremberg*	1961	Memory
	Hotel Rwanda	2004	Genocide, Culture
	Battle of Algiers	1966	Terrorism, Insurgency, Culture
Alternatives	*Gandhi*	1982	Ethics
	District 9	2009	Ethnic Conflict
	Wag the Dog	1997	Diversionary War

Note: *300* can also be used to discuss the influence of domestic politics and the importance of symbols. The use of *300* must come with warnings about its cultural insensitivity and bastardization of history.

Although we have largely refrained from suggesting documentaries, we find two that are especially noteworthy for their success in the classroom. The first, *The World According to Sesame Street* (2006), examines international co-productions of the children's television show, touching on issues that range from gender norms and human rights to nationalism and conflict resolution. The second, *The Invisible War* (2012), provides a powerful indictment of sexual assault in the U.S. military, and has already become required viewing for officers in the U.S. Army.

Once the major theories are introduced, instructors are free to delve into particular issue areas such as migration, environmental politics and international political economy, among many others. Those interested in nuclear strategy, for example, enjoy an embarrassment of riches, beginning with the phenomenal *Dr. Strangelove or: How I Learned to Stop Worrying and Love the Bomb* (1964). Additional options include another comedy co-starring Peter Sellers, *The Mouse That Roared* (1959), and *Thirteen Days* (2000), a dramatization of the Cuban Missile Crisis.

One important aspect of this pedagogical approach is to give the students freedom to engage a film and its relation to global politics on their own terms. The final project for the class asks students to choose from a list of key topics covered in most IR textbooks. Students are then responsible for identifying a film that helps to illustrate their topic, and writing a long paper that explains how they would use this film to communicate the lesson to their classmates. Most students jump at a chance to connect their topic to a favorite film, quickly finding the assignment is not as simple as they had thought. To help, the students are provided a long list of movies that potentially have a connection to IR concepts.

Originality is highly valued in this assignment. The best papers are those that use movies that do seem to illustrate a concept very well at first glance, but constructing an argument, linking it to the film and then explaining this connection is a tough process that in some ways makes the student understand the entire point of the class and the method used to teach the class. We have also found that this assignment encourages students to remain engaged to the very end of the course, while requiring them to demonstrate proficiency in understanding, applying and synthesizing the discipline's foundational concepts.

SCIENCE FICTION LITERATURE IN THE IR CLASSROOM

Novels—however thrilling the plot or beautiful the prose—are admittedly less attractive to many undergraduate students than the films discussed above. At the same time, our experiences and those of others who have taught similar literature-based courses demonstrate that this approach can work, particularly when students have the ability to self-select into the class based upon their own interests. Although works from any number of literary genres might profitably appear in the IR classroom, in this section we narrow our focus to science fiction in order to present a more cohesive set of recommendations and suggested texts. This choice also reflects what seems to be a growing cottage industry of IR scholars drawing upon the sometimes overlapping genres of science fiction and fantasy in both their research and their teaching (Weldes 2003; Nexon and Neumann 2006; Ruane and James 2008; Dixit 2012).

The notion that science fiction might provide insight into the study of political life is not as far-fetched as it initially sounds. Indeed, for a genre purportedly focused on the future, science fiction has long been recognized for its ability to speak to concerns of the present (Neumann 2001). At the same time, science fiction provides scholars and teachers of IR with more than just a mirror to reflect issues in the 'real world'. As Dixit (2012) notes, 'In popular culture, science fiction has a benefit of being considered "not real", and as such, its representations of international relations and security can take on varied forms' (p. 291).

Since 2012, Lobasz has taught a 'Social/Science/Fiction' seminar for first-year students in the Honors Program at the University of Delaware.[1] The purpose of the course is to intersperse classic or otherwise well-regarded science fiction novels with social science articles in order to explore the challenges and possibilities entailed with alien encounter. 'Aliens' in this case refers not to the actual or potential existence of extraterrestrial life, but to a more prominent theme in IR: the Other. The course is structured such that students alternate reading journal articles and book chapters with six to seven science fiction novels. Like the film course discussed above, students should be encouraged to focus less on matters of plot and characterization, and more on the relevance that these novels have for exploring themes of the course. The idea is less 'to seek out new worlds' than to strive for a more nuanced understanding of our own, and of the fears and wonder that accompany, as astronomer and science fiction author Carl Sagan memorably titled his only novel, *Contact*.

The course begins with Hall (1996), and consideration of who (or what) 'counts' as an alien. The next two to three weeks focus on 'Alien Attack', and typically include *The War of the Worlds* by H.G. Wells and *Ender's Game* by Orson Scott Card. Read in conjunction with Lasswell (1941), students consider how states, intergovernmental organizations and non-state actors might relate to an unprecedented common external threat.

Both novels depict humanity as facing existential peril from aliens. Both also recognize humans themselves as fully capable of annihilating peoples and species, which can spark student discussion of circumstances in which mass killing and population removal is considered horrifying and those in which it appears unexceptional.

The next section, 'Alien Anthropology', pairs Geertz's (1972) classic 'Deep Play: Notes on the Balinese Cockfight' and a chapter on contrasting accounts of Captain Cook's last voyage (Hacking 1999) with Card's *Speaker for the Dead* and Le Guin's *The Left Hand of Darkness*. In *Speaker for the Dead*, set three millennia after the events of *Ender's Game*, human colonization of the universe is overseen by the Starways Congress. The bulk of the relevant plotline concerns various species' struggles toward mutual intelligibility. Interspecies relations in *The Left Hand of Darkness* are more advanced than those in *Speaker*, but they are no less regulated and with no fewer chasms in cross-cultural communication. Difference in *Left Hand* is not only political and cultural but also sexual and reproductive.[2] The novel suggests that genuine communication requires an understanding of the Other that is born through empathy and, ultimately, love. In addition to discussing the preconditions necessary for communicating across vast differences, students can also compare and contrast the foundational assumptions and policies of the Starways Congress versus those of its counterpart organization in Le Guin's world, the Ekumen. Which approach is more ethical? More likely? What, if anything, do the two approaches lack?

'Translations and Unknowable Aliens' serves as the concluding theme, in which students read *Wild Seed* by Octavia Butler, *Watchmen* by Alan Moore and Dave Gibbons, and *His Master's Voice* by Stanislaw Lem in conjunction with Malgrem's (1993) 'Self and Other in SF: Alien Encounters'. *Wild Seed*, set in the era of the transatlantic slave trade, departs from previously assigned novels in that the main characters are alien but not extraterrestrial. One promising avenue for class discussion concerns the nature of power relations within the novel's formal and informal modes of slavery and servitude. How should we understand the relationships between and among slaves, slave traders and owners, freed slaves and non-slaves? Students might also examine the role that race, gender, social class and ability play within systems of domination and subordination, and the degrees of communication and companionship possible therein.

If the immortal antagonist of *Wild Seed* is ultimately unknowable, as Butler suggests, so too is he incapable of truly understanding what it means to be human. *Watchmen*, widely regarded as a graphic novel masterpiece, includes a character faced with similar challenges.[3] In Moore and Gibbons' alternate history set in 1985 New York, the U.S. has won the Vietnam War, Richard Nixon remains president, and the Cold War is on the verge of going nuclear. While all of the main characters experience alienation—a major theme of the book—Doctor Manhattan stands apart as the most alien. Indeed, as the Doomsday Clock counts down to nuclear Armageddon, the super-human Doctor Manhattan grows increasingly distant from his human origins, and from humanity itself. Class discussion at this point can return to the Hall (1996) chapter to revisit the question of what makes one human, and the extent to which shared identities and interests are prerequisites to understanding.

Finally, *His Master's Voice* expands upon the issues raised by *Wild Seed* and *Watchmen* to ask what would happen if alien and human modes of communication were radically incommensurable. The novel takes place at a secret government installation in the Nevada desert where the U.S. Department of Defense has sequestered a group of scientists, mathematicians and other academics to study and ultimately translate a message from outer space. While *His Master's Voice* is a challenging text, and many students are likely to miss Lem's dry humor, this richly philosophical account of a Manhattan Project-like endeavor helps to weave together a number of the threads that have been picked up and dropped throughout the course. Promising topics include threat construction, bureaucratic politics, research ethics and, most importantly, the prospect of encountering and the possibilities for communicating across radical difference.

As with more traditional discussion-based seminars, the success of such a course is largely dependent upon students' willingness to complete the assigned reading on time. Instructors should consider incorporating multiple strategies to reinforce timely completion of reading assignments such as requiring regular written response pieces and other short writing assignments and making class participation a significant component of students' final grades. Lobasz has had success with requiring students to post their reading responses to a shared class weblog, and to provide substantive comments to posts written by their peers. Each week the students had the choice of whether to respond to specific questions posted by the instructor, or to pursue their own avenues of inquiry. Given that the class blog was viewable by the public, read and commented upon by their peers and made up a significant portion of their grade for the course, the assignment provided a powerful incentive for students to keep up assigned reading.

Of course, care should also be taken to ensure that students are given enough time to read particularly challenging works. As students are working their way through a novel such as *His Master's Voice*, for example, instructors will want to limit class discussions to no more than three chapters at a time, and may even wish to build in time to watch a thematically relevant movie or television episode in order to give students a chance to catch up on their reading. Instructors might also consider being frank with students about the relative amount of effort and time likely to be demanded by each book. Students who begin *Speaker for the Dead* with the expectation that it will be as quick and easy to digest as its prequel, *Ender's Game*, will be unpleasantly surprised and unlikely to have budgeted a sufficient amount of time to complete their assignment.

Student response to this class has been overwhelmingly positive, with many students reporting in their formal course evaluations that it had 'opened [their] eyes', 'changed the way [they] think', and 'made [them] ask different kinds of questions'. Although classroom discussions of cultural and political difference and of the power relations attached to these differences can become emotionally and politically fraught in some contexts, we found that introducing these topics through fictional narratives and imagined aliens can help lessen both defensiveness and immediately polarized reactions.

LESSONS FROM THE FIELD

Our enthusiasm does not come without reservations, and we offer the following recommendations based on our experiences teaching non-traditional material.

Films and Novels should be Explicitly Tied to Course Themes and Objectives

Weber (2001, p. 282) cautions against a casual or loosely planned approach to incorporating popular films, which may leave students feeling bored or directionless. Tempting as it may be, instructors should resist the urge to assign a book or movie simply because it is popular, or a personal favorite. Relatedly, one should also resist attempts to turn classes into book clubs or film appreciation societies. As important and enjoyable as these texts are in their own rights, the point of incorporating fiction is not to conduct comprehensive literary or cinematic analyses but to provide students with another avenue for engaging with global politics. This is not the forum in which to get lost in plot nuances or character details. Students resent the waste of their time, and rightfully so. Instructors must come prepared to demonstrate, or to help students recognize, the text's relevance for understanding global politics.

One might deliver a brief introductory lecture, as described in the film section above, or circulate discussion questions prior to class so that students have a preliminary framework with which to appreciate the political elements of the text.

A simple checklist might be in order. Does the film or text communicate class concepts better than any lecture could? If I describe the use of the film to a lay person, would they question the film based on preconceived notions? (Put more simply, will someone laugh?) Could the tone or execution of the film or text overwhelm the students and distract them from focusing on the lesson? Is the connection between the text and the concept so clear that it might seem odd to teach the concept again without the aid of the text? Answering affirmative to these questions should help the instructor avoid clichés and traps.

Avoid the Clichéd and Simplistic

Beware narratives that fail to offer more than a plucky group of misfits who must band together to defeat the enemy, for example, or that hew too closely to 'Great Man' accounts of history. There are few heroes in IR, and heroic myths place undue emphasis upon individuals at the expense of the collective actors typically analyzed in IR courses.

Those who assign Orson Scott Card's *Ender's Game* and *Speaker for the Dead*, discussed in some detail above, must take care that students focus more on the important questions raised by the texts and less on the military and political genius of the 6-year-old protagonist. The same warning must be put forth for the Middle Earth movies or novels. Is the story so unrealistic and implausible that the lesson will be overwhelmed by the protagonist? If the answer is no, you have grounds to proceed. If not, reconsider.

Encourage Critical Engagement

Instructors should take advantage of the fact that, as Weber (2001) found, students' 'critical analytical skills are often keenly developed when applied to visual media' (p. 282). These skills help students recognize that cultural artifacts not only represent but also participate in politics. To paraphrase Cox (1981, p. 128), film and literature are also for someone and for some purpose.[4] Classic examples of works with an explicit political message that we have already discussed include *Casablanca* (1942), meant to encourage

U.S. entry into World War II; *Dr. Strangelove* (1964), a satire of mutual assured destruction (MAD) and Cold War hysteria; and *The Fog of War* (2003), which presents 11 'lessons' that former Secretary of Defense Robert McNamara believes should inform U.S. foreign policy.

Instructors might invite students to consider how and to what end a text elides the horrors of war, celebrates militarism, or features substantial military collaboration. Does it matter that *The Hunt for Red October* (1990) was vetted by and filmed with the assistance of the U.S. Navy, or that the Pentagon pulled out of *Thirteen Days* (2000), a docudrama about the Cuban Missile Crisis, due to its bellicose but historically accurate portrayal of Air Force General Curtis LeMay?

Encourage Cultural Engagement

Film and literature provide a unique opportunity to transverse culture in a way a textbook cannot. These modes of communication can transport the student to a new location, time or planet, moving beyond the simple constructs of the textbook. We can expand past the limited connect of the major textbooks that largely are written and supported by Western white males. While the publishing and movie-making industry is also dominated by Western white males, the stranglehold this group has over pedagogy and knowledge is vast compared to the ability of movies and texts to overcome these challenges.

The *Ender's Game* series, for example, explores the Universe and examines the impact of culture on extraterrestrial interactions with groups such as Indians, the Polish, Mayans and the Portuguese playing a key role in the novels. *Munich* is unique in its exploration of Israeli attitudes and concepts of revenge. *All Quiet on the Western Front* is entirely from the point of view of the Germans, a fact missed by many. Recent films like *District 9* and *Elysium* communicate a dystopian future through the perspective of South Africa or a multicultural Latino California.

CONCLUSION

IR scholars are in the unique position to be able to use non-traditional films and novels over more conventional academic sources in order to engage and challenge their students. While textbooks have long held their place at the forefront of classroom learning material, we argue that supplementing these resources with film and literature can represent a more successful pedagogical strategy, offering an accessible platform for all levels of students to have a more thorough grasp of the discipline's central questions. We are among the many in a growing circle of IR scholars who have used such methods to illustrate the field's theoretical debates and further push the boundaries of student learning and comprehension.

Instructors who choose to incorporate non-traditional material would do well to keep our lessons from the field in mind. Texts should be explicitly tied to the course themes and objectives, clichés and simplicity should be avoided, and students' critical engagement should be sought. Beyond this, the IR classroom represents possibility. Try something new and different in your courses. Explore the bounds of knowledge and student engagement. Attempting these sorts of innovations might just revive your interest in teaching IR and engage your students in a new way of thinking that is both more inclusive and effective than traditional methods alone.

As with any classroom teaching, course curriculum and design are at the purview of the individual instructor, and as such, our methods and advice are by no means set in stone. The lesson should be the standard on which you seek to expand your instruction methods and reach. Remain true to the goal, but feel free to explore the sources you use to communicate lessons and create a renewed sense of engagement in the course material for students.

NOTES

* We would like to thank Samantha Smith Kelley for her assistance.
1. The inspiration for this course, as well as the title, were drawn from a course first taught by Patrick Thaddeus Jackson at American University.
2. This is also true, to varying degrees, of *Speaker for the Dead* and *Wild Seed*.
3. Note that *Watchmen* is a remarkably rich and dense text, and that our treatment hardly scratches the surface of characters, plots, themes and visual motifs present.
4. On the constitutive role of popular culture within world politics, see Neumann and Nexon (2006, pp. 14–20).

BIBLIOGRAPHY

Blanton, Robert G. (2012), 'Zombies and International Relations: A Simple Guide for Bringing the Undead into Your Classroom', *International Studies Perspectives*, **14** (1), 1–13.
Cox, Robert W. (1981), 'Social Forces and World Orders: Beyond International Relations Theory', *Millennium: Journal of International Studies*, **10** (2), 125–55.
Dixit, Priya (2012), 'Relating to Difference: Aliens and Alienness in *Doctor Who* and International Relations', *International Studies Perspectives*, **13** (3), 289–306.
Drezner, Daniel (2011), *Theory of International Politics and Zombies*, Princeton, NJ: Princeton University Press.
Geertz, Clifford (1972), 'Deep Play: Notes on the Balinese Cockfight', *Daedalus*, **101** (1), 1–37.
Grayson, Kyle, Matt Davies and Simon Philpott (2009), 'Pop Goes IR? Researching the Popular Culture–World Politics Continuum', *Politics*, **29** (3), 155–63.
Gregg, Robert W. (1998), *International Relations on Film*, Boulder, CO: Lynne Reiner Publishers.
Hacking, Ian (1999), *The Social Construction of What?* Cambridge, MA: Harvard University Press.
Hall, Stuart (1996), 'The West and the Rest: Discourse and Power', in Stuart Hall, David Held, Don Hubert and Kenneth Thompson (eds), *Modernity: An Introduction to Modern Societies*, Malden, MA: Blackwell Publishers, pp. 184–227.
Hunt, Lynn (2007), *Inventing Human Rights*, New York: W.W. Norton & Co.
Inayatullah, Naeem (2003), 'Bumpy Space: Imperialism and Resistance in *Star Trek: The Next Generation*', in Jutta Weldes (ed.), *To Seek out New Worlds*, New York: Palgrave Macmillan, pp. 53–78.
Jackson, Patrick Thaddeus and Daniel H. Nexon (2003), 'Representation Is Futile? American Anti-Collectivism and the Borg', in Jutta Weldes (ed.), *To Seek out New Worlds*, New York: Palgrave Macmillan, pp. 143–68.
Lasswell, Harold D. (1941), 'The Garrison State', *The American Journal of Sociology*, **46** (4), 455–68.
Malmgren, Carl D. (1993), 'Self and Other in SF: Alien Encounters', *Science Fiction Studies*, **20** (1), 15–33.
Neumann, Iver B. (2001), '"Grab a Phaser, Ambassador": Diplomacy in Star Trek', *Millennium: Journal of International Studies*, **30** (3), 603–24.
Neumann, Iver B. and Daniel H. Nexon (2006), 'Harry Potter and the Study of World Politics', in Daniel H. Nexon and Iver B. Neumann (eds), *Harry Potter and International Relations*, Lanham, MD: Rowman & Littlefield, pp. 1–27.
Nexon, Daniel H. and Iver B. Neumann (eds) (2006), *Harry Potter and International Relations*, Lanham, MD: Rowman & Littlefield.

Ruane, Abigail E. and Patrick James (2008), 'The International Relations of Middle-Earth: Learning from *The Lord of the Rings*', *International Studies Perspectives*, **9** (4), 377–94.

Simpson, Archie W. and Bernd Kaussler (2009), 'IR Teaching Reloaded: Using Films and Simulations in the Teaching of International Relations', *International Studies Perspectives*, **10** (4), 413–27.

Valeriano, Brandon (2013), 'Teaching International Politics with Film', *Journal of Political Science Education*, **9** (1), 52–72.

Waalkes, Scott (2003), 'Using Film Clips as Cases to Teach the Rise and "Decline" of the State', *International Studies Perspectives*, **4** (2), 156–74.

Weber, Cynthia (2001), 'The Highs and Lows of Teaching IR Theory: Using Popular Films for Theoretical Critique', *International Studies Perspectives*, **2** (2), 281–7.

Weldes, Jutta (1999), 'Going Cultural: *Star Trek*, State Action, and Popular Culture', *Millennium: Journal of International Studies*, **28** (1), 117–34.

Weldes, Jutta (ed.) (2003), *To Seek out New Worlds: Exploring Links between Science Fiction and World Politics*, New York: Palgrave Macmillan.

34. Promoting course based writing in the discipline
Brian Smentkowski

All of us have heard a version of this story: a student submits a political science paper, seemingly confident that his or her ideas, arguments and conclusions are sound, but upon receipt of the graded work is upset to find a lower-than-expected grade and comments critical of the writing style. The distressed student argues that this is a political science class, not an English class; that the ideas should matter more than the method of expression; that he or she is a good writer and the instructor's disagreement is a mere matter of stylistic opinion.

What is the instructor's response? It depends, but at the core it usually includes a defense of the principle that we all must become fluent—or at least highly proficient—in the language of the discipline and that there is a standard for professional communication. To this end, we commonly concede that some of the ideas might, in fact, be 'good', but that it is the author's responsibility to convince the reader that this is the case. The reader should not have to work harder to see the point than the writer has to work to make the point. In an ideal world, the instructor's comments and feedback should help students see this, guided by references to specific flaws and methods to avoid making the same mistake twice. Ideally, our imperative as instructors should be to prepare students as competent communicators in our field. We cannot assume students possess an innate ability to communicate effectively in the discipline; this can and should be learned (Sherman and Waismel-Manor 2003). But how do we accomplish this? How do we help students realize that writing is both something we teach as a skill while serving as a vehicle to teach additional skills?

This chapter maps out a route to enhancing writing in the discipline by addressing the dynamics and expectations of the field and the curriculum, the types of research and writing common within and across subfields, bringing best practices into the learning environments and providing practical advice for engaging student learning through writing.

WHY WRITING MATTERS

It is instructive to recall that writing is, in its pristine form, evidence of our thinking. When we ask students to 'put that in writing', what we are saying is, 'that sounds like a good idea; tell me more'. Pedagogically, this is a sound way to share the value of writing with students. All too often, students complain about what they 'have to' write. And all too often instructors 'have them write' *x* number of papers of various lengths. Writing is expected and assigned with little to no justification save that 'it is important'. Consequently, it is easy to tokenize the process and the product—to revere it as the epitome of professional communication without articulating its purpose writ large (in the discipline) and small (per assignment). Absent a plausible rationale and sense of shared value and purpose, writing is a task; it is done because it is required, not because it is the most effective way to demonstrate learning, skills or professional development.

Articulating why writing matters is important. Reminding ourselves and our students that writing is a revelatory and purposeful process—not just a slamming of keys until a magical page number is satisfied—reconnects us with our thoughts and how we share them convincingly with others. It reveals not only what we are thinking, but how our ideas and arguments develop. But there is no one-size-fits-all solution to enhancing writing in the discipline. Much of what we write and expect our students to write is bound by the traditions and methods of specific areas of inquiry.

As writing is an expression of thought, and thought is rooted in cognition, Bloom's revised taxonomy is useful for two reasons: 1) it illustrates the progression of cognitive ability inherent in the curricular hierarchy, and 2) it is adaptable to the progression of expressive ability from lower order to higher order thinking and writing skills (Anderson, Krathwohl and Bloom 2001). As the capacity for development increases, so too should the expectations of student performance. At the lower level, where 'remembering' and 'understanding' correspond loosely with introductory material, writing assignments can be tailored to enable students to share what they know in descriptive form, whereas at the top of the pyramid students can reasonably be expected to deploy higher order thinking skills to generate an original, empirical work. Based upon the argument above that writing provides evidence of thinking, the expectation of student writing should increase with the demands for higher order thinking.

DESCRIPTION, EXPLANATION AND PRESCRIPTION: AN ORGANIZING CONSTRUCT

Political scientists, like other academics, have historically valued writing. Whether in furtherance of developing one's own voice (Gentry 2010), to enhance and demonstrate learning gains, or to establish a public presence amidst new media, technology and audiences (Lawrence and Dion 2010), political scientists have maintained a core commitment to writing as part of the research and learning process. In the past, research was (not inappropriately) documented and evidenced in written form and the process of inquiry, discovery and analysis associated with research also provided evidence of learning.

One of the most effective methods of improving teaching is to identify key student learning outcomes associated with a class and then adopt the best methods of accomplishing them. The class is then about goal attainment. It is equally plausible to have a goal-oriented approach to writing in political science, where the goals include description, explanation and prescription.

Description

Description is pervasive in student writing because it is relatively concrete. Identify something and describe it. Do not worry about explaining it (yet). It is often the first toe in the water for emerging political analysts grappling with new concepts, relationships and events. Assignments that permit students to describe aspects of the political world yield direct and often 'right or wrong' results that are more robust than mere opinion but less risky than explanation. Because description can be a building block for further analysis, it is useful to distinguish between discrete descriptive analysis, for which the end game is a better understanding of phenomena in and of itself, and applied descriptive analysis, in which description is deliberately the precursor to explanation.

A common assignment in constitutional law classes involves the authorship of case briefs. While it is true that something can be done with almost any information, case briefs have historically been used by some to teach students how to identify and record essential aspects of a case: date, title, citation, decision, opinions and the legal principles applied or developed in a case. Constitutional scholars also routinely engage in content analysis of cases, just as students in political communication may undertake an analysis of news coverage of a political event or seek to determine the presence of media bias in news coverage. As a precursor to explanatory analysis, students completing a literature review for a research design will commonly write and share annotated bibliographies, in which they describe key findings, methods and theories.

Explanation

Explanation is often regarded as the ultimate goal of political science. We do not just want to know something; we want to explain what it is and why it is. It is inherently robust and predicated upon the application of the scientific method and causality. It yields answers, typically derived from theories, from which hypotheses are stated and tested, the results of which constitute truths unless and until they are falsified through an equally robust analysis.

Teaching and learning explanatory analysis is challenging, with bona fide analyses limited due to time, cost and limited opportunity to develop a genuine command of political phenomena in any given semester. The core concepts are a central part of the foundation of scope and methods classes in political science, and students in such classes will often produce somewhat speculative research designs that demonstrate a command of the relationship between the literature and one's critical assessment of it, as well as the progression from an idea, to a research question, to methods of testing it and how results could be interpreted. In upper division classes, senior seminars, independent studies and honors contracts, the movement into Bloom's 'creating' category is frequently emphasized by requiring students to engage in independent research that seeks to answer a question or chart a compelling course for doing so.

Prescription

Prescriptive political science is a less common but equally valid goal of writing in the discipline. Prescriptive work is characterized by the proposal of a remedy to a political issue. Whereas descriptive writing neither tests nor values, and whereas explanatory writing is purely empirical, prescriptive writing in political science is normative; it addresses questions of good and bad, right and wrong, ought and ought not, and concludes with a logically derived recommendation for change. While an empiricist might use probabilistic models to predict the outcome of judicial decisions, a political theorist interested in the ethical foundations of such decisions might plausibly address the 'what ought I to do' as a citizen living under such rules. Whereas a descriptive analysis of an institutional crisis might tell the story of what happened during a particular event (say, emergency management preparation), a prescriptive and normative assessment of the same event would yield a recommendation for change.

While prescriptive writing is acceptable and common in certain subfields (theory and public administration), the discipline in general has traditionally operated on the side of empiricism, choosing to explain political phenomena but not to change it.

Objectivity

To the extent that there is a common thread running through these types of writing, it is an attempt to be objective. Purely descriptive work is patently neutral—it simply records and reports 'what is' based upon political phenomena and the literature. Genuinely empirical work is neutral as well; it seeks to let the data and results speak for themselves, regardless of whether the story is good or bad. Prescriptive work, despite the infusion of normative inquiry, can be objective as well. It can be predicated upon the articulation of and fidelity to a classic syllogism and rooted in logical consistency. Students engaging in such work would do well to recall Gerald Gunther's analysis of the writings of John Marshall (1969, p. 5): '*McCulloch*'s greatness lay precisely in its justification of the most expectable part of its conclusion. *McCulloch* illustrates what many given to cheering or condemning the Supreme Court forget: that with the Court, because it is a court, lasting impact ultimately turns on the persuasiveness of the reasons it articulates, not on the particular result it reaches'.

That last line is vital and, I would argue, one of the most important insights we can and should share with our students. All too often students believe they need to write to the presumed ideology of their professors—that they have to agree with them 'or else'. Reassuring students that it usually is less about the conclusion than the persuasiveness of the reasoning used to arrive at it and the care with which arguments are assembled and presented that determines a 'good' paper, is worth the effort. As a former student who stands 180 degrees away from me ideologically once said, 'I thought you would question and object to my conclusion, so I was careful to make sure that I didn't give you any ammunition'.

WHERE AND HOW TO INTRODUCE WRITING

For any instructional innovation to work, clarity and consistency are mandatory. We—the students and the faculty—need to be on the same page of the script throughout the course of the semester. For all intents and purposes, the syllabus constitutes the script. It is our roadmap to student success. A good syllabus is more than a description of a class coupled with an agenda and a statement of policies and how grades will be calculated; it is the foundation of a learning community. It is where we explain not only what we will do in a class, but why. For writing—or any assignment, for that matter—to be genuinely purposeful, students need to know why, among a myriad of instructional options, they 'have to write a paper'. But the message cannot be constrained by a 'day one' document.

While the syllabus can and should be used as a touchstone throughout the semester, it rapidly fades as instructions for assignments begin to appear. It is therefore essential that writing assignments include a rationale and justification. The syllabus can clearly state how the material, exercises and assignments were selected to help students accomplish articulated learning outcomes and the instructions for each writing assignment can and should articulate with equal clarity how and why it will accomplish a specific goal. It is important to move beyond the 'that you will write' paradigm and narrative, and to a 'why you will write' position. This consistency, from the big picture in the syllabus to the fine print of the student learning outcomes, attained through a clarity of purpose for every writing assignment, not only helps align course and assignment goals but keeps the students more willfully engaged in their learning.

ASSIGNMENTS AND APPROACHES

Writing has always been purposeful. As our understanding of teaching, learning, writing and the multi-modality of expressing knowledge and skill has evolved; as writing in and across the curriculum initiatives began to flourish on college campuses; and as the discipline has become increasingly aware of the link between effective communication and professional preparation, engagement and even democratic citizenship, many institutions and departments responded by taking deliberate steps to require writing in the classroom. Importantly, and promisingly, the combination of institutional and departmental guidelines and guidebooks both reinforces an ethos that values writing and provides best practices for using writing effectively in the learning environment.

Every fall and spring, the Department of Government and Justice Studies at Appalachian State University offers PS 3001: Writing in Political Science. As stated in the Political Science Undergraduate Course page (http://gjs.appstate.edu/academics/undergraduate-program/courses-political-science),

> This course concentrates upon different writing traditions within political science. It requires students to apply the rhetorical knowledge gained in previous writing courses to the discipline of political science. Students will be expected to read and analyze texts in one or more of the sub-disciplines of political science as well as write effectively in one or more of the writing traditions of political science (e.g., research paper, policy analysis, briefing memo, text review). In addition to effective communication, the course emphasizes critical thinking, local to global connections, and community responsibility within the context of political science. Prerequisite: must be majoring in political science.

Operationally, the designation and title are applied to various subject area classes in the discipline that the instructor and department agree to be writing intensive, either in the form of how students communicate (the students will write several papers) or how they learn to communicate (the students will learn how to write a research design). As such, and for example, the department may address writing in the discipline in Dr. Nancy S. Love's Democracy in the Public Sphere, a political theory class that examines the public sphere in European Enlightenment philosophy and liberal democratic politics; in Dr. Carrie Blanchard Bush's public administration class on Leadership; or in Dr. Ellen M. Key's Judicial Decision-Making class. All carry the PS 3001: Writing in the Discipline title, but each addresses writing in the discipline from the standpoint of her respective subfield.

Segmented Model

Accordingly, Dr. Love's syllabus lists eight course objectives, half of which pertain to the political theory subject area and half of which pertain to writing. The writing specific course objectives include:

- how to design and execute a research paper;
- how to edit your own and colleagues' writing;
- how to find and cite relevant source materials;
- how to write effectively as a political scientist and an engaged citizen.

Her syllabus is punctuated with a number of 'On Writing' topics/sessions, ranging from 'choosing a research topic' to 'preparing an annotated bibliography' and 'composing an argument', to 'drafting, editing and revising' a final manuscript. Each 'On Writing' session includes a specific set of readings, and as each writing-related session concludes, students submit their corresponding work.

Over the years, I have come to regard this method as 'the segmented model', wherein students submit discrete segments of their work after completing the requisite amount of immersion in a specific category of information but before proceeding to the next step (Baglione 2008). This keeps the cumulative learning aspect of the class alive and well while at the same time abiding by what higher education has learned about Just In Time Teaching (JITT). If the students can learn and produce and receive feedback on each segment of their work, they then see writing as less threatening. Indeed—and a word of caution goes with this metaphor—they see the final product as the assembly of each of the pieces, with each piece being vetted and refined before inclusion in the final product. They keep the big picture in mind but focus less on 'writing a paper' than on 'completing a section' of it.

In a similar fashion, in my Introduction to Political Science classes, I have discovered that the single most effective method of teaching students how to develop and write a research design followed the segmented model. On the one hand, scope and methods is one of the best places in the curriculum to address writing, as the class exposes students to 'what we do' and 'how we do it'. It makes sense to emphasize writing and the scientific method given the emphasis on the word 'science'. And there's the rub: on the other hand, there's the science—the math, the models, the holy grail of empirical explanation. So, if left to their own devices amidst a nebulous statement that sometime around the end of the semester a final paper will be due which will require them to convince me they know what kinds of data and methods should be employed to test their hypotheses, the drop rate would exceed an equally high failure rate for the class. Instead, I partition out what we cover, what they learn and what they submit in a logical and patient process. I do this in the form of a rubric so they see what is required at every turn, what my expectations are, and the basis for their grade in each compartment. And each area includes a rationale that links it to the bigger picture: the completed research design and proposal. Each segment is read and commented upon, but not graded, as the emphasis is on development. My goal as the instructor is not to punish them for getting it wrong the first time, but rather to pinpoint and solve problems so that the student can confidently complete the section and progress to the next one.

An added bonus to teaching about research and writing in this way is that, in one segmented assignment, students can provide evidence of accomplishing key student learning outcomes, such as exposure to the literature, hypothesis testing and methods, while also learning how to communicate effectively in the discipline.

Revise and Resubmit

Another tried-and-true method of engaging and enhancing student writing is through the 'revise and resubmit' process. Some topics and writing assignments do not lend themselves to the segmented model: the concepts and arguments are too interconnected. But when a lot (grade-wise) is riding on a single paper, students understandably desire and deserve feedback prior to final submission. Developmentally, early feedback that permits the author to correct mistakes, clarify arguments and ultimately produce a superior document is more pedagogically meaningful than a single, final grade that provides no foundation or opportunity for reflection, growth or improvement. Using and sharing rubrics that compartmentalize main, gradable properties and expectations simplify the efforts of the instructor and clarify the goals of the students.

Peer Readers

Similar to the revise and resubmit process is the use of peer readers. Dr. Bush's syllabus informs students that they will 'work individually and in groups to practice good writing techniques'. The use of other students as reviewers, often in the form of writing circles, is important because it stimulates and requires engagement, time-on-task and the development of sound critical techniques. Students learn more about discovering weaknesses, diagnosing problems and developing both solutions and a slightly thicker skin through this interactive process. The role of the instructor is sometimes to facilitate and moderate discussion but certainly to establish, share and enforce the rules of the game. Effective writing circles are inclusive, civil, productive, fair and linear—they foster the development and progression of ideas and expression.

TYPES OF WRITING ASSIGNMENTS

Much of this chapter has focused on the value of writing, distinctions based upon research traditions (description, explanation and prescription) and how we integrate writing into the curriculum, the discipline, the syllabus and assignments. In the final analysis, it is instructive to consider the different types of writing we can bring into the classroom.

Journals constitute a low-risk but highly effective method of engaging students with material, experiences and their own ideas. Journals can provide a platform for students to develop their knowledge base, their values, their thoughts and their responses to political phenomena. In the modern era, virtually all learning management systems include a function that permits a student to develop an electronic portfolio of world affairs and their responses to them, for example, and for journal entries to be seen by the instructor only, to be shared in defined groups or with the entire class.

A key component of an academic journal is critical reflection. The journal is not a diary; it is supposed to reveal thoughts and responses to political affairs, and for its author to grow from his or her entries. All too often, however, students and even faculty believe that journals in general and reflection in particular cannot be graded; the best you can do is see if the work—any work—has been done and mark it off accordingly. Research by Ash and Clayton (2004, 2005, 2009) provides a foundation for developing and assessing critical reflection through their DEAL model. Adapted from their work in international service learning, the DEAL model incorporates a series of prompts for students to reflect critically as they Describe an experience, Examine the experience and engage in Articulated Learning. For example, in international service learning, a student would describe when and where an experience occurred and then examine the academic concepts relevant to the experience and the academic skills marshaled to make sense of the experience (Clayton 2013).

Compared to critical reflection journals, descriptive reports appear dry, but they are by no means less significant. Unlike journal writing, which requires a considerable amount of critical introspection and efforts to relate experience to context, on a purely descriptive plane students may be expected to report on a political event in order to document a command of it. As faculty gradually drift away from the notion that exams are the only way to test knowledge, we find (and have actually always found) that students can 'show what they know' and learn through the writing process. Through report writing, we see in real time what we know, what we do not and what we need. Being able to compose purely and accurately descriptive reports is also valued and valuable in applied subfields such as public administration.

Prescriptive (policy) analysis augments the descriptive efforts, above, by requiring the author to define a problem, identify stakeholders and stakeholder interests, examine arguments, analyze reasons for success or failure, and propose remedies. It is analytical, predicated upon reason and evidence, and prescriptive. Unlike the mainstream of political science writing, it is more 'professional' and often geared towards a different and frequently non-academic audience of policy makers and administrators (Pennock 2011).

Reaction papers and think pieces require a greater investment of higher order cognitive energy than report writing and are occasionally prescriptive. In constitutional law classes, for example, students may be asked to write a case brief (purely descriptive), but they may also be asked to write a reaction paper on a controversial subject such as the death penalty. Alternatively, the student may be asked to contemplate the plausibility of a theory of constitutional interpretation. In any of these scenarios, the ability of the student to 'go deep' is paramount. The question of whether the work is prescriptive is situationally dependent: if the writing prompt is cast in terms of a controversial statement—'react and respond to the assertion that marriage is a right reserved exclusively for heterosexual couples'—it is indeed difficult to avoid a prescription for change if one takes the counter argument position.

Taking the reaction paper and think piece scenario one step further, we inevitably encounter persuasive writing. Whereas the goal of the think piece traditionally is to engage in and reveal depth of thought, persuasive essays require students to convince the reader that he or she is right about something. A common writing assignment in judicial politics classes requires student role-playing. A case—pending, decided or imaginary—is given to the students, and the students are required to assume the role of a Supreme

Court Justice, an interest group leader writing an amicus brief, lawyers for petitioners and respondents, and the like. In such a scenario, students would write a decision as a Justice or an argument based upon case precedent and a desired outcome for the competing lawyers or interested non-parties, well aware of the Gunther argument above, championing the persuasiveness of reasoning. In international relations classes, students likewise role-play as representatives of nation states in Model United Nations events. Role-playing is arguably less common in political theory and philosophy, but the value of reason and persuasion is virtually inestimable. Whereas quantitative political scientists can argue that the numbers do not lie and actually compute mathematical proofs of political relationships, political theorists (save mathematical logicians) ordinarily rely on the quality of reasoning deployed to develop an argument.

But how do we best teach a student to be persuasive? Given that most undergraduates enter a classroom relatively unprepared to make strong persuasive arguments, one typical approach is to show a class what constitutes a good and bad argument— including concrete examples. Then, faculty can demonstrate persuasive style, starting with a topic sentence and showing how latter sentences should emphasize the key points of the topic sentence. Supporting evidence can be introduced and shown to play a reassuring role in forming persuasive arguments. Then, as with teaching counter argumentation, students can be asked to critique examples of persuasive writing from previous semesters. This activity will help them fine-tune their own understanding of how to best make a point. Then they should be free to attempt writing their own persuasive papers.

Finally, we arrive at empirical research writing, which has occupied the lion's share of this chapter. Suffice it to say, as the discipline has embraced its scientific moniker, the desire/ability/necessity to genuinely explain political behavior and events has become our ultimate goal. Articles are routinely accepted or rejected depending on their degree of methodological rigor and explanatory ability. We want our students to be capable and competent in all writing styles, but we insist they understand that which makes us a science. Whether in scope and methods classes, advanced political methodology classes or upper division classes in the discipline's subfields (to a lesser extent in political theory), political science seeks to advance knowledge based upon, vetted through, and replicated according to the scientific method.

PRACTICAL ADVICE: A TOOLKIT FOR STUDENTS AND FACULTY

In order to enhance and advance writing in the discipline, it is necessary to establish a culture of shared value, exposure and experience, and to align our expectations of students with their expectations of faculty. As this chapter has demonstrated, this requires effective communication in the syllabus, in the assignments, in our feedback instruments and comments, and verbally. It requires us to be engaged and learner centered. By adopting a learner-centered approach to learning through writing, embracing the classroom and focusing on providing developmental (as opposed to remedial) support for writing, we can help students advance through the curriculum as effective communicators.

Creating a Culture of Shared Value and Experience

The key to creating a culture of shared value is to take dedicated time to discuss why writing matters. Through class discussions and explanations of assignments, students should be exposed to why basic grammar and argumentation are essential skills to develop in political science. As I often share with students, even the most brilliant of arguments can be defeated by a few misplaced commas or over-utilized, incorrect grammatical tools. Further, students should be exposed to a broad cross-section of the literature. As political scientists know, the discipline's subfields have slightly different expectations. Providing examples of qualitative and quantitative research, behavioral and institutional analyses, comparative and international politics and political theory sensitizes students not only to the diversity of the discipline but also to the diversity of expression within it. Likewise, requiring exposure to journals throughout a program or course can heighten a student's awareness to nuanced differences. Perhaps the best way to expose students is to provide and discuss examples of how research and writing are done in the discipline. One of my personal favorites is to have students read 'Appendix: Notes on Method' in Fenno's (1978) *Home Style: House Members in their Districts* and 'Appendix B: On Methodology' in Taagepera and Shugart's (1989) *Seats and Votes: The Effects and Determinants of Electoral Systems*. It is important for students to see how radically different writing and research techniques can produce equally superior results. If you can bear to do so, the easiest way to show students the writing process is to share your own work. Provide a copy of a first draft, the editor comments and the final product. Let students see how the revise and resubmit process works, not only as an operational paradigm but also as an improvement mechanism. Creating a sense that we all play by the same rules is revealing, refreshing and instructionally valuable.

Practical Advice for Writing in the Discipline

From research question to conclusion, ideas should communicate clearly and convincingly. They should build from something and lead to what comes next. The reader should never fail to see the forest for the trees. The key is to develop a good *political science* voice, and this requires appropriate usage of terminology and theoretical reference points as well as an ability to make critical distinctions among and between arguments in the literature. With energetic students, time must be spent helping them realize that it is important to avoid too many tangents when writing. It is easy to run adrift by following a tangent that, while interesting and productive, is not necessarily clearly associated with the original argument. This does not mean that we should abandon a good idea—a good tangent—but that we should know when to set it aside as a topic for further and future inquiry. If faculty show students how to write in a linear fashion (progressing logically from a major premise to a minor premise and then and therefore to the conclusion), they will be better prepared to write clearly and defend their thesis. With that said, it is still imperative that students demonstrate their meaning and significance and use the literature to frame arguments and debates. Remind them, however, that quotes are great as a foundation for or defense of one's own argument, but not as the argument itself. Sitting down to write a paper is at once intimidating and tedious. Tell students to organize their thoughts in a way that works for them. Again, writing is an individualized activity and everyone has his or her own method.

Practical Advice for Grading Writing and Providing Feedback

The joy of teaching is often offset by the dread of grading. All too often, the papers come in at the end of the semester and the students and faculty alike are astonished to find that some of the work was unsound from the opening line. This is a crushing blow. To avoid this, consider adopting a revise and resubmit policy so that students may receive less punitive feedback on a draft version of a paper instead of a low grade on the final product. Consider as well the segmented model presented above, in which students submit work and receive feedback on specific sections, one at a time. If faculty want to assure the best chance for student success in writing, they should provide a sufficient amount of time for students to process information and to develop their ideas and arguments before submitting written work. Likewise, faculty should give themselves enough time to provide meaningful feedback.

Empowering the students to learn from one another and to refine their own editorial eye sensitizes them to reader responses, which is crucial to critically assessing and improving one's own work. Groups that meet periodically can review the strengths and weaknesses of arguments, assertions and observations in a non-threatening and developmental conversational tone. This not only improves student writing but also conditions students to the vital role constructive criticism plays in the writing process. Taking the time to meet with students one on one about their ideas and progress is important because it demonstrates a personal commitment to their success and provides an opportunity for students not only to see what the instructor perceives to be major strengths and weaknesses but also to talk about the process and goals of writing and resources that may be necessary to proceed with confidence.

The use of rubrics is regularly discussed within the political science discipline. Both the intercept and the slope coefficient are steep, however, as the development of rubrics, especially for the first time, consumes a lot of up-front energy, but they yield substantial dividends later. The best way to think about it is that the time and effort invested into rubric development subtracts from the time and effort invested into grading itself (Rhodes 2010). A good rubric also shows students exactly what is expected and how it will be evaluated for a writing assignment as a whole and for each of its constituent parts (Stevens and Levi 2012). Especially when they are shared and discussed in advance with students, rubrics help keep the student and the professor on the same page of the pedagogical and assessment script, thusly minimizing unpleasant surprises.

CONCLUSION

Our overarching goal as instructors is to help our students succeed at all levels of their academic career and beyond. Long after our mastery of content fades, our ability to investigate and share remains. As such, writing is a professional skill and a life skill. When words fail us, we have the opportunity to retreat, reflect and patiently develop sound arguments built upon evidence and reason. For students it is vital to develop their own voice but to locate it in the conventions and format of the discipline and its constituent subfields. By doing so, students and faculty can genuinely use the written word as an expression of thought and thinking, and to progress from consumers to producers of knowledge.

REFERENCES

Anderson, Lorin W., David R. Krathwohl and Benjamin S. Bloom (2001), *A Taxonomy for Learning, Teaching and Assessing: A Revision of Bloom's Taxonomy of Educational Objectives*, New York: Longman.
Ash, Sarah L. and Patti Clayton (2004), 'The Articulated Learning: An Approach to Reflection and Assessment', *Innovative Higher Education*, **29** (2), 137–54.
Ash, Sarah L. and Patti Clayton (2005), 'Integrating Reflection and Assessment to Improve and Capture Student Learning', *Michigan Journal of Community Service Learning*, **11** (2), 49–60.
Ash, Sarah L. and Patti Clayton (2009), *Learning through Critical Reflection: A Tutorial for Students in Service-Learning*, Raleigh, NC: PHC Ventures.
Baglione, Lisa (2008), 'Doing Good and Doing Well: Teaching Research-Paper Writing by Unpacking the Paper', *PS: Political Science & Politics*, **41** (3), 595–602.
Clayton, Patti (2013), 'Reflection and International Service-Learning', Paper presented at Appalachian State University, Boone, North Carolina.
Fenno, Richard F. (1978), *Home Style: House Members in their Districts*, New York: Little, Brown and Company.
Gentry, Bobbi (2010), 'Improving Student Writing in the Political Science Classroom: Strategies for Developing Student Voice and Originality', Paper presented at the Southern Political Science Association Conference, Atlanta, Georgia.
Gunther, Gerald (1969), *John Marshall's Defense of McCulloch v. Maryland*, Palo Alto, CA: Stanford University Press.
Lawrence, Christopher and Michelle Dion (2010), 'Blogging in the Political Science Classroom', *PS: Political Science & Politics*, **26** (3), 529–33.
Pennock, Andrew, (2011), 'The Case for Using Policy Writing in Undergraduate Political Sciences Courses', *The Teacher*, January, 141–6.
Rhodes, T. (2010), *Assessing Outcomes and Improving Achievement: Tips and Tools for Using Rubrics*, Washington, DC: Association of American Colleges and Universities.
Sherman, Daniel and Israel Waismel-Manor (2003), 'Get it in Writing: Using Politics to Teach Writing and Writing to Teach Politics', *PS: Political Science & Politics*, **36** (4), 755–7.
Stevens, D.D. and A.J. Levi (2012), *Introduction to Rubrics*, Sterling, VA: Stylus.
Taagepera, Rein and Matthew Soberg Shugart (1989), *Seats and Votes: The Effects and Determinants of Electoral Systems*, New Haven, CT: Yale University Press.

35. Best practices in undergraduate lecturing: how to make large classes work
Kinga Kas and Elizabeth Sheppard

LECTURING TO LARGE CLASSES: AN INTRODUCTION

Lecturing is certainly one of the oldest forms of university teaching still in use today. As a historical 'relic' it has certainly been the object of numerous critiques of those colleagues interested in effective teaching and learning methods who claim that students learn more ineffectively in these settings (National Research Council 2000). However, faced with the current realities of universities, this type of teaching languishes as it responds to a number of dilemmas higher education is faced with. The democratization of higher education (both in Europe and in the USA) has led to increased numbers: for example in the USA, undergraduate enrollment increased by 37 percent between 2000 and 2010 (US Department of Education 2012). Thus, the need to teach equivalent information to more students especially in the first years of undergraduate education (core courses etc.) has increased exponentially. This context has been compounded by the financial crisis hitting universities around the world, limiting funds particularly in certain domains like the social sciences. As such, larger classes are often part and parcel of budget saving measures, and in some cases they are the only answers to not closing down departments or degrees. For some universities, it may also be a response to managing classroom logistics and the lack of classroom space particularly in universities in major cities in which space is at a premium and budgets or the lack of space do not allow for constructing new buildings. As a result, it is not going to disappear any time soon, despite the progress made in teaching methods (see other chapters in this book), in particular works on active learning.

We would argue, in fact, that in a way the economic constraints imposed on universities today throughout the world, bring us full circle back to the original purpose and meaning of lecturing. The scarcity and price of books today in many regions, including Central and Eastern Europe, lead us to take a quick glance at this original meaning to remind us why this indeed is one of the earliest and most permanent forms of teaching in higher education.

WHAT IS LECTURING?

A quick analysis of the etymology of the word in dictionaries leads us back to its antique roots. Inspired most certainly from antiquity and the idea of 'picking out words' ('Lecture' n.d.), by the 1520s it comes to mean the 'action of reading (a lesson) aloud', while the definition of 'a discourse on a given subject before an audience for purposes of instruction' is from the 1530s (Brown and Race 2002, pp. 13–20). Historically books were rare and valuable, which led the professor, and this type of teaching, to be the main source of information (Brown and Atkins 2002). While lecturing is not a uniquely 'large classroom' phenomena, given these origins, its use is generally associated with large classrooms, which is the definition we will be employing here.

Many of us can remember sitting in a large lecture hall, listening to an aged professor read from his or her book, not even bothering to look up and make eye contact with their audience. This is in many ways the 'stereotypical' image of lecturing many hold on to. However, advancements in the pedagogical tools and increased reflection on our teaching methods allow us today to question the best practices in the domain. This chapter attempts to provide a glimpse and tips on how lecturing could be improved in today's higher education.

Our chapter endeavors to delve into these challenges and hurdles in this type of classroom configuration. Our starting point in the first section is the idea that, while lecturing has proven to be one of the less effective learning tools (Chickering and Gamson 1987), and most of us prefer small seminar type classes, any academic career will, by necessity, involve lecturing to large classes. Indeed, lecturing has become increasingly prevalent as the recent economic crisis put universities under substantial financial pressure, a response to which was shrinking student–faculty ratios, as we have seen in our own university systems. In addition, many professors, particularly younger colleagues, have no say in what type of classes they teach, and, thus, cannot find work-arounds to lecturing. Therefore, given that lecturing is an inescapable classroom format, it is imperative to consider how it can be improved.

Our second section looks beyond this, seeing how, within large classes, new alternative formats and tools can be experimented with. Both newly arrived colleagues and those of us that have been teaching for many years can benefit from reflexive thinking on our practices and our solutions to those hurdles, enabling us simultaneously to share our own best practices and integrate the progress made in teaching and learning research. We argue that large lecture classes do not prohibit innovation – in fact, they may function as a good laboratory for numerous innovative activities and techniques, on the condition they be adapted to the size and type of public.

IMPROVING LECTURING: MAKING THE BEST OF IT

The pitfalls of large classes are well documented: even a quick tour of any major university website with teaching resources for colleges (particularly in the USA) illustrates the anxiety this type of teaching can cause for newer colleagues and the desire and need for resources (e.g. Center for Teaching Excellence, University of Maryland or the Center for Teaching and Learning, Stanford University). Unfortunately, it is not possible to provide a recipe with a list of ingredients that will result in an ideal undergraduate teacher. However, there are several factors that, once incorporated into the teaching system, will greatly contribute to a more positive output. These tools cannot perhaps be considered as guarantors, but they are certainly conditions for successful lecturing.

When speaking of good practices in undergraduate teaching, we follow Chickering and Gamson's (1991) widely used list of best practices that is based on the understanding that successful teaching rests and depends on the contribution of both teachers and students. Or, in other words: teaching is tied to learning (Katz and Henry 1988, p. 2). Our responsibility as teachers is to implement our share in this contribution and also keep in mind that it is only with the participation of our students that we can become successful in our work. Below, we focus on connecting with students, maintaining their interest and giving a dynamic lecture, and we suggest a number of solutions to these issues that could potentially make lecturing both a good learning experience for students and a good teaching experience for the instructor.

CLASSROOM MANAGEMENT, COMMUNICATION AND OTHER LECTURING BASICS

Classroom management, communication and behavioral problems (widely experienced by any professor teaching a first year core course with large numbers) are common issues that are the most prevalent in the large setting of a lecture hall. From boredom to chatting online in the modern classroom (which has replaced the incessant chatter we ourselves probably fell prey to in our day), handling these large classes is a multifaceted challenge. Instructors are universally concerned with issues of classroom management. If those who teach in high school and to younger children certainly dedicate a large part of their career to this subject, as evidenced by the large amount of literature, notably the works of C.M. Charles (Charles and Senter 2007), university instructors are not exempt from considering the issue. However, different considerations are required according to the audience in question. While classroom management includes disciplinary issues that either are regulated by universities' honor codes or can be taken care of by setting down rules in syllabi (and then following them in practice), it is much more than that, for it also entails organizing the learning environment and motivating students. Thus, classroom management cannot be boiled down to one single concept (Charles and Senter 2007; Wolfgang 2008). The propositions that follow seek to highlight a number of the elements key to classroom management that instructors face in large classrooms as well as provide insights based on real world experiences, proposing solutions and reflections on such problems. According to the extended interpretation, which we are applying here, effective classroom management involves clear communication of behavioral and academic expectations, as well as a cooperative learning environment (Allen 1986).

Especially at undergraduate level, where students gain their first experience of higher education, accessibility of faculty members and communication with them is an essential point of motivation for students. Maintaining contact with large classes is clearly a bigger challenge than with a small number of students, especially as large classes are, by definition, anonymous, where it is very difficult or nearly impossible for the lecturer to remember all the names. However, in large classes it seems even more important that lecturers adopt an active approach, and in addition to encouraging students to communicate problems, it is important to seek out students with difficulties, offering assistance and intellectual support. One way to do this is to emulate the example of US colleges, where graduate assistants often shoulder this task. In large freshmen classes with students who are unfamiliar with the educational setting or lack courage and confidence to speak up, the accessibility of teaching staff may also help improve retention rates.

In other words, students must be visible and not just outside the classroom. Instructors should make an effort to 'see' the students in the classroom: '[m]aking eye contact and circulat[ing] around the classroom [is] a way of drawing students in and reducing the feel of a large classroom environment' (Loewenberg Ball and Thurnau 2009). Teachers should be aware that students in all parts of the room need to be integrated visually, not merely those students who are in the front rows, present and willing to learn, and in the direct field of vision of the instructor. Not only words but also nonverbal behavior should be used to facilitate interaction. For example, 'a bigger room often requires bigger gestures if you want the impact to reach all the way to the back of the room' (Tait 2011). Familiarizing ourselves with the venue, knowing what practices are most suitable for the type of course we are giving, and having the personal touch by recognizing students, are all essential factors if we want to become successful in an undergraduate classroom (Armstrong 2007).[1]

As such, knowing the layout of the room is important to an instructor in large classrooms, since teaching methods may vary depending on the technology and disposition of the room itself. For large courses, for example, the ability to walk around keeping eye contact with students and approaching them while being heard (which often implies either a voice that carries or technological aids), can be key in getting points across. However, not all lecture halls may allow for this. Similarly, giving instructions clearly gains even more importance in a large class.

Instructors often experience students yawning, chatting or, in general terms, demonstrating a lack of concentration. For lectures to have any positive effect on learning, it is important that the instructor gets across to students, which means grabbing and holding onto students' attention. There are various ways to achieve this. For example, one may start each class with a joke or ask a question that is directly relevant for students. This may involve asking about their participation in upcoming social events at the universities or discussing their future plans and career. Answers tend to be surprisingly honest and give teachers an insight of the expectations and aspirations of their students. Moreover, asking students about their future plans may help them beyond the classroom, since undergraduates in their first two years are often unclear about what they would do with their degree in their pocket and need guidance to work out future possibilities.

Using Technology to 'Spice Up' Lectures and Increase Participation

Many studies (Howe and Strauss 2000; Howe and Strauss 2007; Oblinger 2003; Fraud 2000) have contrasted the behavior of today's students in the classroom with that of their predecessors. Amongst other factors, modern students regularly use digital media in their lives and learning. Thus, we may be able to grab and hold their attention as well as foster their learning in general, if we engage them through media platforms and information technologies that are popular with them. It is standard fare today to use PowerPoint or Prezi as 'supporting actors' in our lectures in the hope that more information will be transmitted and remembered on the part of the students. However, our experience leads us to advise instructors to use them only after careful consideration of their purpose. Slides should be guides, i.e. outlines, to help students to focus and follow classes, and this should be emphasized with students lest they treat slides as substitutes for lectures (or attendance). While it is advisable to summarize the major steps of every lecture at its beginning, slides have an advantage of structuring the class throughout. However, slides with too much information are too heavy. Additionally, fancy or too small fonts, a lot of animation, etc. are also likely to disorient students rather than help them in their learning.

Lectures with slides, or any lectures really, can be interspersed with short videos, maps or other visual content that enables students to take a break without leaving the classroom when attention and enthusiasm wane and a pause is welcome. This is an effective way to overcome the constraints on human attention and need not exceed 20 minutes (Vander Zanden n.d.). Polk (2009) suggests incorporating a brief intermission – a short non-content related video or a funny image – that gives the students the opportunity to regroup and reengage after the 'clip of the day'. For our part, we often use a short 2–3 minute video, a news clip of current events related to the subject that engages the student with the subject matter and the world around them – this enables them to regroup, to reconsider and discuss the subject at hand in a more informal way.

Technology also helps with the challenge of class participation, which is a two-edged sword in large classes. While we do want students to feel free to interact and ask questions, if all of them do so in a large classroom it can be disruptive. We have all had the experience of trying to manage a classroom of 200 students with what seems like a sea of hands raised. Precious classroom time can be wasted on questions that are often redundant or even sometimes inappropriate when the student has not done the assigned work. Many classrooms today benefit from tools such as clickers (or audience response systems – see Chapter 25 of this book) or Twitter, which can be adapted to large classes as a complement to lecturing. We ourselves have used Twitter in particularly large classes to allow students to ask questions when the class size can render them fairly anonymous. Using Twitter or similar tools not only may help to deal with the large volume of student comments but may also assist students who are less likely to speak up in large lecture classes.

In order to facilitate discussions with large groups, our students are often asked to sign up for Twitter. A sheet is handed out at the beginning of the semester informing them of the 'how to' aspects for those who are less connected and less familiar with Twitter. This includes ground rules such as not to post inappropriate comments and to remember that private information should not be shared and that everyone's opinion should be respected – and that we do not use Twitter as a tool to insult classmates or the professor. There are numerous ways to include Twitter in the classroom and to use it as a tool to keep the discussion going outside teaching hours, as many colleagues' blogs and websites indicate. For our part, we have mainly used it as a tool to promote interaction with students to avoid the silence of big classrooms in first year courses where students often hesitate to ask questions in front of 200 of their colleagues and thus their questions might get lost in the crowd. The questions are posted to the class account, and thus the professor can take the time to read and respond to the stream during the class – or in the case of time constraints, he/she can reply via Twitter or other media, outside of class hours. Twitter is also useful to inform students of certain changes or to provide links to information in real time. This is particularly important for us in our introduction courses in international relations or international political economy, since both courses use real world up-to-date examples and thus can benefit from up-to-date information given directly to students who do not necessarily watch the news or read newspapers, despite our constant encouragement.

We have to keep in mind that students (and many of us) cannot envisage life without technology nor the possibility of studying without it. We personally have a hard time banning technology from the classroom as it is a tool that younger faculty also grew up with and use regularly for their work. As such, using technology is a natural step, and more adapted to the learning processes of students today. Additionally, studies and experience show us, particularly around exam correction time, that even the best students retain only a portion of what is said during a lecture at best – at worst, as many of us have experienced, students do not listen, do not take notes and do not retain any information (Hake 1998).

The above-mentioned characteristics of the attention problematic require professors to extend their lectures beyond the 1–3 hours' formal period of lecturing with technology that allow students to have access to the lecture beyond the classroom. Online forums and boards such as Moodle, in which classroom notes, PowerPoints and/or other types of information can be shared, are a useful tool. We have found that study questions posted online, with an adapted forum, can allow for pinpointing those areas in which students need more information and clarification or those areas in which perhaps they simply demonstrate more interest. This also allows for an interaction in real time amongst students themselves and between students and professor. Quizzes such as map quizzes or reading quizzes, for which we do not have the classroom time, can also be proposed on line, charting students' progress and allowing for assessment throughout the semester. For classes in international relations or international political economy that also benefit from an interactive approach integrating current events, forums can allow professors to encourage students to read recently published articles and react to them without much effort.

As professors, we use significant amounts of technology in our daily classes and have noticed the improvement both in our own lectures and in student learning. It should be added that, while initially this is an added effort and workload for the professor, long term, once they have created certain habits and learned the ropes, it makes the professor's job easier and more interesting. However, we cannot stress how strongly we feel that technology is an aid or complement to lecturing – technology does not replace learning but makes it better if it is applied with care and its relationship to classroom material is clearly elaborated. If used well, technology may help students to acquire certain skills beyond the acquisition of knowledge. Nonetheless, a good lecture remains a dynamic one that is well prepared and that engages our students. Technology cannot help a lecture if the professor reads from PowerPoints, for example, the way that past generations read from their notes. The basics of lecturing or public speaking essential to classroom management, such as engaging your audience with your eyes, etc., are still relevant.

Assessment in Large Lecture Classes

One of the greatest weaknesses of large lecture classes is that, given 'activities' in class and the focus on knowledge transmission, they tend to rely on only summative assessment – a midterm exam or often only one final exam. Such an approach is problematic because it does not prepare students for these exams and it robs instructors of feedback that would help them identify problematic points in learning and understanding and act upon these issues. In recognition of this problem, in France in particular, for example, more and more classes are moving away from the single final exam format to a continuous assessment format, allowing instructors more lead way and giving students more opportunities to express themselves. This, however, also means that classroom activities as well as learning objectives must change to align aims, learning tasks and activities with each other.

On occasions when this is not possible, and the lecturing format cannot be abandoned, there still remains some leeway for instructors to find assessment tasks that engage students with the material. For certain classes, we substitute the final exam with a portfolio or similar exercise – this allows instructors to measure progress and can also avoid certain of the pitfalls of 'cookie cutter' type exams. Student portfolios consist of a collection of relatively small-scale assignments, like short writing tasks completed by a student during their progress through the course. Often a portfolio includes a reflective commentary such as a learning journal. Learning journals give students the opportunity to reflect in detail on their researches on a topic and also on their relationships with the course topic. They often complement a portfolio.[2] In cases where end-of-term exams as the form of assessment are mandated by the university and, therefore, it is impossible to abandon them in favor of other assessment tasks, instructors may also introduce formative assessment tasks throughout the term, if only on a voluntary basis for extra credit added to the exam mark.

ALTERNATIVES TO LECTURING

'[W]hen the class size is large, many instructors hesitate to use activities that could be quite productive even—or sometimes especially—in large groups', and 'tend to over-rely on lecture and to count on a Q & A session or large class discussion for interaction, when in reality only a small percentage of people actually get to participate in those when the class is large' (Tait 2011). However, if the format and circumstances permit, and despite large class size, experienced instructors may seek to go beyond the 'lecturing format', which reduces '[s]tudents' opportunities for learning', as 'their role is mainly that of spectators in large lecture classes' (Loewenberg Ball and Thurnau 2009).

If instructors can transform large classes into an environment where the chance for successful interaction is maximized, large classes may turn out to be not that large in the end. Finding effective ways to involve students in large classes requires truly knowing the audience, the instructor's limits (including time constraints and the required material that the instructor may be mandated to pass on) and the general layout as a foundation for innovation. We stress that any good innovative solutions need to be implemented with clearly thought out goals and with knowledge of pedagogic principles, working perhaps with a mentor or a group of colleagues. Below we suggest a number of original approaches to experiment with in large classes. This is far from an exhaustive list, but it allows us to cover some essentials that are, in our experience, essential to the teaching and learning process.

One option is to break down large classes into smaller units. For example, small groups can be created within the large mass.

> While having a group of fifty, we can make ten groups of five. As long as the framework for learning is very clear, we don't have to be in control of that fifty. As long as each group has

clear objectives, clear outlines of what's expected to be achieved, how it's going to be assessed at the end, then it's manageable, and the group has to take some responsibility. (Bishop 2004)

As for the optimum size of small classes, there is a consensus that, in general, the number of students should be between five and eight per group. Below five, diversity and variety of interaction diminishes; above eight, the contribution of some students might decline (Booth 1996). Naturally, this optimum is not something that can be achieved in each and every case, but at least it gives us an indication of the size of small groups to be formed when the possibility arises. Teamwork will be useful to help undergraduate students acquire skills that can improve their individual learning and that they will be able to use later in the workplace. In order to be able to carry out good individual work, students have to learn how to share and discuss ideas, incorporate knowledge from others, and also give opinions and evaluate other people's work. Teamwork and collaboration will teach them to reason, to argument and to exercise critical thinking, which are all essential elements for later independent work.

Furthermore, different types of groups can be created for different purposes, such as informal learning groups (ad hoc temporary clustering of students within a single class session), formal learning groups (teams established to complete a specific task) and study teams (long-term groups with stable membership whose primary responsibility is to provide members with support, encouragement and assistance in completing course requirements and assignments) (Davis 1993). Teamwork in class is often embodied in role playing games and reasoning the pro and cons of an issue related to the learning subjects, but it can be encouraged in out-of-class, university related activities as well. Codde recommends students 'from different races and cultures to share their viewpoints on topics discussed in class', to 'participate in groups when preparing for exams and working on assignments' and 'to join at least one organization on campus' (Codde 2006, p. 2).

One way to turn a class of 80 students into workable units is to create problem-solving groups of ten students as Dzurjanik did with his 'Pillars of European Civilization' course (Dzurjanik 2013). This approach works best with problems that have not one but many correct answers. He used group work to complement learning, not to replace it entirely. Classes started with a short lecture that was followed by a problem-solving task related to the lecture, and then a debriefing session culminating in the revision of classroom material that was not clear for students. To perform this third task, the results of the problem-solving exercise (often presented in short student lectures or summaries) serve as a direct input, providing the instructor with immediate feedback. It is also worth tweaking the format from class to class to keep student interest throughout the course (Dzurjanik 2013), for a task that is executed in the same format, no matter how originally innovative, loses its novelty with students by the twelfth iteration.

Besides teamwork, individual work may also be (re)introduced into large classes. The two most frequently used forms of individual work are presentation in class and essay writing. However, in the case of large classes, these tasks can prove extremely time consuming for both students and lecturers (individual presentations, even short ones, for 30 or 50 and more – often a lot more – students, just like advising and correcting essays, can take up an unmanageable amount of time). Therefore, a compromise solution should be found that allows students to work individually throughout the term yet does not overwhelm the instructor. Below, we present a few examples of the many assessment tasks that may help complement evaluation in large lecture classes.

A viable option for presentations is parallel presentations to groups of peers who have previously worked out (or have been given) clear assessment criteria. While peer assessment may not be a reliable tool of summative assessment or grading, it may fulfill the tasks of formative assessment. By applying the criteria themselves when marking sample assignments (either anonymized student work or pieces written by the lecturer), students understand more clearly what is expected of them. We have also asked students at times to exchange small pieces of writing and discuss them amongst themselves according to given criteria. In the case of essays, position papers, summaries or other written assignments, different students may be assigned to do this task on different weeks. We have, for example, substituted midterm exams with review essays. With large classrooms, we break down the class into different groups that do these at varying times during the semester. This avoids the instructor having to grade 200 works at once.

Introducing Active Learning into Large Classes

Now we provide some general guidance as to how active learning should be introduced into large classes. First, active learning can be looked upon as a continuum from simple activities that take only a few minutes to complex tasks that cover several weeks and practically revise the course (Bonwell and Sutherland 1996). Instructors may want to start with simpler or shorter active learning exercises, and only then proceed to introducing more complex and longer tasks once they have some experience with shorter exercises. Loewenberg Ball and Thurnau (2009), for example, suggest starting to engage students in a large class by a simple task – for instance, asking them to discuss a question with their neighbors. They claim that it is 'not always necessary to elicit responses; instead teachers should show a slide summarizing points that usually come up in such discussions and ask students if they came up with anything that is not on the list' (Loewenberg Ball and Thurnau 2009). Simpler methods also include a quick monitoring technique known as the muddiest point question (in order to find out what was the concept hardest to capture for the students in the given class), an anonymous in-class writing activity called 1 minute paper (where the lecturer asks a question related to the material of the given class in order to get feedback from what students think or understood) or the empty outline task (where students complete in a short amount of time an outline related to in-class presentations). One minute assignments as an informal writing activity can be a very useful feedback tool especially at the beginning stage (first and second year), from two aspects: on the one hand, because of the limited space on the paper or card and limited time, they force students to focus and summarize, while on the other hand they give very quick feedback to teachers on what students learn and withhold as essential knowledge (Bean 2001). We have particularly used the 1 minute essay in our classes to assess where students are in our lectures and in the concepts and to allow for continuous assessment throughout the semester. The application card may help to teach concepts and theories by asking students to find real life or hypothetical examples (Angelo and Cross 1993). These tasks may also be used well in traditional lecture classes, which often suffer from a lack of feedback loop in between summative assessment tasks.

Other, more complex, tasks include case studies, team debates, role plays, simulations (see chapters 15, 23, 26 and 27 of this book) and problem-based learning (see this book, Chapter 30). All promote the task of translating abstract political concepts and theories into real world examples. As opposed to simple memorization, 'case studies prompt students to examine facts, to question their meaning and examine alternative perspectives to thinking about the world in which they live' (Gunter 2008, p. 17).

However, teachers have to make sure that selected topics are related to students' interest, knowledge, personal context or background, otherwise they might lose focus and enthusiasm and thus the potential for deep learning as well. The same conditions are valid in the case of team debates, role plays and simulations: the 'silent classroom' will awaken and become active if students can in some ways identify with the subject of the debate or simulation.[3] It is therefore highly advisable to lecturers to consult the classroom on subjects and questions that are likely to hold interest for students and can therefore motivate them more easily to cooperate and to participate. Even more complicated and therefore more challenging a task is so-called problem based learning (PBL), where students are confronted with applying previously gained knowledge from building up a project from A to Z. Because of its complexity, however, PBL may be more appropriate for students at a more advanced stage of the university curriculum, although with some modifications it may work with freshman as well (see Chapter 30 of this book).

Second, as general guidance, it is important to set the tone for active learning from the very beginning, preferably from the first class, so that students get the idea and taste of it, as well as the expectations that are set for them during the semester. There are several tricks that can contribute to creating the right atmosphere and establishing a non-threatening environment, which is of crucial importance in the case of undergraduates, in order to overcome fear of participation, willingness to remain invisible, and passivity. One such trick is to reduce the space between the lecturer and the students – this gains significance especially in large classrooms. Lecturers are invited to walk up and down in the room amongst the aisles, so everyone is involved, feeling that they have the lecturer's attention. Also, using a cordless microphone can facilitate good hearing and participation in a large class.

Third, the idea of teaching today is not to feed students pre-packaged information and assignments but to make them use the gained knowledge actively – making it their own, being able to express it, discuss it and relate it to practice. However, student learning can only be optimized if undergraduate instructors not only set rules out clearly but also explain to students how these tasks will have to be carried out – before expecting students to perform such exercises – as individuals or teams. Students will need guidance and advice. It often happens that teachers – when giving out these types of tasks for the first time – have to sacrifice a part of the lecture in order to explain to the students what is expected from them.[4] It may also be necessary to run 'test sessions' or 'mock versions' of active learning exercises with no or minimal weight toward the final grade. Finally, active learning should be introduced gradually into the curriculum if students are not likely to have met such tasks before.

Once classroom activities are changed to fulfill new – hopefully more skills-oriented – learning outcomes, assessment methods must change to harmonize with the new goals and activities.

CONCLUSION

We have seen through the above discussion what tools, skills and practices teachers have at their hands to become successful in their work. However, research shows that teachers do not necessarily excel in all kinds of teaching environments. The London School of Economics and Political Science organizes an institution-wide study of students' opinions about all courses during each academic year. Students are requested to provide background information about themselves, to give their views of each course, and to grade their satisfaction with the teaching provided by individual teachers involved. This last component of the data gathering assesses opinions separately about three different teaching modes: lecturing, seminars and class (small-group) teaching. One of the interesting outcomes of this research is the different levels of satisfaction sometimes shown for the same teacher, even within the same course, according to the mode of teaching being assessed (LSE 2011). For individual teachers, students may experience a higher level of satisfaction with one mode of their teaching than with another. In other words, teachers do not usually excel in all kinds of teaching environments, at least not at the same level. Well, the challenge may be for us to change the outcome of the next reports – for the better.

NOTES

1. Armstrong's (2007) list contains additional practices, under 'Top Ten Tips for Teaching Undergraduates'.
2. University of Reading (n.d.) provides several useful assessment methods especially adapted for large classes.
3. Sheppard (2005) and Simon (2005) give a good insight into the difficulties of conducting case studies and role plays, respectively.
4. Discussions with young professors or PhD students during the summer university organized by the ECPR Teaching and Learning Standing Group in Piestany in 2012 confirm this point.

REFERENCES

Allen, James D. (1986), 'Classroom Management: Students' Perspectives, Goals, and Strategies', *American Educational Research Journal*, **23** (3), 437–59.
Angelo, Thomas A. and K. Patricia Cross (1993), *Classroom Assessment Techniques: A Handbook for College Teachers*, San Francisco, CA: Jossey-Bass.
Armstrong, Catherine (2007), 'Top Ten Tips for Teaching Undergraduates', available at http://www.jobs.ac.uk/careers-advice/working-in-higher-education/961/top-ten-tips-for-teaching-undergraduates/ (accessed 10 May 2014).
Bean, John C. (2001), *Engaging Ideas: The Professor's Guide to Integrating Writing, Critical Thinking, and Active Learning in the Classroom*, San Francisco, CA: Jossey-Bass.
Bishop, Pam (2004), 'How "Small" is a "Small Group"?', available at http://www.nottingham.ac.uk/pesl/themes/ldawinners/85/howsmalx991/ (accessed 15 May 2014).
Bonwell, C.C. and T. Sutherland (1996), 'The Active Learning Continuum: Choosing Activities to Engage Students in the Classroom', *New Directions for Teaching and Learning*, **17** (67), 3–16.
Booth, Alan (1996), 'Changing Assessment to Improve Learning', in Alan Booth and Paul Hyland (eds), *History in Higher Education: New Directions in Teaching and Learning*, Oxford: Blackwell Publishers, pp. 261–75.
Brown, G. and M. Atkins (2002), *Effective Teaching in Higher Education*, London: Routledge.
Brown, Sally and Phil Race (2002), *Lecturing: A Practical Guide*, London: Routledge Falmer.

Charles, C.M. and Gail W. Senter (2007), *Elementary Classroom Management*, fifth edition, Boston, MA: Allyn and Bacon Publishers.

Chickering, Arthur W. and Zelda F. Gamson (1987), *Seven Principles for Good Practice in Higher Education*, AAHE Bulletin, March, no. 3.

Chickering, Arthur W. and Zelda F. Gamson (1991), 'Seven Principles for Good Practice in Undergraduate Education', in Arthur W. Chickering and Zelda F. Gamson (eds), *Applying the Seven Principles for Good Practice in Undergraduate Education*, New Directions for Teaching and Learning 47, San Francisco, CA: Jossey-Bass, pp. 63–9.

Codde, Joseph R. (2006), 'Applying the Seven Principles for Good Practice in Undergraduate Education', available at https://www.msu.edu/user/coddejos/seven.htm (accessed 14 May 2014).

Davis, Barbara Gross (1993), *Tools for Teaching*, San Francisco, CA: Jossey-Bass.

Dzurjanik, Peter (2013), 'Problem Solving Class as a Tool for Effective Large Group Teaching', in Ľudmila Adamová and Petra Muráriková (eds), *Innovating Teaching and Learning: Reports from University Lecturers*, Opladen: Barbara Budrich Publishers, pp. 53–62.

Fraud, Jason (2000), 'The Information-Age Mindset: Changes in Students and Implications for Higher Education', *EDUCAUSE Review*, **35** (5), 15–24.

Gunter, Michael M. Jr. (2008), 'Teaching with Case Studies: Bringing Practical Relevance to Political Theories', in Kinga Kas and Malte Brosig (eds), *Teaching Theory and Academic Writing: A Guide to Undergraduate Lecturing in Political Science*, Opladen: Budrich UniPress, pp. 15–20.

Hake, Richard (1998), 'Interactive Engagement vs. Tradition Methods: A Six-Thousand Student Survey of Mechanics Test Data for Introductory Physics Courses', *American Journal of Physics*, **66** (1), 64–74.

Howe, N. and W. Strauss (2000), *Millennials Rising: The Next Great Generation*, New York, NY: Vintage.

Howe, N. and W. Strauss (2007), *Millennials Go to College*, second edition, Great Falls, VA: LifeCourse Associates.

Katz, J. and M. Henry (1988), *Turning Professors into Teachers: A New Approach to Faculty Development and Student Learning*, New York: ACE/Macmillan.

'Lecture' (n.d.), in *Etymology Online*, available at http://www.etymonline.com/index.php?term=lecture (accessed 10 May 2014).

Loewenberg Ball, Deborah and Arthur F. Thurnau (2009), 'Strategies for Engaging Students in Large Classes', *Center for Research on Learning and Teaching (CRLT)*, available at http://www.crlt.umich.edu/sites/default/files/resource_files/Prof_Ball_Summary.pdf (accessed 10 May 2014).

LSE (London School of Economics and Political Science) (2011), 'Effective Course Evaluation: The Future for Quality and Standards in Higher Education', available at http://www.lse.ac.uk/newsAndMedia/aroundLSE/archives/2011/effectiveEvaluationReport.pdf (accessed 14 May 2014).

National Research Council (2000), *How People Learn: Brain, Mind, Experience, and School: Expanded Edition*, Washington, DC: The National Academies Press.

Oblinger, Diana (2003), 'Boomers, Gen-Xers, and Millennials: Understanding the "New Students"', *EDUCAUSE Review*, **38** (4), available at https://net.educause.edu/ir/library/pdf/erm0342.pdf (accessed 14 May 2014).

Polk, Thad (2009), 'Engaging Students in the Classroom and Beyond', available at http://www.crlt.umich.edu/faculty/Thurnau/ThurnauVideos and full text at http://www.crlt.umich.edu/sites/default/files/resource_files/Prof_Polk_Summary.pdf (accessed 14 May 2014).

Sheppard, Elizabeth (2005), 'Motivating the Troops: The Challenge to First Time Teachers', in Gabriela Gregušová (ed.), *How to Teach Political Science: The Experience of First Time University Teachers*, Teaching Political Science 1, Paris: epsNet/Sciences Po Paris, pp. 13–16.

Simon, Eszter (2005), 'Role Play in Foreign Policy Analysis', in Gabriela Gregušová (ed.), *How to Teach Political Science: The Experience of First Time University Teachers*, Teaching Political Science 1, Paris: epsNet/Sciences Po Paris, pp. 57–60.

Tait, Kelly (2011), 'Facilitating Large Group Discussions and Activities: Make Numbers Count', available at http://news.nasje.org/2011/01/26/facilitating-large-group-discussions-and-activities-make-numbers-count/ (accessed 14 May 2014).

University of Reading (n.d.), 'Engage in Assessment: Assessing a Large Number of Students', available at http://www.reading.ac.uk/engageinassessment/assessing-large-groups/eia-assessing-large-groups.aspx (accessed 12 May 2014).

US Department of Education (2012), *The Condition of Education*, Washington, DC: NCES.

Vander Zanden, Brad (n.d.), 'Preparing an Effective Presentation', available at http://web.eecs.utk.edu/~bvz/presentation.html (accessed 15 April 2014).

Wolfgang, Charles H. (2008), *Solving Discipline and Classroom Management Problems*, New York: Wiley Global Education.

36. Political science and the scholarship of teaching
Jeffrey L. Bernstein

INTRODUCTION

In 2006, I was working with advanced undergraduates on a teaching collaboration (more details on this work are provided in Gutman et al. 2009). The students were working as quasi-teaching assistants in my introductory American Government course, facilitating student simulations of the legislative process. The students in the course were required to read and synthesize articles – from diverse genres, ideological positions and levels of quality – on pressing political issues. The students would write papers on these political issues, and then would engage in simulations in which they attempted to change (or beat back changes in) policy on these issues.

One day, over breakfast with two of the facilitators, I asked them a simple question. Was I 'better' than our introductory level students at the tasks required to write the papers – reading material, synthesizing perspectives, and weighing the quality of methods and arguments? Yes, of course, my students replied. I am the professor, they are intro students who don't know about these issues (or about political science). I clearly am better than them at the tasks required to do these papers.

Fine, I said, are *you* better than these intro students? Yes, the facilitators replied. They had learned things in their years as political science majors that made them better than the students they were coaching in the class, most of whom had never taken a political science class before. They could see evidence of this when they were working with the students in class. OK, I said to the facilitators, am *I* better than *you* at these tasks? A final yes – as the professor, with a Ph.D. and years of experience working in the field, I was better at these tasks than these high-achieving undergraduates, extraordinary as they were.

And then we came to the final question: what do I do better than you, and what do you do better than the students in our class? This question led to a fascinating discussion, about the skills we learn in political science, and how those skills lead me to perform a fairly mundane, yet important, activity in our discipline. (As an aside, I would highly recommend having these types of discussions – they can be truly illuminating.) In graduate school, and as a practicing political scientist, I learned to analyze quantitative models. I learned how to read between the lines of authors' arguments to find the points that were not adequately supported by data, or that did not make correct analytical inferences. I learned enough about the literature in my field to put arguments about policy matters into a theoretical framework. When I confront a new political issue about which I know very little, I take the skills I have as a political scientist and bring them to bear on this new context. This ability to transfer my knowledge and skills (Halpern and Hakel 2003) makes me 'better' than my students at this task.

This opening vignette reflects some of my perspective on the scholarship of teaching and learning. As a point of departure, I take the words of historian David Pace (2004):

At the core of the entire project of a scholarship of teaching and learning is the belief that disciplinary thinking is crucial to learning. Therefore, a central goal of this work is to define as clearly as possible the kinds of thinking that students typically have to do in each academic field and to devise strategies for introducing students to these mental operations as effectively as possible. (p. 1179)

In essence, what Pace argues here is that those of us teaching political science must find ways to do what I asked my students to consider. Following on the principles of backward design (Wiggins and McTighe 1998), we need to identify the knowledge and skills that our students should gain when they leave our classes, and then design our classes (and our curricula) to help students gain this knowledge and skill set. For example, if we want students to be able to weave multiple sources into one coherent summary of the literature, we need to teach them how to do it in class, provide opportunities to practice that skill in class and give assignments to require students to do it. Doing so will help students to gain these skills we find so important.

The type of work I describe above has been done by scholars in many fields, often fitting under the genre of 'expert-novice studies'. These include Wineburg (2001) in history, Bowen (1994) in chemistry and Sandefur (2007) in math; Chi, Glaser and Farr (1988) offer an impressive collection of such studies in their edited volume. In my work on experts and novices in political science (Bernstein 2010, 2013), I follow these examples and attempt to map out what experts do when they approach a task, and then compare it to what novices do. Following the principles outlined above by Pace, this work is aimed at helping to make visible the hidden moves that experts make when performing disciplinary tasks, and to help us figure out how best to teach these skills to students. I trust readers will agree that we would be making great progress as teachers if we were able to do this successfully.

I present the work above as an example of what we can learn from doing the scholarship of teaching and learning; one of my goals in this chapter is to enable others to perform their own inquiries on the teaching and learning process in our discipline, perhaps guided by the kinds of questions my students' facilitators and I discussed. But moving beyond that, I argue here that we need to find ways not only to help our students, and improve our own teaching, but also to help good teaching build upon good teaching in the academy at large. In our 'research' – what Boyer (1990) calls the scholarship of discovery – scholarly works build upon scholarly works, enabling scholars to stand on the shoulders of those who have done earlier work. This is how fields grow and move toward answers to important questions. Simply put, we need to use the scholarship of teaching and learning to help college teaching improve itself, writ large.

This chapter proceeds as follows. In the next section, I introduce the scholarship of teaching and learning, and differentiate it from other terms currently in vogue to describe similar work. I then discuss two aspects of the scholarship of teaching and learning that might make this work particularly enticing, and welcoming, for political scientists. I then proceed to discuss some considerations that should guide scholars as they begin their investigations of student learning. I conclude with some arguments for why we need to do this work, and why we need to move with some alacrity. My hope is that this chapter will encourage political scientists to explore work done in this field, and to consider dipping a toe into the water and beginning their own inquiries of teaching and learning in our discipline.

THE SCHOLARSHIP OF TEACHING AND LEARNING: WHAT IT IS, AND WHAT IT IS NOT

The scholarship of teaching and learning begins from Boyer's (1990) perspective that teaching is scholarly work. As such, like all good scholarship, scholarly work in teaching and learning must be based on evidence (however conceived), must build upon work that has come before it, and must be made public in such a way that others can then use it. Regarding evidence, nobody would attempt to make an argument about a scholarly matter without data to support their claims. Likewise, when it comes to teaching, if we make an argument that a particular teaching technique works best, we must be prepared to use evidence of student learning to document that it does. Second, scholarly work in teaching and learning builds upon work that has come before it. Doing the scholarship of teaching and learning requires that we learn from the literature in the field (on teaching and learning in general, as well as on teaching and learning in our disciplines) and use that work to inform what we do. Finally, the scholarship of teaching and learning requires that we go public in our inquiries, whether through presentations at conferences, teaching portfolios (Bernstein et al. 2006) or publications. When we go public with our work, and subject our work to peer review, we transform our teaching into a true act of scholarship.

The *scholarship of teaching and learning* is different from ideas like *good teaching* or *scholarly teaching* (McKinney 2004). All of us have obligations to be *good teachers* – to run effective classes, lead discussions well, design fair and reasonable tests, etc. Places like faculty development centers provide strong resources to faculty who wish to improve their skills in any of these areas (Bernstein and Ginsberg 2009). Moving beyond good teaching, at the next level McKinney argues that we also have an obligation to be *scholarly teachers* – to read and keep up with the literature on teaching and learning, and to have our classroom work informed by the writings of the leading scholars in these fields. While relatively few of us do this on a regular basis, the obligation to do so seems intuitively strong. We would never claim to be doing good research if we were ignoring developments in the professional literature – it is hard to claim we are being the best teachers we can be if we do not keep up with the literature on teaching and learning.

The scholarship of teaching and learning is differentiated from good teaching and scholarly teaching largely by whether or not one is going public as a *producer* of knowledge on teaching and learning. By performing one's own inquiries on student learning, using evidence to inform such investigations, subjecting the results to peer review and going public, one helps others to learn and advances the field of teaching and learning (generally and/or within one's discipline). To be sure, few would argue that all faculty members have an obligation to be scholars of teaching and learning in the way I would argue that we all have an obligation to be good teachers, or even scholarly teachers. Professional pressures, or different levels of interest in this area, might lead some to focus on other areas of scholarship, or other aspects of one's job. Ideally, however, at the institutional level, we have much to gain from a flourishing scholarship of teaching and learning. As Hutchings and Shulman (1999, p. 14) argue:

> [T]he scholarship of teaching *is* a condition – as yet a mostly absent condition – for excellent teaching. It is the mechanism through which the profession of teaching itself advances, through

which teaching can be something other than a seat-of-the-pants operation, with each of us out there making it up as we go. As such, the scholarship of teaching has the potential to serve *all* teachers – and students. (emphasis in original)

While some (e.g. Clegg 2008) are skeptical of the degree to which this work has achieved its potential, most would suggest that this work continues to hold the potential (if not yet actualized) to serve larger purposes within the academy.

FEATURES OF THE SCHOLARSHIP OF TEACHING AND LEARNING

Having offered a broad overview of the scholarship of teaching and learning, I now turn to a brief discussion about two aspects of this work. The fact that the scholarship of teaching and learning values the importance of academic disciplines as strongly as it does makes it especially appealing to political scientists. Furthermore, the perceived methodological biases in the work, while a potential turnoff to some, can also make members of our discipline feel at home in this movement. I discuss each of these points in turn.

The Scholarship of Teaching and Learning Values the Disciplines

One of the criticisms that is often leveled at the teaching and learning literature is that it sometimes appears to take a 'one size fits all' approach, doling out advice for how to teach better, regardless of context. The scholarship of teaching and learning literature generally does not do this. Instead, the scholarship of teaching and learning shows appreciation for the idea that, while good teaching has much in common across the disciplines, teaching itself is a fundamentally different act if one is teaching physics, poetry or political science. For example, a recent spate of edited volumes (Chick, Haynie and Gurung 2012; Gurung, Chick and Haynie 2008; Huber and Morreale 2002; McKinney 2013) provide examples of the scholarship of teaching and learning across the disciplines, showing how what constitutes good teaching (and what constitutes evidence of good teaching) differs across disciplinary boundaries.

The attention to teaching and learning across the disciplines reflects Lee Shulman's (1987) notion of 'pedagogical content learning', in which he posits that effective teaching occurs at the intersection of knowing how to teach and knowing the content of one's discipline. At this intersection, we see the unique skills required to teach in a particular field. Ideally, I not only know how to lead effective discussions, and how to understand the tension between majority rule and minority rights, but I also know specifically how to lead discussions about majority rule and majority rights. Leading such a discussion does involve elements common to leading all discussions, but it is also different from leading discussions of *Beowulf*.

The discipline-centric nature of the scholarship of teaching and learning suggests that we should see discussions of teaching and learning within each discipline. This has occurred in recent years, with the growth of the American Political Science Association Teaching and Learning Conference, as well as the publication of the *Journal of Political Science Education*. These forums, along with the relevant sections of *PS: Political Science*

& Politics, provide opportunities for discipline-based discussions of teaching and learning to occur. Additionally, as the assessment movement gathers steam and society asks for more evidence of the value of higher education, teaching may well come to matter more and more. Finally, to cite one example, my reading of anecdotal evidence suggests that, due to the oversupply of job candidates, and the changing pressures on research-intensive universities, very few schools are ignoring teaching in hiring, and in tenure and promotion decisions. If this continues, we will see even more opportunities for discussion of teaching and learning within the discipline.

The Scholarship of Teaching and Learning, of Necessity, Values Methodological Pluralism

A criticism that is often leveled at the scholarship of teaching and learning is that it privileges social science methodology, leading those who are not social scientists to feel marginalized (e.g. Chick 2013; Grauerholz and Main 2013). While reasonable people may disagree on whether or not this marginalization does occur, one thing that is beyond dispute is that the scholarship of teaching and learning does privilege, or at least broadly tolerate, social scientific methods. Surveying students on their learning, and statistically analyzing the results, is something that is familiar to most social scientists. The 'methods anxiety' that people from the humanities (and, to a lesser extent, the natural and physical sciences) feel as they approach the scholarship of learning is likely to be felt to a much smaller extent by those trained as political scientists.

More than this, however, is the fact that the scholarship of teaching and learning (ideally) respects the methodological standards used in the disciplines. The double-blind, control group studies common in the natural sciences and the medical field can be held up as the methodological standard when evaluating work on teaching and learning in those fields; scholars in those fields will find these studies useful. In contrast, political scientists might be most comfortable with quasi-experiments, tests of statistical significance and 95 percent confidence intervals. Humanities scholars might be most comfortable with thick, narrative descriptions that highlight student learning. Scholars of teaching and learning may have 'data' that are physical representations of student work, while in literature, the student work may look more like an essay. Since the practitioners in each field are the leaders in teaching and learning discussions in those fields, the methodological standards in each field can prevail.

With this said, the scholarship of teaching and learning also values the exchange of methods that are common when different methodological traditions come together. Described most graphically in Huber and Hutchings's (2005) analogy of 'methodological trading zones', scholars of teaching and learning have much to learn from others in their communities about different ways to gather evidence to document student learning. Since the field of political science is a methodologically pluralistic one, we can learn from other studies about how to use methods outside our own individual comfort zones – these can include things like observation of student activity in class, analyzing transcripts of class discussions or various other techniques. Like all good research, the scholarship of teaching and learning calls for fitting the appropriate research method to the research question at hand, rather than fitting the research question into the methods we frequently employ.

GETTING STARTED

For readers who have read the chapter to this point and are interested in getting started with their own scholarship of teaching and learning project, this section lays out a few practical steps for beginning this kind of investigation. The interested reader is encouraged to range more broadly in the literature before beginning this work; Weimer (2002) and McKinney (2007) provide useful introductions to the topic and guidance on getting started with this work that go into more detail than this short chapter can.

Identify an Interesting Teaching/Research Question

As with our work in the scholarship of discovery, it all begins with a question (see Hutchings 2000 on the role of questions in the scholarship of teaching and learning, and for a useful typology of such questions). Good questions start with observation. Look at your students. Where do they struggle? What are the weaknesses in their papers? What concepts do they seem to have trouble applying? What are they unable to do? Think about possible interventions. Then, marry the two. Would doing X help to solve problem Y? Will my students show a greater ability to understand the budget process by using a simulation? Will a particular assignment help my students to better understand how election results turn out the way they do? For most of us, these questions (what Hutchings 2000 calls 'what works?' questions) provide a valuable way to enter this work. And, the nice thing about entering the work in this way is that it is motivated by real issues with which our students struggle; any information we can glean from these investigations will help improve our teaching, and our students' learning.

In my own case (see Bernstein 2010), I became interested in how students learn to make use of multiple, contradictory sources when studying a political issue. Following on Wineburg (2001), I knew that experts do things with sources that novices do not do – for Wineburg's historians this included such behaviors as considering the author and perspective of an article's author *before* reading the article, reading sources in the order in which they were written and, most importantly, engaging sources in dialogue with one another, rather than viewing each as completely separate entities. If I could observe how experts engaged sources in studying an issue, and compared it to what novices did, I would be able to identify the differences, and then find ways to teach novices to mimic expert practice in their own work.

Think Broadly about Data

Once a research question is in place, the next step is to think about data. What evidence can be found that would reveal learning is taking place? There are many possibilities – survey data of students, close analysis of papers, exams or problem sets, interviews with students, analysis of audiotapes or videotapes of classroom discussions, etc. The only limitation is the imagination of the investigator; overviews of the scholarship of teaching and learning, like McKinney (2007), can help expand this imagination by highlighting multiple possible methods. In thinking about data, the main goal is to consider how to document what students are learning. If the innovation is intended to help students develop a better understanding of a concept, for example, then the best way to determine if their understanding has improved is by seeing how well they can write about it, or answer questions about it on an exam. To the extent possible, studies that use 'authentic assessments' (assignments that students do as part of a class, rather than special data collection conducted solely for the purpose of research) are preferred, since they do not add any extra burden to student participants, and the work that students do on those assignments would represent their best efforts (since they know the assignment is being graded).

For my project, I chose to use 'think-alouds'. Used by Wineburg (1991, 2001; see also Chase and Simon 1973; Ericsson and Simon 1984; Sandefur 2007), these think-alouds presented students with an array of source materials and asked them to think aloud about the material. They would read the sources aloud, and process their thoughts verbally; if they were silent too long, I would jump in with a prompt such as, 'What are you thinking now?' By audiotaping these sessions, I could learn the hallmarks of expert thinking, and then compare that to what I saw from the novices. As patterns would emerge, I would get closer and closer to answering my research question.

Think about the Intended Audience

As one goes about these kinds of investigations, it is worth giving some thought to who is the intended audience for the study. One question to consider is whether the study is intended for people who are teaching in the discipline, or for those who are teaching more broadly. Some investigations (such as studying how students understand the United Nations, or how they can learn to write policy papers) might best be aimed at political science audiences, while studies that focus more generally on the affordances and constraints of simulations, or how to lead better discussions, might be aimed at a more general audience. One audience is not better than the other; the goal is to be clear, as early as the study design stage, about who the audience is, and how to aim that study (through the literature review and the discussion) at the right audience.

Human Subjects

Because many investigations of teaching and learning use students as sources of data, most of these investigations (such as my own) require review by the Institutional Review Board (IRB) of the investigator's campus. While seemingly tedious and time-consuming, such reviews are important, because our students represent a vulnerable population. Since students in our classes might not feel free to decline to participate in our studies when asked, it is important that we put procedures in place to protect the legitimate rights of our students to choose not to participate, or to withdraw from the study when they do. The researcher is advised not only to build in safeguards to ensure the interests of human subjects are protected, but also to ensure that time is allotted, before data collection commences, to have the research proposal reviewed by the IRB. At some fortunate schools, investigations in the scholarship of teaching and learning might have been granted blanket approval from the IRB, assuming certain safeguards are put in place. When that is the case, the burdens on the researcher can be significantly lessened.

It is worth pointing out that going through the IRB process can help to minimize the risk that students will tell us what they think we want to hear in their responses to surveys, or other data collection instruments. When I do surveys of my current students, my IRB requires that I take safeguards so that I do not know which students have consented to participate, and which have not, until after the semester ends and grades have been submitted. I also cannot see any data from my students (aside from regular course-based assessments) until that time. I tell students this, emphasizing to them that they need not fear for their grades if they tell me things they might think I do not want to hear. I also emphasize to them that, as a scientist, I value objective and honest data. My sense is that I have been successful in generating such authentic data, in large part because students have reason to trust their interests are protected.

Trade and Share

A final piece of advice for someone considering doing work in the scholarship of teaching and learning is to learn from others – both about good research questions, as well as about methodology. On methodology, the idea of the methodological trading zone (Huber and Hutchings 2005) is worth keeping in mind. More generally, however, work in the scholarship of teaching and learning provides multiple opportunities for productive collaborations with a wider range of colleagues. While it is useful to share my work on simulations in political science teaching with my disciplinary colleagues, my work benefits even more from sharing it with colleagues who use simulations in other fields, or who just value the same kinds of things I value in the classroom. Research can be a lonely endeavor; work in the scholarship of teaching and learning can break down the pedagogical solitude that Lee Shulman (1993) argues is problematic in higher education teaching through transcending disciplinary silos.

WHY SHOULD WE DO THIS WORK?

The foregoing discussion has offered a window into the scholarship of teaching and learning, and how we can get started in it. In this final section of the chapter, I offer a few ideas for *why* we ought to engage in this work. The first, and most important, reason for political scientists to engage in the scholarship of teaching and learning is because it will enable us to enhance our teaching, and our students' learning. Historically within higher education, professors have taught the way they themselves learned, and pass that on to their students, many of whom do not learn the same way we did. Careful attention to the teaching and learning process will enable us to make sure that our students are learning course material. Putting our own work under the microscope, and gathering data on how well we are doing, will help us to do what we do better. It is difficult, and potentially gut-wrenching, to expose one's own work in this way. That point cannot be overemphasized – it takes a strong constitution to gather data that show how we may be falling short in the classroom. It is hard to do this, and humbling, and frustrating. But, in the end, the rewards are well worth it.

A second motivation for doing this work concerns some of the pressures we face in the academy. As the cost of higher education goes up, we are increasingly pressured to show the value of what colleges and universities do (see Bernstein 2012). This most directly reflects itself through the movement to require more 'assessment' of student learning.

Assessment can be important, when done well. It forces us to lay out what our student learning outcomes are, and to find ways to measure if our students are achieving these outcomes.

Assessment generally comes down from the top – it is usually the Provost's Office that gets pressured from outside accrediting bodies to undergo assessment as part of the accreditation process. Faculty have a choice when accreditation comes to the door – we can sit on the outside, or play active roles in the process. I would argue that, if we do not get involved, and if we do not play an active role in specifying what students should learn, and how we measure whether they have learned that, then these determinations will be made by administrators above us. Assessment is simply too important to be left to administrators. Nobody knows what political science students should be learning, and how to assess that learning, better than a group of political scientists. If we do not come forward as part of this process, someone else will, invariably to our detriment.

A third reason to do work in the scholarship of teaching and learning concerns the type of culture we want to see in our departments and universities. When scholars investigate teaching and learning, and engage in discussion with others about issues we confront in the classroom, we generate more knowledge about the teaching and learning process. This ideally feeds back into our classroom – when faculty lounges and water coolers become 'trading zones' for innovation in teaching, we improve our practice. We also help to make our departments more 'student centered', and create a situation where our departments value good work in the classroom. I write this chapter from the perspective that my readers wish to improve their teaching, and wish to teach in departments that value good teaching. Scholarly investigation of teaching and learning holds one of the critical keys for making this happen. It is one that we should pursue aggressively, before it is too late.

REFERENCES

Bernstein, Daniel, Amy Nelson Burnett, Amy Goodburn and Paul Savory (2006), *Making Teaching and Learning Visible: Course Portfolios and the Peer Review of Teaching*, Bolton, MA: Anker Publishing.

Bernstein, Jeffrey L. (2010), 'Using Think-Alouds to Understand Variations in Political Thinking', *Journal of Political Science Education*, **6**, 49–69.

Bernstein, Jeffrey L. (2012), 'Defending Our Lives: The Scholarship of Teaching and Learning in an Academy Under Attack', *International Journal for the Scholarship of Teaching and Learning*, **6** (1), article 2.

Bernstein, Jeffrey L. (2013), 'Plowing through Bottlenecks in Political Science: Experts and Novices at Work', in Kathleen McKinney (ed.), *SoTL in and Across the Disciplines*, Bloomington, IN: Indiana University Press, pp. 84–92.

Bernstein, Jeffrey L. and Sarah M. Ginsberg (2009), 'Toward an Integrated Model of the Scholarship of Teaching and Learning and Faculty Development', *Journal for Centers for Teaching and Learning*, **1**, 57–72.

Bowen, Craig W. (1994), 'Think-Aloud Methods in Chemistry Education: Understanding Student Thinking', *Journal of Chemical Education*, **71**, 184–90.

Boyer, Ernest L. (1990), *Scholarship Reconsidered: Priorities of the Professoriate*, Princeton, NJ: The Carnegie Foundation for the Advancement of Teaching.

Chase, W.G. and Herbert A. Simon (1973), 'Perception in Chess', *Cognitive Psychology*, **4**, 55–81.

Chi, Michelene T.H., Robert Glaser and Marshall J. Farr (eds) (1988), *The Nature of Expertise*, Hillsdale, NJ: Lawrence Erlbaum Associates.

Chick, Nancy L. (2013), 'Difference, Power and Privilege in the Scholarship of Teaching and Learning: The Value of Humanities SOTL', in Kathleen McKinney (ed.), *SoTL in and Across the Disciplines*, Bloomington, IN: Indiana University Press, pp. 15–33.

Chick, Nancy L., Aeron Haynie and Regan A.R. Gurung (2012), *More Signature Pedagogies*, Sterling, VA: Stylus.
Clegg, Sue (2008), 'The Struggle for Connections', Keynote Address at the Annual Meeting of the International Society for the Scholarship of Teaching and Learning, Edmonton, Alberta, Canada.
Ericsson, K. Anders and Herbert A. Simon (1984), *Protocol Analysis: Verbal Reports as Data*, Cambridge, MA: MIT Press.
Grauerholz, Liz and Eric Main (2013), 'Fallacies of SOTL: Rethinking How We Conduct Our Research', in Kathleen McKinney (ed.), *SoTL in and Across the Disciplines*, Bloomington, IN: Indiana University Press, pp. 152–68.
Gurung, Regan A.R., Nancy L. Chick and Aeron Haynie (2008), *Exploring Signature Pedagogies: Approaches to Teaching Disciplinary Habits of Mind*, Sterling, VA: Stylus.
Gutman, Ellen E., Erin M. Sergison, Chelsea Martin and Jeffrey L. Bernstein (2009), 'Engaging Students as Scholars of Teaching and Learning: The Role of Ownership', in Carmen Werder and Megan Otis (eds), *Engaging Student Voices in the Study of Teaching and Learning*, Sterling, VA: Stylus Press, pp. 130–45.
Halpern, Diane F. and Milton D. Hakel (2003), 'Applying the Science of Learning to the University and Beyond', *Change*, **35** (4), 36–41.
Huber, Mary Taylor and Pat Hutchings (2005), *The Advancement of Learning: Building the Teaching Commons*, San Francisco, CA: Jossey-Bass.
Huber, Mary Taylor and Sherwyn Morreale (eds) (2002), *Disciplinary Styles in the Scholarship of Teaching and Learning: Exploring Common Ground*, Washington, DC: American Association for Higher Education and The Carnegie Foundation for the Advancement of Teaching.
Hutchings, Pat (2000), 'Introduction: Approaching the Scholarship of Teaching and Learning', in Pat Hutchings (ed.), *Opening Lines: Approaches to the Scholarship of Teaching and Learning*, Menlo Park, CA: Carnegie Publications, available at http://www.carnegiefoundation.org/elibrary/approaching-scholarship-teaching-and-learning (accessed 14 June 2014).
Hutchings, Pat and Lee S. Shulman (1999), 'The Scholarship of Teaching: New Elaborations, New Developments', *Change*, **31**, 10–15.
McKinney, Kathleen (ed.) (2013), *SoTL in and Across the Disciplines*, Bloomington, IN: Indiana University Press.
McKinney, Kathleen (2007), *Enhancing Learning through the Scholarship of Teaching and Learning: The Challenges and Joys of Juggling*, San Francisco, CA: Jossey-Bass.
McKinney, Kathleen (2004), 'The Scholarship of Teaching and Learning: Past Lessons, Current Challenges, and Future Visions', *To Improve the Academy*, **22**, 3–19.
Pace, David (2004), 'The Amateur in the Operating Room: History and the Scholarship of Teaching and Learning', *American Historical Review*, **109**, 1171–92.
Sandefur, James (2007), 'Problem Solving: What I have Learned from my Students', in Ki Hyoung Ko and Deane Arganbright (eds), *Enhancing University Mathematics: Proceedings of the First KAIST International Symposium on Teaching*, CBMS Issues in Mathematics Education 14, Providence, RI: American Mathematical Society, pp. 117–28.
Shulman, Lee S. (1987), 'Knowledge and Teaching: Foundations of the New Reform', *Harvard Educational Review*, **36**, 1–22.
Shulman, Lee S. (1993), 'Teaching as Community Property: Putting an End to Pedagogical Solitude', *Change*, **25** (6), 6–7.
Weimer, Maryellen (2002), *Learner-Centered Teaching: Five Key Changes to Practice*, San Francisco, CA: Jossey-Bass.
Wiggins, Grant and Jay McTighe (1998), *Understanding by Design*, Alexandria, VA: Association for Supervision and Curriculum Development.
Wineburg, Samuel S. (1991), 'Historical Problem Solving: A Study of the Cognitive Processes Used in the Evaluation of Documentary and Pictorial Evidence', *Journal of Educational Psychology*, **83**, 73–87.
Wineburg, Sam (2001), *Historical Thinking and Other Unnatural Acts: Charting the Future of Teaching the Past*, Philadelphia, PA: Temple University Press.

37. Getting students to talk: best practices in promoting student discussion
Michael P. Marks

This chapter is based on the simple premise that students often learn best through active participation facilitated through classroom discussion. Although lectures and instructor-led lessons play an important role in imparting analytical concepts and empirical facts, the passive assimilation of information does not provide a complete learning experience. Moreover, despite the fact that most instructors are aware of the benefits of engaged student discussion, encouraging active participation can be difficult especially when the benefits of passive learning through such means as massive open online classes have been touted as a partial solution to the problem of access to higher education. Instructors can benefit from maintaining a toolkit of practices that promote student discussion with the aim of reinforcing course concepts through active learning (Meyers and Jones 1993).

Student discussion is useful in a variety of disciplines but is arguably more essential in the social sciences and humanities than in the physical and natural sciences. Although students certainly can benefit from collaboration and group learning in science classes, critical discussion of analytical concepts and theoretical claims in the humanities and social sciences is an integral element in advancing knowledge even at the undergraduate level (Kramer and Korn 1999). In political science classes in particular students benefit from actively participating in the discussion of theoretical approaches as well as policy issues. Intensive classroom discussion mimics the verbal give-and-take professional academics engage in at conferences and workshops as well as workplace dynamics students eventually will encounter in their careers in business, government, non-profit organizations, journalism and the law. Promoting productive student discussion, however, is not a straightforward task and involves more than simply interrupting lectures periodically to ask a few closed-ended questions. This chapter offers suggestions for promoting opportunities for useful student discussion that advances the learning process.

PROVIDING STUDENTS WITH MATERIAL TO DISCUSS

The most obvious way to encourage useful and worthwhile student discussion is to provide students with materials, subject matter and exercises that generate reflection on course themes. Simulations and role-playing exercises provide students with excellent opportunities for involved discussion (Boatright, Giner and Gomes 2013; Frombgen et al. 2013; Biziouras 2013). I employ a case study method in two upper-level courses on international relations. Since students have had the opportunity for hands-on learning utilizing case studies, discussion of the cases engages their active participation and utilizes the information they have generated themselves in the course of investigating the subject matter of the cases and its relationship to concepts covered in class. The questions I pose about the case studies are designed to elicit discussion not only of the facts of each case but of how they relate to course concepts as well as themes developed throughout the term. That way, students are not just reacting to each case but are also engaging analytical concepts that recur during the class and are reinforced during weekly discussion sessions.

In-class writing also can stimulate student discussion (Fulwiler 1987; Tomasek 2009). Writing assignments done in class can be short and the writing itself does not have to consume a great deal of time to generate useful examination of course themes. Students can be assigned to write one paragraph about some aspect of politics and then use what they have written to discuss the topic under investigation. The purpose is not for each student to contribute in turn but to use what they have written to expose multiple ways of thinking about a topic. While in-class writing assignments can get students to *talk*, they do not necessarily encourage students to *discuss* topics unless they are carefully designed to do so. The types of writing assignments that get students to talk, as opposed to discuss an issue, are those that simply ask students to answer a question to which there are a finite number of responses. A better in-class writing assignment would be one that invites discussion by exposing an issue to critical examination. This could happen even in introductory classes. For example, instructors could ask students to write a short paragraph in which they suggest an answer to this question: 'Political parties, interest groups and social movements all promote democratic participation. Which form of collective interest articulation most promotes the principle of democratic participation and why?' A question of this nature encourages students to critically examine how and why certain forms of political participation advance the principles of democracy. Students can discuss the merits of political parties, interest groups and social movements in a manner that engages a variety of ways of thinking about politics, thus promoting collective learning as opposed to individual responses. Students can agree and disagree with each other instead of simply offering a one-time contribution.

Having students bring something to class to talk about also can be an easy way to generate student-led discussion. In political science and international studies courses an obvious item to ask students to bring to class is a news article related to recently covered topics (Knowlton and Barefoot 1999). This strategy can work at any point in the course, even at the beginning of the term when students are just becoming familiar with basic course themes. For example, in my introductory comparative politics course on the politics of advanced industrial societies I dedicate the first week of the semester to introducing and identifying the basic concepts of politics and democracy. Aspects of politics that are introduced are the notion of interests, the nature of political authority, forms of political participation and political ideologies. For the third class session of the semester, I ask students to bring to class a news article on some recent issue of politics somewhere in the advanced industrial world. Students volunteer to summarize their articles and then other students are asked to identify aspects of politics and democracy based on the previous days' lectures. Even though students have not yet read any assigned course texts, they come to the third class session of the semester prepared to discuss newly introduced concepts. Students also get an early opportunity to see how classroom discussion aids understanding key themes and thus are prepared to participate for the duration of the course.

It is important to plan exercises of this nature so that they are coordinated with other course lectures, discussions and exercises and in order that they build on lessons that have been developed over the course of the term. In my upper-level class on European politics, for instance, the course is divided into two broad themes, European integration and the foreign policy of the European Union and its member states. Because there is a natural pause between these two large themes, I build in two weeks between them for students to use recent developments in European politics to reflect on and discuss the theoretical course readings using empirical evidence found in news accounts or current events. Since this exercise is built into the class and listed in the syllabus, students see it as integral to the development of course themes. More importantly, students understand it is their responsibility to tease out concepts that will be useful using factual material to give substance to the abstract concepts covered in analytical course texts.

Similar to exercises in which students bring a news article to class to discuss, meaningful classroom discussion can be generated through short weekly assignments that do not require a large time commitment from students in terms of preparation but can yield appreciable results. Students can be given a short weekly assignment to write a one- or two-paragraph summary of one of the assigned readings for the week along with a suggested discussion question. These types of weekly chapter summaries and suggested discussion questions are useful in ways that spontaneous discussion of course readings may not be. They permit shy students to initiate the discussion through a written submission rather than having to raise their hands. Exercises of this nature also allow the instructor to select the questions that are most likely to generate relevant discussion of weekly readings and direct the discussion using student questions so as to follow a logical progression of thoughts.

ASKING DIRECTED QUESTIONS ABOUT COURSE MATERIALS AND READING ASSIGNMENTS

In order to generate discussion it is necessary to ask students questions (Larkin and Pines 2005). One way to get students feeling comfortable talking in a group is to ask them closed-ended questions about factual material under investigation. However, closed-ended questions only go so far. Questions that elicit information that merely reproduces the content of course materials is not the same thing as generating the type of discussion that prompts investigation of analytical concepts. 'How' questions take the conversation a step further because they encourage longer responses by students. Asking students, for example, how parliamentary systems differ from presidential systems requires students to describe a set of political phenomena and thus allows them to feel comfortable responding in long form.

The best questions for encouraging discussion, as opposed to responses, however, are questions that ask 'why?' These questions elicit answers that encourage students to explain issues in terms of the theories, analytical concepts and frameworks for analysis that are covered explicitly or implicitly in most political science classes. Open-ended 'why' questions are the most likely to foster extended student discussion, but they should be directed towards illuminating themes laid out in course readings or covered in class exercises. It is fair to assume that most students in a political science course have an inclination to be curious about and interested in politics, but a question that is pitched at too high a level of abstraction may intimidate students rather than encourage them because it represents a metaphysical mystery rather than a question about a specific theory of politics. In an introductory international relations class, for example, students are more likely to respond with answers that generate useful discussions to the question 'why do some scholars argue that bipolarity is more likely to create stability than multipolarity?' than the question 'why do some scholars think instability is possible in international relations?' The latter question may in fact engage the relationship between the abstractions of power and stability, but at the undergraduate level the open-ended yet more directed question about distributions of power is more likely to draw on course readings in a way that helps students understand them.

While open-ended questions obviously are useful for stimulating discussion, perhaps the deadliest of the open-ended questions and the one that often elicits little more than blank stares is the question posed in the form of 'what did you think of the reading by author X?' Students are likely to have thought a lot about any given reading, including the fact that it may be poorly written, overly long, confusing or, as is often thought of by students, boring. Asking students their general impression of any given reading is tantamount to querying them about their dislike for said reading or their feeling towards the assignment, which is not the same thing as asking them questions about specific empirical or analytical claims made in the text. This is not necessarily to say that students cannot be queried about their overall reaction to a course reading, but that a preliminary probing of students' impressions should be followed up by more detailed questions about the text.

A good way to encourage enhanced active engagement in assigned texts is to make them manageable and to ask probing questions about them. It is often tempting to assign students a large amount to read over the duration of a week either because there is a lot of material to cover in any given class, or because students should be learning outside of the classroom, or because federal guidelines require a certain number of credit-hours be allocated to work performed beyond the time allotted for class sessions (Joliffe and Harl 2008). However, some of the best student discussion can revolve around an intensive interrogation of a single text of relatively short length. A time-honored practice in both political philosophy and international relations classes alike is to devote an entire class session (or more) to the Melian Dialogue from Thucydides' *History of the Peloponnesian War* (Foran 2001; Bald 2004). This passage comprises a few short pages but invites students to immerse themselves in multiple themes of politics, morality and war and their relevance in a variety of historical settings. Instructors might be tempted to assign more than just this single passage for a day's discussion to convince themselves and students alike that they did sufficient 'work' for the class. However, often if students devote themselves to just one thing they are more likely to think critically about that one thing and be eager to discuss it in a meaningful way than if they are confronted with multiple concepts that are discussed only in a superficial fashion.

OPTIMIZING CLASSROOM CONFIGURATION AND TECHNOLOGY

Seemingly, small things can matter when attempting to encourage classroom discussion. Although instructors can be successful encouraging discussion in classrooms set up for lecture format, classroom configuration can play a role facilitating such discussion (Weinstein 1992). It is likely students will be more inclined to talk, and talk to each other, when a classroom is arranged in a seminar style with tables or desks organized so that students face each other. This is not necessarily to say that students sitting in rows will not be capable of carrying a sustained discussion. However, students typically associate rows of desks with lecture classes (and therefore passive learning), while they associate tables or desks facing each other with a seminar or colloquium format. Moreover, when students are facing each other rather than sitting in rows they can talk to each other instead of directing comments at the instructor or at the backs of each others' heads.

Of course, not all classrooms are set up for a seminar format and in fact may not be appropriate for a course that uses a combination of lectures and discussions. Under these circumstances, modular furniture that can be rearranged can be useful in order to create an architecture conducive to student discussion in classes in which lectures predominate but occasional student discussion takes place. Indeed, asking students to rearrange furniture, despite their occasional reluctance to get up and move, can stimulate friendly banter that carries over to discussion of course readings. Tables arranged in rows can easily be rearranged to create an outer layer of tables facing inward that recreates in part a seminar style feel.

In addition to classroom configuration, what students see in the classroom can have a subtle impact on how receptive they are to discussion. Visual presentation software such as PowerPoint has become an increasingly common feature in classroom use, supplementing or completely replacing chalkboard or dry erase board presentations. As virtually every educator can attest, however, there are obvious drawbacks to relying on technological teaching aids and visual presentation software (Moore, Watson and Fowler 2007; Petrina 2007). Most obviously, when confronted with ready-for-notetaking information displayed clearly and prominently at the front of the classroom, students may be inclined to write down what they think is important and dispense with spontaneous discussion, even if it is instructor generated, since it is not presented in visually displayed text and therefore seemingly not important for subsequent evaluation.

On the other hand, interactive classroom technology such as classroom response systems ('clickers') have proven immensely useful for getting students to actively participate in classroom discussions (d'Inverno, Davis and White 2003; Beatty 2004; Duncan 2005; Caldwell 2007). This type of technology, which can be incorporated into large lecture classes and small seminar courses alike, keeps students engaged in course material. When used thoughtfully by instructors, clickers can yield immediate responses to open-ended questions posed to a class that then lead to discussion of the results displayed on screens or monitors throughout the classroom. Even simple visual aids that require no electronics or expensive technologies can help foster worthwhile discussion. I bring a decidedly low-tech roll-down map of Europe to every class session of my upper-level European politics course. Students frequently point to the map and suggest empirical examples of analytical concepts using geographic information on the map to find applications of conceptual themes.

Internet accessibility in classrooms also can have a positive effect on student discussion by providing a means to look up information relevant to classroom discussion. The ready availability of information provided by in-class online access gives instructors the ability to improvise when it would be helpful to supplement course materials with additional facts. Students also can have an interactive experience in the classroom by finding information online and using it to lead discussion in a useful direction. Many campuses now have Wi-Fi available as well as smart classrooms so students can use their own laptops and mobile devices to go online when appropriate to find information that can contribute to discussion.

AVOIDING THE PERILS OF CONTROVERSY: MAKING CONNECTIONS BETWEEN THEORY AND PRACTICE

Not all discussion is useful discussion. Some of the most animated classroom discussion in political science classes is not always the most productive and can be among the least useful ways of promoting student learning. Specifically, although it may be tempting to draw on students' natural interest in politics, discussions centering on controversial issues that invite students to air their partisan preferences can accomplish little in the way of learning new concepts (for a contradictory opinion, see Hess 2009). At a minimum, partisan arguments in the classroom do not replicate the type of work that scholars undertake in their own academic pursuits nor the atmosphere that is cultivated in most workplace environments students will encounter. Scholars are capable of advancing arguments about causality in politics without injecting their personal preferences. Just because students are talking about politics does not mean they are accomplishing anything productive if their discussion amounts to little more than uninformed repetition of what is 'right' or 'wrong' in the policies of a government, party or individual. It is of course tempting to engage students' interest in politics in order to get them to talk in the classroom. Many students in political sciences classes are there because they are interested in the subject matter. Furthermore, a dry, dull, one-way lecture that does not draw out students' passion for politics will do little to stimulate learning. Still, students are well served by grasping what political scientists understand, namely, that arguing about politics and airing one's partisan preferences is not the same thing as engaging in political science.

On the other hand, in light of students' obvious interest in politics, there are ways of promoting useful discussion of topical issues that relate to class themes. In my comparative politics class on the politics of advanced industrial societies, for example, a question I ask students over the course of the semester is what policies or practices (depending on the theme for the week) are most consistent with the principles of democracy. I then ask them why they answer as they do, using the theories of politics they have been learning about in class. This way students can have an 'opinion', as it were, about politics that even draws on their latent political preferences but is grounded in the approaches to the comparative study of democracy covered in class. What policies and practices are most consistent with democracy is a question that can be analytically answered but allows students to come away with an idea for what they might advocate for advancing democratic governance drawing on an objective analysis of politics.

Because controversial topics can detract more than they aid in generating useful classroom discussion, a way to avoid a descent into partisan arguments is to stress the connections between theory and practice. Moving from an abstract concept to its application in the practice of politics can help students understand the benefits of objective scholarship at the same time they see how issues they care about can be explained. To take a recent example from a comparative politics course I teach, a student asked in his weekly chapter summary question why socialist parties enjoy as little electoral success as they do in the USA compared to other advanced industrial democracies. The ensuing discussion delved into the perennial question of 'why no socialism in the USA?', which allowed students to evaluate the strength of competing theories that have been advanced to answer this question. Having addressed this part of the issue, students who were attracted to the platform of European socialist parties were able to suggest changes to the American political system that might permit greater electoral success by socialist parties. The controversial question of whether President Obama could or should be labeled a socialist (a question that was raised in student weekly chapter assignment submissions) was then tackled in the context of the larger question of how to characterize political parties across various countries using the tools of comparative politics, what students had learned about party families and the recurrent question of why there are no electorally viable socialist parties in the USA.

Discussion of the connections between theory and practice can also narrow the gap between students' interest in learning facts and the need to grasp abstract concepts. Despite the wide availability of a broad range of news sources, many students report not reading the news nor following current events. In political science classes in particular many students expect to learn factual material about *what* transpires in the world of politics, although instructors may be more inclined to emphasize *why* political actions occur. Discussion of course materials can present an opportunity to use news articles and current events to provide the factual information students express an interest knowing about to illustrate the theories of politics that are covered in readings and classroom lectures. In many of my courses, I regularly e-mail students links to news articles about current events and then refer to them during discussion of theoretical readings to give students empirical examples to illustrate the concepts under discussion.

INVENTING STRATEGIES FOR AN INCLUSIVE CLASSROOM

Honoring diversity through inclusive practices is essential to encouraging active participation by all students in a class (Schwarz 2006; Udvari-Solner and Kluth 2008; Lee et al. 2012). It probably goes without saying that every effort should be made, particularly in political science classes, to avoid judgments about the aggregate behavior of demographic groups that might touch on negative stereotypes and generalizations. Students also should not be singled out nor asked to speak as a representative of a certain gender, ethnic, racial, religious, national or cultural group. Neither should they be made to feel intimidated because of their identity or membership in such groups. On the other hand, pointed efforts at avoiding discussion of cultural politics when they are relevant to the subject matter also can have the unintended effect of making students feel as if issues that may be of importance to them are being needlessly avoided. Even despite the best efforts of instructors, students in the course of discussion can make inopportune or unintentionally offensive comments that can intimidate other class members. Most instructors have encountered such awkward situations in which students, almost always unintentionally, have evoked negative cultural stereotypes when discussing issues involving politics. These are the oft-mentioned 'teaching moments' where instructors can defuse a potentially unsettling incident by using what might be considered offensive comments to highlight legitimate ways of thinking about political identities using course readings and the tools of political science analysis.

Aside from the obvious steps instructors should take to provide an inclusive classroom environment that is conducive to student discussion, there are other strategies faculty can use to accentuate more subtle forms of diversity. To the best of their abilities, instructors should endeavor to memorize the names of students as early in the term as possible. Students respond well when addressed by name, which is why it helps to ask students to address each other by their name as well. The diversity that matters also involves encouraging students who are not already familiar and comfortable with each other to engage in participatory classroom discussions. For example, a good practice is to break up groups of friends and form new groups each time small group discussion takes place. In my two upper-level foreign policy courses that involve simulations and role-playing exercises, when students are assigned to groups I make efforts to assign students to different groupings or pairings from one case study to the next. This can be challenging especially with smaller classes, so I keep lists for each case study of student groups and pairs and then shuffle students around so that for each exercise as many new groupings as possible can be formed. Diversity is also important here, which is why I take pains to maintain gender parity as much as possible in creating groups and pairs of students who work together.

Ironically, useful discussion can also occur when lack of diversity is addressed in a pointed and potentially provocative way. For example, the tenets of gender theory can be put to a test during simulation and role-playing exercises by explicitly creating groups of students on the basis of gender diversity and gender homogeneity. I have taught classes in which students engage in exercises using game theory simulations. On at least one occasion students requested that they be allowed to form all-male, all-female and mixed-gender groups so as to test propositions about cooperative versus conflictual behavior. Particularly fruitful post-game discussion engaged students in an analysis of the propositions of gender theory and its application to cases of simulated cooperation and discord. When students take the lead in addressing potentially controversial topics, the ensuing discussion in fact may be more productive than when instructors set up the lesson to be discussed.

An inclusive classroom that encourages student discussion is also one in which instructors acknowledge their own role in respecting students' input and honoring their contributions to the learning process. While it is expected that faculty members in most cases enter the classroom with more knowledge of the subject matter, instructors who needlessly use their command of the material to intimidate students (inadvertently or not) will be frustrated in their efforts to include students in the proceedings. A silent classroom devoid of student participation may be one in which the instructor has adopted a subtly hostile or threatening attitude. Similarly, instructors who dominate the discussion or answer their own questions likely will silence student involvement in discussions.

CONSIDERING THE STUDENT'S ROLE

Students potentially can be enticed to contribute to student discussion if instructors make a classroom participation grade an element in students' final course grade, although research shows that the wisdom for this strategy is not evident for every type of class (Meyer 2009; Miller 2009). Several pitfalls present themselves when a classroom participation grade is at stake. First, discussion of concepts may be essential in small seminar style courses, but in larger lecture classes in which student discussion takes place only sporadically, efforts to prompt discussion at every turn by students seeking to boost their classroom participation grade may be detrimental. Too much student volunteering to talk (in the hope it will improve a student's grade) can keep an instructor from covering all the material necessary for students to understand course concepts.

There is also an important line between the quality and frequency of student contributions to classroom discussion. When students are informed that classroom participation will be part of their final course grade, their first impulse frequently is to talk in class as often as possible in order to conform to the instructor's expectations. Yet talking a lot in class is not the equivalent of making positive contributions to other students' learning. The best student discussions are ones that isolate analytical concepts and empirical evidence and subject them to systematic evaluation without straying off to tangential topics that may arise from student contributions that are made eagerly but not with respect for the themes under investigation. In both cases, where one or more students dominate the discussion or make contributions that are not positive in terms of advancing understanding of the material, the best strategy from my experience is to address the students in question in private rather than in the classroom. This may sound like an obvious suggestion, but on occasion instructors in their frustration can single out students in ways that are not productive. Most students who dominate classroom discussion are aware of their behavior and in most cases respond favorably to instructors who, after all, have their best interests at heart. Private conversations such as these actually can reinforce the role of faculty members as mentors and strengthen their relationship with students.

The last tool for promoting student discussion is perhaps the most ironic and counterintuitive. Instructors can encourage students to actively engage course themes by leaving them alone to work on a group assignment where they must discuss a course reading, simulation or role-playing exercise. Students have to discuss concepts when there is no teacher there. Of course, the obvious potential drawbacks to this method are that students either will fall silent among themselves or will be tempted to talk about things unrelated to the course. Instructor direction is therefore essential to ensure that students left to their own devices are in fact using class time wisely and are discussing course materials in a worthwhile fashion.

An easy means of prompting worthwhile discussion in the absence of the instructor is to assign a writing project to be done as part of discussion of a chosen topic or theme. For example, students could be instructed to come up with a list of all the potential causes of a real or hypothetical historical event. An exercise of this nature can be conducted even in a large lecture class at the beginning of the term. In my introductory international politics course, for instance, I often begin the semester by making a list of common questions people ask about international relations. Students can be divided into groups and be instructed to come up with a list of all the potential causes for aspects of international relations they can think of. Students can also be asked to solve a real or hypothetical political problem and draw up a list of solutions. For example, students in a comparative politics course could be asked to imagine themselves as writing the constitution for a newly democratic country and resolve debates about what type of electoral system should be instituted. The strategy of leaving students to themselves to discuss course themes is eminently useful in classes that use simulation and role-playing exercises. Exercises can be set up so that students are divided into groups to plan strategies for negotiation sessions, develop positions for debates, formulate responses to interviews or work as a team to come up with policy options. Assignments of this nature should be designed to engage course concepts and thereby stimulate useful discussion of topics after the simulations and role-playing exercises have concluded. Students are more likely to approach concepts as 'experts' having adopted the role of principal actors during exercises of this nature.

CONCLUDING THOUGHTS: IT'S NOT ALWAYS ABOUT DISCUSSION

As important as student discussion is for active learning, there can be dangers in assuming that just because students have been given the opportunity to participate learning is taking place. It is worth remembering that students need to be taught material worth discussing and that lectures have their place as well. Discussion works best when material that has been presented to students in a cogent fashion can be subjected to critical analysis. Even in seminar classes where lectures give way to examination of assigned texts, instructors should take care to ensure that the discussion does not proceed aimlessly. Presentation of new material must precede in-depth investigation with active student participation.

Students also have an expectation that it is the instructor's responsibility to teach. As much as educators hope that students will take ownership of the learning process, students respect the authority of the professor and can at times not trust that what they learn from each other is as relevant as what is imparted by the instructor. Based on my own observations, students are more likely to take notes when the instructor is talking than when other students are discussing course material. While faculty members would like to think that undergraduate students can be as animated and interested in course readings as graduate students, the reality is that many contemporary undergraduates expect guidance and look to instructors to serve as authorities on what is to be learned. As in any educational endeavor, excellent teaching is a prerequisite to useful student discussion.

REFERENCES

Bald, S. (2004), 'Melian Dialogue', in Karen A. Mingst and Jack L. Snyder (eds), *Essential Readings in World Politics* (second edition), New York: W.W. Norton Company, pp. 18–19.
Beatty, I. (2004), 'Transforming student learning with classroom communication systems', *EDUCAUSE Center for Applied Research Bulletin*, **2004** (3), pp. 1–13.
Biziouras, N. (2013), 'Midshipmen form a coalition government in Belgium: Lessons from a role-playing simulation', *PS: Political Science & Politics*, **46** (2), 400–405.
Boatright, R.G., N.M. Giner and J.R. Gomes (2013), 'Teaching redistricting: Letting the people draw the lines for the people's house', *PS: Political Science & Politics*, **46** (2), 387–94.
Caldwell, J.E. (2007), 'Clickers in the large classroom: Current research and best-practice tips', *CBE Life Sciences Education*, **6** (1), 9–20.

d'Inverno, R., H. Davis and S. White (2003), 'Using a personal response system for promoting student interaction', *Teaching Mathematics and its Applications*, **22** (4), 163–9.

Duncan, D. (2005), *Clickers in the Classroom: How to Enhance Science Teaching Using Classroom Response Systems*, New York: Addison-Wesley.

Foran, J. (2001), 'The case method and the interactive classroom', *Thought & Action*, **17** (1), 41–50.

Frombgen, E., David Babalola, Aaron Beye, Stacey Boyce, Toby Flint, Lucia Mancini and Katie Van Eaton (2013), 'Giving up control in the classroom: Having students create and carry out simulations in IR courses', *PS: Political Science & Politics*, **46** (2), 395–9.

Fulwiler, T. (1987), *Teaching with Writing*, Portsmouth, NH: Boynton/Cook.

Hess, Diana E. (2009), *Controversy in the Classroom: The Democratic Power of Discussion*, New York: Routledge.

Joliffe, D.A. and A. Harl (2008), 'Studying the "reading transition" from high school to college: What are our students reading and why?', *College English*, **70** (6), 599–617.

Knowlton, S.R. and B.O. Barefoot (eds) (1999), *Using National Newspapers in the College Classroom*, Columbia, SC: University of South Carolina.

Kramer, T.J. and J.H. Korn (1999), 'Class discussions: Promoting participation and preventing problems', in Baron Perlman, Lee I. McCann and Susan H. McFadden (eds), *Lessons Learned: Practical Advice for the Teaching of Psychology*, vol. 1, Washington, DC: The American Psychological Society, pp. 99–104.

Larkin, J.E. and H.A. Pines (2005), 'Asking questions: Promoting student–faculty interchange in the classroom', *Observer*, **18** (11), available at http://www.psychologicalscience.org/index.php/publications/observer/2005/november-05/asking-questions-promoting-student-faculty-interchange-in-the-classroom.html (accessed 14 June 2014).

Lee, Amy, Robert Poch, Marta Shaw and Rhiannon Williams (2012), *Engaging Diversity in Undergraduate Classrooms: A Pedagogy for Developing Intercultural Competence. ASHE Higher Education Report*, vol. 38, no. 2, San Francisco, CA: Jossey-Bass.

Meyer, K.R. (2009), *Student Classroom Engagement: Rethinking Participation Grades and Student Silence* (doctoral dissertation), Athens, OH: Scripps College of Communication of Ohio University.

Meyers, C. and T.B. Jones (1993), *Promoting Active Learning: Strategies for the College Classroom*, San Francisco, CA: Jossey-Bass.

Miller, B.M. (2009), 'Should class participation be graded?', *Perspectives on History*, **47** (8), available at http://www.historians.org/publications-and-directories/perspectives-on-history/november-2009/should-class-participation-be-graded (accessed 14 June 2014).

Moore, A.H., E. Watson and S.B. Fowler (2007), 'Active learning and technology: Designing change for faculty, students, and institutions', *EDUCAUSE Review*, **42** (5), 42–61.

Petrina, S. (2007), *Advanced Teaching Methods for the Technology Classroom*, Hershey, PA: Information Science Publishing.

Schwarz, P. (2006), *From Disability to Possibility: The Power of Inclusive Classrooms*, Portsmouth, NH: Heinemann.

Tomasek, T. (2009), 'Critical reading: Using reading prompts to promote active engagement with text', *International Journal of Teaching and Learning in Higher Education*, **21** (1), 127–32.

Udvari-Solner, A. and P.M. Kluth (2008), *Joyful Learning: Active and Collaborative Learning in Inclusive Classrooms*, Thousand Oaks, CA: Corwin Press.

Weinstein, C.S. (1992), 'Designing the instructional environment: Focus on seating', in Michael R. Simonson and Karen A. Jurasek (eds), *14th Annual Proceedings of Selected Research and Development Presentations at the 1992 Convention of the Association for Educational Communications and Technology*, Association for Educational Communications and Technology, ERIC Document Reproduction Service No. ED 348039, available at http://eric.ed.gov/?id=ED348039 (accessed 21 November 2014).

Index

'4S' applied activities 344–7

academic dishonesty 285–7
  see also plagiarism
Academic Learning Compacts 79
accountability 3, 19–20, 333, 335, 342, 393–4
accrediting bodies 8, 12, 75–6, 97, 109, 124, 241, 442
active learning 63, 158, 173, 175–7, 211–12, 214, 226, 236, 238–40, 256, 261, 265, 267, 295, 301, 305, 315–16, 323, 327–9, 332, 338, 348, 351, 353, 357, 370–71, 375, 380–82, 384, 430–31, 444, 453
  see also simulations
activism 197–9, 201, 204
Adeney, K. 223
adult learners 29–31
  see also lifelong learning; practitioner education
affirmative action programs 186
Alkadry, M.G. 33
Allen, Brooke 212
Allen, Marcus D. 189
Allendoerfer, M.G. 265
al-Qaeda 252–3
Ambrosio, Thomas 309
American Association for Higher Education (AAHE) 6
American Association of Colleges and Universities (AACU) 67
American Association of State Colleges and Universities (AASCU) 7, 65
American Democracy Project 7, 65
American Library Association (ALA) 123
American Political Science Association (APSA) 3–4, 6–8, 12, 21–3, 40, 43, 64, 66, 145, 187, 217
  Task Force on Civic Education 66–7
  Task Force on Graduate Education 36, 38
  Task Force on Mentoring 41
  Teaching and Learning Conference 12, 66, 74–5, 158, 176, 187–8, 209, 217, 258, 437
analytical skills 9, 11, 111, 176–7, 180, 190–91, 228, 247, 316, 325, 388, 406–7
Anastasi, J. 268
Anderson, J. 30
Angelo, T.A. 109

Annals of the American Academy of Social Sciences 358
Arendt, Hannah 239–40
Aristotle 119
Asal, V. 268, 309
Ash, Sarah L. 417
Ashe, F. 151
Association of American Colleges (AAC) 3
Association of American Colleges and Universities (AAC&U) 3, 7, 9
at-risk students 62, 263
attendance 282, 284, 288, 335, 341, 346–7, 425
audience response system (ARS) *see* clickers

backward design 435
Baldwin, David 280
Banta, T.W. 96, 109
Baranowski, Michael W. 158
Barnett, N. 146
Barnett, R. 31
Barrows, Howard 372
Battistoni, Richard 66
Baum, L. 266
BBC 129
Bean, John C. 334
Beaumont, E. 67–8
Beckham, M. 384, 386–7
Behnke, Ralph R. 332
Bell, Derrick 192
Bennett, Andre 208
Bennion, Elizabeth A. 41
Bernstein, Jeffrey L. 212
bibliographies 36, 54–5, 125, 127–8, 412, 415
Biggs, John 129–30
bin Laden, Osama 252–3
blended learning 221–2, 229–31
blogs 90, 121, 125–6, 203, 240, 291, 405, 426
Bloom's *Taxonomy* 48, 51–3, 97–9, 101, 354–5, 364, 370, 375
  Revised 97, 411–12
Bogason, P. 30–31
Bologna Process 132–41, 144–5
Borin, P. 388
Bos, A. 229
Bowen, Craig W. 435
Boyer, Ernest L. 435–6
Boyer Commission 389, 395
Boyer Model of Scholarship 63

Boyte, Harry 66
Brabazon, Tara 121, 123
brainstorming 328, 377, 381
Brans, M. 30–31
Breuning, Marijke 4–5, 11–12
Bridge, David 309
Brintnall, Michael 64
British Social Attitudes Survey 223
Brown, K.E. 29
Brown, Wendy 233
Brown v. Brown (1954) 191
Brunell, L.A. 270
Buchler, Melissa J. 39
Buckley, F. 86, 293–4
building-block model 5–6, 8, 11
bullying 294
bureaucrats 28–9, 32
Bush, Carrie Blanchard 414, 416
Bush, George W. 6, 253, 400–401
BUSINESSEUROPE 133
Butler, J. 196
Butler, Octavia 404

Cabrera, L. 268
Campbell, Patricia 125, 127
Campbell, R. 198
Campus Compact 65
Camus, Albert 117
capstone courses 5–6, 9–10, 16–25, 62, 78, 97, 360, 388–90
Card, Orson Scott 403–4, 406
careers 9, 16, 18, 25, 28, 74–5, 77, 91, 95, 144–5, 265, 384
Carey, S. 223
Carlson, J. 225–6
Carnegie Foundation 7, 18, 65
case briefs 412, 417
case studies 47, 88, 100, 118, 126, 151, 175, 199, 214, 223, 230, 251–3, 319, 342, 351, 360, 363, 371, 431, 444–5, 451
case-based learning 32
cell phones 50, 121, 239, 249, 285, 295, 299, 347, 381, 449
Centellas, Miguel 226, 230, 335–6
charettes 357, 359–60, 366
Charles, C.M. 424
Chi, Michelene T.H. 435
Chickering, Arthur W. 62, 423
Childs, S. 198
Churches, Andrew 51
citizenship 4–5, 8–9, 18, 20, 60, 64–9, 77, 82, 114, 119, 190, 192–3, 247, 249, 291, 414
  see also civic education; global citizenship
civic education 4, 6–8, 11–12, 19, 64–6, 240
  see also citizenship

civic engagement 7, 9–11, 19, 30, 60–61, 64–70, 81–2, 85, 151, 190, 259, 268–9, 272, 330, 362, 365
civil rights 111, 169–70, 174, 188–9, 191–2
Clark, A. 151
class sizes 25, 48, 78, 161, 191, 280, 319, 348, 388, 426, 428
classroom management 253, 424–8
classroom-based experiential learning 351, 357
Clayton, Patti 417
clickers 226–7, 240, 291, 297–302, 342, 345, 448
Clinton, Bill 6
Clinton, Hillary 252
closed-ended questions 297, 444, 446
'closing the loop' 19, 75–6, 109
Codde, Joseph R. 429
codes of conduct 279, 285, 334
Coen brothers 126
Colby, Anne 7
Cole, Alexandra 229
collaborative learning 48, 62, 327, 329, 331, 337, 355, 362, 372, 444
  see also group work
collective action 177, 245, 251, 311
Collegiate Learning Assessment 11
Committee on Institutional Cooperation (CIC) 42
Commons Simulation 319–22
communication skills 77, 80, 147, 150, 190, 203, 270, 327, 369, 382, 389, 414
  written *see* writing skills
community colleges 255–64
community service 6–7, 62, 268–9, 351, 355, 357, 359, 362, 364
community-based learning 9, 363–5
Confederation of British Industry (CBI) 146, 148
conferences 23, 42–4, 91, 151, 188, 252–3, 340, 357, 359–60, 393, 436, 444
  see also American Political Science Association, Teaching and Learning Conference
confidence 29, 56, 90, 147–9, 263, 299, 311, 316, 345, 362, 384, 391
conflict and conflict resolution 173–83
  see also war
Conflict Resolution Quarterly 176
Consortium for Inter-Campus SoTL Research 66
constructive alignment 95–6
constructive criticism 420
  see also feedback
controversial topics 235, 244–53, 299, 417, 449

cooperative learning 329, 332–3, 341, 352, 355, 424
  see also group work; Team-Based Learning
Cope, Jonathan 122–3, 125–6
Cottell, Phillip G. 332
Council for Industry and Higher Education (CIHE) 147
Council of Europe 133
Council on Undergraduate Research 384
course assessment 78, 95–109, 151, 200, 241
coursework 81, 88, 90, 189, 201, 203, 209, 218, 287, 384, 387, 389, 396
Cox, Robert W. 406–7
Craig, J. 32–3, 148
creativity 62, 89, 146, 148, 159, 162, 221–2, 229, 256, 259, 261, 263, 266, 297, 327, 336, 360, 384, 389, 393
critical legal studies (CLS) 192
critical race theory (CRT) 191–2
critical theory 122, 124–5
critical thinking 4–6, 8–11, 16, 31–2, 62, 77, 111, 120, 146, 148, 176–7, 180, 190–91, 208, 234–5, 247, 252, 294, 316, 325, 351–2, 355, 362, 388, 406–7
Croco, S.E. 268
Cross, K. Patricia 109, 332
cumulative learning 415
current events 271, 319, 446, 450
curriculum mapping 81, 96
curriculum reform 3–12, 16, 92–3, 189–90
Curtis, S. 147, 150–51

Dacia Simulation 309–10
Daddow, O. 229
Dahlgren, L. 146
Dahlgren, M.A. 146
Damron, D. 298
Daniel, Sir John 57
Danielson, Mary Ann 280
Darling, J. 270
data collection 180–81, 191, 208, 212–14, 348, 440–41
DEAL model 417
Deardoff, M.D. 86
debates 23, 28, 161, 203, 226, 239, 244–5, 250, 298, 312, 352, 360, 431
debriefing 268, 307–8, 316–18, 321–5, 338, 365–6, 429
deep learning 10–11, 62, 65, 68, 85, 93, 175, 226, 228, 369, 371, 375, 378, 431
Delgado, Richard 192
Detmering, Robert 126
Dewey, John 65, 352–4
Dicklitch, Susan 268, 364
Dickson-Dean, Camille 50

digital literacy *see* information literacy
digital natives 121–3, 129
Diploma Supplement 134–5
Diplomacy (game) 308–9
disabled students 241, 279, 343
discrimination 205, 244
discussion 23, 102, 112, 118–19, 201–2, 239–40, 248, 265, 282, 299, 311, 324, 334, 405, 437, 439, 444–53
  see also online discussion forums
dissertations 91, 215, 218, 221, 225, 229
distance learning 47–58, 69, 211
distribution model 3–4, 8, 11–12
diversity 6, 9, 19, 77, 185–94, 205, 235, 251, 258–62, 450–51
Drake, H. 150
Duerst-Lahti, G. 196
Duffy, Thomas T. 372
Dzurjanik, Peter 429

Economic and Social Research Council (ESRC) 35–6, 38
ECTS system 134–5
Educational Testing Service (ETS) major field test 80–81
Ehrlich, Thomas 365
Eichmann, Adolf 239–40
Eisenberg, Michael 122–3, 129
Elazar, Daniel J. 161
e-learning 50–56
  see also online courses
elections 67, 291
  see also voter turnout
emotions 352–3
Empirical Investigations of Theoretical Models (EITM) 217
employability 144–52, 221, 223–4, 231, 329, 338
empowerment 151, 177, 196–8, 201, 203–4, 206, 336, 394, 420
Engert, S. 270
Enterline, Andrew 392
entrepreneurship 114, 138
environmental studies 115–16
Erasmus 36, 42–3, 136–7, 150
ethics 5, 18, 29, 32, 36, 77, 117, 182, 218, 304
ethnicity 6, 10, 39, 41–2, 77, 160, 185–9, 235, 249, 375, 450
  see also diversity; race
Europe 2020 Strategy 137
European Association for Quality Assurance in Higher Education (ENQA) 133, 135
European Association of Institutions in Higher Education (EURASHE) 133

European Commission 133, 136–7, 144, 149
  see also Erasmus
European Conference of National Political Science Associations (ECNPSA) 138–9
European Consortium for Political Research (ECPR) 43, 217
  summer schools 36
European Court of Justice 137
European Cultural Convention 133
European Higher Education Area (EHEA) 132–6, 138, 145
European Political Science 87
European Political Science Network (epsNET) 138
European Students' Union (ESU) 133
European Union (EU) 127, 133, 137, 144, 151, 306, 364, 375–9, 446
European University Association (EUA) 36, 133
Eurostat 133
Eurostudent 133
Eurydice 133
Excel 211, 214, 309
exchange studies 137–8, 361
  see also mobility; study abroad
exit interviews 5, 78, 80–81
experiential learning 18, 65, 77, 81, 85, 174–6, 179, 204, 351–66
  see also service learning
Experiential Learning Cycle 355
extracurricular activities 61–3
extroverts 336

Facebook 125, 291–2
Farmer, D.W. 109
Farr, Marshall J. 435
federalism 255, 344
feedback 9, 50, 54, 87–8, 92–3, 95, 109, 211, 263, 291, 295–6, 301, 306, 311–12, 333, 336–7, 342–4, 351, 365, 373, 378–9, 393–4, 410, 415–16, 420, 430
  from students 108–9, 225, 296, 298–9, 308, 331, 347
  see also peer evaluation
Feeley, Maureen 329, 333
fellowships 42, 386, 390
feminism 196–200, 204, 206, 233, 248
Fenno, Richard F. 419
fiction see novels
field-based learning 351, 357
  see also service learning
films 126, 177–8, 200, 235, 239–40, 244, 250, 259, 269–72, 289, 399–403, 405–8, 426
  see also YouTube
Fink, L.D. 333, 340

first-generation students 10, 61, 63, 262
fish bowl discussion 334
Flanagan, Richard 122–3, 125–6
flipped classroom 52, 261
focus groups 100
forgery 287
Formicola, Jo Renee 332
Foster, M. 270
Foucault, Michel 117
Fraser, Dorothy 246
Fratantuono, Michael J. 325
Fredericks, Marcel 247
free riders 308, 331, 335, 342–3, 347
Freeman, Alan 192
Fry, Roger 355
Fulbright program 42–3

Gaff, Jerry G. 39, 43
Gainey, Randy R. 251
games 175, 239, 305, 308–9, 315, 325, 327, 351, 451
  see also role play; simulations
Gamson, Zelda 62, 423
Gaylen, Krista 50
Geertz, Clifford 404
gender 41–2, 49, 61, 77, 187–8, 191, 205, 235, 237, 248–9, 450–51
  gender politics 196–206
Gibbons, Dave 404
Gibbons, M. 31
Gingrich, Newt 6
Glaser, Robert 435
Glazier, Rebecca A. 158, 176, 268, 271
global citizenship 125, 265, 268–9
globalization 116, 119, 127, 189, 265, 268, 270
goals see learning objectives
Google 121–2
Gormley-Heenan, Cathy 48
Grade Point Averages (GPAs) 80
graduate research 36, 208–18
graduation rates 61, 64, 79–80, 100
Greenan, John 247
Gregg, Robert 270, 400–401
Grossman, M. 151
group work 113, 147, 177, 214, 322, 327–38, 351, 369, 380, 382, 401, 428–9, 444, 451–2
  see also team-based learning; Team-Based Learning
guest speakers 200
Gump, W. Robert 315
Gunther, Gerald 413

Hale, S. 29, 32
Hall, Stuart 403–4

Hamann, Kerstin 96
Harding, T.B. 29
Hare, William 245
Harris, John 247
Hartlaub, Stephen 5, 280
Hartley, M. 66
Harvard Business School 251
Hawthorne, Nathaniel 117
Head, Alison 122–3, 129
Head, N. 296
Healey, M. 229, 385, 388, 394–5
Hedley, Mark 245, 248
Heller, Joseph 56
Hemery, J. 30
Hensel, N. 384, 386–7
Herbert, Jon 148
Herring, Susan 121
Hesli, Vicki L. 37
Hewitt, J. 225, 228
hidden curriculum 47
higher-order thinking skills 300, 327, 343, 352, 411
high-impact practices (HIPs) 3, 9–11, 16, 63, 65, 68
Hildreth, R.W. 330
Hmelo-Silver, Cindy 372
Hobbes Game 309
Holland, J. 198
Holmes, A. 151
homework 214–15, 282, 284–5, 347
homosexuality 244
Huber, Mary Taylor 438
Hudson, William 66
Hughes, L. 230
human rights 17, 162, 269–70, 322, 364
Hung, Woei 375
Huntington, Samuel P. 252
Hutchings, Pat 436–8
Hy, R. 230
hybrid courses 211, 213, 240, 270

Ibsen, Henrik 249
immigration 188–9
Information Industry Association 123
information literacy 121–30
information obesity 122–3, 129
information overload 291
innovative teaching approaches 11, 39, 53, 55, 85–6, 92–3, 136, 140–41, 148, 163, 174, 187–8, 197, 225, 255–6, 259, 263–4, 266, 301, 408, 413, 423, 439, 442
inquiry-based learning *see* Problem-Based Learning
Institute for Public Policy Research 57
institutional culture 62–3, 79

Institutional Review Boards (IRBs) 218, 440–41
integrated learning 11, 112
Interactive Data Library 223
Intercultural Development Inventory (IDI) 98
interest groups 111, 115, 249, 319, 418, 445
International Political Education Database (IPED) 86, 301
international relations
    simulations in 304–13, 363–4
    teaching 265–72
International Studies Perspectives 74, 82, 176, 315
internationalization 132–41, 189, 265
internships 8–11, 16, 18, 21, 28, 62, 68, 79–81, 100, 149–50, 351, 357, 359, 361
    see also placement learning
interpersonal skills 327–9, 332, 334, 337
interpretive analysis 208
Inter-University Cooperation Programs (ICPs) 137
interviewing skills 203–4, 225, 364, 389
introductory level courses 4–6, 11, 97, 157–63, 257, 259, 265, 281, 298, 415, 434, 447
introverts 294, 300, 336, 446
Ipsos MORI 223
IR Model 48–9, 51, 53–6
Ishiyama, John 4–6, 11–12, 21, 38, 40, 44, 77–8, 280
IT skills 55, 77
iTunes 297

Jackson, Steven F. 309
Jacobson, Trudi 129
Jenkins, A. 388, 394–5
Jenkins, Shannon 365, 385
Jenne, Erin J. 42
jobs skills *see* employability
Johansson, Kristina 19
Johnson, D. 329, 332, 334, 337
Johnson, F.P. 332
Johnson, Paula R. 325
Johnson, R. 329, 334, 337
Jonassen, David H. 375
Journal of Peace Education 176
Journal of Political Science Education 12, 66, 74, 82, 176, 209, 315, 358, 437
journals *see* learning journals; *individual journals*
jury service 119
Just In Time Teaching (JITT) 415

Kafka, Franz 117
Kagan, Robert 253
Kam, C.D. 298

Karukstis, K. 393, 396
Kassiola, Joel 233–4
Kaussler, Bernd 400
Kelly, Marisa 21, 76–8
Kelly, R.M. 196
Kern, R. 280
Key, Ellen M. 414
King, Alison 52
King, Martin Luther 117
King, Paul E. 332
Klinger, J. 29
Klunk, Brian E. 21, 76–8
Knickrehm method 331–2
Knight, A.B. 333, 340, 345
Kolb, David A. 355
Korzybski, Alfred 122
Koulish, R. 268
Krathwohl, David R. 354
Krook, Mona Lena 196–200, 203–4, 206
Kuh, G. 31
Kustra, E. 388

labor market 35–6, 38, 134–6, 140–41, 144, 210
    see also careers
Lambert, Richard 145–6
Lantis, Jeffrey S. 308
laptops 121, 284–5, 298–9, 346, 381, 449
Lasswell, Harold D. 403
Lawless, K.A. 325
Le Guin, Ursula K. 400, 404
Learn and Serve America program 65
learner-centered education *see* student-centered learning
learning community 10, 60, 70, 111–13, 413
learning journals 201–2, 229, 252, 416–17, 428
learning transfer 17–18
lectures 17, 47–8, 50, 109, 128, 158, 176, 191, 200, 211, 223–4, 226–7, 230, 235, 238, 240, 265–6, 288, 295–7, 305, 324–5, 332, 338, 345–6, 348, 352, 369, 378, 381, 401, 406, 422–32, 444–6, 448–9, 452
Lee, Donna 151
Lee, Janet 197, 199, 201–2, 204–5
Lees-Marshment, Jennifer 148
Lem, Stanislaw 404–5
LeMay, Curtis 407
Leston-Bandeira, C. 147, 225
Levintova, E. 175
liberal education 3, 8–9
Liberal Education for America's Promise (LEAP) 9–10
life skills 261, 420
lifelong learning 18, 25, 124–5, 134–5, 137, 356
Lightfoot, Simon 48, 296
Lisbon Strategy 137

Lisle, James 280
Lispky, M. 32
literature *see* novels
literature reviews 54, 212, 236, 389, 412, 440
Loewenberg Ball, Deborah 430
London School of Economics 37
Lopez, Linda 4, 11–12
Love, Gregory 335–6
Love, Nancy S. 414–15
Lusk, Amy B. 250

Mackey, Thomas 129
Magna Charta Universitatum 141
Malgrem, Carl D. 404
Manrique, C. 230
Marcum, Anthony S. 39
Marie Curie Fellowship 42
Markowitz, Linda 245, 248
Marshall, John 413
Marx, Karl 117
Massive Open Online Courses (MOOCs) 47, 57
math aversion 212, 222, 227
McCartney, Allison Rios Millet 66, 269, 364
McDonald, M. 268
McGlynn, Adam 188
McKinney, Kathleen 436, 439
McNamara, Robert 407
media 116, 129, 200, 412
media literacy *see* information literacy
memoranda 229–30, 245, 251–2
memorization 69–70, 284, 297, 352–3, 355, 357, 370, 372, 431, 451
mentoring 35, 40–42, 44, 215–16, 230, 384, 390–94
methods education
    graduate 208–18
    undergraduate 221–31
Michaelson, Larry 333, 340–42, 345–47
Middle States Commission on Higher Education 124
military 29, 119, 174
Miller, H.T. 33
Miller, S. 151
Miller, Steven I. 247
Miller, William J. 40, 44
Millis, Barbara J. 332
minorities 10, 61, 63, 160, 248, 250
mission statements 18, 20, 65, 70, 76, 78
mobile phones *see* cell phones
mobility 35–6, 42–4, 134, 136–7
    see also study abroad
Model United Nations 7, 269, 329, 363–4, 418
Monforti, Jessica Lavariega 188
Moodle 427

Moore, Alan 404
Moore, Joi L. 50
motivation 60–61, 63, 68–9, 149, 162, 269, 306, 316, 323, 330, 352, 362
Mott, J. 298
Moust, Jos H. 375
movies *see* films
Moynihan, Daniel Patrick 245
multiculturalism 186–7
  see also diversity
multidisciplinary approaches 111–20, 123
multiple choice tests 48, 50, 101, 103–4, 108, 333, 342, 344, 348
Münch, Richard 138
Murakami, Michael 208

Napieralski, E.A. 109
National Archives of Ireland 202
National Center for Education Statistics 187
National Election Studies 223
National Science Foundation 390
National Society for Experiential Education 356
National Survey of Senior Seminars and Capstone Courses 21
National Survey of Student Engagement (NSSE) 10, 62
National Task Force on Civic Learning and Democratic Engagement 67
National Union of Students 148
networking skills 36–7, 40, 203
  see also interpersonal skills; social skills
Neumann, Iver B. 400
New Public Management 29
Newmann, William 311
Nexon, Daniel H. 400
Nicholson, L. 196
non-traditional texts 399–408
  see also films; novels
Notman, F. 300
novels 118, 235, 399–400, 403–8
numeracy skills 147–8, 222, 227
  see also math aversion
Nyström, S. 146

Obama, Barack 6, 67, 124, 253, 450
objectionable language 244–5, 249
objectivity 198, 413
Olsen, Mancur 331
one-to-one support 221–3, 230–31
online courses 47–58, 213, 226, 240, 270, 351
online discussion forums 291–5, 300–301
open-ended questions 20, 247, 323, 333–4, 345, 347, 380, 446–8
Osborne, J. 393, 396

Ostrom, Elinor 6, 66
outcomes-based model 7–9, 11
overseas study *see* study abroad

Pace, David 434–5
Palomba, C.A. 96, 109
Parker, Paul 5
Pascarella, E.T. 61
passive learning 240, 297, 304, 306, 332–3, 348, 353, 448
Patterson, A.S. 269
Payne, Brian K. 251
Peace Corps 182
peer evaluation 331–2, 343, 347, 365, 416, 430
peer learning 301, 333
peer pressure 138, 285, 345
peer support 221–2, 224, 230, 357, 359
performance assessment in Europe 85–93
Perrine, Rose M. 280
Pindant, D.G. 29
placement learning 85–8, 90, 149–50, 357, 359
  see also internships
plagiarism 88, 287
Pleschová, Gabriela 38
podcasts 229–30, 240, 291, 295–7, 300–301
POLFORSK program 36
political apathy 6–7, 66–7, 119
political engagement model 6–8, 11, 67–8
Political Engagement Project (PEP) 7
Political Studies Association (PSA) 43, 86, 145, 148
political theory 4, 17, 30, 65, 117, 139, 173, 233–42, 414–15, 418–19
Polk, Thad 426
pop culture 118, 235, 399, 401
pop quizzes 54, 162, 285
portfolios 5, 16, 21–2, 78, 86, 88–90, 100–101, 103, 428
post-positivism 245, 247
PowerPoint 240, 425–7, 448
Powner, L.C. 265, 268
practitioner education 28–33
Prague Declaration 124
Prensky, Marc 121, 123
presentations 18, 20, 77, 88, 90–91, 101, 150, 177, 214, 235, 282, 316, 351, 371
pressure groups 144, 149
Prezi 425
Problem-Based Learning 85, 316, 357, 359, 361–5, 369–82, 388, 431
problem-solving skills 16, 52, 148, 175, 286, 306, 328, 330, 335, 355, 362, 369, 388
professional associations 35, 43–4, 65, 87

professional development 30, 35–45, 65, 255, 257–8
program alignment 24–5
program assessment 16, 19–21, 23, 74–82, 95–6, 151
Provost's Office 442
PS: Political Science & Politics 66, 74–5, 82, 176, 315, 437–8
Public Achievement 330
public administration 4, 6, 28, 30, 32, 85, 139, 208, 213, 215, 413–14, 417
public policy 4–6, 30, 61, 65, 187, 191, 196, 199–200, 204, 320, 327, 355, 365
public service 4, 9, 20, 23, 28–9, 33
publishing 37, 40, 44, 215–18, 256, 436
punishing language 280–81

quality assurance 135, 140–41
Quality Assurance Agency for Higher Education 127–8
questionnaire 78, 100, 128, 223, 227, 229
  see also surveys
Quinn, B. 29, 31–2

R (software) 211, 214–15
race 10, 42, 160, 185–9, 191–2, 201, 205, 235, 237, 244, 247, 450
  see also diversity; ethnicity
Radford, Simon 309
Raiffa, Howard 316
Ralph, J. 296
Ramazanoglu, C. 198
Ramsden, Paul 48–9
rational choice 208, 245
Readiness Assurance Process (RAP) 341–7
referencing 128–9
Reinalda, Bob 133
Reinharz, S. 198
Reitman, Jason 126
religion 61, 111, 118, 160–61, 180–81, 194, 235, 241, 354, 450
  see also diversity
research *see* graduate research; undergraduate research
retention rates 11, 41, 63–4, 80, 100
revise and resubmit policy 416, 419–20
rewarding language 280–81
Ritter, G. 196
Rivera, Sharon Werning 308
Robbins, Lord Lionel 56
Roberts, M. 229–30
Robinson, A. 150
Robles, Alfredo 280
Rodgers, P. 230
Rofe, J.S. 86

Rogers, A. 29
role play 48, 86, 175–6, 178–83, 239, 253, 265, 306, 316–17, 329, 351, 358–9, 418, 431, 451–3
  see also simulations
rote memorization *see* memorization
Roth, Philip 249
Rowe, M. 32
Roy, D. 388
rubrics 9, 20, 23, 81, 89, 92, 102–6, 159, 169–72, 241, 337, 365, 415–16, 420
Ryan, M. 222, 229

Sagan, Carl 403
Salmon, Gilly 48, 51–4
Saltmarsh, J. 66
Sandefur, James 435
sandwich years 90, 149
satire 271, 407
Savery, John R. 372
scaffolding 93, 125, 262–3, 357, 373–4, 375
Schmidt, Henk G. 375
Schneider, M. 229
scholarship of teaching and learning (SoTL) 12, 63, 66, 74, 82, 266, 268, 366, 434–42
Schüttemeyer, Suzanne 138
Schwartz-Shea, Peregrine 208–9
science fiction 118, 235, 400, 403–5
self-assessment 79–80, 108–9, 202, 332, 337
self-reporting 10–11, 98, 100, 307
seminars 5, 9–10, 16–25, 37, 44, 48, 78, 150, 191, 200, 203, 226, 238, 295, 364, 390–91, 423, 448, 452–3
Serafin, Ana Gil 280
service learning 3, 6–7, 10–11, 16, 18, 21–2, 65–8, 77, 79, 85, 100, 175, 240, 268–9, 351, 355, 359, 361–5, 417
sexism 197–8, 202
Shirky, Clay 47, 57
Shugart, Matthew 419
Shulman, Lee S. 436–7, 441
shy students *see* introverts
Simon, Eszter 38, 40, 44, 86
Simons, Janet Thomas 308
Simpson, Archie W. 400
Simpson, Dick 40
simulations 28, 48, 68, 85–6, 88, 91–2, 100, 150, 157–63, 165–72, 175, 178–83, 239–40, 265–70, 272, 299, 304–13, 315–25, 329–30, 334, 337, 351, 359, 361–4, 431, 434, 451, 453
  see also active learning; Model United Nations
Simulations and Gaming 176
smart classrooms 449

SMART goals 97
Smith, K. 329, 334, 337
social networking sites 47, 68, 121, 125–6, 229, 249, 291
  see also Facebook; Twitter
social skills 329, 334, 355
  see also interpersonal skills
Socratic method 239, 362
software 52–3, 100, 210–11, 214–15, 217, 226, 240, 282, 298–9, 309, 361, 448
Sommer, B. 298
Sorbonne Declaration 133
Spade, David 253
Spellings Commission Report 19
Spencer, A. 270
SPSS 211, 214
standardization 7–9, 36, 81, 87, 100, 141, 325, 378
Standing Conference of National and University Libraries (SCONUL) 123
Stata 214–15
statistics 139, 187, 210–12, 214, 221, 227, 346
Stefuriuc, Irina 36–7, 43
stereotyping 193, 202, 249, 363, 423, 450
Stevens, Christy 125, 127
Stice, James E. 158
Stone, Oliver 126
Stover, W. 226
strategic learning 62
student culture 63–4, 68–9, 235
student demographics 185–7, 251
student engagement 9–10, 61–4, 66–70, 81, 87, 204, 227, 265–7, 272, 293, 296, 300–301, 330, 349, 351
student organizations 68–9, 395
student-centered learning 28, 87, 95, 136, 226, 229, 231, 236, 256, 298, 330, 362, 369–72, 418
  see also active learning
study abroad 8–11, 42–3, 62, 79, 97–8, 137–8, 150, 189, 268, 361
  see also mobility
support networks 221–2, 230–31
  see also one-to-one support; peer support
surveys 5–6, 10, 20, 78, 80–81, 103, 179, 208, 223, 229, 307–8, 346
  see also questionnaire
Swansbrough, Robert 327, 330
Sweet, M. 340
syllabus design 279–89
Syme-Taylor, V. 29

Taagepera, Rein 419
Tarsi, Melinda 126

Taylor, Michael 332
Taylor, M.Z. 297
teacher training 35, 38–41, 44
teacher-centered methods 85, 136
teaching assistants 39–40, 159, 171, 248, 282
Team-Based Learning 261, 340–49
  see also group work
technology 47–8, 52, 54–5, 77, 116, 176, 182, 190–91, 210–11, 240, 266, 269–72, 291–302, 316, 345, 411, 425–7, 448
  see also software; virtual learning environments
tenure 40, 79, 186, 208, 212, 215–16, 249, 256, 438
Terenzini, P.T. 61
terrorism 29, 252–3, 320
textbooks 86, 109, 127, 185–6, 188–9, 226, 234, 260, 282, 298, 356, 399–400, 407
theses 16, 18–19, 21–3, 37, 78, 100, 357, 359, 361, 385, 388, 390, 393, 396, 419
think tanks 129, 144, 149
Thomas, G.D. 268
Thoreau, Henry David 117
Thorlakson, Lori 37
Thurnau, Arthur F. 430
Thurston, A. 294
time-management skills 149–50, 261
Tjosvold, Dean 280
transfer students 76
transferable skills 140, 151, 190, 208, 217
Travelling Scholar 36, 42–3
Trudeau, R.H. 293
trustworthiness of sources 128–9, 222
Tucker, Debbie L. 280
tutoring 62, 89, 261, 328–9, 357, 359
Twigg, Judyth 311
Twitter 125, 291, 426
Tymon, A. 152

Ulbig, S.G. 300
undergraduate research 10–11, 18, 77, 221–31, 345–9, 384–96
Undergraduate Research Opportunity Program (UROP) 390
UNESCO 124, 133
United Nations (UN) 127
United States Institute of Peace 176
US Census Bureau 185–7
US Department of Education 7, 67
US State Department 43

Valeriano, Brandon 399, 401
van der Wende, Marijk C. 132
videoconferencing 270
videos *see* films

virtual learning environments (VLEs) 50, 55, 223, 227, 229–30, 292–3, 296, 351
volunteering 6, 67, 357, 363
voter education 7, 204
voter turnout 6, 60, 66–7, 119, 196
  see also political apathy
Vygotsky, L.S. 93

Wahlke Report 3–6, 8, 16
Wald, K. 226
Wallace, Sherri L. 189
war 173, 175, 177–8, 270
  see also conflict and conflict resolution
Webber, Sheila 129
Weber, Cynthia 406
Wedig, Timothy 329–30
Weimer, Maryellen 439
Weinberg, Adam S. 250
Wells, H.G. 403
Western Political Science Association 217
Wetherly, P. 146
Whitehead, Alfred North 48

Whitlock, M.A. 29
Whitworth, Andrew 122, 124, 129
Wikipedia 121–2
Wilson, Harold 56
Wineburg, Sam 435, 439–40
women *see* feminism; gender
Woodworth, James R. 315
work placements *see* internships; placement learning
workshops 39–40, 44, 128–9, 225–6, 230, 357, 359, 361, 380, 390–91, 393, 444
Wrage, S. 29, 32
Wright, B.D. 95, 109
Wright, Richard 117
writing skills 23, 77, 81, 104, 114, 120, 147–8, 190, 234–5, 262, 291, 384, 410–21, 445
Wyman, Matthew 148

Young, Candace 79
YouTube 239, 289, 297

Zurkowski, Paul 123